Y0-CLW-879

THE RELATIONS OF THE UNITED STATES AND SPAIN

DIPLOMACY

THE RELATIONS OF THE UNITED STATES AND SPAIN

DIPLOMACY

BY
FRENCH ENSOR CHADWICK
REAR-ADMIRAL U. S. NAVY
AUTHOR OF "CAUSES OF THE CIVIL WAR"

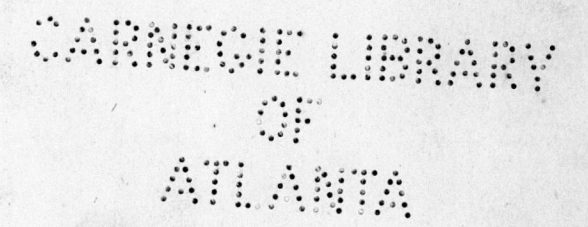

NEW YORK
CHARLES SCRIBNER'S SONS
1909

Copyright, 1909, by
Charles Scribner's Sons

Published December, 1909

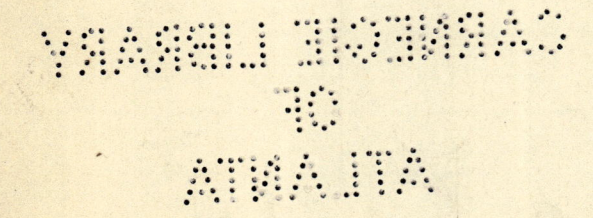

TO
JOHN BIGELOW AND SIDNEY WEBSTER

"Wise friends are the best book of life."—CALDERON.

CONTENTS

CHAPTER		PAGE
	INTRODUCTION	3
I.	THE ATTITUDE OF SPAIN IN THE AMERICAN REVOLUTION	13
II.	DISCONTENT AND INTRIGUE IN THE SOUTH-WEST AND THE TREATY OF 1795	29
III.	THE TRANSFERS OF LOUISIANA	42
IV.	CESSION OF LOUISIANA AND QUESTION OF THE FLORIDAS	61
V.	WAVERING BETWEEN WAR AND PEACE.—PROPOSED ALLIANCE WITH GREAT BRITAIN ABANDONED FOR INTRIGUE WITH FRANCE	86
VI.	THE EFFECT IN AMERICA OF NAPOLEON'S INVASION OF SPAIN.—EVENTS IN THE FLORIDAS	108
VII.	THE FLORIDA TREATY AND JACKSON'S INVASION	121
VIII.	THE RECOGNITION OF SOUTH AMERICAN INDEPENDENCE	148
IX.	THE HOLY ALLIANCE AND THE INVASION OF SPAIN	156
X.	THE DEVELOPMENT OF THE MONROE DOCTRINE	179
XI.	THE PANAMA CONGRESS	205

CONTENTS

CHAPTER		PAGE
XII.	Cuban Conditions.—The Lopez Expeditions.—British and French Interference	224
XIII.	The Case of the Black Warrior.—The Ostend Manifesto	251
XIV.	The Effort of 1865 Toward Reform in Cuban Administration.—Cuban Revolt	273
XV.	The Earlier Diplomacy of the Ten Years' War	287
XVI.	The Firm and Correct Stand of General Grant's Administration.—The "Virginius"	306
XVII.	The "Virginius"	323
XVIII.	The Carlist War.—The Accession of Alfonso XII.—Mr. Fish's Number 266	358
XIX.	The End of the Ten Years' War	387
XX.	The Filibustering Cases.—The "Alliança" Incident.—The Annual Message of 1895	411
XXI.	Cases of American Citizens.—Weyler Succeeds Campos.— Weyler's Proclamations.— Cuba in the Senate.—The Spanish Minister Uses the Newspapers.—Señor Cánovas.—Senate Debate	427
XXII.	The Attitude of the Cleveland Administration Defined.—The Case of the "Competitor"	451
XXIII.	The Case of the "Competitor."—The Annual Message of 1896.—The Action in Congress	468
XXIV.	Cuba in Congress.—The New Administration.—Reconcentration	486

CONTENTS

CHAPTER		PAGE
XXV.	THE NEW AMERICAN ADMINISTRATION.—A LIBERAL SPANISH GOVERNMENT.—MR. MCKINLEY'S FIRST ANNUAL MESSAGE	508
XXVI.	CUBAN RELIEF.—HAVANA RIOTS.—THE INTERCEPTED LETTER AND RESIGNATION OF DUPUY DE LOME.—DESTRUCTION OF THE "MAINE" .	529
XXVII.	THE FIFTY MILLION BILL.—EXCHANGE OF VIEWS AT MADRID.—SPAIN'S FATAL PROCRASTINATION .	544
XXVIII.	THE REPORT ON THE "MAINE" BEFORE CONGRESS.—RESOLUTIONS IN CONGRESS.—SPANISH PROPOSITIONS	561
XXIX.	SPAIN'S PRACTICAL ACCEPTANCE OF AMERICAN DEMANDS.—COLLECTIVE NOTE OF THE FOREIGN POWERS.—THE PRESIDENT'S MESSAGE.—THE JOINT RESOLUTION OF CONGRESS.—THE DECLARATION OF WAR	572
	INDEX	589

THE RELATIONS OF THE UNITED STATES AND SPAIN

DIPLOMACY

INTRODUCTION

THIS book is the outcome of a study of the causes of the war of 1898 between the United States and Spain. Beginning as a preliminary chapter of the war, it was soon found that these causes were of such long growth and of such intricate character that it was vain to hope to bring them into short compass. The attempt at compression was abandoned and the book is thus an effort to bring before the reader the story of more than a hundred years of what has been really a racial strife; on the part of one race for actual domination over regions in which apparently it could not brook a division of rule; on the part of the other for the preservation of the *status quo*.

The late war was thus but the culmination of difficulties which had their seed in the peace of 1763. They sprung into life twenty years later with the advent on the world's stage of the American Union; remained in full vigor for half a century thereafter with scarcely an interval of repose, and waxed and waned for seventy-five years more, until finally war came in 1898 to remove the last cause of friction. Few of the 115 years from 1783 to 1898 were free from bitterness of feeling. The war was thus but a final episode in a century of diplomatic ill-feeling, sometimes dormant but more often dangerously acute.

One of the races involved is essentially practical, untrammeled by the conventions and conservatism natural to an old civilization; protestant in the large sense of ignoring generally the ways of the past, and with its natural and racial protestantism accentuated by a democratic development of nearly three hundred years. The other, offspring of all the ancient races of the Mediterranean, was in the grip of antiquity, with the inherited traits of the most ancient civilizations of the Mediterranean world and naturally antagonistic in all its ways of thought and action to a people which, from its point of view, was an upstart without traditions; whose ancestors were barbarians when of literature, art and law Spain had possessed for a thousand years all that the ancient world had to give.

But it was more than antiquity, more than an old civilization, which produced the differences which made it impossible for the North American Anglo-Saxon to live near his Spanish neighbor without friction. The chief cause was in the absolute racial unlikeness itself, and though racial differences are somewhat modified by more modern conditions, the basis of this unlikeness, this racial temperament, still has an influence over the relations of men, immeasureable in degree, and more potent, though so intangible, than any other force in humanity.

Of the many races which have gone to make up the varying type of men in the Spanish Peninsula, the early Afro-Semitic and the Saracen have made the strongest impress upon the national character, and have given it mainly its qualities, good and bad; its tribal tendencies, its artistic temperament, its courtesy, its fanaticism, its fatalism, its gloomy pride and conservatism, and, not least, its cruelty. For the Iberian, the earliest known occupant of the Peninsula, was a Semite, and we have to-day his counterpart in the men of the Kabyl tribes of the Atlas. Says one who of Anglo-Saxons perhaps knows best the Spanish people: "Not alone in physique do these tribes resemble what the early Iberian must have been, but in the more unchanging peculiarities of character and institutions the likeness is easily traceable to the Spaniards of to-day. . . . The village granary (*posito*) still stands in the Spanish village as its counterpart does in the Atlas regions; the town pasture and communal tillage land continue on both sides of the straits to testify to the close relationship of the early Iberians with the Afro-Semitic races, which included the Egyptian or Copt, the Kabyl, the Touareg, and the Berber. The language of the Iberian has been lost, but enough of it remains on the coins of the later Celtiberian period to prove that it had a common root with the Egyptian and Saharan tongues, which extend from Senegal to Nubia on the hither side of the negro zone."[1]

Wave after wave of Semitic blood added itself to the kindred strain of the original Iberian. The Phœnician came for six

[1] Hume, *The Spanish People*, 3-4.

hundred years and he again was followed and displaced by his near relative, the Carthagenian, who was dominant in all the coasts of the land for two hundred and fifty more, when their power sank in the final defeat of Hannibal and in the victory of Scipio Africanus, 202 years before Christ. Cadiz, the last stronghold of Carthagenian power, was then abandoned and Rome ruled the land as long as there was Roman power.

In the north the Celt had preceded the Phœnician, and Goth and Vandal and Visigoth had followed the Roman and left marked traces; but all the varied races of the Peninsula were engulfed 300 years after the downfall of the Romans by the last and greatest of the historic invasions from Africa (A. D. 711) when Arab and Berber began a conquest which was for a time to include all Spain, and was to hold its fairest provinces for a longer period than any other race within man's knowledge. Islam did not rule the greater part of Spain for 500 years and these fairest provinces 300 years longer without leaving more than a memory. It made a deep impress on the blood as well as the thought and history of Spain, and, added to the Iberian-Phœnician-Carthagenian strain, accentuated the already strong Semitic qualities of the race, and made the man of the Peninsula closely akin in temperament and mental qualities to the Oriental and very different even from his closest neighbor north of the Pyrenees. During the most of this period, nearly as long as from the conquest of England by the Norman to the present day, the Moor-Berber was the dominant race, physically and intellectually, and after the last remnant of their dominion had passed there continued to live in Spain, subject to the Spanish Christians, a host of men of Moorish blood, a great portion of whom became merged into what came to be known only four centuries since as the Spanish nation.

It is clearly impossible that the great Moorish power which so long ruled the Peninsula, built great cities, reared a great and at the time an unapproached civilization, could have been represented only by the comparatively small remnant of 500,000 Moors driven to Africa in the early part of the XVIIth century by the mad religious fury which came into being with the closing years of Ferdinand and Isabella and reached its acme under Philip II. Says an able historian: "When we compare the inconsiderable number of exiles with the original large Moorish population of the lands recovered during the reconquest we can realize how great a proportion of the Mudejares must have become Christians and have merged indistinguishably with their conquerors. Mediæval toleration had won them over and its continuance would in time have completed the process. Not only would an infinite sum of human misery have been averted, but Spain would to some extent have escaped the impoverishment and debility which served as so cruel an expiation."[1]

The impress of the Moor differed from that of the Romans as a national migration differs from military occupancy. The Moors were a resident race; the Romans a governing class. However great the effect of Roman language, laws, and methods upon Iberia, and it was of course very great and lasting, there could not be a blood mixture in any degree commensurable with that due to the presence for so much longer a period of the millions who had so much of race feeling common with the Iberian native to the soil.

It thus could not be otherwise than that this latest comer and longest stayer should leave a great mark, and that we have in the Spaniard, a man in whom so much is not understandable until we reckon with him, not as a European, but as the Moro-Iberian which he is; a man apart, and differentiated from the other races of Europe. Looked at so, much becomes explicable which is otherwise strange, and has defied the effort of the Anglo-Saxon to understand the philosophy of the acts and ways of the conglomerate race of the Peninsula, which, in its incapacity for government, its regionalism, its chronic state of revolution, its religiosity, its fatalism and procrastination, its sloth in material development, have made the Spanish nation an enigma to the northern mind.

But with whatever shortcomings, the race has, or certainly has had, great qualities. It did a work in the exploitation of America which in its energy and its earlier results; in the actual work of building cities; in exploration; in the missionizing of savage races, surpassed for a century and a half that done or even attempted by any other race of the time. Though the basis of this energy was chiefly a *fames auri* of a most sordid type; though no great part of the Spanish migration had for cause such motives as those of the

[1] Lea, *The Moriscos of Spain*, 360.

founders of New England, or even the more prosaic desire to colonize a new land in a true sense, this energy must remain one of the marvels of accomplishment. One can only wonder to-day at the immensity of the force, whatever its basis, which made, so long since, great and important places of Mexico, Caracas, Lima, Havana; which built the walls of Cartagena and Panama, penetrated to Bogotá, to Quito, and to the inmost recesses of Paraguay, when the colonies of France and England were but in their infancy.

The Spaniard left a mighty impress upon the New World; an impress in many ways Roman in character. While so like the Roman in building up a world empire, there is also a striking analogy in Rome's decay. As did Rome, so Spain sent her lieutenants to rule the provinces and build their fortunes in greed and oppression. She laid the heavy band of tribute upon the western world for the benefit of Spain alone and in large degree became the rapacious metropolis as was Rome; and faction and anarchy, as in her great exemplar, ruled at home until she stands to-day shorn of her ancient power, but still, like Rome, preserving to the last her gladiatorial games.

But while leaving this material impress in America, the Spaniard has also left much of the spiritual in the lofty courtesy, temperance, and the strong and kindly family feeling of his race, for which the Anglo-Saxon would be the better man. No one nation has all the virtues, and while the more marked of the Spaniard may not be those of the Anglo-Saxon, he has a large share of those of his own kind, and it is hoped that wherever the one race may be associated with the other, it will be, not to supplant but to unite the admirable qualities of both.

The marriage of Fernando of Aragon and Isabella of Castile, whose destruction of the Moorish power and the establishment of the Inquisition brought them the title of the "Catholic Kings," was the first step toward solidifying Spain. Until then the Peninsula was a collection of diverse petty kingdoms with its fairest parts still in Moorish control, and all at sword's point with one another. "Castilians hated Aragonese, Catalans detested Castilians, Navarrese had nothing whatever in common with either nation. Galicians were a race akin to the Portuguese, but had no fellow-feeling with the half-Moorish Andalusians and Valencians. There was, indeed, still no Spain, either ethnologically or politically, for the country consisted of half a score of separate dominions each with its own laws, customs, traditions, prejudices, and racial distinctions," [1] and much of this remains to this day.

The religious fanaticism instigated and fomented by Fernando and Isabella had for its object chiefly the unification of the Spanish people through the establishment of a great and moving sentiment which should be common to all. It was, in one respect, unfortunately only too successful. It wakened the old Iberic spirit of fanaticism which the race had in common with its African ancestors, whose descendants on the southern shore of the Mediterranean had ranged themselves under the banners of Islam, and developed the spirit of mysticism and religious exaltation which made Spain the depository in its own eyes of the only true religion, and raised it to an exaltation which demanded that it should not only carry this religion to the heathen of newly discovered America, but that it should force the heretic parts of Europe into the true way. Nor was the futility of this felt or in any great degree recognized until the stern lesson of the loss in 1588 of the missionizing fleet known as the Spanish Armada and the defeat in the Netherlands forced the conviction upon the Spanish king and nation that they were unequal to the task.

The elevation of Charles I to the imperial throne as Charles V, while flattering to pride, drew Spain into the innermost whirlpool of European politics and made her merely the money chest of widespread and interminable wars in which she had no real concern, and which brought her to the depth of ruin and poverty from which she never had the political or commercial ability to rise. She was trailed in the wake of the so-called Holy Roman Empire, hugging the delusion that she was leading when she was only dragged, bled white by the incessant demands of one who was practically a foreign ruler. Her sons and her treasure were spent in Flanders and Italy, not for the purposes of the King of Spain, but for those of the Roman emperor, who completed the ruin of the country by leaving as a heritage to Spain the Netherlands, which had come to him through his Austrian father, Philip. It was this heirship which continued to Spain her unfortunate linking with a political

[1] Hume, *The Spanish People*, 310.

system which was in no sense hers, and which, combined with the economic effects of the expulsion of the Moriscos under the edict of September 22, 1609, by Philip III, and the growth of the Inquisition into the most terrible national flail known in history,[1] gave the final blow which sank Spain into the deepest depths of political, moral, and economic ruin.

The extraordinary obliquity of mind which in the thought of many not only of the time but still for centuries to come placed Spain as a great power is illustrated by the remark of James I: "The King of Spain is greater than us all together." This was said not only when her navy had been ruined, and when she had been defeated in the Netherlands, but at a time when she was in direst poverty, without commerce, bereft of everything but her fanaticism and spirit of adventure and of her ardor for literature and art, which last were to make her really great in the noblest fields. Jews and Moriscos had been slaughtered and driven from the country of which they were the main wealth producers; the export of gold and silver was prohibited and the use of these metals for any other purposes than as coin forbidden; certain goods could not be sent to America, as it was supposed that the American demand made them dear in Spain; articles of food were taxed an eighth of their value; and above all, trade was ruined by a tax, termed the *alcabala*, of ten per cent, rising later to fourteen, on every sale and which necessarily crushed commercial movement of every kind. Labor, which had been the perquisite of the Jew and of the Moor, was despised by the "Old Christian," misery and squalor stalked through the land, while the court was given over to reckless extravagance. Says Hume: "The religious fervor which first demonstrated itself in Isabel the Catholic, the exaltation induced by the Inquisition, and the ascetic mysticism which was at once the chief characteristic and the main policy of Philip II, provided for the Spanish people the direction for which their spirit yearned. Priests and friars were ever present. In court, in camp, and in every-day life the atmosphere of rigid unified religion enveloped all things and persons. Hard, severe, and ascetic as a protest against Moorish grace, cleanliness, and elegance, and equally against the sensuous beauty with which the Italians

[1] See Lea, *History of the Inquisition in Spain*, passim.

had invested their worship, the Spanish mind revelled in the painful self-sacrificing side of religion which appealed to their nature. They became a nation of mystics in which each person felt his community with God, and, as a consequence, capable of any sacrifice, any heroism, any suffering in this cause. The ruling idea was one of celestial knighthood, of daring adventure to rescue the cause of the suffering Christ even as the now-waning knights-errant had undertaken to rescue ill-treated ladies. Saint Teresa de Jesus, Saint Ignatius de Loyola and his marvellous company, and Saint Juan de la Cruz, with their visions and their ecstasies, were merely types; there was hardly a monastery without its fasting seer or its saintly dreamer, hardly a nunnery without its cataleptic miracle worker, hardly a barren hill-side without its hermit, living in filth and abject misery of the flesh, but with the exalted conviction of his personal community with God. Not churchmen alone, but laymen and soldiers too, were swayed by the strange thought, and went forth to work or war in a spirit of sacrifice, relieved by orgies of hideous immorality. Philip himself, living like a hermit and toiling like a slave in his stone cell, practising rigid mortifications, and undergoing the voluntary suffering in which he gloried, was beloved by his people, because he was moved by the same instinct that they were. He led them, it is true, but he did so because they wished to tread the same road."[1]

The three hundred years after Philip II, which so altered most of Europe, wrought but slow changes in Spain, harrowed as was its people by poverty, misrule, and frequent anarchy. Democratic in its impulses as are all its kindred races, the theocratic rule of centuries fitted that of Spain but illy to adjust itself to the realities of democracy as developed in other European countries. Intensely provincialized both by reason of ignorance and by the barriers set by nature between the various kingdoms of Spain; with difficult and infrequent communications; segregated from the rest of Europe by a lofty mountain range; holding with overweening pride the conviction of a superiority of race which, it was felt, only accident had thwarted; unable by race characteristics to develop a sane and wholesome polity, Spain, almost equally with Turkey, had become a synonym for ineptitude

[1] Hume, *The Spanish People*, 375–376.

in government and for maladministration in such governmental systems as the nation was able to form.

It was this inability or slowness of adaptation to the world's new conditions which caused the century just ended to be darkened with struggles in Spain's American dependencies, for what appeared to Anglo-Saxons for generations inherent rights. These dependencies, less enthralled as to thought in the last hundred years than the mother country, demanded more than, unhappily, the mother country could see its way to give. The practical political knowledge which should have developed in Spain as elsewhere in Europe came a century too late, and was acted upon only when the last of the numerous brood to which she had given birth had snapped the ties which had so long been weakening through the misrule which did not vary, in principle or in practice, during a period of three hundred and fifty years.

A notable Spaniard himself says: "If some day a mature judgment of our decadence and fall (*vencimiento*) be written, there will be placed as first of all their causes *the evident inferiority of our aptitude for administration and government*. One will then see how small are the matters which fix the attention of historians and statisticians in the incapacity and small emotions which have been so largely the peculiar attribute of our governors. At the moment when vast territories and complicated interests demand elevated intelligence and large ability we appear before the world with the admirable court of artists, captains, mystics, colonists, navigators, and even political writers of value, but without lighting upon a single man skilled in government; a Cromwell, Sully, Richelieu, Colbert, Louvois, etc., in whom the ancient personal strength has happened to be cast in the new moulds of modern nations."[1]

But it has not been a Cromwell or Richelieu that has been needed; it has been chiefly a want of political aptitude in the race itself, without which the individual leader is of but small avail.

Great leadership is but the exponent of national feeling and aspiration. There was a nucleus of such in Spain a hundred years since and in its encouragement was Spain's need and safety. But

---

[1] Don Pablo de Alzola, quoting Don Fernando de Silvela, *Revista Contemporanea*, V, 111 (1898).

this encouragement was denied her. Spanish effort in the earlier part of the nineteenth century to keep step with the spirit of democracy awakened by the French revolution was stifled, not by Spaniards but by the France of Louis XVIII and the Holy Alliance. The utmost evils which could be attributed to the Napoleonic designs of 1808 and the sufferings from the savage devastation of Spanish cities and the shameless rapacity of French generals at this melancholy period, could not equal in unhappiness to the Spanish people the results of the atrocity of the French invasion of 1823. This invasion, the only reason for which was the suppression of the liberal movement and the constitution, re-established absolutism in the person of an incapable and degraded monarch, Fernando VII, and dealt Spanish liberalism a blow which rent the country with anarchic strife, stunted the moral and material growth of the kingdom, and fastened upon Cuba the despotic régime embodied in the king's decree of 1825.

It must thus be recognized that the vast evils befalling Spain and her island dependencies throughout the nineteenth century, evils so great that no qualifying words can express their enormity, were not all of her own making. France, Russia, Austria, and Prussia were the culpable partners in a crime which, more than all things else together, fastened woe upon a brave people and made certain the continuance of the evil elements of the country.

Without this action Spain, with her more liberal forces free to develop, might in some degree at least have advanced politically with the rest of Europe. Cuba might have been to-day a Spanish Canada and the Philippines a Spanish India. But these things were not to be. Racial peculiarities, regionalism, religious bigotry, and the ignorance which went hand in hand with fanatical subservience to priestly rule were possibly sufficient to have prevented such a change; but the French invasion, or to speak more truly, the invasion by the Holy Alliance, made this change impossible, and by its reinstallation of absolutism made certain anarchy at home and loss of empire abroad. Spanish history when truly written will recognize this great fact.

CHAPTER I

THE ATTITUDE OF SPAIN IN THE AMERICAN REVOLUTION

The difficulties between the United States and Spain began with the advent of the former as an independent power. These difficulties, as already mentioned,[1] were a heritage of the peace of 1763. By the preliminary articles, dated November 3, 1762, of the definitive treaty signed February 10, 1763, a treaty which ended the great colonial wars of the middle of the eighteenth century, France yielded Canada to Great Britain and the latter took over Florida in exchange for Havana, which had fallen in 1762 to the English and colonial forces under Lord Albemarle and Admiral Pocock. On the same day, with the adoption of the preliminary articles of the treaty, the French king "ceded to his cousin of Spain and to his successors, forever, in full ownership and without exception or reservation whatever, from pure impulse of his generous heart and from the sense of the affection and friendship existing between these two royal persons, all the country known under the name of Louisiana." This act had been so unforeseen that the Spanish ambassador, who had had no instructions in the subject, accepted the gift conditionally, that is, *sub spe rati*, subject to the ratification of his Catholic Majesty. On the 13th of the same month the latter accepted the donation,[2] but it was not until by letter of April 21, 1764, to the Governor of Louisiana that the transfer was made public. Thus so easily, and apparently with no other cause than to recompense Spain for the loss of Florida, was signed away an empire.

The definitive treaty gave no indication of this transfer, but proceeded in Article VII to assign limits as if it had not been made: "The limits of the British and French territories in that part of the world shall be fixed irrevocably by a line down the middle of the river Mississippi, from its source to the river Iberville,

[1] Introduction. [2] Gayarré, *History of Louisiana*, II, 92.

and from thence by a line drawn along the middle of this river and the lakes Maurepas and Pontchartrain to the sea; and for this purpose the Most Christian King cedes in full right, and guarantees to his Britannic Majesty, the river and port of Mobile, and everything he possesses or ought to possess on the left side of the river Mississippi, except the town of New Orleans and the island in which it is situated, which shall remain to France; provided the river Mississippi shall be equally free, as well to the subjects of Great Britain as to those of France, in its whole breadth or length, from its source to the sea, and expressly that part which is between the said island of New Orleans and the right bank of that river, as well as the passage both in and out of its mouth. It is furthermore stipulated that the vessels belonging to the subjects of either nation shall not be stopped, visited, or subjected to the payment of any duty whatsoever."

In this clause rested later the claim of the United States to the right of navigation of the river as successor to all the rights of Great Britain under the treaty of 1763.

Spain in exchange for the restitution of Havana and Cuba ceded "Florida, with Fort St. Augustin and the bay of Pensacola, as well as all that Spain possesses on the continent of North America to the east or to the south east of the river Mississippi, and in general everything that depends on said countries and lands." By this treaty all the North American continent east of the Mississippi, except the island of New Orleans, became British territory.

But this was not the whole of the rearrangement of North American boundaries. By British royal proclamation of October 7, 1763, the ceded territories were divided into four governmental districts—Quebec, East Florida, West Florida, and Granada, which last included the whole of the British West Indies; a fifth district comprising the region between the Alleghany and the Mississippi was set aside for the Indians. In this last vast area British subjects were prohibited from making "any purchases or settlements whatever, or taking possession of any of the lands above reserved, without our special leave or license."[1] Naturally

[1] For text of this proclamation, see *Annual Register*, 1763, Winsor, "*Narrative and Critical History*," VI, ch. IX, Hart and Channing, *American History Leaflets*, No. 5.

the English colonists paid practically no attention to this attempt to set new bounds to the ancient charters, and the westward movement across the Alleghanies, already begun, went forward with constant acceleration.[1]

The provinces known as East Florida and West Florida were divided by the Appalachicola River; both had at first the thirty-first parallel of latitude as a northern boundary, but this, for West Florida, was changed the next year to 32° 28', marking the mouth of the Yazoo, a change which later gave rise to no little discussion.

Spain by the treaty came into the greatest potential heritage with which a nation was ever dowered. Her possessions included three-fourths the habitable parts of North and South America; the richest and greatest islands of the West Indies were hers; she stretched from frozen north to frozen south through 110 degrees of latitude, holding within her grasp the richest mines then known of the world, and far richer which were yet to be discovered. Never had race or nation such opportunities. But this great estate was in hands powerless to use it; the gift from France of half a continent was in itself a cause of terror and foreboding, as bringing Spain into direct and hated contact with the Anglo-Saxon, a contact she had hoped to avoid through the continuance of a buffer state under the dominion of France.

Spain saw in the American Revolution her supposed opportunity for safeguarding her American interests, in weakening the dominion of the English race through the revolt of the colonies, and gave secretly to France 1,000,000 of the 3,000,000 francs handed by the French in 1776 to the American Commissioners. As the war progressed, "and the issue was independence, Spain was no longer inclined to help on a movement which would be a dangerous precedent to her own colonies, and which, if successful, would build up on her borders a sovereignty in its political principles very hostile to her traditions, and occupied by a people whose energy and aggressiveness would be made more formidable by a successful war. This was the second attitude assumed by Spain

[1] Eleven years later, in 1774, this was followed by a parliamentary act known as the Quebec bill, the passing of which was largely influenced by the revolutionary commotions of the period in Boston and which extended the jurisdiction of the Quebec government to the Ohio. The colonies affected vigorously protested against this as a violation of their ancient charters.

to our Revolution; an attitude of annoyance, of displeasure, of anxiety, causing her to repel any advance made by us with a sullen though adroit persistence." [1]

The treaty of alliance, signed February 6, 1778, between France and the United States had included a secret article enabling the King of Spain to become a party to the alliance, but Spain did not move until April 29, 1779, when she made a secret convention with France to become a party to the war with Great Britain, a provision of which was that the war should continue until Gibraltar should be taken. Six days later she made proposals of alliance with England, but these being refused, she declared war May 3, 1779. Article 4 of the secret convention, notwithstanding Spain's real dislike to such an outcome, engaged the Spanish King "not to lay down his arms until" the independence of the United States "is recognized by the King of Great Britain, it being indispensable that this point shall be the essential basis of all negotiations for peace which may be instituted hereafter," an article instigated not by French altruism for the benefit of the United States but by the determination to continue the war to the completion of England's humiliation.

The proposal and request of the King of France in the same article, that on the day the King of Spain should declare war against England he should recognize the "sovereign independence" of the United States ended with the proposition. The policy of Spain was moved by very different views from that of France. The latter was already disinherited of her American continental possessions; the former was potentially a great American power, and, as mentioned, there was wisdom enough in Spain to cause her ministers to dread the formation of a new and independent empire, protestant in religion and moved by a spirit of intense democracy. Said Florida Blanca, the Spanish minister of state, to the French ambassador Montmorin, "The King, my master, will never acknowledge their independence until the English themselves shall be forced to recognize it by the peace. He fears the example which he should otherwise give to his own possessions." [2] From this attitude Spain did not move.

---

[1] Wharton, *Diplom. Cor. of the American Revolution*, I, 427.
[2] Bancroft, *United States*, V, 307, Ed. 1890.

Spain thus, inasmuch as she became a party to the war, had a common interest with the United States. But she was powerless to aid effectively in such a contest. Her fleet was what it always had been and continued to be—ill-manned, ill-equipped and in bad repair. Such resources as she had were swallowed in the siege of Gibraltar, and the slight efforts she made in America were all directed to the later despoilment of the colonies. She was never an ally of the United States, morally or by treaty.

In 1779 an agent, Don Juan de Miralles, was sent from Cuba, who, through the French minister, Gerard, addressed a memorial to Congress, May 19, on the subject of the seizure by American privateers of three vessels under the Spanish flag.[1] This was followed by a letter to Congress, November 24, 1779, stating that he "was commissioned with sufficient authority by order from his Excellency Don Diego Joseph Navarro, Governor and Captain-General of the island of Cuba, dated at the Havana, the 19th and 22d of July last," to announce formally the fact of the declaration of war by Spain published in Havana July 22, 1779, and to urge upon Congress the capture of St. Augustine, Florida, in order that it might be restored to Spain and also that assault upon this place might withdraw some of the British forces from the defence of Pensacola and Mobile.[2] This letter presents Spain in the extraordinary attitude of a suppliant for favors rather than as a friend who had come to aid in a great struggle, and it was, indeed, to this former attitude that with scarcely any exception she held throughout.

Though Mr. John Jay, sent as envoy to Madrid in the hope of effecting an alliance, reached Cadiz January 22, 1780, it was not until May 10 of that year that he was able to have audience with the Count of Florida Blanca, minister of foreign affairs, who intimated that the chief difficulty in the way of any treaty laid in the pretensions of the United States to the navigation of the Mississippi. This had already been made plain when a committee of Congress reported (February 2, 1780) a communication from the French government, the presentation of which was significant of the later antagonistic attitude of France herself. By this the King of Spain

[1] *Diplom. Cor.*, III, 170.   [2] *Diplom. Cor.*, III, 412–415.

made known the "articles which his Catholic Majesty deems of great importance to the interests of his crown, and on which it is highly necessary that the United States explain themselves with precision and with such moderation as may consist with their essential rights.

"That the articles are:

"(1). A precise and invariable western boundary of the states.

"(2). The exclusive navigation of the river Mississippi.

"(3). The possession of the Floridas; and

"(4). The lands on the left or eastern bank of the river Mississippi.

"That in the first article it is the idea of the cabinet of Madrid that the United States extend to the westward no farther than settlements were permitted by the royal proclamation bearing date the [seventh] day of [October,] 1763.

"On the second, that the United States do not consider themselves as having any right to navigate the Mississippi, no territory belonging to them being situated thereon.

"On the third, that it is probable that the King of Spain will conquer the Floridas during the course of the present war; and in such event every cause of dispute relative thereto between Spain and the United States ought to be removed.

"On the fourth, that the lands lying on the east side of the Mississippi, whereon the settlements were prohibited by the aforesaid proclamation, are possessions of the crown of Great Britain, and proper objects against which the arms of Spain may be employed for the purpose of making a permanent conquest for the Spanish crown. That such conquest may probably be made during the present war; that therefore it would be advisable to restrain the Southern states from making any settlements or conquests in those territories; that the council of Madrid consider the United States as having no claim to those territories, either as not having had possession of them before the present war, or not having any foundation for a claim in the right of the sovereignty of Great Britain, whose dominion they have abjured."[1]

It cannot be said that Spain did not state her position with absolute clearness. It is also the first hint of an understanding

[1] *Diplom. Cor.*, III, 489.

between France and Spain that when peace came the Alleghanies should be the boundaries of the United States, an understanding in which there is little doubt that there was also bound up the hope of France to recover to herself the main part of the great territory so recklessly yielded in 1763.

In his despatch of November 6, 1780, to the President of Congress,[1] Jay detailed the events connected with his mission. The use of the word "events" was a figure of speech, as, in fact, there were no events; there was practically simple inaction on the part of Spain. Her aid was confined to that of guaranteeing bills drawn against Mr. Jay to the extent of some fourteen thousand dollars to be payable in three years. Florida Blanca also, in a note of June 7, 1780,[2] suggested the possibility of becoming responsible for bills to the extent of a hundred thousand pounds, if "Congress should engage to build without delay some handsome frigates and other smaller vessels of war" for Spain, to be manned by Americans and sailed under Spanish colors and to be used for the interception of the British East Indian commerce.

The proposition in itself was an absurdity such as could only have been devised by Spanish officialdom of the period. Even if Congress had been in a situation to "build, equip, and man" them, two years at least would have elapsed before the squadron of "four good frigates and some other lighter vessels" could be made ready. Jay endeavored to impress upon the Spanish minister of state that money was necessary in the beginning to undertake such work and that no funds were available; that what Congress desired was a loan outright for the repayment of which the credit of the United States would be pledged.

The situation of the American minister became very embarrassing as it was only by courtesy of the bankers that the bills drawn against him, small in actual amount as they were, were not sent to protest. His notes to the minister of foreign affairs were left unanswered and his treatment altogether was one of extreme humiliation and anxiety.

Throughout the whole period Spain held rigidly to her views already expressed regarding the navigation of the Mississippi, and in a conference which took place September 23, 1780, the

[1] *Diplom. Cor.*, IV, 112 *et seq.*   [2] *Ibid.*, IV, 115.

Spanish attitude was expressed in the notes of Mr. Jay as follows: "The count . . . made several observations tending to show the importance of this object to Spain and its determination to adhere to it, saying with some degree of warmth that unless Spain could exclude all nations from the Gulf of Mexico they might as well admit all; that the king would never relinquish it; that the minister regarded it as a principal object to be obtained by the war; and *that obtained*, he should be perfectly easy whether Spain procured any other cession; that he considered it far more important than the acquisition of Gibraltar; and that if they did not get it, it was a matter of indifference to him whether the English possessed Mobile or not." [1]

In such manner, with almost absolute indifference on the part of Spain to the cause of the United States, with cynical disregard of the straits to which the war in which both were engaged subjected the latter, and with no thought but of despoiling them, did Jay's efforts at negotiation stagger on from month to month. The plain truth as to financial assistance was no doubt Spain's own chronic poverty. But while thus poverty-stricken at home, without resources in money, energy, or excess of population, she was greedily grasping to extend an empire already vastly greater than her ability to populate or control, and nearly the whole of which was to slip from her hold within the next forty years.

But the spell of supposed Spanish power was still over the world, and so eager was youthful America to form an alliance with this decrepit government, that Congress withdrew from its position regarding the Mississippi, and Jay was informed under date of May 28, 1781, that "a reconsideration of that subject determined Congress on the 15th day of February last to recede from that instruction (of October 4, 1780) so far as it insisted on their claim to the navigation of that river below the thirty-first degree of north latitude and to free port or ports below the same.[2] This was a complete yielding of the position taken in the letters of October 6 and 17, 1780, the latter of which had been drawn by Madison[3] and represented an attitude from which he never swerved. The former of these directed a strict adherence to the preceding in-

[1] *Diplom. Cor.*, IV, 146.   [2] *Ibid.*, IV, 453.
[3] Madison, *Writings*, edited by Hunt, I, 82.

structions as to boundaries and an insistence on the navigation of the Mississippi for the citizens of the United States in common with the subjects of his Catholic Majesty as well as a free port or ports below the northern limit of West Florida for the use of the former. The letter of October 17 entered at length into the demands of Spain, the occupancy of territory east of the Mississippi and north of the thirty-first degree of latitude by right of conquest, and stated "particularly and ably the right of the United States to the free navigation of the river Mississippi, and enumerates the various reasons which induce them (Congress) to decline relinquishing it." [1]

"The minister, however, did not at any time enter into the merits of these arguments nor appear in the least affected by them. His answer to them all was that the King of Spain must have the Gulf of Mexico to himself; that the maxims of policy adopted in the management of their colonies required it; and that he had hoped the friendly disposition [!] shown by this court toward us would have induced a compliance on the part of Congress." [2]

Jay had received, May 18, a copy of the resolution of the 15th of February, 1781, through Mr. Lovell. It had been brought to Cadiz by the *Virginia*. "It is remarkable," says Jay, "that none of the journals or gazettes nor the letters from Congress which Mr. Lovell gave me reason to expect ever came to my hands. But as all the papers brought by the *Virginia* passed through the hands of the governor of Cadiz, and afterward through the post-office, the suppression of some of them may be easily accounted for." [3] As Jay had not received the copy of the resolution officially, he thought he was justified in delaying to bring the matter before the Spanish minister, though it became evident that the latter was aware of the existence of the resolution. "My only difficulty," said Jay, "arose from this single question, whether I could prudently risk acting on a presumption either that Spain did not already or would not soon be acquainted with the contents of this instruction. If such a presumption had been admissible, I should, without the least hesitation, have played the game a little further, keeping this instruction in my hands as a trump card, to prevent a separate peace between Spain and Great Britain, in case such an event

[1] Jay to President of Congress, October 3, 1781, *Diplom. Cor.*, IV, 738.
[2] *Ibid.*
[3] *Ibid.*, 740.

should otherwise prove inevitable. Had Spain been at peace with our enemies, and offered to acknowledge, guarantee, and fight for our independence, provided we would yield them this point (as once seemed to be the case), I should for my own part have no more hesitation about it now than I had then. But Spain being now at war with Great Britain to gain her own objects, she doubtless will prosecute it full as vigorously as if she fought for our objects. There was and is little reason to suppose that such a cession would render her exertions more vigorous or her aid more liberal. The effect which an alliance between Spain and America would have on Britain and other nations would certainly be in our favor, but whether more so than the free navigation of the Mississippi is less certain. The cession of this navigation will, in my opinion, render a future war with Spain inevitable, and I shall look upon my subscribing to the one as fixing the certainty of the other." [1]

This was both sound policy and sound sense, in which Jay was supported by Franklin, who, with a prescience far beyond that of Congress, wrote Jay from France, October 2, 1880: "Poor as we are yet as I know we shall be rich, I would rather agree with them to buy, at a great price, the whole of their right on the Mississippi than to sell a drop of its waters. A neighbor might as well ask me to sell my street door." [2] Jay felt obliged, however, to mention the fact of the change in the views of Congress, and did so in conversation May 23, following this up by a note of July 2, 1781, stating "that Congress, in order to manifest in the most striking manner the sincerity of their professions to his majesty, and with a view that the common cause may immediately reap all advantages naturally to be expected from a cordial and permanent union between France, Spain, and the United States, have authorized me to agree to such terms relative to the point in question as to remove the difficulties to which it has hitherto given occasion." [3]

It was not until July 11 that Jay received the official information of the action of Congress, February 15, conveyed in a letter from the President of Congress of May 28. Nothing came from the Spanish minister but two short notes acknowledging the reception of those of Mr. Jay; but as an issue of a conference at St. Ildefonso

[1] *Diplom. Cor.* IV, 743. [2] *Ibid.*, IV, 75.
[3] *Ibid.*, VI, 747.

September 19, 1781, Mr. Jay submitted, on September 22, propositions for a basis of amity and alliance[1] which included two of extreme importance, as follows:

"VI. The United States shall relinquish to his Catholic Majesty, and in future forbear to use or attempt to use, the navigation of the river Mississippi from the thirty-first degree of north latitude—that is, from the point where it leaves the United States—down to the ocean."

"VIII. That the United States shall guarantee to his Catholic Majesty all his dominions in North America."

Jay, however, most fortunately and wisely added on his own responsibility a statement that this offer must necessarily be limited by the duration of the pending circumstances, "and consequently that if the acceptance of it should, together with the proposed alliance, be postponed to a general peace, the United States will cease to consider themselves bound to any propositions or offers which he may now make on their behalf."[2] He was upheld throughout by a resolution in Congress April 30, 1782,[3] which might be read as a withdrawal of the offer itself, an interpretation no doubt intended by Madison, its introducer and a vehement opponent of such concession.

Nothing could have been more fortunate than Spain's vacillations and procrastination. They saved the United States from an unhappy situation whose only solution later was war or a dismemberment of the newly formed Confederation and the erection of a separate sovereignty west of the Alleghanies.

A forcible indication of Spain's intentions appeared in the Madrid *Gazette* of March 12, 1782, which mentioned the arrival of a letter from the commander-in-chief at Havana giving news of an expedition of sixty-five militia and sixty Indians which had left St. Louis January 2 and had seized the post of St. Joseph on Lake Michigan, "which the English occupied at two hundred and twenty leagues distant from that of the above-mentioned St. Louis. . . . They made prisoners of the few English they found in it. . . . Don Eugenio Purre took possession, in the name of the king, of that place and its dependencies, and of the river of the Illinois; in con-

[1] *Diplom. Cor.*, IV, 760–762.   [2] *Ibid.*, IV, 761.
[3] *Ibid.*, V, 380.

sequence whereof the standard of his majesty was there displayed during the whole time."[1] As Jay well said, it was not necessary for him to swell his letter with remarks on this subject; the meaning was self-evident: it was carrying out the views as to the occupancy of the lands east of the Mississippi expressed in the fourth proposition of Spain in the communication laid before Congress February 2, 1780.[2] The Spanish action, however, was more than offset by Clark's expedition and his capture of Kaskaskia, in southwestern Illinois, and it was this little border army which gave the United States the claim of actual conquest and occupancy of this region which became of such importance in the discussion of the final settlement of our boundaries. The one real success of the Spanish arms was in the capture by Galvez, the young governor of Louisiana, of the British posts in West Florida, that at Pensacola falling May 9, 1781, a success which gave Congress much concern as giving Spain a claim to the region in the coming negotiations for peace.

Franklin was of one mind with Jay as to the attitude of Spain. "I am surprised," he writes, "at the dilatory, reserved manner of your court. I know not to what amount you have obtained aids from it, but if they are not considerable it were to be wished you had never been sent there, as the slight they put upon our offered friendship is very disreputable to us, and of course hurtful to our affairs elsewhere. I think they are short-sighted and don't look very far into futurity, or they would seize with avidity so excellent an opportunity of securing a neighbor's friendship, which may hereafter be of great consequence to their American affairs. If I were in Congress I should advise your being instructed to thank them for past favors and take your leave."[3] He gave this advice a little later in any case. He wrote April 22, 1782: "Here you are greatly wanted, for messengers begin to come and go and there is much talk of a treaty proposed, but I can neither make nor agree to propositions of peace without the assistance of my colleagues. I wish, therefore, that you would resolve upon the journey and render yourself here as soon as possible. You could be of infinitive service. Spain has taken four years to consider

[1] *Diplom. Cor.*, V, 363.   [2] *Supra.*, 18.
[3] Franklin to Jay, January 19, 1782, *Diplom. Cor.*, V, 119.

whether she would treat with us or not. Give her forty, and let us in the meantime mind our own business."[1]

Jay accepted Franklin's advice, and in June, 1782, left Madrid for Paris, leaving Mr. Carmichael as chargé d'affaires. The dismal failure of the final attack on Gibraltar, September 13, 1782, paved the way to a general pacification. Peace negotiations began with both France and her Spanish ally, secretly and actively opposed to the broad and generous treatment of the United States by Great Britain. Both allies would gladly have seen the United States hemmed in by the Alleghanies, and both lent their efforts to this. Count d'Aranda, the Spanish ambassador at Paris, charged with the Spanish negotiations for peace, soon made known the reason for Spain's unwillingness to enter into alliance with the United States on the bases offered by stating Spain's real expectancies. He insisted, "First, that the western country had never belonged to, or been claimed as belonging to, the ancient colonies. That previous to the last war it had belonged to France, and after its cession to Britain remained a distinct part of her dominions, until, by the conquest of West Florida and certain ports on the Mississippi and Illinois, it became vested in Spain. Secondly, that supposing the Spanish right of conquest did not extend over *all* that country, still it was possessed by free and independent nations of Indians whose lands we could not with any propriety consider as belonging to us."[2] A few days later Count d'Aranda sent Mr. Jay a map "with his proposed lines marked on it in red ink. He ran it from a lake near the confines of Georgia, but east of the Flint River, to the confluence of the Kanawha with the Ohio, thence round the western shores of Lakes Erie and Huron, and thence round Lake Michigan to Lake Superior."[3]

The evident association of France with Spain, to despoil the United States of territories into parts of which had already begun the stream of settlers from Virginia and North Carolina, brought a separate settlement between Great Britain and the United States, and the signing of a provisional treaty, November 30, 1782, effected without the knowledge of France or Spain as to details, and in direct, and as we now know, necessary disregard of the explicit

[1] *Diplom. Cor.*, V, 320.
[2] Jay to Livingston, November 17, 1782, *Ibid.*, VI, 22.   [3] *Ibid.*, 23.

instructions of Congress to "make the most candid and confidential communications upon all subjects to the ministers of our generous ally, the King of France, and to undertake nothing in the negotiations for peace or truce without their knowledge and concurrence, and ultimately to govern yourselves by their advice and opinion."[1]

The action of France in supporting Spain's claims, and in urging, even so early as 1781, the presentation of the American "demands with the greatest moderation and reserve, save independence,"[2] cannot now be regarded as due to a mere desire to please Spain. Such support can only be understood when we recognize that French statesmen had already begun to look to Spain for the restitution of Louisiana, which had been given her twenty years before, and which was to be forced from her by France twenty years later. Vergennes himself attempted its recovery for France, and "Spain was willing to return it, but asked a price which, although the mere reimbursement of expenses, exceeded the means of the French treasury."[3]

Had the instructions from Congress been followed, the new republic would have ended with the Alleghanies; Canada would have been bounded by the Ohio, and Spanish North America would have reached east to Georgia and the Kanawha. The large views of the British government of the period on one hand, the independent action of the American commissioners on the other, saved the United States from so serious a situation. The Spanish and French Bourbons were thwarted in reality by the adhesion of England to the old colonial charters.[4] It is true that there were intrigues later, on the part of British officials in Canada, to restore the Quebec boundary of 1774; and Spain, as will be seen, conspired to separate Kentucky and the South-west from the Union, but with slight adjustment the lines consented to by Shelburne were to stand until carried to the Pacific, at the expense of the power which had desired to restrain the Union to, roughly, what are now New England and the Atlantic states north of Florida.

The time has come for Americans to recognize the magnanimity, taking the word in its broadest sense, of the English ministry

---

[1] Secret Journals, *Diplomatic Correspondence*, IV, 477 and 505.
[2] Report of Conference to Congress, May 28, 1781, *Dip. Cor.*, IV, 453–457.
[3] Adams, *United States*, I, 353.   [4] Winsor, *The Westward Movement*, 213.

which made the peace of 1783. The names of Shelburne, Oswald, Jay, Franklin, and Adams are those of the men who stood at the parting of the ways and guided so fortunately the affairs of the two great branches of the Anglo-Saxon race at a most critical period for both. The first held, following the views of Adam Smith and Dr. Price, that it was "better by far for England that North America should become a powerful sovereignty, controlled by men of English blood, embracing the whole Mississippi Valley, than that that fertile valley should be subjected to the paralyzed power of Spain; and that the English-speaking people of America should in this way be so weakened as to be permanently dependent upon an alliance with France. It was on these principles that the peace of 1782–3 was negotiated."[1]

The deep disappointment of Spain was expressed in a paper submitted to the king by the Spanish negotiator, Count d'Aranda, "The independence of the English colonies has been recognized. It is for me a subject of grief and fear. France had but few possessions in America, but she was bound to consider that Spain, her most intimate ally, had many, and that she now stands exposed to terrible reverses. From the beginning France has acted against her true interests in encouraging and supporting this independence, and so I have often declared to the minister of that nation."[2]

It was not until February 22, 1783 that the Spanish government was able to bring itself to declare its acceptance of the situation. The foreign minister, Florida Blanca, then informed La Fayette, who at the moment was at Madrid, in a note which carried a

[1] Wharton, Introduction to *Diplomatic Correspondence*, p. 328. "It is impossible," says Lecky, "not to be struck with the skill, hardihood, and good fortune that marked the American negotiation. Everything the United States could with any shadow of plausibility demand from England they obtained, and much of what they obtained was granted them in opposition to the two great powers by whose assistance they had triumphed."—Lecky, *England in the XVIII Century*, V, 199, ed., 1893. This treaty, made with such secrecy, had also, by securing America on the side of peace, the very important result of saving Gibraltar to Great Britain. The British cabinet had "actually resolved to exchange Gibraltar for Guadeloupe when the news of the accomplished peace with America induced them to reconsider their determination."—Lecky, IV, 284. Fitzmaurice, *Life of Shelburne*, III, 305–306, 314.

[2] John Basset Moore, *American Diplomacy*, 18.

threat, that it was "his majesty's intentions to abide for the present by the limits established by the treaty of the 30th of November 1782, between the English and Americans; yet the king intends to inform himself particularly whether it can be in any way inconvenient or prejudicial to settle that affair amicably with the United States."[1]

Spain for twelve years more was to occupy the same sinister position. "All this while she was seeking to lure any one who would act in concert with her, both among the wild tribes of the South-west and among the almost as wild frontiersmen of the outlying settlements of the confederacy and the later Union."[2]

[1] Count of Florida Blanca to La Fayette, February 22, 1783, *Diplom. Cor.*, VI, 261.
[2] Winsor, *The Westward Movement*, p. 327.

CHAPTER II

DISCONTENT AND INTRIGUE IN THE SOUTH-WEST AND THE TREATY OF 1795

By the provisional treaty between the United States and Great Britain, which was to go into effect when terms of peace should be concluded between Great Britain, France, and Spain, the northern boundary of West Florida was established at the parallel of thirty-one degrees. A separate secret article however provided that, should Great Britain recover West Florida, its northern boundary should run due east from the mouth of the Yazoo in latitude 32° 28', a line established by England in 1764 for her own administrative purposes. The concession was yielded by the American commissioners as a compromise with the British negotiator, Oswald, who had endeavored to extend this boundary to the Ohio.[1]

The provisional treaty between Great Britain, France, and Spain, of January 20, 1783, made definitive as also that with the United States, September 3, 1783, yielded the Floridas to Spain without assignment of limits. When the British and American understanding came to be known, Spain naturally took her stand upon the line 32° 28' as the boundary not only established in 1764, but recognized by both England and the United States. She claimed the territory by right of conquest during the war, and when the conquest was made, the more northerly line was undoubtedly that in force. There is no gainsaying the fact of the strength of Spain's contention.

Spain during the war had also extended her posts northward and was in occupancy at Natchez and Walnut Hills, (now Vicksburg.) Settlers from the American side had been moving in under Spanish control. As soon as the secret article became known, Spain at once demanded that this region should be regarded as within the boundaries of Florida as ceded to herself, and held to her contention

[1] *Diplom. Cor.*, VI, 567.

by the continuation therein of her military posts. The American confederacy thus found itself, in 1784, with every river of its territory, leading to the Gulf of Mexico, in the hands of a power which did not dissemble its unfriendliness; and, what was of deeper importance, it was itself threatened by dissolution and civil war. The almost anarchy of the four years succeeding the revolution was Spain's opportunity, and she did not hesitate to use her advantage.

Spain's first envoy, Señor Gardoqui, with the title of chargé d'affaires, a title the modesty of which was in itself indicative of Spanish reluctance to deal with the new nation, did not arrive in the United States until May 15, 1785, nearly six years from the first effort of Congress to enter into diplomatic relations with his country. He carried plenary powers to arrange all questions of dispute, but his mission was destined to be chiefly one of intrigue for separation of the western country from the Union. He was already well known to Mr. Jay, to whom he had given much assistance in his difficulties while near the Spanish court.

It was the era of the most picturesque episode of American history—the great crossing. From 1769, when that fine type of courage and self-reliance, Daniel Boone, had gone into Kentucky, a stream of daring and independent frontiersmen had been pouring over the Alleghanies, and the region which is now Kentucky and Tennessee had nearly a hundred thousand people who, in reason and by right, looked upon the Mississippi as their proper highway to the ocean. To close this only outlet meant to them either war between the United States and Spain or the setting up of an independent West, which would settle the difficulty in its own way either by hostile operations against Spain on its own account, by a recognition of Spanish sovereignty or, as was in the minds of some, by reuniting with Great Britain.

The chaotic condition of the affairs of the American confederacy, the widespread belief, preceding the almost fortuitous forming of the constitution, in the disruption of the existing weak union of the states, and the leaning toward Spain of some of the most influential men of the West, gave Gardoqui good grounds for believing that it was possible to unite again the western country, south of the Ohio, to Louisiana. The withholding of any concession of the navigation of the great highway of the people, combined with dissatisfaction with their political status, was Gardoqui's main hope toward bringing this about. His attitude was a perfectly reasonable one. It could not be otherwise when feeling was such that Sevier, the ex-governor of Franklin, the short-lived state of a year, set up, in 1786, from the western portion of North Carolina, could write the governor of Louisiana, September 12, 1788, informing him that the inhabitants of Franklin were unanimous "in their vehement desire to form an alliance and treaty of commerce with Spain, and put themselves under her protection,"[1] Sevier continued, begging "for ammunition, money and whatever other assistance Miro could grant, to aid the contemplated separation from North Carolina;" "which," said Sevier, "has refused to accept the new constitution proposed for the confederacy, and therefore a considerable time will elapse before she becomes a member of the Union, if that event ever happen."[2]

Intrigue had begun indeed, before the arrival of Gardoqui. Miro, the acting governor at New Orleans, had entered into a treaty, May, 1784, with representatives of the various tribes of the then South-west, headed by a half-breed named McGillivray, the product of a Scotch father and an Indian mother, who desired to put his people under the protection of Spain, in anticipation of the setting up of an independent government by the western Americans.[3]

Washington, who, in addition to his other great qualities, was the greatest practical statesman of the revolutionary period, expressed in the same year after a trip to the West covering nearly seven hundred miles, his deep sense of the danger, in a letter to Governor Benjamin Harrison of Virginia. "The western states," he said, "(I speak now from my own observation) stand as it were upon a pivot. The touch of a feather would turn them any way."[4]

It was in such conditions, of which the above is necessarily but the barest sketch, that Jay, elected by Congress, May 7, 1785, secretary for foreign affairs, received from Congress, July 21,

[1] Gayarré, *Louisiana*, 257.   [2] *Ibid.*, 258.
[3] See McGillivray to Miro, *Ibid.*, 159.
[4] Washington to Harrison, October 10, 1784, *Correspondence*, IX, 63.

powers to treat with the Spanish envoy; limited, however, by instructions "that he enter into no treaty, compact or convention whatever, with the said representative of Spain, which did not stipulate our right to the navigation of the Mississippi, and the boundaries as established in our treaty with Great Britain." Gardoqui was equally explicit, his letter to Jay, May 25, 1786, stating that "the king will not permit any nation to navigate between the two banks belonging to his majesty."[1] The result was an impasse in dealing with which Jay, for once, failed to reach the high standard of judgment and statesmanship which so distinguished his fine career. On August 3, 1786, he addressed Congress in a speech advising, as the negotiation seemed otherwise impossible of accomplishment, acceptance of a treaty; one of the articles of which would stipulate that the United States would forbear the use of the navigation of the Mississippi, below their territories, but that on account of this the treaty should be limited to twenty-five or thirty years.

Jay's arguments were: "1. Because unless that matter can in some way or other be settled, the treaty, however advantageous, will not be concluded. 2. As that navigation is not *at present* important, nor will probably become much so, in less than twenty-five or thirty years, a forbearance to use it while we do not *want it* is no great sacrifice. 3. Spain now excludes us from that navigation and with a strong hand holds it against us. She will not yield it peaceably and therefore we can only acquire it by *war*. Now, as we are not prepared for a war with any power; as many of the states would be little inclined to a war with Spain for that object at this day, and as such a war would for those and a variety of obvious reasons be inexpedient, it follows that Spain will, for a long space of time yet to come, exclude us from that navigation. Why, therefore, should we not (for a valuable consideration, too) consent to forbear to use what we know is not in our power to use? 4. If Spain and the United States should part on this point, what are the latter to do? Will it after that be consistent with their dignity to permit Spain forcibly to exclude them from a right which, at the expense of a beneficial treaty, they have asserted? They will find themselves obliged either to do this, and be humiliated, or they

[1] *State Papers*, I, 249.

must attack Spain. Are they ripe and prepared for this? I wish I could say they are."[1]

The navigation interests of the North, ignoring the situation in the Western country, demanded the trade facilities which Spain was willing to offer, and were ready to sacrifice the West to these. The North felt that its own interests were being sunk, for what appeared to it a contest for an abstract right which it would require years to make into concrete value. The ocean-carrying trade was perishing under British orders in council which forbade American vessels to carry fish to the West Indies or any but British ships to carry American goods to Britain. Spanish-American ports were closed to all but Spanish vessels. The proposed treaty with Spain would open Spain and the Canaries to American products, to the lumber, tar, fish, grain, and flour which America was ready to supply so cheaply, and in such quantities. Why should this potentially great and lucrative traffic, the only one which could bring money into a country destitute of mines of gold and silver, be forgone for the benefit, still in the far future, of a small community of widely scattered frontiersmen, who would be occupied, for years to come, chiefly in fighting the Indians?

In the vote taken August 29, 1786, on the motion to repeal the instructions of a year before, exacting the right of navigation, every member present from the seven Northern states voted "aye"; every Southern member present (all the states of the South being represented except Delaware) voted "no." The motion was entered in the journal as carried. An objection brought forward next day, that the Articles of Confederation required the assent of nine states to treaties, brought a storm of debate in which the North and South were as rigidly and oppositely arrayed as they were to be seventy-five years later.

Madison, greatly depressed, wrote Jefferson: "To speak the truth, I almost despair even of [having the convention of 1786 called at Annapolis fulfill the first intent, the accomplishment of a commercial reform]. You will find the cause in a measure now before Congress, of which you will receive the detail from Colonel Monroe. I content myself with hinting that it is a proposed treaty with Spain, one article of which shuts up the Mississippi twenty-five

[1] Congress, *Secret Journals*, IV, 53–54.

or thirty years; passing by the other Southern states, figure to yourself the effect of such a stipulation on the Assembly of Virginia already jealous of Northern politics, and which will be composed of about thirty members from the Western waters; of a majority of others attached to the Western country from interests of their own, of their friends or their constituents, and of many others who, though indifferent to the Mississippi, will zealously play off the disgust of its friends against federal measures. Figure to yourself its effect upon the people at large on the Western waters, who are patiently waiting for a favorable result to the negotiation with Gardoqui, and who will consider themselves as sold by their Atlantic brethren. Will it be an unnatural consequence if they consider themselves as absolved from every federal tie, and court some protection for their betrayed rights? This protection will appear more obtainable from the maritime power of Britain, than from any other quarter; and Britain will be more ready than any other nation to seize an opportunity of embroiling our affairs. . . . As far as I can learn the assent of nine states in Congress will not at this time be got to the projected treaty, but an unsuccessful attempt by six or seven will favor the views of Spain, and be fatal I fear to an augmentation of the federal authority, if not to the little now existing. My personal situation is rendered by this business particularly mortifying. Ever since I have been out of Congress I have been inculcating on our assembly a confidence in the equal attention of Congress to the rights and interests of every part of the republic, and on the Western members in particular, the necessity of making the Union respectable by new powers to Congress if they wished Congress to negotiate with effect for the Mississippi." [1]

On September 16, 1788, the adoption of a resolution by the expiring Congress of the old confederacy that the subject "be referred to the federal government which is to assemble in March next," gave the death blow to Spain's contention. She was now to deal with a concrete government instead of with the representatives of thirteen loosely bound states.

Gardoqui returned to Spain in 1789, with nothing accomplished in the way of a treaty, leaving behind him a state of extreme tension, which Señores Saunders and Viar, who, together, were now

[1] Madison to Jefferson, August 12, 1786, *Writings*, II, 262.

the representatives of Spain near the American government, proceeded to increase by threatening letters respecting the "United States meddling with the affairs of nations who are, by treaties solemn and ratified, allied with Spain,"[1] these nations and allies being the Indians of the South-west.

The South was wiser than the North. The West's only practical outlet, in a day which knew only the creeping transport to the Atlantic seaboard of the slow-moving wagon over almost impossible mountain roads, was the Mississippi. It knew no other sea than the great river, and no other ship but the flatboat. The government of the Union must stand by their demands or the hundred thousand of population now in Tennessee and Kentucky would arrange the question in their own way, by setting up an independent government which would win the right of navigation by force of arms, or by becoming a part of the Spanish dominions. The West was seething with intrigue, and no conspirator was more deeply immersed than James Wilkinson, a Marylander, a soldier of the revolution, who was later to become general-in-chief of the American army; was to be allied with Burr's adventure; was long the paid agent of Spain, and was to play a part in American history as ignoble as that of Benedict Arnold, but more fortunate than his brother traitor through the long burial of the proofs of his villainy in the archives of Simancas.[2]

The constant and rapid flow of population across the mountains and down the Ohio added to the difficulties of the situation. There were but so many more voices to be raised in protest against the trying conditions now also accentuated by the difficulties with the Indians of the South-west, whom Spain, as mentioned, had taken under her protection. It was clear that an agreement or war must come. This was as plain to Spain as to Washington and his cabinet, and December 16, 1791, the Spanish minister for foreign affairs made known the readiness of Madrid to negotiate. William Carmichael, chargé d'affaires at Madrid, and William Short, chargé at Paris, were appointed the American commissioners, with lengthy instructions dated March 18, 1792,

[1] *State Papers*, I, 265.
[2] For copies of Wilkinson's treasonable correspondence see Gayarré, *Louisiana* (Spanish Domination).

which demanded the parallel of thirty-one degrees as a boundary, the free navigation of the river, and a place of deposit for American goods near the mouth.[1]

But Gardoqui was again the commissioner for Spain, and the American commissioners found Spanish views, as expressed by him, unchanged. In their despatch of May 5, 1793, they stated very clearly the impressions which Gardoqui had received in the United States. "He still sees them divided among themselves and without efficient government. . . . He saw some individuals of the Western country, or going to settle there, who treated their adhesion to the rest of the Union as visionary. From hence he has formed opinions, which he has not concealed from us, that the United States do not desire this navigation or the limits we ask, or at least do not desire it so generally as that they could be brought to make any general effort to obtain it. . . . He did not conceal from us that he thought it impossible the Northern, Middle, and Southern states should ever be brought to act in concert with respect to a foreign enemy out of their territory; and even if they should, that they had no means of acting efficaciously until they should have a marine —an event he regarded as never to take place, or at least to be so far off as not to be worthy of present consideration."[2]

Gardoqui's impressions did not differ so greatly from those of American statesmen at this moment. In 1794 it was the opinion of Randolph, who had succeeded Jefferson as secretary of state, that "the people of Kentucky either contemning or ignorant of the consequences, are restrained from hostility by a pack-thread. They demand the conclusion of the negotiations or a categorical answer from Spain. . . . What if the government of Kentucky should force us either to support them in their hostilities against Spain, or to disavow and renounce them, war at this moment would not be war with Spain alone. The lopping off of Kentucky from the Union is dreadful to contemplate, even if it should not attach itself to some other power."[3]

This other power was now England. Simcoe wrote to the Lords of Trade (September 1): "It is generally understood that above

---

[1] *State Papers*, I, 252–257.
[2] Carmichael and Short to secretary of state, *Ibid.*, I, 262–263.
[3] Winsor, *The Westward Movement*, 542–543.

half the inhabitants of Kentucky and the Western waters are already inclined to a connection with Great Britain." Thurston, a Kentucky observer, had just before written to Washington that a powerful faction was scheming to place the country under British protection.[1]

The French minister, Genêt, who arrived in 1793, had views which looked to reuniting Louisiana with France. He was enlisting in the West men in the French service, to act against Spain, which was now (1794) at war with France; and was commissioning officers, among whom, as major general, was George Rogers Clark, now through drink but the shadow of a once great figure.

The whole so-called civilized world was, however, in one of its periodic throes of social reconstruction; the French revolution was in full progress; the French nation was spreading its new-found views with the sword; America, which had but just come to its real birth, in the newly formed constitution, was still with the unformed mind and the weakness of infantile conditions, and apparently, to the European observer, and to many patriotic but despairing Americans, ready for despoilment.

On November 24, 1794, in the month and year in which the new treaty between Great Britain and the United States was signed in London by John Jay and Lord Grenville, Thomas Pinckney, American minister in London, was commissioned envoy extraordinary to attempt to conclude the long abortive negotiations at Madrid. He arrived June 28, 1795, and found changed conditions. Godoy, Duke of Alcudia, soon to be known as Prince of the Peace, from the peace with France signed at Bale, July 22, 1795, was now an all powerful minister. The treaty with Great Britain, in which was seen a possible alliance between that country and the United States, and the former's threatening posture toward Spain, were taken to heart by Godoy,[2] and on October 27, 1795, was signed a treaty which conceded all the United States could fairly ask and more than could have been hoped. It stands a memorial of elevation of mind and breadth of view not generally accorded the young favorite of Charles IV and his queen, and who was far more the statesman and able man of affairs than history has generally allowed. Free ships were to make free goods; a convention was

[1] Winsor, *The Westward Movement*, 542–543.   [2] Godoy, *Memoirs*, I, 458.

arranged to consider the claims for depredations upon American shipping in the war just ended between Spain and France; the claim of the United States to a southern boundary of 31° was agreed to; the joint navigation of the Mississippi in its whole length, assured; a right of deposit of American merchandise at New Orleans without duties was granted, and after three years, if the right at New Orleans should be withdrawn, another place should be substituted; both nations were "expressly to restrain by force all hostilities on the part of the Indian nations living within their boundary; so that Spain will not suffer her Indians to attack the citizens of the United States, nor the Indians inhabiting their territory; nor will the United States permit these last mentioned Indians to commence hostilities against the subjects of his Catholic Majesty, or his Indians, in any manner whatever"; all places held by Spain in what now became American territory were to be evacuated within six months.

Article 7 stipulated that "in all cases of seizure, detention or arrest, for debts contracted, or offenses committed, by any citizen or subject of the one party, within the jurisdiction of the other, the same shall be made and prosecuted by order and authority of law only, and according to the regular course of proceedings usual in such cases. The citizens and subjects of both parties shall be allowed to employ such advocates, solicitors, notaries, agents, and factors as they may judge proper in all their affairs, and in all their trials at law, in which they may be concerned before the tribunals of the other party; and such agents shall have free access to be present at the proceedings in such causes and at the taking of all examinations and evidence which may be exhibited in the said trials."[1] This article was to bear a momentous part in Spanish-American diplomatic discussion throughout the whole of the next century.

[1] For the text of this treaty see *State Papers*, I, 546–549. The treaty with Great Britain (1794) did not stand on so high a plane. It set aside the principle of exemption from seizure of enemy goods in neutral ships and made all materials for ship-building contraband. When the treaty was made public in 1795, the Spanish minister to the United States, the Marquis de Yrujo, very properly took strong exception to the articles (17 and 18) dealing with these subjects, as abrogating express stipulations with Spain; as also to article 3, which stipulated that Great Britain should have the right of free navigation of the Mississippi from its source to the ocean. (For this protest see *State Papers*, I, 14.)

Washington, when the treaty had passed the Senate, "expressed the hope that it would prove soothing to the inhabitants of the Western waters. . . . He little knew that Judge Innes, in whom he had confided all along to quiet the discontent, was deep in the nefarious plot of Sebastian—the former being a circuit judge of the United States, and the other the Chief Justice of Kentucky. The infamous Sebastian engaged to give his services to Spain to subserve her interests and subvert those of his own country, for a yearly pension of $2,000, and he received the stipend regularly. After thus debasing himself, Sebastian, accompanied by Power,[1] in the spring of 1796 sailed from New Orleans for Philadelphia, and thence passed westward with propositions from Carondelet [who had succeeded Miro in 1791 as governor of Louisiana]: To prepare Kentucky for a revolution, and to give them money to organize the project $100,000 will be sent to Kentucky. When independence is declared, Fort Massac [near the junction of the Ohio and Mississippi] shall be occupied by Spanish troops, and $100,000 shall be applied in supporting the garrison. The northern bounds of Spanish territory are to be a line running east from the mouth of the Yazoo River to the Tombigbee, while all north of such a line shall, except the reservation recently fortified at the Chickasaw bluff, belong to the revolted state, which shall enter into a defensive alliance with Spain. The new treaty of San Lorenzo shall not be observed; but the new state shall enjoy the navigation of the Mississippi. Ten thousand dollars were to be sent in sugar barrels up the river to Wilkinson, now the general-in-chief of the American army!" part of which safely arrived; the remainder being lost through the murder by the boatmen of the messenger in charge. "Neither Wilkinson nor Judge Innes thought it prudent to bring the felons to justice and they were hurried off beyond the Mississippi."[2]

Such, even now, was the uncertainty of the outcome of the treaty; but events were rapidly altering Western conditions. The sweep of population across the Alleghanies was in full progress, and the conspirators had to deal with new forces, whose prepossessions were for the Union, backed as they now were by a treaty which promised at least all that Kentucky demanded.

[1] Thomas Power, who professed to be a wandering naturalist in America.
[2] Winsor, *The Westward Movement*, 556-557.

The treaty was, however, really but a stop-gap to difficulties; the situation was of a character which forbade permanent quiet. Jefferson, as vice-president, in 1798 was writing Madison: "Very acrimonious altercations are going on between the Spanish minister and the executive, and at the Natchez something worse than mere altercation. If hostilities have not begun there it has not been for want of endeavors to bring them on by our agents."[1]

Much more than the questions of the south-west frontier was involved; the many seizures of American vessels by those of Spain, and the reception in her ports and condemnation there of those seized by French privateers and cruisers, were subjects of bitter correspondence in which right certainly laid with the United States. Spain was, however, under the heel of France, and it is at the door of the latter the iniquities complained of should be laid, instead of at that of the moribund state, which was practically powerless. More than three hundred American vessels had been seized by France in the latter half of 1796, and Spanish ports were used by the French privateers as their own. Spain was helpless.

But the main difficulty was in the impossibility that the men who settled Kentucky and Tennessee should accept the dominancy by the King of Spain of the right of way to the sea. An able historian sums up the feeling which had grown in the South and West: "Of all foreign powers Spain alone stood in such a position as to make violence seem sooner or later inevitable, even to the pacific Jefferson; and every Southern or Western state looked to the military occupation of Mobile, Pensacola, and New Orleans as a future political necessity. By a sort of tacit agreement the ordinary rules of American politics were admitted not to apply to this case. To obtain Pensacola, Mobile, and New Orleans, the warmest states-rights champions in the South, even John Taylor of Carolina and John Randolph of Roanoke, were ready to employ every instrument of centralization. On the Southern and Western states this eagerness to expel Spain from their neighborhood acted like a magnet, affecting all without regard to theories or parties. . . . They could not endure that their wheat, tobacco, and timber should have value only by the sufferance of a Spanish official and a corporal's guard of Spanish soldiers at New Orleans and Mobile.

[1] Jefferson to Madison, January 25, 1798, *Writings*, VIII, 191.

Hatred of the Spaniard was to the Tennesseean as natural as hatred of an Indian, and contempt for the rights of the Spanish government was no more singular than for those of an Indian tribe. Against Indians and Spaniards the Western settler held loose notions of law; his settled purpose was to drive both races from the country and to take their lands. . . . In the end far more than half the territory of the United States was despoiled of the Spanish empire, rarely acquired with perfect propriety. To sum up in a single word, Spain had immense influence over the United States; but it was the influence of the whale over its captors—the charm of a huge, helpless, and profitable victim." [1]

[1] Henry Adams, *History of the United States*, I, 338–340.

CHAPTER III

THE TRANSFERS OF LOUISIANA

A FEW years, however, were to bring a complete and unexpected change of situation. Bonaparte had appeared on the stage of world politics and had become the boldest and most impressive actor upon it; and upon no country did his action have more momentous influence than upon the United States. On September 30, 1800, was signed the treaty between France and the United States nominally ending the difficulties which had brought about a *quasi* war between the two countries, and the next day, October 1, was signed at St. Ildefonso a treaty by which Spain ceded to France "the colony or province of Louisiana with the same extent it now has in the hands of Spain, that it had when France possessed it, and such as it ought to be according to the treaties subsequently passed between Spain and other states."[1]

The price paid by Napoleon was the easy promise to erect for the heir presumptive of the Duchy of Parma, the nephew and son-in-law of Charles IV of Spain, a kingdom of which Tuscany was to form the chief part, and to procure the consent of Austria and other states thereto. This treaty was preliminary to another signed at Madrid, March 31, 1801, which definitely fixed the status of the new kingdom of Etruria, which was to be regarded as the property of Spain and an inalienable appanage of its royal house.[2] Its fifth article arranged to carry into execution the preliminary agreement of the preceding year regarding the cession of Louisiana.

Talleyrand had been the *deus ex machina* in bringing about this change, which, in a way so unforeseen by himself and to his deep

[1] Treaty of St. Ildefonso, October 1, 1800, *State Papers*, II, 576.
[2] Art. 6 of treaty, *Ibid.*, II, 511.

vexation, was to be so momentous to the United States. So early as 1798 in his instructions to Guillemardet, French minister to Madrid he had said: "There are no other means of putting an end to the ambition of the Americans than that of shutting them up within the limits which nature seems to have traced for them; but Spain is not in a condition to do this work alone. She cannot, therefore, hasten too quickly to engage the aid of a preponderating power, yielding to it a small part of her immense domains in order to preserve the rest. Let the court of Madrid cede these districts (the Floridas and Louisiana) to France, and from that moment the power of America is bounded by the limits which may suit the interests and the tranquility of France and Spain to assign her. The French republic, mistress of these two provinces, will be a wall of brass forever impenetrable to the combined efforts of England and America. The Court of Madrid has nothing to fear from France." [1]

The scheme of a buffer state, however, between the United States and the Spanish provinces was not a sufficient bait. It failed, and the subject did not move again until the conquering will of Napoleon, now First Consul, came into the question. He failed, however, to add the Floridas to the cession, the King of Spain through sentiment holding with unexpected tenacity to these as being part of the national domain originally settled by Spain.

Rumors of the transfer of Louisiana, as arranged by the treaties mentioned between Spain and France, had begun to come to the United States early in 1801 through Mr. Rufus King, United States minister in London,[2] and these rumors were sufficiently convincing to cause Madison, Jefferson's secretary of state, to instruct Livingston, United States minister to France, and then about to sail, respecting the anxiety of the United States government to obtain the Floridas, or if it should not be possible to obtain both, at least West Florida.[3]

Mr. King was able, November 20, 1801, to send a copy of the treaty of March 31, 1801, the fifth clause of which removed any

[1] Instructions données au Citoyen Guillemardet, May 20–June 19, 1798, *Archives des Aff. Étr.* MSS. Henry Adams, *United States*, I, 355 et seq.
[2] King to Madison, March 29 and June 1, 1801, *State Papers*, II, 509.
[3] September 28, 1801, *Ibid.*, II, 510.

doubt of the cession.[1] Livingston, at Paris, could get nothing but false or evasive replies from Talleyrand, who was French minister of foreign affairs. Livingston wrote April 24, 1802: "The minister will give no answer to any inquiries I make on the subject. He will not say what their boundaries are, what are their intentions, and when they are to take possession. And what appears very extraordinary to me, is that by a letter I have just received from Mr. Pinckney [American minister to Spain] I find that he still supposes the Floridas are not included in the cession; and he writes me that he has made a proposition to purchase them, which lies before the minister with whom he is to have a conference on the subject. You may, however, be fully assured that the Floridas are given to France; that they are at this moment fitting out an armament from here to take possession. This will be commanded by General Bernadotte."[2]

So late as June 2, 1802, even Señor d'Azara, the Spanish minister at Paris, was unable, though willing to give what information he could, to state in reply to a letter of Livingston, whether the Floridas had been included in the cession to France.[3]

Mr. Madison wrote, May 11, 1802, to Mr. Charles Pinckney in Madrid: "We are still without a line from you since your arrival in Madrid and feel an increasing solicitude to hear from you on the subject of Louisiana. . . . What the intentions of Spain may be we wait to learn from you. Verbal information, from unofficial sources, has led us to infer that she disowns the instrument of cession, and will rigorously oppose it. Should the cession actually fail from this or any other cause, and Spain retain New Orleans and the Floridas, I repeat to you the wish of the President that every effort and address be employed to obtain the arrangement by which the territory on the east side of the Mississippi, including New Orleans, may be ceded to the United States, and the Mississippi made a common boundary, with a common use of its navigation for them and Spain. The inducements to be held out to Spain were intimated in your original instructions on this point. I am charged by the President now to add that you may not only receive and transmit a proposition of guarantee of her territory beyond the Mississippi, as a condition of her ceding to the United

[1] *State Papers*, II, 511.   [2] *Ibid.*, II, 515.   [3] *Ibid.*, II, 519.

States the territory including New Orleans on this side, but, in case it be necessary, may make the proposition yourself, in the forms required by our constitution. You will infer from this enlargement of your authority how much importance is attached to the object in question, as securing a precious acquisition to the United States as well as a natural and quiet boundary with Spain."[1]

By September Livingston was convinced that the Floridas were not included in the cession,[2] and he had, acting upon his instructions, informed Joseph Bonaparte "that we had no wish to extend our boundary across the Mississippi."[3]

This proposition conveyed by Madison of guarantee to Spain, so startling from our present point of view, is proof of the limited vision of the administration; a limitation the narrowness of which is accentuated by Jefferson's extraordinary statement two years later in a letter to Dr. Joseph Priestly: "Whether we remain in one confederacy, or form into Atlantic and Mississippi confederacies, I believe not very important to either part."[4] It is no excuse to say that the statesmen named were not above their fellows in this respect; that no one dreamed at the time of a trans-Mississippi empire; the fact remains that it required Napoleon himself to open their minds to the true destiny which lay before their country and rouse an ideal before which even the scruples of Jefferson on the constitutional question involved gave way. That Jefferson's views as to the trans-Mississippi and the proposition to guaranty the vast region to Spain came to naught, was an enormous good fortune which came to the United States through Napoleon alone.

The authority to give this extraordinary promise was somewhat modified a year later by instructions saying: "The guarantee of the country beyond the Mississippi is another condition which it is well to avoid if possible, not only for the reasons you already possess, but because it seems not improbable, from the communication of Mr. King, that Great Britain is meditating plans for the emancipation and independence of the whole of the

[1] *State Papers*, II, 517.
[2] Livingston to Madison, September 1, 1802, *Ibid.*, II, 525.
[3] Livingston to Jefferson, October 28, 1802, *Ibid.*, II, 525.
[4] Letter to Priestly, January 29, 1804, *Writings*, VIII, 295.

American continent south of the United States, and consequently such a guarantee would not only be disagreeable to her, but embarrassing to the United States. Should war indeed precede your conventional arrangements with France, the guarantee, if admitted at all, must necessarily be suspended and limited in such a manner as to be applicable only to the state of things which may be fixed by a peace";[1] a modification induced by information from Mr. Addington to Mr. King that if war should happen "it would, perhaps, be one of their first steps to occupy New Orleans."[2] Addington at the same time disclaimed any desire on the part of England of permanent possession.

The thought of the possession of New Orleans and the Floridas by what was now in Europe an all-conquering France, stirred even the pacific Jefferson to something of a warlike impulse. In a letter of April 18, 1802, to Livingston in Paris, he said: "There is on the globe one single spot, the possessor of which is our natural and habitual enemy. It is New Orleans. . . . France placing herself in that door assumes to us the attitude of defiance. Spain might have retained it quietly for years. Her pacific dispositions, her feeble state, would induce her to increase our facilities there, so that her possession of the place would hardly be felt by us, and it would not perhaps be very long before some circumstance might arise which might make the cession of it to us the price of something of more worth to her. Not so can it ever be in the hands of France. The impetuosity of her temper, the energy and restlessness of her character, placed in a point of eternal friction with us, and our character, which, though quiet and loving peace and the pursuit of wealth, is high-minded, despising wealth in competition with insult or injury, enterprising and energetic as any nation on earth, these circumstances render it impossible that France and the United States can continue long friends when they meet in so irritable a position. They as well as we must be blind if they do not see this; and we must be very improvident if we do not begin to make arrangements on that hypothesis. The day that France takes possession of New Orleans fixes the sentence which is to restrain her forever within her low

[1] Madison to Livingston and Monroe, May 28, 1803, *State Papers*, II, 562.
[2] King to secretary of state, April 2, 1803, *Ibid.*, II, 551.

water-mark. It seals the union of two nations who in conjunction can maintain exclusive possession of the ocean. From that moment we must marry ourselves to the British fleet and nation. We must turn all our attention to a maritime force, for which our resources place us on very high grounds; and having formed and cemented together a power which may render reinforcement of her settlements here impossible to France, make the first cannon which shall be fired in Europe the signal for tearing up any settlement she may have made, and for holding the two continents of America in sequestration for the common purposes of the united British and American nations."[1]

Jefferson's abstractions and French leanings were scattered to nothingness by the danger which the real common sense at the base of his character made clear to him. He also wrote Mr. Dupont de Nemours, a French gentleman returning from America to France and whom he selected to carry the despatches giving these views: "I wish you to be possessed of the subject because you may be able to impress on the government of France the inevitable consequence of their taking possession of Louisiana; and though, as I here mention, the cession of New Orleans and the Floridas to us would be a palliation, yet I believe it would be no more, and that this measure will cost France, and perhaps not very long hence, a war which will annihilate her on the ocean and place that element under the despotism of two nations—which I am not reconciled to the more because my own would be one of them."[2] Brave phrases which were, however, but the expression of a passing feeling, and which in the bitter years of national humiliation, soon to come at the hands of both France and Great Britain, it had been well to have changed to action. They were the more extraordinary, too, as coming from one whose ideas of a naval force were bounded by trifling gun-boats, and whose use for dry docks was principally to lay up therein the few frigates we possessed, unmanned and dismantled.

While, however, using the bold words which were to be carried by Dupont to Napoleon, and while bent upon precipitating a crisis by threats the more astonishing as coming from a man who

[1] Jefferson, *Writings*, VIII, 143 (Putnam's, 1897).
[2] Jefferson to Dupont de Nemours, April 25, 1802, *Works*, IV, 435.

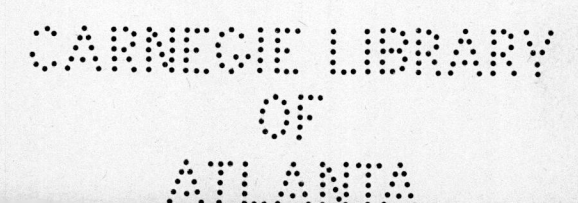

had apparently been bent upon reducing to nullity the little navy we had, Jefferson weakly attempted to influence Talleyrand by a message derogatory both to his own character and good sense; representing the overthrow of the Federal party as an American rehabilitation of Talleyrand, whose astonishing venality in his demand of payment for his services from the American commissioners who negotiated the French treaty of 1800, had been exposed in the previous administration;[1] a message which in itself could be read as nullifying the thunder carried by Dupont, even had Napoleon, an impossible supposition, been disposed to notice it.

The transfer of Louisiana to French authority had been delayed by the inability or unwillingness of Napoleon to meet the conditions of the treaty of March, 1801, regarding the new kingdom of Etruria, in such manner at least as would satisfy the awakened conscience of the weak-minded king, supported as he now was by Godoy, who had returned to power after the treaty of October 1, 1800. Talleyrand, however, was directed by Napoleon, July 27, 1801, to demand of Spain the authorization to take possession of Louisiana,[2] and in preparation for its occupancy detailed directions were given October 21, 1801, to Berthier, minister of war, to complete arrangements for an imposing expedition which was fitting out at Flushing, Havre, Brest, Lorient, Rochefort, Cadiz, and Toulon to crush the government by the blacks under Toussaint l'Ouverture in Santo Domingo,[3] but which was later to form the garrison of the transatlantic empire repossessed by France. Napoleon's brother-in-law, Leclerc, was designated as commander-in-chief, with Villaret, Joyeuse, and Latouche-Treville, in command of the fleet of thirty-three ships of the line and twenty-one frigates, besides transports, the main body of which left Brest November 22, 1801. On January 29, 1802, they were, except those driven back by gales to European ports (among which was the Spanish admiral in command of the contingent which Spain was ordered by Napoleon to furnish) finally assembled in Samaná Bay.

Napoleon, moved by the prospect of the certain subjugation of Santo Domingo, reversed the solemn declaration in his

---

[1] *Cf.* Adams, I, 412. [2] Napoleon's *Correspondence*, VII, 210.
[3] *Ibid.*, VII, 297, 320.

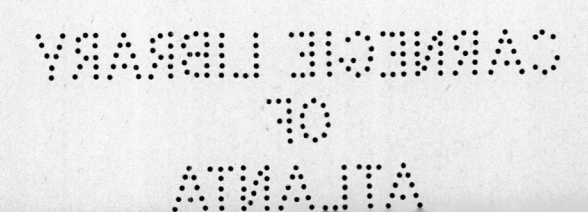

proclamation of November 8, 1801, to the people of the island, "that whatever your origin and color, you are all Frenchmen; you are all free and all equal before God and the Republic."[1] In this reversal he stifled his instincts, which were those of an intense democrat, dug the grave of French dominion in the new world, and brought the Anglo-Saxon and Spaniard face to face in the battle for supremacy. For it was the resistance of the blacks to this decree, in which was swallowed the over-sea resources of France, which was the great determinant of the destiny of Louisiana.

Almost at the same moment with the issuance of this decree, Napoleon gave orders respecting a new armament to the minister of marine, saying: "My intention, citizen minister, is to take possession of Louisiana with the shortest delay; that this expedition be made with the greatest secrecy; that it shall appear to be directed to Santo Domingo. The troops which I intend sending being upon the Scheldt, I desire that they shall leave from Antwerp and Flushing; finally, I desire that you inform me as to the number of men you think necessary to send, both of infantry and artillery, and that you give me a project of organization for this colony, both military and administrative, the works that we shall have to undertake and the batteries we shall have to construct in order to have an anchorage and a shelter for ships of war against superior forces. In order to do this, I desire that you have prepared for me a chart of the coast, from St. Augustine and Florida to Mexico, and a geographical description of the different cantons of Louisiana, with the population and resources of each canton."[2] He followed this quickly with instructions to St. Cyr, French ambassador at Madrid, to press Spain to deliver Louisiana,[3] and by additional orders for the preparation of an expedition which was to be commanded by General Victor.[4]

St. Cyr, in making known Napoleon's wishes to Spain, presented, July 22, 1802, a note giving a promise of most binding character, which a few months later Napoleon was to entirely ignore. The note said: "His Catholic Majesty has appeared to wish that France

[1] Napoleon's *Correspondence*, June 14, 1802, VII, 315.
[2] *Ibid.*, June 4, 1802, VII, 485.
[3] *Ibid.*, July 25, 1802, VII, 532.
[4] *Ibid.*, August 24, 1802, VIII, 4.

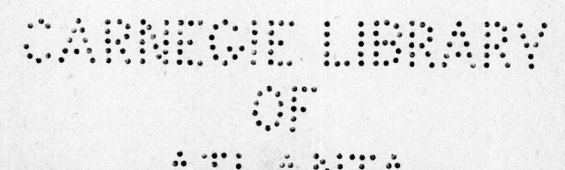

should engage not to sell or alienate, in any manner, the property and the enjoyment of Louisiana. Its wish in this respect is perfectly conformable with the intentions of the Spanish government; and its sole motive for entering therein was because it respected a possession which has constituted a part of the French territory. I am authorized to declare to you, in the name of the First Consul, that France will never alienate it." [1]

The preparation for the new expeditionary force, which was never to leave, pressed forward,[2] and October 15, 1802, the order was signed at Barcelona by the king for the delivery of Louisiana to France. That Napoleon had no immediate views beyond French occupancy is evident by his still decided desire to add Florida to the concession. The bribe of Parma and two other duchies had been held before the new King of Etruria, if in return the King of Spain would but annex Florida to Louisiana.[3] The exchange was pressed later in a letter from Napoleon to the King of Spain himself,[4] but the imperious will of the First Consul was finally thwarted by Godoy, upheld as he was by the British minister, John Hookham Frere. Napoleon was informed by General Beurnonville, his new minister at Madrid, in January, 1803, that "The Prince [Godoy] told me that the British minister had declared to him, in the name of his government, that his Britannic Majesty, being informed of the projects of exchange which existed between France and Spain, could never consent that the two Floridas should become an acquisition of the Republic; that the United States of America were in this respect of one mind with the Court of London; and that Russia equally objected to France disposing of the estates of Parma in favor of Spain, since the Emperor Alexander intended to have them granted as indemnity to the King of Sardinia. In imparting to me this proceeding of the British minister, the prince had a satisfied air, which showed how much he wishes that the exchange, almost agreed upon and so warmly desired by the Queen of Spain, may not take place." [5]

[1] The Spanish minister to the secretary of state, *State Papers*, II, 569.
[2] Napoleon *Correspondence*, August 24 and November 23, 1802, VIII, 4, 106.
[3] *Ibid.*, August 29, 1802, VIII, 12.
[4] *Ibid.*, November 27, 1802, VIII, 111.
[5] Beurnonville to Talleyrand, January 17, 1803, *Archives des Aff. Etr.*, MSS., quoted by Adams, I, 402.

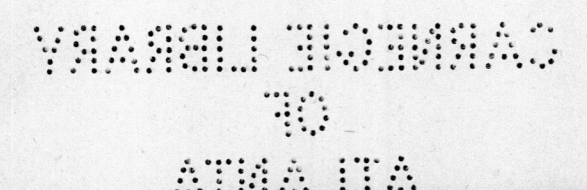

Two anxious years had been passed during which the Jefferson administration saw itself apparently powerless between the grinding of the French and Spanish millstones of state policy; the motive power of both was, however, altogether the mind and will of the most forceful genius that has ever appeared among mankind. In the meantime the South-west was in warlike mood through the action of the Spanish intendant at New Orleans in closing the Mississippi by annulment, October 16, 1802, of the right of deposit at New Orleans. The administration, in November, 1802, received information that this had been done by proclamation, without an equivalent establishment being arranged for as required by the treaty of 1795. By one of the curiosities of Spanish administration, the officials of the superior departments were independent of one another, and apparently the governor was in nowise a party to the transaction; there seems little doubt that the intendant was acting of his own motion, and it is more than likely that, foreseeing the almost certain transfer to France, he was merely desirous of acting as a marplot and of bringing between the United States and her new neighbor a burning question which might easily develop into flame. It is clear that the Spanish minister to the United States, the Marquis of Casa Yrujo, son-in-law of Governor McKean of Pennsylvania, was not only not forewarned, but that he was markedly averse to the intendant's action. He wrote him sharply, at the same time disclaiming to the American government the intendant's act.

Madison wrote Pinckney, minister to Spain, November 27, 1802,[1] saying: "This proceeding is so direct and palpable a violation of the treaty of 1795, that, in candor, it is to be imputed rather to the intendant solely, than to instructions of his government. The Spanish minister takes pains to impress his belief, and it is favored by private accounts from New Orleans, mentioning that the governor did not concur with the intendant. But from whatever source the measure may have proceeded, the President expects that the Spanish government will neither lose a moment in countermanding it, nor hesitate to repair every damage which may result from it. You are aware of the sensibility of our Western citizens to such an occurrence. This sensibility is justified by the interest

[1] *State Papers*, II, 527.

they have at stake. The Mississippi is to them everything. It is the Hudson, the Delaware, the Potomac, and all the navigable rivers of the Atlantic states, formed into one stream."[1]

Nor did Madison exaggerate. The one great and incomparably cheapest method of transport was by water, and the great trade artery of the West into which flowed all the others of the more settled Western country was the Mississippi. It was, from the standpoint of the day, vital. The Western country was then so distant from the East in communication, that its isolation is now hardly conceivable. There were many who thought it impossible that there should not be several Anglo-Saxon nations to the North American Continent, south of Canada. And such thought was not wholly unjustified by the conditions. The Alleghanies formed a barrier which separated countries facing in wholly different directions. One looked east toward the Atlantic, to which all its natural highways tended; the other west and south, its interests governed thitherward by inexorable natural conditions. The dream of a south-western empire, which undoubtedly was in the minds of many, had a realistic base which might in time have developed into reality, had not the steam motor, of which there was then a faintest dawn visible to a few far-seeing and wisely imaginative men, come to keep step with the growth of the American Republic and bring its widely separated borders into neighborhood.

It was thus not without cause that the House resolved, January 7, 1803, that it viewed the news of the Spanish intendant's action "with deep sensibility," and expressed its "unalterable determination to maintain the rights of navigation and commerce through the river Mississippi as established by existing treaties."[2] Happily, the Marquis of Casa Yrujo came, April 19, 1803, to the secretary of state to announce that the Spanish government had given orders for the re-establishment of the right—action which caused doubts in Madison's mind of the actuality of Spain's transfer of Louisiana to France.[3]

The President's message, December 15, 1802, barely touched upon the momentous change of masters in Louisiana, of which

[1] Madison to Pinckney, November 27, 1802, *State Papers*, II, 527.
[2] *Ibid.*, II, 471. [3] *Ibid.*, II, 556.

there was yet no sign of actual transfer. He said: "The cession of the Spanish province of Louisiana to France, which took place in the course of the late war, will, if carried into effect, make a change in the aspect of our foreign relations which will doubtless have just weight in any deliberations of the legislature connected with the subject." Nothing of Jefferson's views on this momentous subject, beyond this meaningless phrase, was given to the public, nor was there, respecting France, anything of belligerency in his announcements regarding the navy, such as appeared in his personal letters to Livingston and Dupont de Nemours. His message stated that "a small force in the Mediterranean will be necessary to restrain the Tripoline cruisers, and the uncertain tenure of peace with some other of the Barbary powers may eventually require that force to be augmented," but far more stress was given to the proposal of the message (amazing in the reason assigned) "to add to our navy yard here a dock within which our vessels may be laid up dry and under cover from the sun."

But the political turmoil which was the product of the intendant's action roused an energy and an apprehension in the administration which no mere transfer of half a continent had been able to produce. Madison wrote Pinckney at Madrid, January 10, 1803: "The House has passed a resolution explicitly declaring that the stipulated right of the United States on the Mississippi will be inviolably maintained. The disposition of many members was to give to the resolution a tone and complexion still stronger. To these proofs of the sensation which has been produced, it is added that representations expressing the peculiar sensibility of the Western country are on their way from every quarter of it to the government. There is, in fact, but one sentiment throughout the Union with respect to the duty of maintaining our rights of navigation and boundary. The only existing difference relates to the degree of patience which ought to be exercised during the appeal to friendly modes of redress;"[1] all of which had much better have been said to our minister in France, which government was now, as by this time Jefferson was well assured, master of the situation.

The temper and tone of Congress were such that action by the

[1] *State Papers*, II, 528.

Executive was imperative. Jefferson thus putting aside his warlike views of a few months before, sent on January 11, 1803, a message to the Senate, saying: "The cession of the Spanish province of Louisiana to France, and perhaps of the Floridas, and the late suspension of the right of deposit at New Orleans, are events of primary interest to the United States. On both occasions such measures were promptly taken as were thought most likely amicably to remove the present and prevent future causes of inquietude. The objects of those measures were to obtain the territory on the left bank of the Mississippi, and eastward of that if practicable, on conditions to which the proper authorities of our country would agree; or at least to prevent any changes which might lessen the exercise of our rights. While my confidence in our minister plenipotentiary is entire and undiminished, I still think that these objects might be promoted by joining with him a person sent from hence directly, carrying with him the feelings and sentiments of the nation, excited on the late occurrence, impressed by full communications of all the views we entertain on this interesting subject. . . ." He therefore nominated Livingston as minister plenipotentiary and Monroe as minister extraordinary and plenipotentiary to France, and, as Spain was still in possession "and the course of events may retard or prevent the cession to France being carried into effect," Pinckney and Monroe were nominated as envoys to Spain, to enter into a treaty or convention with either power as events should demand, "for the purpose of enlarging and more effectually securing our rights and interests in the river Mississippi and in the territories eastward thereof."

There is no word, nor is there hint, either in the message or in the elaborate instructions of March 2, 1803, to the several envoys named, of any desire to go beyond the Mississippi. The instructions accepted as almost a certainty that the Floridas also had been ceded to France and outlined in seven articles the proposed basis of a treaty. France was to be induced to cede "the territory east of the Mississippi, comprehending the two Floridas, the island of New Orleans, and the islands lying to the north and east of that channel of the said river, which is commonly called the South Pass, together with all such other islands as appertain to either West or

East Florida—France reserving to herself all her territory on the west side of the Mississippi." The boundary above the thirty-first degree of latitude was to be the middle of the channel; the navigation of the river in its whole length and breadth was to be free to both nations; there was to be equality of treatment in fiscal matters; French citizens were to be allowed for ten years to deposit their goods at New Orleans and other ports on the ceded shore of the Mississippi; it was to be expected, though such provisions could not be made in the treaty, that the inhabitants of the ceded territory would be incorporated with the citizens of the United States on an equal footing without unnecessary delay. In the observations upon this plan there is a hint of objection on the part of Spain, and care was to be taken to conserve the treaty of 1795 between Spain and the United States. It may seem somewhat strange to the American public of this day, that the subject which, after that of the cession itself, gave most concern to the American Department of States, was the possible attitude of Great Britain in regard to the free navigation of the river to which, by the treaties of 1783 and 1794, she had a clear right in so far as the United States could give such right.

Should France refuse to cede any territory, it "remained to explain and improve the existing right of deposit by adding the privileges of holding real estate for commercial purposes, of providing hospitals, or residences for consuls or other agents; and should not a cession of the Floridas be obtainable, to arrange for the right of deposit on rivers of the United States passing through the Floridas, and for their free navigation." "The President," says the instructions, "has made up his mind to go as far as fifty millions of *livres tournois*, rather than lose the main object." [1]

To this dwindled our demands after the exciting debates in the Senate at the end of February and beginning of March, 1803, on resolutions which proposed authorizing the President to take immediate possession of such places as he might deem fit and convenient for places of deposit, and authorizing him to call into active service any number of militia of South Carolina, Georgia, Ohio, Kentucky, Tennessee, and Mississippi, not to exceed fifty thousand, for effecting these objects.[2] Gouverneur Morris, one

[1] *State Papers*, II, 540. [2] *Abridgment Debates*, II, 670.

of the senators from New York, and certainly one of the ablest and most acute minds this country has produced, said: "I have endeavored to show that, under the existing circumstances, we are now actually at war, and have no choice but manly resistance or vile submission; that the possession of this country by France is dangerous to other nations but fatal to us; that it forms a natural and necessary part of our empire. . . . I have no hesitation in saying that you ought to have taken possession of New Orleans and the Floridas the instant your treaty was violated. You ought to do it now. Your rights are invaded—confidence in negotiation is vain; there is therefore no alternative but force. You are exposed to imminent present danger. You have the prospect of great future advantage. You are justified by the clearest principles of right. You are urged by the strongest motives of policy. You are commanded by every sentiment of natural dignity." [1]

There were some who deprecated such extreme measures, but the sense of the Senate was expressed in resolutions, passed unanimously, authorizing the President, "whenever he shall judge it expedient, to require the executives of the several states to take effectual measures to arm and equip, according to law, and hold in readiness to march at a moment's warning, eighty thousand effective militia," also to appropriate for them pay and subsistence, and to erect arsenals at such points on the Western waters as he might deem necessary.[2]

The turmoil in Jefferson's mind showed in the suggestion which he had advanced to extend the domination of the Anglo-Saxon alliance, and which he forecast, over both Americas. Spain seems to have been lost sight of in the mental shuffle which he was experiencing. How serious for the moment he was in the expression of such views is shown by the propositions laid before the cabinet, April 8, 1803, at a time when "a French prefect was

[1] *Abridgment of Debates*, II, 684. Senator Morris also said in this speech: "When we have twenty ships of the line at sea, and there is no good reason why we should not have them, we shall be respected by all Europe. . . . The expense compared with the benefit is moderate, nay, trifling. . . . Whatever sums are necessary to secure the national independence must be paid. . . . If we will not pay to be defended we must pay for being conquered." (*Annals of Congress*, 1802, 1803, 199.) His words were soon to have most melancholy significance.

[2] *Ibid.*, 692, *Annals of Congress*, 1802, 1803, 255.

actually in New Orleans and the delivery of Louisiana to Bonaparte might from day to day be expected," of an alliance with England in case France, as he expressed it, "refused our rights." He suggested "three inducements which might be offered to Great Britain: '1. Not to make a separate peace. 2. To let her take Louisiana. 3. Commercial privileges.' The cabinet unanimously rejected the second and third concessions; but Dearborn and Lincoln were alone in opposing the first, and a majority agreed to instruct Monroe and Livingston, 'as soon as they find that no arrangements can be made with France, to use all possible procrastination with them, and in the meantime to enter into conferences with the British government, through their ambassador at Paris, to fix principles of alliance, and leave us in peace until Congress meets; and prevent a war until next spring.'"[1]

Madison, in the instructions dated ten days later, directed the two ministers in case France "instead of friendly arrangements or views, should be found to meditate hostilities, or to have formed projects which will constrain the United States to resort to hostilities," that co-operation of England was to be sought with the expectation that the support of the United States would induce her to begin again a war which had but so lately closed, and which was not to end or be suspended except by mutual consent. Should the right of navigation of the Mississippi not be disputed by France but the right of deposit denied, it should be left to Congress to decide between an "instant resort to arms" or further procrastination.[2]

War anew between France and Great Britain was now imminent. The very disquieting remarks of Napoleon, March 13, 1803, to Lord Whitworth, the British ambassador, and the active preparations in both countries, combined with the almost certain action of England, which would be to occupy New Orleans,[3] must have rendered the peace-loving Jefferson anxious indeed. Livingston in Paris pressed the subject of purchase of territory east of the river with increased persistence, knowing now that he would have to share with a colleague any honor which might come from suc-

[1] Cabinet Memoranda of Jefferson, April 8, 1803; Jefferson MSS., quoted by Adams, *United States*, II, 1, 2.
[2] *State Papers*, II, 555–556.
[3] Letter of Mr. King to secretary of state, April 2, 1803, *State Papers*, II, 551.

cess later. "The affairs of New Orleans gave me two very important strings to touch: I endeavored to convince the government that the United States would avail themselves of the breach of the treaty to possess themselves of New Orleans and the Floridas; that Britain would never suffer Spain to grant the Floridas to France, even were she so disposed, but would immediately seize upon them as soon as the transfer was made; that without the Floridas, Louisiana would be indefensible, as it possesses not one port even for frigates; and I showed the effect of suffering that important country to fall into the hands of the British, both as it affected our country and the naval force of all Europe. These reasons, with the probability of war, have had, I trust, the desired effect. Mr. Talleyrand asked me this day, when pressing the subject, whether we wished to have the whole of Louisiana. I told him no; that our wishes extended only to New Orleans and the Floridas; that the policy of France, however, should dictate (as I have shown in an official note) to give us the country above the river Arkansas, in order to place a barrier between them and Canada. He said that if they gave New Orleans the rest would be of little value, and that he would wish to know "what we would give for the whole." I told him it was a subject I had not thought of; but that I supposed that we should not object to twenty millions, provided our citizens were paid."[1]

Though Talleyrand even the next day was denying that Louisiana was theirs and that his proposition was only personal,[2] Napoleon himself had already decided the question. On Easter Sunday, April 10, 1803, he had announced to two of his ministers his intention to give Louisiana to the United States. One was Barbé Marbois who had been consul-general of France in America, had married an American wife, and had American predilections. The story told by Marbois at great length, though strongly colored, has enough verisimilitude for acceptance. Napoleon said: "I know the full value of Louisiana, and I have been desirous of repairing the fault of the French negotiator who abandoned it in 1763. A few lines of a treaty have restored it to me and I have scarcely recovered it when I must expect to lose it. . . . [The British] sail

[1] Livingston to Madison, April 11, 1803, *State Papers*, II, 552.
[2] Livingston to Madison, April 13, 1803, *Ibid.*, 552.

over those seas as sovereigns, whilst our affairs in Santo Domingo have been growing worse every day since the death of Leclerc. The conquest of Louisiana would be easy. . . . I have not a moment to lose in putting it out of their reach. . . . I think of ceding it to the United States. . . . They only ask of me one town in Louisiana, but I already consider the colony entirely lost, and, it appears to me, in the hands of this growing power, it will be more useful to the policy and even the commerce of France than if I should attempt to keep it."[1]

Marbois was as cordial in agreement with the First Consul as the other minister—who, as an officer of the French army had been also in America during the Revolution—was opposed. The conference lasted late into the night without determination. The ministers remained at St. Cloud, and early next morning Napoleon summoned Marbois, read to him the disquieting despatches from London, and said: "I renounce Louisiana. It is not only New Orleans that I will cede, it is the whole colony without reservation. I know the price of what I abandon, and I have sufficiently proved the importance that I attach to this province, since my first diplomatic act with Spain had for its object the recovery of it. I renounce it with the greatest regret. To attempt obstinately to retain it would be folly. I direct you to negotiate this affair with the envoys of the United States. Do not even await the arrival of Mr. Monroe;[2] have an interview this very day with Mr. Livingston; but I require a great deal of money for this war, and I would not like to commence it with new contributions. . . . If I should regulate my terms according to the value of these vast regions to the United States, the indemnity would have no limits. I will be moderate in consideration of the necessity in which I am of making a sale. But keep this to yourself. I want fifty millions [francs] and for less than that sum I will not treat."[3]

It is not the province of this work to treat of the details which passed between Marbois and the American envoys. The latter were wise enough to exceed their instructions, particularly as it was found as they "advanced in the negotiations, that M. Marbois was

[1] Barbé Marbois, *History of Louisiana*, 263.
[2] Monroe, however, arrived the evening of this same day, April 11.
[3] Barbé Marbois, *Louisiana*, 274.

absolutely restricted to the disposition of the whole; that he would treat for no less portion, and of course it was useless to urge it. On mature consideration, therefore, we finally concluded a treaty [signed April 30, 1803,] on the best terms we could obtain for the whole." [1] These terms were the payment of sixty millions of francs and undertaking the payment of the claims of the American citizens against France for the illegal capture and condemnation of vessels, which were estimated at twenty millions more; much less, it should be said, than the amount of claims admitted in principle, and falling far short of the reality.

Thus, for a sum of $15,360,000, came into the hands of the United States a territory in extent a great empire, and with its possession passed a danger which included the alternative of a war with France or the possession of Louisiana by Great Britain. It seems strange that the vast potentialities involved should have been haggled over by the American negotiators for a moment. Napoleon was not a man with whom to chaffer and at any moment might have changed his mind or raised his price. The truth is that the possibility of so great a coup had never entered the minds of the Americans. It came with an absolute unpreparedness which staggered them. The purchase of Louisiana was in fact forced upon us, so far as the great country across the Mississippi was concerned. It was not the work of Jefferson or Madison or Livingston (who in his own words had never thought of it) or of Monroe. It was wholly the act of Napoleon, who recognized that Spain's forced gift was now, in the circumstances, in the nature of the proverbial white elephant, and he preferred that the country should be in the hands of a friend rather than almost certainly fall to the foe with whom he was again about to go to war.

[1] Livingston and Monroe to Madison, May 13, 1803, *State Papers*, II, 559.

CHAPTER IV

CESSION OF LOUISIANA AND QUESTION OF THE FLORIDAS

But it remained to deal with Spain. The territory was ceded to the United States in the terms of the Spanish cession to France, which were quoted in the first article of the new treaty, viz.: "With the same extent that is now in the hands of Spain, and that it had when France possessed it, and such as it should be after the treaties subsequently entered into between Spain and other states;" an ambiguity which the American ministers vainly attempted to have removed, and which again brought Spain and the United States to the verge of war.

The treaty arrived in Washington July 14, 1803. On September 4, the Marquis de Casa Yrujo addressed a note to the secretary of state informing him that the knowledge of the treaty had come to the King of Spain through his ambassador in Paris, and calling attention to the solemn engagement entered into by Napoleon never to alienate the territory.[1] Yrujo wrote again, September 27, reiterating the statement of his previous note that France had no power to make such transfer, and calling attention to the fact that France had not even fulfilled the stipulations of the treaty by which it was transferred to herself by Spain.

There can be no doubt that, as between France and Spain, all of the rights of the question were with the latter. She had been bullied into the transfer in the first instance; there had never been a delivery of the promised equivalent, and there was the solemn engagement of France not to sell or alienate the territory. But this, as a diplomatic question, did not affect the United States, though the latter was unquestionably somewhat in the attitude of a receiver of stolen goods. Napoleon's promise was no part of

[1] *State Papers*, II, 569.

the treaty of St. Ildefonso and had not been known to the United States; nor was the latter in any wise concerned with the arrangement regarding Etruria. The recriminations of Spain could apply to France alone.

Mr. Madison in answering Yrujo's note, October 4, 1803, with, it must be acknowledged, somewhat of casuistry, said: "The repugnance manifested in these communications on the part of his Catholic Majesty to the cession of Louisiana, lately made by the French Republic to the United States, was as little expected as the objections to the transaction can avail against the solidity."[1] He referred to the communication of Mr. Cevallos to the American plenipotentiary at Madrid in a note of the 4th of May, 1803: "By the retrocession made to France of Louisiana this power has recovered the said province with the limits which it had and saving the rights acquired by other powers. The United States can address themselves to the French government to negotiate the acquisition of territory which may suit their interests."[2] The administration regarded this as an explicit and positive recognition (which it was) of the right of the United States and France to enter into the transaction which had taken place. M. Pichon, the French minister, of course supported Jefferson; he cited the facts that the promise was made fifteen months after the signature of the treaty and that, notwithstanding the failure of Great Britain at the peace of Amiens, March 27, 1802, to acknowledge the King of Etruria, the Court of Madrid had ordered the transfer of Louisiana to France in the following October.[3] The objections were regarded, however, as so serious that it was feared delivery would be refused and steps were taken to use forces if necessary, consisting "of the regular troops near at hand, as many of the militia as may be requisite and can be drawn from the Mississippi territory, and as many volunteers from any quarter as can be picked up. To them will be added five hundred mounted militia from Tennessee, who it is expected will proceed to Natchez."[4] Jefferson had thought in case the Spanish authorities should resist the transfer "to take by surprise New Madrid, St. Genevieve, St. Louis, and all the other small posts, and that all this should be made as much as possible

---

[1] *State Papers*, II, 569.   [2] *Ibid.*, II, 570.   [3] *Ibid.*, II, 572.
[4] Madison to Livingston, November 9, 1803, *Ibid.*, II, 572.

the act of France, by including Laussat, with the aid of Clark, to raise an insurrectionary force of the inhabitants, to which ours might be only auxiliary." [1]

But such forcible action was unnecessary. Spain was powerless. Napoleon treated her as an appanage of France, and his promise to Charles IV as a promise made to himself and to be broken at will. Spain thus interposed no real obstacle, but it was not until February 10, 1804, after a note of "sharp remonstrance" from France,[2] that the Spanish minister of foreign affairs stated that he had orders to declare to the American government "that his majesty has thought fit to renounce his opposition to the alienation of Louisiana made by France, notwithstanding the solid reasons on which it was founded; thereby giving a new proof of his good feeling and friendship toward the United States." [3]

Though the Spanish decree ordering the delivery of the colony to France was dated October 15, 1802, the chargé d'affaires of France at Washington had orders to combine the proceedings of the two cessions, that from Spain to France and that from France to the United States, without leaving such an interval as would justify an expedition on the part of the English.[4] It was thus not until the 30th of November, 1803, that M. Laussat, the commissioner of the French government, took over the government which he administered a short three weeks only, or until December 20, when he in turn ceded his authority to the United States commissioners, one of whom was Governor Claiborne of Mississippi Territory, the other the unspeakable Wilkinson. It certainly was one of the most curious of the turns of fortune that should have caused this archtraitor to play such a part. He had conspired, and was still to conspire, to separate the West from the East, and deliver it into the hands of Spain; he was in Spain's pay as her secret agent, and was now to sign his name to the letter addressed by the two commissioners on this notable day to the secretary of state, saying: "We have the satisfaction to announce to you that

[1] Jefferson to Gallatin, October 29, 1803, *Writings*, VIII, 274.
[2] Talleyrand to Spanish minister in Paris, January 3, 1804, **Archives des Aff., Étr., MSS.**, Adams, II, 277.
[3] Don Pedro Cevallos to Mr. Pinckney, *State Papers*, II, 583.
[4] Barbé Marbois, *History of Louisiana*, 321.

the province of Louisiana was this day surrendered to the United States by the commissioner of France, and to add that the flag of our country was raised in this city midst the acclamations of the inhabitants." [1] History presents few stranger incidents and providence, in its treatment of individuals, as judged from mortal standpoint, has seldom seemed more at fault.

No mention at the time was made of West Florida, but it was one which almost immediately became a burning dispute. Certain facts are clear: that French claims previous to 1763 extended to the Perdido River, which was fixed as a boundary between French and Spanish possessions in 1719; that France ceded all her possessions east of the Mississippi and island of New Orleans to Great Britain; that Spain ceded Florida to Great Britain in exchange for Havana, which the latter had captured in 1762; that Great Britain had organized the region bordering on the Gulf of Mexico, east of the Iberville River and of Lake Ponchartrain, into two governments, East and West Florida; that Spain owned again nothing east of this dividing line until 1783 when Great Britain in the general peace ceded to her both the Floridas.

The first phrase of the San Ildefonso treaty describes the ceded territory as "the colony or province of Louisiana with the same extent that it now has in the hands of Spain." This much in any case is perfectly definite and by no twist of meaning could cover West Florida. The second descriptive phrase of its extent, "that it had when France possessed it, and such as it ought to be according to the treaties subsequently passed between Spain and other states," would seem as clear. The words "when France possessed it," modified as they were by the succeeding words, could only apply to the other boundaries of this vast area, and not to the boundaries "subsequently passed between Spain and other states," viz., Great Britain and the United States. That Livingston himself earlier held the view that West Florida was not included in the cession to France is most clear. He writes, July 30, 1802, that he had received verbally from the Spanish ambassador at Paris " . . . his explicit assurance that the Floridas are not included in the cession; and I have been applied to, by one of the ministers here, to know what we understand, in America, by Louisiana. You can easily conceive

[1] *State Papers*, II, 581.

my answer. Since the possession of the Floridas by Britain and the treaty of 1763, I think there can be no doubt as to the precise meaning of the terms. In the meantime all that can be done here will be to endeavor to obtain a cession of New Orleans either by purchase or by offering to make it a port of entry to France on such terms as shall promise advantages to her commerce. . . . If to this we could add a stipulation that she shall never possess the Floridas, but on the contrary, in case of a rupture with Spain and a conquest of them, cede them to us, our affairs in that quarter would stand as well as I would wish; and the colonies that France might attempt to establish on the west side of the Mississippi would be too feeble to injure us. I find them very anxious to have the ports of Pensacola and St. Augustine, as they dread our having command of the Gulf. I confess this appears to me no very important object, and if they would be content with these, and give us West Florida and New Orleans, even at a large price, we should not hesitate. . . . "[1]

September 1, 1802, he writes to the secretary of state: "I have every reason to believe the Floridas are not included. They will for the present at least remain in the hands of Spain."[2] Even so late as May 12, 1803, Livingston writes: "I am satisfied . . . if they could have concluded with Spain we should also have had West Florida." Eight days later he completely changed his attitude, if not his mind, moved by a conversation with Marbois which conveyed the idea that Mobile was a part of the cession, unconscious that Napoleon himself was the instigator of the attitude of his ministers in the remark to Marbois who went to him bearing the request of the American commissioners to define the boundary: "If an obscurity did not already exist, it would perhaps be good policy to put one there."[3] Calling upon Talleyrand, the minister for foreign affairs, he writes the result: "I asked the minister what were the east bounds of the territory ceded to us. He said he did not know; we must take it as they received it. I asked him how Spain meant to give them possession. He said according to the words of the treaty. But what did you mean to take? I do not know. Then you mean that we shall construe it our own way? I

[1] Livingston to Madison, *State Papers*, II, 519.
[2] *State Papers*, II, 525. [3] Marbois, *Louisiana*, 283.

can give you no direction; you have made a noble bargain for yourselves, and I suppose you will make the most of it."

This, Livingston advised Madison to proceed to do. "Now, sir, the sum of this business is to recommend to you, in the strongest terms, after having obtained the possession that the French commissary will give you, to insist upon this as part of your right; and to take possession, at all events, to the river Perdido. I pledge myself that your right is good. . . . It may also be important to anticipate any designs that Britain may have upon that country. Should she possess herself of it, and the war terminate favorably for her, she will not readily relinquish it. With this in your hand, East Florida will be of little moment, and may be yours whenever you please. At all events proclaim your right and take possession."[1]

This was followed, June 7, by a letter signed by both Livingston and Monroe forwarding the ratification by the First Consul of the treaty and conventions of April 30, 1803, saying: "We are happy to have it in our power to assure you that on a thorough examination of the subject we consider it incontrovertible that West Florida is comprised in the cession of Louisiana. West Florida was a part of Louisiana when it was in the hands of France, and it was not in her hands in any other situation. The transfer of the whole was on the same day, the 3d of November, 1762, that being the day of the secret convention between France and Great Britain. The treaty of 1783 between Britain and Spain, by which the Floridas were ceded to the latter, put Louisiana in her hands in the same state it was in the hands of France; and the remaining or third member of the article in the treaty of St. Ildefonso between France and Spain, under which we claim, by referring to that of 1783 (as to that between Spain and the United States of 1795) and of course in the above character, only tends to confirm this doctrine. We consider ourselves so strongly founded in this conclusion that we are of opinion the United States should act on it in all the measures relative to Louisiana, in the same manner as if West Florida was comprised within the island of New Orleans, or lay to the west of the river Iberville, and to the lakes through which its waters pass to the ocean.

[1] Livingston to Monroe and Madison, May 20, 1803, *State Papers*, II, 560.

Hence the acquisition becomes of proportionally greater value to the United States."[1]

This was enough for Jefferson and Madison, although the latter, in a despatch to Pinckney at Madrid, July 29, 1803, had stated his understanding that the Floridas were not ceded, and directing Pinckney to await Monroe's arrival before beginning negotiations looking to a purchase.[2] Jefferson particularly, at the moment, had an elevated faith in Monroe's judgment and abilities for which we of later generations do not seem to find altogether adequate justification, and which Jefferson himself was later to come to doubt, and Madison was instructed by Jefferson to claim as the two plenipotentiaries advised, though in his letter to Livingston, January 31, 1804, he says: "It does not appear that in the delivery of the province by the Spanish authorities to M. Laussat, anything passed denoting its limits either to the east, the west, or the north; nor was any step taken by M. Laussat, either while the province was in his hands or at the time of his transferring it to ours, calculated to dispossess Spain of any part of the territory east of the Mississippi. On the contrary, in a private conference he stated positively that no part of the Floridas was comprised in the eastern boundary—France having strenuously insisted to have it extended to the Mobile, which was peremptorily refused by Spain. We learn from Mr. Pinckney that the Spanish government holds the same language to him. To the declaration of M. Laussat, however, we can oppose that of the French minister, made to you, that Louisiana extended to the river Perdido; and to the Spanish government, as well as to that of France, we can oppose the treaty of St. Ildefonso, and [that] of September 30, 1803, interpreted by facts and fair inferences. . . . As the question relates to the French government, the President relies on your prudence and attention for availing yourself of the admission by M. Marbois that Louisiana extended to the river Perdido, and for keeping the weight of that government in our scale against that of Spain. With respect to the western extent of Louisiana, M. Laussat held language more satisfactory. He considered the Rio Bravo or del Norte,[3] as far as the 30th degree of north latitude, as its true boundary on that side."[4]

[1] *State Papers*, II, 564.
[2] *Ibid.*, II, 614.
[3] The Rio Grande.
[4] *State Papers*, **II, 574.**

In the question of the ownership of West Florida, it is impossible not to think the United States greatly in the wrong, and that our action redounds to the credit of no one of the American administration connected with it. Madison's despatch, just cited, which was equally, of course, Jefferson's, was a piece of pettifoggery unworthy of high-minded statesmen. The President, the secretary of state, and the negotiators were equally in the wrong and wrong in the face of seemingly patent facts. Livingston "was forced at last to maintain that Spain had retroceded West Florida to France without knowing it, that France had sold it to the United States without suspecting it, that the United States had bought it without paying for it, and that neither France nor Spain, although the original contracting parties, were competent to decide the meaning of their own contract."[1] Not only was the American administration wrong in making and pressing the demand, but it was to do so in vain. It was to cover its diplomacy with humiliation, bring the country to the verge of war with France and Spain, and lose Texas; the whole through an unworthy demand which seemed to become an obsession. It was moved by the fact that they had met the wishes of the Southwest but half way; the great empire so unexpectedly thrust upon us was not felt to be an offset to the failure to acquire the control of all the rivers of the United States entering the Gulf of Mexico, and the Livingston-Monroe despatch of June 7 was eagerly taken as a basis for an immoral and unjust claim. It can have but one defence; a false view of its necessity.

How truly aright is such judgment as applied to the conduct of the American government, is shown not only by Livingston's earlier statements but by the instructions which were issued by Decrès, the minister of marine and of the colonies, to Victor and Laussat, November 26, 1802. The former was to command the expeditionary army, which was never to reach Louisiana; the latter was to be the prefect whose only duty, as determined by the fates, was to deliver Louisiana to the United States. These instructions bounded Louisiana "on the west by the Rio Bravo, [Rio Grande] from its mouth to about the 30° parallel; the line of demarcation stops after reaching this point and there seems never

[1] Adams, *United States*, II, 246, 247.

to have been any agreement in regard to this part of the frontier. The farther we go northward, the more undecided is the boundary. . . . There also exists none between Louisiana and Canada." Decrès quoted the treaty of 1763, when Florida became a British possession, fixing "its terms as still binding upon all the interested parties." "'It is agreed'" said the seventh article of this treaty, "'that in the future the boundaries between the states of his Most Christian Majesty and those of his Britannic Majesty shall be irrevocably fixed by a line drawn down the middle of the Mississippi River from its source to the river Iberville, and from there by a line down the middle of that river and of the lakes Maurepas and Pontchartrain to the sea. New Orleans and the island on which it stands shall belong to France.' Such is still to-day the eastern limit of Louisiana. All to the east and north of this limit makes part of the United States or West Florida." [1]

"Nothing could be clearer. Louisiana stretched from the Iberville to the Rio Bravo; West Florida from the Iberville to the Appalachicola. The retrocession of Louisiana by Spain to France could restore only what France had ceded to Spain in 1762. West Florida had nothing to do with the cession [to Spain] of 1762, or of the retrocession [to France] of 1800, and being Spanish by a wholly different title could not even be brought in question by the First Consul, much as he wanted Baton Rouge, Mobile and Pensacola." [2]

The eagerness to press the claim, thus caused the administration to put aside the much greater claim westward, the already acknowledged right to the territory later to become Texas. This, by the understanding between France and Spain, and by the terms of the transfer from France to the United States, was unquestionable. The mouth of the Rio Grande and a few intervening posts between that region and New Orleans had but to be occupied and Texas would have become an appanage to the United States in 1803 instead of a state of the Union forty-five years later at the expense of an unfair and despoiling war.

---

[1] *Instructions secrètes*, November 26, 1802, *Archives de la Marine*, MSS., Adams, II, 6, 7.

[2] Adams, II, 7. See Señor Don Pedro Cevallos to Monroe and Pinckney, February 24, 1805, *State Papers*, II, 644.

Jefferson throughout was dominated by the Western feeling that every river of the United States passing through Spanish territory must be in American hands throughout its length. Expansion westward seemed so vague and still so distant that it did not seem to him to come within the domain of practical politics. The result was the introduction, November 30, 1803, by John Randolph, now the spokesman, but soon to become the bitter enemy of the administration, of a bill giving effect to the revenue laws of the United States within the ceded territory, which passed and, February 24, 1804, received the President's signature. The fourth section directed that the territories ceded to the United States by the treaty, "and also all the navigable waters, rivers, creeks, bays and inlets lying within the United States which empty into the Gulf of Mexico east of the River Mississippi, shall be annexed to the Mississippi district and shall together with the same constitute one district and be called the District of Mississippi." The eleventh section authorized the President, "whenever he shall deem it expedient, to erect the shores, waters, and inlets of the bay and river of Mobile, and of the other rivers, creeks, inlets, and bays emptying into the Gulf of Mexico east of the said river Mobile, and west thereof to the Pascagoula inclusive, into a separate district and to establish such places within the same as he shall deem expedient to be the port of entry and delivery for such district."

This, so far as words had meaning, was a frank declaration that the United States had determined to take over the territory the cession of which was so strenuously denied, and denied justly, by both France and Spain. The intent of the bill was, moreover, accentuated by the fact that its introducer had declared officially in October, 1803, that Mobile belonged to the United States. An elaborate brief sent Livingston by Madison two days after the adjournment of Congress supported the claim in the fullest degree.[1] The situation logically meant war.

It was impossible that such action should pass unnoticed by Spain, and the Spanish minister, a few days after the publication of the act, called at the Department of State, "with the gazette in his hand and entered upon a very angry comment on the eleventh section which was answered by remarks . . . calculated to as-

[1] Madison to Livingston, March 31, 1804, *State Papers*, II, 575.

suage his dissatisfaction with the law, as far as was consistent with a candid declaration to him that we considered all of West Florida westward of the Perdido, as clearly ours by the treaty of April 30, 1803, and that of St. Ildefonso."[1]

Yrujo naturally was not to be satisfied with such an explanation, and followed it by notes of, in Madison's words, "a rudeness which no government can tolerate,"[2] but which in reality the gross indignity to Spain of the passage of such an act justified. It was the end of good-will between the Spanish minister and the American secretary of state; turned Yrujo, himself half American by long residence and marriage, into an enemy of the American government; made him an intriguer with the press, and ended his career in America with a bitterness of feeling between the administration and himself such as has rarely existed toward a diplomatic official. He was to defy every effort toward removal, and remained a thorn in the side of the department of state, until on his own request he was, in 1807, transferred to Milan as minister near the court of Eugéne Beauharnais. The injustice involved in the Mobile act was finally too much even for the administration, and on May 30, 1804, a proclamation was issued which, after reciting the terms of the act, overrode the law, and by an executive usurpation of authority declared the "shores, waters, inlets, creeks, and rivers lying *within the boundaries of the United States*, a collection district, with Fort Stoddert as a port of entry."[3]

The Mobile act had further the effect of setting aside the Spanish ratification of the "Spanish claims convention" of August 4, 1802, covering the question of damages to American shipping during the quasi war with France in which Spain, then an ally of France, had agreed to consider the claims for captures made by Spanish cruisers while reserving for later action those made by the French and brought into Spanish ports. Very improperly, and for wholly insufficient reasons, action upon this had been delayed in the American Senate until January 4, 1804. The time for ratification having long since expired, it was necessary to ask a renewal of ratification by Spain. This request was naturally met by a refusal, unless the Mobile act should be revoked, and in addition the abandonment of the reserved claim for the French spoliations was now demanded.

[1] *State Papers*, II, 576. [2] *Ibid.*, II, 576. [3] *Ibid.*, II, 583.

French influence had begun to be felt in the latter demand. It could be easily foreseen that Napoleon would now allow no Spanish money to go into other coffers than his own, and, besides, Spain had begun to see that it was possible, even as a matter of legal right, that she should be absolved from such an obligation. Yrujo had obtained an opinion from five eminent American lawyers upon an hypothetical case which he stated as follows: "The Power A lives in perfect harmony and friendship with Power B. The Power C, with reason or without, commits hostilities against the subjects of Power B, takes some of their vessels, carries them into the ports of A, friend of both, where they are condemned and sold by the official agents of Power C *without Power A being able to prevent it*. At last a treaty is entered into by which the Powers B and C adjust their differences, and in this treaty the Power B renounces and abandons to Power C the right to any claim for the injuries and losses occasioned to its subjects by the hostilities from Power C. Query: Has the Power B any right to call upon the Power A for indemnification for the losses occasioned in its ports and coasts under the conditions mentioned?" The treaty thus cited was the convention of 1800 with France, the erasure of the second article of which released France from indemnity for American claims of that date.

An opinion was given, November 15, 1802, by Jared Ingersoll, William Rawle, J. B. McKean, and P. S. Duponceau; ten days earlier one had been sent by Edward Livingston, of New York, which may be taken as a short résumé of the later and more elaborate paper. Livingston said, "According to the above statement, I have no doubt that B, having abandoned his rights to indemnity against C, would have no claim whatever against A, more especially as the case supposes it out of the power of A to have prevented the transaction."[1]

Spain had a strong case, made stronger also by the ninth article of the treaty of cession of Louisiana which released France in full of all indemnities, the payment of these being taken over by the United States government. Notwithstanding the attitude of Spain thus bolstered both by American legal opinion and by the interested friendship of France which was now becoming ap-

[1] For these and the Spanish argument, see *State Papers*, II, 604, 605.

parent, Madison issued instructions on April 15, 1804, to Monroe to proceed to Madrid and, acting jointly with Pinckney, to press these claims as well as the claim to West Florida. "The objects to be pursued" he said, "are 1st, an acknowledgment by Spain that Louisiana, as ceded to the United States, extends to the river Perdido; 2d, a cession of all her remaining territory eastward of that river, including East Florida; 3d, a provision for arbitrating and paying all the claims of citizens of the United States not provided for by the late convention, consisting of those for wrongs done prior to the last peace, by other than Spanish subjects within Spanish responsibility; for wrongs done in the Spanish colonies by Spanish subjects or officers, and for wrongs of every kind for which Spain is justly responsible, committed since the last peace." This was followed by the first hint of withdrawal from any claim to extend to the Rio Grande. Madison continued, "On the part of the United States, it may be stipulated that the territory on the western side of the Mississippi shall not be settled for a given term of years, beyond a limit not very distant from that river, leaving a spacious interval between our settlements and those of Spain, and that a sum in no event to exceed two million dollars shall be paid by the United States to be applied to the discharge of awards to their citizens. It may also be stipulated, or rather may be understood, that no charge shall be brought by the United States against Spain for losses sustained from the interruption of the deposit at New Orleans." The interval of non-settlement was suggested as that between the Sabine and Colorado Rivers. "No final cession" was "to be made to Spain of any part of the territory on this side of the Rio Bravo, but in the event of a cession to the United States of the territory east of the Perdido; and in that event, in case of absolute necessity only."[1]

During these months Pinckney had been pressing Spain, "in that positive and decided manner which the circumstances of Europe and the particular situation of Spain seemed . . . to warrant,"[2] and which bade fair to disturb President Jefferson's dream of unbroken peace. In regard to the spoliations he justly said: "There has been such a treatment to the vessels, cargoes,

[1] *State Papers*, II, 627.
[2] Pinckney to Madison, August 2, 1803, *Ibid.*, II, 597.

and in many instances persons of our citizens, as no man could believe who has not an opportunity to examine the archives of our mission to this court. The individual sufferings have been incredible and the property lost of immense value. There is scarcely a part or port of his Catholic Majesty's dominions in Europe and America, that has not been the scene and witness of their sufferings—sufferings such as I believe no people ever endured from a nation to whose coasts they went under the solemn protection of treaties, the laws of nations, and in many instances, express royal orders or permissions from the king,"[1]

Previous to this he had already hinted strongly at the probability of war, and when, on July 2, 1804, Cevallos declined a ratification of the convention of 1802 unless the French claims were withdrawn and the Mobile act revoked,[2] Pinckney wrote: "I shall proceed without delay to give your Excellency that decisive answer to yours of the 2d, and to take those definite measures which my instructions and duty now make necessary"; but before doing so he wished to know specifically if his Majesty would not ratify the convention except under the conditions stated by Cevallos. If so, he requested the return of the ratification and papers sent Cevallos some time since at Aranjuez. He proceeded: "On Tuesday, I send a courier with circular letters to all our consuls in the ports of Spain, stating to them the critical situation of things between Spain and the United States, the probability of a speedy and serious misunderstanding, and directing them to give notice thereof to all our citizens, advising them so to arrange and prepare their affairs as to be able to move off within the time limited by the treaty. Should things end as I now expect, I am also preparing the same information for the commander of our squadron in the Mediterranean, for his own notice and government and that of all the American merchant vessels he may meet."[3]

Señor Cevallos replied to this outburst that he could not conceive how Pinckney's instructions could authorize him to proceed to such extremes. He referred to the opinions of the dis-

[1] Charles Pinckney to Señor Cevallos, June 22, 1804, *State Papers*, II, 618.
[2] *State Papers*, II, 619.
[3] Charles Pinckney to Señor Cevallos, July 5, 1804, *State Papers*, II, 620.

tinguished jurists of the United States, upholding the Spanish contention regarding depredations by French ships; showed that Spain was merely demanding a satisfactory explanation of such clauses of the Mobile act as infringed the rights of the Spanish crown, and stated that the king had resolved to transfer the negotiation to Washington.[1] Pinckney's reply was to despatch his circular letter, which created a panic among American traders in the Mediterranean, and to inform Cevallos that so soon as he could arrange his affairs he would ask for his passports.[2]

Pinckney, in conversation with Cevallos, now listened to some severe remarks and some rough truths upon the attitude of the United States: that the Spanish government had ten times more trouble with them than with any other nation, and for his part he did not wish to see the trade with the United States extended. Spain had nothing to fear from the United States and had heard with contempt the threats of senators like Ross and Gouverneur Morris. The Americans had no right to expect much kindness from the king; in the purchase of Louisiana they had paid no attention to his repeated remonstrances against the injustice and nullity of that transaction, whereas if they had felt the least friendship they would have done so. They were well known to be a nation of calculators bent on making money and nothing else."[3]

Though Cevallos talked so severely and apparently boldly, he was much alarmed, and he appealed to the minister of France, now Spain's ally, or, to speak more in accord with facts, her master. "The French representative wrote to Talleyrand that Pinckney had terrified the secretary beyond reason,"[4] and a few days later reported Señor Cevallos as saying, "If the emperor would but say a word and let the United States understand that he is not pleased at seeing them abuse the advantages which they owe to their strength and to the nearness of their resources over an ally of France, this would reconcile all difficulties and save his Majesty

---

[1] Cevallos to Pinckney, July 8, 1805, *State Papers*, II, 620.
[2] *State Papers*, II, 621.
[3] Charles Pinckney to Madison, July 20, 1804, MSS. State Department, Adams, II, 283.
[4] Vandeul to Talleyrand, July 26, 1804, *Archives des Aff. Étr.* MSS., Adams, II, 284.

the necessity of exacting satisfaction for an insult which is as good as inflicted." [1]

On the arrival in the United States of the correspondence between Pinckney and Cevallos, giving the news of the strained relations thus established, Yrujo sent a note to Madison repeating the objections made by Cevallos, which was answered by expressing surprise that the Mobile act should have given rise to complaint and declaring that the President had a right to expect that such an act, "depending essentially for its effect in the particular case on his discretion, would have been left to the regular exposition and execution, before it should become the object of criticism and complaint from any foreign government," [2] ignoring the fact that the President, who controlled the diplomacy of the government, was also part of the law-making power, and having affixed his signature as such to the document, the law was in part of his own making and had to be taken by Spain according to the letter and not as later amended by the President's own authority. Madison assured the Spanish minister that the operation of the act should only be within the acknowledged limits of the United States and "should not extend beyond them until it should be rendered expedient by friendly elucidation and adjustments with the Spanish government." Yrujo was informed of Monroe's mission and that "in the meantime the President concurs" with the Spanish government "in the expediency of leaving things precisely *in statu quo*." [3]

Monroe was thus, on October 25, 1804, ordered to Madrid "without delay," with directions to press the demands in his instructions of April 25, 1804, except that the indemnities for the interruption of deposit at New Orleans might be tacitly waived, and if Spain refused to cede the territory east of the Perdido, and should require as indispensable to an acknowledgment of the American title to West Florida an acknowledgment by the United States that their pretensions should not go west of the Colorado, the joint negotiators, after reasonable endeavors to effect their object, were to acquiesce. [4]

[1] Vandeul to Talleyrand, August 6, 1804, MSS., *ibid.*, 285.
[2] Yrujo to Madison, October 13; Madison's reply, October 15, 1804, *State Papers*, II, 624, 625. [3] *Ibid.*, 625.
[4] Madison to Monroe, *State Papers*, II, 631.

At the moment that Pinckney was threatening Spain with war, and the American government giving him good reasons, in the passage of the Mobile act, to suppose that it wished war, a powerful influence, personified in Talleyrand, was exerted to defeat the negotiations which Jefferson had so much at heart. Talleyrand had become bitterly inimical to the United States, first, through the exposure of his venality in connection with the commission of 1797 charged with the settlement of the difficulties of that period between France and the Union;[1] and, secondly, through mortification on account of the miscarriage of his work in the reannexation of Louisiana to France, the result of which had inured wholly to the benefit of the United States. The recovery of Louisiana by France had been Talleyrand's work, begun by him in 1797, when minister for foreign affairs under the Directory, necessarily dropped in 1799 on his dismissal from office, and taken up again on his restoration in 1800 by Napoleon, in whom Talleyrand found a chief like-minded with himself. He had failed to acquire the Floridas, which had been included in his designs, but he had succeeded as to Louisiana, only to see it pass almost immediately to the nation, the limiting of whose power by making Louisiana and the Floridas, in the possession of France, "a wall of brass forever impenetrable to the combined efforts of England and America," had been one of his chief arguments in the earlier negotiation.[2]

He had thus, in these months of stormy diplomacy, and while Madison was engaged in the preparation of arguments for the pressure of the claims for the actions of French privateers in Spain, written Admiral Gravina, the Spanish ambassador at Paris, on July 27, 1804: "Certainly if I had been informed that the ministers of his Catholic Majesty had carried their condescensions to the United States so far as to engage Spain to be responsible to it for the indemnities for pretended violations made by France, I should most assuredly have received from my government an order to manifest the discontent which France would have experienced by a *condescension so improper*, a discontent that would have been expressed more strongly toward the government of the

---

[1] *State Papers*, II, 204–238.
[2] Instructions au Citoyen Guillemardet (minister to Spain), May 20, June 19, 1798, *Archives des Aff. Étr.* MSS., Adams, I, 357.

United States than toward Spain. Besides, the explanations which have already been given to your court, . . . and those which I have authorized to be again made to the government of the United States by the chargé d'affaires of his Imperial Majesty, ought to leave the presumption that, from the opinion which his Majesty has adopted on this question, *that as it has already been the subject of a long negotiation, and of a formal convention between France and the United States, it cannot again become the subject of a new discussion.*" [1]

This was followed by instructions to General Turreau, the French chargé d'affaires at Washington, regarding Louisiana, that "if the Mississippi and Iberville trace with precision the eastern boundary of that colony, it has less precise limits to the westward. No river, no chain of mountains separates it from the Spanish possessions. . . . Spain already appears to fear that the United States, who show an intention of forcing back the western limits of Louisiana, may propose to advance in this direction to the ocean, and establish themselves on that part of the American coast which lies north of California." [2]

A week later Turreau was fully instructed as to the attitude of France upon the question of the claims against Spain,[3] and on August 30, 1804, a note assured the Spanish ambassador at Paris that in the treaty of cession and in the negotiations which preceded it "France could not even take upon herself to indicate what ought to be [the precise western limit of Louisiana] for fear of wounding upon this point the pretensions of one or other power directly interested. . . . Nevertheless, as the Americans derive their rights from France, I have been enabled to express to his Imperial Majesty's minister plenipotentiary near the United States the chief bases on which the emperor would have planted himself in the demand for the demarcation of boundaries; starting from the Gulf of Mexico, we should have sought to distinguish between settlements that belong to the kingdom of Mexico, and settlements that had been formed by the French or by those who succeeded

[1] Cevallos to Pinckney and Monroe, February 16, 1805, *State Papers*, II, 643. Italics in original.
[2] Talleyrand to Turreau, August 8, 1804, *Archives des Aff. Etr.* MSS., Adams, II, 295.   [3] *Ibid.*, 296.

them in this colony. This distinction between settlements formed by the French or by the Spaniards would have been made equally in ascending northward. All those which are of French foundation would have belonged to Louisiana. . . . The great spaces which sometimes exist between the last French settlements and the last Spanish missions might have left still some doubts on the direction of the boundary to be traced between them, but with the views of friendship and conciliation which animate their Majesties, these difficulties would have been soon smoothed away." [1]

It was a misfortune to the United States that the administration of its government was at this period almost completely in the hands of lawyers, seldom good administrators, and those in power displayed to the full the defects of their training. Jefferson and Madison had as their antagonists three of the ablest statesmen—Napoleon, Talleyrand, and William Pitt—the world has produced, and two of these were the most unscrupulous of history. To discuss with these two legal technicalities based upon the loose phraseology of a treaty the understanding of which by France and Spain, so far as the eastern boundary of Louisiana was concerned, had time and again been stated, was to fly in the face of fate. This, however, Monroe, as their agent, proceeded to do.

Monroe had already left London on October 8, 1804, for Paris, en route for Madrid, with Madison's voluminous instructions of April 15, 1804, for his guidance. On his arrival in France, though in nowise accredited to its government and despite the evident and just dissatisfaction of Livingston, still minister (though General Armstrong had arrived to succeed him), and with the fatuous idea that he might bring Napoleon to assist him in his Spanish negotiation, he addressed a letter to Talleyrand setting forth the object of his journey as "due to the candor which the President will never fail to observe in his transactions with the emperor," and repeating the well-worn arguments as to the ownership of West Florida.[2] One can well imagine the smile upon the saturnine countenance of Talleyrand, upon the reception of the document.

Monroe left Paris on December 8, for Madrid without a formal

[1] Talleyrand to Gravina, *Archives des Aff. Etr.* MSS., Adams, II, 299.
[2] Monroe to Talleyrand, November 8, 1804, *State Papers*, II, 634.

reply, but he had learned from "an informal but authentic source" that a report had been made to the emperor, "the substance of which was that West Florida was not comprised by the terms of the treaty or intention of the parties . . . and also that the claim on Spain by the United States for vessels condemned then taken by French privateers was precluded by our treaty with France of 1800." [1]

Monroe, who knew, as did his colleagues in diplomacy and every member of the American administration, that upon the attitude of Napoleon depended his success, might well have spared his government and himself the humiliation which he invited by proceeding on his mission in the face of such information. Napoleon had, in fact, determined that if Spain ceded Florida, the United States must pay money, and that the money should be for the benefit of France.[2]

Of all this Monroe had been informed, but with his slow mentality and dogged persistence of character, he held the course laid out for him by the two men, Jefferson and Madison, he most trusted, and who were equally at fault in pursuing a course which the dullest should have known, long before the negotiations were closed, could end only in failure.

While Monroe was now at least conscious that the French government did not uphold the American pretensions, he was far from

[1] Monroe to Madison, Bordeaux, December 16, 1804, *Writings*, IV, 277.
[2] On September 21, 1804, Livingston had written Madison. "While Spain wishes to limit us as much as possible [in the question of boundaries], France wishes to make our controversy favorable to her finances. Yesterday Marbois again spoke to me on the subject of purchasing the Floridas and giving sixty millions [of francs] for them and even pressed the matter very strongly upon me. You see by this which way the wind sets. The distresses of Spain make them fear that she shall not be able to comply with her engagements and the threatening war and internal expenses render the state of the Treasury here very precarious." (Monroe's *Writings*, IV, 305). On December 24, 1804, Armstrong wrote Madison: "This country has determined to convert the negotiation into a sale, to draw from it advantages merely pecuniary to herself, or in other words to her agents. It is this venality which explains her present reserve, the degree of excitement displayed by the emperor on reading the note, and the marked incivility with which Mr. Monroe was treated by Talleyrand. Since his departure repeated intimations have been given me that if certain persons could be sufficiently gratified, the negotiation should be transferred hither, and brought to a close with which we should have no reason to find fault." (MSS. State Department.)

knowing the acrimony of the language of the report of which he had been informed. "Only," said Talleyrand, "in case the United States should desist from their unjust pretensions to West Florida, and return to forms of civility and decorum, . . . could the emperor allow himself to second at the court of Madrid the project of the acquisition of the two Floridas." [1]

Backed by such views and by the knowledge soon to come, of a letter of similar tenor to the American minister at Paris, December 21, 1804, which was a reply to Monroe's own to Talleyrand, and which specifically stated that France had laid no claim to West Florida by the treaty of retrocession, but two years later had endeavored, without effect, to open negotiations for its cession,[2] the Spanish minister of state could well afford to treat the American negotiators with perfect ease of mind. Spain's enemies were now by treaty enemies of France, for even while Monroe was on his month's journey from Paris to Madrid, where he arrived January 2, 1805, Spain had declared war with England.

It was not until January 28, 1805, that the negotiation was opened with a note from Monroe and Pinckney devoted to the claim of the Rio Perdido on the east (which was unjust) and the Rio Bravo on the west (which was just), as the boundaries of the Louisiana cession; and to the propriety of Spain's yielding the remainder of the Floridas to the United States for a money consideration. Appended to this paper was a project of a convention, drawn in accordance with Madison's instructions, already mentioned, but including the claims arising from the suppression by the Spanish intendant, in 1802 and 1803, of the right of deposit at New Orleans.[3]

Thus began a futile four months' discussion aggravated by the pressure to their limit of the American claims for depredations, a pressure scarcely to be avoided by the American negotiators in the face of their instructions backed as they were by a private letter from Madison to Monroe saying "Spain must also, sooner or later, swallow the claim for French injuries. All she can expect is

[1] Rapport a l'Empereur, November 19, 1804, *Archives des Affaires Étrangères*, etc. MSS., Adams, *United States*, II, 312.
[2] Talleyrand to Armstrong, *State Papers*, II, 435.
[3] *State Papers*, II, 636-639.

to have the pill wrapped up in the least nauseous disguise." Madison wrote as if France herself was not to be considered, and as if he were backed by battle-ships instead of by the petty gun-boats which were Jefferson's ideal of naval power for the United States. He informed Monroe that Pinckney's recall had been asked by the Spanish government and that Bowdoin was to succeed him. "He [Pinckney] is well off in escaping reproof, for his agency has been very faulty as well as feeble," words which we of this day may well think should apply even more forcibly to Madison himself and to his chief. The vanity of Godoy, who was regarded as all-powerful, was to be appealed to as his special weakness. "Such a resource is not to be neglected. But the main one will lie in a skilful appeal to the fears of Spain and the interest which France as well as Spain has in not favoring a coalition of the United States with Great Britain.[1]

The demand for the inclusion of the French claims brought at once from Señor Cevallos the disclosure of the note from the French government to its ambassador at Madrid forbidding its becoming the subject of a new discussion.[2] The sharpness of the Spanish note, particularly in regard to the question of the deposit, caused the American negotiators to fear an end of the negotiation, and they requested a conference. Señor Cevallos followed this with a temperate discussion of the eastern boundary of Louisiana.[3]

By this time Monroe had also Talleyrand's note of December 21, 1804, to Armstrong, emphatically denying the right of France, by the treaty of St. Ildefonso, to West Florida and consequently the right of the United States. Monroe had written Armstrong twice during February to sound the French government in the general question of Florida, sending copies of his correspondence with Cevallos; these last, however, were not shown to the French foreign office in view of the very emphatic declaration which Armstrong received and conveyed in a letter of March 12, 1805, to Monroe, that the French government declared that the claim for French spoliations within Spanish territory must be abandoned, and that in the event of rupture with Spain "we can neither doubt nor

[1] Madison to Monroe, November 9, 1804, *Works*, II, 208.
[2] February 16, 1805, *State Papers*, II, 643, *Supra.* 78.
[3] February 24, 1805, *Ibid.*, II, 644.

hesitate; we must take part with Spain, and our note of December 21, 1804, was intended to communicate and impress this idea."[1]

The remainder of the negotiation was but a beating of the air. Though the American negotiators, in a note of April 9, made a distinct threat of war, saying if Spain was indisposed to "adjust these important concerns . . . on fair and equal terms," that "the United States are not unprepared for or unequal to any crisis that may occur," and declaring that they had submitted with unexampled patience to the injuries of which they complain,"[2] Señor Cevallos, feeling secure under the ægis of Napoleon took no notice of the threat and proceeded four days later to discuss the western boundary of Louisiana, which he said "should be by a line beginning on the Gulf between the river Caricut, or Cascassia, and the Armenta, or Marmentoa, (and) should go to the north, passing between the Adaes and Natchitoches, until it cuts the Red River." The boundary thence only was to be a subject of negotiation.[3]

Monroe at this time could write in his diary, "No other alternative presented itself to me than to abandon the object and return to London, or to submit to the terms which it was sufficiently understood France was willing to accept, and seemed in some measure to dictate, which amounted to this: that we should create a new loan of about seventy millions of livres, and transfer the same to Spain, who would immediately pass them over to France, in consideration of which we should be put in possession of the disputed territory, under stipulations which should provide for the adjustment of the ultimate right there, and reimbursement of the money by instalment in seven years."[4]

Notwithstanding this conviction and the passing of four months in unavailing discussion, the American envoys on May 12, 1805, made one more effort in a statement of what they termed their "ultimate conditions." These were, in case Spain would cede all territory east of the Mississippi and arbitrate the claims of the citizens and subjects of each power under the convention of August 11, 1802, the United States would waive all other claims and cede all right to territory west of the line formed by the Rio

[1] *State Papers*, II, 636.   [2] *Ibid.*, II, 659.   [3] *Ibid.*, II, 662.
[4] Monroe's diary at Aranjuez, April 22, 1805, MSS. State Department.

Colorado to its headwaters, thence to the south-westerly source of the Red River, thence along the highland forming the watershed of the Mississippi and Missouri and of the Rio Bravo, thence north, with a belt of thirty leagues on each side of the line, or on the American side only, to "remain neutral and unsettled forever."![1]

The Spanish minister of state, denying the claim of the United States to the territory which they offered to cede for the Floridas, and declaring the propositions wholly unjust to Spain and inadmissible,[2] the American envoys, on May 18, 1805, stated that they considered the negotiations closed. Three days later, Monroe had audience of their Spanish Majesties, left Madrid May 26, reached Paris June 20, remained there until July 17, in the vain hope that the French government would relent, and reached his post at London July 23, conscious of humiliating failure. Pinckney was recalled in October and G. W. Erving was sent from London to take charge of the legation as chargé d'affaires. Pinckney's successor, James Bowdoin, did not leave the United States until the following summer, and then only to touch at Santander, proceed to London for consultation with Monroe, and thence to France, where he was to be associated with General Armstrong in Paris, to which capital any further negotiation in Spanish matters was now transferred, the presence of a minister at Madrid being regarded undesirable in what had become very strained relations. How strained, may be judged from the reception by Godoy, in December, of Mr. Erving's remonstrances against the seizures of American ships in flagrant violation of the treaty of 1795. Receiving Erving with "the good-natured courtesy which marked his manners," he asked, "How go our affairs? Are we to have peace or war?" As to the seizures the prince said it was impossible for Spain to allow American vessels to carry English property. "But," said Erving, "we have a treaty which secures us that right"; to which Godoy replied, "Certainly, I know you have a treaty, for I made it with Mr. Pinckney"; and proceeding to announce that the free goods provision would be no longer respected, said: "You may choose either peace or war. It's the same thing to me. I will tell you candidly that if you will go to war this is certainly the moment and you may take our possessions from us. I advise you to go to war now, if you

[1] *State Papers*, II, 665.   [2] *Ibid.*, 666.

think this is best for you; and then the peace which will be made in Europe will leave us two at war."[1]

There was in this a hint of the foreboding which Godoy—far the cleverest Spaniard of his time—must have had of the storm which was soon to break upon Spain from France. He may have hoped that an American war would bring difficulties to France, in which would lie safety to the peninsula which itself was soon to be much more seriously threatened than was distant Florida.

[1] Erving to Madison, December 7, 1805, MSS. State Department, Adams, III, 38.

CHAPTER V

WAVERING BETWEEN WAR AND PEACE. PROPOSED ALLIANCE WITH GREAT BRITAIN ABANDONED FOR INTRIGUE WITH FRANCE

HAD Jefferson had a tithe of Napoleon's foresight and decision he would now have acted as Armstrong advised in a letter sent to Monroe while still at Madrid. "It is simply," he said, "to take a strong and prompt possession of the northern bank of the Rio Bravo, leaving the eastern limit *in statu quo*. A stroke of this kind would at once bring Spain to reason and France to her rescue, and without giving either room to quarrel. You might then negotiate and shape the bargain pretty much as you pleased." [1]

But the timidity of character common to both Jefferson and Madison stood in the way of such action, politically wise and morally just. While deprecating even the possibility of war, they had been pressing the claim to West Florida to the very verge of hostilities, and this, though assured by statement after statement, official and unofficial, from Frenchman and Spaniard of its baselessness. Nor was Madison blind to the truth and meaning of such statements. He could write Jefferson: "If [France] should persist in disavowing her right to sell West Florida to the United States, and above all can prove it to have been the mutual understanding with Spain that West Florida was no part of Louisiana, it will place our claim on very different ground—such probably as would not be approved by the world, and such certainly as would not with that approbation be maintained by force." [2]

Jefferson, every effort of whose administration thus far had been toward the unjust despoilment of Spain, could write: "That our relations with Spain should be of a peaceable and friendly character

---

[1] Armstrong to Monroe, May 4, 1805, MSS. State Department.
[2] Madison to Jefferson, March 27, 1805, Jefferson MSS., Adams, III, 55.

has been our most earnest desire. Had Spain met us with the same dispositions, our idea was that her existence in this hemisphere and ours should have rested on the same bottom; we should have swam or sunk together. We want nothing of hers and we want no other nation to possess what is hers. But she has met our advances with jealousy, secret malice, and ill-faith. Our patience under this unworthy return of disposition is now on its last trial. And the issue of what is now depending between us will decide whether our relations with her are to be sincerely friendly or permanently hostile. I still wish and would cherish the former but have ceased to expect it." [1]

It is impossible to reconcile the conduct of the American executive and the sentiment of these letters. Gallatin, secretary of the treasury, and in many ways the most solid mind of the administration, said: "The demands from Spain were too hard to have expected, even independent of French interference, any success from the negotiation." Though he had been steadily opposed to any increase of expenditures for the navy, he now said that which was the only real solution of the problem of the preservation of American dignity. "Perhaps a law making efficient provision for building a dozen of ships of the line would be the most dignified and most forcible mode of reopening the negotiation." He could not help, however, hedging somewhat in remarking, "But it will be a doubt with some whether the remedy be not worse than the disorder." [2]

Deeply moved by the humiliation which his diplomacy had brought, Jefferson's thoughts now turned again to a British alliance. On August 7, 1805 he wrote Madison the suggestion, and asked that he would consult the secretaries of war and of the navy, [3] and himself on the same date [4] wrote Gallatin, on whose judgment he had special reliance. Jefferson's views, given more fully in a later letter to Madison, were that "the treaty should be provisional only, to come into force on the event of our being engaged in war with either France or Spain during the present war in Europe. In that event we should make common cause and England should

---

[1] Jefferson to Bowdoin, April 27, 1805, *Writings*, VIII, 351.
[2] Gallatin to Madison, August 6, 1805, *Writings*, I, 238.
[3] Jefferson, *Writings*, VIII, 375.   [4] *Ibid.*, VIII, 375.

stipulate not to make peace without our obtaining the objects for which we go to war, to wit: the acknowledgment by Spain of the rightful boundaries of Louisiana (which we should reduce to our minimum by a secret article), and, second, indemnification for spoliations, for which purpose we should be allowed to make reprisal on the Floridas, and *retain them* as an indemnification. Our co-operation in the war (if we should actually enter into it) would be a sufficient consideration for Great Britain to engage for its object; and it being generally known to France and Spain that we had entered into treaty with England would probably insure us a peaceable and immediate settlement of both points." [1]

Gallatin's reply to Jefferson's request for an opinion, delayed by the illness and death of a child, did not come until September. A strong criticism of the character of our diplomacy with Spain, and an appeal for peace, it carried Jefferson's wavering mind with it. Gallatin held that the failure of the American negotiators of the treaty of cession of Louisiana to demand exact boundaries was a failure for which Spain was not responsible and which should not be remedied by war. Nor were the spoliations in the circumstances sufficient justification for war. As to the policy of war he was even more emphatic. He dreaded the expense; he saw melting away the yearly surplus which was rapidly reducing the debt, and could only expect a disrupture of the orderly system of federal finance of which he was the careful nurse. He asked, "What are both Floridas worth? For this is exactly what we may gain . . . what would be the cost of one year's war, not merely the positive expense, but the national loss? . . . In case of rupture it is to be expected that France and Spain will seize or sequester property to an immense amount; Amsterdam, Antwerp, and even Bordeaux, Cadiz, and Leghorn are filled with our merchants' property, exclusive of vessels which might be there at the time." Gallatin discussed "boundaries," the "*status quo*," the question of "Mobile," the "convention of 1802," "new aggressions" by French and Spanish privateers ("often armed in Cuba and who uniformly take their prizes there and plunder them"), and finally "preparations" which meant the building of a navy. He would apply the surplus of two millions a year ("and it is a very low

[1] Jefferson, *Writings*, VIII, 377.

calculation"), which he considered would be lost in case of war, wholly "to the building of ships of the line . . . that the act would have a favorable effect on our foreign relations, and even on the pending negotiation, is also certain. Nor indeed, supposing Congress to be at all events averse to a war with Spain for the present, would it be an undignified course to make efficient provision for the preparation of a force which would prevent a repetition of wrongs which the United States did not at this moment feel prepared properly to resent"[1]—wise words to which, almost at the moment of their writing, a deeper significance was to be given by the beginning of a series of events to which the previous "wrongs" mentioned were but as trifles.

Scarcely anything could be more surprising, in the face of Gallatin's long-continued opposition to such a course, than this turning of his thoughts to a powerful navy, truest statesmanship as this was. His argument was for this and for three or four years of peace. His wish for the latter, which the mere beginning of naval preparation would have assured with honor, was fulfilled by supinely cowering with dishonor; his suggestion for the former was unheeded. The result to America was humiliation which should have entered as iron into the soul of her rulers.

Without entirely dropping the idea of a British alliance, Jefferson, who had received and now leaned to Armstrong's suggestion of the occupancy of Texas, wrote Madison: "Supposing a previous alliance with England to guard us in the worst event, I should propose that Congress should pass acts (1) authorizing the executive to suspend intercourse with Spain at discretion; (2) to dislodge the new establishments of Spain between the Mississippi and Bravo; (3) to appoint commissioners to examine and ascertain all claims for spoliation."[2]

But news was about reaching America which brought an end to any idea of a British alliance, and as Jefferson was not of the fibre to hold long to the bold views which he had thus expressed, he turned to the underhand proposals of France which had been sufficiently accurately expressed in the quotation already given from Monroe's diary.[3]

[1] Gallatin to Jefferson, September 15, 1805, *Writings*, I, 241–254.
[2] Jefferson to Madison, September 16, 1805, *Works*, IV, 587. [3] *Supra*, 83.

Some words of explanation are now necessary to the understanding of our relations with Great Britain which had so great a bearing upon those with Spain.

The United States at this period was, through her neutrality, practically the world's carrier. Nations at this period were still wholly under the bondage of the idea that the trade of colonies should be the perquisite of the parent state, the first break in which was the opening by France of her colonial ports to neutral commerce in 1793, she being then at war with England and her own carriers swept from the sea. So long as this neutral trade continued the colonies prospered as in peace, and the trade of the European continent kept pace with this prosperity, but the gainer above all was the American ship-owner. England invoked "the rule of 1756" which in substance was "that a neutral has no right to deliver a belligerent from the pressure of his enemies' hostilities by trading with his colonies in time of war in a manner not allowed in time of peace." The effect was decree and counter decree under which American ships were seized or detained in hundreds by France, Spain, and England. It is impossible to detail here the complexities of this subject, with which it was difficult for the ship-owner himself to keep pace. In 1800, however, it was possible for American ships to bring cargoes from the Dutch and Spanish colonies to the United States and re-export such goods to Holland and Spain. The direct voyage was not allowed, but it soon became a question as to what constituted an actual re-export from America. In February, 1800, Sir William Scott (later Lord Stowell) gave a momentous decision in the matter. The ship *Polly* had brought a cargo from Havana to Marblehead, had landed and paid duty upon this, had repaired, effected a new insurance and had reshipped the cargo and sailed for Bilboa. She was seized and brought in as a prize, but Scott held that she had not made a continuous voyage and the ship was released. During the remainder of the war, closed by the short peace of Amiens, American shipping prospered amazingly, and when war broke again, protected by Scott's decision, it was again the great carrier. Practically every merchant flag had disappeared from the seas except those of the United States and Great Britain, and the former had largely taken over that which naturally would have been the trade of British ships. "So far was the rule of 1756 relaxed that the ports of the United States of America became so many entrepots for the manufactures and commodities of France, Spain, and Holland, from whence they were re-exported under the American flag to their respective colonies; they brought back the produce of those colonies to the ports of America; they reshipped them for the enemies' ports of Europe; they entered freely all the ports of the United Kingdom, with cargoes brought directly from the hostile colonies; thus, in fact, not only carrying on the whole trade of one of the belligerents, which that belligerent would have carried on in time of peace, but superadding their own and part of ours. . . . One single American house contracted for the whole of the merchandise of the Dutch East India Company at Batavia, amounting to no less a sum than £1,700,000 sterling. The consequence was that while not a single merchant ship belonging to the enemy crossed the Atlantic or doubled the Cape of Good Hope, the produce of the Eastern and Western worlds sold cheaper in the markets of France and Holland than in our own. . . . The commerce of England became every month more languid and prostrate, till reduced, as justly observed, . . . 'to a state of suspended animation.'"[1]

It was not in human nature for England to sit calmly and see the world's carrying trade pass to other hands and make prosperous her enemies, while, moreover, she was, in her view, fighting the battle of the world's freedom. Thus on July 23, 1805, the very day Monroe reached London from Madrid and Paris, worn with the knowledge of a great failure, Scott reversed his decision of three years before, and held as fair prize the *Essex*, which had sailed from Barcelona, had landed her goods at Salem, given bond only for the payment of duties on goods not exported, and, reladen with the same cargo, had sailed for Havana. The voyage was held by Scott as in effect a direct voyage, a decision, be it said, which was to have a weighty bearing against British shipping in the American civil war.

The immediate effect of Sir William Scott's decision was the seizure of a large number of American ships. Fifty were known to have been carried to ports in the British islands and as many were

[1] *London Quarterly Review*, March, 1812, 5–7; Moore, *Digest*, VII, 384.

believed to have been libelled in the West Indies.[1] The American loss was enormous and the situation one of despair to the American commercial world. The new rule was but the beginning of further restrictions, of decrees by Napoleon and orders in council by Great Britain which were as sentences of death to the American carrying trade.[2]

But the *Essex* decision had a secondary effect of much greater consequence than mere monetary loss. Added to the already overbearing conduct of British naval commanders, who carried on the right of search and impressment even in our own waters and were practically blockading New York; with Englishman, Frenchman, and Spaniard as naval officer, privateer, or pirate seizing American ships in every part of the world, the American executive naturally gave up the hope of an English alliance and turned to France, knowing that in the terms she was willing to make was the only road to the peaceable possession of the Floridas. Qualms of conscience wholly disappeared; there was to be a complete negation both of morals and bold words despite Madison's expressions of lofty morality ("entirely" approved by Jefferson) in a despatch to Armstrong of June 6, 1805, in which he spoke of the venal suggestions emanating from the French functionaries," and Jefferson's bold remark that "considering the character of Bonaparte, I think it material at once to let him see we are not of the powers who will receive his orders."[3] The occasion was at the meeting of the cabinet, on Jefferson's initiative and following his suggestions,[4] November 12, 1805; the results are set down in Jefferson's own hand:

"Present the four secretaries; subject, Spanish affairs. The extension of the war in Europe leaving us without danger of a sudden peace, depriving us of the chance of an ally, I proposed we should address ourselves to France, informing her it was a last effort at amicable settlement with Spain and offer to her or through her: (1) A sum of money for the rights of Spain east of Iberville, say the Floridas; (2) To cede the part of Louisiana from the Rio

[1] Monroe to British secretary for foreign affairs, September 25, 1805.
[2] For an admirable analysis of the maritime difficulties of the period, see Admiral Mahan, *Sea Power in Its Relations to the War of* 1812.
[3] Jefferson to Madison, August 27, 1805, *Writings*, VIII, 377.
[4] Jefferson to Madison, October 23, 1805, and to Robert Smith, secretary of the navy, October 24, 1805, *Ibid.*, VIII, 380, 381.

Bravo to the Guadeloupe; (3) Spain to pay within a certain time spoliations under her own flag, agreed to by the convention (which we guess to be a hundred vessels, worth two millions), and those subsequent (worth as much more), and to hypothecate for these payments the country from Guadeloupe to the Rio Bravo; Armstrong to be employed. The first was to be the exciting motive with France, to whom Spain is in arrears for subsidies, and who will be glad also to secure us from going into the scale of England; the second, the soothing motive with Spain, which France would press *bona fide* because she claimed to the Rio Bravo; the third to quiet our merchants. It was agreed to unanimously, and the sum to be offered fixed not to exceed five million dollars. Mr. Gallatin did not like purchasing Florida under an apprehension of war, lest we should be thought in fact to purchase peace. We thought this overweighted by taking advantage of an opportunity which might not occur again of getting a country essential to our peace and to the security of the commerce of the Mississippi. It was agreed that Yrujo should be sounded through Dallas whether he is not going away, and if not he should be made to understand that his presence at Washington will not be agreeable and that his departure is expected. Casa Calvo, Morales, and all the Spanish officers at New Orleans are to be desired to depart with a discretion to Claiborne [Governor of Louisiana] to let any friendly ones remain who will resign and become citizens, and also women receiving pensions to remain if they choose." [1]

The day after this meeting, in which the President and his counsellors had decided to succumb to the covert overtures of France made months before, arrived from General Armstrong definite propositions. The French situation gave an earnest of its intentions. Napoleon in August had changed his menace from England to Austria; his vast schemes demanded money; this his ally Spain could only supply through the concessions for which the United States would pay. An unsigned note in Talleyrand's handwriting was handed to the American minister advising that Spain be frightened by vigorous language and conduct, "to unite in reclaiming the good offices of France." Said the note: "The more you refer to the decisions of the emperor the more sure and easy will be the

[1] *Cabinet Memoranda*, Jefferson MSS., Adams, III, 78.

settlement. . . . The following conditions will probably be acceptable to France and all her efforts will be given to have them executed." France and Spain to have the same trade privileges in the Floridas as in Louisiana; the boundary to be the Colorado and a line northwardly including the headwaters of all rivers entering the Mississippi, with thirty leagues on each side to be unoccupied forever; the debts due from Spain (excluding the French spoliations) to be paid by bills on the Spanish colonies; ten million dollars to be given by the United States to Spain.[1]

On September 4, Napoleon was in Paris *en route* for Austria. Talleyrand's agent reappeared; Armstrong objected to the proposals as sacrificing the country between the Colorado and Rio Bravo; as accommodating Spain in the payment of her debts beyond what she herself required; as sacrificing part of West Florida; as abandoning the *entrepôt* claim and that for the French spoliations. Finally, ten millions was an enormous sum for East Florida. What, declared Armstrong, is to prevent our occupancy to the Rio Bravo, the holding of the Floridas as indemnity for Spain's debt, or laying an embargo on Spanish commerce? He was answered: "I see where the shoe pinches. It is the enormous sum of ten millions of dollars; but say seven. Your undisputed claims on Spain amount to two and a half or three millions." On September 10, 1805, Armstrong sent his despatch.[2]

In a cabinet meeting, November 14, terms were agreed upon by which territory extending to the Rio Bravo (Texas) was to remain unsettled for but thirty years, and meanwhile to be hypothecated by Spain to the United States as a guarantee for the payment, by December 31, 1807, of $4,000,000 indemnity, for spoliations under her flag prior to November 1, 1805.[3] But on November 19, these were abandoned and Napoleon's proposition was accepted in full except that five millions instead of seven should be paid; for this last the authority of Congress was necessary.[4]

Jefferson at once acted upon Talleyrand's advice as energetically as the latter could have hoped. On the opening of Congress, December 3, 1805, he sent a message which was taken by the

[1] Armstrong to Madison, September 10, 1805, MSS. State Department.
[2] *Ibid.*   [3] Cabinet decision on Spain, Jefferson's Writings, VIII, 383.
[4] For the cabinet memoranda in full, see Adams, 111, 106.

public as equivalent to advising a declaration of war against Spain. Nothing of the diplomatic correspondence of the year had been made public; nothing other than the message was in the hands of Congress to enable it to read the mind of the executive. The message said: "With Spain our negotiations for the settlement of differences have not had a satisfactory issue. Spoliations during the former war, for which she had formally acknowledged herself responsible, have been refused to be compensated, but on conditions affecting other claims in nowise connected with them. Yet the same practices are renewed in the present war and are already of great amount. On the Mobile our commerce passing through that river continues to be obstructed by arbitrary duties and vexatious searches. Propositions for adjusting amicably the boundaries of Louisiana have not been acceded to. While, however, the right is unsettled, we have avoided changing the state of things by taking new coasts or strengthening ourselves in the disputed territories in the hope that the other powers would not, by a contrary conduct, oblige us to meet their example and endanger conflicts of authority the issue of which may not be entirely controlled. But in this hope we have now reason to lessen our confidence. Inroads have been recently made into the territories of Orleans and the Mississippi. Our citizens have been seized and their property plundered in the very parts of the former which had actually been delivered up by Spain, and this by the regular officers and soldiers of that government. I have therefore found it necessary at length to give orders to our troops on that frontier to be in readiness to protect our citizens and to repel by arms any similar aggressions in future. Other details necessary for your information of the state of things between this country and that shall be the subject of another communication.

"In reviewing these injuries from some of the belligerent powers, the moderation, the firmness and the wisdom of the legislature will all be called into action. We ought still to hope that time and a more correct estimate of interests as well as of character will produce the justice we are bound to expect. But should any nation deceive itself by false calculations and disappoint that expectation we must join in the unprofitable contest of trying which party can do the other most harm. Some of these injuries may perhaps admit a peaceable remedy. Where that is competent it is always the most desirable. But some of them are of a nature to be met by force only and all of them may lead to it. I cannot therefore but recommend such preparations as circumstances call for. The first object is to place our seaport towns out of danger of insult. Measures have been already taken for furnishing them with heavy cannon for the service of such land batteries as make a part of their defence against armed vessels approaching them."

It is not surprising that the seaboard was thrown by such a document into a state of anxious expectancy and that sea insurance doubled. The President continued his message with a statement of what was desirable for defence—"a competent number of gunboats, and the number, to be competent, must be considerable"; and such an organization of the militia "as would enable us on any sudden emergency to call for the services of the younger portion" were recommended. No word of a navy was uttered beyond discussing whether it was advisable to limit the complement of the few frigates to two-thirds the full number as the law now required.

Six days later, on December 9, a second message promised in the first was sent as a confidential document with the papers relating to the late abortive negotiation, and next day additional documents illustrating the seizures and plunders of American property in Cuba, Puerto Rico, West Florida, and Louisiana. The documents, said the message, "authorize the inference that it is the [Spaniards'] intention to advance on our possessions until they shall be repressed by an opposing force." No recommendation, however, was made, the President confining his warlike fervor of a few days before to the remark that "considering that Congress alone is constitutionally invested with the power of changing our condition from peace to war, I have thought it my duty to await their authority for using force in any degree which could be avoided."[1]

There was no hint in the message of the entirely new direction which his diplomacy had taken, and which he was confident would solve the anxious situation which he so graphically detailed in his message of December 3, and which in reality was but a play en-

[1] The message and accompanying documents are in *State Papers*, II, 613–669; those regarding depredations, in *ibid.*, 669–695.

acted for the supposed benefit of the French government, to be taken to heart by Spain in the new negotiation now proposed to be set on foot.[1] For the benefit of Congress, John Randolph (the chairman of the committee to which the message was referred) was informed privately that what was really wanted was an appropriation of $2,000,000 to carry out what was now considered a compact with France, a request which Randolph bitterly opposed, as laying the burden of initiative upon Congress and not upon the administration which had brought about the situation and which should be courageous enough to say what it wanted and what it intended doing. Madison told Randolph "that France would not permit Spain to settle her differences with us; that she wanted money and that we must give her money or take a Spanish or French war." "From that moment," said Randolph, "all the objections I had to the procedure were aggravated in the highest possible degree. I considered it a base prostration of the national character to excite one nation by money to bully another out of its property." [2]

It is out of place to discuss the party schism which now occurred, the causes of which laid deeper than in distaste for Jefferson's proposal, so properly stigmatized by Randolph. The latter, however, failed in his opposition, and a bill was passed, signed by the President, February 13, 1806, appropriating the money.

But more than this was necessary to propitiate Napoleon. Santo Domingo had now almost entirely escaped from the grasp of France, but, as the richest island of the time, the trade of which, inward and outward, had at times amounted to $140,000,000, Napoleon held to its possession with a fixity of purpose which made abhorrent to him the support given the insurgent blacks by the trade with the United States. The American ships left their home ports armed, a procedure in itself a necessary precaution against the swarm of piratical rovers in the Caribbean, but there was frequently a superfluous equipment which found its way to the Haytians. In a despatch from Armstrong of August 10, 1805, was enclosed a note from Talleyrand written in terms of deep indignation, which closed with "his Majesty charges me, sir, to

---

[1] See Jefferson to Gallatin, November 24, 1805, Gallatin's *Writings*, I, 264.
[2] Randolph's speeches, April 5 and 7, 1806, *Annals of Congress*, 1805–1806, pp. 947, 985.

request, in his name, that they interdict every private adventure which, under any pretext or designation whatever, may be destined to the ports of St. Domingo occupied by the rebels." [1]

This note was soon followed by another in much more peremptory terms, saying, "This complaint obliges his Majesty to consider as good prize everything which shall enter the port of St. Domingo occupied by the rebels, and everything coming out," ending with: "This system of impunity and intolerance can no longer continue (*ne pourroit durer davantage*), and his Majesty is convinced that your government will think it due from its frankness promptly to put an end to it." [2]

Despite the strong opposition which came from ship-owners and from the men of more independent spirit in Congress, Napoleon's mandate, aided by the South's fears of the rebel negroes, was obeyed and on February 28, 1806, a bill received the President's signature declaring forfeited any American ship, including cargo, "which shall be voluntarily carried or shall be destined to proceed," to Santo Domingo. The law was limited to one year.

France propitiated at every point, the way to Florida now seemed clear, and on March 13, 1806, Madison wrote Armstrong and Bowdoin in Paris, directing them to express the views of the administration in a way "which, without any improper condescensions on the part of the United States, will best conciliate the French government to our objects"; the latter was to be informed "that no direct communication on the subject has been made to the Spanish government." [3] But the sacrifice was in vain. Napoleon was now holding Florida as a bait for an American alliance. When, on May 1, 1806, Armstrong made known to the French foreign office his instructions just received, and when next day Talleyrand carried the subject to Napoleon, the latter placed in Talleyrand's hands a formal declaration from Charles IV, that on no account would he alienate the Floridas. This, no doubt, was a part of the play arranged by the arch-schemer himself, for when the French ambassador in Madrid, urged by Talleyrand, and making the mistake of supposing constancy in Napoleon's wishes

---

[1] *State Papers*, II, 726.
[2] Talleyrand to Armstrong, August 16, 1805, *Ibid.*, II, 727.
[3] *Ibid.*, III, 539.

or plans, obtained from Godoy, in June, an agreement to refer the negotiation of the questions in dispute to Paris, he met stern rebuke from the emperor for his meddlesomeness. The subject passed beyond the influence of the American minister to cause a recall, until Napoleon nearly two years later was to offer the Floridas to America if she would join with France.

The autumn of 1806 found Napoleon, through the battle of Jena, master of Prussia, from whose capital, on November 21, he issued the famous Berlin decree, followed a year later by the yet more drastic decree from Milan which practically annulled neutral rights and carried despair to the American ship-owner. These were his answers to Jefferson's attempts at propitiation. He was determined if possible, now that the French navy had been engulfed at Trafalgar, to force the United States to take sides against England.

The great numbers of sequestered ships soon to be held in French ports could, the American minister was informed, only be released when the American government should take sides with France,[1] and on February 2, 1808, the French army now occupying Spain, Napoleon directed Champagny, now foreign minister, to "Let the American minister know that whenever war shall be declared between America and England, and whenever . . . the Americans shall send troops into the Floridas to help the Spaniards and repulse the English, I shall much approve of it. You will even let him perceive that in case America should be disposed to enter into a treaty of alliance, and make common cause with me, I shall not be unwilling to intervene with the court of Spain to obtain the cession of these same Floridas in favor of the Americans."[2] Armstrong besought "the government to select its enemy, either France or England," but "in either case do not suspend for a moment the seizure of the Floridas"[3] and informed the state department a week later that the emperor was determined "that the Americans should be compelled to take the positive character either of allies or enemies," ending with the significant words: "If I am right in supposing that the emperor has definitively taken his ground I cannot be wrong in concluding that you will immediately take yours."[4]

[1] Champagny to Armstrong, January 15, 1808, *State Papers*, III, 249.
[2] Napoleon, *Correspondence*, XVI, 301.
[3] Armstrong to Madison, February 15, 1808, MSS., State Department.
[4] Armstrong to Madison, February 22, 1808, *State Papers*, III, 250.

Before this was received the administration had taken its ground, but not in the sense intimated by Armstrong. On May 2, 1808, Madison wrote, referring to Champagny's note of January 15: "To present to the United States the alternative of bending to the views of France against her enemy, or of incurring a confiscation of all the property of their citizens carried into the French prize courts, implied that they were susceptible of impressions by which no independent and honorable nation can be guided," [1] a sentiment conveyed to the French government in a note of July 4, from Armstrong, who six days later, in a note declining more definitely the alliance, expressed the satisfaction of the administration in hearing of the emperor's approval of "a cautionary occupation of the Floridas," which had come to the American government through the French minister at Washington. [2] Napoleon threw over the subject as if never in question. He directed the foreign minister: "Answer the American minister that you do not know what he means about the occupation of the Floridas, and that the Americans, being at peace with the Spaniards, cannot occupy the Floridas without the permission or request of the King of Spain." [3]

Intrigue at least with France was ended. On December 31, 1808, the two millions appropriated for the purchase, but in reality as a bribe to Napoleon, lapsed and the American minister was informed: "From this and other considerations it is deemed expedient at present to suspend the negotiation in relation to that subject." [4]

There were, however, during 1805 and 1806, other serious causes of trouble with Spain besides the attempts of the American administration to close the questions of Florida and Louisiana. Two men, both of fervid imagination and reckless in scheme, appeared in the troubled world of Spanish-American politics. One, Miranda, can be granted a spirit of patriotism; the other, Aaron Burr, ex-vice-president of the United States, and slayer of Hamilton, looked to the dismemberment of the western country from the Union, and

[1] Madison to Armstrong, *State Papers*, III, 252.
[2] Champagny to Turreau, February 15, 1808, *Archives des Aff. Étr.* MSS., Adams, IV, 308.
[3] Napoleon, *Correspondence*, XVII, 326.
[4] Robert Smith, secretary of state to Armstrong, March 15, 1809, *State Papers*, III, 542.

the setting up of an independent empire which should include Mexico. Burr intrigued with the British minister, Jackson, who lent himself to his views. Failing, however, the support of the money and fleet requested of the British government, which in no wise accorded with its minister, Burr turned to the Spanish minister for aid in Louisiana, the population of which was deeply disaffected and ready to return to the mastership of either France or Spain. Should circumstances favor, the fault was largely with the federal administration, which, besides being indifferent to their demands for self-government, had sent a governor unfitted for such a post, and retained in command of its forces a traitor in the pay of Spain. The French prefect of a few weeks thus describes Claiborne, the governor, and Wilkinson, the general. "The first, with estimable private qualities, has little capacity and much awkwardness, and is extremely beneath his place; the second, already long known here in a bad way, is a flighty, rattle-headed fellow, often drunk, who has committed a hundred impertinent follies."[1] That Wilkinson was deep in Burr's conspiracy, though he was later, but very tardily, to assist in revealing it, is undoubted. To what point his Spanish connections would have led him is, of course, but wild conjecture with such a character. Spain had full knowledge of Burr's plans and was apprehensive as to Mexico and the Floridas. That there was hope in the heart of the Spanish minister at Washington of a gain to Spain through Wilkinson's association with Burr's project may be supposed from his despatch home of December 4, 1806. "I wrote to the governors of both Floridas and to the viceroy of Mexico, giving them a general idea of this affair and recommending them to watch the movements of Colonel Burr and his adventurers. This is an excess of precaution since by this time they must not only know through the New Orleans and Natchez newspapers of the projects attributed to Colonel Burr, but through the confidential channel of the No. 13 [Wilkinson] of the Marquis of Casa Calvo's cipher with the Prince of Peace, who is one of the conspirators, and who is to contribute very efficaciously to the scheme in case it shall be carried into effect."[2]

[1] Laussat to Decrès, April 8, 1804, Gayarré, III, 10; Adams, III, 298.
[2] Yrujo to Cevallos, MSS., *Spanish Archives*, Adams, III, 263.

The conspiracy dwindled to but a picturesque episode and left the Louisianians unsettled and uncertain. It did one good, however; it opened the eyes of the administration to the serious character of the feeling of the French-Spanish population. Fifteen hundred Spanish troops were in the Red River region, with a strong garrison at Bayou Pierre and a force close to Natchitoches. There was evidently now no intention on the part of Spain of yielding Texas except under pressure.

Francisco de Miranda, born at Carácas June 9, 1756, had been an officer in the Spanish army, which he left in 1783 under strong suspicion of disloyalty. He then passed some time in the United States and became very friendly with Hamilton, whom he imbued with his ideas of independence for the South American provinces. He went to Europe and was general of a division under Dumouriez in the French republican army. Obliged to leave France, he went to England, then (1798) at war with France and Spain, and interested Pitt in his schemes, as also Mr. Rufus King, the American minister at London, who regarded the situation of affairs between the United States and Spain as very serious and Miranda's projects as offering a welcome aid to the former in case of war. England's action depended entirely on Spain's attitude toward France.[1]

Miranda came to the United States in November, 1805, with numerous letters of introduction which gave him an excellent standing with the prominent men he sought to meet; among them Jefferson and Madison. All were undoubtedly sympathetic, though he was informed by Madison that the United States could not aid or countenance any secret enterprise and would interfere in case of infraction of the law. Madison's attitude was represented very differently to William Smith, surveyor of the port of New York and a warm friend of Miranda's, and to a Mr. Samuel Ogden, who both, moved by the impression of the government's favor, gave him aid, Ogden furnishing him the ship *Leander* in which he was to sail with his expedition. He left New York February 1, 1806, his almost last act being to write a most compromising letter to Madison, which gave the impression that the latter was fully informed of the expedition and was in sympathy with its purpose. Miranda touched Jamaica, purchasing there two schooners in which thirty-

[1] King to Madison, April 6, 1798, King, *Life and Correspondence*, II, 653.

six Americans of the expedition were placed, and proceeded to the Venezuelan coast.

The Spanish minister at Washington had, however, been fully informed of Miranda's preparations, and had despatched swift vessels to warn the officials of the Spanish main. The result was the capture of the schooners, the escape of the *Leander*, and the failure of the expedition, which had no real result except to deeply compromise the administration and give grounds for Spanish resentment, of which every advantage was taken by the Spanish minister, now so completely *persona non grata* that the action he desired had to be taken through the representative of France.

Smith was removed from office; both he and Ogden were indicted and tried. Though the judge charged strongly against them, the jury found them not guilty. Both claimed that the scheme had the secret support of the government. Madison, however, though both he and Jefferson were unwise in the outwardly cordial treatment given Miranda, must be believed in the statement "that the government proceeded with the most delicate attention to its duty," adding, "I do not believe that in any instance a more unexceptionable course was ever pursued by any government." [1]

Not only Madison's word but circumstances speak for the truth of this. That the American executive should hazard the friendship and good offices of France in the subject of Florida, so near the heart of the President, by favoring the schemes of an adventurer, the success of which meant the enmity of France, was not in reason. Miranda's adventure, though appearances favored Spain's strong animadversions, cannot be regarded as important other than as being the forerunner of the great revolt which was to begin four years later, with all the horrors which have ever accompanied the civil strifes of the Spanish race.[2]

It has been seen how completely the concession to France in the matter of Florida failed of its purpose. The American govern-

[1] Madison to Monroe, March 10, 1806, *Works*, II, 220.

[2] Miranda returned to England, where his views would have met with success but for the invasion of Spain. He reappeared in Venezuela in 1810, was dictator in 1812, and surrendered to the Spanish forces July 25 of that year; imprisoned at Cadiz, he died there July 14, 1816. See an admirable history of his picturesque life, by W. S. Robertson, An. Rep. Am. Hist. Assn., 1907, vol. I.

ment was left with the consciousness that it had lent itself to an immoral scheme and, moreover, that it had done so uselessly. Beset with the idea that he must obtain Florida at any cost, Jefferson, in his intrigue with Napoleon, stifled conscience and threw over any constitutional scruples, such as he expressed as to the acquirement of Louisiana, which may have remained. He was ready to despoil Spain by a money payment to her oppressor, hugging the idea of treating the warring powers of Europe with impartial neutrality while all, in effect, were waging war against his country. It was with too much truth that the French minister could write "that [the United States] is disposed to suffer every kind of humiliation, provided it can satisfy both its sordid avarice and its projects of usurpation over the Floridas." [1]

Great Britain had begun a course which called for war even more strongly than did that of France and Spain, and which in a few years was to bring war, with a vast expenditure of treasure and, except for the conduct of the navy and the saving victory of New Orleans, still vaster humiliation. New York was practically at times a blockaded port. In 1806 two British frigates, the *Cambrian* and *Leander*, were boarding and searching every entering vessel. Shot were freely used to bring them to, and so carelessly that a man in a coasting sloop, in line with the vessel brought to, was killed. Many ships were seized, and if not condemned at Halifax, whither they were sent, were subjected to almost interminable delays and great costs. A thousand seamen were being impressed from American ships yearly. The European world was now in the throes of war, and passive America was one of the victims. Spain, February 19, 1807, had followed Napoleon's Berlin decree of November 21, 1806, and American merchant-men were a natural prey; they were equally the victims of the British orders in council, and the whole was crowned, June 22, 1807, by the attack of the British ship *Leopard* upon the practically defenceless frigate *Chesapeake*, which has just left the capes of Virginia for Tripoli, the killing of three men, the wounding of eighteen, and the removal of four. The ignoble answer to all these insults was, on December 22, 1807, the embargo, which forbade American ships to go to sea, and brought American foreign commerce to a stand-still.

[1] Turreau to Talleyrand, September 4, 1807, *Archives des Aff. Etr.* MSS., Adams, IV, 141.

There are some things worse than war, and among them was the course of Jefferson's administration at this period. Jefferson's failure to appreciate the degradation to which his policy was bringing the country was a mental shortness of vision, a defective judgment such as makes it impossible to rank him as a statesman, if a statesman be "one with broad, sagacious views and distinguished ability in dealing with questions arising in public affairs."[1] With national insult and injury which an unsuccessful war could hardly exceed, he held to the view that a navy was "a ruinous folly,"[2] and the only approach to armament to which he could bring his mind (and he had his way) was to build a great number of petty and useless gun-boats which could not go to sea with safety without striking their one gun into the hold, and lay up the few frigates (which later were to save the country's good name) to "serve as receptacles for enlisting seamen, to fill the gun-boats occasionally."[3]

The only true and statesman-like course which the administration could have taken was that suggested by Gallatin: to expend the yearly surplus of from two to three millions in line of battle ships. Trafalgar had been fought.[4] The navy of France, already inefficient and demoralized through the loss of trained officers by the revolution, and through inability, on account of the superior force of England, to keep the sea and acquire the sea-habit so necessary to efficiency, was now powerless; that of Spain was always at the period a negligible quantity. The action for America, even had Trafalgar not been, was to arm; to occupy Texas to the boundaries set in the instructions by France to her agent when Louisiana was transferred; to have let come war with Spain or with both Spain and France if it would. Spain's depredations against our commerce, her militant attitude in what should have been non-debatable territory, her unwarrantable impositions against American cargoes in transit at Mobile fully justified such a course.

The bare fact of putting afloat such a naval force as the proposed Florida expenditure would have provided, would have made both Napoleon and Canning (the latter now the *deus ex machina*

[1] *Standard Dictionary.*
[2] Letter to Paine, September 6, 1807, *Writings*, IX, 136.
[3] *Cabinet Memoranda*, October 22, 1807, Jefferson, MSS., Adams, IV, 159.
[4] October 21, 1805.

Britannica) our friends. The one would have curried favor in the hope of such naval assistance; the other would have recognized the impolicy and danger of driving to the wall a power whose seamen had shown themselves as able and daring sailors as the English, and of a temper and training which made meeting them a very different proposition to that in which the British navy, since the French revolution, had won such easy renown.

Whether with or without a war, a navy would have saved us the six years of humiliation which were to intervene between 1806 and 1812; it would have saved the embargo which was to tie to the wharves in rotting idleness more than a million tons of shipping which had been engaged in foreign trade; to bring grass-grown streets in our greatest ports, and to strain the sentiment of the several sections of the Union to the point of separation. It would have saved the war of 1812, the capture and burning of Washington, and the shameful ineptitude, with one brilliant exception, of our army commanders in that contest; it would have saved Texas and the war with Mexico. There would have been a cessation of British impressment, and there would have been no such orders in council as those directed to the destruction of American commerce; or had these come before America was ready with her ships, there would have been, as soon as these were afloat, quick renunciation.

England was now losing an empire on the river Plate by the surrender by General Whitelock at Buenos Ayres, July 7, 1807, of an army of twelve thousand men sent to conquer the country; the first effort toward the revolt of Spanish America, as just seen, had failed; Spain, by February, 1808, was occupied by a French army. On March 19 the old King Charles IV abdicated in favor of his worthless son known as Fernando VII. By April both were in France in the clutches of Napoleon, the former never to return to Spain, the latter to be a willing prisoner in exile until 1814. For five years Spain, occupied as a battle-field by French and English, was, as a nationality, effaced. But the schemes wrought by Napoleon's vast imagination had reached too far. The insurrection of the second of May, 1808, at Madrid, was the signal of his own coming defeat and the forerunner of a movement which carried "the vast Spanish empire into the vortex of dissolution. . . .

Spain, France, Germany, England were swept into a vast and bloody torrent which dragged America, from Montreal to Valparaiso, slowly into its movements, while the familiar figures of famous men—Napoleon, Alexander, Canning, Godoy, Jefferson, Madison, Talleyrand, emperors, generals, presidents, conspirators, patriots, tyrants, and martyrs by the thousand—were borne away by the stream, struggling, gesticulating, praying, robbing, each blind to everything but selfish interest, and all helping more or less unconsciously to reach the new level which society was obliged to seek. Half a century of disorder failed to settle the problems raised by the *Dos de Maio*, but from the first even a child could see that in the ruin of a world like the empire of Spain, the only nation certain to find a splendid and inexhaustible booty was the republic of the United States."[1]

[1] Adams, IV, 301.

CHAPTER VI

THE EFFECT IN AMERICA OF NAPOLEON'S INVASION OF SPAIN—EVENTS IN THE FLORIDAS

THE United States thus had already been drawn into the seeth stirred by the magic wand of the great emperor when came Napoleon's invasion of Spain which was to bring his own ruin and that of the Spanish dominion in America.

The revolt against his domination of the peninsula found expression, after the fateful second of May, 1808, in the formation of juntas in every province of Spain, as well as in London, each of these assuming authority as the government of the kingdom. Out of these by a natural survival, due to escape to Cadiz before the victorious advance of the French hosts, grew what became known as the Central Junta, which though it soon became odious to the Spaniards themselves, offered a semblance of nationality sufficient for England to recognize it as government and form with it an alliance about which gathered such forces as Spanish revolt against the French could offer. The coming into existence of the junta saved European Spain but it wrecked the Spanish empire beyond the seas.

The junta, discredited as a body, was finally forced to appoint a committee of five, known as "The Regency," which assumed collectively, as had the junta itself, the designation of "Majesty" and exercised in Fernando's name the authority of the absent prince, whom the junta had declared king, and issued decrees as if he were present. It ordered the election of a cortes with one member for every 50,000 of population in Spain, but only allowed one member for each of the Spanish provinces of America, though these had been declared integral members of the Spanish kingdom. As the peninsular provinces were allowed 208 members besides a deputy from each provincial junta and one from each city which had sent deputies to the Cortes of 1789, it will be seen how great was the departure from a theory of equality which had been thrice enunciated in a few months. The formation of provincial juntas in America in imitation of those in Spain was but a natural and proper act of self-preservation forced upon them by the apparent fact that Spain was to become French and by the beginnings of an assumption of authority by the latter in America itself. The new juntas in the beginning, in an access of loyalty, and in their fear of French domination, had declared for Fernando and had enthusiastically allied themselves with the central junta at Cadiz, demonstrating their faith by contributions of many millions.[1] Appeals were made for reforms most of which were self-evidently rightful. Among them: no distinction between the provinces of the Peninsula and those of America in national representation; freedom to cultivate whatever they could produce; freedom to manufacture, to trade with other nations, to trade with one another and with the Spanish possessions in Asia; freedom to trade from all portions of Spanish America and the Philippines with other parts of Asia; suppression of monopolies; freedom to work the quicksilver mines; equal eligibility of all persons of Spanish or Indian descent to office; that half the nominations in the kingdoms of Spanish America be given to natives; that the order of the Jesuits be restored (the last on account of the success of the society in civilizing the Indians). Through the remonstrances of Cuba, the council of regency had passed a decree permitting the American provinces to trade with foreign nations in their own productions in cases where there was no market for them in Spain. "This decree, morally just and politically wise and necessary, did not suit the interests and was offensive in the highest degree to the merchants of Cadiz,[2] on whom the regency were in a great measure dependent for the means of continuing their new, feeble, and slippery government. This decree was therefore revoked on the 17th of June [1810]. And the regency had even the ridiculous folly to pretend that it was not authentic, but

[1] Estimated at ninety millions of dollars, fifty-five of which came from Mexico, Walton, *Dissensions of Spanish America*, 137.

[2] Spain at this time had the monopoly, by decree, of the trade with the Spanish-American possessions. This was earlier confined to the one port of Seville; later the sole right to trade was transferred to Cadiz.

an imposition on the public."[1] It ordered "the arrest of its minister of the Indies and the first official of the secretariat of this ministry, and sent to America viceroys and royal commissioners empowered to replace the juntas which had been established in these states, commanding them in a jargon of affected royalty 'to reassemble in whole or in part all authority, to suspend or set aside employees of whatever class or grade, to use whatever funds pertain to my royal exchequer, to pardon or punish as you may find good, and give such orders as you may think proper, which shall be complied with as if from my royal person, so that in no case may there be doubt of your powers for want of sufficient expression.' "

But the actions of the regency developed into still greater madness when, on July 27th, 1810, the formation of the Carácas junta was proclaimed treasonable, and the ports of the province declared in a state of blockade until the inhabitants should recognize the regency of Cadiz as the true and legitimate representatives of Fernando VII.

The success of the population of the river Plate region against the British in 1807 had prepared the way for independent action when Spain, by 1810, had apparently become permanently a province of the French empire. The new military spirit along with the spread of free ideas in the seven months of British occupation of Montevideo, the active trade which had sprung up under their auspices, and the general liberalism of their policy made it impossible to cling to what was apparently a dying cause and which at the same time was insistent in continuing the ancient despotism.

Though certain to come with time, unless there had been an absolute transformation of Spanish political character, the great movement of Spanish-American secession was thus precipitated, not by the American provinces, but by Spaniards of Spain, claiming at the time to rule the empire in the name of the absent king; and thus, with their country in the throes of an agony almost that of death, and which would have resulted in its extinction as a sovereign state but for English aid, they began a contest the last shot in which was to be fired eighty-eight years later. With fatuous light-mindedness and folly they led Spain to despoilment;

[1] *Annual Register*, 1810, p. 225.

one by one, amid the horrors of a civil strife rarely matched in history, were to drop away all the provinces of her vast American empire, leaving for the moment only Cuba and Puerto Rico protected awhile by the slave power of the United States which was to forbid the action of their sister provinces which would have set them free.

The influence of the occupancy of Spain by the French, while thus reaching far beyond Europe, had perhaps the most momentous of its effects through making the greater part of South America permanently Spanish in character instead of Anglo-Saxon. For the Spanish revolt against Napoleon and the establishment of even a nominal national government brought peace between Great Britain and the Spanish people; the ten thousand men assembled at Cork, under Sir Arthur Wellesley (soon to be Duke of Wellington), for the purpose of invading the Spanish possessions, were diverted to the Peninsula, and supremacy in the southern continent was lost to Great Britain through her new attitude.[1]

Thus, August 1, 1808, Wellesley and his army were landed in Portugal instead of in South America. Thenceforward Spain, or that which was accepted by England as the Spanish government, had to be dealt with as an ally of Great Britain, and the latter in some degree at least had to be reckoned with by the United States during the tightening of their grip upon the Floridas. The revolt of the South American provinces now about to develop through the ineptitude and folly of the Cadiz regency could but have the sympathy of the American government and people; a sympathy which brought in its train numerous complications which came through the material assistance rendered the provinces by the many privateers fitted out and manned in the United States and sailing under the flags of the new states.

Señor Valentino de Foronda had succeeded the Marquis de Casa Yrujo as envoy to the United States and his time during 1808 and 1809 was taken up in the presentation of complaints of raids and

---

[1] Wellesley himself, influenced by Miranda, inclined to the invasion of Venezuela. The British cabinet apparently wavered between this and the river Plate. Had political circumstances favored, simultaneous attacks would have been made upon both. See W. S. Robertson, *Francisco de Miranda and the Revolutionizing of Spanish America*, An. Rep., Amer. Histor. Assn., 1907, pp. 406–410.

plots. In 1810 the Chevalier Don Luis de Onis was accredited as minister, but the American government, now holding a position of strict neutrality until the question of occupancy of the Spanish throne should be decided, refused to receive him as such. Such Spanish consuls as had been received before the invasion of Spain, were continued, but none others received an exequatur. Erving, chargé d'affaires in Spain, left Madrid in May, 1810, and there were no recognized diplomatic officials in the two countries, until 1814, when the same official was appointed minister to Spain. De Onis against whom were charges of complicity in the intrigues for dismemberment of the American South-west, besides being so unfortunate as to write a depreciatory letter concerning the American government to the captain-general of Carácas, February 2, 1810, which was made public,[1] was, after much undignified wrangling, received by the United States in 1815.

Until the expulsion of the French from Spain, however, the uncertainty whether Napoleon or Fernando was to be the putative master of Spanish America brought to the Floridas, even more than to the other American provinces of Spain, the natural unrest which came from want of headship. The population was chiefly an extraordinary mixture of adventurers, filibusters, and men of piratical inclinations and life, a large proportion of whom were fugitives from justice. These, with fugitive slaves, and Indians sensitive as to the future of their lands, made a restless community which could scarcely be expected in the circumstances of Spanish anarchy to remain quiescent under the weak domination of a nominal government.

The result was a convention in the spring of 1810 of the inhabitants of West Feliciana, which declared independence of Spain. The fort at Baton Rouge was seized and a proposal transmitted to Washington by the insurgent president, John Rhea, for incorporation with the United States. The answer was a proclamation, October 27, 1810, by Madison, now President, taking possession of West Florida, which while claiming the region justly to be our own, stated that a crisis had "at length arrived, subversive of the order of things under the Spanish authorities, whereby the failure of the United States to take said territory into its possession

[1] *State Papers*, III, 404.

may lead to events ultimately contravening the views of both parties, whilst in the meantime, the tranquillity and security of our adjoining territories are endangered and new facilities given to the violators of our revenue and commercial laws and of those prohibiting the introduction of slaves." [1]

Madison unquestionably had inward doubts of the justice of his claim of actual title, however much the necessities of the case demanded such action, and the necessity did exist, unless anarchy were to be tolerated. Madison's doubt was shown by the mention in the proclamation that the situation would "not cease to be a subject of fair and friendly negotiation and adjustment." It was ordered that the district be considered a part of the territory of Orleans, soon to become the state of Louisiana.

The hint of events "contravening the views of both parties," meant the possibility of British occupancy. In any case Great Britain could not look kindly upon such action as that now taken against the interests of her ally, and Mr. Morier, the British chargé d'affaires, addressed a note of protest, December 15, 1810, to the secretary of state saying that "such are the ties by which his [Britannic] Majesty is bound to Spain, that he cannot see with any indifference, any attack upon her interests in America." [2]

The Spanish governor of Florida, Don Vicente Folch, reinforced Madison's action by writing the secretary of state from Mobile, on December 2, 1810, that he had decided "on delivering this province [West Florida] to the United States under an equitable capitulation, provided I do not receive succor from the Havana or Vera Cruz, during the present month; or that his Excellency, the Marquis of Someruelos (on whom I depend) should not have opened directly a negotiation on this point. The incomprehensible abandonment in which I see myself, and the afflicted situation to which this province sees itself reduced, not only authorize me, but force me to have recourse to this determination, the only one to save it from the ruin which threatens it.' [3]

President Madison, "taking into view the tenor of these several communications" and "the posture of things with which they are connected," as he phrased a confidential message sent to Congress

[1] *State Papers*, III, 396, 397.   [2] *Ibid.*, III, 399.   [3] *Ibid.*, III, 398.

January 3, 1811, and moved by apprehension of the Floridas passing from Spain to another power, which power was England, advised an act which was passed by Congress in secret session authorizing the President to take possession of East Florida, in case the local authority should consent or a foreign power attempt to occupy it. Two commissioners, George Matthews and John McKee, were appointed with instructions, dated January 26, 1811, from Monroe, secretary of state, that if they should find the local authority inclined to surrender East Florida and the remaining portions of West Florida, the surrender was to be accepted, with the engagement of "re-delivery to the lawful sovereign," should such a stipulation be insisted upon. Effective measures were to be taken "in case of the actual appearance of any attempt to take possession by a foreign power." The aid of military and naval forces was assured in case of need. Any stipulation as to redelivery was not to impair the title of the United States to the country west of the River Perdido.[1]

Mr. Augustus J. Foster had been transferred in April, 1811, from Sweden as British minister to the United States, with instructions to protest against the occupation of West Florida. With the added reason now given by the action of the President and Congress, he followed up Morier's expostulation, July 2, 1811, with "the solemn protest of his Royal Highness [George, Regent], in the name and on behalf of his Majesty, against an attempt so contrary to every principle of public justice, faith, and national honor, and so injurious to the alliance existing between his Majesty and the Spanish nation."[2]

Affairs between America and England were now tending toward war. A few weeks before Foster's arrival, the British sloop of war *Little Belt* had been almost destroyed off the capes of the Chesapeake by the *President* in a night action, claimed by the Americans to have been brought on by a first shot from the former, and the new minister found the American government in any but a mood to be expostulated with on the subject of Spain's possessions. He was thus vigorously answered by Monroe, secretary of state, on November 2, 1811, intimating that it was impossible to be unmindful of the possibility of the occupancy of Florida by another

[1] *State Papers*, III, 571, 572.   [2] *Ibid.*, III, 543.

power.[1] Foster had already given vent to his feelings in a letter, July 5, to the British minister for foreign affairs, "It was with real pain, my lord, that I was forced to listen to arguments of the most profligate nature, such as that other nations were not so scrupulous; that the United States showed sufficient forbearance in not assisting the insurgents of South America, and looking to their own interests in the present situation of that country"[2]— words which scarcely came well from the minister of a power in whose diplomacy the word *Copenhagen* had but a short time before been written in deepest black.

Matthews read as the spirit of his instructions much more than appeared in the letter and the result was the seizure, March 18, 1812, of Fernandina by some two hundred adventurers under the name of insurgents, organized with Matthews's aid and backed by a force of gun-boats, stationed in the near-by waters of the St. Mary's to enforce the non-importation act then in force and prevent the illegal traffic of which Fernandina, a nest of smugglers, was a centre. The Spanish garrison of an officer and ten men surrendered, the independent flag of the "patriots" was raised, and Matthews with a company of the regular army crossed the river, March 19, and took possession of Amelia Island subject to the President's approval. But his action was more vigorous than desired. On April 4, Matthews was informed that it was not "the policy of the law, or purpose of the executive to wrest the province forcibly from Spain," but to occupy it (with the consent of the authorities) to prevent its falling into the hands of any foreign power, "and to hold that place under the existing peculiarity of the circumstances of the Spanish monarchy for a just result in an amicable negotiation with Spain." Matthews's powers were revoked, and transferred to the governor of Georgia, with, however, practically no change in the situation.[3]

President Madison regarded the event as making "a most distressing dilemma,"[4] but, as Monroe mentioned to Serrurier, the French minister, "there would be more danger in retreating than in advancing; and so, while disavowing the general's too precipi-

---

[1] *State Papers*, III, 544.
[2] MSS., British Archives, Adams, VI, 38.
[3] *State Papers*, III, 572. See also McMaster's *United States*, III, 537–540.
[4] Madison to Jefferson, April 24, 1812, *Works*, II, 532.

tate conduct, they would maintain the occupation."[1] The fear of Great Britain's possible course justified the action. On June 18, 1812, the United States declared war against England, and, in anticipation of her occupancy of Florida, a bill was introduced in Congress authorizing the President to establish a government over the whole of the Floridas. It passed the House June 25, 1812, and, though lost in the Senate, the occupation of Fernandina was maintained until May 16, 1813.

Nor in the circumstances of a scattered freebooting population of whites of many races, of warlike Indians and fugitive slaves, was the action, in the face of the oncoming war, unjustified. Law, at the best uncertain in its justice, is a mirror with many reflections, and among these stands out boldly as a rule of conduct that of self-preservation. We have not arrived at the point of altruism which leads a nation, unless under stress of force, to sacrifice a course it deems necessary to its safety.

The events of the war now beginning were soon to go far toward justifying the proposed action. On July 23, 1814, Pensacola, Fort St. Michael, and Fort Barrancas, the latter six miles distant from the town at the entrance of Pensacola Bay, were occupied, regardless of Spain's neutrality, by a British force of some hundred "colonial marines," under a Lieutenant-Colonel Edward Nichols, supported by Captain W. H. Percy, the senior officer of the *Hermes* and *Carron*, sloops of war. Among the officers of the marines were a Captain Woodbine and Lieutenant Ambrister, both of whom were to be heard of later. Nichols hoisted the British flag in the forts along with the Spanish and issued a proclamation which, while appealing to Kentuckians to "range yourselves under the standard of your forefathers or be neutral," was described four years later by the American secretary of state as inviting "all the runaway negroes, all the savage Indians, all the pirates, and all the traitors to their country whom they knew or imagined to exist within reach of their summons, to join their standard and wage an exterminating war against the portion of the United States immediately bordering upon this neutral and thus violated territory of Spain."[2]

---

[1] *Archives des Affaires Étrangères*, MSS., Adams, VI, 242.

[2] J. Q. Adams, November 28, 1818, to minister at Madrid, *State Papers*, IV, 539.

The picture was not overdrawn. Pensacola was held by the English in amicable sufferance on Spanish part, and was made the central point of distribution of arms to the Indians, the movement being but a belated item of the endeavor by British officials to combine all the Western tribes in war against the United States. The battle of the Thames, October 5, 1813, and the death of Tecumseh, broke the Indian power of the Northwest; on March 27, 1814, an equally destructive blow had been struck against the Creeks, who by a treaty made August 9, 1814, by General Jackson in command of the American army, were forced to cede the greater part of their lands within the limits of the Union to the United States.

The Creek war brought upon the borders of Florida and at Mobile an army which, now used to expel the British forces in the vicinity, was to inflict a little later upon the British expedition, intended to wrest New Orleans and Louisiana from the United States and effect their return to Spain,[1] the most signal defeat in the annals of the British army.

The English commander, shortly after Jackson's arrival at Mobile, left Pensacola with four sloops of war and a strong detachment of white troops and Indians. On September 15 an attack was made upon Fort Bowyer at the entrance to Mobile Bay, which was repulsed with the loss of the senior officer's ship the *Hermes*. Jackson, on the arrival of reinforcements, moved upon Pensacola and, November 7, occupied the place and took possession of the Spanish posts, the whole of the British forces leaving the bay the next day after blowing up Fort Barrancas. By November 11 Jackson was again in Mobile with his army.

Monroe had written, October 21, 1814, warning Jackson against "measures which would involve this government in a contest with Spain." This was not received by Jackson until his expedition had been accomplished, but had it been otherwise it is very sure that such an impetuous and headstrong character, whose only

[1] "You will discountenance any proposition of the inhabitants to place themselves under the dominion of Great Britain, and you will direct their disposition toward returning under the protection of the Spanish crown rather than to the attempting to maintain what will be much more difficult to secure substantially, their independence as a separate state."—Instructions to Ross, September 6, 1814, MSS. British Archives, Adams, VIII, 314, 315.

government was his own judgment, would have given such instructions no heed. And in this case he was entirely in the right. So strongly, however, did affairs in Florida occupy his mind that it was with the utmost difficulty and with much delay that the seriousness of the threat against New Orleans was brought to his perception, a passiveness which was to be nobly retrieved the 8th of the following January.

Peace came and Colonel Nichols had returned to Florida in April, 1815. Of his own motion, as his action was entirely disavowed by the British government, he made an offensive and defensive treaty between Great Britain and the Seminoles, "declared by his Britannic Majesty a free and independent people," and prompted them to demand the return of the lands ceded by the treaty made by Jackson, as in accord with the ninth article of the treaty of peace with Great Britain. He built a powerful fort on the Appalachicola River, 15 miles above its mouth and 120 miles east of Pensacola, armed with a number of cannon, among which were one 32-pounder and three twenty-fours, and stored with 2,500 muskets and accoutrements, 500 carbines, 500 swords, 400 pistols, 300 quarter casks of rifle powder and 763 barrels of common powder,[1] and this while the governor of Pensacola in whose jurisdiction the fort was, had not powder enough to fire a salute.[2]

Nichols left for England during the summer, carrying with him the chief Francis and other Indians who received in London attention which extended to the giving by the government of a uniform to the prophet Francis, the presentation of other gifts and a reception by the prince regent. These acts, and the great value of the arms and stores in the Appalachicola fort, show, despite the asseverations to Mr. Adams the American minister,[3] a certain governmental interest, besides a powerful financial support far in excess of ordinary individual means.

The fort, occupied on the departure of Nichols by a large number of escaped negroes from Georgia, became known as Negro Fort and was soon the centre of raids upon the Georgia frontier. General Jackson, who commanded the Southern military division,

[1] Parton, *Jackson*, II, 399.
[2] Captain Amelung to Jackson, June 4, 1816, *State Papers*, V, 557.
[3] Adams to Monroe, September 19, 1815, *Ibid.*, IV, 554.

was ordered, March 15, 1816, to call the attention of the Spanish governor at Pensacola to the situation, and he demanded, under the treaty of 1795, a suppression of the nuisance, a demand which, though made by Jackson in friendly terms, assured the governor that if not put down by Spanish authority the United States would be compelled, in self-defence, to act.[1] The governor declared his good-will and perfect accord with Jackson's views, and that he had proposed to the captain-general of Cuba, under whose jurisdiction he was, to take action, but that he could not act until he should receive orders and the necessary assistance.[2]

General Edmund P. Gaines, second in command to Jackson in the district and, under him, charged with the preservation of its peace, had, in order to overawe the negroes, built Fort Scott close to the Florida boundary, at the junction of the Flint and Chattahoochee Rivers which form the Appalachicola. The difficulty of transport through the wild and roadless region made it necessary to send supplies by water from New Orleans. The first convoy sailed thence, June 24, 1816, under the command of Sailing-Master Jairus Loomis of the navy. Gaines thinking trouble probable, ordered Colonel Clinch, in command at Fort Scott, to go down the Appalachicola to the vicinity of the negro fort, to secure the safe passage of the convoy; a message was sent Loomis to await notice of the arrival, near the fort, of these troops. He arrived off the Appalachicola River July 10. While lying at the mouth of the river a boat was fired upon, July 15. Two days later an armed boat under Midshipman Luffborough was sent in with four men for fresh water. The boat was attacked, the midshipman and two men killed; one man escaped, and one, Edward Daniells, was carried off prisoner and, as later known, tarred and burned to death.

On July 16 Clinch with 116 men had started down the river. While on the way he was joined by a large body of Seminoles, who were at enmity with the negroes and who agreed to act in concert with him. The Indians, scouting in advance, seized a negro with a fresh scalp from a white man, and learned from him of the attack upon the boat's crew and the retirement of the attacking

[1] Jackson to Governor Zuniga, April 23, 1816, *State Papers*, IV, 556.
[2] Zuniga to Jackson, May 26, 1818, *Ibid.*, V, 556.

party to the negro fort. Word was sent to Loomis, but fifteen miles away, to come up the river and assist in an attack. The negroes hoisted the British union jack and under it a red flag, and opened fire with their heavy guns, with, however, no effect. All the negroes of the vicinity had on Clinch's advance hurried to the fort, which now contained 100 men and 234 women and children. Loomis arrived July 27, and opened fire without effect until a shot heated in the galley fire was fired. The result was the explosion of the 10,000 pounds of powder in the fort and the destruction of nearly all its inmates. Two hundred and seventy were killed instantly. But three were unharmed, among them the leader Garçon, who, delivered over to the Seminoles, was put to death. An unwise promise by Colonel Clinch to the Indians to give them, for their aid, the arms found in the fort, caused the distribution among them of the many hundreds of muskets and pistols later to be used effectively against the United States, and the possession of which, no doubt, had influence in encouraging the Indians to the hostilities soon to come.[1]

[1] Condensed from Parton, *Jackson*, II, 402–407.

CHAPTER VII

THE FLORIDA TREATY AND JACKSON'S INVASION

FERNANDO VII, released by the overthrow of Napoleon, had returned to Spain in 1814. He refused to accept the revolutionary "liberal" constitution formed at Cadiz in 1812, and urged, it must be said, by a large proportion of the Spanish people, reverted to absolutism as it was understood by the most absolute of his predecessors. The Jesuits were brought back, the monastic orders restored to all their ancient privileges, the inquisition reinstated, and the prisons filled with political prisoners. "The king's crowning act was to decree the death penalty to any one who dared *even to speak* in favor of the constitution."[1]

It was with such a government, now also faced by the revolt of the Spanish-American world, that the United States had to deal. The Chevalier Luis de Onis, after much unseemly wrangling, had been received at Washington in December, 1815, as minister. He was to demand the return of West Florida to Spanish jurisdiction, and call attention to the fitting out in United States ports of privateers and expeditions on behalf of the revolted provinces.[2]

There is no doubt of the great extent of such procedure or of the great damage to Spain. Such vessels under the flags of the new-born sovereignties, manned largely by Americans, swarmed in the western seas, with little inquiry on the part of United States authorities as to the validity of those which frequented our ports and sold their captured goods with impunity. The great booty available to such freebooters, the chaotic state which was the natural result of a world everywhere at war, brought into being a great number of such rovers whose deeds were as often as not pirati-

[1] Hume, *Modern Spain*, 192.
[2] De Onis to Monroe, December 30, 1815, *State Papers*, IV, 422–424.

cal and whose extirpation took years of effort and long occupied the attention of the greater part of the American navy. Baltimore and Charleston were the two ports more particularly concerned in this great scandal. Regarding the former: "The misfortune," said Adams, when he became the American secretary of state in 1817, "is not only that this abomination has spread over a large portion of the merchants and population of Baltimore, but that it has infected almost every officer of the United States in the place. They are all fanatics of the South American cause. Skinner, the postmaster, has been indicted for being concerned in the piratical privateers. Glenn, the district attorney, besides being a weak, incompetent man, has a son said to be concerned in the privateers. . . . The district judge, Houston, and the circuit judge, Duval, are both feeble, inefficient men over whom William Pinkney [one of the most noted lawyers of the time], employed by all the pirates as their counsel, domineers like a slave-driver over his negroes."[1]

The correspondence which ensued between the American secretary of state and the Spanish minister reiterated the claims of the United States to West Florida. Monroe affirmed that there was not only no doubt as to the justice of the claim, but that the United States government had "never doubted, since the treaty of 1803," that the western boundary of Louisiana "extended to the Rio Bravo (Rio Grande)."[2] He showed that the enterprises to aid the revolutionists of New Spain (Mexico), of which De Onis complained, had been forestalled by the American authorities wherever such authority extended, and gave, in a report of the United States attorney for the district of Louisiana, the names of

[1] Adams, *Memoirs*, IV, 318, 319. Adams continues: "The grand jury indicted many, and the petit jury convicted one man, but every one of the causes fell through upon flaws in Glenn's bills of indictment. The conduct of the juries proves the real soundness of the public mind; . . . the political condition of Baltimore is as rotten as corruption can make it. Now that it has brought the whole body of European allies upon us [the Holy Alliance] in the form of remonstrances, the President is somewhat concerned about it, but he had nothing but directions altogether general to give me concerning it. I must take the brunt of the battle upon myself and rely upon the justice of the cause." The editor appends a note: "These proceedings formed much of the staple of the argument of the British government in justification of its own course during the late civil war. It will appear from this passage how little the American government was disposed to justify them."

[2] *State Papers*, IV, 430.

a number of persons presented for attempting violation of neutrality, and a list of vessels libelled for illegal outfits and a number of those captured by illegally fitted out privateers, which were restored to their owners.[1]

The European world being now at peace and our own government freed from the incubus of war, serious effort was making to preserve neutrality in connection with Spanish America, and a statute was passed, March 3, 1817, in accord with the recommendation of President Madison's special message, December 26, 1816, to strengthen the neutrality act, imposing a fine not to exceed $10,000, forfeiture of the vessel, and imprisonment not exceeding ten years on any engaged in fitting out vessels in American ports to cruise against powers with which the United States was at peace.[2]

The American occupancy of West Florida; the necessary temporary occupancy of East Florida; the glaring evidence of Spain's inability to control the scant and unwholesome mixture of Indians, lawless adventurers, and negroes which formed the chief part of the population, made it clear to Spain that the Florida provinces were lost, and the Spanish government soon recognized the policy of giving Florida for as much of Texas as the American government might be willing to yield, and as a set-off to the still unadjusted claims of the United States for commercial depredations.

De Onis, in his note of December, 1815, and in conference, had stated the desire of Spain to arrange pending differences, and Mr. Erving, now American minister at Madrid, was thus directed to present the points on which the United States sought redress and indemnity, these being "spoliations on their commerce, the suppression of the right to deposit at New Orleans, and the refusal of the Spanish government to settle the boundaries of Louisiana on just principles." To these were added the encouragement given in East Florida to the Indian tribes in Georgia and on the southern frontier to make war on the United States; the aid given them; the aid afforded Great Britain by permitting supplies to pass through East Florida to its Indian allies and allowing her to establish a place of arms in Florida to

[1] *State Papers*, IV, 432.
[2] The extent of the difficulties arising in this subject may be judged by the complaints of the Spanish minister in 1817, *Ibid.*, IV, 184-201.

support the Indians; and allowing the frigate *Essex* to be attacked by two British frigates in Valparaiso Bay.[1]

Cevallos, the Spanish foreign minister, in a note of September 15, 1816, informed the American minister that De Onis was empowered to enter upon the negotiations which were to end in the treaty known as that of 1819. The Spanish project of conditions, first developed, included the return of the whole of Louisiana west of the Mississippi in exchange for both of the Floridas.[2]

Monroe was now, since March 4, 1817, President. John Quincy Adams, minister to England, had come thence to be secretary of state, the best-equipped and ablest statesman who during our history has held the office. A war of correspondence ensued with De Onis in which De Onis ably upheld the Spanish view.[3] On two of the contentions he held impregnable positions: 1. That France had never claimed West Florida as part of the territory ceded by the French-Spanish treaty of 1800, and 2. That the claims against Spain for French depredations on American commerce were unjust in view of the French-American treaties of 1800 and 1803. The United States stood on equally firm ground as to the western limit of Louisiana, which was understood by France to extend to the Rio Grande and thus include Texas, as certainly as France understood that the eastern boundary was to be the Iberville and Lake Pontchartrain.

On January 16, 1818, Adams, in a short despatch to De Onis, laid down the American proposals: Spain was to cede all territory east of the Mississippi; the western boundary of Louisiana to be the Colorado, to its source and from thence to the northern limits of Louisiana, or to leave that boundary unsettled for future arrangement; the claims for spoliations, whether Spanish or French, to be arbitrated as agreed in the convention of 1802; the Florida lands from the east to the Perdido River to be answerable for such claims; no Spanish grants of lands subsequent to August 11, 1802, to be valid; Spain to be exonerated from the payment of any debts.

These proposals did not differ materially from those made in 1805 [4] and were in accord with the views expressed by President

---

[1] *State Papers*, IV, 433, 434.
[2] Pizarro to Erving, August 17, 1817, *Ibid.*, IV, 445.
[3] *Ibid.*, 452-463.   [4] *Ibid.*, 464.

Monroe from the beginning of the American ownership of Louisiana, as to the desirability of exchanging part at least of Texas for the Floridas. Adams was of another mind and held, until overborne in the cabinet, to the whole of Texas. The ensuing correspondence embodied the ablest statement of the American claims yet made in one of the best papers written by Adams during his term of office, in which he held firmly to the Rio Grande as a boundary by all historical evidence.[1]

But the negotiations were to have a road beset with dangers. On June 29, 1817, there landed at Amelia Island, on the northeast point of Florida, on the Atlantic, a force of fifty adventurers gathered chiefly in Baltimore by an erratic Scotchman of rank and fortune, a Sir Gregor McGregor, who announced himself "commander-in-chief of all the forces both naval and military, destined to effect the independence of the Floridas, duly authorized by the constituted authorities of the republics of Mexico, Buenos Ayres, New Granada, and Venezuela."[2] He demanded and received the surrender, June 29, 1817, of the Spanish garrison under Don Francisco de Morales, the civil and military commandant on the island. He issued a proclamation declaring Florida in a state of blockade,[3] and shortly after, accompanied by the British intriguer, Captain Woodbine, of Nichol's late command, who had arrived from Nassau, left for New Providence to gather recruits, leaving in charge R. Hubbert, a man who had been sheriff of New York City. Woodbine, accompanied by Lieutenant Ambrister, had previously to this made his appearance on the Appalachicola in an endeavor to arouse the Indians. Going in an

[1] Adams to De Onis, March 12, 1818; De Onis to Adams, March 23, 1818, *State Papers*, IV, 468–486. This paper and De Onis's reply form a complete history of the claims of the contending parties in this celebrated and momentous question. As to Adams's attitude, he himself says, "in all the negotiations conducted by me while secretary of state, whether with Spain, France, or England, I insisted invariably upon all the claims of the United States to their utmost extent; and whenever anything was conceded, it was by direction of the President himself, and always after consultation in cabinet meetings, and that it was especially so in the negotiation of the Florida treaty."—*Memoirs*, VIII, 186; see also his diary for February, 1819. It would seem clear that the loss of Texas at this time was due to Monroe, supported by the other members of the cabinet.

[2] *State Papers*, IV, 144.
[3] *Niles's Register*, September 6, 1817, p. 28.

armed vessel elsewhere for supplies, he left Ambrister as his agent, to the latter's final great undoing.

A thousand miles away, in distant Mexico, was a "Commodore" Aury who, "with a few small schooners from Aux Cayes [in Hayti], manned in a great measure with refugees from Barataria, and mulattoes, and reinforced by a few more men, French and Italians, who had been hanging loose upon society in and about New Orleans," had set up a semblance of government at Galveston, under the Mexican flag. From this station, "fed and drawing all its resources from New Orleans, . . . an active system of plunder was commenced on the high seas, chiefly of Spanish property, but often without much concern as to the national character" of the prizes, the cargoes of which, including every sort of merchandise, from jewelry and laces to slaves, were chiefly surreptitiously carried into Louisiana.[1]

Aury transferred himself to Matagorda, and hearing of McGregor's venture sailed for Fernandina with a force of one hundred and fifty men. Arriving in October with his "squadron of privateers and prizes," he found Sheriff Hubbert and the others of McGregor's supporters entirely out of funds, and refused them aid unless "on condition of being made commander-in-chief; and that as "General" McGregor never had any commission whatever, the flag of the Florida republic must be struck and that of the Mexican hoisted; and that Fernandina should be considered as a conquest of the Mexican republic (under which he was commissioned) without its being necessary that any other part of the province of East Florida should be conquered."[2]

McGregor's force of necessity yielded. Hubbert died through intemperance and mortification of spirit, and his party, mostly American, English, and Irish sailors, were without a leader and under the heel of Aury's followers, "composed chiefly of brigand negroes," though as the Americans were reported by Captain Henley of the navy as apparently "much worse than any others," sympathy need not be wasted.

The President's duty under the joint resolution of January 15,

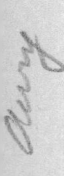

[1] Chew, collector of the port at New Orleans, to Crawford, secretary of the treasury, August 1, 1817, *State Papers*, IV, 134.
[2] McIntosh to Crawford, October 30, 1817, *Ibid.*, IV, 138.

1811, empowering him to occupy any part of the territory of Florida, in the event of an attempt to occupy it on the part of any foreign power, was clear. In Spain's powerless condition the action taken was a kindness to the Spanish government. A naval force under Captain J. D. Henley and an army detachment under Major James Bankhead were sent, and December 22, 1817, Aury, after protest, surrendered. The American flag was hoisted, and Aury with his squadron withdrew.

The incident had but a six months' life, but it illustrated in full the desperate condition of Spain, and her inability to preserve the peace in the wild region bordering the Gulf of Mexico, at this period the happy hunting ground of the most lawless of the world's adventurers. In all the region of Florida, as large as England and Wales, there were but about ten thousand persons. The whole coast was a nest of piracy. It was vain to hope that Spain, bled to her last resources by the futile endeavor to put down an insurrection which extended over a third of the parts of the world peopled by men of European blood, should have the vigor to restrain the wild population inhabiting her lands on the southern borders of the United States. She did not even attempt it.

Meanwhile the restlessness of the Indians under the loss of their lands had burst into flame. Almost the whole of the southern tribes were within the limits of Florida, whence, with the assistance of the many escaped Georgia negroes, murders and depredations began against the American settlers on the frontier, and continued through the spring and summer of 1817. It is fair to presume that the latter were by no means guiltless of impositions against the Indians. On November 21 an attack by American troops upon the Indian village known as Fowltown, brought on by a detachment sent by General Gaines from Fort Scott to seize and bring to the fort the chief and few warriors in the village, began the Seminole war. Nine days later the burning of the village was followed by the massacre or torture to death of forty soldiers accompanied by seven women and children on their way up the Appalachicola to Fort Scott.

The war department, as yet not informed of an Indian outbreak, had, November 12, ordered General Gaines to go to Amelia Island to take charge of the operations in contemplation against the filibusters. As soon as it was informed of these events General Jackson was directed, December 20, to take personal command at Fort Scott and carry the war to a conclusion.

The earlier orders to Gaines had at first deprecated, in the event that hostilities should occur, crossing the Spanish line, but later he was instructed, in case the Indians should refuse reparation, to "consider himself at liberty to march across the Florida line and attack them within its limits should it be found necessary, unless they should shelter themselves under a Spanish post. In the last event you will immediately notify this department." [1] Jackson had proposed, in a letter written before the reception of his orders, to improve upon the orders to Gaines, which latter were wholly justifiable. He wrote, January 6, 1818, to President Monroe, urging the seizure of the whole of East Florida to be "held as an indemnity for the outrages of Spain," and saying, "Let it be signified to me through any channel (say Mr. J. Rhea) that the possession of the Floridas would be desirable to the United States and in sixty days it will be accomplished." [2]

President Monroe was ill when the letter reached him. He took but little note of its contents, and it was inexplicably disregarded. In any case, without going into the intricacies of a much-vexed and undecidable question, Jackson came to understand that his suggestion was approved, and his action was prompt. Authorized by his orders to call upon the governors of the adjacent states for as many of the militia as he thought necessary (there was in reality but one state, Georgia, adjacent to Florida, and the militia of this was already called out), Jackson took the matter into his own hands and enlisted a thousand mounted men in Tennessee and Kentucky. He did not arrive at Fort Scott, four hundred and fifty miles from Nashville, until March 9, 1818, after great hardships from the weather and such want of provisions as to threaten famine. On March 16 he was, now with a force of two thousand white troops and friendly Indians, at the negro fort which he at once gave orders to rebuild. By the 26th he marched, determined to occupy St. Marks. He swept away the Indian villages in his

[1] Secretary of war to Gaines, December 16, 1817, *State Papers*, Military Affairs, I, 689.
[2] Parton, *Life of Andrew Jackson*, II, 433, 434.

path, captured "the greatest abundance of corn, cattle, etc." "In the council houses of Kenhageestown, . . . more than fifty fresh scalps were found."

St. Marks was occupied April 6, Jackson giving as his reasons that "Fort St. Marks could not be maintained by the Spanish force garrisoning it. The Indians and negroes viewed it as an asylum if driven from their towns and were preparing to occupy it in this event. It was necessary to anticipate their movements, independent of the position being deemed essential as a depot on which the success of my future operations measurably depended. In the spirit of friendship, therefore, I demanded its surrender . . . until the close of the Seminole war." During the negotiation "circumstances transpired convicting" the Spanish commandant of a disposition to favor the Indians and of having taken an active part in aiding and abetting them in their war. "I hesitated," continues Jackson, "no longer, and as I could not be received in friendship I entered the fort by violence." Three companies of infantry were "ordered to advance, lower the Spanish colors, and hoist the star-spangled banner on the ramparts of Fort St. Marks. The order was executed promptly and no resistance attempted on the part of the Spanish garrison. The duplicity of the Spanish commandant in professing friendship for the United States while he was aiding and supplying her savage enemies, . . . appropriating the king's stores to their use, issuing ammunition and munitions of war to them, and knowingly purchasing of them property plundered from citizens of the United States, is clearly evinced by the documents accompanying my correspondence."[1]

An inventory of Spanish property was taken and the garrison shipped to Pensacola, the commanding officer being provided with a letter from Jackson, in which he declared that he came "not as the enemy but the friend of Spain," with the additional statement that his "possession of the garrison of St. Marks will be referred to our respective governments for amicable adjustment."[2]

A Scotch trader named Arbuthnot, who in Jackson's mind, at least, was guilty of inciting the Indians to war, was found at the Spanish fort and seized. A few days later another British subject, Ambrister, the lieutenant of the "notorious" Woodbine, was

[1] Jackson's report, *State Papers*, Military Affairs, I, 702.   [2] *Ibid.*, 704.

captured on his way to join the Indians. A court-martial was convened at St. Marks, April 26, for the trial of these men for inciting the Indians to war, and "aiding, abetting, and comforting the enemy." Arbuthnot was sentenced to be hanged, Ambrister to be shot. They were executed April 29. Like measures were taken with two notable Indians, who, lured aboard a supply transport from New Orleans by the hoisting of the British flag, were seized and hanged by Jackson's order; one of these was the prophet Francis, but just lately returned from England, and against whom but little could be said; the other a murderous chief who had taken part in all the late horrors and who well deserved his fate.

As to the equity of the execution of Arbuthnot there has been much controversy. His name has come down declared by many as that of a man of character and ability (which he undoubtedly was), against whom there was nothing but that he was a trader supplying the Indians with such arms and ammunition as they could buy, and acting as their agent in correspondence with British and Spanish authorities. But the mere fact that he was a foreign trader among the Indians on the soil of a nationality peculiarly jealous of such intrusion goes for much. There can be little doubt that Adams was correct in declaring him "only the successor of Nichols."

There was no doubt about Ambrister; he pleaded guilty and threw himself upon the mercy of the court. But aside from questions of equity, there was no need for action of such haste and severity. Jackson was in the territory of a friendly power; to seize and execute in this territory the subjects of another friendly power, even under the circumstances, which, it may be granted, were difficult, and thus bring upon his government the burden of explanation, was a violation of every principle of international law and good sense. It aroused violent feeling in the English press and public, and but for the firmness of the British cabinet, which held the conduct of these two men "unwarrantable" and as not calling for interference,[1] would have brought war. "Such," said Lord Castleraugh in 1819, to Rush, the American minister, "was the temper of Parliament and such the feeling of the country that he believed *war might have been produced by holding up a fin-*

[1] J. Q. Adams, *Memoirs*, IV, 312.

*ger"; "*and he even thought that an address to the crown might have been carried for one *by nearly an unanimous vote.*" [1]

While scouring the region, Jackson received, May 23, 1818, a protest from the Spanish governor at Pensacola "remonstrating" (using Jackson's words) "against my proceedings, and ordering me and my forces instantly to quit the territory of his Catholic Majesty, with a threat to apply force in the event of non-compliance." No one could thus throw down the gauntlet to Jackson and escape the acceptance of such a challenge. Says Jackson, "This was so open an indication of hostile feeling . . . that I hesitated no longer. . . . I marched for and entered Fort St. Michael, Pensacola, with only a show of resistance on the 21st of May." [2] The governor fled to Fort Barrancas, six miles distant, at the mouth of the bay. Jackson demanded its surrender. "This is the third time," says Jackson, in a letter of May 23, 1818, to the governor, D. José Masot, at Fort Barrancas, "that the American troops have been compelled to visit Pensacola from the same causes. Twice had the enemy been expelled, and the place left in quiet possession of those who had permitted the irregular occupancy. This time it must be held until Spain has the power or will to maintain her neutrality. . . . If the peaceable surrender be refused, I shall enter Pensacola by violence and assume the government until the transaction can be amicably adjusted by the two governments. The military in this case must be treated as prisoners of war." [3]

The action against the fort is described in Jackson's report: "I marched for and invested it on the evening of the 25th of May, and on the same night pushed reconnoitring parties under its very guns." Cannon were planted. "A spirited and well-directed fire was kept up the greater part of the morning and at intervals in the afternoon" of May 27. In the evening the Spanish commandant offered to capitulate, and next day articles were signed "more favorable," says Jackson, with extraordinary naïveté, "than a conquered enemy would have merited, but, under the peculiar circumstances of the case, my object obtained, there was no motive for wounding the feelings of those [whom] military pride or honor had prompted to the resistance made." [4] The Spanish troops were to

[1] Rush, *The Court of London*, 1819–1825, 120. The italics are Rush's.
[2] *State Papers*, Military Affairs, 1, 708.   [3] *Ibid.*, 712.   [4] *Ibid.*, 708.

leave the fort with the honors of war and to be transported with their families and goods to Havana at the expense of the United States government. Article 19 stated that "This capitulation is made under the confidence that the general of the American troops will comply with his offer of returning integral this province in the state in which he receives it, as explained in his official letter." [1]

Jackson appointed his aide-de-camp as collector of the port, organized the district as if an American province, and marched homeward, leaving the American administration with a problem of the utmost difficulty and danger to adjust with England, whose subjects had been so harshly dealt with, and with Spain against whom actual operations of war had thus been undertaken.

Nor had Jackson proposed to end with the seizure of Pensacola. On August 7, 1818, he wrote General Gaines, directing him that if there was evidence that the Indians had been excited to war, and furnished with supplies by the Governor of St. Augustine, and "should you deem your force sufficient, you will proceed to take and garrison Fort St. Augustine with American troops and hold the garrison prisoners until you hear from the President of the United States, or transport them to Cuba as . . . you may think best." [2]

The Spanish minister promptly demanded reparation. On July 18, 1818, he wrote Adams: "General Jackson, with the American forces under his command, has not only violated the Spanish territory under the pretext of pursuing and chastising the Seminole Indians, but has taken possession by force of arms of the fort and bay of St. Mark, driven the Spanish garrison from these places, and sent them as prisoners to Pensacola, the capital of West Florida. Not satisfied with this enormous outrage, he marched against the latter place, and has by open rupture and bloodshed violated the peace existing between Spain and the United States. He demanded the surrender of Pensacola as if war had been declared between the two nations, and on the refusal of the Spanish governor to surrender or deliver up the place the American commander, availing himself of his superior force, attacked it, and bombarded the castle of Barrancas, whither the

[1] *State Papers*, Military Affairs, 719, 720.
[2] *Ibid.*, Military Affairs, I, 744.

governor had retired with his small garrison and such of the inhabitants as chose to follow him. Having surrounded that fortress, he gave orders for the assault and carried it. The governor with all his people were made prisoners of war, and were sent off, as it appears, by the American general, to Havana, who proceeded to extend his authority over the whole of West Florida by hoisting on its forts the flag of the United States." Proceeding to exonerate the Spanish governor from blame, he said, "Neither he nor the Governor of East Florida was notified of the war against the Seminole Indians, . . . nor was any call made upon them to seek and punish those Indians" in case of aggression. "Notwithstanding the total omission of all this, which was to have been expected as a regular and necessary consequence of the stipulations of the existing treaty, the aforesaid governor granted no favor to the Indians, but forbade them to enter the Spanish territory; and when a small number came to Pensacola to receive the annual presents, the governor allowed only a few of them to enter the place without their arms. . . . He further took every necessary precaution to prevent their being supplied with arms and ammunition within his Majesty's territories. . . . It would be inferred that the war . . . has been merely a pretext for General Jackson to fall, as a conqueror, upon the Spanish provinces, unprovided as they now are, and reposing in perfect security, for the purpose of establishing therein the dominion of this republic upon the odious basis of violence and bloodshed. . . . I am persuaded that the government of the United States cannot have authorized this hostile, bloody, and ferocious invasion of the dominions of Spain." Señor de Onis concluded: "It is therefore my duty to protest, and I do hereby solemnly protest, in the name of the king, my master, against these public acts of hostility and invasion, and I demand, through you, of the President, in the name of my sovereign, the prompt restitution of the fort and bay of St. Mark, also of Pensacola, Barrancas, and other places in Florida. . . . In like manner, I demand the faithful delivery of all the artillery, warlike stores, and property, both public and private, taken at Pensacola and other forts and places, by the American commander, indemnity for all the injuries and losses sustained by the Crown of Spain and the subjects of his Catholic Majesty in consequence of this act of invasion, and a satisfaction proportioned to the enormity of these offences, together with the lawful punishment of the general and the officers of this republic by whom they were committed." [1]

There was no question of the strength of Spain's case as thus stated, nor was it exaggerated. The administration was deeply embarrassed. The President and all the cabinet, except Adams, were of the opinion that Jackson acted not only without but against his instructions; that he had committed war against Spain, which could not be justified and in which if not disavowed the administration would be disavowed by the country.[2] "I insisted," said Adams, "that the character of Jackson's measures was decided by the intention with which they were taken, which was not hostility to Spain but self-defence against the hostility of Spanish officers. I admitted that it was necessary to carry the reasoning upon my principles to the utmost extent it would bear to come to this conclusion. But if the question was dubious it was better to err on the side of vigor than of weakness—on the side of our own officer, who had rendered the most eminent services to the nation, than on the side of our bitterest enemies and against him. . . . Calhoun [secretary of war] bore the principal argument against me." [3]

Adams overbore opposition, and, July 23, 1818, replied to the Spanish minister in the President's name, not only upholding Jackson's action, but, analyzing the attitude of the Spanish officials in Florida, declared that "a conduct not only so contrary to the express engagements of Spain, but so unequivocally hostile to the United States, justly authorizes him to call upon his Catholic Majesty for the punishment of those officers who, the President is persuaded, have acted contrary to the express orders of their sovereign." The despatch ended: "I am instructed by the President to inform you that Pensacola will be restored to the possession of any person duly authorized on the part of Spain to receive it; that the fort of St. Mark, being in the heart of the Indian country and remote from any Spanish settlement, can be surrendered only to a force sufficiently strong to hold it against the attack of the hostile Indians, upon the appearance of which force it will also be restored. In communicating to you this decision I am

[1] *State Papers*, IV, 496, 497. [2] Adams, *Memoirs*, IV, 108.
[3] Adams, *Memoirs*, V, 113.

also directed to assure you that it has been made under the fullest conviction, which he trusts will be felt by your government, that the preservation of peace between the two nations indispensably requires that henceforth the stipulations of Spain to restrain by force her Indians from all hostilities against the United States should be faithfully and effectually fulfilled." [1]

The receipt from De Onis of this note at Madrid brought a note from Señor Pizarro, the Spanish minister of foreign affairs to Mr. Erving, declaring that his Majesty was convinced that it was incompatible with the honor of the crown to pursue further negotiations until proper amends were made for Jackson's action and that the incident was of primary importance "capable of producing an essential and thorough change in the political relations of the two countries,"[2] words which could only mean a threat of war, a threat, however, soon practically withdrawn by a note from De Onis, October 18, 1818, informing Adams that he had received new instructions to resume negotiations, and also that the king had, on July 9, 1818, ratified the long-pending convention of August 11, 1802. Jackson's aggressive action had been taken to heart, and instead of retarding was to be "among the most immediate and prominent causes" producing the treaty. [3]

Adams replied to Pizarro in one of the ablest and most effective state papers ever issued from the department of state. He showed that Colonel Nichols did not consider the peace between the United States and Great Britain as having put an end to his military occupations or negotiations with the Indians in Florida; that on his departure for England he had left the fort, which he called the British post on the Appalachicola, amply supplied with military stores and ammunitions, to the negro department of his allies; that this fort was a post "whence to commit depredations, outrages, and murders, and as a receptacle for fugitive slaves and malefactors"; that the Spanish governor explicitly admitted, in answer to General Jackson, in April, 1816, that he " had neither sufficient force nor authority without orders from the governor-general of the Havana to destroy it"; that the intrusion of Arbuthnot as an Indian trader, was contrary to the policy observed

[1] *State Papers*, IV, 497–499.
[2] Pizarro to Erving, August 29, 1818, *Ibid.*, IV, 523.
[3] Adams, *Memoirs*, IV, 278.

by all European powers in this hemisphere, and by none more rigorously than by Spain, of excluding all foreigners from intercourse with the Indians; that it was for Spain to explain how, consistently with her engagements to the United States, she could grant such a license to a foreign incendiary whose principal, if not only, object appeared to have been to stimulate hostilities which Spain had expressly stipulated, by force, to restrain; that Jackson had, on his approach to St. Marks, been informed direct from the Spanish governor that the hostile Indians had threatened to seize the fort and that he feared he had not strength to defend it; that Arbuthnot "the British Indian trader from beyond the seas, the firebrand by whose touch this negro-Indian war had been rekindled, was found an inmate of the commandant's family"; that the commandant had permitted councils of war to be held by the savages; that Spanish storehouses had been appropriated to their use; that the fort was an open market for cattle known to have been robbed from citizens of the United States; that information had been afforded from the fort by Arbuthnot of the strength and movements of the American army; and that ammunition and all necessary supplies had been furnished the Indians. The governor of Pensacola was declared to have been equally disregardless of the obligations of the treaty. Adams declared that the President would neither inflict punishment nor pass censure upon Jackson for conduct the motives of which "were founded in purest patriotism, of the necessity for which he had the most immediate and effectual means of forming a judgment, and the vindication of which is written in every page of the law of nations as well as in the first law of nature—self-defence." He demanded an inquiry into the conduct of the Spanish Governor of Pensacola and the commandant at St. Marks, and the infliction of a suitable punishment "for having, in defiance and violation of the engagements of Spain with the United States, aided and assisted these hordes of savages . . . which it was their official duty to restrain." He asked most pertinently, "What . . . was the character of Nichols's invasion of his Majesty's territory, and where was his Majesty's profound indignation at that? Mr. Pizarro says his Majesty's forts and places have been violently seized on by General Jackson. Had they not been seized on, nay, had not the principal of his forts been blown up by Nichols and a British fort on the same Spanish territory been erected during the war, and left standing as a negro fort, in defiance of Spanish authority, after the peace? Where was his Majesty's profound indignation at that? Has his Majesty suspended formally all negotiation with the sovereign of Colonel Nichols for this shameful invasion of his territory, without color or provocation, without pretence of necessity, without shadow or even avowal of a pretext? Has his Majesty given solemn warning to the British government that these were incidents of transcendent moment, capable of producing an essential and thorough change in the political relations of the two countries? . . . Against the *shameful invasion* of the territory; against the violent seizure of forts and places; against the blowing up of the Barrancas and the erection and maintenance, under British banners, of the negro fort on Spanish soil; against the negotiation by a British officer, in the midst of peace, of pretended treaties, offensive and defensive, and of navigation and commerce, upon Spanish territory, between Great Britain and Spanish Indians, whom Spain was bound to control and restrain—if a whisper of expostulation was ever wafted from Madrid to London, it was not loud enough to be heard across the Atlantic nor energetic enough to transpire beyond the walls of the palaces from which it issued and to which it was borne." He declared the connection between Nichols and Arbuthnot "established beyond all question," as also, as shown by documents, that between Ambrister, Woodbine, and McGregor, whose object "was the conquest of Florida from Spain by the use of those very Indians and negroes whom the commandant of St. Marks was so ready to aid and support in war against the United States." The Spanish minister of state was to be informed that if necessity should again compel the United States to take possession of the Spanish forts and places in Florida that another unconditional restoration of them must not be expected.[1]

This paper, accompanied by documents, copies of which were sent to all American legations abroad, " silenced European comment and convinced Spain herself."

Before Adams had completed his despatch, Congress had met, and the question was taken up with extreme bitterness against

[1] Adams to Erving, November 28, 1818, *State Papers*, IV, 539–545.

Jackson and particularly by Clay, the outcome of whose action was a mortal enmity between the two which was to have later deep effect upon American domestic politics. But public feeling was with Jackson, and though the majority of the House committee and the committee of the Senate made strongly adverse reports, commenting with great severity upon Jackson's acts, the majority of the House, after a debate of twenty-seven days which occupied the attention of the country, was against the finding and that in the Senate was never brought to a vote.

The negotiations of the treaty with Spain being, as mentioned, renewed, De Onis, in his note of October 24, 1818, proposed a line beginning on the Gulf of Mexico between the rivers Mermento and Calcasia, crossing Red River in latitude 32°, thence north to the Missouri, thence to the source of this river.[1]

Adams replied, October 31, with what was "to be considered as the final offer upon the part of the United States," which was a line beginning at the mouth of the Sabine, to follow that river to latitude 32°; thence north to the Red River; thence following this river to its source, "touching the chain of the Snow Mountains in latitude 37° 25'; thence to the summit of these, following the chain to latitude 41°; thence west to the "South Sea." All claims provided for in the convention of 1802; all condemnations by French consuls in Spanish ports of captures by French privateers; all indemnities for suspension of deposit at New Orleans; all claims of citizens against Spain which had been presented to the notice of the United States government from 1802 to the date of the treaty were to be renounced, the United States undertaking to satisfy all these classes of claims to an extent not exceeding five millions of dollars.[2] De Onis's proposition to abrogate Article 15 of the treaty of 1796, which stipulated that the flag should cover the property, was accepted with the modification that (as it appears in the final draught) "if either of the two contracting parties shall be at war with a third party, and the other neutral, the flag of the neutral shall cover the property of enemies whose government acknowledges this principle, and not of others.[3]

[1] *State Papers*, IV, 526.   [2] *Ibid.*, 530.
[3] Art. 12 of treaty, *Ibid.*, IV, 623–625.

The treaty followed the foregoing outline with the exception that the line should follow the Red River to longitude 100° and should then go due north to the Arkansas and follow the south bank of that river to latitude 42°, and thence on that parallel to the Pacific Ocean, or, in Adams's old-fashioned phrase, to the "South Sea," a concession due wholly to Adams's initiative and pressure which preserved to the United States the great Northwest beyond what was then called the "Stony Mountains."

On February 22, 1819, the treaty was signed, but the signature was but the forerunner of other difficulties, the first, but least, being an opposition led by Clay to giving up the Rio Grande as a boundary. Monroe's nervous anxiety to come to an understanding regarding Florida would, but for Adams, have given an even less satisfactory result; had he not been so pressing, and have allowed the matter to rest yet awhile in abeyance, Spain shortly, almost beyond question, in view of the insurgency of Mexico, would have yielded to the full limit claimed by the United States. As it was, however, Texas, thus surrendered, passed to Mexico and became the subject of war a quarter of a century later.

The more vexing question to the administration was that of late grants of lands by the King of Spain covering nearly the whole of Florida, lands the sale of which, by express understanding on the part of the United States as well as of Spain, were to be used to extinguish the claims against the latter. Adams had proposed the date of 1802 as that after which all grants should be void. To this De Onis very reasonably demurred and suggested the date of January 24, 1818, as being that upon which Spain had first expressed her willingness to yield Florida. This was accepted by Adams with the distinct understanding on the part of both negotiators that three immense grants made after this date were void. The unworthy character of these acts is well shown in the *cedula* of February 6, 1818, signed by the king after the date mentioned, and with the full understanding that Florida was about to pass from his possession. The *cedula* cited the petition of Count of Puñon Rostro, "My governor of the Floridas," submitted November 3, 1817, who, "prompted by the desire of promoting by all possible means the improvement of the extensive waste and unsettled lands possessed by your Majesty in the Americas," humbly requested the grant of a region which comprised several million acres. The king, taking the premises into consideration, antedated the decree to December 17, 1817, and "judged fit to grant to him the same . . . to the end that the said Count of Puñon Rostro may forthwith carry his plans into execution in conformity with my beneficent desires in favor of the agriculture and commerce of the said territories which require a population proportioned to the fertility of the soil and the defence and security of the coast."[1] One grant, dated March 10, 1818, was of land in West Florida, west of the Perdido and already in possession of the United States.[2]

Mr. Forsyth, newly appointed minister to Spain, sailed in March from Boston for Cadiz in the sloop of war *Hornet*, carrying with him the treaty ratified by the Senate, February 24. His instructions included a reference to the grants which were giving such disturbance of mind to Mr. Adams, who severely blamed himself for his failure to examine more closely Mr. Erving's report enclosing the copy of the decree just quoted, which would perhaps have caused him to take greater precautions.[3] Mr. Forsyth carried with him a form of declaration stating that both plenipotentiaries had agreed upon the date of January 24, 1818, as the date subsequent to which all grants of land made by his Majesty should be null and void, and that the ratifications were exchanged under the explicit declaration and understanding that the three mentioned were so included and would be so held by the United States. He was also instructed that "it is not anticipated that any objection will be made to receiving the declaration; if, however, there should be, you will nevertheless exchange the ratifications."[4]

The President had directed the insertion of this last in Mr. Forsyth's instructions, "for he considered the treaty of such transcendent importance to this country that if we should not get an inch of land in Florida the bargain would still be inexpressibly advantageous to us. The removal of all apprehension of a war with Spain, the consolidation of our territorial possessions, the command of the Gulf of Mexico, the recognized extension to the South

---

[1] *State Papers*, IV, 525.
[2] Adams, *Memoirs*, IV, 291. For details of these grants, see Forsyth to Spanish minister of foreign affairs, October 18, 1819, *State Papers*, IV, 668.
[3] Adams, *Memoirs*, IV, 287 *et seq.*   [4] *State Papers*, IV, 652.

Sea, and the satisfaction of so large an amount of the claims of our citizens upon Spain were objects of paramount consideration, and the attainment of them would raise our standing and character so high in the estimate of the European powers that the land was of very trifling comparative consequence. Besides, as Onis admits that he signed the treaty with the understanding that the grants were annulled, and De Neuville [the French minister, who seems to have acted throughout as *amicus curiæ*] certifies that such was the mutual understanding, if the fact be that they were made before the 24th of January, the fraud will be so palpable that when we have got possession of the country we shall have the means of doing ourselves justice in our own hands." [1]

On May 18, 1819, Mr. Forsyth notified the Spanish minister of foreign affairs of his readiness to exchange ratifications. [2] Receiving no reply, he addressed him again June 4, recalling that the sloop of war *Hornet* was awaiting the treaty at Cadiz and that her return without it would produce "the most unfavorable impressions." [3] It was not until June 19 that the American minister received an answer stating that his Majesty, "reflecting on the great importance and interest of the treaty, he is under the indispensable necessity of examining it with the greatest caution and deliberation before he proceeds to ratify it." [4] The animated reply of Forsyth two days later was the first of a series which went much beyond the usual bounds of diplomatic language. On August 10, in a communication largely given to a criticism of Forsyth's manner, he was informed that the king "is of opinion that a final decision cannot be taken thereupon without previously entering into several explanations with the government of the United States, to some of which your government has given rise," and that he had selected a person to go to the United States "possessing the qualifications necessary for bringing this interesting trust to a happy conclusion." [5]

The *Hornet*, meanwhile, had reached the United States. The treaty fell by limitation unless ratified within six months from February 22, but in a despatch from Adams of August 18, 1819, Forsyth was authorized to extend the time "in case the exchange shall be immediate" and the ratified treaty arrive in Washington "before

[1] Adams, March 9, 1819, *Memoirs*, IV, 290.
[2] *State Papers*, IV, 654.   [3] *Ibid.*, 654.   [4] *Ibid.*, 654.   [5] *Ibid.*, 656.

the meeting of Congress on the first Monday in December"; that if it should not so arrive "a full communication will be made by the President to Congress of all the transactions relating to the treaty, and such measures be adopted by that body as they shall think required by the exigency of the case; that whatever their determination may be, the Spanish government will be responsible to the United States for all damages and expenses which may arise from the delay or refusal of Spain to ratify, and from the measures to which the United States may resort to give efficacy to their rights; and that, for the indemnities to which they will be justly entitled for this violation of faith by Spain, the United States will look to the territory west of the Sabine River."[1]

Adams rightly held that the delay of Spain was wholly unjustified. A distinguished authority has stated: "Had the Spanish government, no matter for what motives, promptly disavowed the treaty as made in excess of instructions, the United States would have had no ground for substantial complaint no matter what might have been the reasons for such disavowal."[2] But the word of the king had been given, "Obliging ourselves, as we do hereby oblige ourselves and promise on the faith and word of a king, to approve, ratify, and fulfil, and to cause to be immediately observed and fulfilled *whatsoever may be stipulated and signed by you*, to which intent and purpose I grant you all authority and full power, in the most ample form, thereby as of right required." In Adams's view, it was thus the duty of the Spanish government to ratify the treaty at once, quoting in support Vattel and Martens: "*Whatever he* [the plenipotentiary] *promises within the terms of his commission and according to the extent of his powers is binding upon his constituent.*"[3]

[1] *State Papers*, IV, 657.
[2] Wharton, *Inter. Law Digest*, II, par. 161-a.
[3] *State Papers*, IV, 657–660. The measures referred to by Adams involved taking possession of Florida. At the cabinet meeting, August 10, 1819, it was unanimously agreed that in case the ratification should be withheld it would be proper to recommend such action to Congress.—Adams, *Memoirs*, IV, 406. The President thus in his annual message, December 7, 1819, "submitted to the consideration of Congress whether it will not be proper for the United States to carry the conditions of the treaty into effect in the same manner as if it had been ratified by Spain." This, however, was qualified by a suggestion that if a law for carrying the treaty into effect be adopted, it should be contingent, leaving the responsibility for action upon the executive. —*State Papers*, IV, 627.

The *Hornet*, carrying the declaration of proposed action in Adams's despatch, arrived again at Cadiz September 17, 1819, but left there after a stay of but three hours for Gibraltar, as Cadiz was at this time desolated by yellow fever. The captain, bearing the despatch, did not reach Madrid until September 30, and October 2 its tenor was laid before the Spanish foreign minister, requesting an "immediate, explicit, and unequivocal reply. Should this reply not be made before the 10th of the current month, I give formal notice to your excellency that the proposal will be considered as rejected and the proper communication will be made to the President."[1]

The answer was made October 8, the only noteworthy remark being that the king regarded it indispensable to send to the United States a person possessing his confidence who, "by smoothing the obstacles or removing the difficulties which have hitherto opposed the accomplishment of his beneficent intentions, may fully convince the federal government of the frankness and loyalty, as well as the honor and dignity which it is his Majesty's desire to maintain in his relations of amity and union with that government."[2] While considering the business of the treaty thus "at rest," Forsyth continued his correspondence by a note, October 10, requesting authenticated copies of the Spanish grants, which, being peremptorily refused, he followed, October 18, by a lengthy and threatening note respecting the grants which, on November 10, was returned to him as not "conceived in fit and becoming terms."[3]

The *Hornet* sailed from Malaga, October 20, 1819, for the United States bearing news of the continued unsatisfactory state of the treaty. Her arrival in Spain had already produced great anxiety at Madrid,[4] which the correspondence just mentioned did nothing to allay. So serious was the aspect that the Spanish minister called upon Count Bulgary, the Russian chargé d'affaires, requesting him to visit Mr. Forsyth and ask that he might not insist upon sending in again the returned note, and explaining that General Vives had been selected as minister to the United

---
[1] *State Papers*, IV, 663. [2] *Ibid.*, IV, 664.
[3] *Ibid.*, IV, 668–672.
[4] Forsyth to secretary of state, October 10, 1819, *Ibid.*, IV, 666.

States, with competent powers, and that everything would be amicably arranged, the future discussions to be transferred entirely to Washington.[1]

The cause of the Spanish minister's reference to the Russian representative at Madrid lay in the fact that the Russian emperor, Alexander, the foremost spirit of the Holy Alliance and particularly concerned with the affairs of Spain, feared lest the peace be broken with the United States and the aims of the alliance now incubating at Aix-la-Chapelle be thwarted. A note to Poletica, the Russian minister at Washington, after expressing the supposition that he was doubtless informed how far the President's last instructions to Mr. Forsyth were positive, said, "The emperor will not now take upon him to justify Spain; but he charges you to plead with the government at Washington the cause of peace and concord." [2]

Not only was Russia concerned, but France had made the strongest remonstrances to the Spanish cabinet. De Neuville, the French minister at Washington, informed Adams that the French government was assured that it was the king's "most earnest desire and settled determination to finish this transaction with the United States; that the real obstacle was not 'the affair of the grants.' The great stumbling block was South America. The proposition which we had made to England and were ready to make to France and Russia, for a joint recognition of the independence of Buenos Ayres, had been made use of to persuade the King of Spain that if he should ratify the treaty the next day we should recognize the South Americans and make common cause with them. His jealousy, being thus excited, had been much strengthened by exaggerated representations from this country of a miserable plundering expedition into the province of Texas which had been carried on last summer by people from the United States. De Neuville's instructions are, therefore, to use all his influence with the government of the United States to prevail upon them to take no precipitate measure which might produce war, but to wait until the Spanish minister shall come, with the perfect assurance that

[1] Forsyth to Adams, January 3, 1820, *State Papers*, IV, 674.
[2] Nesselrode to Poletica, November 27, 1819, *Ibid.*, IV, 676.

we shall obtain the ratification without needing the application of force."[1]

Vives left Madrid January 25, 1820, and presented his credentials in Washington April 12. A month earlier (March 9) the House committee on foreign affairs had submitted a bill to authorize the President to take possession of the whole of Florida and establish a temporary government.[2] On April 14 Vives presented a note "opening and almost closing the negotiation,"[3] in which, while dwelling upon "the system of hostility which appears to be pursued in so many parts of the Union against theSpanish dominions," he proposed, by command of the king, as a subject "to be taken into full consideration," besides "the scandalous system of piracy established in and carried on from several of their ports," that the United States should give a pledge that the integrity of his Catholic Majesty's possessions should be respected. "And, finally, that they will form no relations with the pretended governments of the revolted provinces of Spain."[4]

Adams replied, in a short and sharp note, that "it is indispensable that before entering into any new negotiation between the United States and Spain that relating to the treaty already signed should be closed. If upon receiving the *explanations* which your government has asked, and which I am prepared to give, you are authorized to issue orders to the Spanish officers commanding in Florida, to deliver up to those of the United States who may be authorized to receive it immediate possession of the province according to the stipulations of the treaty, the President, if such shall be the advice and consent of the Senate, will wait (with such possession given) for the ratification of his Catholic Majesty till your messenger shall have time to proceed to Madrid; but if you have no such authority, the President considers it will be at once an unprofitable waste of time, and a course incompatible with the dignity of this nation, to give explanations which are to lead to no satisfactory result and to resume a negotiation the conclusion of which can no longer be deferred."[5]

Vives in reply assured Adams that he was not authorized to de-

[1] Adams, *Memoirs*, IV, 453.
[2] *State Papers*, IV, 690.
[3] Adams, *Memoirs*, V, 70.
[4] *State Papers*, IV, 680.
[5] Adams to Vives, April 21, 1820, *Ibid.*, 682.

liver Florida, despite his statement of authority to Gallatin, the American minister in France, whom he met in Paris on his way to America.[1] The fact was that he was so authorized should he be satisfied as to conditions. The whole question hinged in reality, not upon the question of grants, but upon the attitude of the United States toward the revolted South American provinces. It was attempted to make clear to Vives that acceptance of the Spanish proposal meant departure from the attitude of neutrality of the United States to which the government had steadily held despite certain clamor in and out of Congress.

But events in Spain were hastening a settlement independently of the Washington negotiations. A revolution begun in January, 1820, ended in the unwilling acceptance by Fernando, March 7, of the Cadiz constitution of 1812. The determination of the United States government to occupy Florida was of course known, and the new government was reconciled to such an event.[2] The question of imminency, however, was soon removed by the reception of President Monroe's special message of May 9, 1820, forwarding the Spanish correspondence. Recognizing in this the difficulties of the new Spanish government, he declared that "the United States would not be justified in their own estimation should they take any steps to disturb its harmony. When the Spanish government is completely organized . . . there is just ground to presume that our differences with Spain will be speedily and satisfactorily settled."[3]

Monroe's forecast was correct. The Cortes met July 6. On October 5, by an almost unanimous vote, it advised the king to cede the Floridas to the United States, and declared null and void the cessions of land of which the United States had made complaint.[4] On October 24, 1820, the king signed the order of transfer, and February 19, 1821, the Senate a second time consented to the ratification of the treaty, and on February 22, 1821, after a struggle of two years, the ratifications were exchanged. The formal act of transfer was signed July 10, 1821, by Governor Don José Coppinger

[1] *State Papers*, IV, 679.
[2] Forsyth to Adams, May 20, 1820, *Ibid.*, IV, 690.
[3] Message, *Ibid.*, IV, 676, 677.
[4] Forsyth to Adams, October 5 and 12, 1820, *Ibid.*, IV, 694-701.

on the part of Spain and Mr. Robert Butler, commissioner, on the part of the United States. General Andrew Jackson was appointed governor, an office in which he quickly showed his more unfortunate and unhappy characteristics.

CHAPTER VIII

THE RECOGNITION OF SOUTH AMERICAN INDEPENDENCE

WHILE the greatest cause of difficulty between Spain and the United States had thus been removed by the ratification of the treaty, there yet remained the question of the revolted Spanish-American provinces; one which was not finally to be at rest for three-quarters of a century to come.

In 1810, when the victory of Napoleon appeared to be complete, the principal inhabitants of Carácas, in the name of Fernando VII, deposed the Spanish colonial officials and elected a supreme junta. On April 25, 1810, the president and vice-president of this junta addressed to the secretary of state of the United States a letter accrediting Don Juan Vicente Bolivar and Don Telesforo Ozea as bearers of the intelligence that Venezuela had severed her allegiance to Spain. Several papers were later presented, the first recorded acknowledgment of which is in a letter of Monroe, secretary of state, of December 19, 1811, mentioning the reception of a copy of the declaration of independence, "and that the President had received it with the interest the matter deserved." [1]

President Madison mentioned the subject in his message, November 5, 1811, with an expression of general interest in the events now developing in South America, and the select committee to which this part of the message was referred reported a joint resolution December 10, to the effect that the United States beheld "with friendly interest the establishment of independent sovereignty by the Spanish provinces in America . . . and that when these provinces shall have attained the condition of nations . . . the Senate and House of Representatives will unite with the executive

[1] Moore, *International Law Digest*, I, 75.

in establishing with them . . . such amicable relations and commercial intercourse as may require their legislative authority."[1] No action was taken upon the resolution, which in the circumstances was nowise unfriendly to Spain, which was, at the moment, practically a French province.

The destruction of Carácas and 20,000 of the inhabitants in 1812 by an earthquake caused the temporary failure of the revolution,[2] and Miranda, who had reappeared from England as a leader, submitted, July 26, 1812, on a basis of a general amnesty which was not regarded by the Spanish general. Miranda a little later, through the inactivity of Bolivar, fell into the hands of the Spaniards, was sent to Spain, and died in imprisonment July 14, 1816; his fate a sad blot upon the latter's reputation. The Spanish forces, under General Morillo thenceforward until 1819, were in the ascendancy.

On June 28, 1810, Mr. Joel Poinsett was appointed agent to Buenos Ayres, where a junta on the call of the viceroy May 25, 1810, had organized a government declaring the country independent of the French government in Spain, but still subject to the authority of Fernando VII. Full independence of Spain was not declared until July 9, 1816. Poinsett's instructions stated that "the real as well as ostensible object of your mission is to explain the mutual advantages of commerce with the United States, to promote liberal and *stable* regulations, and to transmit seasonable information on the subject."[3]

The revolution in Chile also began in 1810. The whole of South America was thus, with the exception of the viceroyalty of Peru, thenceforward in a revolutionary state. No movement toward revolt took place in the latter until 1819, or in Mexico until 1821.

In 1817 a commission, composed of Cæsar A. Rodney, John Graham, and Theodoric Bland, was appointed to go to South America to report upon the general situation, but more particularly

[1] Resolution in *State Papers*, III, 508.
[2] On May 8, 1812, the United States Congress voted $50,000 to purchase provisions for relief of citizens who had suffered by the earthquake in Venezuela, an act which was carried into effect, Mr. Alexander Scott being designated as the agent of distribution.
[3] House Rep. 72, 20 Cong., 2 Sess.; Moore, *Digest*, 1, 215.

that in Buenos Ayres and Chile. The commission sailed from Hampton Roads in the frigate *Congress*, December 4, 1817, and on arriving at Montevideo, found it in possession of a Portuguese army, Uruguay being claimed as part of Brazil which was then an integral part of the Portuguese dominions. Mr. Bland was the only one to cross the Andes and visit Chile. Separate reports were made by these gentlemen, November, 1818, as also by Mr. Poinsett, the special agent to Buenos Ayres.[1]

The result was the determination not as yet to recognize the independence of the provinces visited, President Monroe's annual message November 16, 1818, stating that "there is good cause to be satisfied with the course heretofore pursued by the United States in regard to this contest, and to conclude that it is proper to adhere to it, especially in the present state of affairs." The fact that the treaty with Spain was then pending would appear, despite many assertions to the contrary, to have had but little weight in this determination. Long before the conclusion of the treaty, the views of the United States government were known to Spain, as Adams, the secretary of state, on December 12, 1818, desired the French minister de Neuville "to write to the Duke of Richelieu and state to him that we hope France will soon be prepared to move with us in the formal acknowledgment of the government of Buenos Ayres; that we have given the same notice to Great Britain; that we have patiently waited without interfering in the policy of the allies [2] on the subject, and as they have not agreed upon anything, and the fact of the independence of Buenos Ayres appears established, we think it necessary that it should be recognized." "The French minister," says Adams, "appeared to be startled."[3]

There was good reason that the French minister should appear as Mr. Adams mentioned, for there was then incubating the scheme of establishing a Bourbon prince as king of the southern part of South America, which culminated in an express offer of support from France. On June 18, 1819, the French minister for foreign affairs wrote: "With a view to the attainment of an object so desirable to the South Americans as their independence of the

---

[1] For these interesting papers see *State Papers*, IV, 348.
[2] The Holy Alliance. [3] Adams, *Memoirs*, IV, 190.

crown of Spain . . . the French government offers to undertake the task of obtaining the assent of all the courts thereto, upon the elevation of the Prince of Lucca and Etruria [1] to the throne of South America; for the accomplishment of which latter object all the requisite aid should be offered, both in naval and military forces, so as to enable him not only to command respect, but even to repel any power that might oppose itself to his elevation. . . . The French government agrees to take charge of the diplomatic relations upon the subject; and promises to grant to the Prince of Lucca all the support, assistance, and protection which would be granted even to a French prince." [2]

This proposal was accepted November 12, 1819, by the oligarchy at Buenos Ayres, calling itself a congress, but with a most important reservation—its acceptance should be provisional upon the friendly attitude of Great Britain; a proviso fatal to the project, as the latter emphatically dissented, seeing in such a scheme the destruction of her rapidly increasing South American commerce. How large a part this intrigue on the part of France was to play in her motives for the occupancy of Spain by her armies six years later has not come to light, but that it was an element in the designs of the Holy Alliance as to the future of the South American provinces there can be little doubt. It was, however, never to emerge from the early eclipse caused by British policy.

Mr. Clay, a warm advocate of the South American cause, partly from genuine sympathy, partly as an opponent to the administration, had already, March 24, 1818, in order to force the administration's hands, moved in the House and supported by an impassioned speech an amendment appropriating $18,000 for an outfit and a year's salary for a minister to the government of Rio de la Plata. This was rejected by a vote of 115 to 45.[3] Along with the very natural and proper sympathy for the South Americans, which had been throughout exhibited by the people of the

[1] Then eighteen years old, and nephew of the King of Spain.

[2] Memorandum of Baron de Reyneval in reply to a note from Don José Valentin Gomez, the Argentine commissioner in Paris, to the French minister of foreign affairs (*British and Foreign State Papers*, VI, 1091). The new kingdom was to include Argentina, Uruguay, Entre Rios, Corrientes, and Paraguay.

[3] Debates in Congress, VI, 136–169.

United States, there was influence of a more sinister sort which was used to promote the feeling that independence should be granted; the influence of the profits of privateering and of the prospective exclusive privileges hoped for by certain men of standing and political influence.[1]

Two years later, Clay moved in the House, April 4, 1820, an appropriation for such minister or ministers as the President might, with the concurrence of the Senate, send to any of the South American governments that had established and were maintaining their independence against Spain. This motion was carried by a vote of 80 to 75, but had no result. A motion for an appropriation made February 5, 1821, in the next session of Congress, was defeated, but a motion was carried declaring that the House "participates with the people of the United States in the deep interest which they feel for the success of the Spanish provinces of South America, which are struggling to establish their liberty and independence, and that it will give its constitutional support to the President of the United States whenever he may deem it expedient to recognize the sovereignty and independency of any of the said provinces."[2]

On January 30, 1822, the House requested the President to lay before it the reports of the agents sent to the revolted states. In doing this, the President sent a message to both houses of Congress, March 8, in which, while stating tersely the situation in the several continental provinces, he said: "When we regard, then, the great length of time which this war has been prosecuted, the complete success which has attended it in favor of the provinces, the present condition of the parties, and the utter inability of Spain to produce any change in it, we are compelled to conclude that its fate is settled, and that the provinces which have declared their independence and are in enjoyment of it ought to be recognized. . . . Should Congress concur in the view herein presented they will doubtless see the propriety of making the necessary appropriations for carrying it into effect."[3]

[1] See Adams, *Memoirs*, V, 56.
[2] Davis, *Treaty Notes*, Treaty Vol. 1776–1887. Moore, *International Law Digest*, I, 84. Debates in Congress, VII, 93–95.
[3] *State Papers*, IV, 819.

On March 9, 1822, the day after the President's message was sent, Señor Don Joaquin de Anduaga, now the Spanish minister, sent a vigorous protest, asking: "What is the present state of South America, and what are its governments, to entitle them to recognition? Buenos Ayres is sunk in the most complete anarchy, and each day sees new despots produced, who disappear the next. Peru, conquered by a rebel army, has near the gates of its capital another Spanish army aided by part of its inhabitants. In Chile, an individual suppresses the sentiments of its inhabitants, and his violence presages a sudden change. On the coast of Firma [Venezuela] also the Spanish banners wave, and the insurgent generals are occupied in quarrelling with their own compatriots. In Mexico, too, there is no government. . . . Where then are those governments which ought to be recognized? Where the pledges of their stability? Where the proof that those provinces will not return to a union with Spain, when so many of their inhabitants desire it? and, in fine, where the right of the United States to sanction and declare legitimate a rebellion without cause, and the event of which is even not decided? . . . I think *it my duty to protest, as I do solemnly protest, against the recognition of the governments mentioned of the insurgent Spanish provinces of America, by the United States, declaring that it can in no way now, or at any time, lessen or invalidate in the least the rights of Spain to said provinces, or to employ whatever means may be in her power to reunite them to the rest of her dominions.*" [1]

The Spanish minister's statement as to interior anarchic conditions was not far from the truth, but they were conditions which were to obtain yet for a generation and more. But exteriorly the case was hopeless. On April 6, 1822, Adams replied: "In every question relating to the independence of a nation, two principles are involved: one of *right*, and the other of *fact;* the former exclusively depending upon the determination of the nation itself, and the latter resulting from the successful execution of that determination. The right has recently been exercised, as well by the Spanish nation in Europe, as by several of those countries in the American hemisphere which had for two or three centuries been connected as colonies with Spain. In the conflicts which have attended these

[1] *State Papers*, IV, 845–846. The italics are Señor Anduaga's.

revolutions, the United States have carefully abstained from taking any part respecting the right of the nations concerned in them to maintain or newly organize their own political constitutions, and observing, wherever it was a contest by arms, the most impartial neutrality. But the civil war in which Spain was for some years involved with the inhabitants of her colonies in America has, in substance, ceased to exist. Treaties equivalent to an acknowledgment of independence have been concluded by the commanders and viceroys of Spain herself with the republic of Colombia, with Mexico, and with Peru; while in the provinces of La Plata and Chile, no Spanish force has for several years existed to dispute the independence which the inhabitants of those countries had declared.

"Under these circumstances, the government of the United States, far from consulting the dictates of a policy questionable in its morality, has yielded to an obligation of duty of the highest order, by recognizing as independent states, nations which, after deliberately asserting their right to that character, had maintained and established it against all the resistance which had been or could be brought to oppose it. This recognition is neither intended to invalidate any right of Spain, nor to affect the employment of any means which she may yet be disposed or enabled to use, with a view of reuniting those provinces to the rest of her dominions. It is the mere acknowledgment of existing facts, with a view to the regular establishment with the nations newly formed of those relations, political and commercial, which it is the moral obligation of civilized and Christian nations to entertain reciprocally with one another." [1]

Adams's note of April 6 was in accord with Jefferson's pronouncement, as secretary of state, to Gouverneur Morris, minister to France: "We surely cannot deny to any nation that right whereon our own government is founded, that every one may govern itself according to whatever form it pleases, and change these forms at its own will; and that it may transact its business with foreign nations through whatever organ it thinks proper, whether king,

[1] *State Papers*, IV, 846. For an extended and interesting résumé of the question of the Spanish-American provinces, see Adams's instructions, May 27, 1823, to Anderson, minister to Colombia, *State Papers*, V, 888–890.

convention, assembly, committee, president, or anything else it may choose. The will of the nation is the only thing essential to be regarded."[1]

We shall see in how small regard this principle, now universally accepted, was held at the moment with which we are dealing by the powers of continental Europe, which had taken upon themselves the general superintendence of the world's affairs.

Nor as already mentioned was there, throughout the Florida negotiations, any deception on the part of the United States or concealment of its attitude. "During the negotiation, . . ." says Adams, "repeated and very earnest efforts were made, both by Mr. Pizarro at Madrid, and by Mr. Onis here, to obtain from the government of the United States either a positive stipulation or a tacit promise that the United States would not recognize any of the South American revolutionary governments; . . . the Spanish negotiators were distinctly and explicitly informed that this government would not assent to any such engagement, either express or implied."[2]

On May 4, 1822, an act was approved appropriating $100,000 "for such missions to the independent nations of the American continent as the President of the United States may deem proper."

More than a year passed before, in accord with this action, R. C. Anderson, of Kentucky, was appointed minister to Colombia and C. A. Rodney, of New Jersey, to Argentina. H. Allen, of Vermont, was appointed to Chile in 1824, and Joel R. Poinsett, of South Carolina, to Mexico in 1826.

[1] Jefferson to Morris, March 12, 1793; Moore, *American Diplomacy*, 143.
[2] Adams to Lowndes, Chairman House Com. on Foreign Relations, December 21, 1819, *State Papers*, IV, 674.

CHAPTER IX

THE HOLY ALLIANCE AND THE INVASION OF SPAIN

In the period just discussed there was, besides the difficulties between Spain and the United States, a second potent element of danger which, in one of the most extraordinary political combinations in history, threatened, through Spain, the peace not only of Europe but of both Americas. The movement was absolutism gone mad.

The treaty of alliance between Austria, Russia, Prussia, and England signed at Chaumont, France, March 1, 1814, confirmed and made permanent at Vienna, March 25, 1815, reaffirmed and added to at Paris, November 20, 1815, dealt chiefly with the relations of the allies with France; it gave little hint of the extraordinary document signed September 14, 1815, by the emperors of Austria and Russia and the King of Prussia themselves, and not, as is usual, by their ministers of state. To this latter paper was given the name, written in the document itself, of the Holy Alliance, suggested by Madame Krudener, a religious enthusiast and a friend and guide of the Emperor Alexander's, himself at this time a religious *exalté* with very advanced liberalistic views. In itself it can be regarded as but a religious rhapsody, a foolish effervescence in its author of altruism worked to fever heat by the immense success of the allied armies.

This convention, apparently so harmless, solemnly declared the conviction of the monarchs of the necessity of founding their conduct upon the sublime truths of the Christian religion; and their fixed resolution, "both in the administration of their respective states and in their political relations with every other government, to take for their sole guide the precepts of that holy religion: viz., the precepts of justice, Christian charity, and peace"; that they should consider each other as fellow countrymen, regarding themselves toward their subjects and armies as "fathers of families," "as merely delegated by Providence to govern three branches of one family," exhorting their people "to strengthen themselves every day more and more in the principles and exercise of the *duties which the Divine Saviour has* taught to mankind"; finally stating that all powers "who shall choose solemnly to avow the sacred principles which have dictated the present act . . . will be received with equal ardor and affection into this holy alliance."[1]

---

[1] The full text of the convention was as follows:

"In the name of the Most Holy and Indivisible Trinity.

"Their Majesties the Emperor of Austria, the King of Prussia, and Emperor of Russia, having, in consequence of the great events which have marked the course of the last three years in Europe, and especially of the blessings which it has pleased Divine Providence to shower down upon those states which place their confidence and their hope on it alone, acquired the intimate conviction of the necessity of founding the conduct to be observed by the powers in their reciprocal relations upon the sublime truths which the holy religion of our Saviour teaches.

"They solemnly declare that the present act has no other object than to publish, in the face of the whole world, their fixed resolution, both in the administration of their respective states and in their political relations with every other government, to take for their sole guide the precepts of that holy religion; namely, the precepts of justice, Christian charity, and peace, which, far from being applicable only to private concerns, must have an intimate influence on the councils of princes, and guide all their steps, as being the only means of consolidating human institutions and remedying their imperfections. In consequence their Majesties have agreed upon the following articles:

"Art. 1. Conformably to the words of the Holy Scriptures, which command all men to consider each other as brethren, the three contracting monarchs will remain united by the bonds of a true and indissoluble fraternity, and considering each other as fellow countrymen, they will, on all occasions and in all places, lend each other aid and assistance; and regarding themselves toward their subjects and armies as fathers of families, they will lead them in the same spirit of fraternity with which they are animated, to protect religion, peace, and justice.

"Art. 2. In consequence, the sole principle in force, whether between said governments or between their subjects, shall be that of doing each other reciprocal service, and of testifying, by unalterable good-will, the mutual affection with which they ought to be animated, to consider themselves all as members of one and the same Christian nation, the three allied princes looking on themselves as merely delegated by Providence to govern three branches of the one family, namely, Austria, Prussia, and Russia; thus confessing that the Christian world, of which they and their people form a part, has in reality no other sovereign than Him to whom alone power really belongs, because in Him alone are found all the treasures of love, science, and

There is no need to impute to Alexander, the author and moving spirit of the document of the 14th of September, any but the best of motives. Master "of the unbroken might of Russia," the semi-Asiatic empire which now for the first time felt itself really a European power, he was enthusiastically moved by the idea of a personal mission to dominate Europe for Europe's good, the mechanism being autocracy tempered by a compound of the teachings of Rousseau and of the Christian religion.

All powers were requested to join the alliance, two excepted: Turkey, naturally, as not Christian, and Spain, the conduct of whose king at this time was regarded by the monarchs as derogatory to kingship. All the sovereigns of Europe but the two excluded ones, and the pope and the Prince Regent of Great Britain, became signers; the last named, though a fervent supporter of a

infinite wisdom, that is to say, God, our Divine Saviour, the Word of the Most High, the Word of Life. Their Majesties consequently recommend to their people, with the most tender solicitude, as the sole means of enjoying that peace which arises from a good conscience, and which alone is durable, to strengthen themselves every day more and more in the principles and exercise of the duties which the Divine Saviour has taught to mankind.

"Art. 3. All the powers who shall choose solemnly to avow the sacred principles which have dictated the present act, and shall acknowledge how important it is for the happiness of nations, too long agitated, that these truths should henceforth exercise over the destinies of mankind all the influence which belongs to them, will be received with equal ardor and affection into this Holy Alliance.

"Done in triplicate and signed at Paris, in the year of grace, 1815, 14th (26th) September.

"[L. S.] Francis.
"[L. S.] Frederick William.
"[L. S.] Alexander."

(*Annual Register*, 1816, 381–382; also Hansard, First Series, XXXII, 355.) The original, says Capefigue, was entirely in the handwriting of the Emperor Alexander, with corrections by Madame Krudener. Strangely enough the fundamental idea, thus expressed, had come from the British foreign minister, Lord Castlereagh, one of the British representatives in the negotiation of the many treaties of the period. Writing Lord Liverpool, the prime minister, he said: "Although the Emperor of Austria is the ostensible organ, the measure has entirely originated with the Emperor of Russia, whose mind has latterly taken a deep religious tinge. Since he came to Paris he has passed a part of every evening with a Madame de Krudener, an old fanatic, who has considerable reputation amongst the few highflyers in religion that are to be found at Paris. The first intimation I had of this extraordinary act was from the emperor himself, and I was rather surprised to find it traced back to a con-

general idea of the union, being prevented by the constitutional objection to the British monarch becoming a personal signatory.

Notwithstanding its apparent harmlessness, however, the first article stating that the monarchs "*will on all occasions, and in all places, lend each other aid and assistance*" came to have in the light of later years a deep significance. This, combined with the statement that the three sovereigns looked upon themselves as "merely delegated by Providence to govern three branches of one family"; that these branches were the most important of the European continent; that they had just settled the affairs of Europe to their satisfaction, was to mean later, whatever the first intent, more than was first understood by the rest of mankind, and more, no doubt, than the imperial author himself foresaw.

But what became known as the Holy Alliance, its soul, in fact, was not the rhapsodic document of Alexander and Madame

versation with which I was honored with the emperor when leaving Vienna. You may remember my sending home a project of declaration with which I proposed the congress should close, in which the sovereigns were solemnly to pledge themselves in the face of the world to preserve to their people the peace they had conquered, and to treat as a common enemy whatever power should violate it. The emperor told me that this idea, with which he seemed much pleased at the time, had never passed from his mind, but that he thought it ought to assume more formal shape and one directly personal to the sovereigns. . . . Prince Metternich came to me the following day with the project of the treaty since signed. He communicated to me in great confidence the difficulty in which the Emperor of Austria felt himself placed; that he felt great repugnance to be a party to such an act, and yet was more apprehensive of refusing himself to the emperor's application; that it was quite clear his mind was affected . . . the King of Prussia . . . felt in the same manner. . . . As soon as the instrument was executed between the sovereigns, without the intervention of their ministers, the Emperor of Russia brought it to me, developed his whole plan of universal peace, and told me the three sovereigns had agreed to address a letter to the prince regent to invite him to accede, of which intended letter his Imperial Majesty delivered to me the enclosed copy. The Duke of Wellington happened to be with me . . . and it was not without difficulty that we went through the interview with becoming gravity. . . . The fact is that the emperor's mind is not completely sound."—Lord Castlereagh to Lord Liverpool, September 28, 1815. Wellington, *Supplementary Despatches, etc., of the Duke of Wellington*, XI, 175.

The Emperor Alexander published, on Christmas Day, 1815, a manifesto of much the same character, which, accompanied by a copy of the treaty, was read in all the Russian churches. The manifesto ended: "May this sacred union be confirmed between all the powers for their general good; and (deterred by the union of all the rest) may no one dare to fall off from it."—Hansard, XXXII, 358.

Krudener, but the sixth article of the treaties of November 20, 1815, made by England with Austria, Prussia, and Russia severally. These while, as a whole, concerned with the questions of France, now to be occupied for three years longer as a conquered territory, said, in the article mentioned: "to consolidate the connections which at the present moment so closely unite the four sovereigns for the happiness of the world, the high contracting parties have agreed to renew their meetings at fixed periods, either under the immediate auspices of the sovereigns themselves, or by their respective ministers, for the purpose of consulting upon their common interests and for the consideration of the measures which at each of those periods shall be considered the most salutary for the repose and prosperity of nations, and for the maintenance of the peace of Europe." [1]

It was this agreement which became the real basis of the attempt to rule Europe, and even America, by a series of "congresses" of the allied sovereigns, from the logical effect of which the world was to be saved by the revolt of Great Britain from their demands, and by the decisive pronouncement of the American government in 1823, known as the "Monroe doctrine."

As agreed in 1815, under this article, the four allied powers met October 1, 1818, at Aix-la-Chapelle; present, the sovereigns of Russia, Prussia, and Austria in person. The Government of Great Britain was represented by Lord Castlereagh (still foreign minister) and the Duke of Wellington; that of Austria by Metternich; the Russian, by Capo d'Istria and Nesselrode; the Prussian, by Hardenburg and Bernstorff. As the meeting was to arrange for the withdrawal of the armies of occupation, which during this period had remained in France at that unhappy country's expense, the Duke of Richelieu was allowed to be present on its behalf. Though the affairs of France were foremost, appeals came to this "court extraordinary" from all Europe: from Denmark; from Bernadotte of Sweden, whom the congress forced to fulfil the stipulations of the treaty of Kiel, and from the host of German rulers on questions left undetermined by the congress of Vienna.

1. The question of the evacuation of France settled, the French

[1] Hansard's *Parliamentary Debates*, First Series, vol. XXXII, 272.

king was now a free sovereign, and he demanded admittance to the quadruple alliance; but this was so especially directed to arranging the affairs of France, that matters were compromised by the signing, November 15, 1818, of two protocols. The first, a secret document, renewing the quadruple alliance for the purpose of watching over France, was communicated in confidence to Richelieu. It stated: "1. That the subscribing courts are firmly resolved never to depart, neither in their mutual relations, nor in those which bind them to other states, from the principle of intimate union which has hitherto presided over all their common relations and interests, a union rendered more strong and indissoluble by the bond of Christian fraternity which the sovereigns have formed among themselves. 2. That this union . . . can only have for its object the maintenance of the general peace, founded on a religious respect for the engagements contained in the treaties and for the whole of the rights resulting therefrom. 3. That France, associated with other powers by the restoration of the legitimate monarchical and constitutional powers, engages, henceforth, to concur in the maintenance and consolidation of a system which has given peace to Europe, and which can alone insure its duration." The fourth section arranged for future meetings of the representatives of the alliance, "and in the case of these meetings having for their object affairs specially connected with the interests of the other states of Europe, they shall only take place in pursuance of a formal invitation on the part of such of those states as the said affairs may concern, and under the express reservation of the right of direct participation therein, either directly or by their plenipotentiaries." This important reservation was, as will be seen, soon to be thrown to the winds, as was also "the religious respect" for the engagements in treaties.

The second protocol to which France was made a party was a declaration of the same date, explanatory of the high principles governing the self-appointed keepers of the world's peace. It declared that "the convention of the 9th of October, which definitely regulated the execution of the engagements agreed to in the treaty of peace of November 20, 1815, is considered by the sovereigns who concurred therein as the accomplishment of the work of peace, and as the completion of the political system destined to insure its stability. The intimate union established among the monarchs who are joint parties to this system by their own principles, no less than by the interest of their people, offers to Europe the most sacred pledge of its future tranquillity. The object of this union is as simple as it is great and salutary. It does not tend to any new political combination—to any change in the relations sanctioned by existing treaties. Calm and consistent in its proceedings, it has no other object than the maintenance of peace and the guarantee of those transactions on which the peace was founded and consolidated."

Promising "the strictest observation of the principles of the right of nations . . . the repose of the world will be constantly their motive and their end. . . . They solemnly acknowledge that their duties toward God and the people whom they govern make it peremptory upon them to give to the world, as far as in their power, an example of justice, of concord, and of moderation; happy in the power of concentrating from henceforth all their efforts to protect the arts of peace, to increase the internal prosperity of states, and to awaken those sentiments of religion and morality, whose influence has been but too much enfeebled by the misfortune of the times." [1]

To these documents were appended, among others, the names of Castlereagh and Wellington, the British representatives. Great Britain was thus still a party to the union.

The association was, in fact, the first great peace society, but it had its own special views as to what constituted peace, and reckoned not at all with the aspirations of the millions of whom they declared themselves the Heaven-appointed directors. With the conjunction of France and the acquiescence of the British representatives, it thought itself secure in the re-establishment of the ancient despotisms which made the sovereign the only source of law.

The *deus ex machina* in the alliance was now, as in fact always, Metternich, the impersonation of the idea of autocratic power, and whose vast and overpowering self-esteem was such as banished from his mind the thought that he could be mistaken and made him blind to the possibility that there should be any aspirations in the mass of men which needed to be regarded. His dominant idea and whole principle of action was that all concession in the direc-

[1] *Annual Register*, 1819, 135.

tion of constitutional or popular government must come from the fountain head of power and authority, the monarch. Ruling completely the mind of his own emperor, he became equally the master of the thoughts of the Emperor Alexander and the King of Prussia. He was the mover of the conference of the German states at Carlsbad in 1819, and the author of the despotic "Carlsbad" decrees, the outcome of this conference, which "are held to have fettered opinion and postponed constitutional liberty in Germany for a generation."[1] Metternich soon, by holding before Alexander the enormity of the German agitation for greater freedom and taking advantage of the assassination, March 23, 1819, of the reactionist journalist Kotzebue, by Karl Sand, as a text, completely subordinated the emperor's mind to his own and turned him from liberalism to completest despotism.

Few in history have lived lives of, at the time, apparently, so great personal success, only to dwindle in the estimate of posterity to a character fraught with evil, with a want of judgment and foresight, and with the narrowness, ever an accompaniment of a despotic mind, which should class him among the flails of mankind. It was due to his influence, as he himself so well depicts in his correspondence, that the three monarchs upon whom the well-being of Europe so largely turned, stepped back into the despotism which the French revolution and Napoleon, who though a despot was a democrat, had done so much to overturn. Germany has reason to remember much; but to Italy his memory and the memory of his policy, which bound her so long in chains during the years of dawning liberty in Europe, must ever be her darkest thought.[2]

Before adjournment of the meeting at Aix, in 1818, it was known at Washington that the mediation of the allies had been solicited by Spain, and agreed to be given by them for the purpose

[1] *Cambridge Modern History*, X, 367.
[2] It is not surprising that two such antipodal minds as Metternich and Canning should not think well of one another; that Metternich, who was to see his ideals overthrown by Canning, should speak of the latter as "the malevolent meteor hurled by an angry Providence upon Europe," and that Canning should say in a letter to Lord Granville, British ambassador at Paris: "You ask me what you shall say to Metternich [then expected at Paris]. In the first place you shall hear what I think of him—that he is the greatest r[ascal] and l[iar] on the continent, perhaps in the civilized world."—Canning to Granville, March 11, 1825. Stapleton, *Canning and His Times*, 427.

of restoring Spanish dominion in South America, under certain conditions of commercial privileges to be guaranteed to the inhabitants. Spain now offered a general amnesty to the insurgents on their submission; the admission of native Americans, "endowed with the requisite qualifications," to office in common with European Spaniards, and "regulation of the commerce of the provinces with foreign states according to free principles and conformably to the present political situation of these countries and Europe,"[1] the offer being dependent upon the support of the alliance. She had until this refused to open the Spanish-American ports to trade, though in great degree powerless to prevent their rapidly growing commercial intercourse with Great Britain and the United States.

It was proposed by some of the powers that the United States should be invited to join in this mediation. The ministers of the United States to France, England, and Russia were immediately instructed to make known that the United States would not take part in any plan not founded on a basis of total independence of the colonies. Great Britain, while concurring at this moment in the plan of restoring Spanish authority, declared as a condition of her participation that there should be no resort to force. To this France and Russia, after some hesitation, assented. A proposition to prohibit commercial intercourse, in case mediation should not be accepted by the South Americans, was negatived by England, as transferring, of course, the whole trade to the United States. As a last expedient it was proposed that the Duke of Wellington should go to Madrid with the joint powers of all the allied sovereigns to arrange terms, but this failed, as the duke insisted that, if he should go, a previous entry should be made upon the protocol at Aix-la-Chapelle that no force, in any result of his embassy, should be used against the South Americans. Spain declined any mediation which would not guarantee the restoration of her authority.[2]

The Emperor Alexander, ever since 1815 much concerned with the affairs of Spain and her insurgent provinces, moved particularly by this blot upon the universal peace of which he now regarded

[1] *Annual Register*, 1818, 161.
[2] Adams, secretary of state, to Thompson, secretary of the navy, May 20, 1819, 17, MS., Dom. Let. 304, Moore, *International Law Digest*, VI, 375–376.

himself the great supporter, was personally desirous of securing the United States as a member of the alliance; and Poletica, the Russian minister at Washington, was instructed to approach the American government. The attitude of the latter is defined in a despatch to the American minister at St. Petersburg. "It has been suggested," says Mr. Adams, "as an inducement to obtain their compliance, that this compact bound the parties to no specific engagement of anything. That it was a pledge of mere principles—that its real as well as professed purpose was merely the general preservation of peace—and it was intimated that if any question should arise between the United States and other governments of Europe, the Emperor Alexander, desirous of using his influence in their favor, would have a substantial motive and justification for interposing if he could regard them as his *allies*, which, as parties to the Holy Alliance, he would. . . . No direct refusal has been signified to Mr. Poletica. It is presumed that none will be necessary. His instructions are not to make the proposal in form unless with a prospect that it will be successful. . . . As a general declaration of principles . . . the United States not only give their hearty assent to the articles of the Holy Alliance, but will be among the most earnest and conscientious in observing them. But . . . for the repose of Europe as well as of America, the European and American political systems should be kept as separate and distinct from each other as possible. If the United States as members of the Holy Alliance could acquire the right to ask the influence of its most powerful member in their controversies with other states, the other members must be entitled in return to ask the influence of the United States, for themselves or against their opponents; in the deliberations of the league they would be entitled to a voice, and in exercising their right must occasionally appeal to principles which might not harmonize with those of any European members of the bond. This consideration alone would be decisive for declining a participation in that league, which is the President's absolute and irrevocable determination, although he trusts that no occasion will present itself rendering it necessary to make that determination known by an explicit refusal." [1]

[1] Adams to Middleton, minister to Russia, July 5, 1820, MS. Instructions to Ministers, IX, 18, Moore, *Digest*, VI, 376–379.

The foregoing sufficiently defines the attitude of the American and British governmental mind during the years 1818 to 1820. During this period an expedition was attempted to be organized in Spain for the reconquest of the South American provinces, independently of aid from the alliance. This "continued to be postponed from time to time, for the equipment of a single squadron was now an effort which exhausted all the resources of this great kingdom—once by its powers and riches the tyrant or the terror of Europe. The Spanish marine, since the fatal alliance formed with France in the year 1796, and the long series of national misfortunes which had resulted from this step, had sunk into the last stages of decay. The navy had been annihilated, the arsenals emptied, and the forests of the kingdom destroyed. In the present emergency therefore the government had found it necessary to make application to Russia to furnish vessels for the South American expedition, and a considerable number had arrived at Cadiz. But these ships, which were built only of pine, and had already seen much service, were soon discovered to be in so bad a state that considerable repairs were requisite to fit them for the voyage";[1] one which, it should be said, never came to pass. The yellow fever broke out, the troops became mutinous, and the country, in an inconceivable state of destitution and misrule, broke into the revolution of January, 1820, which, as mentioned, forced the king to accept the constitution of 1812 and a Cortes.

A note, April 19, 1820, from Señor Zea Bermudez, the Spanish minister at St. Petersburg, informing the Russian government of the adoption of a constitution in Spain, and expressing a desire to know how the emperor viewed this, caused the immediate issuance of a Russian circular note stating that "the revolution of the Peninsula fixes the attention of two hemispheres; the interests which it is about to decide are the interests of the universe. . . In the course of long conferences, relative to the differences with Rio de la Plata, and to the participation of the colonies, they [the

---

[1] *Annual Register*, 1819, page 179. Five ships of the line and three frigates were purchased for which the enormous sum of 54,000,400 *pesetas* (about $10,500,000) was paid. The chief persons involved in the transaction were the king, Ugarte, Taticheff, the Russian minister, and Equia, the minister of war. *The Cambridge Modern History*, X, 209.

allied sovereigns] let it be sufficiently understood that these institutions would cease to be a means of peace and happiness if, instead of being granted by kindness, as a voluntary concession, they should be adopted by weakness as a last resource of salvation. . . . In unison, therefore, with his allies, his majesty cannot but desire to see granted to the Peninsula, as to its trans-marine provinces, a government which he considers as the only one that can yet justify some hope in this stage of calamities. But in virtue of his engagements of the 3d–15th of November, 1818, his majesty is bound to mark, with the most forcible reprobation, the revolutionary measures set in action to give new institutions to Spain . . . [the powers] have doubtless deplored, as he has, the outrage which has recently tarnished the annals of Spain. We repeat it, this outrage is deplorable. It is deplorable for the Peninsula; it is deplorable for Europe; and the Spanish nation now owes the example of an expiatory deed to the people of two hemispheres. Till this be done the unhappy object of their disquietude can only make them fear the contagion of their calamities."

He proposed that the plenipotentiary of Spain at each of the five courts be informed that these courts "have desired that in Europe, as in America, institutions conformable to the progress of civilization, and to the wants of the age, might procure to all Spaniards long years of peace and happiness. . . . They have wished that all institutions should become a real blessing by the legal manner in which they should be introduced. They now wish the same.

"This last consideration will convey to the ministers of his Catholic Majesty with what sentiments of affliction and grief they have learned of the events of the 8th of March, and those which preceded it. According to their opinion the salvation of Spain, as well as the welfare of Europe, will require that this crime should be disavowed, this stain effaced, this bad example exterminated. . . . If these salutary counsels be listened to; if the Cortes offer to their king, in the name of the nation, a pledge of obedience; if they succeed in establishing, upon durable bases, the tranquillity of Spain and the peace of Southern America, the revolution will have been defeated at the very moment when it thought to obtain a triumph."

This long document, of which but portions have been given, ended with an ominous warning: "If, on the contrary, alarms, perhaps too reasonable, be realized, at least the five courts will have discharged a sacred duty; at least a new occurrence will have developed the principles, indicated the object, and displayed the scope of the European alliance."[1]

Spain's example was followed by Naples, July 2, and Portugal, August 12, each of which, as the result of revolutionary procedures, adopted the Spanish constitution; the autocratic cabal thus saw itself faced by a widespread movement subversive of the reconstructed feudalism which they thought secured by the overthrow and imprisonment of Napoleon.

The Russian note, however, brought from the British cabinet in May, 1820, a circular note to the other four powers which boded ill for the Metternich system. Although the great majority of the thirteen then composing the cabinet were Tories, the ultra-Toryism of seven of them, including the Duke of Wellington, the lord chancellor, and Lord Bathurst, being "unqualified by liberal opinions upon any subject whatever of external or internal policy,"[2] one member, George Canning, now about to leave it, was of very different mind, and his powerful and liberal character was the saving leaven in this community of reaction.

Canning, two years before, had taken exception to the proposal of the congress at Aix for "continued meetings at fixed points." At a cabinet meeting where there were but six, Castlereagh and Wellington being of the absent members and, as members of the congress, supporting the proposition, Canning announced his opposition. "He thinks," said Lord Bathurst in a letter to Lord Castlereagh, "the system of periodical meetings of the four great powers, with a view to the general concerns of Europe, new and of

[1] *Annual Register*, 1820, 725. It was this document which, judging by its form and style almost certainly emanated from Metternich, gave the new and dangerous tone to the Holy Alliance. The new compact of 1818 did not include any such principle as that now enunciated by the Emperor Alexander. In fact it was expressly stipulated that meetings affecting either states should "only take place in pursuance of a formal invitation on the part of such of those states as the said affairs may concern," and expressly arrange for their participation. (See page 161.)

[2] Stapleton, *Life of Canning*, I, 127.

very questionable policy; that it will necessarily involve us deeply in all the politics of the continent, whereas our true policy has always been not to interfere except in great emergencies, and then with a commanding force. He thinks that all other states must protest against such an attempt to place them under subjection; that the meetings may become a scene of cabal and intrigue; and that the people of this country may be taught to look with great jealousy for their liberties if our court is engaged in meeting with great despotic monarchs, deliberating upon what degree of revolutionary spirit may endanger the public security and therefore require the interference of the alliance. . . . I do not subscribe to Canning's opinions, nor did any of the cabinet who attended, but if this is felt by him, it is not unreasonable to apprehend it may be felt by many other persons, as well as by our decided opponents."[1] There can thus be little doubt that the note of May, which sounded so discordantly in the concert in which all had heretofore gone so smoothly, was, while over the signature of Castlereagh, the work of Canning. Every phrase of strength has the ring of his decided and liberal temper. Beginning with the milder view that it appeared "advisable studiously to avoid any reunion of the sovereigns —to abstain, at least in the present stage of the question, from charging any ostensible conference with commission to deliberate on the affairs of Spain,"—it proceeded, after a general consideration of the Spanish situation and of that of Portugal, for the protection of whose European dominions Great Britain was bound by treaty, to announce publicly certain fundamental principles which must govern British conduct, declaring that "the notion of revising, limiting, or regulating the course of such experiments, either by foreign council or by foreign force, would be as dangerous to avow as it would be impossible to execute," that "in this alliance, as in all other human arrangements, nothing is more likely to impair, or even to destroy, its real utility, than any attempt to push its duties and its obligations beyond the sphere which its original and understood principles will warrant. It was a union for the reconquest and liberation of a great portion of the continent of Europe from the military dominion of France, and having subdued the conqueror

[1] Bathurst to Castlereagh, October 20, 1818. Stapleton, *Canning*, I, 55–58.

it took the state of possession, as established by the peace, under the protection of the alliance. It never was, however, intended as a union for the government of the world, or for the superintendence of the internal affairs of other states. . . . We shall be found in our place when actual danger menaces the system of Europe; but this country cannot, and will not, act upon abstract and speculative principles of precaution. The alliance which exists had no such purpose in view in its original formation. . . . It was never so explained to Parliament; if it had, most assuredly the sanction of Parliament could never have been given to it; and it would now be a breach of faith were the ministers of the crown to acquiesce in a construction being put upon it, or were they to suffer themselves to be betrayed into a course of measures, inconsistent with those principles which they avowed at the time, and which they have since uniformly maintained both at home and abroad."[1] It was this stand, undoubtedly due to Canning's influence, which determined the British attitude at Troppau and Laybach, and later at Verona.[2]

The domination by Austria of a large part of Italy, and the treaty of the former with Naples, of June 12, 1815, by which the latter had bound itself not to introduce changes "irreconcilable either with ancient monarchial institutions, or with the principles adopted by his Imperial and Apostolic Majesty for the interior government of his Italian provinces,"[3] caused, however, through the dominating influence of Metternich, a putting aside of Spanish affairs for the moment in favor of immediate attention to those of Naples. The allies thus met, October 9, 1820, at Troppau in Austrian Silesia; the sovereigns of Austria, Russia, and Prussia being present as well as their ministers. Sir Charles Stewart,

[1] Laid before Parliament, April 21, 1823, *Hansard*, VIII, N. S. 1136–1139.
[2] *The Cambridge Modern History*, X, 12, remarks: "It was only in 1822, on the eve of the Congress of Verona, that the long process of [Castlereagh's] disillusionment culminated in the determination to make that open breach with the system by which, in his untimely death, the credit fell to George Canning."

There is nothing to show in Castlereagh's private correspondence such a change of mind as the above would indicate, and much to show that Canning was throughout the moving spirit of discontent. Everything points to Castlereagh's disappointment in the trend taken by the various conferences as the cause of the unsettlement of his mind.

[3] *Annual Register*, 1820, 732.

brother of Lord Castlereagh and British ambassador at Vienna, was present, but with instructions to observe only and do nothing.

In the first days of the meeting Metternich succeeded so completely in bringing to his own views the Emperor of Russia, that there was not now a vestige left of the liberalism which in its uncertainty had been Metternich's nightmare. "To-day," said Alexander, speaking at Troppau, "I deplore all I said and did between the years 1815 and 1818. . . . You have correctly judged the condition of things. Tell me what you want, and what you want of me, and I will do it."[1] Austria thus had a free hand. The representatives of France and England were not admitted to the conferences, as they were only empowered "to report," not "to decide," and the three powers on November 19, 1820, signed a protocol, binding themselves "by peaceful means, or if need be by arms, to bring back the guilty state into the bosom of the great alliance," in case of a change of government by revolution which threatened "immediate danger" to other states. To this France later gave a qualified adhesion.

This protocol was followed, December 8, 1820, by a circular note giving a "Short View of the First Results of the Conferences," which stated that the "monarchs assembled at Troppau resolved to invite the King of the Two Sicilies to an interview at Laybach; a step the sole object of which was to free the will of the king from all external constraints, and to place his Majesty in the situation of a mediator between his misled people and the states whose tranquillity was threatened. As the monarchs are resolved not to recognize governments which had been produced by open rebellion, they could not enter into negotiations except with the king alone."[2] All this was in accord with the principles announced in the Berlin *Gazette*, that "there cannot be a thought of bringing a constitution which is the product of unlawful power more or less near to the monarchial principles. The monarchial principle rejects every institution which is not determined upon and accomplished by the monarch himself of his own free will";[3] a principle which, denying the right of revolution, was the basis of the action of the allies during the next three years.

[1] *The Cambridge Modern History*, X, 28.
[2] *Annual Register*, 1820, 736
[3] *Ibid.*, 1820, 734.

Great Britain, however, in a lengthy instruction of December 16, 1820, to her ambassador at Vienna, opposed *in toto* such claims, declaring that the country could not "charge itself as a member of the alliance with the moral responsibility of administering a general European police of this description."[1]

The congress moved in January, 1821, to Laybach, where it sat in utmost secrecy, not even a secretary being allowed at the meetings, nor a stranger permitted in the town. The first result was a manifesto from Austria which stated the "firm determination" of the sovereigns announced to the King of Naples, now present, "not to allow the continuance of a system which had been forced upon the kingdom of the Two Sicilies by a faction without a name and without authority"; and "that if this state of things did not end . . . by a spontaneous disavowal of those who exercised the power at Naples, it would be necessary to have recourse to arms." It declared that the Emperor of Russia, "convinced of the necessity of struggling against an evil so serious, would lose no time in joining his forces to those of Austria. In the whole of the transactions which have taken place, the monarchs have only had in view the safety of the states they are called upon to govern and the tranquillity of the world. . . . The inviolability of all established rights, the independence of all legitimate governments, the integrity of all their possessions, these are the bases from which their resolutions will never deviate."

The paper ended with a phrase such as flowed so smoothly from the pen of Metternich, and which marked in him a faculty which made him so easily the master mind of the Pecksniff family: "They [the monarchs] will bless the period when, set free from all other causes of anxiety, they can devote exclusively to the happiness of their subjects all the means and the power which have been conferred on them by Heaven."[2]

The result was the movement into Italy, begun February 4, 1821, of an Austrian army of 85,000 men. The quick defeat of the Neapolitan army, and the restoration in Naples of absolutism, was followed soon by a like suppression of revolution in Piedmont, which, March 10, 1821, had also declared for the Spanish constitu-

[1] *The Cambridge Modern History*, X, 29.
[2] *Annual Register*, 1820, 739–745; Frankfort *Gazette*, February 19, 1821.

tion. For forty-five years longer Italy was to seethe with discontent, her sons to undergo imprisonment and death, and to suffer a tyranny as ruthless and vindictive as that which later stirred America to sympathy for Cuba. The Austrian action in Italy was but a prelude to like designs as to Spain and the revolted provinces in America.

The Neapolitan question had continued to arouse British feeling, which found strong and earnest expression in Parliament, Canning himself, in a speech of March 20, 1821, qualifying the congress of the allies as "the self-constituted, usurping, tyrannical and insolent tribunal at Laybach."[1] On January 19, the foreign office issued a circular despatch to its missions abroad, declaring that it had acted with all possible explicitness, even before the conclusion of the treaty of alliance of 1815. The note continues: "It should be clearly understood that no government can be more prepared than the British government to uphold the right of any state or states to interfere where their own immediate security or essential interests are seriously endangered by the internal transactions of another state. But as they regard the assumption of such right as only to be justified by the strongest necessity, and to be limited and regulated thereby, they cannot admit that this right can receive a general and indiscriminate application to all revolutionary movements, without reference to their immediate bearing upon some particular state or states, or to be made prospectively the basis of an alliance. They regard its exercise as an exception of the greatest value and importance, and as one that can only properly grow out of the circumstances of the special case; but at the same time consider that exceptions of this description never can, without the utmost danger, be so far incorporated into the ordinary diplomacy of states or into the institutes of the law of nations."[2]

Before the breaking up of the congress at Laybach, May 13, 1821, it was resolved to meet again at Verona, in the fall of the next

---

[1] Hansard, IV (1821), 1378.
[2] *Ibid.*, IV (1821), 286. The mild character of this note, compared with that of January, 1820, shows the absence of the master mind of Canning, who had now resigned from the cabinet, as not wishing to take part in the action against Queen Caroline.

year. In the meantime Greece had revolted, and Russia was eager for war with Turkey. The new congress thus found itself faced with a new question which threatened the destruction of the compact which governed it; a danger which was overcome by the influence of Metternich with the Emperor Alexander, who yielded to Metternich's arguments and appeals, backed as they were by those of Castlereagh, to hold to the principles of the alliance and preserve the peace of Europe. The main question thereafter was the status of Spain, and of her revolted American dependencies.

On October 25, 1820, Fernando VII had appealed by letter to Louis XVIII for help in what he termed his captivity, and begged the French king to obtain for him the aid of the allied powers.[1] A French army had already been moved to the Pyrenees, establishing what was termed a *cordon sanitaire*, nominally as a protection against the introduction of the yellow fever then so prevalent in Spain; the force, however, was gradually increased to 100,000 men, and when there was no longer the pretext of the prevention of contagion, the name was changed to that of the army of observation; French money assisted Fernando in secretly promoting a counter revolution.[2] An "army of the faith," an outcome of the suppression of the religious communities, and the forces of the "regency" set up at Seo de Urgel on the theory that Fernando was a captive, ravaged the north of Spain. They were, however, but two of the many bands which, with the aid of discord in the Cortes, made anarchy throughout the Peninsula, until in December, 1822, the liberal forces dispersed the army of the faith and drove those of the Urgel regency to take refuge in France. The situation now, though serious, might, with the advice and moral support of the British government, and the aid, both sentimental and real, of the English people, have brought a permanent reconstruction of Spain on more sensible lines than those of the Cadiz constitution, but the action of the allies forestalled such a possibility.

Canning had succeeded Lord Castlereagh as foreign minister, on the latter's suicide, which had occurred August 12, 1822. Wellington thus alone represented Great Britain, at the conference

[1] *The Cambridge Modern History*, X, 222.   [2] *Ibid.*, 225.

which met at Verona in October, though the British ambassador at Vienna was at hand as an observer. Neither, however, under the changed conditions in the British foreign office, would have been present had not Spanish interests been too deeply involved for England to ignore the proceedings. No stranger was allowed to remain in Verona, "without a most satisfactory explanation to the Austrian authorities . . . nor was permission to pass through the town easily obtained." [1]

Wellington carried with him the instructions which Castlereagh had drawn up for himself, and which included a rigid abstinence from any interference in the internal affairs of Spain.[2] One of Canning's first acts was to supplement this by a note which involved a threatening warning, saying: "If there be a determined project to interfere by force or by menace in the present struggle in Spain, so convinced are his Majesty's government of the uselessness and danger of any such interference, so objectionable does it appear to them in principle, as well as utterly impracticable in execution, that, when the necessity arises (I would rather say), when the opportunity offers, I am to instruct your Grace at once frankly and peremptorily to declare that, to any such interference, come what may, his Majesty will not be a party." [3]

On October 20 the Duke of Montmorency, the French representative, addressed three questions to the conference: 1. Would the powers break off diplomatic relations with Spain should France find herself obliged to do so? 2. If war should occur between France and Spain, under what form and by what acts would the powers give France the moral support which would give her measures the weight and authority of the alliance and inspire a salutary dread in the revolutionists of all countries? 3. What effective assistance would be given by the powers in case France should demand it?

The Emperor Alexander was only too eager to move 150,000 Russians wherever needed; an offer which, however, apart from the effect which it would have had upon England, suited at the moment neither Austria nor France. The continental allies

[1] *Annual Register*, 1822, 218.
[2] Correspondence presented to Parliament, April, 1823, Hansard, N. S. **VIII** (1823), 904 *et seq*. In the writer's view such instructions were due to feeling in Parliament rather than to Castlereagh's convictions. [3] *Ibid.*, 905.

thus answered, on October 30, that they would act as should France in regard to their ministers in Spain; but the British representative protested at length against such action, and refused an answer to the hypothetical questions of France, of the grounds for which the British government was wholly ignorant. Nor indeed were they ever discoverable, if ever they existed. The movement was in fact, though France was now a constitutional monarchy, one of absolutism face to face with liberalism in a struggle for supremacy which if successful would have left England and the United States alone as constitutional governments.

On December 14, 1822, the plenipotentiaries of Austria, Prussia, and Russia (Metternich, Bernstorff, and Nesselrode) addressed instructions to the representatives of these powers at Madrid, the general tenor of which appears in the following from Count Nesselrode: "In vain," he says, "will malevolence endeavor to represent [the intentions of the allies] in the light of foreign interference which seeks to dictate laws to Spain. To express desire of seeing a protracted misery terminate, to snatch from the same yoke an unhappy monarch and one of the first among European nations, to stop the effusion of blood, and to facilitate the re-establishment of an order of things at once wise and natural, is certainly not attacking the independence of a country, nor establishing a right of intervention against which any power whatever would have reason to protest."

The French government, now deeply concerned by the attitude of England, and brought to a wavering state of mind which might have arrested the movement had the other continental powers consented, did not send its instructions until December 25, declaring that "his Majesty's government is intimately united with the allies in the firm resolution to repel by every means revolutionary principles and movements."[1]

On January 5, 1823, the French minister, followed next day by the representatives of the other continental allies, presented notes, in accord with their instructions, demanding the abrogation of the constitution of 1812, and the release of the king, whom it suited them to regard as a prisoner; refusal on the part of the Spanish government was to cause the withdrawal of the several ministers.

[1] For these documents, see *The Annual Register*, 1822, 565 *et seq.*

It was but natural that such demands should be received with deep indignation by Spain's new government, and on January 14, 1823, the Russian minister withdrew, followed on the 15th by the Prussian minister and on the 16th by the minister of Austria. The French minister left a few days after.

On January 28, 1823, Chateaubriand, the French minister for foreign affairs, and who fitly impersonated its light-headed policy, addressed Mr. Canning a note setting forth voluminously the weak reasons for the action of France. The character of the note may be judged by the declaration that the question "was at once wholly French and wholly European," thus combining the opinions of two other of the French ministers, one of whom had declared it wholly the former, and one wholly the latter. Canning immediately answered in noble words, such as were to be expected from the leader of the government of liberty-loving England: "We disclaim for ourselves and deny for other powers the right of requiring any changes in the internal institutions of independent states, with the menace of hostile attack in case of refusal." [1]

The same day that this despatch was written the French Chambers opened with the king's speech, in which he said:

"I have made every endeavor to guaranty the security of my people, and preserve Spain herself from these extreme misfortunes. The blindness with which the representations made at Madrid have been rejected leaves little hope of preserving peace. I have ordered the recall of my minister. One hundred thousand Frenchmen, commanded by a prince of my family, by him whom my heart delights to call my son, are ready to march, invoking the God of St. Louis for the sake of preserving the throne of Spain to a descendant of Henry IV, of saving that fine kingdom from its ruin and of reconciling it with Europe. If war is inevitable, I shall use all my endeavors to confine its circle, to limit its duration: it will be undertaken only to conquer the peace which the state of Spain would render impossible. Let Fernando VII be free to give to his people the institutions which they cannot hold but from him, and which, in insuring their tranquillity, would dissipate the just inquietudes of France." The British ambassador was not present.

[1] Canning to Sir Charles Stuart, ambassador at Paris, January 28, 1823, Hansard, VIII (1823), 923.

On May 23, 1823, the French army, under the Duc d'Angoulême, entered Madrid, and by September the occupation of Spain was complete from the Pyrenees to Cadiz, meeting with an opposition so slight that any action by England in aid of Spain, which probably would have been forthcoming had Spain been as strong in deeds as she was in protests, was made impossible.

On March 23, 1823, however, a note was sent by Canning to the British ambassador at Paris which forewarned France that England considered the question of the separation of the colonies from Spain as substantially decided by the course of events, although the formal recognition of their independence by England might be hastened or retarded by external causes, as well as by the internal condition of the colonies themselves; and that as England disclaimed all intention of appropriating to herself the smallest portion of the late Spanish possessions in America, she also felt satisfied that no attempt would be made by France to bring any of them under her dominion, either by conquest or by cession from Spain.[1]

[1] Rush, *The Court of London*, 362.

CHAPTER X

THE DEVELOPMENT OF THE MONROE DOCTRINE

CIRCUMSTANCES had made the relations of Great Britain and the United States with Spain curiously similar. They were the two great commercial powers, and the ships of both had now been coming and going in the Spanish-American ports for a dozen years with, in general, but limited hindrance from Spain herself, who in this long period had been practically powerless to prevent the great trade which had naturally developed under freedom and which England also claimed as her right by a treaty of 1810.

The commerce of both countries had, however, suffered severely by the declaration of the blockade of the ports of the Spanish main. By a formal treaty between Bolivar and Marshal Morillo in the cessation of hostilities in 1820, it had been stipulated that, if the war should be renewed, it should be conducted on the principles applicable to wars between independent nations. On the renewal of hostilities in 1821 a blockade of 1,200 miles of coast had been declared June 6, the only Spanish force available being a frigate, a brig, and a schooner, used chiefly in transporting supplies from Curaçao to Puerto Cabello, which latter was still in Spanish hands. Not only did Spain reclaim the right of colonial monopoly and prohibitions which had excluded foreigners from all trading, but on September 15, 1822, Marshal Morales, now Spanish commander-in-chief, issued a decree of most brutal and sanguinary character, condemning to death, after undergoing summary trial, all foreigners in the service, military or civil, of the enemy; those "having a share in any printing office; or being editors or compilers of any journal, pamphlet, or work relative to the present war, the affairs of revolted America, the Roman Catholic religion, or that shall be in any manner offensive to the nation, its government, or subjects. . . . Whatever property they possess, whether real or personal or in movables, shall be forfeited to the use of the public treasury." Any other foreigners found in the country "shall be condemned to labor at the public works for three years, and all their property . . . confiscated."[1]

The protests of the American and British naval commanders on the coast were of course immediate and energetic, as they had been also against the pretended blockade.

Even more serious were the depredations of the privateers, which, said the American secretary of state, "have been by their conduct distinguishable from pirates only by commissions of the most equivocal character from Spanish officers . . . swarms of pirates and of piratical vessels, without pretence or color of commission, have issued from the island of Cuba, and the immediate neighborhood of Havana. . . . These piracies have now been for years continued under the immediate observation of the government of the island of Cuba, which, as well as the Spanish government, has been repeatedly and ineffectually required to suppress them . . . when pursued by a superior force the pirates have escaped to the shores, and twelve months have elapsed since the late Captain General Mahy refused to Captain Biddle the permission to land even upon the desert and uninhabited parts of the island where they should seek refuge from his pursuit.[2] . . . From the most respectable testimony we are informed that these atrocious robberies are committed by persons well known, and that the traffic in their plunder is carried on with the utmost notoriety. They are sometimes committed by vessels equipped as merchant vessels, and which clear out as such from the Havana. It has also been remarked that they cautiously avoid molesting Spanish merchant vessels, but attack without discrimination the defenceless vessels of all other nations."[3]

This is a severe arraignment, but not more severe than was warranted. While, however, the action of the United States for a time was confined to protests, Great Britain, despite the fact

[1] *British and Foreign State Papers*, X, 938.
[2] Nevertheless they were so pursued into the tortuous and deep bays of Cuba which afforded so admirable a refuge.
[3] Adams to Nelson. Instructions, April 28, 1823, *State Papers*, V, 408.

1822] ENGLAND AND SPAIN IN THE WEST INDIES 181

that she was at the time Spain's earnest supporter, in the press, in Parliament, and in diplomacy, against the aggressions of France and the allies, was taking vigorous action as to reprisals in the West Indies, re-enforcing her fleet in those waters, and demanding compensation for losses already suffered. Canning was at the same moment instructing the British minister at Madrid, Sir William á Court, to give to the Spanish government all aid possible short of a promise of warlike support in her affairs with France, and pressing her vigorously and effectively as to her procedure in South America. "Our difficulty," he said in a private and confidential letter to the minister, December 3, 1822, "arises from the double character in which Spain presents herself in Europe and America; fighting for her independence in the former, and in the latter exercising a tyranny and assuming a tone of arrogance not to be endured; proposing new ties of friendship here, and there prohibiting our accustomed intercourse; holding out her European hand for charity, and with her American one picking our pockets."

Canning admitted in this letter that an attack by France "coinciding in point of time with our operations in the West Indies would produce an appearance of concert, utterly remote from the truth, indeed, but likely to impose upon Europe; and sure to be felt most deeply and resentfully by Spain. To avoid this appearance would be a great object; but seriously and sincerely (you may assure the Spanish minister) it is not in our power to avoid it unless Spain will speedily, instantly, do us justice. Let the Spanish government send off orders without delay to her governors of Puerto Rico and Puerto Cabello (to Cuba, I trust, strict orders will already have been sent), and to her naval officers in the West Indies, to execute the projects for which our armament is destined. Let these orders (or duplicates of them) be sent hither, to be forwarded to our officers in those seas, and to be then delivered to their several destinations, and they may, perhaps, yet be in time to prevent a blow being struck in anger; but there is no time to spare, and I assure you, and beg you to impress upon M. San Miguel, that the patience of our mercantile interests here is exhausted by the long series of injuries which they have endured. . . . Let Spain do us justice fully and handsomely, and so enable us to behave toward her with that singleness of conduct which it is as much our desire, as it is her interest, that we should pursue." [1]

Spain's concession to the British demands was immediate. The decree of January 27, 1822, opening the trade of Cuba to the world, was on January 9, 1823, extended by the Cortes for the term of ten months, "in favor of all those nations which the government may think proper to include therein," and a sum of 40,000,000 reals (about $2,000,000) assigned in the "Great Book" for the indemnification of such British claims as should be established by a mixed board of British and Spanish arbitrators, setting against such claims reclamations of Spanish subjects against Great Britain.[2] Finally by decree of February 9, 1824, (absurd in the situation) freedom of commerce was extended to all Spanish America.

The future of Cuba was at this time regarded by the American government as in the balance. The situation was anomalous and threatening in high degree. France a month after the compact with England just mentioned had entered Spain with a great army. What was to be the end? Was she again to attempt to reduce Spain to a French overlordship? Having done this was she to extend her conquests to South America, and establish there new kingdoms under her influence? Would she occupy Cuba as a part of the Spanish territory? These were all questions, and very vital questions, in which Great Britain was almost as deeply interested as was the United States. Already by 1823 French consuls were established in Spanish West Indian ports, whereas formal recognition of the British and American commercial agents employed by these countries was denied.[3]

[1] Stapleton, *George Canning and His Times*, 385-387.
[2] *British and Foreign State Papers*, X, 867. The American claims of like nature were not settled until February 17, 1834. By a convention of that period $500,000 were allowed, interest to be paid, at five per cent., by Spain, on any unpaid sum until the full payment should be completed. (Senate Doc. 147, 23 Cong., 2 Sess., 1835.) The final payment was not made until October, 1908.
[3] Two years later the American minister, pressing the Spanish minister of state on this subject, reports, as the result, "that although Spain was willing as far as possible to overlook and keep out of sight, in all her relations with us, the unpleasant circumstance of our recognition of the independence of the colonies, yet that she did not think it politic to admit into any of the American possessions an authorized public agent of a power which openly avowed the policy of encouraging the separation of these possessions from

Writing April 28, 1823, the French army now in Spain with scarcely a show of resistance, Mr. Adams said: "In the war between France and Spain now commencing, other interests, peculiarly ours, will, in all probability, be deeply involved. Whatever may be the issue of this war, as between these two European powers, it may be taken for granted that the dominion of Spain upon the American continents, north and south, is irrecoverably gone. But the islands of Cuba and Puerto Rico still remain nominally, and so far really, dependent upon her, that she yet possesses the power of transferring her dominion over them, together with the possession of them to others. . . . Cuba, almost in sight of our shores, from a multitude of considerations has become an object of transcendent importance to the commercial and political interests of our Union. Its commanding position with reference to the Gulf of Mexico and the West Indian seas; the character of its population; its situation midway between our southern coast and the island of St. Domingo; its safe and capacious harbor of the Havana fronting a long line of our shore destitute of the same advantage; the nature of its productions and of its wants, furnishing the supplies and needing the returns of a commerce immensely profitable and mutually beneficial,—give it an importance in the sum of our national interests with which that of no other foreign country can be compared, and little inferior to that which binds the different members of this Union together. Such indeed are, between the interests of that island and of this country, the geographical, commercial, moral, and political relations, formed by nature, gathering in the process of time, and even now verging to maturity, that, in looking forward to the probable course of events for the short period of half a century, it is scarcely possible to resist the conviction that the annexation of Cuba to our federal republic will be indispensable to the continuance and integrity of the Union itself. It is

the mother country; that our ministers and consuls on the continent were constantly holding a language favorable to the insurgents; that our consuls in the islands would no doubt do the same, and that if they were formally recognized there would be no means of preventing them; but that at present the authorities would have the right, if the consuls conducted themselves imprudently, to proceed against them in the usual forms of law."—Mr. Alexander H. Everett to the Department of State, September 25, 1825, House Ex. Doc., 121, 32 Cong., 1 Sess., p. 24.

obvious, however, that for this event we are not yet prepared. Numerous and formidable objections to the extension of our territorial dominions beyond sea present themselves to the first contemplation of the subject; obstacles to the system of policy by which alone that result can be compassed and maintained are to be foreseen and surmounted both at home and abroad; but there are laws of political as well as of physical gravitation, and if an apple, severed by the tempest from its native tree, cannot choose but fall to the ground, Cuba, forcibly disjoined from its own unnatural connection with Spain, and incapable of self-support, can gravitate only toward the North American Union, which, by the same law of nature, cannot cast her off from its bosom.

"In any other state of things than that which springs from this incipient war between France and Spain, these considerations would be premature. . . . Whether the purposes of France or of her continental allies extend to the subjugation of the remaining ultra-marine possessions of Spain or not has not yet been sufficiently disclosed. But to confine ourselves to that which immediately concerns us—the condition of the island of Cuba—we know that the republican spirit of freedom prevails among its inhabitants. The liberties of the constitution are to them rights in possession; nor is it to be presumed that they will be willing to surrender them because they may be extinguished by foreign violence in the parent country. A Spanish territory, the island will be liable to invasion from France during the war, and the only reasons for doubting whether the attempt will be made are the probable incompetency of the French maritime force to effect the conquest and the probability that its accomplishment would be resisted by Great Britain. In the meantime, and at all events, the condition of the island, in regard to that of its inhabitants, is a condition of great imminent and complicated danger. . . . Were the population of that island of one blood and color, there could be no doubt or hesitation with regard to the course which they would pursue as dictated by their interests and their rights; the invasion of Spain by France would be the signal for *their* declaration of independence. That even in their present state it will be imposed upon them as a necessity is not unlikely; but among all reflecting men it is admitted . . . that they are not competent to a system of permanent self-dependence . . . in the event of the overthrow of the Spanish constitution, that support can no longer be expected from Spain—their only alternative of dependence must be upon Great Britain or the United States."

Mr. Adams mentioned the hope of the United States government that the connection with Spain should continue for the time being if possible, an expression of which had already been conveyed to the Spanish government; but the withdrawal of Great Britain from the Holy Alliance; her disapproval of the war undertaken by France; her determination to defend Portugal from a like invasion; the certainty of the revival of natural resentments and jealousies made her entry into the conflict very probable. "The prospect is that she will soon be engaged on the side of Spain; but in making common cause with her, it is not to be supposed that she will yield her assistance upon principles altogether disinterested and gratuitous. As the price of her alliance, the two remaining islands of Spain in the West Indies present objects no longer of much possible value or benefit to Spain, but of such importance to Great Britain that it is impossible to suppose her indifferent to them."

The independence of Mexico and the annexation of the Floridas, the internal condition of Cuba, the precariousness of its dependence on Spain, and the need of Spain to secure by some equivalent the support of Great Britain seemed to Adams to form a remarkable concurrence of reasons to predispose the latter to annex the island. He acknowledged that an indirect communication from the French government mentioning that, some two years before, Great Britain had offered Gibraltar in exchange, was probably a mistake; but he did not wholly rely upon Canning's late declaration to the French government, confidentially communicated to the American government, that Great Britain would hold it disgraceful to avail herself of the distressed situation of Spain to obtain possession of any of her American colonies. They did not forbear to avail themselves of Spain's distress by sending two successive squadrons to the West Indies to make reprisals. They obtained an immediate revocation of the fictitious blockade proclaimed on the Venezuelan coast and pledges of reparation for captures so made; also an acknowledgment of many long-standing claims of British subjects and promises of payment as part of the national debt. For the payment of these, said Adams, "the island of Cuba may be the only indemnity in the power of Spain to grant, as it will undoubtedly be to Great Britain the most satisfactory indemnity which she could receive. The war between France and Spain changes so totally the circumstances under which the declaration above mentioned was made, that it may, at the very outset, produce events under which the possession of Cuba may be obtained by Great Britain without ever raising a reproach of intended deception against the British government for making it. . . . The question both of our right, and our power to prevent it if necessary by force, already obtrudes itself upon our councils." He closed with: "It will be among the primary objects requiring your most earnest and unremitting attention to ascertain and report to us every movement of negotiation between Spain and Great Britain upon this subject. . . . We scarcely know where you will find the government of Spain upon your arrival in the country, nor can we foresee with certainty by whom it will be administered. Your credentials are addressed to Ferdinand, the King of Spain, under the constitution. You may find him under the guardianship of a Cortes, in the custody of an army of [the] faith, or under the protection of the invaders of his country. So long as the *constitutional* government may continue to be administered in his name, your official intercourse will be with his ministers, and to them you will repeat what Mr. Forsyth has been instructed to say, that the wishes of your government are that Cuba and Puerto Rico, may continue in connection with independent and constitutional Spain."[1]

While the American government was thus nervous as to the intentions of that of Great Britain, the latter was equally so as to those of the former. The hastening of the powerful British naval force to the Caribbean was not alone to repress Spanish aggression against British commerce; it was also to prevent American action against Cuba. Said Canning, "whatever they might do in the absence of a British squadron, they would hardly venture in the face of one to assume the military occupation of the island."[2] A

---

[1] Instructions to Mr. Nelson, newly appointed minister to Spain, April 28, 1823, House Ex. Doc. 121, 32 Cong., 1 Sess.
[2] Stapleton, *Official Correspondence of Canning*, I, 48.

little later, in May, 1824, Great Britain even went so far, though this action was directed mainly against the Holy Alliance, and thus for the moment in support of the United States, as to offer to Spain "to guarantee to her the secure possession of Cuba."[1]

So long as the action of the allies was confined to Spain the United States had only an abstract interest, but it soon became clear that the designs of the alliance went far beyond and touched the deepest interests of America, North and South, and in the most concrete manner, by their intention to call a congress to consider the return of the late Spanish-American colonies to their allegiance. The secrecy of the movement had withheld this knowledge from the government of the United States; the first note of warning came from England, and the first step toward a correspondence which led to the momentous declaration in the annual message of President Monroe to Congress, December 2, 1823, was in a conversation of August 16, 1823, between Mr. Richard Rush, the United States minister in London, and Mr. George Canning, the British minister for foreign affairs, in which Canning introduced the subject. In a note to Rush, on August 20, Canning asked: "Is not the moment come when our governments might understand each other as to the Spanish-American colonies? And if we can arrive at such an understanding, would it not be expedient for ourselves, and beneficial for all the world, that the principles of it should be clearly settled and plainly avowed?

"For ourselves we have no disguise.

"1. We conceive the recovery of the colonies by Spain to be hopeless.

"2. We conceive the question of the recognition of them, as independent states, to be one of time and circumstances.

"3. We are, however, by no means disposed to throw any impediment in the way of arrangement between them and the mother country by amicable negotiations.

"4. We aim not at the possession of any portion of them by ourselves.

"5. We could not see any portion of them transferred to any other power with indifference.

[1] Canning, in letter to George IV, February 1, 1825, Stapleton, *George Canning and His Times*, 424.

"If these opinions and feelings are as I firmly believe them to be, common to your government with ours, why should we hesitate to mutually confide them to each other and to declare them in the face of the world?

". . . Such a declaration on the part of your government and ours would be at once the most effectual and the least offensive mode of intimating our joint disapprobation of such projects.

". . . Do you conceive that under the power which you have recently received you are authorized to enter into negotiation and to sign any convention on the subject? Do you conceive, if that be not within your competence, you could exchange with me ministerial notes upon it?

"Nothing could be more gratifying to me than to join with you in such a work, and, I am persuaded, there has seldom in the history of the world occurred an opportunity when so small an effort of two friendly governments might produce so unequivocal a good and prevent such extensive calamities."[1]

Here was a long step toward the Monroe Doctrine, which though preceded, by a month, as will be seen, by Adams's announcement to the Russian minister at Washington, went far to justifying Canning's boast later of calling a new world into existence to redress the balance of the old.

Three days later, August 23, 1823, Canning wrote Rush: "I have received notice but not such notice as imposes upon me the necessity of any immediate answer or proceeding—that as soon as the military objects in Spain are achieved . . . a proposal will be made for a congress, or some less formal concert and consultation, specially upon the affairs of Spanish America. I need not point out to you all the complications to which this proposal, however dealt with by us, may lead."[2]

On September 18, in an interview with Rush, Canning said that events "were hourly assuming new importance and urgency, under aspects to which neither of our governments could be insensible. . . . He had the strongest reasons for believing that

---

[1] Moore, *Digest*, VI, 389, 390; Ford, Mass. Hist. Soc. *Proceedings*, January, 1902, 415, 416.
[2] Enclosed with Mr. Rush's No. 326, August 28, 1823; Ford, Mass. Hist. Soc. *Proceedings*, January, 1902, (XV) 416.

the co-operation of the United States with England, through my [Rush's] instrumentality, afforded with promptitude, would ward off altogether the meditated jurisdiction of the European powers over the new world."

Rush, with an exhibition of initiative rare in any public servant, declared himself ready to stand upon his general powers as a minister plenipotentiary. "I would put forth, with Great Britain, the declaration to which he had invited me," but it must be with the understanding that England would immediately recognize the independence of the revolted provinces. This Canning was not prepared to do, among the objections being "still that of the uncertain condition, internally of these new states, or at any rate of some of them."[1]

Rush's views of British altruism at the moment were not complimentary. "Since the present year set in, she has proclaimed and until now cautiously maintained her neutrality under an attack by France on the independence of Spain, as unjust, as nefarious, and as cruel, as the annals of mankind can recount[2] . . . Britain has been from the very beginning, positively or negatively, auxiliary to the evils with which this Alliance under the mark of Christianity, has already affected the old, and is now menacing the new world. It is under this last stretch of ambition that she seems to be roused, not, as we seem forced to infer after all we have seen, from any objections to the arbitrary principles of the combination, for the same men are still substantially at the head of her affairs; but rather from the apprehensions, which are now probably coming upon her, touching her own influence and standing through the formidable and encroaching career of these Continental potentates. She at last perceives a crisis likely to come on, bringing with it peril to her own commercial prospects on the other side of the Atlantic, and to her political sway in both hemispheres."[3]

This, as has been shown, is but partially just. While England's

[1] Rush to Adams, September 19, 1823, *Court of London*, 388–403.
[2] Mr. Rush did not overdraw the iniquity of French action, which in effect was that of Russia, Austria, and Prussia also. Any strictures from either of these governments upon future American action in regard to Cuba lose all force in face of the enormity of this invasion.
[3] Rush to President Monroe, September 15, 1823, Ford, Mass. Hist. Soc. *Proceedings*, XV, 421.

commercial interests in South America, now equalling a fourth of her trade with continental Europe,[1] were at stake and she was ruled, as nations always have been, by self-interest, enough has been quoted to show that the despotic character of the alliance was deeply resented on principle alone. Canning's defence in Parliament of abstention from a more warlike attitude was sound. He had already gone far. The reason for caution was clear enough also to Rush, who, in the same despatch and with more justice, said, "The former war of twenty years more than once shook her prosperity and brought hazards to her existence, though for the most part she was surrounded by allies. A second war of like duration with no ally in Europe might not have a second field of Waterloo for its termination." She thus sought an ally in the United States and found, if not an ally, a power willing to relieve her of the whole burden.

The despatches of Mr. Rush naturally created deep interest and even alarm in the mind of the President. Adams was absent from Washington, and Monroe wrote Jefferson, October 17, 1823:

"I transmit to you two despatches which were received from Mr. Rush, while I was lately in Washington, which involve interests of the highest importance. They contain two letters from Mr. Canning suggesting designs of the Holy Alliance against the independence of South America, and proposing a co-operation between Great Britain and the United States in support of it against the members of that alliance. The project aims, in the first instance, at a mere expression of opinion, somewhat in the abstract, but which it is expected by Mr. Canning will have a great political effect by defeating the combination. By Mr. Rush's answers, which are also enclosed, you will see the light in which he views the subject and the extent to which he may have gone. Many important considerations are involved in this proposition. 1. Shall we entangle ourselves at all in European politics and wars, on the side of any power, against others, presuming that a concert by agreement, of the kind proposed, may lead to that result? 2. If a case can exist in which a sound maxim may and ought to be departed from, is not the present instance precisely that case? 3.

[1] Lord Lansdowne's and the Earl of Liverpool's speeches, March 15, 1824, Hansard, N. S., X, 970–1003.

Has not the epoch arrived when Great Britain must take her stand either on the side of the monarchs of Europe or of the United States, and in consequence either in favor of despotism or of liberty, and may it not be presumed that, aware of that necessity, her government has seized on the present occurrence as that which it deems the most suitable to announce and mark the commencement of that career?

"My own impression is that we ought to meet the proposal of the British government, and to make it known, that we would view an interference on the part of the European powers, and especially an attack on the colonies by them, as an attack on ourselves, presuming that if they succeeded with them they would extend it to us. I am sensible, however, of the extent and difficulty of the question, and shall be happy to have your and Mr. Madison's opinions on it. I do not wish to trouble either of you with small objects, but the present one is vital, involving the high interests for which we have so long and so faithfully and harmoniously contended together. Be so kind as to enclose to him the despatches with an intimation of the motive." [1]

Both Jefferson and Madison favored co-operation with England. Jefferson said:

"The question presented by the letters you have sent me is the most momentous which has ever been offered to my contemplation since that of independence. That made us a nation; this sets our compass and points the course which we are to steer through the ocean of time opening on us. And never could we embark upon it under circumstances more auspicious. Our first and fundamental maxim should be, never to entangle ourselves in the broils of Europe; our second, never to suffer Europe to intermeddle with cisatlantic affairs. America, North and South, has a set of interests distinct from those of Europe, and particularly her own. She should therefore have a system of her own, separate and apart from that of Europe. While the last is laboring to become the domicile of despotism, our endeavor should surely be to make our hemisphere that of freedom.

"One nation, most of all, could disturb us in this pursuit; she

[1] Monroe to Jefferson, Oct. 17, 1823, received Oct. 23, Ford, Mass. Hist. Soc. *Proceedings*, January, 1902, 375; Moore, *Digest*, VI, 393.

now offers to lead, aid, and accompany us in it. By acceding to her proposition, we detach her from the bands, bring her mighty weight into the scale of free government, and emancipate a continent at one stroke, which might otherwise linger long in doubt and difficulty. Great Britain is the nation which can do us the most harm of any one, or all on earth; and with her on our side we need not fear the whole world. With her, then, we should most sedulously cherish a cordial friendship and nothing would tend more to knit our affections than to be fighting once more, side by side, in the same cause. Not that I would purchase even her amity at the price of taking part in her wars.

"But the war in which the present proposition might engage us, should that be its consequences, is not her war, but ours. Its object is to introduce and establish the American system of keeping out of our land all foreign powers—of never permitting those of Europe to intermeddle with the affairs of our nations. It is to maintain our own principle, not to depart from it. And if, to facilitate this, we can effect a division in the body of the European powers, and draw over to our side its most powerful member, surely we should do it. But I am clearly of Mr. Canning's opinion, that it will prevent instead of provoking war. With Great Britain withdrawn from their scale and shifted into that of our two continents, all Europe combined would not undertake such a war, for how would they propose to get at either enemy without superior fleets?[1] Nor is the occasion to be slighted which this proposition offers of declaring our protest against the atrocious violations of the rights of nations by the interference of any one in the internal affairs of another, so flagitiously begun by Bonaparte, and now continued by the equally lawless alliance calling itself holy.

"But we have first to ask ourselves a question. Do we wish to acquire to our own confederacy any one or more of the Spanish provinces? I candidly confess that I have ever looked on Cuba as the most interesting addition which could ever be made to our system of states. The control which, with Florida Point, this island would give us over the Gulf of Mexico and the countries and isthmus bordering on it, as well as all those whose waters flow into it, would fill up the measure of our political well-being. Yet,

[1] Jefferson here recognizes for once the meaning of a navy.

as I am sensible that this can never be obtained, even with her own consent, but by war, and its independence, which is our second interest (and especially its independence of England), can be secured without it, I have no hesitation in abandoning my first wish to future chances, and accepting its independence, with peace and the friendship of England, rather than its association at the expense of war and her enmity.

"I could honestly, therefore, join in the declaration proposed, that we aim not at the acquisition of any of those possessions, that we will not stand in the way of any amicable arrangement between them and the mother country, but that we will oppose, with all our means, the forcible interposition of any other power, as auxiliary, stipendiary, or under any other form or pretext, and most especially their transfer to any power by conquest, cession, or acquisition in any other way. I should think it therefore advisable that the executive should encourage the British government to a continuance in the dispositions expressed in these letters by an assurance of his concurrence with them as far as his authority goes; and that as it may lead to war, the declaration of which requires an act of Congress, the case shall be laid before them for consideration at their first meeting, and under the reasonable aspect in which it is seen by himself. . . ."[1]

Madison wrote: "I have just received from Mr. Jefferson your letter to him, with the correspondence between Mr. Canning and Mr. Rush, sent for his and my perusal, and our opinions on the subject of it.

"From the disclosures of Mr. Canning it appears, as was otherwise to be inferred, that the success of France against Spain would be followed by an attempt of the holy allies to reduce the revolutionized colonies of the latter to their former dependence.

"The professions we have made to these neighbors, our sympathies with their liberties and independence, the deep interest we have in the most friendly relations with them, and the consequences threatened by a command of their resources by the great powers, confederated against the rights and reforms of which we have given so conspicuous and persuasive an example, all unite

[1] Jefferson, *Writings*, X, 315, Sen. Doc. 26, 57 Cong., 1 Sess.; Moore, *Digest*, VI, 394.

in calling for our efforts to defeat the meditated crusade. It is particularly fortunate that the policy of Great Britain, though guided by calculations different from ours, has presented a co-operation for an object the same with ours. With that co-operation we have nothing to fear from the rest of Europe, and with it the best assurance of success to our laudable views. There ought not, therefore, to be any backwardness, I think, in meeting her in the way she has proposed, keeping in view, of course, the spirit and forms of the constitution in every step taken in the road to war, which must be the last step if those short of war should be without avail.

"It cannot be doubted that Mr. Canning's proposal, though made with the air of *consultation* as well as concert, was founded on a predetermination to take the course marked out whatever might be the reception given here to his invitation. But this consideration ought not to divert us from what is just and proper in itself. Our co-operation is due to ourselves and to the world; and while it must insure success in the event of an appeal to force, it doubles the chance of success without that appeal. It is not improbable that Great Britain would like best to have the merit of being the sole champion of her new friends, notwithstanding the greater difficulty to be encountered, but for the dilemma in which she would be placed. She must, in that case, either leave us, as neutrals, to extend our commerce and navigation at the expense of hers, or make us enemies, by renewing her paper blockades and other arbitrary proceedings on the ocean. It may be hoped that such a dilemma will not be without a permanent tendency to check her proneness to unnecessary wars.

"Why the British cabinet should have scrupled to arrest the calamity it now apprehends, by applying to the threats of France against Spain the small effort which it scruples not to employ in behalf of Spanish America is best known to itself. It is difficult to find any other explanation than that interest in the one case has more weight in its casuistry than principle had in the other."

Mr. Madison's suggestions now went far beyond the bounds laid down in the rules of American statesmanship, saying: "Will it not be honorable to our country, and possibly not altogether in vain, to invite the British government to extend the 'avowed disapprobation' of the project against the Spanish colonies to the enterprise of France against Spain herself, and even to join in some declaratory act in behalf of the Greeks? On the supposition that no form could be given to the act clearing it of a pledge to follow it up by war, we ought to compare the good to be done with the little injury to be apprehended to the United States, shielded as their interests would be by the power and the fleets of Great Britain united with their own. These are questions, however, which may require more information than I possess and more reflection than I can now give them.

"What is the extent of Mr. Canning's disclaimer as to 'the remaining possessions of Spain in America?' Does it exclude future views of acquiring Puerto Rico, etc., as well as Cuba? It leaves Great Britain free, as I understand it, in relation to other quarters of the globe." [1]

Beginning August 19, 1823, Rush wrote six despatches and letters which, in the time preceding the President's annual message, could have influenced the declaration. His first was received October 9; the last, from London, October 10, was received November 19. Adams, on November 13, found Monroe "altogether unsettled in his own mind as to the answer to be given Mr. Canning's proposals, and alarmed far beyond anything I could have conceived possible, with the fear that the Holy Alliance are about to restore immediately all South America to Spain, Calhoun stimulates the panic, and the news that Cadiz has surrendered to the French has so affected the President that he appeared entirely to despair of the cause of South America." Two days later the subject was resumed. "Calhoun is perfectly moon-struck by the surrender of Cadiz, and says the holy allies, with ten thousand men, will restore all Mexico and all South America to the Spanish dominion. I did not deny that they might make a temporary impression for three, four, or five years, but I no more believe that the holy allies will restore the Spanish dominion upon the American continent than that Chimborazo will sink beneath the ocean." [2]

Rush's despatch of October 10, received November 16,[3] ex-

[1] Madison to Monroe, Oct. 30, 1823, *Works*, III, 339; *Digest*, VI, 396.
[2] Adams, *Memoirs*, VI, 185, 186.
[3] For this see Ford, Mass. Hist. Soc., *Proceedings*, January 1902, (XV,) 424. Ford gives date of reception as November 19, Adams as the 16th, VI, 187.

pressed deep disappointment in an apparent change in Canning, inasmuch as the latter now said nothing on the South American subject beyond remarking that consuls were about to be sent. "Not another word," said Rush, October 22, "has he said to me on it since the 26th of last month. . . . and he has gone now out of town to spend the remainder of this and part of the next month."[1]

Canning's conduct which thus left to Adams and Monroe full initiative, was to be explained later. It was not, however, until November 24 that he stated to Rush that as the latter had been unable to act "he had deemed it indispensable, as no more time was to be lost, that Great Britain herself should come to an explanation with France." This explanation had been made, October 9, 1823, when Prince Polignac, the French ambassador, was informed with great plainness that Great Britain would recognize the independence of the South American colonies "in case France should employ force in aid of their resubjugation," or if "Spain herself, reverting to her old colonial system, should attempt to put a stop to the trade of Britain with those colonies," this right to trade having been established by a convention so far back as 1810 as an equivalent for British mediation offered at that time.

Canning had disclaimed to Polignac any desire of appropriating any portion of the Spanish possessions, or of taking part in any conflict between these and Spain, but stated that Great Britain could not wait indefinitely for an accommodation.

The attitude of Canning, of which, in fact, the French government had had full knowledge since March, 1823, brought from her ambassador the declaration "that this government believed it to be utterly hopeless to reduce Spanish America to the state of its former relations with Spain;

"That France disclaimed on her part any intention or desire to avail herself of the present state of the colonies, or of the present situation of France toward Spain, to appropriate to herself any part of the Spanish possessions in America, or to obtain for herself any exclusive advantages;

"And that like England, she would willingly see the mother country in possession of superior commercial advantages by amic-

[1] Rush to Monroe, Ford, Mass. Hist. Soc. *Proceedings*, January, 1902 (XV), 428.

able arrangements, and would be contented, like her, to rank, after the mother country, among the most favored nations;

"Lastly, that she abjured in any case any design of acting against the colonies by force of arms."

Polignac proceeded, however, to say that as soon as "the King of Spain should be at liberty" they would be ready to enter upon the question of the best arrangement between Spain and her colonies, "in concert with their allies and with Great Britain among the number." He "could not conceive" the meaning of an acknowledgment of simple independence so long as there existed no government offering any appearance of solidity, and that such acknowledgment in such a state of things appeared "nothing less than a real sanction of anarchy." He ended by saying that "it would be worthy of the European governments to concert together the means of calming in those distant and scarcely civilized regions passions blinded by party spirit, and to endeavor to bring back to a principle of union in government, whether monarchial or aristocratical, people among whom absurd and dangerous theories were now keeping up agitation and disunion." Mr. Canning contented himself with saying that, however desirable "a monarchial form of government, in any of these provinces might be, . . . his government could not take upon itself to put it forward as a condition of their recognition."[1]

The day after Canning's interview with the French ambassador, British consuls to the ports of Spanish South America were instructed and commissions to report upon conditions in Columbia and Mexico were ordered.

All this, however, was unknown at Washington, but both Britain and America were at this juncture fortunate in having as ministers for foreign affairs men of absolute courage and firmness and of highest quality of statesmanship. Both had the same end in view; the overthrow of the assumption of despotic rule by a congress of monarchs who claimed the right to allow no change of form of government unless the change should come from the head of the state, and who demanded the right to arrange the affairs of other states as seemed to them best. Meanwhile, thus in ignorance of what was transpiring in London, Adams held firm

[1] Rush to Adams, November 26, 1823, *The Court of London*, 409 *et seq.*

for no concert of action with Great Britain except upon the basis of recognition of independence of the South American states.[1]

The note of the coming action of the United States had, however, been sounded by Adams more than a month before Canning had acted. On July 17, 1823, he informed Baron Tuyll, the Russian minister, "that we should contest the right of Russia to *any* territorial establishment on this continent and that we should assume distinctly the principle that the American continents are no longer subjects for *any* new colonial establishments."[2]

A communication from Baron Tuyll, October 4, declaring the intention of the Russian government "faithful to the political principles which it follows in concert with its allies, "not to receive any agent of the revolted provinces; and another, October 15, enclosing a copy of a despatch from Count Nesselrode, stating the intention of the allies "to insist with energy on the necessity of [Spain's] preventing the future from reproducing the errors of the past, of confiding the destinies of Spain to strong, monarchical and wholly national institutions,"[3] afforded, Adams thought, "a convenient opportunity for us to take our stand against the Holy Alliance, and at the same time to decline the overture of Great Britain. It would be more candid as well as more dignified to avow our principles explicitly to Russia and France than to come in as a cockboat in the wake of the British man-of-war."[4]

The "political principles" mentioned in the Russian note of October 4 had reference, said Baron Tuyll, later, in a conversation with Adams, November 8, "to the right of supremacy of Spain over her colonies."

In the cabinet meeting of November 21 Adams expressed his desire to reply to the Russian notes declaring "our dissent from the principles avowed in these communications; to assert those upon which our own government is founded, and, while disclaiming all intention of attempting to propagate them by force, and all inter-

---

[1] Conversations with Addington, British minister, November 17 and 19, Adams, *Memoirs*, 188, 191.

[2] Adams, *Memoirs*, VI, 163. Whatever the expressions of like character from Americans of prominence, this was the first official declaration. It covered in a few words the later pronouncement fathered by Monroe.

[3] For these, see Ford, Mass. Hist. Soc., January, 1902 (XV), 400, 404.

[4] Adams, *Memoirs*, VI, 179.

ference with the political affairs of Europe, to declare our expectation and hope that European powers will equally abstain from the attempt to spread their principles in the American hemisphere, or to subjugate by force any part of these continents to their will." [1]

Adams's draught of the reply to Baron Tuyll was objected to by the President and all the other members of the cabinet as perhaps in some of its phrases offensive and therefore dangerous in what was by all regarded so critical a moment; how critical, in the minds of the men of the period, is shown by the thoughts passing in Adams's own mind when he wrote in his diary: "If. . . . the Holy Alliance should subdue South America, however, they might set up the standard of Spain, the ultimate result of their undertaking would be to recolonize them, partitioned out among themselves. Russia might take California, Peru, Chile; France, Mexico—where we know she has been intriguing to get a monarchy under a prince of the house of Bourbon as well as at Buenos Ayres. And Great Britain as a last resort, if she could not resist this course of things, would take at least the island of Cuba for her share of the scramble. Then what would be our situation—England holding Cuba; France, Mexico?" [2]

But discussed and amended as the draught was, Adams's force and courage carried the day, and when, on November 27, it was read to Baron Tuyll it was a full exposition of the policy of the United States. It declared that their neutrality would be maintained "as long as that of Europe, apart from Spain, shall continue," and gave as a conclusion the declaration "That the United States of America, and their government, could not see with indifference the forcible interposition of any European power, other than Spain, either to restore the dominion of Spain over her emancipated colonies in America, or to establish monarchical governments in those countries, or to transfer any of the possessions heretofore or yet subject to Spain in the American hemisphere to any other European power." [3]

---

[1] Adams, *Memoirs*, VI, 194.   [2] Adams, *Ibid.*, VI, 207.
[3] For this paper, showing the omitted paragraphs, see Mr. Ford's paper in Mass. Hist. Soc. *Proceedings*, January, 1902 (XV), 405–408. For the long and interesting discussion in the cabinet, Adams, *Memoirs*, VI, 199–212.

It is remarkable in view of the anxiety which he had expressed in his letter to Jefferson, and the character of the replies of Jefferson and Madison, that Monroe, when he read, November 21, the sketch of his annual message to Congress, now so soon to meet, laid much more stress upon the situation in Europe itself, and spoke "in terms of the most pointed reprobation of the late invasion of Spain by France and of the principles upon which it was undertaken by the open avowal of the King of France." Monroe was carried away, too, by the strong popular sympathy for the Greeks in their struggle for independence and the draught "also contained a broad acknowledgment of the Greeks as an independent nation and a recommendation to Congress to make an appropriation for sending a minister to them."[1] Such a message, declared Adams, would be a summons to arms against all Europe and for objects exclusively European. "It would have the air of open defiance of all Europe. . . . The aspect of things was portentous, but if we must come to an issue with Europe let us keep it off as long as possible."[2]

The message of the President on December 2 dealt finally with two phases of the question of European action in the Americas. The first had reference to the gradual advance of Russia on the north-west coast of North America; the second to the affairs of the now independent Spanish-American provinces. The two declarations are as follows:

"At the proposal of the Russian imperial government, made through the minister of the emperor residing here, a full power and instructions have been transmitted to the minister of the United States at St. Petersburg to arrange, by amicable negotiation, the respective rights and interests of the two nations on the north-west coast of this continent. A similar proposal has been made by his Imperial Majesty to the government of Great Britain, which has likewise been acceded to. The government of the United States has been desirous, by this friendly proceeding, of manifesting the great value which they have invariably attached to the friendship of the emperor and their solicitude to cultivate the best understanding with his government. In the discussions to which this interest has given rise, and in the arrangements by which they may terminate, the occasion has been judged proper for asserting as a

[1] Adams, *Memoirs*, VI, 194.   [2] *Ibid.*, 195.

principle in which the rights and interests of the United States are involved, that the American continents, by the free and independent condition which they have assumed and maintain, are henceforth not to be considered as subjects for future colonization by any European powers.[1] . . .

"In the wars of the European powers in matters relating to themselves we have never taken any part, nor does it comport with our policy so to do. It is only when our rights are invaded or seriously menaced that we resent injuries or make preparation for our defence. With the movements in this hemisphere we are, of necessity, more immediately connected, and by causes which must be obvious to all enlightened and impartial observers. The political system of the allied powers is essentially different in this respect from that of America. This difference proceeds from that which exists in their respective governments. And to the defence of our own, which had been achieved by the loss of so much blood and treasure, and matured by the wisdom of their most enlightened citizens, and under which we have enjoyed unexampled felicity, this whole nation is devoted. We owe it, therefore, to candor, and to the amicable relations existing between the United States and those powers, to declare that we should consider any attempt on their part to extend their system to any portion of this hemisphere as dangerous to our peace and safety. With the existing colonies or dependencies of any European power we have not interfered and shall not interfere. But with the governments who have declared their independence and maintained it, and whose independence we have, on great consideration and on just principles, acknowledged, we could not view any interposition for the purpose of oppressing them, or controlling in any other manner their destiny, by any European power, in any other light than as the manifestation of an unfriendly disposition toward the United States. In the war between these new governments and Spain we declared our neutrality at the time of their recognition, and to this we have adhered and shall continue to adhere, provided no change shall occur which, in the judgment of the competent authorities of this government, shall make a corresponding change on the part of the United States indispensable to their security.

[1] Paragraph 7, message of December 2, 1823.

"The late events in Spain and Portugal show that Europe is still unsettled. Of this important fact no stronger proof can be adduced than that the allied powers should have thought it proper on any principle satisfactory to themselves, to have interposed, by force, in the internal concerns of Spain. To what extent such interposition may be carried, on the same principle, is a question in which all independent powers whose governments differ from theirs are interested, even those most remote, and surely none more so than the United States. Our policy in regard to Europe, which was adopted at an early stage of the wars which have so long agitated that quarter of the globe, nevertheless remains the same, which is, not to interfere in the internal concerns of any of its powers; to consider the government *de facto* as the legitimate government for us; to cultivate friendly relations with it, and to preserve those relations by a frank, firm, and manly policy, meeting, in all instances, the just claims of every power, submitting to injuries from none. But in regard to these continents, circumstances are eminently and conspicuously different. It is impossible that the allied powers should extend their political system to any portion of either continent without endangering our peace and happiness; nor can any one believe that our southern brethren, if left to themselves, would adopt it of their own accord. It is equally impossible, therefore, that we should behold such interposition, in any form, with indifference. If we look to the comparative strength and resources of Spain and those new governments, and their distance from each other, it must be obvious that she can never subdue them. It is still the true policy of the United States to leave the parties to themselves, in the hope that other powers will pursue the same course."[1]

The message was received in England with great and general satisfaction. "That event," said Brougham, "which is decisive of the subject in respect to South America, is the message of the President of the United States to Congress." The French administration journal, *L'Étoile*, denounced the message and called Monroe a dictator, but the London *Times* hastened to defend him.

"We shall hear no more," said the London *Courier* of December 24, "of a congress to settle the fate of the South American states.

[1] Paragraphs 48 and 49, message of December 2, 1823.

Protected by the two nations that possess the institutions and speak the language of freedom—by Great Britain on one side and the United States on the other—their independence is placed beyond the reach of danger."[1]

Rush wrote: "The most decisive blow to all despotic interference with the new states is that which it has received in the President's message. . . . It was looked for here with extraordinary interest, . . . and I have heard that the British packet which left New York at the beginning of this month was instructed to wait for it and bring it over with all speed. It is certain that this vessel first brought it, having arrived at Falmouth on the 24th instant. On its publicity in London . . . the credit of all the Spanish-American securities immediately rose, and the question of the final and complete safety of the new states from all European coercion is now considered as at rest."[2]

There was one dissentient in England, however, to the extreme ground taken in the message, that "unoccupied parts of America are no longer open to colonization from Europe." Canning, while pleased with the demand of non-interference which was in accord with what he had so vigorously maintained—"that foreign powers had no right, either directly or indirectly, to interfere forcibly between Spain and her American colonies, and that they had consequently no right to aid Spain in her attempt to recover them"—held that "the United States has no right to take umbrage at the establishment of new colonies from Europe on any such unoccupied parts of the American continent."[3] The Pacific Northwest, which was about to become the subject of negotiation between Russia, Great Britain, and the United States, was in Canning's mind. The matter at stake was the great region west of the Rocky Mountains, and which, north of the parallel of 49°, to Alaska, was to be lost to the United States by the compromise of 1848.[4] But Canning's main object was gained. The pro-

[1] Quoted by McMaster, *United States*, V, 48.
[2] Rush to Adams, December 27, 1823, Ford, Mass. Hist. Soc. *Proceedings*, XV, 436.
[3] Stapleton, *Canning and His Times*, 396.
[4] For a discussion of the situation, see Adams to Rush, July 22, 1823, *State Papers*, V, 447. Prominent men of the period were, so late as 1829, curiously wanting in prescience respecting this subject. It was to some "the

posal to hold a conference at Paris to advise Spain in regard to her late South American possessions sank to inanition through the American pronouncement and the attitude of England; to Spanish continental dominion in America it was a death-blow. It was impossible for the continental European powers to think of oversea military action in the face of the British and American fleets. Such hopes were sunk in the waters of Trafalgar beyond the possibility of resurrection.

decree of nature herself that the Rocky Mountains shall be the western boundary of this republic."—*Register of Debates in Congress*, V, 1828–29, pp. 134–137.

CHAPTER XI

THE PANAMÁ CONGRESS

THE recognition by the United States of South American and Mexican independence; the declaration of President Monroe and the friendly attitude of Great Britain toward the new states which led to complete recognition in 1825, despite the opposition of George IV, who himself favored the Holy Alliance,[1] brought an increased political activity in Spanish America, and the project of what to-day would be termed a pan-American congress took form in a circular addressed to the Spanish American states by Bolivar in December, 1824, in which the concurrence and representation of the United States was earnestly desired.

The ministers of Mexico, Central America, and Colombia, in the spring of 1825, requested interviews with Mr. Clay, who had become secretary of state upon the accession of Mr. John Quincy Adams to the presidency, to ask if such concurrence could not be had. They were received separately on the same day, and asked to state later, more explicitly and more officially than they were then able to do, the objects of the congress and the powers to be given the representatives composing it. They were informed "that of course" the United States could not make themselves a party to the existing war with Spain nor to councils for deliberating on the means of its further prosecution."[2]

Mexico and the South American states were now bound together by treaties of "perpetual union, league, and confederation,"[3] and it was understood that one of their aims was the wresting from Spain of Cuba and Puerto Rico, the continued occupancy of

[1] See the king's memorandum to Lord Liverpool, January 27, 1825, Stapleton, *George Canning and His Times*, 416–419.
[2] Clay to President Adams, December 20, 1825, *State Papers*, V, 835.
[3] For these treaties, see *State Papers*, V, 840–846.

which afforded a base for military and naval action by Spain or her supporters against themselves. Already, however, the United States had begun to look askant at the idea of the independence of these islands or their possession by any power other than Spain. Two, and certainly powerful, reasons were that the character of the population rendered "extremely problematical their capacity to maintain independence," and that a premature declaration would probably result only in the afflicting repetition of the disastrous scenes of St. Domingo."[1] A third reason not yet acknowledged, and to be of overpowering influence, was the possible effect upon our Southern states of the declaration of negro freedom in Cuba, which would certainly follow independence gained by the aid of the new nations, all of which had abolished slavery.

Vera Cruz had fallen to the Mexican forces November 18, 1825, and so great had been the sensation in Havana that a fast ship was sent to Spain to make known the news, and "implore the king immediately to terminate the war and acknowledge the new republic as the only means left of preserving Cuba to the monarchy."[2]

The good offices of the United States were now earnestly turned to inducing Spain to accept the actualities of the situation. "True wisdom," said Clay, "dictates that Spain, without indulging in unavailing regrets on account of what she has irretrievably lost, should employ the means of retaining what she may yet preserve from the wreck of her former possessions. . . . Not a solitary foot of land from the western limits of the United States to Cape Horn owns her sway; not a bayonet in all that vast extent remains to sustain her cause. . . . If she can entertain no rational hope to recover what has been forced from her grasp, is there not great danger of her losing what she yet but feebly holds? . . . The armies of the new states, flushed with victory, have no longer employment on the continent, and yet while the war continues, if it be only in name, they cannot be disbanded without a disregard of all the maxims of just precaution. . . . Will they not strike wherever they can reach? And from the proximity and great value of Cuba and Puerto Rico, is it not to be anticipated that they will aim, and aim

[1] Middleton, minister to Russia, to Count Nesselrode, January 2, 1825, *State Papers*, V, 917.
[2] Clay to Middleton, December 26, 1825, *Ibid.*, V, 850.

a successful blow, too, at those Spanish islands? . . . It is not, then, for the new republics that the President wishes you to urge upon Spain the expediency of closing the war. . . . It is for Spain itself, for the cause of humanity, for the repose of the world that you are required, with all the delicacy which belongs to the subject, to use every topic of persuasion to impress upon the councils of Spain the propriety by a formal pacification of terminating the war. . . . The United States are satisfied with the present condition of those islands in the hands of Spain with their ports open to our commerce, as they are now open. This government desires no political change of that condition. The population itself of those islands is incompetent at present, from its composition and amount, to maintain self-government. The maritime force of the neighboring republics of Mexico and Colombia is not now, nor is it likely shortly to be, adequate to the protection of those islands, if the conquest of them were effected. The United States would entertain constant apprehension of their passing from their possession to that of some less friendly sovereignty; and of all the European powers this country prefers that Cuba and Puerto Rico should remain dependent on Spain. If the war should continue . . . and those islands should become the object and theatre of it, their fortunes have such a connection with the prosperity of the United States that they could not be indifferent spectators; and the possible contingencies might bring upon the government of the United States duties and obligations, the performance of which, however painful it should be, they might not be at liberty to decline. A subsidiary consideration," continued Clay, ". . . is that as the war has been the parent cause of the shocking piracies in the West Indies, its termination would be, probably, followed by their cessation."[1] A despatch of the same tenor was sent to the American minister in Russia instructing him to endeavor "to engage the Russian government to contribute its best exertions toward terminating the contest."[2]

Neither appeal, however strongly backed by reason, met with acceptance. The Spanish minister said that "the king would never abandon his claim to those his ancient and rightful posses-

[1] Clay to Everett, minister to Spain, April 27, 1825, *State Papers*, V, 866.
[2] Clay to Middleton, May 10, 1825, *Ibid.*, V, 846.

sions."[1] The reply of Russia was almost equally unsatisfactory; no separate negotiation could be instituted until the ulterior views of Spain were known.[2]

An agreement made at the end of 1824, on request of Fernando, for 35,000 of the French troops to remain in Spain, had been followed in the summer of 1825 by the presence in West Indian waters of a powerful French squadron. Mexico, believing that it portended an invasion and seizure of Cuba, "promptly called upon the government of the United States . . . to fulfil the memorable pledge of the President of the United States in his message to Congress of December, 1823."[3] The American minister to France was at once directed "in the most conciliatory and friendly manner" to request an explanation of the presence of so powerful an armament at such a time, and as rumors of designs by France upon Cuba had reached the United States, to say "that we could not consent to the occupation of [Cuba and Puerto Rico] by any other European power than Spain under any contingency whatever."[4]

It was not until November that the explanations requested of the Spanish-American republics were received. While it appeared from these that the United States were not expected to violate any of their neutral obligations toward Spain, it is clear that the views expressed and the attitude taken by the United States were well known to the newly appointed Spanish-American envoys and to their governments, and raised hopes in some at least, as expressed by the "explanations," that "one of the subjects which will occupy the attention of the congress will be the resistance or opposition to the interference of any neutral nation in the questions and war between the new powers of the continent and Spain," and "that as the powers of America are of accord as to resistance, it behooves them to discuss the means of giving to that resistance all possible force that the evil may be met if it cannot be avoided; and the only means of accomplishing this object is by a previous concert as to the mode in which each shall lend its co-

[1] Everett to Clay, September 25, 1825, *State Papers*, V, 867.
[2] Nesselrode to Middleton, August 20, 1825, *Ibid.*, V, 850.
[3] Clay to Poinsett, minister to Mexico, November 9, 1825, *Ibid.*, V, 854.
[4] Clay to Brown, minister to France, October 25, 1825, *Ibid.*, V, 855.

operation." It was hoped that upon this and upon the question of colonization in America by European powers the United States representatives would be specially instructed.[1]

Mr. Clay, in reply to the Mexican and Colombian ministers, said: "In your note there is not recognized so exact a compliance with the conditions on which the President expressed his willingness that the United States should be represented at Panamá as could have been desired," but that though there had not been the full understanding desirable as to the precise questions to be discussed, and as the want of adjustment of these preliminaries could only cause delay, "the President was determined at once to manifest the sensibility of the United States to whatever concerns the prosperity of the American hemisphere, and the friendly motives which have actuated your government in transmitting the invitation" to send commissioners to the Congress. "While they will not be authorized to enter upon any deliberations, or to concur in any acts inconsistent with the present neutral position of the United States, and its obligations, they will be fully empowered and instructed upon all questions likely to arise in the congress on subjects in which the nations of America have a common interest."

President Adams thus notified Congress in his first annual message, December 6, 1825, that "the invitation has been accepted, and ministers on the part of the United States will be commissioned to attend at these deliberations, and to take part in them so far as may be compatible with that neutrality from which it is neither our intention nor the desire of the other American states that we should depart." This was followed by a special message to the Senate, nominating R. C. Anderson, of Kentucky, and John Sergeant, of Pennsylvania, envoys extraordinary and ministers plenipotentiary "to the assembly of American nations at Panamá, and William B. Rochester, of New York, to be secretary to the mission." The question of commercial relations; the "consentaneous adoption of principles of maritime neutrality"; the hope that "the doctrine that free ships make free goods, and the restrictions of reason upon the extent of blockade may be established by general agreement with far more ease . . . than by

[1] Señor Olregon, minister from Mexico, and Señor Salazor, minister from Colombia, to Mr. Clay, Nov. 3 and Nov. 2, 1825, *State Papers*, V, 836.

partial treaties or conventions with each of the nations separately. An agreement between all the parties represented at the meeting that each will guard, by its own means, against the establishment of any European colony within its borders," were the first mentioned reasons for action. As additional motives were suggested the moral influence of the United States in advancing religious liberty and "the indirect influence which the United States may exercise upon any projects or purposes originating in the war in which the Southern republics are still engaged and which might seriously effect the interests of this Union, and the good offices by which the United States may ultimately contribute to bring that war to a speedier termination"; and finally, in a general way to show interest and good-will.

There can be no doubt that the President's action was sound statesmanship. If the congress was to take place, the interests of the United States were so involved in its possible action that it was necessary that it should appear if but as a moderator. Though no hint appeared in the presidential papers, congressional opposition hinged almost wholly upon the question of slavery. It was known that whatever the other results expected of the congress by the Spanish-American states, an agreement to invade Cuba and Puerto Rico was a certainty. Bolivar's organ, the *Official Gazette of Colombia*, for February, 1825, stating in detail the objects of the congress, had made this clear. These were as follows:

"1. To form a solemn compact or league by which the states whose representatives are present will be bound to unite in prosecuting the war against their common enemy, Old Spain, or against any other power which shall assist Spain in her hostile designs, or may otherwise assume the attitude of an enemy.

"2. To draw up and publish a manifesto setting forth to the world the justice of their cause, and the relations they desire to hold with other Christian powers.

"3. To form a convention of navigation and commerce applicable both to the confederated states and to their allies.

"4. To consider the expediency of combining the forces of the republics, to free the islands of Puerto Rico and Cuba from the yoke of Spain, and in such case what contingent each ought to contribute for this end.

"5. To take measures for joining in a prosecution of the war at sea and on the coasts of Spain.

"6. To determine whether these measures shall be extended to the Canary and the Philippine Islands.

"7. To take into consideration the means of making effectual the declaration of the President of the United States, respecting any ulterior design of a foreign power to colonize any portion of this continent, and, also, the means of resisting all interference from abroad with the domestic concerns of the American governments.

"8. To settle, by common consent, the principles of those rights of nations, which are in their nature controvertible.

"9. To determine on what footing shall be placed the political and commercial relations of those portions of our hemisphere which have obtained, or shall obtain, their independence, but whose independence has not been recognized by any American or European power, as was for many years the case with Hayti." [1]

But, it must be said again, the policy of the United States was now dominated by a question of transcendent importance, both ethically and practically, to the peace of the country. To touch the question of slavery politically was to set the South afire. The new republics had all abolished slavery; if they freed Cuba and Puerto Rico they would also free the blacks in these islands. The likelihood of such a situation was regarded as unendurable, and a storm of protest broke from the Southern members in the Senate against the proposed meeting and the possibilities which the concurrence of the United States at Panamá might open.

The Senate committee on foreign affairs, to which the message had been referred, made, on January 16, 1826, an adverse report of great length, which, while carefully refraining from touching on the question of slavery and abstaining "from any remark as to the nominations," recommended a resolution that it was not "expedient at this time for the United States to send any ministers to the congress of American nations assembled at Panama." [2]

The true reasons were, however, brought forward in a debate of great bitterness opened February 1. "When," said Berrien, of Georgia, "we look to the situation of those islands, to the commanding position they occupy with reference to the commerce of the West Indies, we cannot be indifferent to a change in their condition. But when we reflect that they are in juxtaposition to a portion of the Union where slavery exists; that the proposed change is to be effected by a people whose fundamental maxim it is that he who would tolerate slavery is unworthy to be free; that the

[1] Debates of Congress, VII, p. 422.   [2] *State Papers*, V, 857–865.

principle of universal emancipation must march in the van of the invading force; and that all the horrors of a servile war will too surely follow in its train—these merely commercial considerations sink into insignificance—they are swallowed up in the magnitude of the dangers with which we are menaced. Sir, under such circumstances the question to be determined is this: With a due regard to the safety of the Southern states, can you suffer these islands to pass into the hands of buccaneers drunk with their new-born liberty? Cuba and Puerto Rico must remain as they are. To Europe the President had distinctly said: 'We cannot allow a transfer of Cuba to any European power.' We must hold a language equally decisive to the South American states. We cannot allow their principle of universal emancipation to be called into activity in a situation where its contagion 'from our neighborhood would be dangerous to our quiet and safety.'"[1]

Said Benton: "The relations of Hayti with the American states (these United States inclusive), and the right of Africans in this hemisphere, are two other questions to be 'determined.' . . . Our policy toward Hayti, the Old San Domingo, has been fixed, Mr. President, for three and thirty years. We trade with her, but no diplomatic relations have been established between us. We purchase coffee from her and pay her for it, but we interchange no consuls or ministers. We receive no mulatto consuls or black ambassadors from her. And why? Because the peace of eleven states in this Union will not permit the fruits of a successful negro insurrection to be exhibited among them. It will not permit black consuls and ambassadors to establish themselves in our cities and parade through our country and give their fellow-blacks in the United States proof in hand of the honors which await them for a like successful effort on their part. It will not permit the fact to be seen and told that for the murder of their masters and mistresses they are to find friends among the white people of the United States. No, Mr. President, this is a question which has been determined here for three and thirty years. . . . It is one which cannot be discussed in this chamber this day; and shall we go to Panamá to discuss it?"[2]

[1] Benton, *Abridgment of Debates*, VIII, 421 *et seq.*
[2] *Ibid.*, VIII, 469.

These speeches can stand for all those from men of the South. There was but the one note, whether from Hayne of South Carolina, from Benton of Missouri, or White of Tennessee. All dreaded the influence of freedom to the blacks, at our doors, in Cuba.

The situation was thus a delicate one, whether from the standpoint of home or foreign policy. In case the islands were invaded by the allied Spanish-American republics we were faced by the danger of foreign intervention, which we had declared we should resist; if, in the face of this declaration, intervention should be withheld and Cuba and Puerto Rico freed from Spain, their freedom would be accompanied by the freedom of the blacks, which the Southern senators declared could not be endured.

Notwithstanding, the Southern opposition in the Senate was overborne, and, on March 14, 1826, the nominations of the President were confirmed. The debate was now transferred to the House on the question of the necessary appropriations. On March 17, 1826, Adams sent a message. Every consideration of good statesmanship upheld the President in the views which he set forth at much length. His altruistic spirit shone out in advice which was both sound sense and sound policy. He declared that the republics "had given us notice that in the novelty of their situation, and in the spirit of deference to our experience, they would be pleased to have the benefit of our friendly counsel. To meet the temper with which this proposal was made with a cold repulse, was not thought congenial to that warm interest in their welfare with which the people and government of the Union had hitherto gone hand in hand through the whole progress of their revolution. To insult them by a refusal of their overture, and then invite them to a similar assembly to be called by ourselves, was an expedient which never presented itself to the mind. I would have sent ministers to the meeting had it been merely to give them such advice as they might have desired, even with reference to *their own* interests, not involving ours. I would have sent them had it been merely to explain and set forth to them our reasons for *declining* any proposal of specific measures to which they might desire our concurrence, but which we might deem incompatible with our interests or our duties. In the intercourse between nations, temper is a missionary more powerful than talent. Nothing was ever lost by kind treatment; nothing can be gained by sullen repulse and aspiring pretensions."

He referred to the Monroe declaration and the proposition to consider at Panama the measures to make it effectual, but "the purpose of this government is to concur in nothing which would import hostility to Europe or justly excite resentment in any of her states." As to Cuba and Puerto Rico: "The invasion of both these islands by the united forces of Mexico and Colombia is avowedly among the objects to be matured by the belligerent states at Panama. The convulsions to which, from the peculiar composition of their population, they would be liable in the event of such an invasion, and the danger therefrom resulting of their falling ultimately into the hands of some European power other than Spain, will not admit of our looking at the consequences to which the congress at Panama may lead with indifference. It is unnecessary to enlarge upon this topic, or to say more than that all our efforts in reference to this interest will be to preserve the existing state of things, the tranquillity of the islands, and the peace and security of the inhabitants. And lastly, the congress at Panamá is believed to present a fair occasion for urging upon all the new nations of the South the just and liberal principles of religious liberty. . . ."[1]

It was not until April, and after long debate, that the appropriation was passed. The congress met at Panama June 22, 1826. But there were present only the representatives of Colombia, Mexico, Central America, and Peru. Mr. Anderson died at Cartagena on his way from Bogota, and Mr. Sergeant never set out from the United States. On July 15 was signed a treaty of "union, league, and perpetual confederation" between the four states represented, to which any other might accede within a year; the renewal of the congress annually in time of war, and biennially in time of peace, was agreed upon; a convention was made fixing the contingent of each for the common defence, and an agreement was established regarding the employment of these contingents, and certain declarations made regarding the treaties which had been made by Colombia with the states represented and the United

[1] *State Papers*, V, 882–886.

States. The congress was then adjourned to Tucubaya, a short distance from the city of Mexico, but it never again met. The league naturally fell apart as soon as it became evident that it was no longer in the power of Spain to continue the contest against the continental provinces, and that the United States was determined to discountenance action against the islands.

American slavery was thus the bulwark of what remained of Spanish dominion in the Americas. Whatever of self-interest there was in this attitude of the United States government, there can be no question that its action throughout worked for the good of Spain, or what Spain supposed was such. The advice given to this now beggared and distracted country was thoroughly sound, and saved the islands yet many years to the Peninsula, but the doing so was the establishment of what was to become a sore "thorn in the flesh" to both Spain and the United States.

While there was this willingness on the part of the United States to have Cuba remain Spanish, there was a general consensus among American statesmen of the period as to the desirability of acquiring the island for the Union. Adams, as already seen, expressed this view as a necessity and as being "indispensable to the continuance and integrity of the Union itself,"[1] a forecast which, of course, though Adams himself was strongly adverse to slavery, had reference to the necessity of the retention of slavery in the island on account of the South. Jefferson, in his letter to Monroe respecting Canning's proposals as to the Holy Alliance, was, as mentioned, almost equally emphatic.[2]

Jefferson had, however, at a much earlier date, expressed such views, in which he gave free rein to an imagination which went far beyond that of to-day, and to views of strategy such as only the author of the gunboat system of defence could have held. Napoleon at the moment held Spain; in Jefferson's mind this meant also the over-lordship of the Spanish-American provinces. He thus, in a letter to Madison, of April 27, 1809, said: "[Napoleon] ought the more to conciliate our good-will, as we can be such an obstacle to the new career opening on him in the Spanish colonies. That he would give us the Floridas to withhold intercourse with the residue of those colonies cannot be doubted, but that is no price, because

[1] Adams to Nelson, April 28, 1823. *Supra.* 183.   [2] *Supra.* 192.

they are ours in the first moment of the first war, and until a war they are of no particular necessity to us. But, although with difficulty, he will consent to our receiving Cuba into our Union to prevent our aid to Mexico and the other provinces. That would be a price, and I would immediately erect a column on the southernmost limit of Cuba and inscribe on it *ne plus ultra* as to us in that direction. We should then have only to include the North in our confederacy, which would be, of course, in the first war, and we should have such an empire for liberty as she has never surveyed since the Creation; and I am persuaded no constitution was ever before so well calculated as ours for extensive empire and self-government. . . . It will be objected to our receiving Cuba that no limit can be drawn to our future acquisitions. Cuba can be defended by us without a navy, and this develops a principle which ought to limit our views. Nothing should ever be accepted which requires a navy to defend it." [1]

Notwithstanding such views, all the efforts of the American government were turned for many years to the preservation of the *status quo*, as stated so explicitly in the despatches of Clay to the American minister in France.[2] Great Britain equally had been made aware that a seizure of Cuba would mean war.[3]

In 1827 suspicions were again aroused in Washington by the reception from the American minister at Madrid of a translation of a confidential despatch from the Count de la Alcudia, the Spanish minister at London, to the minister of state saying:

"I deem it my duty to give you notice, for the information of the king, our lord, that this government despatched a frigate some time ago to the Canary Islands with commissioners on board who were instructed to ascertain whether any preparations were making there for an expedition to America, and also the state of those

---

[1] Jefferson to President Madison, April 27, 1809, *Works*, V, 443. No document can illustrate more fully Jefferson's inconsistency of character. Doubting but a few short years before the constitutionality of the acquirement of Louisiana, he was now coveting the possession of a great island; opposed to a navy, he was reaching for territory which only a navy could defend; a lover of peace, he was looking to war to secure British America.

[2] *Supra.* 208.

[3] Clay to A. H. Everett at Madrid, April 13, 1826. House Ex. Doc., 121, 32 Cong., 1 Sess.

islands and the dispositions of the inhabitants. The result of these inquiries was that the said islands were in a wholly defenceless situation, provided with few troops, and those disaffected and ready for any innovation.

"The frigate then proceeded to the Havana, where the commissioners found many persons disposed to revolt; but in consequence of the large military force there, and the strength of the fortifications, they considered it impossible to take possession of the island without the co-operation of the authorities and the army. In consequence of the information thus obtained, measures have been taken in both these islands to prepare the public opinion, by means of emissaries, in favor of England, to the end that the inhabitants may be brought to declare themselves independent, and to solicit the protection of the British. The latter are prepared to assist them, and will in this way avoid collision with the United States. The whole operation is to be undertaken and is to be conducted in concert with the revolutionists here [at London] and in the islands, who have designated a Spanish general, now at this place, to take command of the Havana when the occasion shall require it.

"The Duke of Wellington communicated to me the above information, which is also confirmed by an intimation which he gave to Brigadier-General Don Francisco Armenteros when this officer took leave of him to go to the Havana. The duke then advised him, if he should discover any symptoms of disaffection in the authorities, to give immediate notice to the king, as it would be a grievous thing for his majesty to lose the Havana.

"I have thought it my duty to make these circumstances known to your excellency. . . ."[1]

In conveying to the Spanish minister of state the knowledge of the existence of such information, the American minister declared again "the settled principle" of his government, "that the island of Cuba must in no event and under no pretext pass into the possession of, or under the protection of, any European power other than Spain." The American minister at the same time recalled that while France "had for three or four years past a consul at

[1] Enclosure from A. H. Everett, minister at Madrid, August 17, 1827. House Ex. Doc., 121, 32 Cong., 1 Sess., p. 20.

Havana," and that Spain was "bound by treaty to admit a consul for the United States in all" ports in Spanish dominions "where such agent is admitted for any foreign power," the United States had been for more than two years soliciting in vain the fulfilment of this contract. "In the meantime, the British government have, under the name of commissioners for attending to the execution of the slave-trade convention, two acknowledged political agents at the Havana. One of them (Mr. Kirby) was a particular friend of the late Mr. Canning, . . . and is doubtless the manager of the present intrigue for revolutionizing the island."

Mr. Everett also recalled that while there had been an immediate arrangement with Great Britain, for the reclamations of the British government for depredations committed, "under precisely the same circumstances, upon the rights and property of British subjects and citizens of the United States," there had not even been a formal reply to the American demand for a similar arrangement. American ships, too, said the minister, pay a tonnage duty in the peninsular ports of twenty reals against the one real paid by all others. "A proposition made . . . in the name of the government nearly two years ago, to treat on this subject, remains unanswered," and the minister had been privately informed that it was even determined to raise, instead of diminishing, the tonnage duty on American ships, the result being to drive them to Gibraltar, which thus became a base for smuggling cargoes into Spain. He also complained of the enormous tonnage duties in Cuba, which, as nine-tenths of Cuban commerce was with the United States, was practically a discrimination against the commerce of the latter.[1]

The communication, however, which so aroused American suspicions may be taken to have had as a basis the French occupation of Spain, which was to continue yet two years at the request of Fernando himself, whose murderous activity against the liberals needed such support.[2] The mere fact that the revelation had been

---

[1] Memorandum from Mr. A. H. Everett, American minister, to Spanish minister of state, Madrid, December 10, 1827. House Ex. Doc. 121, 32 Cong., 1 Sess., p. 22.

[2] The cost, of course, was borne by Spain. On December 30, 1828, a treaty was signed at Madrid by which she acknowledged for this a debt of 80,000,000

made by the Duke of Wellington, himself a member of the British cabinet, but as a grandee of Spain, and the chief instrument of her release from the Napoleonic dominion, naturally friendly to the Spanish nation, goes far to show that the action of the British government was merely precautionary against the results to the islands which would come from a long-continued French occupation. The scheme had no further development.

The complaints of the American minister in his memorandum as to the non-reception of consuls were but the repetition of those of two years before, when the recognition by the United States of the Spanish-American republics, and the danger of admitting the authorized agents of a power friendly to independence, were made the grounds of refusal. "Spain," it was said, "would perhaps be disposed to concede this point if the United States would furnish any pledges or guarantees, by way of security, respecting their future relation with the islands," which was enlarged into meaning a guarantee by treaty of Spain's continued possession, a proposal which naturally was declined.[1]

For the next twenty-five years, the government of the United States was haunted by the idea that Cuba would be seized by Great Britain or France, and the reiteration of American antagonism to such action, brought about by this impression, went far toward preserving the island to a country now racked throughout its length and breadth by insurrection, brigandage, and misrule, and one whose incapacity to govern itself so clearly demonstrated its unworthiness, at the time, to govern any other. The heavy financial responsibilities of Spain to both France and England, caused by the support of the French army and by the engagement to pay the indemnities for injuries to British commerce, and for which the possession of Cuba and Puerto Rico seemed the only secure guarantee, made the fears of the United States not at all

---

francs to France. Spain was to pay annually 2,400,000 francs (3 per cent.) in interest and 1,600,000 francs annually until the debt should be redeemed. *British and Foreign State Papers*, XVI, 989.

[1] A. H. Everett to Clay, September 25, 1825. House Ex. Doc. 121, 32 Cong., 1 Sess., p. 25. See also Señor Bermudez to Mr. Nelson, July 12, 1825, who in addition declared that the thought of ceding Cuba and Puerto Rico to any power had never been entertained, and that it was firmly determined to keep them under Spanish sovereignty. *Ibid.*, 14.

unreasonable. Not only did the United States stand between any such possible demands of the two powers mentioned, but her interposition with the new American republics had undoubtedly saved the islands from invasion and capture. The American government thus continued to press Spain, in her own interest and that of general peace, not to persevere in the assertion of her claims over her former colonies,[1] and when this danger was past, to reiterate from time to time its general attitude in the Cuban question.

Thus on July 15, 1840, the American minister was directed: "Should you have reason to suspect any design on the part of Spain to transfer voluntarily her title to [Cuba], whether of ownership or possession, and whether permanent or temporary, to Great Britain or any other power, you will distinctly state that the United States will prevent it at all hazards, as they will any foreign military occupation for any pretext whatsoever; and you are authorized to assure the Spanish government that, in case of any attempt, from whatever quarter, to wrest from her this portion of her territory, she may securely depend upon the military and naval resources of the United States to aid her in preserving or recovering it."[2]

Slavery was again an element of the question, for Great Britain had, in 1830, abolished slavery in all her possessions. The slave-trade in Cuba had remained, however, in full vigor, despite the nominal concurrence of Spain in the efforts toward its destruction by a treaty which agreed to a complete closure of the trade by May, 1820, a concurrence for which she received from England £400,000 as compensation for loss to the crown. The trade flourished in Havana, despite the efforts at capture by British ships; and the presence there of numerous men-of-war whose duty was largely the prevention of the trade, the irritation of the British government with Spain on the subject, and the pressure upon it of the British abolition societies, was a principal element in again causing apprehension on the part of the United States. In 1843 Web-

[1] Van Buren, secretary of state, to Van Ness, minister at Madrid, October 2, 1829, and October 13, 1830. House Ex. Doc. 121, 32 Cong., 1 Sess., 26, 28.
[2] Mr. Forsyth, secretary of state, to Mr. Vail, minister to Spain, July 15, 1840. MSS. Inst. Spain, XIV, 111. Moore, *International Law Digest*, VI, 450.

ster, moved by rumors of British action, wrote in almost the same words as those just quoted.[1] Though Webster became satisfied that reports had been greatly exaggerated, he was convinced that "enough, however, of danger and alarm still exists in that quarter to render caution and vigilance on the part of this government indispensably necessary."[2] Webster's successor, Mr. Upshur, was of like opinion, and he sent, a little later, the same warning.[3]

Four years later the successful war with Mexico, with the annexation of Texas and California, despite the opposition of those who feared the slave power, caused the pro-slavery administration in 1848 to reach out for Cuba. "If Cuba were annexed to the United States," said Buchanan, secretary of state, Polk being President, "we should not only be relieved from the apprehensions which we can never cease to feel for our own safety and the security of our commerce while it shall remain in its present condition, but human foresight cannot anticipate the beneficial consequences which would result to every portion of our Union. This can never become a local question. . . .

"Desirable, however, as the possession of the island may be to the United States, we would not acquire it except by the free consent of Spain . . . it is supposed that the present relations between Cuba and Spain might incline the Spanish government to cede the island . . . upon the payment of a fair and full consideration. We have received information from various sources, both official and unofficial, that among the Creoles of Cuba there has long existed a deep-rooted hostility to Spanish dominion. The revolutions which are rapidly succeeding each other throughout the world have inspired the Cubans with an ardent and irrepressible desire to achieve their independence. Indeed we are informed by the consul of the United States at Havana that 'there appears every probability that the island will soon be in a state of civil war.' He also states that 'efforts are now being made to raise money for that purpose in the United States, and there will be attempts to induce

---

[1] Daniel Webster, secretary of state, to Robert C. Campbell, consul at Havana, January 14, 1843; copy furnished the Spanish minister at Washington and to Washington Irving, American minister at Madrid, January 17, 1843. Moore, *International Law Digest*, VI, 37–40.
[2] Webster to Irving, March 14, 1843. *Ibid.*, 41.   [3] *Ibid.*, 41.

a few of the volunteer regiments now in Mexico to obtain their discharge and join the revolution.' I need scarcely inform you that the government of the United States has no agency whatever in exciting the spirit of disaffection among the Cubans. . . . I have warned [the consul] to keep a watchful guard both upon his words and actions, so as to avoid even the least suspicion that he had encouraged the Cubans to rise. . . . I stated also that the relations between Spain and the United States had long been of the most friendly character; and both honor and duty required that we should take no part in the struggle which he seemed to think was impending. I informed him that it would certainly become the duty of this government to use all proper means to prevent any of our volunteer regiments now in Mexico from violating the neutrality of the country by joining in the proposed civil war. . . ." Orders, says Buchanan, were given June 10, directing that the transports carrying troops from Mexico should proceed directly home, and "in no event to touch at any place in Cuba."

After dealing at length with the advantages to Spain, Cuba, and the United States, of annexation, Buchanan continued:

"Cuba, justly appreciating the advantages of annexation, is now ready to rush into our arms. . . . The President believes that the crisis has arrived when an effort should be made to purchase the island. . . . At your interview with the minister for foreign affairs you might introduce the subject by referring to the present distracted condition of Cuba, and the danger which exists that the population will make an attempt to accomplish a revolution. This must be well known to the Spanish government. . . . In order to convince him of the good faith and friendship toward Spain with which this government has acted, you might read to him the first part of my despatch to General Campbell [consul at Havana] and the order issued by the secretary of war. . . . You may then touch delicately upon the danger that Spain may lose Cuba by a revolution in the island, or that it may be wrested from her by Great Britain, should a rupture take place between the two countries, arising out of the dismissal of Sir Henry Bulwer, and be retained to pay the Spanish debt due to the British bondholders. You might assure him that whilst this government is entirely satisfied that Cuba shall remain under the dominion of Spain, we should in any event resist its acquisition by any other nation. And, finally, you might inform him that, under all these circumstances, the President had arrived at the conclusion that Spain might be willing to transfer the island to the United States for a fair and full consideration."[1] A hundred million dollars was named as the limit of the sum which might be offered.

The proposal, whatever consideration it might have been given by the government had it been free to act, was rejected, the Spanish minister for foreign affairs finally declaring "that it was more than any minister dare, to entertain such a proposition; that he believed such to be the feeling of the country that, sooner than see the island transferred to any power, they would prefer seeing it sunk in the ocean";[2] to this attitude Spain, unfortunately for herself, held to the end. The next American administration declared, less than a year after President Polk's offer, that any proposal for the transfer of Cuba must come from Spain.[3]

Though successive later administrations pushed the project of purchase to the very eve of the civil war, Buchanan, a Northern man himself, being its most prominent advocate, the question of the extension of territory southward which was, or might become, slave—advocated so strongly by Southern statesmen, and by some of the North, there being no more prominent advocate than the Pennsylvanian Buchanan—could now and thenceforward only arouse bitter antagonism from the rapidly growing antislavery sentiment in the North. There was no time between 1848 and 1861 when the annexation of Cuba could have assumed probability without fierce resistance from the now rapidly increasing opponents of the extension of slave territory. The question, in fact, never assumed a serious form, nor, despite the efforts in the next decade, 1850–1860, could it have done so.

[1] Mr. Buchanan to Mr. Saunders, minister to Spain, June 17, 1848. House Ex. Doc. 121, 32 Cong., 1 Sess. Moore, *Digest*, I, 584, and VII, 921.

[2] Saunders to Buchanan, December 14, 1848. House Ex. Doc. 121, 32 Cong., 1 Sess. Moore, *Digest*, I, 588.

[3] Clayton, secretary of state, to Barrington, minister to Spain, August 2, 1849. MS. Inst. Moore, *Digest*, I, 587.

CHAPTER XII

CUBAN CONDITIONS: THE LOPEZ EXPEDITIONS: BRITISH AND FRENCH INTERFERENCE

In May, 1825, the French army occupying Spain in the interest and at the request of Fernando VII, the imperious and savage edicts relating to Spain herself and the revolted South American colonies, were followed by a decree with reference to the authority of the Captain-General of Cuba:

"His majesty being formally persuaded that at no time and under no circumstances will the principle of rectitude and love to his royal person, which characterizes your excellency, ever be weakened; and his majesty, desiring to obviate any difficulties which might arise in extraordinary cases from a division of authority and the complication of command and control by the respective officers, and to the important end of preserving in that precious island his legitimate sovereign rule and the public peace, has been pleased, in accordance with the judgment of his council of ministers, to invest your excellency with full authority, conferring all the powers which by royal decree are conceded to the governors of cities in a state of siege. His majesty consequently invests your excellency with full and unlimited authority to detach from that island, and to send to this Peninsula, all officials and persons employed in whatsoever capacity, and of whatsoever rank and class or condition, whose presence may appear prejudicial, or whose public or private conduct may inspire you with suspicion, replacing them in the interim with faithful servants of his majesty who are deserving of the confidence of your excellency, and furthermore to suspend the execution of any orders or general regulations issued in whatever branch of the administration to whatever extent your excellency may consider convenient to the royal service; such measures to be always provisional, and a report thereof to be sent by your excellency for the sovereign approval of his majesty. In dispensing to your excellency this signal proof of his royal favor and the high confidence which his majesty places in your perfect loyalty, he hopes that, worthily co-operating, you will use the greatest prudence and circumspection together with indefatigable activity, and trusts that your excellency will be endowed through this same favor of his royal goodness with a greater responsibility, redouble your vigilance in seeing that the laws are observed, that justice is administered, and that the faithful subjects of his majesty be rewarded; at the same time punishing without delay or hesitation the misdeeds of those who, forgetting their obligations and what they owe to the best and most beneficent of sovereigns, violate the laws and give vent to sinister machinations by the infraction of said laws and of the administrative ordinances relating thereto."

This decree, which was to remain the constitution under which Cuba was governed for a large part of the century, was the natural outcome of the despotism which had returned to Spain; but its immediate cause was the discontent between insulars and peninsulars, which began to show itself prominently as early as 1821 in connection with the elections for the Cortes, under the short-lived revival of the constitution, and brought the island to the verge of insurrection, through a conspiracy more serious than the space generally allotted to it in Cuban history would lead one to suppose. That in 1826 there were 11,000 troops in the island illustrates this fact.

All this time Spain was continuing the downward course of the earlier part of the century, the question of a successor to Fernando VII coming to rack the country with insurrection and civil war. The Cortes, in 1789, on request of Charles IV, had secretly agreed to the abolition of the Salic law established by Philip V in 1713, but the agreement, had never been published as legalization required. Fernando had no heir. In 1829 he married as his fourth wife his niece, Maria Cristina of Naples, and on March 31, 1830, the queen being pregnant, he published a decree restoring the ancient law of succession in either male or female line, in accordance with the secret petition of the Cortes mentioned. It was a signal for revolt even before the birth of the expected child. On October

10, 1830, a princess, to become known as Isabella II, was born. In January, 1832, there came still another princess; by this time the King was sinking to his end and no more children could be expected. On September 18, 1832, Fernando, now on his deathbed, under pressure of the president of the council of Castile, Calomarde, signed the revocation of the decree of 1789 which he had sanctioned two and a half years before, and his daughter was legally no longer heir. Doña Carlota, sister of the queen, and wife of the king's youngest brother (reputed a son of Godoy's), extorted the revocation from Calomarde and destroyed it; caused the dying king privately to sign a cancellation of the revocation, and on October 6, 1832, to sign a decree appointing his wife, Maria Cristina, sole regent. Fernando revived sufficiently to return from La Granja to Madrid, and on the last day of 1832 the revocation was "publicly withdrawn by the king with every solemnity and formality." His brother, Don Carlos, was sent to Portugal, and later when sent for to swear allegiance to the baby princess who, as heir, received the oath of allegiance of the Cortes June 20, 1833, refused to come, claiming the heirship for himself. On September 29, 1833, Fernando died, leaving his widow guardian of his two children and Queen-Governess of Spain; and, through this action, leaving also a long heritage of civil war which was to devastate his country and retard its progress toward light.

The government of the Regent Maria Cristina, in its manifesto of October 4, 1833, made no concessions to freedom or to the demands of modern progress. But there was liberalism enough in Spain to force a half-hearted step toward constitutionalism, and an edict put forth in April, 1834, established a parliament; but it was one which could only discuss subjects submitted by the queen's ministers. In two and one-half years a third of Spain was in the hands of the Carlists, and the rest in the throes of a revolution. On August 13, 1836, under the threat of the insurrectionary troops, the constitution of 1812 was re-established "pending the manifestation by the Cortes of the will of the nation," and Spain, or so much of the distracted country as was not overrun by the Carlist forces, was once more under a constitutional regimen.

Under the letter of the constitution Cuban representation in the Spanish Cortes was again possible, and the members allowed to the island, and who were elected under pressing orders from the home government, presented themselves for admission to the Cortes, which began its sittings October 24, 1836. The Cortes had sat three months, with the demands of the Cuban and Puerto Rican representatives for admission before it, when finally the following law was passed in secret session, January 16, 1837, and promulgated April 18:

"The Cortes, under the power conceded by the constitution, has decreed: It not being possible to apply the constitution which has been adopted for the Peninsula and the adjacent islands, to the ultramarine provinces of America and Asia: these will be ruled and administered by special laws fitted for their respective situations and circumstances and calculated to secure their happiness; consequently the deputies of the said provinces will not be seated in the Cortes."[1]

The cause of the denial was laid mainly at the door of the Captain-General Tacon, who, "despot by instinct, by education, and interest, hated liberty." This is the true beginning of Cuban revolt. The island remained under the despotic rule of men sometimes good, more frequently bad, who built an absolute and despotic power upon a foundation which had its beginning in the earliest days of Spanish colonization and, despite appearances, was never really changed until the final year of Spain's dominion.

While of such great importance in the relations of Cuba and Spain, the benefits proposed to themselves by the inhabitants of the Antilles through representation were, viewed in their true light, really illusionary. This was clearly seen by Saco, who of Cuban publicists has shown the highest qualities of statesmanship. The small proportion of representatives which could have been allowed on any basis proposed would have been then, as they were later, powerless to effect reform in Cuban laws or administration. The only real panacea for Cuban feelings and for Cuban misgovernment was in local self-government, in the autonomy which fifty years later they were to spurn, though at this period it was not even thought of. For the moment, at least, they would have been satisfied with the representation allowed by the constitution which the Cortes violated, combined with an opening, to even a moderate degree, of

[1] Sedano, *Estudios Politicos*, 162.

administrative career to the natives of the island. One at least of the later captains-general, Concha, in his *Memorias*, advocated such reform, and it was to his initiative that, in 1863, the establishment of the "Ministerio de Ultramar" was due; but though he afterward filled the post, he made no endeavor to bring into active being his just and excellent views of the burning question. Cuba remained what it always had been, less the recognition of the rights which in theory had been theirs ever since the formulation of the laws of the Indies, and which for two short intervals (in 1810 and in 1821) they had momentarily enjoyed.

The government remained a despotism pure and simple; its code, the *bando* of 1842 of Captain-General Geronimo Valdes, whose "spirit" for many years to come "walked abroad through this old body of laws, customs, regulations, edicts, *bandos*, decrees, circulars, orders, and injunctions which he gathered together and vitalized. The titles of the *bandos* relate to religion and public morality, order, health, security, theatres, cleanliness, and decoration. It required two hundred and sixty-one articles to define the relation of the citizen to the government, or the municipality, with respect to these headings. A special chapter is devoted to the *pedaneos* or petty law officers. The instructions give an insight into the entire lack of personal or civil liberty reserved to the individual. The *pedaneos* and their assistants, the *cabos de rondas*, or roundsmen, were real Paul Prys of the state. The list of cases in which they could acquire fees was a long one, and they could impose fines in compliance with specific articles of the *bando*. They were practically charged with the regulation of both the public and private morals of the community. The regulations are wearisome in their minuteness, from their prohibition of the picador at the bull-fight pricking the animal when in the centre of the ring, to the requirement that the bodega keepers should have a basin of water standing in front of their shops so that the dogs which ran through the streets might drink as they listed, and thus avoid the danger of hydrophobia. But through them all runs the authority from above and it is the very highest authority." [1]

Cuba in 1850 had a population of about 1,200,000, half of whom were whites, a sixth free colored, the remainder, about 450,000,

[1] Pepper, *Tomorrow in Cuba*, 110.

slaves. There were in the island 35,000 Spaniards and 23,000 Spanish troops. The Creole whites were thus ten to one of the Spanish population. The island sent large sums to the Madrid government. Besides, it supported all the Spanish officials in the country from the captain-general down; it paid the army and the navy in the island; paid the interest on the debt incurred; paid largely, if not all, the expenses of Spanish consuls and the Spanish minister in the United States, and also provided the secret-service fund of the legation. Naturally with such a bank to draw upon Spain paid large salaries. In the latter years of her rule the captain-general (later called governor-general) received $50,000 a year with a palace in Havana, a country house, servants, and a secret-service fund; the director-general of the treasury, $18,500; the archbishop of Santiago and the bishop of Havana, $18,000 each; the admiral commanding the naval station, $16,392; the general second in command of the island, and the president of the "audiencia," $15,000 each. Major-generals received $7,500, brigadier-generals $4,500, capitan de navio (corresponding to captains in our navy) $6,300, commanders $4,560, lieutenant-commanders (teniente de navio, 1ª class) $3,370. The ministry of the colonies received $96,800 a year from Cuba. The island was filled with officials from Spain who made their careers a saturnalia of plunder. For the whole population of over 600,000 whites in 1850 there were fewer than 250 schools, and less than 9,000 white and colored children in attendance, nor was the proportion ever materially changed.

The imports in 1847 were over $30,000,000 in value; the exports nearly $28,000,000; the revenue nearly $13,000,000. The chief trader with the island was the United States, notwithstanding the heavy discriminating duties in favor of Spain. The duty on foreign flour was $10 per barrel, though its value in the United States was but $4.50; facts which caused American flour to go by way of Spain and enter Cuba as Spanish flour in Spanish ships.

The natural outcome of the situation, combined with the civil strife of Spain and the volcanic condition of Europe in 1848, was the beginning of the long era of revolt which was to run through the next half of the century. The first actor of importance was

Narciso Lopez, of Venezuela, who had been a major-general in the first Carlist war, a senator of Spain, governor of Valencia, and governor of Madrid; he had also held high office in Cuba. Attempting to organize a revolt of the island in 1848, he was sentenced to death by the authorities, but escaped to the United States.[1]

In 1849 he began in New York the preparation of an expedition. This was promptly suppressed by the American authorities, and a proclamation issued by President Taylor, August 11, 1849, warning "all citizens of the United States who shall connect themselves with an enterprise so grossly in violation of our laws and treaty obligations, that they will thereby subject themselves to the heavy penalties denounced against them by our acts of Congress, and will forfeit their claim to the protection of their country. No such persons must expect the influence of this government, in any form, on their behalf, no matter to what extremities they may be reduced in consequence of their conduct."[2] These extreme expressions were later to be used with effect by the Spanish authorities in defence of high-handed action which was wholly in disaccord with international rules of law as generally understood. If taken literally, they took from American citizens the protections guaranteed by the treaty of 1795.

Lopez, early in 1850, attempted to organize another expedition with Savannah as a base, but finding himself closely observed by the federal authorities, he transferred his endeavors to the more congenial field of New Orleans, where were many fresh from the war with Mexico who favored his cause. Prominent among them was General Quitman, of Mississippi, to whom was offered the leadership, declined by him only because of the secessionist movement of 1850, of which he was a vehement advocate.[3] He assisted Lopez, however, financially and advised his having, at the first, at least 2,000 men to maintain a footing pending re-enforcement. Lopez, over-optimistic as to Cuban readiness to join, gathered at New Orleans, chiefly from Cincinnati and its vicinity, some 750

---

[1] Curtis, *Life of Webster*, II, 547. De Olivart, *Revue Générale de Droit International Public*, tome IV (1897), 586.
[2] House Ex. Doc. 5, 31 Cong., 1 Sess., p. 17.
[3] Claiborne, *Life of Quitman*, II, 56–58.

men. On April 25, 1850, 250 of these, under Col. Theodore O'Hara, the second in command to Lopez, left New Orleans in the bark *Georgiana*, followed, May 2, by the brig *Susan Loud* with 170, the men being furnished with tickets for Chagres (on the isthmus of Panama), the vessels being chartered, advertised, and cleared for that port. Ostensibly the men were bound for California (as in fact a number of them were), to which at this moment there was an exodus from the East, through the furor, then at its height, on account of the lately discovered gold. Lopez followed, May 7, in the small steamer *Creole*, with the remainder of the men. Three-fourths of the force were ex-volunteers of the Mexican war, instigated to adventure by their late experiences. However well known that a gathering for such a purpose was in progress, the actual expedition seems to have left, unsuspected for the moment, and a man-of-war sent later in pursuit was unsuccessful in finding it.[1]

Rendezvous was made off the coast of Yucatan, where the whole of the invading force was taken aboard the *Creole*, the other two vessels, with the passengers for California, being left in charge of their ordinary non-combatant crews. The first intention was to land at Matanzas, but fearing that knowledge of this had got abroad, Cardenas was selected instead, and landing was made there at midnight of May 19. The small Spanish garrison was surprised and the town easily occupied. Lopez called upon the natives for volunteers, without a single response except from the Spanish soldiers, of whom thirty-four joined him. There was, however, some show of friendly feeling in the bringing of some arms and horses. The evident general fear prevented, however, any volunteering of the people.

After twelve hours of disappointment and rumors of powerful Spanish re-enforcements, the men were re-embarked. Lopez desired to make another effort elsewhere, but the men were now unruly and mutinous. A consultation of officers ended in submitting the question to a vote of the men, who refused further effort by a large majority. The ship then left about 9 P. M. (May 20) for Key West, the nearest American port, about a hundred

[1] The sending of this ship caused a question and debate in the Senate as to the President's action. See Curtis, *Webster*, II, 441.

miles distant, and the only one which could be reached with the coal aboard. Before clearing the intricate approaches to Cardenas, she ran ashore some five miles from the town and remained aground until dawn, when after throwing overboard all stores and ammunition she was floated. The Lieutenant-Governor of Cardenas, the commander of the garrison, and several other Spanish officials who had been seized were put ashore in a small boat, the lieutenant-governor on leaving "waving adieu with his handkerchief in handsome style,"[1] and the steamer proceeded with, "as is notoriously the case with volunteer forces making a retrograde movement," a completely demoralized command.[2]

Anchoring some forty miles from Key West during the night, the ship, shortly after getting under way, was discovered by the Spanish war steamer, *Pizarro*, which had been into Key West the day previous in search of her. The *Pizarro* started in pursuit, but the *Creole* entered Key West some six miles ahead, with fuel completely exhausted. The *Pizarro* also came into the port, and her captain demanded the arrest of the men of the expedition.[3]

The *Creole* was at once seized by the port authorities, but the men aboard were allowed to disperse, apparently without any effort at detention. Key West was, however, at this time but a small village, the resort of a lawless class of wreckers, and it may well be that any effort to seize the leader or any portion of the force of more than four hundred well-armed men was regarded impracticable. The Spanish naval commander offered his services to

[1] Lieutenant Hardy of the Kentucky battalion, *An Authentic History of the Cuban Expedition*, 45.

[2] Report of Lieutenant-Colonel Pickett, Kentucky Regiment, *Ibid.*, 70.

[3] The commandant-general of the naval forces of Spain in the Antilles, Francisco Avenero, to the Spanish consul at Key West (House Ex. Doc. 83, 32 Cong., 1 Sess., p. 45.). The loose views of the Spanish commander regarding international law are shown by a remark in his letter to the consul: "You, and the people of Key West, have been witnesses of the high consideration I have shown to the American flag, since, after coming alongside of the aforesaid vessel in the vicinity of the port, I did not capture it, being well assured that the government of the United States, which is as much interested in the punishment of every act of piracy as that of the country most concerned in it, would have taken all the necessary steps in order to have that punishment administered." The words "vicinity of the port" necessarily implied within the port, as the *Pizarro* entered a considerable interval after the *Creole*.

assist, but they were declined.[1] The men gradually found their way elsewhere from this, then, out-of-the-way point, which offered but little means of transportation beyond the small craft of wreckers and spongers. Lopez, arrested at Savannah, was brought before the courts, but was finally released through a failure of evidence that he had violated the neutrality laws. The *Creole* was confiscated.

The *Pizarro* and the brig *Habanero*, acting upon intelligence brought by Havana fishing vessels which had been at the island of Contoy, had seized the *Georgiana* and *Susan Loud* on May 18. All the fifty-two people on board, forty-two of whom were *bona fide* passengers for California, and the other ten the crews of the two vessels, were removed to the Spanish ships and taken to Havana May 20, the vessels themselves, with prize crews, reaching there June 5. The master of the *Susan Loud*, who had called aboard the *Creole* before her departure, and three men of his boat's crew had been forcibly detained there and thus escaped the imprisonment and trial for "piracy" to which the others were at once subjected. A demand for their release, on the ground of capture in neutral waters, made by the American consul and by Captain Randolph of the sloop of war *Albany*, to the Spanish naval commander-in-chief, in whose hands the affair rested, was refused. The case of the Duc d'Enghien was cited as a parallel, but the admiral held that it was not so; "that the duke was a gentleman."

Commodore Charles Morris, acting as a special commissioner under the department of state, was directed to go to Havana, in the steamer *Vixen*, to demand of the governor-general an immediate release of all the prisoners taken at Contoy, and to inform him that the President would "view their punishment by the authorities of Cuba as an *outrage* upon the rights of this country." He was also directed to inform the governor-general that the return of the vessels with damages for their capture and detention was expected. If the demand for release of the prisoners was refused, the commodore was to inquire fully into their treatment and condition, and into the evidence upon which the Spanish authorities relied to establish their guilt.[2]

[1] Admiral Avenero to Señor Calderon de la Barca, Spanish minister at Washington, *Ibid.*, 44.
[2] *Ibid.*, 5–7.

A copy of Commodore Morris's instructions was sent to the American minister at Madrid for his guidance. The latter at once had a conference with the Marquis of Pidal, minister of state, who took the position that "the right of Spain, under the circumstances, thus to capture them, to take them into her own ports, and to try them before her own tribunals, was undoubted by the law of nations, and Spain *insisted on that right.*" Mr. Barringer said that, apart from certain facts, the more important of which was that the prisoners taken at Contoy were *bona fide* passengers for California, that the island of Contoy, near Yucatan, was subject to the sovereignty of Mexico; that such seizure on the territory of a third and friendly power was in derogation of the rights of the United States: "The United States could not recognize such a right or pretension, and protested in the most firm and solemn manner against all proceedings and consequences which had [followed] or might follow from such unlawful capture."

Señor Pidal "argued at some length and with much animation" that the pretension of the United States would deprive "Spain of her right to combat invaders of her territory, except upon that territory itself; . . . it denied her the right to pursue their ships, to beat up their rendezvous, to capture or destroy them in their stronghold . . . that if, instead of three, fifty vessels (as you say this expedition might have been, but for the action of your government) should go out of your ports to-morrow filled with the armed enemies of Spain, and rendezvous at the desert spot of Contoy, and twenty of the fifty should actually make a descent upon the coast of Cuba, Spain might combat the twenty after they had arrived, but she could not send her cruisers to molest the thirty, not yet quite ready to follow—to combat, to capture, if possible, and conduct them into her own ports for trial before her own tribunals. Such a pretension could not be admitted by Spain for a moment. . . . Spain could not make a reclamation or claim indemnity from Mexico for the violation of her supposed territory, which was nothing but a desert, and a capture on it was equivalent to a capture on the high seas. The right to seize, imprison, judge, and punish those found guilty in such cases was indispensable for the defence and safety of nations. . . . [Spain] could never surrender this right, or yield to such a demand. *It was impossible for her to do so.*"[1]

The American minister, in making the more formal demand, did so in the terms of the instructions to Commodore Morris, reiterating that the United States cannot recognize the right of Spain to seize American vessels at anchor on the coast and within the territory and jurisdiction of a friendly power; that, even if guilty of an *intention* to join the expedition of Lopez, this was a crime punishable only by and under the laws of the United States.

Señor Pidal "insisted " in his reply, in "qualifying the expeditionaries as pirates"; that when captured, "I could not regard the said vessels as Anglo-American, nor those who manned them as citizens of the United States, because having undertaken an expedition of piracy, declared such by the law of nations, and by the government of the confederacy itself, and having put themselves on their own account, in war with Spain, they had lost by that sole act their nationality and the right to be regarded and protected as citizens of the Union." From the moment that the conspirators placed themselves beyond American jurisdiction and "in the territory of another power . . . the pursuit and punishment of those who can no longer be considered but as pirates, pertains very specially to the nation against whom they direct themselves."[2] The mind which declared such views as to international law, and established such a definition of piracy, made negotiation very difficult.

The forty-two California passengers and the "foremast hands" of the two vessels were released, but the master of the *Georgiana* and the two mates of the vessels were sentenced to ten, eight, and four years of hard labor. They were sent from Havana to Spain September 10, en route to Ceuta, but the American demands caused their pardon, and November 16, 1850, they were sent home from Cadiz.

Both vessels were confiscated by what was termed, though there was no pretension of a state of war, a prize court. The department of state seems to have treated the cases with an extraordinary apathy, due largely, no doubt, to the ill health of Mr. Webster, so soon to end in death. The last official word at the time is in a

[1] Mr. Barringer, minister at Madrid to Mr. Clayton, secretary of state, August 7, 1850. House Ex. Doc. 83, 32 Cong., 1 Sess. [2] *Ibid.*

letter from him to the President, January 27, 1852, answering the resolution of the House of Representatives calling for information in the matter. He says: "It does not appear that a copy of the judicial proceedings, which resulted in the condemnation of the vessels referred to, has been communicated by the parties interested, or from any other quarter. When a transcript of those proceedings will have been received, the cases shall be examined; and if the result of the examination shall show that the vessels when captured were engaged in a commerce sanctioned by the laws of the United States, a claim for indemnification will be presented to her Catholic Majesty's government."[1]

Such a result gave good ground for Spanish action later. If an American ship could be seized in neutral waters and confiscated; if the claims by the Spanish government in this case could be carried to a successful conclusion, later Spanish governments could feel justified in seizing upon the high seas, or in American jurisdiction itself, any vessel carrying an expedition like that of the *Creole*. The case of the *Virginius* was much less flagrant.[2]

Later the United States put itself upon unmistakable ground and declared "That American vessels on the high seas, in time of peace, bearing the American flag, remain under the jurisdiction of the country to which they belong, and therefore, any visitation, molestation, or detention of such vessel by force, or by the exhibition of force, on the part of a foreign power, is in derogation of the sovereignty of the United States."[3]

The next year Lopez led a third expedition in the steamer *Pampero*, which left New Orleans, without clearance, August 3, 1851, with 480 men, mostly Americans. His second and third

[1] House Ex. Doc. 83, 32 Cong., 1 Sess.

[2] Some publicists hold that Spain's position in the latter case, based upon the theory of self-defence, has much to be said for it, so far as the mere seizure of the ship is concerned. In the present case, however, there was no invading party aboard either ship. If the seizure was justifiable at Contoy, it would have been so anywhere and at any time later; an impossible supposition.

[3] Senate resolution, adopted June 16, 1858. This action was the result of the examination of vessels under the American flag, by British cruisers in search of slavers. See also note of Mr. Cass, secretary of state, to Lord Napier, British minister, April 10, 1858, and Lord Malmesbury, British foreign secretary to Mr. Dallas, American minister, June 8, 1858 (*Foreign Relations*, 1875, Part II, 1191), all being in agreement as to the principle of the Senate resolution.

in command were an exiled Hungarian, Pragay, and Colonel W. S. Crittenden, a member of a distinguished family in Kentucky, and who had served with distinction in the Mexican war. Besides Pragay, there were eight other Hungarians and nine Germans, nearly all of whom occupied leading positions; forty-nine of the expedition were Cubans.

After touching at Key West a landing was made on the night of August 11, 1851, at Playtas, some sixty miles west of Havana, and Lopez, with about 300 men, advanced some six miles to Las Pozas, leaving Colonel Crittenden with the remainder of the force in charge of the baggage. The ship was sent to Florida. Crittenden determining to join Lopez, was attacked on his way, August 13. He retreated to the landing place, whence fifty-two embarked in four boats found in the vicinity, with a vague idea of reaching the Florida coast. They were, however, picked up by a Spanish cruiser and carried to Havana. They were tried by a military court and executed as "pirates" August 16. Among these was Colonel Crittenden.

The main body, after an action August 21 with overwhelming Spanish forces, in which the latter lost heavily (among them a General Enna), was scattered in the forest. Many were killed by the troops, despite a proclamation by Captain-General José de la Concha offering quarter to those surrendering. Lopez was taken by the treachery of a Cuban countryman who had given him shelter, and was garroted at Havana, September 1. There remained but 226 of the 480 who had landed. Of these 135 were sent to Spain, September 8, under sentence of hard labor, leaving under like sentence 25 in hospital and 16 in prison for whom the transport had no room. All those left in Havana were finally released through the action of Commodore Parker, American commander-in-chief in the West Indies, who had been named by the President a special commissioner under the department of state to confer with the captain-general of Cuba. Parker reported: "My opinion is that the Creoles are not in a situation to throw off the Spanish yoke, even if they wished it, and that no invading force coming to this island can expect aid from them."[1]

[1] Commodore Parker to secretary of state, Flagship *Saranac*, Havana, September 12, 1851. Senate Doc., 32 Cong., 1 Sess., Vol. I, p. 33.

An earnest plea for the pardon of those sent to Spain was made through the American minister, at Madrid,[1] which the Spanish government wisely heeded, as removing what otherwise would have been an unending source of irritation; and early in 1852 word was conveyed by the Spanish minister to the department of state of their release.

The criminality of the expedition was condemned in strongest terms by the American government. "No individuals," said President Fillmore, in his annual message, December 2, 1851, "have a right to hazard the peace of the country, or to violate its laws, upon vague notions of altering, or reforming, governments in other states. . . . The government of the United States, at all times . . . has abstained, and has sought to restrain the citizens of the country, from entering into controversies between other powers, and to observe all the duties of neutrality. . . . In the administration of Washington, several laws were passed for this purpose." . . . These, as re-ennacted and strengthened in 1818, with the specific understanding that the action was mainly for the benefit of Spain, were quoted by the President with an expression of laudable pride in the fact that in this subject the United States had not followed but led.[2]

[1] Mr. Webster, secretary of state, to Mr. Barringer, minister, November 25, 1851. Webster, *Works*, VI, 513–517.

[2] It should not be forgotten that such expeditions were not entirely new elsewhere. Six expeditions are said to have been sent from London to the assistance of Venezuela at the end of 1817. All efforts to check illegal preparations for South American service in British ports "could not prevent an Irish and English brigade of two thousand, under one Colonel English, from sailing in June (1818) to reach the insurgent ports before August. And other expeditions sailed for South America at will." (*Recollections of a Service of Three Years . . . in the Republics of Venezuela and Colombia.* By an Officer of the Colombian Navy. 2 vols. London, 1828, I, 6–19; and G. L. Chesterton, *Narrative of Proceedings in Venezuela* . . . 1819 and 1820. London, 1820. Quoted by Paxson, *Independence of South American Republics*, 185.) The British foreign enlistment bill, introduced May 13, 1819, "avowedly based on the recent neutrality act of the United States," was bitterly opposed in Parliament, Sir James Mackintosh, one of the leading members, saying that he considered it "in no other light than as an enactment to repress the rising liberty of the South Americans, and to enable Spain to reimpose the yoke of tyranny which they were unable to bear, and which they had nobly shaken off and from which he trusted God they would finally be enabled to free themselves, whatever attempts were made by the ministers of this or any other country to countenance or assist their oppres-

The arrival at New Orleans of the *Crescent City*, August 21, with the news of the executions, created there, where there was so strong a sympathy with the movement, an intense excitement, with the result that a mob attacked the Spanish consulate, destroying the archives and the furniture, defacing the portrait of the Queen of Spain, and tearing to pieces the Spanish flag. The printing office of the Spanish newspaper, *La Union*, was completely destroyed, and ten Spanish coffee houses and cigar shops wholly or partially demolished. The riot was only suppressed by calling out the militia. The Spanish consul placed himself and the business of his office in the care of the British and French consuls.

The situation, following so immediately upon the difficulties caused by the expedition itself, was of course very serious. The Spanish minister called upon the American government for protection to Spanish citizens, and for satisfaction and indemnification to the sufferers.[1]

The absence from Washington through illness of Mr. Webster, the secretary of state, caused a delay in reply until November 13, when Webster characterized the outrages as "disgraceful acts, and a flagrant breach of duty and propriety," stating that the government "disapproves of them as seriously, and regrets them as deeply, as either Mr. Calderon or his government can possibly do; . . . but the outrage, nevertheless, was one perpetrated by a mob composed of irresponsible persons." All officials, whether national, state, or municipal, "did all which the suddenness of the occasion would allow to prevent it. The assembling of mobs happens in all countries; popular violences occasionally break out everywhere, . . . trampling on the rights of citizens and

sors." [Loud cheers.] (Hansard, First Series, XL, 367-368.) Strong petitions were sent to Parliament against the passage of the act. One was "subscribed by 1,700 of the most respectable individuals connected with the trade of London" (*Ibid.*, 858), a fact which shows how largely the South American question was, in Great Britain, a question of commerce. The resistance to the bill was only overborne by the energy of Canning, who, later, April 26, 1823, when there was a question of its repeal, paid the high compliment to the United States of saying: " If I wished for a guide in a system of neutrality, I should take that laid down by America in the days of the presidency of Washington and the secretaryship of Jefferson." (Hansard, New Series, VIII, 1056.)

[1] Señor Calderon de la Barca to department of state, September 5, 1851. Senate Docs., 32 Cong., 1 Sess., Vol. I, p. 44.

private men; and sometimes on those of public officers and private governments, especially entitled to protection. In these cases the public faith and national honor require, not only that such outrages should be disavowed, but also that the perpetrators of them should be punished, . . . and further that full satisfaction should be made in cases in which a duty to that effect rests with the government. . . . The government of the United States would earnestly deprecate any indignity offered in this country, in time of peace, to the flag of a nation so ancient, so respectable, so renowned as Spain. . . . Mr. Calderon expresses the opinion that not only ought indemnification to be made to Mr. Laborde, her Catholic Majesty's consul, for injury and loss of property, but that reparation is due . . . to those Spaniards . . . whose property was injured or destroyed by the mob; and intimates that such reparation had been verbally promised to him; . . . but while this government has manifested a willingness and determination to perform every duty which one friendly nation has a right to expect from another, in cases of this kind it supposes that the rights of the Spanish consul, a public officer residing here under the protection of the United States government, are quite different from those of the Spanish subjects who have come into the country to mingle with our own citizens, and here to pursue their private business and objects. The former may claim special indemnity; the latter are entitled to such protection as is afforded to our own citizens. . . . In conclusion . . . if Mr. Laborde shall return to his post, or any other consul for New Orleans shall be appointed . . . the officers of this government, resident in that city, will be instructed to receive and treat him with courtesy, and with a national salute to the flag of his ship, if he shall arrive in a Spanish vessel, as a demonstration of respect, such as may signify to him and to his government, the sense entertained by the government of the United States of the gross injustice done his predecessor by a lawless mob as well as the indignity and insult offered by it to a foreign state, with which the United States are, and wish ever to remain, on terms of the most respectful and pacific intercourse."[1]

[1] Daniel Webster, secretary of state, to the Spanish minister, November 13, 1851. (Senate Docs., 32 Cong., 1 Sess., Vol. I, 62-65. Webster, *Works*, VI, 507-512.) This despatch drew a compliment even from Palmerston, at the time British foreign minister. See Curtis, *Life of Webster*, II, 556.

An immediate result of the Lopez expeditions was concurrent action by France and England; announcement being made to the department of state, September 27, 1851, by Mr. Crampton, the British chargé d'affaires, that orders had been given to the British squadron in the West Indies "to prevent by force any adventurers of any nation from landing with hostile intent upon the island of Cuba," followed, October 8, by information from the French minister that like action had been taken by France.

That such surveillance should be submitted to by the United States was impossible. President Fillmore at once wrote Mr. Webster, who was at this time at Marshfield: "Any attempt to prevent such expeditions by British cruisers must necessarily involve a right of search into our whole mercantile marine in those seas . . . and [is] well calculated to disturb the friendly relations now existing." Webster replied that "this could never be submitted to."[1] The French minister, the Count de Sartiges, was informed by the department of state of the gravity with which such action was viewed.[2]

Acting upon the "anxious desire" of the Spanish government that, "through the friendly interest and influence of England, an abnegatory declaration on the part of France and the United States, and England of course, might be made with regard to Cuba,"[3] the British and French ministers at Washington presented identic notes, April 23, 1852, enclosing the draft of a triple agreement which declared that "the high contracting parties hereby severally and collectively disclaim, both now and for hereafter, all intention to obtain possession of the island of Cuba; and they respectively bind themselves to discountenance all attempt to that effect on the part of any power or individuals whatever.

"The high contracting parties declare, severally and collectively, that they will not obtain or maintain for themselves, or for any one of themselves, any exclusive control over the said island, nor assume nor exercise any dominion over the same."[4]

---

[1] Mr. Fillmore to Mr. Webster, October 2; Webster to Fillmore, October 4, 1851. Curtis, *Webster*, II, 551.

[2] Crittenden to De Sartiges, October 22, 1851, Senate Docs., 32 Cong., 1 Sess., I, 76.

[3] Lord Howden to Earl Granville, January 9, 1852, *British and Foreign State Papers*, XLIV.   [4] Senate Doc. 13, 32 Cong., 2 Sess.

Mr. Webster's note in reply was but little more than an acknowledgment of the reception of the proposal, in which he took pains to restate the position of the United States government in the words: "It has been stated, and often repeated, to the government of Spain by this government and under various administrations, not only that the United States have no design upon Cuba themselves, but that if Spain should refrain from a voluntary cession of the island to any other European power, she might rely on the countenance and friendship of the United States to assist her in the defence and preservation of that island." While stating that the President would take the communications into consideration and give them "his best reflections," he recalled that the policy of the United States "has been uniformly to avoid, as far as possible, alliances or agreements with other states, and to keep itself free from national obligations, except such as affect directly the interests of the United States themselves." [1]

After waiting two months, the subject was again brought forward by the British and French representatives in identic notes, July 8, 1852, which laid stress upon the indefeasibility of the Spanish title and the importance of the island with reference to the proposed isthmian canals and its permanent neutrality, which would be assured by the agreement proposed. The notes dwelt also upon the existing Spanish obligations to both countries, saying: "You are no doubt aware that British and French subjects, as well as the French government, are, on different accounts, creditors of Spain for large sums of money. The expense of keeping up an armed force in the island of Cuba of twenty-five thousand men is heavy, and obstructs the government of Spain in the efforts which they make to fulfil their pecuniary engagements. By putting an end to the state of apprehension which is the cause of those armaments, we should increase to Spain the means of meeting those engagements. This consideration is, no doubt, applicable more particularly to Spain, to England, and to France; but there are others which apply more generally to the commercial interests of all nations, and especially to the commercial interests of the United States, which are greater than those of any other nation in Cuba.

[1] Webster to British and French ministers, April 29, 1852. *Ibid.* Also *British and Foreign State Papers*, 44, 122. Moore, *Digest*, VI, 460.

One of these considerations is that, in the present state of things, we cannot reasonably expect Spain to take any measure toward lowering her tariff at Havana. . . . But if, by the guarantee of quiet possession which the proposed declaration of the great maritime powers would confer, Spain should be enabled to diminish her military force in Cuba, she might probably be induced to relieve foreign commerce there from the charges which now press upon it; and of this foreign commerce, as I have observed, the United States have by far the largest share." [1]

Before these could be answered Webster had become very ill; he died October 24, 1852, and the duty devolved upon Mr. Edward Everett who became the new secretary of state, and who, December 1, sent a note dealing with the subject at great length and with a completeness which ended the proposal. He recalled the large extensions of French dominion in the previous twenty years on the northern coast of Africa, and of England throughout the world in the previous fifty years, which had created no uneasiness on the part of the United States, and the acquisition of territory by the last, which had done nothing to disturb the powers of Europe. "But the case would be different in reference to the transfer of Cuba from Spain to any other European power. That event . . . could not but awaken alarm in the United States. . . . M. de Turgot [2] states that France could never see with indifference the possession of Cuba by *any* power but Spain, and explicitly declares that she has no wish or intention of appropriating the island to herself; and the English minister makes the same avowal on behalf of his government. M. de Turgot and Lord Malmesbury do the government of the United States no more than justice in remarking, that they have often pronounced themselves substantially in the same sense. The President does not covet the acquisition of Cuba for the United States; at the same time he considers the condition of Cuba mainly an American question. The proposed convention proceeds on a different principle. It assumes that the United States have no other or greater interest in the question than France or England. . . . No such convention would be viewed with favor by the Senate. Its certain rejection . . . would leave the question of Cuba in a more unsettled condition than

[1] Senate Doc. 13, 32 Cong., 2 Sess   [2] French foreign minister.

it is now, . . . it may well be doubted whether the constitution . . . would allow the treaty-making power to impose a permanent disability upon the . . . government for all coming time, and [referring to previous purchases of territory] prevent it . . . from doing what has been often done in times past. . . . The President . . . has no wish to disguise the feeling that the compact, though equal in terms, would be very unequal in substance. . . . The island of Cuba lies at our doors. It commands the approach to the Gulf of Mexico, which washes the shores of five of our states. It bars the entrance of that great river which drains half the North American continent. . . . It keeps watch at the doorway of our intercourse with California by the isthmus route. If an island like Cuba, belonging to the Spanish crown, guarded the entrance of the Thames and the Seine, and the United States should propose a convention like this to France and England, those powers would assuredly feel that the disability assumed by ourselves was far less serious than that which we asked them to assume. . . .

For domestic reasons . . . the President thinks that the incorporation of the island into the Union at the present time, although effected with the consent of Spain, would be a hazardous measure, and he would consider its acquisition by force, except in a just war with Spain, . . . as a disgrace to the civilization of the age. . . . He has thrown the whole force of his constitutional powers against all illegal attacks upon the island. It would have been perfectly easy . . . to allow projects of a formidable character to gather strength by connivance. No amount of obloquy at home, no embarrassments caused by the indiscretion of the colonial government of Cuba, have moved him from the path of duty in this respect. The captain-general of that island . . . has, on a punctilio in reference to the purser of a private steamship (who seems to have been entirely innocent of the matters laid to his charge), refused to allow the passengers and mails of the United States to be landed from a vessel having him on board. . . . The captain-general is not permitted by his government, three thousand miles off, to hold any diplomatic intercourse with the United States. He is subject in no degree to the direction of the Spanish minister at Washington; and the President has to choose between a resort to force, to compel the abandonment of this gratuitous interruption of commercial intercourse (which would result in war), and a delay of weeks and months, necessary for a negotiation with Madrid. . . .

That a convention such as is proposed would be a transitory arrangement, sure to be swept away by the irresistible tide of affairs in a new country, is . . . too obvious to require a labored argument. . . . Can it be for the interest of Spain to cling to a possession that can only be maintained by a garrison of twenty-five or thirty thousand troops, a powerful naval force, and an annual expenditure for both arms of the service of at least twelve millions of dollars? Cuba, at this moment, costs more to Spain than the entire naval and military establishment of the United States. . . .

"I will but allude to an evil of the first magnitude: I mean the African slave-trade . . . for which it is feared there is no hope of a complete remedy while Cuba remains a Spanish colony. . . .

"The President is convinced that the conclusion of such a treaty . . . would strike a death-blow to the conservative policy hitherto pursued in this country toward Cuba. No administration of this government . . . could stand a day under the odium of having stipulated with the great powers of Europe, that in no future time, under no change of circumstances, by no amicable arrangement with Spain, by no act of lawful war (should that calamity unfortunately occur), by no consent of the inhabitants of the island, should they, like the possessions of Spain on the American continent, succeed in rendering themselves independent; in fine, by no overruling necessity of self-preservation, should the United States ever make the acquisition of Cuba."[1]

This paper, somewhat over-rhetorical and of much length, is distinguished for the frankness and completeness of its exposition of American policy. The fact that Cuba, more than half a century later, is still not a part of the Union, is standing and forcible evidence of the honesty of its statements.

Lord John Russell, who had succeeded Lord Malmesbury as British foreign minister, replied, February 16, 1853. He indulged in some weak and unbecoming sarcasm as to its length and its historic detail. He closed: "While fully admitting the right of the United States to reject the proposal, . . . Great Britain must at once resume her entire liberty; and upon any occasion that

[1] Senate Ex. Doc. 13, 32 Cong., 2 Sess., Moore, *Digest*, VI, 460–470.

may call for it, be free to act, either singly or in conjunction with other powers, as to her may seem fit."

His reply, as also a similar one from the French government, was presented by Mr. Crampton, April 18, 1853, to Mr. Marcy, now secretary of state. The incident was mutually regarded as closed.[1]

A secondary result of the Lopez enterprise was an increased tyranny of conduct in Cuban affairs, and an exasperating interference with American shipping which was to last, in many phases, to the end of Spanish rule. The case recalled by Mr. Everett in his notes to the British and French ministers was that of the *Crescent City*, one of a line of mail steamers between New York and New Orleans, touching at Havana. The ships were commanded by officers of the navy, allowed leave for the purpose, the captain of the *Crescent City* being Lieutenant David D. Porter, later the distinguished admiral.

The captain-general, moved by an offensive article against the government of the island which he stated had appeared in one of the New York papers, though neither the article itself nor its character was ever specified by the Spanish authorities, on September 21, 1852, ordered that the purser, William Smith, of the *Crescent City*, whom he accused as the author, should not be allowed to land in Cuba, and "if, in future, said individual should return in any of the steamers of the company, or any other person employed on them should take the liberty to abuse in a similar manner the

[1] Mr. Everett, now in private life, felt called upon to make a personal reply of great length to Lord John Russell, which might as well have been left unmade. The principal point, beyond the iteration of much he had said in the previous paper, was to recall, in answer to certain banalities in Lord John's paper regarding "duty to our neighbors," the expedition of General Torrijos, in 1831, "fitted out in the Thames, without interruption till the last moment, and though it then fell under the grasp of the police, its members succeeded in escaping to Spain, where, for some time, they found shelter at Gibraltar. It is declared," said Everett, "in the last number of the *Quarterly Review* to be 'notorious that associations have been formed in London for the subversion of dynasties with which England is at peace; that arms have been purchased and loans proposed; that "Central Committees" issue orders from England, and that Messrs. Mazzini and Kossuth have established and preside over boards of regency for the Roman States and Hungary, and for the promotion of revolution in every part of the world.'" (Everett's pamphlet, *Correspondence on the Proposed Tripartite Convention Relative to Cuba*, Little, Brown and Company, 1853, in which appears the whole correspondence).

privileges that the Spanish authorities offer him in the ports of this island, this sole act will be sufficient not to allow entry to the vessel conveying him, whatsoever the losses may be that such a measure may accrue to the company; for although the company may not have it in their power to prevent their subordinates from committing such excesses, their honor and interest must immediately oblige them to immediately withdraw their trust from any one that should attempt to compromit them foolishly." [1]

It would be difficult to cite a more childish exhibition of autocratic and irresponsible power than this order afforded. On October 3 the *Crescent City*, on her arrival at Havana, was peremptorily ordered to leave the port, and was not allowed to land either her mails or the sixty-five passengers she had aboard from New York for Cuba. On her return from New Orleans, October 14, she entered the port, but was again obliged to leave without communicating.

The order was suspended on the ship's arrival, November 16, from New Orleans, but the captain was informed that she would be positively excluded on her return from New York, should Purser Smith be aboard.[2]

The reception of an affidavit from Smith, an old and respected officer of the company, that he was entirely innocent of the offence charged, a copy of which the American secretary of state weakly sent to the Spanish minister,[3] caused a revocation of the order.

The remonstrance made to Spain by the American government before this could be known had brought from the former an emphatic approval of the course of the captain-general, as necessary in the situation of the island, " constantly menaced with invasion by bands of adventurers, who collect in the United States, who there conspire, who there distribute arms and money, who there print incendiary libels, and who, united with some Cubans proscribed by the laws as traitors to the laws of their country, exert themselves to light up the fire of sedition." [4]

The American minister correctly measured the situation when

---

[1] House Ex. Doc. 86, 33 Cong., 1 Sess., 7. [2] *Ibid.*, 14.
[3] Everett to Calderon de la Barca, November 15, 1852, *Ibid.*, 36.
[4] Señor Manuel Bertran de Lis, Spanish secretary of state, to Mr. Barringer, American minister, December 8, 1852, *Ibid.*, 54.

he said: "The policy of the Spanish government, as far as the same can be carried out without an actual interruption of peaceful relations, will be that of non-intercourse between our people and the island of Cuba. . . . The difficulties of adjusting all commercial questions with a people and government so wedded to antiquated and obsolete ideas, may well be inferred from the recent correspondence . . . on the subject of the refusal of [Spain] to . . . place American shipping in the Peninsula and adjacent islands on a footing with that of other nations. The tone assumed, and the policy pursued, toward the United States, . . . may be fairly attributed not only to their devotion to ancient prejudices and notions of government and their want of a true knowledge of our people and institutions, but to expectations of foreign aid for the security of the island of Cuba to the Spanish crown, in the event of a rupture with the United States." [1]

The American minister energetically protested against the exclusion of "any American vessel from the ports of Cuba because she may have one objectionable person on board . . . more especially when that vessel partakes of a public character, by being employed by the government of the United States for the transportation and delivery of the public mail, and is commanded by an officer of the war marine for that purpose. . . . Such a course is a gross violation of that international comity on which is founded almost all commercial intercourse." [2]

The United States executive was directing its efforts, however, against a practically irresponsible authority. Its weakness in not pressing the Spanish government to a disclaimer of the captain-general's conduct in the case of the *Crescent City* had its natural effect in a continuance of like unjustifiable interference with the ordinary and necessary movements of shipping, the mail steamer *Ohio*, for example, from Colon to New York, belonging to a line which at this period was almost the only means of communication with California, being detained nearly three days on putting into Havana for coal, on April 10, 1853, without being able to communicate with the shore. The ship carried the mails, had on board

---

[1] Mr. Barringer to Mr. Everett, December 14, 1852, *House Ex. Doc.* 86, 33 *Cong.*, 1 *Sess.*, 54.
[2] Mr. Barringer to Spanish minister of state, December 12, 1852, *Ibid.*, 57.

four hundred and fifty-six passengers, some fifty of whom were expecting to land at Havana to proceed thence to New Orleans, and two and a half millions of dollars in gold. She had a clean bill of health, and the health officers who came alongside, but not aboard, were informed that the only sick were some few cases of the ordinary Panama malarial fever.

Without making any further investigation, the captain was ordered to remain where he was, not to approach the coal wharf, and not to communicate in any way with the shore. An armed guard was stationed to prevent any passengers from leaving the ship, and the captain was refused permission even to send a letter to the consul. Permission was given to coal from lighters, the small force of the ship only to be employed. The ship, however, was finally set at liberty by the volunteering of a Spanish naval surgeon to come aboard and make a personal examination and assure the authorities as to the safety of the conditions.[1]

The procedure of the authorities in this instance, though showing a high-handed disregard of the ordinary comity which should facilitate the movements of the ships of a friendly power, was evidently the outcome of unreasoning fear, as shown in the failure of the health officers to examine the ship. The protest of the American government, however, but brought a statement from the Spanish minister of state, who, referring to a phrase used by the American minister, said that "the only analogy which, for my part, I encounter between these two cases [of the *Crescent City* and the *Ohio*] is, that in the case of the *Crescent City* the government of your excellency recognized explicitly, as I flatter myself it will on this occasion, the right of the captain-general of the island of Cuba *to take, by virtue of the powers with which he is invested, whatsoever measure, however restrictive may be its character, which he may consider necessary for the preservation of the island whose government is given him in charge.*"[2] The captain-general was thus declared above the law, either municipal or international. It is not to be wondered at that with such powers, and in face of the weakness which had been exhibited by the American

---

[1] *House Ex. Doc.* 86, 33 *Cong.*, 1 *Sess.*, 87.

[2] General Lersundi, minister of state, to Mr. Barringer, June 15, 1853, *Ibid.*, 89. (Italics in original.)

government in the cases of the *Georgiana* and *Susan Loud* and in that of the *Crescent City*, American vessels should be continued to be fired upon, boarded, and sometimes searched on the high seas, as had already occurred in the case of the mail steamer *Falcon*, August 16, 1851,[1] and was to occur, March 31, 1853, in the case of the ship *Harriet*. Ignorance, despotic authority, and a total disregard of international usage and right, seem at this time to have characterized the conduct of the Spanish government toward the United States, both in the Peninsula and in Cuba.

[1] House Ex. Doc. 86, 33 Cong., 1 Sess., 129.

CHAPTER XIII

THE CASE OF THE BLACK WARRIOR: THE OSTEND MANIFESTO

PIERRE SOULÉ, French in birth and rearing; an exiled revolutionist who had come to New Orleans; who had thriven in its Gallic atmosphere, and had become United States senator from Louisiana, was now appointed minister to Spain. His attitude toward the French government, not only in earlier days, but later, when he was accused of holding communication with the new emperor's adversaries;[1] his avowed sympathy with the filibusters shown in a speech in the Senate just before his appointment;[2] the speeches made in Washington in reply to felicitations, and in New York when, cheered and serenaded just before sailing by a vast crowd in which were several Cuban revolutionary associations,[3] made his appointment a wholly improper one, and one to which the Spanish government could most justly have objected.

At no time in American history did the pro-slavery leaders feel themselves more firmly seated; the Mexican war, a distinctively Southern war, had been brought to a triumphant conclusion; Texas had been secured, and there was now a distinct policy of further territorial extension to increase slave territory, and this French "fire-eater," with as little of the American in his mental and psychic make-up as could well be found, was sent to represent the United States at a point where he could only arouse distrust and antagonism, with the hope, on the part of those who caused his appointment by the President, that the threatening bluster which was part of his character would succeed in carrying out their views as to Cuba. An indication of what was to come was given in the speech prepared for his audience on presentation of his credentials, which contained such allusions to other powers

---

[1] Moore, *International Law Digest*, IV, 558.
[2] The speech was made January 25, 1853.
[3] Sedano, *Estudios Politicos*, 119.

that he was requested by the Spanish minister of state to modify it. He thus delivered, on his presentation at the end of October, 1853, a short, and what he called in his despatch communicating the event, an "emasculated and insipid harangue," well satisfied, however, to have been received at all, as he remarks of his presentation that "the strange, though altogether unaccountable, emotion created by my appearance here in the official character which I hold, has happily subsided, and I may now address you, free from the anxiety which I had been, for some time past, laboring under, in anticipation of the obstacles which it was supposed my admittance at this court would have to encounter."[1]

While Soulé's appointment was of this objectionable character, the instructions from Mr. Marcy, July 23, 1853, differed but little in tenor from those of so many of his predecessors in the office of secretary of state. "Nothing will be done," said Mr. Marcy, as to Cuba, "on our part to disturb its present connection with Spain, unless the character of that connection should be so changed as to affect our present or prospective security. While the United States would resist at every hazard the transference of Cuba to any European nation, they would exceedingly regret to see Spain resorting to any power for assistance to uphold her rule over it. . . . While Spain remains, in fact as well as in name, the sovereign of Cuba, she can depend upon our maintaining our duty as a neutral nation toward her, however difficult it may be. . . . Under certain conditions the United States might be willing to purchase [Cuba]; but it is scarcely expected that you will find Spain, should you attempt to ascertain her views upon the subject, at all inclined to enter into such a negotiation. There is reason to believe that she is under obligations to Great Britain and France not to transfer the island to the United States. . . . The sort of joint protest by England and France against some of the views presented in Mr. Everett's letter of the 2d of December would alone be satisfactory proof of such an arrangement. . . . In the present aspect of the case, the President does not deem it proper to authorize you to make any proposition for the purchase of that island. . . . The United States would cordially favor . . . a vol-

[1] For both addresses, see House Ex. Doc. 93, 33 Cong., 2 Sess. (Vol. X), p. 12.

untary separation and, if necessary to effect it, would be willing to contribute something more substantial than their good-will toward an object so desirable to them. . . . On this interesting subject this department is very desirous of obtaining early and full information. . . . On the supposition that no change is to take place in the relations between Spain and Cuba—that arbitrary power by the former is for some time to repress discontent in the latter—this government has a right to demand exemption from the annoyances which are likely to result from such a condition of things. Our flag must be respected, and our commerce relieved from embarrassment by the Cuban authorities. The United States will not submit to have their merchant vessels, though in the vicinity of that island, searched or detained on their lawful voyages. . . . If the unquiet condition of Cuba has rendered it necessary, in the judgment of Spain, to adopt harsh and stringent measures, . . . she is bound to take every precaution to prevent the evils of such a policy from reaching the citizens of other governments. Our past experience shows that when such is the case, these evils are aggravated by the embarrassments thrown in the way of obtaining redress. The captain-general is not vested with the power of holding political intercourse with the governments or consuls of the injured or complaining party . . . it seems to be almost necessary that there should be allowed a qualified diplomatic intercourse between the captain-general of that island and our consul at Havana in order to prevent difficulties, and preserve a good understanding between the two countries." [1]

In the same month Mr. Buchanan, now the American minister to Great Britain, was instructed "to ascertain as fully as possible the views of the British government in regard to Cuba, and what arrangement, if any, she has entered into or contemplates with Spain, either by herself or conjointly with France, relative to that island." He was also directed to bring to the notice of the British government the continuance of the slave-trade. He was told that "in spite of all that has been promised by Spain, and all that has been done by other powers to suppress [it], the possession of Cuba by Spain favors its continuance, and is a formidable obstacle to its suppression." [2]

[1] In full, House Ex. Doc. 93, 33 Cong., 2 Sess.   [2] *Ibid.*, p. 8.

The apprehensions of the American government were natural in view of the sympathetic relations of France and Great Britain, not only in the subject of Cuba, but in general policy, as soon to be shown by allied action in war. The pressure of England upon Spain for a guarantee to long-outstanding Spanish bonds held by British subjects was ominous, and it was known that the interest of the British government in suppressing the continued traffic in Cuba in African slaves and in freeing those already there was not wholly altruistic, such suppression and freedom being considered as "a most powerful element of resistance to any scheme for annexing Cuba to the United States, where slavery exists." [1]

In 1853, however, the British government took a higher plane, and the question of the abolition of the slave-trade was treated apart from that of freeing the slaves already in Cuba, the British ambassador in Spain being informed that "whatever may be the interests of this country [England] not to see Cuba in the hands of any other power than Spain; yet in the eyes of the people of this country the destruction of a trade which conveys the natives of Africa to become slaves in Cuba will furnish a large compensation for such a transfer. For such an exhibition of public feeling the government of Spain should be prepared." [2]

Soulé found the Spanish government "ill inclined to favor any policy which might tend to bring Spain to a closer connection with the United States." The much-desired commercial treaty was impossible. The foreign minister, Calderon, was "no less opposed" to any alteration in the relations between the captain-general of Cuba and the American consul at Havana.[3] Soulé struck, however, upon at least one truth. "France, for reasons unknown to me, is as much opposed as England herself to Cuba becoming ours. She may dissemble for a time and hush down her antipathies; but as long as she bends her neck under the yoke of the man who now holds the rod over her, she will be our enemy

---

[1] Lord Palmerston, British foreign minister, to British ambassador at Madrid, May, 1851, *British and Foreign State Papers*, XLII, quoted by Latané, *Diplom. Rel. U. S. and Span. America*, 125.

[2] Lord John Russell to Lord Howden, January 31, 1853, *British and Foreign State Papers*, XLII, 335.

[3] House Ex. Doc. 93, 33 Cong., 2 Sess., 15.

and join in any crusade which may be set on foot against us."[1] He scented the schemes of the second empire which had now just been established, and which were to culminate in Mexico, though he was ignorant of their form.

Soulé's opportunity for treating the Spanish government forcibly was, however, soon to come in the seizure of the *Black Warrior*, one of a line of mail steamers between New York and Mobile, of which Havana was a port of call for landing and taking passengers and mails, but no cargo. It was an act even more unaccountable and foolish than any of those, so rasping and unnecessary, which had preceded it.

It is clear, from a sifting of all the evidence, that these ships were accustomed to enter the cargo in transit as "ballast," by direction of the collector,[2] and this had been done through the entire period of the *Black Warrior's* eighteen months' service on the line, during which she had touched thirty-six times at Havana. On the morning of February 27, 1854, on arrival of the ship from Mobile, the crew list, bill of health, separate lists of the passengers for Havana and those in transit, together with a manifest, upon which was specified all the ship's stores, the cargo of cotton in transit being entered as "ballast," was handed to the boarding officer, and the ship hauled alongside the coal wharf to coal. Later in the day, on applying to the custom-house for the usual pass obtained for leaving port, the clerk sent by the agent was informed that the ship would not be allowed to sail, as she was entered as "in ballast," whereas the authorities knew that she had cotton on board. Application, made well within the hours allowed for permission to make the proper alteration in the manifest, was refused, though the law was explicit as to this privilege,[3] and the captain and agent were informed that the cargo of the ship was confiscated and must be discharged. On the morning of February 28 lighters were brought alongside by the chief of the custom-house officers afloat, and the captain directed to dis-

---

[1] Soulé to Marcy, December 23, 1853, H. Ex. Doc. 93, 33 Cong., 2 Sess., 16.
[2] Marcy to Soulé, June 22, 1854, *Ibid.*, 110.
[3] Affidavit of Chas. Tyng (agent) and James D. Bullock (commander), *Ibid.*, p. 47. See also *Rules* for captains and supercargoes in full, *Ibid.*, pp. 42–44.

charge his cargo, which the latter refused to do. He was informed by the Spanish official in charge that he would himself discharge the cargo, whereupon Captain Bullock, hauling down his flag, left the ship, the property on board, her officers, crew, and passengers, in the hands of the Spanish authorities and went aboard the United States steamer *Fulton*, Bullock himself being an officer of the navy,[1] as were, as already mentioned, several other commanding officers of the line.

It is impossible to find in any part of the voluminous correspondence of either side, in this remarkable case, an excuse or an impelling motive for the Spanish action, except mere whim. The usage of a year and a half, during all which time it was impossible to think that the authorities should suppose that the steamer was really in ballast only, was suddenly and rudely set aside, with great loss to her owners and inconvenience and injury to the passengers. The news was received with natural and just indignation in the United States, and the case immediately and necessarily became one of first importance.

In compliance with a resolution of the House of Representatives, March 10, 1854, President Pierce transmitted, March 15, all the information in the department of state with reference to the *Black Warrior*, with a message saying: "There have been, in the course of a few years past, many other instances of aggression upon our commerce, violations of the rights of American citizens, and insults to the national flag by the Spanish authorities in Cuba, and all attempts to obtain redress have led to protracted and, as yet, fruitless negotiations. . . . The offending party is at our doors with large powers for aggression, but none, it is alleged, for reparation. The source of redress is in another hemisphere; and the answers to our just complaints, made to the home government, are but the repetition of excuses rendered by inferior officials to their superiors in reply to representations of misconduct. . . . Spain does not seem to appreciate, to its full extent, her responsibility for the conduct of these authorities. In giving very extraordinary powers to them, she owes it to justice and to her friendly relations with this government to guard with

---

[1] Captain Bullock was later to become notable as the chief agent in England of the Southern confederacy.

great vigilance against the exorbitant exercise of these powers, and, in case of injuries, to provide for prompt redress. . . . It is vain to expect that a series of unfriendly acts infringing our commercial rights, and the adoption of a policy threatening the honor and security of these states, can long consist with friendly relations. In case the measures taken for amicable adjustment of our difficulties with Spain shall unfortunately fail, I shall not hesitate to use the authority and means which Congress may grant to insure the observance of our just rights, to obtain redress for injuries received and to vindicate the honor of our flag. In anticipation of that contingency, which I earnestly hope may not arise, I suggest to Congress the propriety of adopting such provisional measures as the exigency may seem to demand." [1]

It is, as the message expresses, extraordinary that the Cuban authorities should have been allowed by the home government to bring the two countries to the verge of war by conduct so unnecessary and so unfriendly, and which could result in good to neither. In all the long category of causes for complaint there is none in which the offending party showed so little of that blessed quality, common-sense; it was but playing into the hands of the now powerful and dominant slavery party of the South.

For want of time an intimation only of this serious difficulty was sent Mr. Soulé in a despatch of March 11, 1854, followed on March 17 by the full statement carried to Madrid by a special messenger. This latter said: "Neither the views of this government nor the sentiments of this country will brook any evasion or delay on the part of her Catholic Majesty, in a case of such flagrant wrong. . . . The damages to the owners of the *Black Warrior* and the cargo are estimated at three hundred thousand dollars, and this amount you will demand as the indemnity . . . you will obtain as early a reply as practicable to your demand. The messenger . . . has instructions to remain a reasonable time at Madrid in order that he may be the bearer of the reply you may receive. . . . The course hitherto pursued by the Spanish government, in regard to our complaints, . . . will not meet the exigency of this case. That course has, in effect, been an evasion of our claims for redress, and resulted in a practical denial of justice. . . .

[1] Message, House Ex. Doc. 93, 33 Cong., 2 Sess., 33–34.

It is expected that Spain will be prepared, when you shall present the demand, to apprise this government of the course she intends to pursue in this matter; and that course will be either a disavowal of the acts of her officials at [in] Cuba, and an immediate tender of satisfaction, or the assumption of the responsibility of upholding their conduct. In a matter of such high import, involving her amicable relations with this country, it is not to be assumed that she has not a full knowledge of the acts of her subordinate officers at Havana." [1]

Such expectancy was not realized. The course of Spanish officialdom was of Oriental slowness, a policy of delay; and when Mr. Soulé, on April 8, 1854, the day after the arrival of the bearer of the despatch, placed the subject before the Spanish minister, the latter had not yet received any information in the matter from the Marquis de Polavieja, the new Captain-General of Cuba. While Mr. Soulé's note was sharp in tone, it was not unjustifiably so. [2]

Waiting three days without a reply, Mr. Soulé, April 11, struck a higher note. He repeated what he had orally stated, that the wrong "bearing upon its face the most glaring evidences of a preconcerted purpose on the part of its perpetrators to harass and offend legitimate interests and high susceptibilities, the United States cannot brook that the reparation due them for the insult offered to their flag and the injury done to the property of their citizens, be in any way evaded or unnecessarily delayed." He then continued, "I must, therefore, insist that those who have been wronged receive an indemnity equal to their losses, namely, three hundred thousand dollars; and that all persons, whatever be their official rank or importance, who have, in any responsible manner, been concerned in the perpetration of the wrong, be dismissed from her majesty's service in the offices they now hold. The noncompliance with these just demands within forty-eight hours after the delivery of this communication into the hands of your excellency, will be considered by the government of the United States as equivalent to a declaration that her majesty's government is determined to uphold the conduct of its officers." [3]

[1] Mr. Marcy to Mr. Soulé, March 17, 1854, House Ex. Doc. 93, 33 Cong., 2 Sess., 32. [2] *Ibid.*, 69. [3] *Ibid.*, 70.

On the day this was written came a reply to the first note, stating that the government was not in possession of the "authentic and complete data, which in good law are indispensable in order to form a correct and equitable judgment of the case." Soulé replied by practically accusing the minister of duplicity. He said that "it is known that letters have been received in Madrid, more than three days since, with Havana dates up to the 13th" of March.[1]

On April 12 the Spanish minister replied again that "whenever the government shall have before it the authentic and complete data, which it lacks at present, it will propose to her majesty a resolution conformable to justice." Señor Calderon went on to say that it would not be surprising "that a manner so peremptory of exacting satisfaction, without listening to the defence of the accused, should suggest to the government of her majesty a suspicion that it is not so much the manifestation of a lively interest in the defence of pretended injuries, as an incomprehensible pretext for exciting estrangement, if not a quarrel, between two friendly powers. . . . Permit me, in conclusion, to impress upon the mind of your excellency that the government of her majesty, jealous also of its decorum, is not accustomed to the harsh and imperious manner with which it has been pressed; which, furthermore, is not the most adequate for attaining to the amicable settlement which is wished for."[2]

Soulé, though perhaps somewhat more precipitate than policy called for, was justified in pressing the matter forcibly by the instructions he had but just received from the secretary of state; but the justification for further pressure for the indemnity was almost at once removed by the action of the owners themselves in submitting to a fine, from which they were later released, and by their taking over the ship, thus enabling the Spanish minister to reply rather exultingly that "the delay . . . has been very quickly justified by events, if the recently received accounts are certain, although unofficial, that the *Black Warrior* had already been delivered to her captain, and thus the principal difficulty was arranged."[3]

[1] House Ex. Doc. 93, 33 Cong., 2 Sess., 72.
[2] Señor Calderon de la Barca to Mr. Soulé, April 12, 1854, *Ibid.*, 73–74.
[3] Señor Calderon de la Barca to Mr. Soulé, April 18, 1854, *Ibid.*, 75.

The Cuban authorities had negotiated directly with the steamship company, conceding privileges theretofore denied, and of more value, perhaps, than their estimate of losses by the detention of the ship;[1] but that such an arrangement removed "the principal difficulty" was, and correctly, far from Mr. Soulé's view. He replied, April 20, "However grievous the outrage perpetrated on the captain and owners of the *Black Warrior* may be, it sinks into insignificance when compared with the insult offered to the dignity of the nation whose colors it bore."[2]

It was not until May 7 that the subject was dealt with at length by the Spanish foreign office by citation of law already well known to all concerned, the letter of which condemned the ship; by a statement, impossible to uphold, that neither the captain "nor the consignee sought to make additions to the false manifest within the legal period of time," and by the rather childlike statement that the fact "that the *Black Warrior* had been several times [thirty-six] permitted to arrive with cargo and to declare herself in ballast, would only seem to prove the credence which was given to her declaration, or the condescension of some of the subordinate officers, which cannot be adduced as an evidence that the regulations had become extinct."[3]

But the tempest had already been swallowed by designs held more important by the American administration than this very gross outrage. The Crimean war had come to remove any apprehension of serious intervention in Cuba, by Great Britain or France, and the American government felt free to act. The secretary of state thus sent, in April, by a special messenger, a confidential despatch dwelling upon the fears of the United States that certain new regulations introducing laborers under a system of apprenticeship, would result in Africanizing Cuba, and empowering the American minister to open anew the question of its sale to the United States, or, if "the pride of Spain might revolt at the proposition to sell the island . . . to a foreign power, it has been

---

[1] Mr. Soulé to Mr. Marcy, May 10, 1854, House Ex. Doc. 93, 33 Cong., 2 Sess., 84.   [2] *Ibid.*, 77.
[3] *Ibid.*, 87. For a complete reply to this document, see Mr. Marcy's despatch No. 16, June 22, 1854, to Mr. Soulé, *Ibid.*, 108–117.

suggested that she might be induced to consent to its independence, and that the United States might essentially contribute to such a result."[1]

No step, however, could be taken in Madrid at the moment, and Mr. Soulé was much concerned as to the silence of the administration in the affair of the *Black Warrior*. His complaints of its position had much justification. "Spain," he said, "doubts no longer but that she has little to fear from our resentment."[2] Soulé wrote of the strange and discrepant impressions produced . . . by the President's proclamation of May 31, 1854, against filibusters, and by the announced departure from the United States of commissioners having charge to reconcile the differences between the Spanish and American governments.[3] The rumor of the commission had a good base, though Soulé was only informed of the fact by a despatch from Washington of the same date as the letter just quoted.[4]

The project of a commission to Madrid was abandoned, but Mr. Marcy was perplexed by the differing reports made to him by the American representatives in Madrid, Paris, and London, regarding the purposes of Spain, France, and Great Britain concerning Cuba. Therefore the President suggested, and it was arranged, that the American ministers to those nations should meet elsewhere in conference and give their combined views.[5] The result was the extraordinary document which has come down in history as the "Ostend manifesto."

The American minister to Great Britain at this period was, as mentioned, Mr. Buchanan, of Pennsylvania; to France, Mr. John T. Mason, of Virginia. The former was already fully committed to the support of the proposal to purchase;[6] the latter, as a strong pro-slavery advocate, was naturally of like mind. The three ministers met, as finally agreed upon, at Ostend, Belgium,

---

[1] Mr. Marcy to Mr. Soulé, April 3, 1854, House Ex. Doc. 93, 33 Cong., 2 Sess., 80–82.
[2] Mr. Soulé to Mr. Marcy, June 19, 1854, *Ibid.*, 106.
[3] Mr. Soulé to Mr. Marcy, June 24, 1854, *Ibid.*, 107.
[4] *Ibid.*, 117.
[5] Mr. Marcy to Mr. Soulé, August 16, 1854, *Ibid.*, 124.
[6] See Mr. Buchanan's despatch, when secretary of state, to Mr. Saunders, June 17, 1848, *Supra*, 221–223.

October 9, 1854, remained there until October 11, and then went to Aix-la-Chapelle, whence, October 18, their report was sent. It is in full as follows:

AIX-LA-CHAPELLE, *October* 15, 1854.

SIR:—

The undersigned, in compliance with the wish expressed by the President in the several confidential despatches you have addressed to us, respectively, to that effect, have met in conference, first at Ostend, in Belgium, on the 9th, 10th, and 11th instants, and then at Aix-la-Chapelle, in Prussia, on the days next following, up to the date hereof.

There has been a full and unreserved interchange of views and sentiments between us, which we are most happy to inform you has resulted in a cordial coincidence of opinion on the grave and important subjects submitted to our consideration.

We have arrived at the conclusion, and are thoroughly convinced, that an immediate and earnest effort ought to be made by the government of the United States to purchase Cuba from Spain at any price for which it can be obtained, not exceeding the sum of $.[1]

The proposal should, in our opinion, be made in such a manner as to be presented through the necessary diplomatic forms to the Supreme Constituent Cortes about to assemble. On this momentous question, in which the people both of Spain and the United States are so deeply interested, all our proceedings ought to be open, frank, and public. They should be of such a character as to challenge the approbation of the world.

We firmly believe that, in the progress of human events, the time has arrived when the vital interests of Spain are as seriously involved in the sale, as those of the United States in the purchase of the island, and that the transaction will prove equally honorable to both nations.

Under these circumstances we cannot anticipate a failure, unless possibly through the malign influence of foreign powers who possess no right whatever to interfere in the matter.

We proceed to state some of the reasons which have brought us to this conclusion, and, for the sake of clearness, we shall specify them under two distinct heads:—

1. The United States ought, if practicable, to purchase Cuba with as little delay as possible.

2. The probability is great that the government and Cortes of Spain will prove willing to sell it, because this would essentially promote the highest and best interests of the Spanish people.

Then 1. It must be clear to every reflecting mind that, from the peculiarity of its geographical position, and the considerations attendant on it, Cuba is as necessary to the North American republic as any of its present members, and that it belongs naturally to that great family of states of which the Union is the providential nursery.

[1] Left blank.

From its locality it commands the mouth of the Mississippi and the immense and annually increasing trade which must seek this avenue to the ocean.

On the numerous navigable streams, measuring an aggregate course of some thirty thousand miles, which disembogue themselves through this river into the Gulf of Mexico, the increase of the population within the last ten years amounts to more than that of the entire Union at the time Louisiana was annexed to it.

The natural and main outlet to the products of this entire population, the highway of their direct intercourse with the Atlantic and Pacific states, can never be secure, but must ever be endangered whilst Cuba is a dependency of a distant power in whose possession it has proved to be a source of constant annoyance and embarrassment to their interests.

Indeed the Union can never enjoy repose, nor possess reliable security, as long as Cuba is not embraced within its boundaries.

Its immediate acquisition by our government is of paramount importance, and we cannot doubt but that it is a consummation devoutly wished for by its inhabitants.

The intercourse which its proximity to our coasts begets and encourages between them and the citizens of the United States has, in the progress of time, so united their interests and blended their fortunes that they now look upon each other as if they were one people and had but one destiny.

Considerations exist which render delay in the acquisition of this island exceedingly dangerous to the United States.

The system of immigration and labor, lately organized within its limits, and the tyranny and oppression which characterize its immediate rulers, threaten an insurrection at every moment which may result in direful consequences to the American people.

Cuba has thus become to us an unceasing danger, and a permanent cause of anxiety and alarm.

But we need not enlarge on these topics. It can scarcely be apprehended that foreign powers, in violation of international law, would interpose their influence with Spain to prevent our acquisition of the island. Its inhabitants are now suffering under the worst of all possible governments—that of absolute despotism delegated by a distant power to irresponsible agents, who are changed at short intervals, and who are tempted to improve the brief opportunity thus afforded to accumulate fortunes by the basest means.

As long as this system shall endure, humanity may in vain demand the suppression of the African slave-trade in the island. This is rendered impossible whilst that infamous traffic remains an irresistible temptation and a source of immense profit to needy and avaricious officials, who, to attain their ends, scruple not to trample the most sacred principles under foot.

The Spanish government, at home, may be well disposed, but experience has proved that it cannot control these remote depositaries of its power.

Besides, the commercial nations of the world cannot fail to perceive and appreciate the great advantages which would result to their people from a dissolution of the forced and unnatural connection between Spain and Cuba, and the annexation of the latter to the United States. The trade of England and France with Cuba would, in that event, assume at once an important and profitable character, and rapidly extend with the increasing population and prosperity of the island.

2. But if the United States and every commercial nation would be benefited by this transfer, the interests of Spain would also be greatly and essentially promoted.

She cannot but see what such a sum of money as we are willing to pay for the island would effect in the development of her vast natural resources.

Two-thirds of this sum, if employed in the construction of a system of railroads, would ultimately prove a source of greater wealth to the Spanish people than that opened to their vision by Cortes. Their prosperity would date from the ratification of the treaty of cession.

France has already constructed continuous lines of railway from Havre, Marseilles, Valenciennes, and Strasbourg via Paris, to the Spanish frontier, and anxiously awaits the day when Spain shall find herself in a condition to extend these roads through her northern provinces to Madrid, Seville, Cadiz, Malaga, and the frontiers of Portugal.

This object once accomplished, Spain would become a centre of attraction for the travelling world, and secure a permanent and profitable market for her various productions. Her fields, under the stimulus given to industry by remunerative prices, would teem with cereal grain, and her vineyards would bring forth a vastly increased quantity of choice wines. Spain would speedily become what a bountiful Providence intended she should be—one of the first nations of continental Europe—rich, powerful, and contented.

Whilst two-thirds of the price of the island would be ample for the completion of her most important public improvements, she might, with the remaining forty millions, satisfy the demands pressing so heavily upon her credit, and create a sinking-fund which would gradually relieve her from the overwhelming debt now paralyzing her energies.

Such is her present wretched financial condition that her best bonds are sold upon her own Bourse at about one-third of their par value; whilst another class, on which she pays no interest, have but a nominal value, and are quoted at about one-sixth of the amount for which they were issued. Besides, these are held principally by British creditors, who may, from day to day, obtain the effective interposition of their government for the purpose of coercing payment. Intimations to that effect have already been thrown out from high quarters, and unless some new source of revenue shall enable Spain to provide for such exigencies, it is not improbable that they may be realized.

Should Spain reject the present golden opportunity for developing her resources, and removing her financial embarrassments, it may never again return.

Cuba, in its palmiest days, never yielded her exchequer, after deducting the expenses of its government, a clear annual income of more than a million and a half of dollars. These expenses have increased to such a degree as to leave a deficit chargeable on the treasury of Spain to the amount of six hundred thousand dollars.

In a pecuniary point of view, therefore, the island is an incumbrance, instead of a source of profit to the mother country.

Under no probable circumstances can Cuba ever yield to Spain one per cent. on the large amount which the United States are willing to pay for its acquisition. But Spain is in danger of losing Cuba without remuneration.

Extreme oppression, it is now admitted, justifies any people in endeavoring to relieve themselves from the yoke of their oppressors. The sufferings which the corrupt, arbitrary, and unrelenting local administration necessarily entails upon the inhabitants of Cuba, cannot fail to stimulate and keep alive that spirit of resistance and revolution against Spain which has, of late years, been so often manifested. In this condition of affairs it is in vain to expect that the sympathies of the people of the United States will not be warmly enlisted in favor of their oppressed neighbors.

We know that the President is justly inflexible in his determination to execute the neutrality laws; but should the Cubans themselves rise in revolt against the oppression which they suffer, no human power could prevent the citizens of the United States and liberal-minded men of other countries from rushing to their assistance. Besides, the present is an age of adventure, in which restless and daring spirits abound in every portion of the world.

It is not improbable, therefore, that Cuba may be wrested from Spain by a successful revolution; and, in that event, she will lose both the island and the price we are willing now to pay for it—a price far beyond what was ever paid by one people to another for any province.

It may also be remarked that the settlement of this vexed question, by the cession of Cuba to the United States, would forever prevent the dangerous complications between nations, to which it may otherwise give birth.

It is certain that, should the Cubans themselves organize an insurrection against the Spanish government, and should other independent nations come to the aid of Spain in the contest, no human power could, in our opinion, prevent the people and the government of the United States from taking part in such a civil war, in support of their neighbors and friends.

But if Spain, dead to the voice of her own interests, and actuated by stubborn pride and a false sense of honor, should refuse to sell Cuba to the United States, then the question will arise: What ought to be the course of the American government under such circumstances?

Self-preservation is the law of states as well as with individuals. All nations have, at different periods, acted upon this maxim. Although it has been made the pretext for committing flagrant injustice, as in the partition of Poland and other similar cases which history records, yet the principle itself, though often abused, has always been recognized

The United States have never acquired a foot of territory except by fair purchase, or, as in the case of Texas, upon the free and voluntary application of the people of that independent state, who desired to blend their destinies with our own.

Even our acquisitions from Mexico are no exception to this rule, because, although we might have claimed them by right of conquest in a just war, yet we purchased them for what was then considered by both parties a full and ample equivalent.

Our past history forbids that we should acquire the island of Cuba without the consent of Spain, unless justified by the great law of self-preservation. We must, in any event, preserve our conscious rectitude and our own self-respect.

Whilst pursuing this course we can afford to disregard the censures of the world, to which we have been so often and so unjustly exposed.

After we shall have offered Spain a price for Cuba far beyond its present value, and this shall have been refused, it will then be time to consider the question; does Cuba, in the possession of Spain, seriously endanger our internal peace and the existence of our cherished Union?

Should this question be answered in the affirmative, then, by every law, human and divine, we shall be justified in wresting it from Spain, if we possess the power; and this upon the very same principle that would justify an individual in tearing down the burning house of his neighbor if there were no other means of preventing the flames from destroying his own home.

Under such circumstances we ought neither to count the cost nor regard the odds which Spain might enlist against us. We forbear to enter into the question whether the present condition of the island would justify such a measure. We should, however, be recreant to our duty, be unworthy of our gallant forefathers, and commit base treason against our posterity, should we permit Cuba to be Africanized and become a second St. Domingo, with all its attendant horrors to the white race, and suffer the flames to extend to our own neighboring shores, seriously to endanger or actually to consume the fair fabric of our Union.

We fear that the course and current of events are rapidly tending toward such a catastrophe. We, however, hope for the best, though we ought certainly to be prepared for the worst.

We also forbear to investigate the present condition of the questions at issue between the United States and Spain. A long series of injuries to our people have been committed in Cuba by Spanish officials, and are unredressed. But recently a most flagrant outrage on the rights of American citizens and on the flag of the United States was perpetrated in the harbor of Havana under circumstances which, without immediate redress, would have justified a resort to measures of war in vindication of national honor. That outrage is not only unatoned, but the Spanish government has deliberately sanctioned the acts of its subordinates and assumed the responsibility attaching to them.

Nothing could more impressively teach us the danger to which the peaceful relations it has ever been the policy of the United States to cherish with foreign nations are constantly exposed, than the circumstances of that case. Situated as Spain and the United States are, the latter have forborne to resort to extreme measures.

But this course cannot, with due regard to their own dignity as an independent nation, continue; and our recommendations, now submitted, are dictated by the firm belief that the cession of Cuba to the United States, with stipulations as beneficial to Spain as those suggested, is the only effective mode of settling all past differences, and of the securing the two countries against future collisions.

We have already witnessed the happy results for both countries which followed a similar arrangement in regard to Florida.

Yours very respectfully,

JAMES BUCHANAN,
J. Y. MASON,
PIERRE SOULÉ.[1]

HON. WM. L. MARCY, *Secretary of State.*

While the signatures to this extraordinary document, which told Mr. Marcy nothing new, were those of Buchanan, Mason, and Soulé, we should know the pen to be the pen of Soulé, whose fervid diction would be unmistakable, even had we not his intimation of authorship in his despatch No. 35, of October 15, 1854, to Mr. Marcy. Two of the signers were Southerners and slave-owners; the first, though a Pennsylvanian, was almost more Southern than the Southerners. The fact of Europe's being in the throes of the Crimean war made the conferrees particularly eager for action. "Now is the moment," said Soulé, "to be done with it; for if we delay its solution we will certainly repent that we let escape the fairest opportunity we could ever be furnished with of bringing it to a decisive test."[2]

But the cooler temperaments of Pierce's administration were not affected by the perfervid oratory of the assembled ministers, and the question of the purchase of Cuba was dropped as impracticable at the time, to be taken up by Mr. Buchanan when he succeeded Mr. Pierce as President, only, however, to be iterated and reiterated through three annual messages to audiences which were deaf to his appeals.

It is particularly remarkable that such a document should have been signed by James Buchanan, a cautious lawyer, an experienced statesman and diplomat, and one reared in the antislavery atmosphere of Pennsylvania Quakerdom. It was the era of the

---

[1] House Ex. Doc. 93, 33 Cong., 2 Sess., 127–132.
[2] Mr. Soulé to Mr. Marcy, October 20, 1854, *Ibid.*, 126.

Kansas-Nebraska act; of *Uncle Tom's Cabin;* of the development of civil war in Kansas; and of the ferment which resulted in the formation of the Republican party. Neither the administration nor the man who two years later was to be elected President, and who was one of the signers of this report, could read these portentous signs. However galling the Spanish situation was to the United States, neither purchase nor war was possible with the consent of the people of the North, who were determined upon no further extension of slave territory.

Mr. Marcy told Mr. Soulé in reply, "to enter upon negotiations in relation to [the transfer of Cuba] whenever a favorable opportunity occurs," but, "should you have reason to believe that the men in power are averse to entertaining such a proposition—that the offer of it would be offensive to the national pride of Spain, and that it would find no favor in any considerable class of the people, then it will be but too evident that the time for opening, or attempting to open, such a negotiation has not arrived." . . . Soulé was also told by Mr. Marcy that "to conclude that, on rejection of a proposition to cede, seizure should ensue, would be to assume that self-preservation necessitates the acquisition of Cuba by the United States; that Spain has refused, and will persist in refusing, our reclamations for injuries and wrongs inflicted, and that she will make no arrangement for our future security against the recurrence of similar injuries and wrongs."

Soulé was also told that the door to the adjustment of the case of the *Black Warrior* should not be regarded as closed, particularly as Señor de Luzuriaga, the new minister for foreign affairs, "has distinctly indicated a willingness to recede from the position of his predecessor." As the minister had declared that Captain-General Pezuela and the intendant of customs had not been removed [as lately had occurred] "for the purpose of evading or defeating any part of our demand for redress, . . . should the government of Spain recede from the ground taken in Mr. Calderon's note . . . of the 7th of May last, disapprove of the conduct of her authorities at Havana, in the case of the *Black Warrior,* disavow their acts, show in an appropriate manner its displeasure toward them on that account, and offer full indemnity for the losses and injuries which our citizens sustained in that affair, you will entertain these propositions and signify the willingness of your government to adjust the case on such terms. . . . It is not expected that Spain will stop at the adjustment of the case of the *Black Warrior*. Our citizens have many other claims, originating from the conduct of her officials in Cuba, which in justice and honor she is bound to adjust." If, however, the cession of the island had "to be hopelessly abandoned for the present," Soulé was informed that the United States "will most pertinaciously insist upon some security against the future misconduct of the authorities at Cuba," the remedy in Mr. Marcy's view being in the enlargement of the powers of the captain-general to enable him to redress wrongs, instead of merely receiving complaints from the consul at Havana. "If," he said, "the feelings of Spain toward this country are such as she proposes—if she desires to perpetuate the relations of peace with the United States—she will yield to our just demands on this subject."

The note from Mr. Marcy closed by saying: "In resuming negotiations with Spain you will, in a firm but respectful manner, impress upon her ministry that it is the determination of the President to have all the matters in controversy between her and the United States speedily adjusted. He is desirous to have it done by negotiation, and would exceedingly regret that a failure to reach the end he has in view in this peaceful way should devolve upon him the duty of recommending a resort to coercive measures to vindicate our national rights and redress the wrongs of our citizens."[1]

This despatch repudiated the "Ostend manifesto" and ended the purposes for which Mr. Soulé regarded himself to be in Spain, and left him, he said, "no alternative but that of continuing to linger here in languid impotence, or of surrendering a trust which, with the difficulties thrown in the way of its execution, I would strive in vain to discharge either to the satisfaction of the government or my own credit. . . . I resign my commission . . . and beg . . . to be relieved from duty, if at all possible, by the end of next January."[2] In the Cortes, the day after this was written, the

[1] Mr. Marcy to Mr. Soulé, November, 13, 1854. In full, House Ex. Doc. 93, 33 Cong., 2 Sess., pp. 134–139.
[2] Mr Soulé to Mr. Marcy, December 17, 1854, *Ibid.*, 140.

Spanish minister for foreign affairs, "with an emphasis full of significancy, repelled the suspicion that the government might be disposed to part with [the island], by declaring that in its judgment 'to part with Cuba would be to part with the national honor.' The declaration was covered with the frantic applause of the assistance in the galleries, and received the spontaneous and undivided sanction of the House." [1]

On February 1, 1855, Mr. Soulé, in audience with the queen, ended his mission, leaving the American legation in charge of the secretary. The momentous questions with which it had been his province to deal were still all in the air. On September 16, the Spanish minister of state had tendered the establishment at Madrid of a mixed commission, on the basis of the convention entered into by the United States with Great Britain, on February 3, 1853, for the adjustment of all claims for reparation and indemnity for injuries suffered by private individuals, now pending between the two governments; but this was declined, as "some of these claims are of such a character as self-respect would not permit us to submit to arbitrament in any form." [2]

---

[1] Mr. Soulé to Mr. Marcy, December 23, 1854, *Ibid.*, 141.

[2] Mr. Marcy to Mr. Soulé, November 13, 1854, *Ibid.*, 136; Mr. Soulé to Señor Luzuriaga, December 15, 1854, *Ibid.*, 140.

It was not until 1860 that a joint convention was agreed upon and the American demands, amounting to $128,635.54 were acknowledged. Spain agreed to pay $100,000 of this within three months after exchange of ratification, withholding the remainder, however, to await a decision in the *Amistad* case, which had been pending since 1839, stipulating that it be submitted to arbitration. The Senate thus rejected the convention.

The very extraordinary case of the *Amistad* was as follows: She cleared in June, 1839, from Havana for the eastern part of Cuba, two whites being in charge of fifty-four recently imported negro slaves. The latter mutinied, murdered the captain and crew, and ordered the two owners to steer toward Africa; this they did during the day when the negroes could observe the sun, but at night they steered for the American coast. On August 26, the schooner was discovered near Montauk Point by Lieutenant Gedney commanding the coast survey vessel, *Washington*, and taken into New London. The Spanish minister demanded the return of the vessel and negroes under Art. IX of the treaty of 1795, which declared that all ships and merchandise, "of what nature soever," rescued from pirates or robbers should, if brought into the port of either state, be restored entire to the true proprietor. The attorney-general advised restoration, but in the meantime complications arose through various libels; the negroes claimed that they had been unlawfully kidnapped in Africa, and brought to Cuba in violation of Spanish law. The vessel and

The question of Cuban annexation, though it was not yet so recognized by all persons, was now practically dead. The Democratic platform of 1856, the year of the election of Buchanan to the presidency, pronounced strongly in favor of the acquirement of the island; that of the newly born Republican party denounced, as strongly, the Ostend manifesto, of which the Democratic candidate was a signer. But Mr. Buchanan's interest did not cease; in each of his annual messages, except the first, with, from our present stand-point, an incomprehensible blindness to an irresistible trend of sentiment, he made a recommendation for its purchase. It is safe to say that by this period even the free gift of Cuba to the United States would have been met, on the part of the North, by a refusal which could not have been overcome. The day had passed when annexation was possible. The passage of half a century has not seen its realization, or even the expression of a wish by the American government or people in its favor.

The statesmanship of the period in both countries was sadly astray. That of Spain refused a great benefit in a royal gift, and in relief from conditions which, for more than a generation, were to waste fearfully the resources of a people already poverty stricken, and prevent Spain's natural development. The statesmanship of the party in power in the United States was reaching out for what the American people were, by 1856, almost sure, and by 1860, certain, to reject. The last action in Congress, looking to nego-

---

cargo were awarded to the owners, by the district court, subject to claims of salvage to one-third the value; the negroes, with one exception, were to be delivered to the President of the United States, to be sent to Africa, in conformity with an act of Congress of March 3, 1819. Carried to the Supreme Court, the decree of the Circuit Court was upheld, excepting that the act of 1819 had not been contravened, and the negroes were ordered set at liberty. The vessel was sold, apparently to satisfy claims of salvage. The demand of the Spanish minister for indemnity for vessel, cargo, and negroes was refused by Mr. Webster, secretary of state. The Spanish minister then demanded the surrender of the negroes as criminals; this was also refused. President Tyler, Buchanan, as secretary of state, President Polk, Fillmore, Pierce, and Buchanan, all recommended favorable consideration of the Spanish claims. (See Moore, V, 852–854, for a statement of the case, and for references to the very voluminous literature of the subject.)

The Spanish claim appears, to the writer, just. In the circumstances, it was not for the United States to decide whether the negroes were legally held as slaves, any more than it was the province of Spain thirty-five years later to decide upon the right of the *Virginius* to an American register.

tiations for the purchase of the island was in a bill introduced in the Senate by Mr. Slidell, of Louisiana. The report in its favor from the committee on foreign relations, ordered printed January 24, 1859,[1] received no further notice. Mr. Buchanan reiterated his recommendation for an appropriation for the purpose, in his annual message in 1860; a painful demonstration of his inability to understand the angry mutterings which in a few short months were to burst into the thunder of the civil war.

[1] *Senate Report*, 351, 35 Cong., 2 Sess.

CHAPTER XIV

THE EFFORT OF 1865 TOWARD REFORM IN CUBAN ADMINISTRATION: CUBAN REVOLT

THE interval of thirteen years, 1855 to 1868, was one of comparative quiet in Spanish-American relations. Spain, on June 17, 1861, had declared her neutrality in the contest between the North and South, thus conceding belligerent rights to the Southern confederacy. She was a signatory to the convention concluded in London between Great Britain, France, and herself, October 31, 1861, for combined action for the redress of grievances against Mexico, which resulted the same year in the expedition so fatal to France, and in which, in the beginning, a Spanish force under Marshal Prim, took part. In April, 1862, an agreement with Mexico having been reached as to the claims of Great Britain and Spain, Prim followed the example of the latter power, and withdrew the Spanish force, though this action was not in accord with the views of the Spanish ministry.[1]

Spain was now wasting her strength in useless adventures in Cochin China, in Santo Domingo (a party in the Spanish half of which desired reannexation to Spain), and in a war, in 1866, against Peru and Chile, in which, May 2, her squadron was bitterly worsted in an attack on Callao. The whole of such inconsiderate action was due to the desire of Marshal O'Donnell, at the head of the ministry, to give employment to possible rivals,[2] of whom Narvaez, Serrano, and Prim were the chief.

Entire deprivation of political rights and emoluments would be serious enough in the present age, even were the autocratic government an ideal one in its administration of justice and finance. But when such a government, furnished by a distant authority, is radically corrupt in all its details, when it exists wholly for the

[1] Hume, *Modern Spain*, 446.   [2] *Ibid.*, 446.

benefit of such distant authority and of the officials it supplies, the governed would be worthy of their slavery were there not discontent and effort at revolution. Cuba, naturally, under such circumstances, so long as slavery continued among us, desired and labored for annexation to the United States whence came her prosperity. With the abolition of slavery in the United States, there developed an antagonism to annexation among many of the Cuban planters themselves, as fearing the economic result of manumission in Cuba. Particularly was this so among Spanish owners of slaves, who became known as "negreros" or slave-dealers. Not that there were not many planters who joined with the abolitionist party, which had existed in the island since 1830, in deprecating slavery and desiring its discontinuance; but the change wrought by the civil war had a distinct effect in causing Cuba to turn to Spain in an endeavor to establish relations which, being bearable, would bind the island more closely to the mother country.

At this epoch the slave-trade to Cuba still continued. In 1863 and 1864 the attention of the captain-general had been called, by the British consul, to eleven disembarkations of slaves, one from a steamer at Cardenas and Sagua amounting to 1,500, and during these years 3,565 imported negroes were seized; chiefly, of course, on the motion of British and American authorities: statements which speak for the magnitude of the traffic.[1]

The abolition of slavery in the United States and the unsettlement of the labor conditions of the South had given a great impetus to the sugar industry of Cuba, and caused the formation of a Spanish party "for whom the cause of slavery and that of Spanish domination were identical and synonymous."[2] It could not be

[1] A despatch of Lord Lyons, February 4, 1864, to Mr. Seward, secretary of state, enclosed a memorandum which was a copy of a despatch from the British minister in Madrid, who, discussing the means of prevention, mentions the number of Africans introduced into Cuba in the twelve months ending September 30, 1863, as estimated at between 7,000 and 8,000, as against 11,254 in the twelve months preceding. He credited the diminution to the efforts of the new governor-general, Dulce, who undoubtedly did his utmost to suppress the traffic. Under the existing laws, the seizure of newly imported slaves by the authorities was prohibited after they had been received on an estate.

[2] Gallenga, *The Pearl of the Antilles*, 12.

otherwise, as severance from Spain, followed by annexation to the United States, now meant death to slavery. Two great parties were thus formed, the one fanatically loyal to Spain and consisting chiefly of Spanish immigrants favoring slavery and the *status quo;* the other, separatist, to which belonged most of the native-born element.

Notwithstanding the facts of the slave-trade so fully established, the anti-reformist party, in a memorial addressed to the crown, June 28, 1865, claimed that the traffic no longer existed. They were unable to see that the question of slavery in Cuba itself had been decided by the outcome of the civil war in the United States.

In the agitation following the expeditions of Lopez, the Spanish element had strengthened itself with the home government by claiming to stand for Spanish dominion and had re-enforced its political position by forming an organization of volunteers which became important by numbers, which rose to some 70,000 or 80,000; and by membership in the clubs throughout the island which, patterned after the Casino Español, of Havana, became points of great political influence and a power which no governor-general could resist, their power extending even, as will appear later, to forcing General Dulce, one of the best-meaning and most able governors of the island during the century, to resign his post and leave for Spain.

On May 12, 1865, there was sent to Marshal Serrano, Duke de la Torre, at that time in the cabinet, a letter signed by over 24,000 residents of the island, among whom were all the most distinguished and important natives, calling for his aid in the Cortes, and detailing the difficulties under which Cuba labored. Serrano had been captain-general; he had left Cuba with the reputation of a kindly and beneficent master, and the appeal was not in vain. He spoke in the senate and answered in terms which gave hope of a change. The enemies of reform appealed to the crown for the retention of the *status quo,* but the outcome was a decree appointing a commission which, in the words of Marshal Serrano in a letter addressed to the signers of the reformist petition, "could inform the government concerning the reforms which, demanded by opinion, it is urgent to establish in that island." He continues: "This decree, recognizing and sanctioning in a solemn manner the right of the American provinces to take part in the formation of the political and economical laws by which they shall be governed, is a very advanced step in the reforms for which the island calls." [1]

It is clear that representation was still looked upon as a panacea which was to bring justice and content to the Antilles, and the sentiment of the many overpowered the wise judgment of Señor Saco, who saw no practical good in the presence of a small knot of representatives, who could not have the numbers or influence in the Spanish Cortes to effect their wishes over those of a great majority formed of peninsular representatives.

The royal decree, authorizing the ministry of ultramar to open an inquiry respecting reforms in Cuba and Puerto Rico was signed the 25th of November, 1865, the inquiry extending to principles on which the special laws governing Cuba and Puerto Rico should be based; the manner of regulating colored and Asiatic labor, and the means of facilitating the importation of such labor; the treaties of navigation and commerce which should be made with other nations, and the reform in the tariff and in the administration of the customs.

Twenty representatives of the government, councilors of state, were to be named from the various departments of the government: sixteen members were to be elected from the fifteen most important ayuntamientos of Cuba, and six from Puerto Rico. Notwithstanding a change in the electoral law in the interest of the party of antireform while the election was pending, the whole representation sent from the Antilles belonged to the reform party. The following [2] were regarded as the bases of their demands:

1. That the exceptional status of the islands cease, and also the discretional powers of the governor-general.

2. Separation of the political and civil power from the military.

3. That the stipulated guaranties be rigorously applied, and that the rights recognized in the constitution of the kingdom be extended to all Spanish subjects.

4. A governor-general to be nominated by the crown, representing the executive power with all its associated faculties.

---

[1] Sedano, *Estudios Politicos*, 260.
[2] From Sedano. *Estudios Politicos*, 300 *et seq.*

5. A captain-general also to be nominated by the crown to command the army.

6. A naval commander-in-chief also to be named by the crown, to command the department.

7. A provincial junta and an insular committee for affairs peculiar to the island.

8. Representation in the Cortes in conformity with the law in force in the Peninsula.

9. Division of the province of Cuba into six districts, with their respective governors, councilors, and provincial committees with the same faculties as those of the Peninsula, saving the variations due to special conditions in the two countries.

10. Municipal governments to be elected and to have such enlargement of attributes as differing circumstances in the two countries demand.

11. That the creation of new municipalities be facilitated when desired.

The abolition of the slave-trade was to be demanded, as also steps toward the abolition of slavery itself. And finally the vicious and complicated financial system was to be one of the main questions considered, and action taken toward seeking to reduce the enormous charges of the customs administration and its personnel, and to adopt a freer regimen which would augment the trade between Cuba and the United States. It was recognized and stated that it was Cuba's relations with this country which chiefly affected her commercial importance; the United States taking sixty-two per cent. of her sugar, England, France, and other powers twenty-two per cent., and Spain but three per cent.

The commission began its sittings October 30, 1866, under the presidency of Señor Cánovas del Castillo, minister of ultramar. In opening the conference Señor Cánovas stated that he had not been the author of the decree of inquiry, but that he had accepted and would accept it in good faith; that the government declared solemnly that it had no preconceived idea, that it gave preference to no system, and that it was disposed to extract from the inquiry all the benefit which could be afforded through the knowledge and true patriotism of the commissioners sent by the islands of Cuba and Puerto Rico, and from the knowledge and experience of those who had been called together with them to consult; that they were authorized to discuss everything which might touch the prosperity of the ultramarine provinces without any limitations other than in the three points which were the bases of the Spanish social organization, viz.: National unity, religious unity, and monarchical unity, which it was not supposed they would wish to discuss. Otherwise they were to have the fullest liberty of discussion and expression.

The studies of the several committees upon the important subjects before the conference were submitted to the minister of ultramar, January 30, 1867.

The commission was inclined to the suppression of customhouses, demonstrating the possibility of the scheme without burdening the producing classes, proving by official data that five per cent. on the income or net production would suffice to meet the charges of the island, and this with scarcely making in the estimate the numerous deductions which, in the opinion of the commissioners, justice demanded. They were also of the opinion that within the limits of six per cent. there would be had a surplus of about $2,000,000, and which, at the same time that taxable wealth would increase, would facilitate a progressive reduction of the rate.

The commission recommended also the reduction of duties and the simplification of the tariff, an indispensable point in order that the productive capacity of the provinces should not decline, demonstrating that the one and the other, far from diminishing the public income, would increase it, the resulting commercial movement compensating the higher tariff. It also called for the suppression of the differential duties and for the removal of all unnecessary obstacles, which restrained the development of commerce. The question of cereals was treated from the point of view of justice to Cuba and of profit to the Castiles, showing that these could obtain greater or less advantages without obliging Cuba to eat bad and dear bread, and saying that the profits which the small number of traffickers attained in this monopoly did not, in the most remote manner, compensate for the sacrifice imposed on the island, if it is possible to have compensation for an injustice.

The commission also petitioned that commerce between the Antilles and the Peninsula should be declared coasting trade.

But the commission did not propose, nor indicate, nor even imagine, the possibility that there would be an amalgamation of the two systems, and that the custom-houses should be left with all their immoralities and other shortcomings, and the direct tax should be laid without previous political or economic organization; that these contributions should be established along with others, and much less that, by this substitution, a ten-per-cent. tax should be established, leaving in force the greater part of the old imposts, when six per cent. had been considered, and was considered, a sufficient substitute for everything and leave a surplus.

The result, fatal in its influence to Spain, was a decree signed February 12, merely changing the system of imposts in Cuba "in such form that, of itself, it sufficed to bring disturbance and discontent to the mind of every inhabitant, and produce the revolutionary sentiment which has brought such woes to the previously peaceful isle of Cuba." [1]

In view of the gravity of the situation, the commission presented a petition that the publication of the decree should be suspended in the Antilles, at least until it would be possible to publish with it others which might explain the intention of the attempted reform and the advantages to be hoped, and though promises were made, "neither were other decrees made nor other reforms attempted as a compensation for the direct impost, nor did the *Official Gazette* publish the reply to the economic interrogatory. The royal decree of February 12 was carried into execution, and, as it caused such perturbation in Cuba, the commissioners received, as was to be expected, bitter denunciations."

Following this failure in fiscal reform, the question of political reforms was taken up, formulated under ten heads,[2] the whole being based upon the supposition that it was conceded that all political rights, established by law for the inhabitants of the Peninsula and adjacent islands, should have extension to Cuba and Puerto Rico. Freedom of the press; right of petition; no restriction of rights to public posts or employments; right of exercising any legal industry or profession; right of acquiring or disposing of property; right of public meeting; no detention or separation from domicile except as the law prescribes; declaring perpetual proscription an

---

[1] Sedano, 306.   [2] Sedano, p. 295, *et seq.*

outrage; that no contract shall reduce any one in possession of freedom to perpetual or temporary servitude; that there should be no confiscation of property without compensation, were the reasonable demands which were brought forward by the reformists and reported upon by a special committee of the commission. Though there was a division of opinion in the committee as to the form which the Antilles representation should take, there was none as to general principles, except that Señores Saco and Bernal wisely favored insular legislatures as opposed to representation in the national Cortes.

That there were Spaniards of standing and authority who favored the desired reforms is shown by the remarks of Marshal Serrano in a report to the government on May 10, 1867, saying: "The result of the deliberation of the Cortes of 1836, and the constitutional precept of 1837, misinterpreted, in fact, by the negation of all political rights of the natives of the Antilles; the repressive measures which the local governor of Cuba made excessive, and the real administrative chaos which succeeded this epoch, and which my predecessor, the Marquis of Havana, has described in such lively colors in the two memorials which he has printed, raised to the highest pitch the discontent and desperation, if I may say so, of almost all the natives of Cuba."

Touching the subject of the danger occasioned by the expeditions which had had their birth in the United States, he added:

"This danger cleared away, and the passions calmed, the Cuban mind began to prepare itself for the establishment of a great national party in which, under the name of the party of reform, all are grouped to-day, animated with hopes which I and many others, on the faith of good Spaniards, have believed we ought to encourage, and which, in my judgment, the patriotism of the government ought not disregard. . . . I flatter myself that I know the tendencies of the Cubans well; I have tried to make friends with them and hear, without prejudice, their complaints and aspirations. I succeeded—I say it with satisfaction; and after my departure from Havana have been in constant communication with many of their most important men; have had sent me a letter which belongs to the whole public, in which are expressed their wishes and which is subscribed by all the most notable

Cubans of all parts of the island. I cannot do otherwise than recognize, nor do less than say to-day to the government of her majesty with all the loyalty of my character and with the impulse of the most intimate conviction, that the complaints of the Cubans are just, that their aspirations are legitimate, that there is no reason why they, Spanish as we ourselves, should have no press, nor any representation in their government, nor a single one of the guarantees to which we in the Peninsula have right; that there is no reason why a military and absolute government, from the highest to the lowest grades, should be the sole regimen of the Antilles; and that now is the precise moment—let the government not forget it—to take advantage of the internal and external circumstances which favor the political reform demanded with insistency by the Spanish of the Antilles, and which it is just and proper to grant them without delay."

Plans for the abolition of slavery in both islands were presented at the last session of the commission, April 27, 1867, but there was nothing to come of the eager anticipation and the severe labors but the increased taxation ordered by the decree of February 12. The elaborate reports to the government slumbered in forgetfulness, the fateful fruit of which was to be war and the ruin of Spanish oversea dominion.[1]

This was the turning-point in the relations of Cuba and Spain. Until now Cuba had been loyal, at least in such degree as never to really endanger the political union between the two countries. Whatever minds were turned to independence or to annexation to the United States, the great majority were loath to part the bonds of the mother country, and sought within the law an alleviation of their conditions. But the absolute failure of the commission, the more than failure, in fact, as the burdens of the Antilles were

[1] The foregoing is chiefly transcript or paraphrase from Señor Don Carlos de Sedano's *Estudios Politicos Sobre Cuba*, 295–320. Señor Sedano was an ex-deputy of the Cortes, strongly opposed to annexation to the United States, and to the insurrection, which developed into the ten years' war, and which was the direct outcome of the treatment of the commissions and of the procrastination, so fatal an element of Spanish character, when the road was opened by the establishment of the republic. No one has treated the subject of Cuba in a more upright, sober, dispassionate, and patriotic way. He was firmly convinced that Cuba should remain Spanish, but was equally convinced of the necessity of reform.

increased, meant war and separation, and the war soon came. Spain was, herself, but a volcano in unrest. By 1867 she was in chaos, "the government was irresistibly swept along the current of reaction until its decrees became such as would have shamed Fernando VII. All loyalty was trampled under foot, all guarantees forgotten, all liberty crushed. Taxes were extorted in advance, municipalities dissolved, the electoral laws altered by decrees, the press and speech, public and private, suppressed. Dismay, almost panic, reigned supreme; ruined shopkeepers put up their shutters in every town, merchants closed their country houses, money wellnigh disappeared from circulation." [1] Prim was an exile in France; in April, 1868, an attempt of the Cortes to meet was violently repressed, and all leaders not favorable to the reactionary ministry were arrested and banished, among them Generals Serrano, Dulce, Cordoba, Zabala, Serrano-Bedoya, Caballero de Rodas, Hoyas, Letona, and Rios Rosas, the president of the Cortes. September 19, 1868, Admiral Topete's squadron, at Cadiz, raised the flag of revolt, and the revolution began which resulted in the dethronement and, ten days later, the deportation of Isabella II, and the installation of Serrano, Prim, Topete, and Sagasta, as the chiefs of a new provisional government.

The call of Amadeo, Duke of Aosta, to the throne, in November, 1870; the death, by assassination, of Prim, December 30 (the very day Amadeo landed on Spanish soil), and Amadeo's abdication, February 11, 1873, are but stations in the sea of discord through which unhappy Spain was passing in these years, and evidences of her unfitness to deal with such questions as the earnest Cubans and their few Spanish friends had endeavored to bring before an ever transitory government.

On May 30, 1866, General Lersundi, a strong supporter of the reactionary government with which the reign of Isabella ended, had replaced the liberal General Dulce as captain-general, and when the pronunciamiento of Yara came, October 10, 1868, and D. Manuel Cespedes, wearied as were so many by an insupportable situation, raised the cry of independence, it found at the head of the affairs of the island one of those least fitted to deal

[1] Hume, *Modern Spain*, 455.

with so difficult a situation; one, too, which might not have been had a ruler more sympathetic with Cuban hopes been at hand.

The time of revolt was sadly ill-chosen. Had it been delayed it is more than probable that Cuban aspirations would have been met by the new government, at the head of which was Cuba's strong friend, Serrano. With him was Prim, a landmark of wisdom and intelligence in Spanish statesmanship; Topete, an honest and liberal-minded sailor; Mateo Sagasta, who was to be the head of Spain's ministry in the disastrous epoch of thirty years later, and Lopez de Ayala, the last as minister of ultramar.

Lersundi, who steadily reported the failure of the insurrection, received notice in November of his relief by General Dulce, but the latter did not arrive until January 4, 1869. His reception by the Spanish element "was as cold as the air which was then blowing from the north, and only a few, but loyal and sincere friends associated with the ideas of reform to which he aspired, were present to visit him aboard." The powers of Havana, the army, the volunteers, the clubs,—all, in fact, which represented the peninsular element, were against him.

General Dulce had returned with extraordinary discretionary powers, and one of his first acts, within a week of his landing, was to declare liberty of press and speech, except that the Catholic dogma and slavery should not be discussed until allowed by the Spanish Cortes.[1] His efforts were sincerely conciliatory, and these, combined with the good-will of the new and liberal ministry, might have succeeded in the endeavors to bring peace, but the fates were against it. While negotiations were favorably progressing between the insurgent leaders and the commissioners of conciliation, who were cordially received in the insurgent camp, both at El Turias and at Ojo de Agua de los Melones, "and when, in the judgment of Peninsulars and Cubans of highest character, the preliminaries of pacification appeared already certain, a most unhappy and never-to-be-sufficiently-lamented deed disarranged all, and made conciliation impossible. The insurrectionist chief, D. Augusto Arango, who incautiously presented himself at the gates of Puerto Principe, alone, unarmed, with two safe-conducts, to hold an interview with the military governor of this city, an-

[1] Decree January 7, 1869, Sedano, *Estudios Politicos*, 367.

nouncing the immediate presentation and submission to the government of 600 or 700 men of the 800 or 1,000 who, for the moment, were in arms in that department, and with which act the insurrection still localized there and in the vicinity of Bayamo, would have ended, was assassinated by a justice of the peace (comisario de barrio), a lieutenant, and four armed peasants."

"This unfortunate occurrence ended attempts at conciliation and aroused a sentiment of exasperation amongst the insurgents. Threats, insults, and provocations followed everywhere; the best and wealthiest families of the island sought refuge in Europe and the United States, and civil war spread throughout all the eastern half of the island with all its horrors." The pacific captain-general was powerless in the hands of the ungovernable organization of the volunteers composed almost wholly of Peninsulars, and who, never taking the field, became an armed political party dominating the towns and all Cuba not in control of the insurrectionists, representing in their views and acts a retrogressive and absolutist policy, before which all reform became mute.

Though the captain-general was nominally the governor of Cuba, the real power was now in the hands of the volunteers, who were in the end, the *de facto* rulers. Dulce had been constrained by them within three months to wholly change his liberal policy for one of inhuman severity. On March 24, 1869, but three weeks after the advent of the new administration at Washington, the following decree was issued:

"Vessels which may be captured in Spanish waters or on the high seas near to the island, having on board men, arms, and munitions, or effects that can in any manner contribute, promote, or foment the insurrection in this province, whatsoever their derivation or destination, after examination of their papers and register shall be *de facto* considered as enemies of the integrity of our territory, and treated as pirates, in accordance with the ordinances of the navy. All persons captured in such vessels, without regard to their number, will be immediately executed."[1]

---

[1] Senate Ex. Doc. 7, 41 Cong., 2 Sess., 12. Almost coincidently with this decree, the brig *Mary Lowell*, with a cargo of arms and supplies, had been seized, March 15, 1869, at Ragged Island, one of the Bahamas, in what was claimed to be British waters.

On April 4, 1869, the Count of Valmaseda, commanding at Bayamo, issued a proclamation declaring:

"1st. Every man from the age of fifteen years upward found away from his habitation (finca), and who does not prove a justified motive therefor, will be shot.

"2d. Every habitation unoccupied will be burned by the troops.

"3d. Every habitation from which does not float a white flag, as a signal that its inhabitants desire peace, will be reduced to ashes.

"Women that are not living at their own homes, or at the house of their relatives, will collect in the town of Jiguani or Bayamo, where maintenance will be provided. Those who do not present themselves will be conducted forcibly."[1]

On April 1 a decree was issued which practically forbade the alienation of property in the island, except with the revision and assent of certain officials, and which declared void all sales made without such assent.[2] This was followed shortly by decrees creating an administrative council for the custody and management of embargoed property, which was extended to the property of all persons, either within or without the island, who might take part in the insurrection by aiding it in any way.

These decrees, issued at the bidding of the volunteers, and all of which went full in the face of the treaty of 1795, in so far as American citizens were involved, drove out of the island, as mentioned, many persons of property who fled to the United States. The men of the escaping families became active members of the Cuban juntas formed in the Union. Although their estates and properties in Cuba were confiscated, many of them had very large resources from investments out of the country, and these were poured into the insurgent exchequer with a lavishness which was highest proof of their earnestness in the cause for which they had given up so much. Of the lofty spirit of these early revolutionists there can be no question.

A Cuban *junta* was organized in New York that issued, sold, or gave away Cuban bonds payable on the independence of the island. The money thus obtained, and that from other sources, was used to fit out and send expeditions to Cuba carrying arms

[1] Senate Ex. Doc. 7, 41 Cong., 2 Sess., 20.   [2] *Ibid.*, 19.

and men, in violation of the laws of the United States. Although the vessels used were, in the main, ordinary tug-boats, and none of them were vessels able to cruise and commit hostilities, as were those built and fitted out in England against the United States during the war of secession, and there was not recognized war between Spain and her Cuban subjects, in which the United States was a professed neutral, yet the use by Cuban rebels of the United States as treasury and arsenal presented much the same principles of law. The Cuban *junta* and a large body of public opinion demanded from President Grant a recognition of the belligerency of the Cubans in arms, such as Great Britain had given to the Confederate government.

CHAPTER XV

THE EARLIER DIPLOMACY OF THE TEN YEARS' WAR

THE President of the United States was now, since March 4, 1869, General Grant; the secretary of state, Mr. Hamilton Fish; the minister to Spain, General Sickles, a prominent officer in the civil war. Mr. John Hay was secretary of legation, than whom the minister could not have had a better right hand. The Cuban insurrection had, by early spring of 1869, taken on so virulent a character, on both sides, that it became a matter of deep concern to the United States government, so many of whose citizens were large proprietors in the island, and so much of whose commercial well-being was involved. The country was fortunate in having in the head of the department of state an official of great ability, of highest character, and of conservative instincts. It was certain that Cuban affairs would be managed with the justice and high-mindedness which were part of Mr. Fish's character.

When Mr. Fish entered the department of state he was confronted by two controversies threatening the peace of the United States. One was the *Alabama* difficulty; the other the questions of Cuba. Each presented belligerent recognition at the threshold. "The secretary was in a dilemma. The rule of action he was about to lay down as that which should have guided the British government in 1861 must control the United States in 1869. That was obvious. But in 1869 the United States was itself the interested observer of an insurrection on the neighboring island of Cuba, and, moreover, the new President was not backward in expressing the warm sympathy he felt for the insurgents against Spanish colonial misrule."[1] Mr. Fish had to formulate for his guidance a rule applicable to both situations. This he did, and adhered to, and, what was of greatest moment, held President Grant to the same.

[1] Charles Francis Adams, *Treaty of Washington*, 108.

Mr. Fish at once protested to the Spanish minister against General Dulce's decree of March 24, saying: "It is to be regretted that so high a functionary as the Captain-General of Cuba should, as this paper seems to indicate, have overlooked the obligations of his government pursuant to the law of nations, and especially its promises in the treaty between Spain and the United States in 1795. Under that law and treaty, the United States expect for their citizens and vessels the privilege of carrying to the enemies of Spain, whether those enemies be claimed as Spanish subjects or citizens of other countries, subject only to the requirement of a legal blockade, all merchandise not contraband of war. Articles contraband of war, when destined for the enemies of Spain, are liable to seizure on the high seas, but the right of seizure is limited to such articles only, and no claim for its extension to other merchandise or to persons not in the civil, military, or naval service of the enemies of Spain, will be acquiesced in by the United States. This government certainly cannot assent to the punishment by Spanish authorities of any citizen of the United States for the exercise of a privilege to which he may be entitled, under the public law and treaties." He hoped that the proclamation would be recalled, or that orders preventing its illegal application to citizens of the United States would be given. "A contrary course might endanger those friendly and cordial relations between the two governments, which it is the hearty desire of the President should be maintained."[1]

This was quickly followed by an energetic note concerning Count Valmaseda's proclamation of massacre. "In the interest of civilization and common humanity, I hope that this document is a forgery. If it be indeed genuine, the President instructs me in the most forcible manner to protest against such a mode of warfare, and to ask you to request the Spanish authorities in Cuba to take such steps that no person, having the right to claim the protection of the government of the United States, shall be sacrificed or injured in the conduct of hostilities upon this basis."[2]

[1] Mr. Fish to Mr. Roberts, April 3, 1869, Senate Ex. Doc. 7, 41 Cong., 2 Sess., 12.
[2] Mr. Fish to Mr. Lopez Roberts, May 10, 1869, Senate Ex. Doc. 7, 41 Cong., 2 Sess., 21.

In June, 1869, two Americans were summarily shot at Santiago. One, Charles Speakman of Indiana, had shipped in good faith as a seaman aboard the schooner *Grapeshot*, ostensibly bound for Falmouth, Jamaica; the other, Albert Wyeth, of Pennsylvania, was a passenger going to Jamaica for his health. Some fifty Cubans with arms were put aboard the *Grapeshot* in the lower bay of New York, whereupon Speakman had requested to leave the schooner, but was assured there was no intention of touching Cuba, but that the Cubans were to be landed at Falmouth. The latter took possession of the schooner off Cape Maysi, ran her ashore, and disembarked, the two Americans being forced to go with them. The force was attacked by the Spaniards and dispersed. The Americans surrendered themselves on the first opportunity, were carried to Santiago, and shot, Speakman on June 16; Wyeth five days later. No attention was paid to protests of the acting consul of the United States,[1] such action, apart from the brutal circumstances, being in distinct contravention of the treaty of 1795, in full force, which assured to American citizens a fair trial and the right to the assistance of counsel.

The consul at Santiago in reporting these cases said: "The country is in a complete state of anarchy; the Catalonian volunteers do not allow the governor to render justice, and he cannot publicly resist them." He pleaded for the presence of an American man-of-war,[2] and Rear-Admiral Hoff, the commander-in-chief of the American naval forces in the West Indies, was himself sent to investigate. He reported: "These men were cruelly murdered owing to the weakness of the Spanish official at this city in yielding to the demands of the Catalan volunteers, and in misconstruing or acting upon the cruel decree of the 24th of March." "In this opinion," said Mr. Fish, "and in the forcible language in which it is expressed, the President fully concurs." The minister was directed to demand full reparation, and finally to "solemnly protest against any longer carrying on the war in Cuba in this barbarous way. . . . Our relations with Cuba are so many and so intimate that we cannot regard this struggle in all its details with

[1] General Sickles to Spanish minister of state, September 6, 1869, House Ex. Doc. 160, 41 Cong., 2 Sess., 104–106.
[2] Consul Phillips to Mr. Fish, June 19, 1869, *Ibid*, 98.

anything but intense interest. Our earnest wish has been, and is, to do our whole duty as a neutral nation to Spain in this emergency. Feeling that we have done so . . . we think we have a right on our part to insist that Spain shall carry on this war hereafter in a manner more in accordance with the humane and Christian sentiment of the age."[1]

The result was a reply from Señor Silvela, the Spanish minister of state, supporting for the moment the conduct of the Santiago officials, but declaring that the captain-general had ordered that reports should be made to himself of such cases, and that mercy and humanity had been enjoined in the conduct of the war,[2] a somewhat different view to that which had been taken a fortnight before by the acting minister Becerra, who promised that "if the facts were as alleged, full reparation would be made to the families of the deceased"; adding, as did Señor Silvela, "that orders have been given to prevent such scenes of cruelty in the future conduct of the war."[3]

On June 2 General Dulce, with every insult possible to one in his position, was forced by the volunteers to resign and leave for Spain. This organization now controlled the political situation, and was violently opposed to any treatment of the insurrectionists which leaned toward humanity, such as General Dulce in several instances had shown. General Caballero de Rosas came to take over the duties of a now most difficult and trying office. On July 7, 1869, he issued a decree closing to trade, whether foreign or coasting, all but the more important ports of the island, from Key Bahia de Cadiz eastward, on the north, and from Cienfuegos eastward, on the south. The second article directed that vessels carrying powder, arms, or military supplies should be seized and confiscated. The sixth and last article, referring to supposed rights under treaties with the United States and other nations, declared the right of search of suspicious vessels on the high seas adjacent to the island.[4]

[1] Mr. Fish to General Sickles, August 10, 1869, Sen. Ex. Doc. 7, 41 Cong., 2 Sess., 40.
[2] Señor Silvela to General Sickles, October 11, 1869, *Ibid.*, 44–45. See Sickles's reply, October 30, *Ibid.*, pp. 46–49.
[3] General Sickles to Mr. Fish, September 14, 1869, *Ibid.*, 43
[4] In full, *Ibid.*, 51.

On July 16 Mr. Fish, in a note to the Spanish minister, said: "[The decree mentioned] purports to be issued in order to put an end to an insurrection in the island of Cuba, which the United States have hitherto treated only as a civil commotion within the dominions of Spain, that did not give rise to what we understood as belligerent rights on the part of either party to the conflict. But the decree of Captain-General de Rosas assumes powers and rights over the trade and commerce of other peoples inconsistent with a state of peace, and which the United States can be expected to allow their vessels to be subjected to when Spain avows herself to be in a state of war, or shall be manifestly exercising the rights conceded only to belligerents in the time of war. . . . In case the success of the revolutionary party should put any of the ports declared to be closed in their possession, the United States, as a maritime nation, will regard an effective blockade to be necessary to the exclusion of their commerce." Respecting the second article, he said: "The transportation on the high seas, in time of peace, of articles commonly known as contraband of war, is a legitimate traffic and commerce, which cannot be interfered with unless by a power at war with a third party, in the admitted exercise of the recognized rights of a belligerent. . . . The United States cannot . . . be indifferent or silent under a decree which, by the vagueness of its terms, may be construed to allow their vessels on the high seas, whatever may be their cargo, to be embarrassed or interfered with. If Spain be at war with Cuba, the United States will submit to those rights which public law concedes to belligerents," otherwise the enforcement of the decree "cannot but be regarded as a violation of their rights that may lead to serious complications." Mr. Fish showed that there was no treaty right, such as the captain-general declared to exist, except in time of war. The treaty "limits and prescribes the manner of exercising a belligerent right when such exists." He requested to be informed "at the earliest practicable moment" if Spain, by the issuance of this decree, claimed the right of a belligerent. Its continuance, he declared, involved "the logical conclusion of a recognition by Spain of a state of war with Cuba." Attention was called to the grave consequences which might ensue from interference with a vessel of the United States on a lawful voyage, and the hope expressed that

Mr. Roberts would "speedily be at liberty to announce the formal abrogation of a decree which causes so much serious apprehension to the government of the United States, and against which this government feels bound most earnestly to remonstrate."[1]

On July 18 the particularly offensive sixth article was withdrawn by the captain-general, and on July 6 a humane decree was issued, ordering respect for the lives, houses, and property of all persons, without distinction; no one was to be imprisoned on mere suspicion, and in case of arrest there was to be an immediate examination. "The greatest care," said the decree "shall be taken that in proceeding in any manner against foreigners, no legal requisite shall be omitted."[2]

Mr. Fish's note became the basis of American action throughout the revolt, and was among the most forcible in argument of his papers against the recognition of the insurgents as belligerents. Such recognition would at once have given Spain the right which the captain-general had so improperly assumed. The sympathy of the American public was naturally almost wholly with the Cubans, as, by long tradition, it was with any people struggling for political freedom; accentuated in this case, however, by the inhuman and ruthless decrees which had been issued by the Spanish authorities. The United States, however, held rigidly to its duties, the President issuing, in July, 1869, to the district attorney and marshal for the southern district of New York, a commission empowering them, or either of them, "to employ such part of the land or naval forces of the United States, or of the militia thereof, for the purpose indicated in the eighth section of the act of April 20, 1818, commonly known as the neutrality act." Orders were at the same time given for the capture of all concerned in expeditions violating such law.[3]

The instructions to General Sickles, when newly appointed minister to Spain, directed him, as soon as opportunity should occur, to proffer the good offices of the United States for the establishment of peace. "On either side," said Mr. Fish, "the war has been one of desolation, and if continued, must result in the entire destruc-

[1] Senate Ex. Doc. 7, 41 Cong., 2 Sess., 51-53.   [2] *Ibid.*, 54-55.
[3] Mr. Fish to Mr. Pierrepont, July 13, 1869, 81 MS., Dom. Let. 385, Moore, *Digest*, VII, 1032.

tion of a large part of the productive capacity of the island, as well as of an immense amount of property and of human life. It is not impossible that the Cubans may be conquered, if Spain devotes her whole energies to the work; but they can never again be contented, happy, fruitful, or quiet subjects of that power. Assuming that Spain may eventually subdue the present insurrection, she will find herself in possession of a devastated and ruined territory, inhabited by a discontented people. The enlightened statesmen of Spain cannot fail to appreciate that the feelings and affections of the entire native population of the island are not only estranged, but that they are deeply hostile to the continuance of Spanish rule. Nor can they fail to recognize the advancing growth of that sentiment which claims for every part of the American hemisphere the right of self-government and freedom from transatlantic dependence. . . . After much consideration, and a careful survey of the question in all its relations, this government has arrived at the conclusion that it is its duty to exert its influence to bring this unhappy strife to a close. Duty to its own citizens, and large property interests, jeoparded by the continuance of the war—the necessity of maintaining quiet within its borders, now seriously disturbed by the continual strife carried on so near its borders—our friendship for Spain . . . our sympathy for the Cubans, who are our neighbors, alike impel the government to this course.

"The President therefore directs you to offer to the cabinet at Madrid, the good offices of the United States, for the purpose of bringing to a close the civil war now ravaging the island of Cuba, on the following bases:

"1. The independence of Cuba to be acknowledged by Spain.

"2. Cuba to pay to Spain a sum, within a time, and in a manner to be agreed upon by them, as an equivalent for the entire and definite relinquishment by Spain of all her rights in the island, including the public property of every description. If Cuba should not be able to pay the whole sum at once in cash, the future payments by instalments are to be adequately secured by a pledge of the export and import customs duties, under an arrangement to be agreed upon. . . .

"3. The abolition of slavery in the island of Cuba.

"4. An armistice, pending the negotiations for the settlement above referred to."

The minister was directed to telegraph in case the good offices of the United States should be accepted; to ask that communication should be allowed between Cubans in the United States and those in the field, and that a conference be held in Washington between the representatives of each party, clothed with full powers to arrange all details.[1]

This despatch was accompanied by a confidential note, in which the minister was informed that while the proposal was "expressed to be for the purpose of bringing to a close the civil war now ravaging the island," and "is not designed to grant any public recognition of belligerent rights to the insurgents, it is, nevertheless, used advisedly, and in recognition of a state and condition of the contest which may not justify a much longer withholding of the concession to the revolutionary party of the recognized rights of belligerency. Should the expression, therefore, be commented upon, you will admit what is above stated with reference to it, and may add, in case of a protracted discussion, or the prospect of a refusal by Spain to accept the proposed offer of the United States, that an early recognition of belligerent rights is the logical deduction from the present proposal, and will probably be deemed a necessity on the part of the United States, unless the condition of the parties to the contest shall have changed very materially."

If the Spanish cabinet should insist, the President was ready to advise to Congress the guarantee of the payment of the sum that Cuba should pay to Spain. Mention was also made of the desirability of arranging a severance also of Puerto Rico from Spain, should the subject be brought forward by the Spanish minister. Mr. Paul S. Forbes, who had personal relations with General Prim and many other influential Spaniards, was named as a special and confidential agent, with, however, advisory powers only.[2]

The American minister confined his action, for the time, to making informally, in his conversation with Marshal Prim, the

[1] Mr. Fish to General Sickles, June 29, 1869, House Ex. Doc. 160, 41 Cong., 2 Sess., 13–16.
[2] *Ibid.*, 16–17. Mr. Forbes arrived before General Sickles, but awaited the latter; he left Spain about August 20, 1869.

president of the council of state, and Señor Silvela, the foreign minister, a general tender of the good offices of his government.

"It was," said Señor Silvela, "the intention of the Spanish liberals, who planned and executed the revolutionary movements which had given to Spain its new political life, to make at the earliest moment provision for granting self-government to Cuba. But this fatal insurrection broke out at the very moment when it was becoming possible to give Cuba all the rights she desired. . . . The liberal party in Spain finds itself, to its own infinite regret, forced into seeming sympathy with the reactionary party in Cuba; and the liberals of Cuba, who ought to be its firm friends, are converted by the fatality of the situation into its bitterest enemies. . . . He considered the insurrection as a most deplorable misfortune and mistake, both for Cuba and for Spain. . . . It has been [the] constant hope and wish of the liberals to grant to the Cubans the administration of their own affairs, and the full fruits of their own labor, preserving their commercial connections and some shadow of their political relations."[1]

Prim was more emphatic: "For his part, if he were alone concerned, he would say to the Cubans, 'Go if you will; make good the treasure you have lost us, and let me bring home our army and fleet, and consolidate the liberties and resources of Spain.'"[2] But in the view of the Spanish ministry the constitution intervened to prevent any definite arrangement until Cuban representatives should have taken their seats in the Cortes.

The Spanish government thus intimated its willingness to accept the good offices of the United States on the following bases:

1. The insurgents to lay down their arms.

2. Spain to grant simultaneously a full and complete amnesty.

3. The people of Cuba to vote by universal suffrage upon the question of their independence.

4. The majority having declared for independence, Spain to grant it, the Cortes consenting; Cuba paying satisfactory equivalent, guaranteed by the United States.[3]

---

[1] General Sickles to Mr. Fish, August 12, 1869, House Ex. Doc. 160, 41 Cong., 2 Sess., 19.
[2] Prim to Sickles; General Sickles to Mr. Fish, August 16, 1869, *Ibid.*, 25.
[3] General Sickles to Mr. Fish (telegram), August 13, 1869, *Ibid.*, 27.

On the reception of the telegram stating these terms, Mr. Fish telegraphed that the first proposition of Spain, that the insurgents should lay down their arms, was incapable of attainment, and that to ascertain the will of the Cubans by a vote was impracticable, because of the disorganization of society, the terrorism which prevails, and the violence and insubordination of the volunteers. "There can be no question," he said, "as to the will of the majority; it has been recognized and admitted. An armistice should immediately be agreed upon to arrest the carnage and destruction of property, and opportunity be granted to communicate with the insurgents, and emancipation of slaves be determined."[1]

Of the good intentions of the Spanish government there can be no doubt. In answer to the American minister's argument, "that Austria had transferred Venice to France, and assented to its immediate transfer to Italy, before peace was declared; that the independence of all the [South] American states had been recognized at one time and another during the progress of hostilities," Prim, the president of the council, said: "The Cuban insurgents hold no city or fortress; they have no ports, no ships; they have no army that presumes to offer or accept battle; and now, before the period of active operations, when Spain will send the ample re-enforcements she holds in readiness, it is only necessary for the Cubans to accept the assurance of the United States, given on the faith of Spain, that they may have their independence by laying down their arms, electing their deputies, and declaring their wish to be free by a vote of the people."

Next day Prim explained to the American minister that "the first proposition of Spain was not a preliminary to an agreement with the United States, but was a condition of concessions to the insurgents; and that the third proposition was a condition of the independence of Cuba." "I again," said Sickles, "urged acceptance on the basis proposed by the United States." Prim said: "Spain desired the good offices of the United States, and was prepared to set Cuba free, but that the consent of Spain must be given in a manner consistent with her self-respect." He repeated, "that an armistice with the insurgents was impossible; that the emancipation of slaves could not be separated from the other questions

[1] House Ex. Doc. 160, 41 Cong., 2 Sess., 25.

now paramount, and that communication with the insurgents would be permitted after agreement with the United States."[1]

The American minister justly regarded the report of the conversation as (using his own words) essential to a correct appreciation of the views of Spain. We here see the outcrop of one of the great obstacles to Spain's happiness, the exaggeration of the sentiment known as *pundonor*, forever a stumbling-block, and which in this instance was to stand for years of bloodshed, for millions of wasted treasure, for misdirected energies which, rightly directed, would have made Spain prosperous and powerful. "It is impossible," said Prim, "to treat with the Cubans now, but the United States, once convinced of the good intentions and good faith of the Spanish government, can then assure the Cubans that, by following the programme I have indicated, they can have their liberty without firing another shot. . . . Here, then, are the successive steps:

"1. A settlement of a basis of agreement which shall assure the government of the United States of the good intentions and good faith of the Spanish government;

"2. The United States to counsel the Cubans to accept this agreement;

"3. Cessation of hostilities and amnesty;

"4. The election of deputies;

"5. Action of the Cortes;

"6. Plebiscit and independence.

"This being all arranged in advance between the two governments, if the United States could be satisfied of the sincerity of these proposals, and would persuade the Cubans to accept them, the object we both desire could be accomplished. There will, of course, be difficulties in the execution of the plan, but they must be met and overcome."[2]

On August 24, 1869, Mr. Fish telegraphed General Sickles: "The propositions of Spain are incompatible with any practicable negotiation. The representatives of the insurrectionary government are necessary parties to a negotiation. Free communication

[1] General Sickles to Mr. Fish (telegram), August 20, 1869, House Ex. Doc. 160, 41 Cong., 2 Sess., 28.
[2] General Sickles to Mr. Fish, August 21, 1869, *Ibid.*, 30.

through the Spanish lines is immediately necessary. The United States cannot ask the insurgents to lay down their arms unless the volunteers are simultaneously effectually disarmed and in good faith disbanded. This, if practicable, would require time. We want to arrest the destruction of life and property and to stop the outrages and annoyances of our citizens. An armistice would effect this immediately, and the terms of the emancipation to be made to Spain by Cuba could then be arranged between them, under the mediation of the United States. You may say that we deem an armistice indispensable to the success of any negotiation. Spain may in honor grant this at the request of the United States and in deference to the wishes of a friendly power whose good offices she is willing to accept. This being done, negotiations can immediately be opened that will probably result in peace and her receiving a fair compensation." [1]

A week later, September 1, Mr. Fish telegraphed: " United States willing to mediate on these terms: First, immediate armistice; second, Cuba to recompense Spain for public property taken; United States not to guarantee unless Congress approve . . . ; third, persons and property of Spaniards remaining on island protected, but they may at option withdraw. To prevent difficulties as well as stop bloodshed and devastation, we must have early decision. These offers withdrawn unless accepted before October 1. Say that anarchy prevails over much of island. Murders of American citizens are committed by volunteers. Confiscation of their property attempted by Spanish authorities." [2]

On September 3, 1869, the American minister, thus pressed, sent a note to Señor Becerra, the Spanish minister of state, *ad interim*, which embodied his instructions of June 29, with the addition of remarks upon the developments in the interval. Señor Becerra was assured that "the good offices of the President will be quite unavailing unless both the antagonists are disposed to listen to friendly counsels. This consideration increased the regret . . . in having to communicate . . . the declaration of . . . the minister of state, that Spain 'can come to no definite decision in regard to the political situation and future government of the island of Cuba until

[1] Mr. Fish to General Sickles, House Ex. Doc. 160, 41 Cong., 2 Sess., 31.
[2] *Ibid.*, 32.

the insurgents lay down their arms and cease the struggle.' The undersigned is instructed to state that these conditions are deemed by the President incompatible with any practicable negotiation. It is not reasonable to hope that either party to a long and sanguinary contest will voluntarily abandon it without guarantees for the future in some measure equivalent to the sacrifices it has made. The United States cannot ask the insurgents to lay down their arms unless the volunteers are simultaneously and effectively disarmed and in good faith disbanded. . . . The excesses which have followed the domination of the volunteers in some parts of the island, sparing neither combatants nor prisoners of war nor unoffending citizens of the United States, have aroused feelings of indignation and horror, which the refinement and sensibility of the Spanish nation will be the first to appreciate." [1]

It was very unfortunate that General Sickles was required by his instructions to hand in his note without delay. Both Prim, president of the council, and Silvela, minister of state, were, at the moment, absent at Vichy. What followed illustrates to the full the ever-present discordance of opinion in Spanish cabinets. Señor Becerra was bitterly opposed to the separation of Cuba from Spain and, besides, was not in the secret of what had gone before. Alarmed and indignant, he published the substance of General Sickles's note and threw Spain into a ferment of excitement. Prim hastened from Vichy, but the attitude of the Cortes had been taken from which there was no withdrawal. This attitude was well expressed in a statement from Señor Becerra to the American minister respecting a rumor that Spain had entered upon negotiations with other powers upon the subject of the note. "As Spain," he said, "will not negotiate with the United States upon a subject like that of Cuba, which relates to its internal policy and government, neither will she negotiate with any other power." [2] Said Prim to Sickles: "Nothing remains to be done but to wait for a year or two until public opinion in Spain becomes calm." [3]

The situation, too, was unfortunately complicated at this moment by the detention of several small gun-boats, orders for thirty of which for services in Cuban waters had been given in the

[1] House Ex. Doc. 160, 41 Cong., 2 Sess., 34–36.   [2] *Ibid.*, 40.
[3] General Sickles in note to author.

United States by Spain. On July 1, 1869, an energetic protest had been made by the Peruvian minister at Washington against their delivery. Spain was still technically at war with Peru, and the latter's minister claimed that even if these boats were for actual use in Cuba, they would thereby release all Spain's other naval forces against the republics on the Pacific coast, in case hostilities should be renewed.[1] However much it was made in the interest of Cuba, as may well have been the case, the President had no option but to comply with the request, which was precisely similar in character to one made by the Spanish minister the year before respecting two monitors sold to Peru, which were detained until released by consent of the Spanish minister, on the assurance that they would not attempt to commit any act offensive to Spanish interests during their voyage to the Pacific.[2]

Despite the views expressed by the president of the council and the minister of state, an irritating situation which was susceptible of immediate arrangement was allowed to continue, apparently through the inertia of diplomacy. "The war between Spain and Peru was," said Prim, "an absurd and foolish war, left by the late government of Spain, and which the present government was determined to close at once. Not another shot will be fired in it, and that the Peruvians know as well as we. We cannot be induced to recommence that war."[3] Though apparently a mere suggestion of action from Spain to the American government was all that was necessary to dissipate the cloud, it was not until December that assurance from Spain was given through the secretary of state at Washington to the Peruvian minister, who withdrew his objection, and the gun-boats were released; there had been, however, the long interval for the incubation of ill feeling, full advantage of which was taken by the Spanish monarchical press, with the result of making it increasingly difficult for the Spanish government to act in accord with the proposals from Washington for the pacification of Cuba.

The acting minister of state requested the withdrawal of the American minister's note of September 3. While accepting the

[1] Señor Freyre, Peruvian minister, to Mr. Fish, secretary of state, House Ex. Doc. 160, 41 Cong., 2 Sess., 55.
[2] Señor Goñi, Spanish minister, to Mr. Seward, secretary of state, May 23, 1868, and November 24, 1868, *Ibid.*, 55.
[3] Mr. Sickles to Mr. Fish, September 25, 1869, *Ibid.*, 51.

good offices of Washington, the bases proposed were rejected. The permanent commission of the Cortes on transmarine affairs opposed treating with any foreign power respecting Cuba, and unanimously assured the government that all means would be at the disposal of the government for putting down the rebellion. An armistice would be agreed to, if necessary, for peace, though such a measure must be left to the discretion of the captain-general in Cuba. It was declared that Spain was ready to give Cuba ample reforms and the widest liberties enjoyed in the Peninsula, with a general amnesty and gradual emancipation of slaves. If these proposals should be rejected, the war would be prosecuted with energy and activity, pardoning, however, the vanquished and prisoners, and striving to prevent all shedding of blood through revenge, and all reprisals, whatever the provocation, from insurgents. Reparation was promised in the cases of Speakman and Wyeth, the cruelty of which had been spoken of by every member of the Spanish government with indignation, and orders were given to prevent such cruelties thereafter.[1]

On September 15, 1869, Mr. Fish sent the following telegram:

If a negotiation were made on the basis of the six successive steps mentioned in your despatch No. 10, August 21, omitting the plebiscit, can the president of the council give assurance that if the United States induced the insurgents to lay down arms, and deputies to the Cortes be elected by Cuba, that the Cortes will grant independence? The plebiscit is impracticable, because, in the present circumstances and conditions of the island, a popular vote can be no indication of the popular will, and this must be borne in mind with reference to any election to be held for deputies. It is doubtful if the insurgents will consent to lay down their arms, but if their early independence can be assured thereby, the United States will make every effort to induce them to do so.[2]

As seen, the views of the two most influential of the men at the moment in power in Spain were not in disaccord with the suggestions from Washington, and they were now receiving some support from public opinion. "Six months ago," said Prim, in an interview, September 23, with the American minister, "the question

[1] Señor Becerra to General Sickles, September 16, 1869, House Ex. Doc. 160, 41 Cong., 2 Sess., 39–41. General Sickles to Mr. Fish (telegram), September 16, 1869, *Ibid.*, 41–42.   [2] *Ibid.*, 41.

could not be discussed in Spain, now it is a general topic of discussion. At first there was but one side, now there are evidently two; a decided sentiment in favor of the emancipation of Cuba is growing up; let the national honor be saved," and he thought there would be no serious difficulty in accomplishing the emancipation of the island. His news from the captain-general was very good; he expected with the assistance of a few additional battalions to break the military power of the insurrection; in the course of the autumn the government expected to be able to begin the work of political reform. The one thing necessary is to bring about as soon as possible the cessation of hostilities. He regarded the election of delegates to the Cortes an absolutely necessary preliminary to the action of the Cortes; no other course was possible without a violation of the constitution; the disarmament of the volunteers would be simultaneous with the cessation of hostilities; he had already taken his measures and given orders to the captain-general for that purpose. Severe and positive orders had been given to prevent the barbarous and cruel executions which had hitherto marked the progress of the war.[1] Captain-General de Rodas, in answering, had avowed his intention of putting a stop to such occurrences, resorting to the punishment of death, if necessary.[2]

General Sickles had declined to withdraw his note of September 3, but now, under the discretion allowed him by a telegram from the department of state, September 23, and with the assurance of Prim that at the moment it embarrassed the Spanish government, Sickles stated that he would withdraw the bases of action proposed from Washington and the tender of good offices from the United States. "We can better proceed in the present situation of things," said Prim, "without even the friendly intervention." [3]

The one step forward was an understanding that a plebiscit would not be insisted upon. But practically, however strong the good-will of the head of the government, nothing happened;

[1] A marked instance of the cruelty shown is to be found in a letter of the American consul at Matanzas, August 18, 1869, giving an account of the shooting, by order of a Colonel Palacios, of over twenty persons, near Bayamo, most of whom belonged to the most prominent families of Santiago. The affair was a cold-blooded massacre. (House Ex. Doc. 160, 41 Cong., 2 Sess., 122.)
[2] General Sickles to Mr. Fish, September 25, 1869, *Ibid.*, 50.
[3] *Ibid.*, 52.

"although," wrote the American minister, "the Cortes have been in session for a month, the Cuban question has not been considered, nor even mentioned, otherwise than incidentally in the public sittings. With every mail from Havana the announcement is repeated that the insurrection is suppressed, yet the embarkation of re-enforcements continues. The consul at Cadiz reports the departure of 1,428 troops since the middle of October."[1] On November 8 the colonial minister declared in the Cortes "that the government would not bring forward any measure of reform for Cuba until the last hostile band was dispersed and the insurgents had lost all hope."[2] Spain, he said again, "is in the position of a man of honor who does not yield what is asked of him by an armed adversary. The first thing is to conquer; if possible, bloodlessly; but if this be impossible, the right of force and the force of right will decide."[3]

On November 21, however, a project for reforms in Puerto Rico was brought forward, indicating what might be done for Cuba. This included local self-government, modified liberty of the press and of public discussion and association, the establishment of public schools, impartial suffrage, gradual but speedy abolition of slavery, civil and political rights without distinction of color, and right of domiciled foreigners to vote for town officials after six months' and for members of the provisional council after one year's residence. The American minister was assured that these reforms would be extended to Cuba when hostilities should cease and deputies should be chosen in compliance with the constitution.[4] A marked sign of the changed attitude in Spain was the appearance in the *Diario*, of Barcelona, of its conclusion that "in our judgment no other resource remains to us but to open negotiations with the United States for the cession to them of our Antilles," a remark copied into the popular organ in Havana of the volunteers, the *Voz de Cuba*, of September 20, 1869, the latter a fact in itself indicative of the new possibilities.

There can be little doubt that adjustment was almost within reach. The action of the British government in directing its

---

[1] General Sickles to Mr. Fish, November 3, 1869, House Ex. Doc., 160, 41 Cong., 2 Sess., 60.
[2] *Ibid.*, 60.   [3] *Ibid.*, 162.   [4] *Ibid.*, 162–164.

ambassador at Madrid, Mr. Layard, to second the American minister in his suggestions to the Spanish government in regard to the abolition of slavery, came to add weight to the American proposals.[1]

In reply to General Sickles's announcement of this support, Mr. Fish wrote: "It becomes more apparent every day that this contest cannot terminate without the abolition of slavery. This government regards the government at Madrid as committed to that result," and the American minister was directed to state that it was expected, if it should appear that the insurrection was regarded as suppressed, as had been frequently stated, that such steps would be taken.[2]

But the great opportunity which promised so fair was lost; the Spanish proviso of antecedent peace called for the impossible. Had the acceptance of the good offices of the United States been continued, had the government of the latter been given at this moment opportunity to act as a mediator, there would have been possibility of the accomplishment of what the more influential of the men in power in Spain were undoubtedly desirous of bringing about. Had the insurgents refused such mediation, they would have lost the American sympathy, which was so strong an element in heartening the insurgent party in continuing the struggle. Had Spain been willing to proceed upon the basis of an armistice, and had such offer been accepted by the insurgents, and had Spain thereupon not carried out the intentions which were to serve as the base of American action, such failure would have been just cause for the United States to intervene forcibly in the contest. The resolution, announced November 8 by the colonial minister, to first conquer a peace was fatal. It was a declaration of war for nine more years.

The fundamental difficulty was in the state of Spain itself. At the end of 1869 the country "found itself a kingdom without a king, with a nerveless regency, an effete Cortes, a constitution disregarded, a ministry divided against itself, an empty treasury, and a population irritated to the point of fury. . . . More conscripts

---

[1] General Sickles to Mr. Fish, December 29, 1869, House Doc. 160, 41 Cong., 2 Sess., 67.
[2] Mr. Fish to General Sickles, January 26, 1870, *Ibid.*, 69.

were needed, and fresh risings took place against the blood tax; powers of suppression were hurriedly granted by the Cortes which practically suspended the constitution; murder, pillage, anarchy, and national decay had reached their apogee in the spring of 1870, when the question of the monarch had to be settled,"[1] as it was soon to be by the choice of the Italian Prince Amadeo; a choice for which Prim's life was to be the forfeit.[2]

[1] Hume, 480.
[2] Amadeo was elected king November 16, 1870, by a vote of 191 out of 311, a majority of 71 of the members present. The whole number of deputies was 344. Besides the 33 absent, 19, of whom 12 were Carlists, voted blank, 63 voted for a republic, 27 for the Duke of Montpensier, and the rest scattering. It appears, therefore, that of the 229 votes cast for candidates for the throne, the Italian prince received 84 per cent. (General Sickles to Mr. Fish, November 19, 1870, *Foreign Relations*, 1871, 731.)

CHAPTER XVI

THE FIRM AND CORRECT STAND OF GENERAL GRANT'S ADMINIS-
TRATION. THE "VIRGINIUS"

By this time Spain had available in Cuba, if the 40,000 volunteers doing garrison duty be included, over 100,000 men; 34,000 had been sent from Spain since the beginning of November, 1868. Of the total force but 7,500 were cavalry, the only arm which could be of real value in such warfare.

Throughout this and the final contest, Spain's great error was in sending to the island vast bodies of infantry, which were wholly ineffective against a mounted enemy such as the Cubans were. Amazing as was her energy in the transport and support of such great masses of troops, equally amazing was its misdirection. There were fourteen men-of-war on the station, including two iron-clads, besides the small gun-boats built and building in the United States. The whole was an astonishing exhibition of effort on the part of a country torn by internal dissensions and with credit at the lowest ebb.

The brutal conduct of officials in Cuba, their disregard of the treaty of 1795, the refusal of Mr. Fish to consent to the issue of a proclamation of recognition of the Cuban rebels as constituting a belligerent government, and the arrest of military enterprises destined for Cuba, created great emotion in Congress and throughout the country. Mr. Fish wrote to General Sickles mentioning the manner in which hostile action against Spanish sovereignty over Cuba had been resisted by the administration, "against a strong sympathetic pressure from without," a pressure so strong that there was a brief time in August, 1870, when the President contemplated the granting of belligerent rights, and had even caused a proclamation to be prepared which he signed and left with Mr. Fish, but which the latter did not issue.[1]

If one may make a safe inference from the notes of Mr. Fish that have been published by Congress, it was his desire and purpose to keep the *Alabama* negotiation and the Cuban difficulties out of the hands of Congress and in his own control, subject, of course, to the orders of the President. In that he was successful, but the emotions in Congress and in the country over the coming seizure of the *Virginius*, and the massacre of many of her crew and passengers, nearly forced his hand.

The President's first annual message, December, 1869, had dealt very shortly with Cuban affairs. Though himself in strong personal sympathy with the aspirations of the insurgents, so much so, in fact, that but for the determined attitude of Mr. Fish he would have yielded to the pressure of those in Congress who had his confidence, and who were eager for action against Spain, he had said in his message, "the contest has at no time assumed the conditions which amount to war in the sense of international law, or which would show the existence of a *de facto* political organization of the insurgents sufficient to justify a recognition of belligerency." Notwithstanding, on January 31, 1870, a joint resolution, granting the insurgents belligerent rights, was introduced in the House by Mr. Fitch, and on February 11 in the Senate by Mr. John Sherman.[2]

The President's sympathies were well known, and the character of the special message on the subject sent to Congress June 13, 1870, must have come with a certain shock of surprise to the

[1] Senate Ex. Doc., 108, 41 Cong., 2 Sess., 245; *Foreign Relations*, 1871, 697; Moore, *International Arbitrations*, II, 1033 (note); *The Atlantic Monthly*, February, 1894; Adams, *Lee at Appomattox, and Other Papers*, 117–123; Rhodes, *United States*, VI, 345.

[2] Mr. Sherman's move was taken with an inconsiderateness unhappily not unusual in our congressional action, and was a forecast of his attitude twenty-seven years later. He was not, in 1870, even aware of the existence of the treaty with Spain, of 1795, and under it, of the necessary consequences of his action if carried through. He admitted that he had not examined the subject closely, and was advised by Mr. Fish, "in connection with the passing of his resolution, to prepare bills for the increase of the public debt and to meet the increased appropriation which [would] be necessary for the army, navy, etc. (Mr. Fish's *Private Journal*, February 19, 1870; John Bassett Moore, in the *Forum*, May, 1896, 295.)

promoters of the resolution. Recalling his previous statement of December, 1869, and mentioning that no signs of advance had been shown, either by the insurgents or the Spanish authorities in Cuba, the President said: "The torch of Spaniard and Cuban is alike busy in carrying devastation over fertile regions; murderous and vengeful decrees are issued and executed by both parties. Count Valmaseda and Colonel Boet, on the part of Spain, have each startled humanity and aroused the indignation of the civilized world by the execution, each, of a score of prisoners at a time; while General Quesada, the Cuban chief, coolly and with apparent unconsciousness of aught else than a proper act, has admitted the slaughter, by his own deliberate order, in one day of upward of six hundred and fifty prisoners of war. A summary trial, with few, if any, escapes from conviction, followed by immediate execution, is the fate of those arrested on either side on suspicion of infidelity to the cause of the party making the arrest. Whatever may be the sympathies of the people or of the government of the United States for the cause or objects for which a part of the people of Cuba are understood to have put themselves in armed resistance to the government of Spain, there can be no just sympathy in a conflict carried on by both parties alike in such barbarous violation of the rules of civilized nations, and with such continued outrage upon the plainest principles of humanity."

The President continued in a remark which it would have been well to have kept in mind in later days, saying with justice: "We cannot discriminate in our censure of their mode of conducting their contest between the Spaniards and the Cubans. Each commit the same atrocities and outrage alike the established rules of war."

Mr. Fish had already declared in a despatch to General Sickles in January, 1870, that the flagrant violations of law by the agents of the insurrectionists had decreased public interest in the United States, and had alienated popular sympathy; that if, instead of employing persons to go in armed bands to Cuba, they had gone thither to take personal part in the struggle, "it is certain that there would have been a more ardent feeling . . . in favor of their course, and more respect for their own sincerity and personal courage."[1] The President dwelt upon this phase, saying: "During the whole contest the remarkable exhibition has been made of large numbers of Cubans escaping from the island and avoiding the risks of war, congregating in this country at a safe distance from the scene of danger, and endeavoring to make war from our shores, to urge our people into the fight, which they avoid, and to embroil this government in complications and possible hostilities with Spain. It can scarce be doubted that this last result is the real object of these parties, although carefully covered under the deceptive and apparently plausible demand for a mere recognition of belligerency.

"It is stated, on what I have reason to regard as good authority, that Cuban bonds have been prepared to a large amount, whose payment is made contingent upon the recognition by the United States of either Cuban belligerency or independence. The object of making their value thus contingent upon the action of this government is a subject for serious reflection."

Citing the action of all previous administrations and recalling the strict rule of public policy expressed by Mr. Monroe, with reference to the Spanish-American revolted provinces, that "as soon as the movement assumed such a steady and consistent form as to make the success of the provinces probable, the rights to which they were entitled by the laws of nations as equal parties to a civil war were extended to them," the President proceeded:

"The question of belligerency is one of fact, not to be decided by sympathies for, or prejudices against, either party. The relations between the parent state and the insurgents must amount, in fact, to war, in the sense of international law. Fighting, though fierce and protracted, does not constitute war; there must be military forces acting in accordance with the rules and customs of war, flags of truce, cartels, exchange of prisoners, etc., and, to justify a recognition of belligerency, there must be, above all, a *de facto* political organization of the insurgents sufficient in character and resources to constitute it, if left to itself, a state among nations, capable of discharging the duties of a state, and of meeting the just responsibilities it may incur as such toward other powers

[1] Mr. Fish to General Sickles, January 26, 1870, House Ex. Doc. 160, 41 Cong., 2 Sess., 69.

in the discharge of its national duties. . . . The insurgents hold no town or city; have no established seat of government; they have no prize courts; no organization for the receiving and collecting of revenue; no seaport to which a prize may be carried, or through which access may be had by a foreign power to the limited interior territory and mountain fastnesses which they occupy. The existence of a legislature representing any popular constituency is more than doubtful. In the uncertainty which hangs about the entire insurrection, there is no palpable evidence of an election, of any delegated authority, or of any government outside the limits of the camps occupied from day to day, by the roving companies of insurgent troops; there is no commerce, no trade, either internal or foreign, no manufactures. The late commander-in-chief of the insurgents, having recently come to the United States, publicly declared that 'all commercial intercourse or trade with the exterior world has been utterly cut off,' and he further added, 'To-day we have not ten thousand arms in Cuba.'

"It is a well-established principle of public law that a recognition by a foreign state of belligerent rights to insurgents under circumstances such as now exist in Cuba, if not justified by necessity, is a gratuitous demonstration of moral support to the rebellion. Such necessity may hereafter arrive, but it has not yet arrived, nor is its probability clearly to be seen. If it be war between Spain and Cuba, and be so recognized, it is our duty to provide for the consequences which may ensue in the embarrassment to our commerce and the interference with our revenue. If belligerency be recognized, the commercial marine of the United States becomes liable to search and to seizure by the commissioned cruisers of both parties—they become subject to the adjudication of prize courts. Our large coastwise trade between the Atlantic and Gulf states and between both and the Isthmus of Panama and the states of South America (engaging the larger part of our commercial marine) passes, of necessity, almost in sight of the island of Cuba. Under the treaty of 1795, as well as by the law of nations, our vessels will be liable to visit on the high seas. In case of belligerency, the carrying of contraband which is now lawful, becomes liable to the risks of seizure and condemnation. The parent government becomes relieved from responsibility for acts done in the insurgent territory, and acquires the right to exercise against neutral commerce all the powers of a party to a maritime war. To what consequences the exercise of those powers may lead is a question which I desire to commend to the serious consideration of Congress."[1]

On June 16 the resolution to recognize insurgent belligerency passed the House by a vote of 80 to 68; but after much discussion and amendment was lost in the Senate.[2]

On June 9 Mr. Fish, in a note to the Spanish minister, summarized the complaints of the United States in regard to the savagery of the orders issued by Spanish commanders in Cuba; to the proclamations forbidding the alienation of American property, and the custody and management of such property which had been embargoed; and to the violations of the seventh article of the treaty of 1795 which forbade such embargo and assured freedom from arrest of citizens of either party to the treaty except by order and authority of law, and likewise assured to persons so arrested the assistance of such counsel and agents as they should judge proper.[3]

Extraordinary powers as to affairs in Cuba had been conferred upon the Spanish minister in August, 1869, to arrest the infractions of the rights secured by the treaty and to obtain the restoration of the properties. Mr. Fish asked, in the same despatch, if these powers were continued, and being informed by the Spanish min-

[1] Senate Ex. Doc. 99, 41 Cong., 2 Sess., 1-5.
[2] General Grant, in combating later Mr. Fish's desire to retire, said: "On two important occasions, at least, your steadiness and wisdom have kept me from mistakes into which I should have fallen. On one of these occasions you led, too, against my judgment at the time—you almost forced me—in the matter of signing the late Cuban message. I see now how right it was, and I desire most sincerely to thank you. The measure was right, and the whole country acquiesces in it." He repeated that he wished to thank me especially for those two occasions. They were, one, preventing the issuing, last August and September, [1869] of the proclamation of Cuban belligerency which he had signed, and which he wrote me a note instructing me to sign (which I did) and to issue (which I did not); and, second, the Cuban message of June 13 [1870]. (Mr. Fish's *Private Journal*, quoted by John Bassett Moore in *The Forum*, May, 1896, 295.)
[3] *Foreign Relations*, 1871, 698-700; also Senate Doc. 108, 41 Cong., 2 Sess., 239-242.

ister, June 24, that in view of the favorable situation in Cuba they had been deemed no longer necessary and had been withdrawn,[1] General Sickles was instructed to present the subject to the Spanish government combined with an extended series of reclamations for offences such as were complained of in Mr. Fish's note of June 9 to Señor Roberts. This General Sickles did in a lengthy note, July 26, 1870, ending: "The treaty of 1795, negotiated on the part of Spain by the Prince of [the] Peace and ratified during the administration of George Washington, recalls some of the earliest traditions of the cordial and uninterrupted friendship which has been so long preserved between the United States and Spain. In the name of these traditions and for the sake of that friendship, I appeal to your excellency to cause such instructions to be given to the authorities in Cuba as will prevent further injuries to citizens of the United States who may be bound within that jurisdiction or who may have property there. . . ."[2]

A long and intricate series of communications passed before an understanding could be effected, February 12, 1871, one of the chief difficulties on the Spanish side being that of arranging satisfactorily concerning those of Cuban birth who, many in good faith, many otherwise, had become citizens of the United States.[3]

On May 5, 1870, the new law had been presented to the Cortes, making Puerto Rico a province of Spain with proportional representation in the Cortes, and establishing a provincial chamber of deputies with, however, very limited powers, subject to approval by the Cortes. The power of the captain-general remained practically the same. No public discussion was allowed as to separation of the island from Spain or as to slavery. A very ineffective and insufficient bill for the emancipation of slaves both in Cuba and Puerto Rico was, however, offered on May 28, 1870, by the minister of the colonies, Señor Moret y Prendergast, which became a law on June 23, the last day of the sitting of the Cortes. All chil-

---

[1] *Foreign Relations*, 1871, 243.   [2] *Ibid.*, 705.
[3] See *Ibid.*, 697–775. The commission, finally organized, sat at Washington. Its labors did not end until January 1, 1883. There were 130 claims presented amounting to $29,946,183.32. Awards were given in favor of 35 claims amounting to $1,293,450.55. See on this subject Moore, *Digest*, VI, 907–913.

dren born after the decree, and all slaves on reaching the age of sixty-five, were to be free.[1]

Though the Captain-General of Cuba on his own authority had, on May 14, 1870, issued a *bando* declaring the emancipation of slaves of the insurgents, and slavery had been declared abolished by the insurgents, February 26, 1869, the Moret law was a dead letter so far as Cuba was concerned, and was not even allowed by the volunteers to be published for nearly two years after the world supposed it to have been in action.[2]

Much, in these months, had happened in the Peninsula. The country by 1870 was anarchic. There was a powerless regency of which Serrano was the nominal but Prim the real head. The question of the year was a new monarch to replace the imitation of government. "Carlist bands sprang up in all parts of Spain; socialist and separatist risings took place in Cataluña, Aragon, Andalusia, and Valencia. Again the blood of Spaniards was shed by Spaniards in almost every great town before comparative order could be restored; and, in the meanwhile, intrigues without end, secret combinations, and active propaganda at home and abroad pushed the interests of rival candidates for the throne."[3] The result was the acceptance, as king, November 3, 1870, by a vote of 191 in a house of 311 members present, of Amadeo, Duke of Aosta, the second son of Victor Emmanuel of Italy. While on his way to Spain in the iron-clad *Numancia*, his chief supporter Prim was shot in Madrid, December 27, and died the day Amadeo landed in Spain, three days later.

Amadeo entered Madrid January 2, 1871, to reign over a distracted government a little more than two years. He resigned his kingship February 11, 1873, and a republic was proclaimed, with Pi y Margall, Salmeron, and Castelar, successively, as presidents. The whole north rose in favor of Don Carlos, and a civil war began which brought anarchy to every part of the Peninsula. The coast, January 31, 1874, was declared blockaded from Cape de Peñas to Fuenterrabia, some two hundred and fifty miles in extent; and on July 18, 1874, the whole of Spain and the ad-

---

[1] Senate Doc. 113, 41 Cong., 2 Sess., 8–12.
[2] Gallenga, *The Pearl of the Antilles*, 17.
[3] Hume, *Modern Spain*, 476.

joining islands was declared in a state of siege. The credit of the country naturally sank until it was "lower than that of any other nation."[1]

In November, 1873, General Jovellar, taking over the governor-generalship, at once announced to the "Inhabitants of the Ever Faithful Island of Cuba," in the name of the government of President Castelar, that, after an experience of five years without any definite results, "it is expedient and even necessary to subordinate all other questions to one alone—to that of war,"[2] a pronouncement which left no hope for a cessation of the ruin and desolation which had been so long the island's fate.

The Cubans in the United States, many of whom were of great wealth, had been continuously active in equipping expeditions and in endeavoring to send men and arms. Some of these efforts were successful despite the earnest and best-intentioned efforts of the American authorities. On October 31, 1873, the steamer *Virginius*, commanded by Captain Joseph Fry, formerly of the United States and later of the Confederate navy, carrying a crew of fifty-two, chiefly of American and British nationality, and one hundred and three Cubans as passengers, and with a considerable cargo of arms and equipments, was, after a long chase, captured some twenty miles from the Jamaican coast by the Spanish steamer *Tornado*.

The *Virginius* and her captor had both been built in Scotland as blockade-runners in the civil war; the former, known as the *Virgin*, being in Mobile at the close of hostilities, became prize to the Federal government. Sold once and taken back by the government for a debt, she was sold again in 1870, at Washington, to one John F. Patterson, of New York, for $9,800.[3] As appeared later, Patterson was but the nominal owner, the real owners being a number of Cubans, of whom General Quesada and José Mora were the representatives.[4] The ship was registered in the New

[1] General Sickles to Mr. Fish, October 27, 1873, *Foreign Relations*, 1874, 845.
[2] *Ibid.*, 850. Jovellar's career was for the moment short. He resigned March 10, 1874, and General José de la Concha, who later had the title of Marquis of Havana, was appointed governor-general in his stead.
[3] Bill of sale, *Ibid.*, 1874, 1001.   [4] *Ibid.*, 1009.

York Custom-House, September 26, 1870, Patterson making oath that he was the "true and only owner," and that "no subject or citizen of any foreign prince or state [was] directly or indirectly, by way of trust, confidence, or otherwise, interested therein, or in the profits or issues thereof."[1] She cleared in due form for Curaçao October 4, 1870, her manifest showing a cargo of one hundred and seventy barrels of bread, two boxes of saddlery, and four trunks of clothing. She was not only to all outward form an American merchant vessel, "but she sailed unsuspected alike by the Spanish minister, the Spanish consul, and their detectives—unsuspected also by the United States."[2] She carried a crew of thirty men, with one, F. E. Shepperd, formerly of the United States and later of the Confederate navy, in command.

After leaving New York she took aboard, some four miles at sea, twenty Cubans, several of them of especial prominence. After lying at Curaçao several days, she left there October 19, 1870, accompanied by the American schooner *Billy Butts*, which had arrived the previous day from New York. Off the island of Buen Ayre, not far from Curaçao, the *Virginius* took from the schooner a considerable quantity of arms and ammunition and four brass field-pieces.[3]

Her career thenceforward was one of desultory wandering in the waters of the Spanish main; at one time in November, 1870, assisting in the capture of a flotilla of armed schooners on the Venezuelan coast, belonging to the party then contending against Guzman Blanco, with, it would appear, the understanding that Blanco would give assistance to the Cuban cause, in men and otherwise, as soon as the Venezuelan revolution should be put down.[4] To some degree at least this contract was carried out, thirty-nine Venezuelans being among those aboard the *Virginius* when, June 21, 1871, she landed men, arms, and other war material at Boca de Cabello, on the south coast of Cuba.[5]

The ship's status became a trying question to the American representatives in Venezuela and Colombia, her papers being

[1] *Foreign Relations*, 1874, 1003.
[2] Mr. Fish to Admiral Polo de Bernabé, Spanish minister, April 18, 1874, *Ibid.*, 1875, part 2, 1207.
[3] *Ibid.*, 1874, 1105.
[4] Testimony of F. E. Shepperd, *Ibid.*, 1010.
[5] *Ibid.*, 1109.

perfectly regular, but her occupation notoriously offensive to Spain, though within the limits of international law, in so far as carrying what would, in time of war, be considered contraband. The demands for her forcible retention made by Spanish authorities upon these national governments (both of which had recognized Cuban belligerency) were resisted by the American ministers upon these grounds.[1]

There were many changes of commanders and such financial difficulties that a bottomry bond was executed, in 1872, by her then captain, Bowen, at Aspinwall (Colon), to pay the ship's indebtedness. Later, at Puerto Cabello, Venezuela, she was advertised for sale and bid in for $17,500. The sale, however, which was to an Englishman, was not completed, as, by the statement of her then captain, Charles Smith, he was informed by the British consul that the British minister telegraphed that she would be seized as a pirate if she hoisted the British flag.[2] The American consuls also did not believe the ship morally entitled to protection, though legally so.[3]

On July 1, 1873, the *Virginius* was at Colon, where also at the time were lying the United States steamship *Kansas* and the Spanish steamer *Pizarro*. The captain of the latter had declared his intention of seizing the *Virginius* as soon as she should put to sea. She was flying the American flag, her papers were declared correct by the American consul, and Commander White, of the *Kansas*, decided to protect her. She was accompanied by the *Kansas*, cleared for action, until the *Virginius* showed that she clearly had the better of the *Pizarro* in speed and was safe from the latter's threat.[4] She later made a second landing on the Cuban coast and put into Kingston, Jamaica, July 10, 1873, where she remained until October 23. She then cleared for Port Limon, Costa Rica, her actual destination being to make a landing of men and arms in Cuba. She sprang a leak soon after leaving Kingston, and Captain Fry, who had served twenty years in the Federal and later in the Confederate navy, and had joined her but a short time before, put into an obscure Haitian port for repairs. The ship left

[1] *Foreign Relations*, 1872, 140, 156–158, 715–716.
[2] *Ibid.*, 1874, 1022.   [3] *Ibid.*, 1024, 1027.
[4] Commander White's action was fully upheld by the navy department.

Hayti, October 30, with a crew of fifty-two, including the captain, and with one hundred and three passengers, most of whom were Cubans. Among these were a brother and a son of Cespedes, the insurgent president. Twenty-six of the crew, including the second mate and twelve of the passengers, were British subjects, one of these being a "General" Ryan, a Canadian.[1] The ship had aboard some five hundred rifles, a large number of revolvers, and a quantity of ammunition, clothing, medicines, and provisions.

When about twenty miles from the Cuban coast the *Virginius* was sighted in the afternoon of October 31 by the *Tornado*, which, on information from the Spanish consul at Kingston, had gone to sea in search of her. After a chase of about seven hours she was captured at 10 P. M., some eighteen miles from Morant Bay, Jamaica.[2] She was carried into Santiago de Cuba, where she arrived at 5 P. M., November 1.

A summary court-martial was convened aboard the *Francisco de Borja* the next day, and on November 4 Ryan and three Cubans were shot as "pirates." On the 7th, with circumstances of the utmost barbarity, Captain Fry and thirty-six others were executed, and on the 8th twelve more, a total of fifty-three, despite the strongest protests from the American and British consuls and in total disregard of treaty stipulations with the United States regarding counsel and trial before a proper court. It was justly characterized as "a dreadful, a savage act."[3]

The transmittal to Jamaica by the American vice-consul of a telegram asking the actual status of the *Virginius* had even been insultingly refused, and a long delay in replying to the vice-consul's protest was put down by the governor, Burriel, "to important and peremptory affairs to which I had to devote myself exclusively; further, the past two days were holidays, upon which the officials do not come to their offices, being engaged, as every one else, in the meditation of the divine mysteries of All Saints', and the commemoration of All Souls' day, as prescribed by our holy religion; consequently it was impossible for me until early this morning to

---

[1] For lists of crew and passengers, see *Foreign Relations*, 1874, 1060, 1082, 1092, 1095. [2] *Ibid.*, 1076.
[3] Mr. Caleb Cushing, American minister, to Señor Ulloa, Spanish minister of foreign affairs, July 21, 1874, *Ibid.*, 1876, 499.

comply with your wishes, as well as my own, to answer your communications." [1]

The British man-of-war *Niobe*, Captain Sir Lambton Lorraine, was hurried from Jamaica, and arrived at Santiago November 7. The second execution took place the day of the *Niobe's* arrival. On November 8 Captain Lorraine had an interview with the governor and protested against the execution. He followed this, next day, November 9, with a written protest in which (under the British ruling in the case of the British yacht *Deerhound*, seized in June, 1873, under very similar circumstances) he declared that Great Britain refused to recognize the right of Spain to pursue and capture a vessel outside of territorial limits even if it had violated Spanish regulations; that the right to treat as prisoners of war the crews of vessels carrying contraband or persons in military service was not recognized in international law; that the views of his government in such a question applied to the *Virginius*, as British subjects were among the crew. He ended saying: "I am instructed to appeal in behalf of these last—the dead must now be omitted—soliciting, as I do, with all the force which such a situation demands, that although there may be no doubt that most of these British subjects have committed offences against the Spanish nation, they have, nevertheless, not offended to such an extent as to merit the punishment of death by any law. Even if legally captured they could not in the view of the British government be treated as prisoners of war, still less as pirates, any Spanish decree to the contrary notwithstanding. But the capture of the *Virginius* on the high seas is a proceeding which . . . her Britannic Majesty cannot regard as justifiable." [2]

On November 11 General Burriel replied to Captain Lorraine: "If by legal proceedings the death sentence be decreed against any one of the prisoners of the *Virginius*, be he of whatever nationality he may, he will be executed without fail. I am not in the habit of allowing myself to be overawed by any one, and I will not take notice of any petition, unless his excellency, the governor, captain-general of the island, orders me to do otherwise." [3] General Burriel's attitude was, in fact, a case, in officialdom, of running amuck.

---

[1] *Foreign Relations*, 1874, 1065.
[2] House Rep. 781, 43 Cong., 1 Sess. (1874).   [3] *Ibid*.

The *Wyoming*, Captain Cushing, hurried from Colon, arrived the night of November 15. Cushing immediately addressed the governor in forcible terms. "So far," he said, "from being a pirate as defined by international law, the *Virginius*, if offending at all, was simply a neutral vessel carrying contraband of war, 'a blockade runner,' or at most a smuggler. She was unarmed, and was lawfully furnished with sea papers entitling her to navigate the high seas in safety from all men . . . a vessel of a neutral country might, under the laws and agreements of nations, attempt to carry in arms and any contraband of war, subject only to the penalty of capture in transportation and confiscation of ship and cargo. No other punishment is permitted by the law of nations, to which each individual state must consent. . . . In the eye of the nations of the earth and their well-defined laws . . . such trial and execution is simply murder. . . . I solemnly protest against the imprisonment or other punishment of any of the living members of the crew or passengers who are either born or naturalized citizens of the United States. . . ."[1]

Not only had the protests of the American, British, and French consuls (there being a French citizen aboard) been flouted in the most unmannerly way, but a telegram from Madrid had been equally ineffective, through, as reported back from Cuba, the cutting of the telegraph lines by the insurgents. This had been sent by President Castelar, November 6, before any knowledge of any execution,[2] "at seven o'clock in the morning, as soon as he read the telegram from Cuba [announcing only the capture], and without reference to any international question, for that indeed had not occurred to him . . . to the captain-general admonishing him that the death penalty must not be imposed upon any non-combatant

---

[1] *Foreign Relations*, 1874, 1099.

[2] The first information regarding the *Virginius* received by the Spanish government was published in the official gazette November 6, and appeared as follows:

"Island of Cuba.—The captain-general, in a telegram of yesterday, the 5th, reports that the steamer *Tornado* captured the pirate *Virginius*, six miles from the coast of Jamaica, having made Bembeta, Hernando Céspedes (son) Quesada, Jesus del Sol, and others to the number of 165, prisoners, some of them being of importance. The horses, arms, and provisions of the *Virginius* were thrown overboard during the chase. The captain-general attaches importance to the occurrence." (*Ibid.*, 922.)

without the previous approval of the Cortes, nor upon any person taken in arms against the government without the sanction of the executive." [1]

Mr. Fish had at once, on receiving the news of the first execution, telegraphed the American minister at Madrid, November 7: "The capture on the high seas of a vessel bearing the American flag presents a very grave question, which will need investigation, and the summary proceedings resulting in the punishment of death, with such rapid haste, will attract attention as inhuman and in violation of the civilization of the age. And if it prove that an American citizen has been wrongfully executed, this government will require most ample reparation." [2]

Already, before the reception of this telegram, General Sickles, also in ignorance of the executions, but recognizing the gravity of the capture in such circumstances, had called upon the minister of state to suggest directing the captain-general in Cuba to await orders from the government before taking any further steps in the case.[3] As seen above, this had already been done. "I learn to-day," said General Sickles in his despatch of November 7, "that many deputies have united in an address to President Castelar, praying him to interpose his authority to prohibit the infliction of the death penalty on any of the persons captured in the *Virginius*. A similar petition has been laid before the parliamentary committee sitting during the recess, and which is invested with certain extraordinary powers. This proceeding is passionately assailed by the reactionary press, which loudly demands the blood of the prisoners." [4]

Having received Mr. Fish's telegram of November 7, General Sickles called upon the minister of state, and stated his hope that the Spanish government, without waiting for a formal reclamation, would take immediate steps to make the reparation which public law and the recognized usage of nations might require. "On the case as it now appeared," he said, "the proceeding of the *Tornado* was as indefensible as if a Spanish commander in the north pursued Don Carlos to Bayonne, seizing him and taking him to Pamplona to be shot. Spanish vessels had no more right to lay hands on an

---

[1] General Sickles to Mr. Fish, November 7, 1873, *Foreign Relations*, 1874, 922.
[2] *Ibid.*, 922.   [3] *Ibid.*, 922.   [4] *Ibid.*, 923.

American vessel at sea than we would have to enter the port of Cadiz and arrest an offender against our laws." [1]

Señor Carvajal was still in ignorance of any executions. He was very glad the American minister had made no formal demand. "It was," he said, "unnecessary. The government would take up the question at once, and decide it on principles of public law, and according to its international obligations, uninfluenced by political opinions or passions in any quarter." [2]

Later on the day of this interview Señor Carvajal called upon General Sickles to state that the colonial minister had received information of the shooting of four of the passengers of the *Virginius*. He expressed his extreme regret, and was confident the act took place before the orders sent by President Castelar on the 6th had been received.[3]

That the Spanish government deeply regretted the action at the moment is beyond doubt. It would, in Spain's situation at home, have required more than such a madness as that so frequently shown by its officials in Cuba to have brought the government to a congratulatory state of mind, however much it may have approved, and finally did approve, in words, the action at Santiago. It was not in reason that it should wish to add a foreign war to the civil strifes now so serious both in the Peninsula and the insurgent island.

The minister of state called upon the American minister, November 8, to express the government's extreme regret in the news of the first execution, and to say that he was confident the act took place before the reception of the orders by President Castelar, of November 6, and that further orders to stay proceedings had been sent.[4] The minister, calling again on November 13, communicated the report of the shooting of the 7th and 8th, "with," says General Sickles's telegram, "profound regret. . . . General Jovelar, the captain-general in Cuba, says he will stop any more slaughter." [5] President Castelar was himself greatly moved. "How deeply," he said to the American minister, "I deplore the execution of the four prisoners at Santiago de Cuba! What a misfortune that my order was not received in time to prevent such an act! . . . Such scandals must cease. A conservative deputation was here this

[1] *Foreign Relations*, 1874.
[2] *Ibid.*, 923.   [3] *Ibid.*, 924.   [4] *Ibid.*, 924.   [5] *Ibid.*, 935.

morning, and I told them frankly that we must put an end to slavery in Cuba; it brutalizes all it touches."[1] He received the later news of further slaughter with "deepest feeling."[2] The foreign minister said in extenuation that the legislation of September, 1873, which forbade death penalties without the approval of the Cortes, in the case of civilians, and of the executive, in military sentences, had failed to become operative in Cuba, and that the authorities had thus followed the prescriptions of the old colonial code. "General Jovellar now held himself responsible for the due observance of this law, which had been extended to Cuba by an executive order, and it was at least certain that the slaughter had ceased."[3]

The sentiments of the members of the government, whether real or, as would seem from later events, assumed, as in the case of the minister of state at least, went for little, whether in the Peninsula or in Cuba. In the latter the decrees from home were, to a great extent, nullified by the will of the volunteers, and later, Burriel himself, as a defence of his action, cited as still existent the decree of March 14, 1869, ordering the immediate execution of all persons captured in Spanish waters or on the high seas under such circumstances as those of the *Virginius*.[4] There was, in truth, but little at the moment which could be called government in either Spain or Cuba, in both of which was civil war with every horror common to Spanish usage in such a strife.

[1] General Sickles to Mr. Fish, November 12, 1873, *Foreign Relations*, 1874, 931.   [2] *Ibid.*, 935.
[3] General Sickles to Mr. Fish, November 13, 1873, *Ibid.*, 933.
[4] Letter of General Burriel to the *Revue des Deux Mondes*, in *La Epoca*, Madrid, April 21, 1874, and in *Foreign Relations*, 1876, 490.

CHAPTER XVII

THE "VIRGINIUS"

On November 12, 1873, Mr. Fish sent a note to Admiral Polo de Bernabé, the Spanish minister at Washington, mentioning that he had information of the shooting, at Santiago de Cuba, of fifty-two of the crew and passengers of the *Virginius*. He added: "This information relates to an act apparently too shocking and cruel to be credible. I am in hopes that more authentic intelligence may have reached you, which would tend to discredit the statement referred to. I will consequently thank you to relieve, as soon as you conveniently can, our natural anxiety upon the subject."[1] The admiral replied at once that he had no information. On the same day Mr. Fish sent a telegram to General Sickles, instructing him as follows: "If the report be confirmed, you will protest, in the name of this government and of civilization and humanity, against the act as brutal, barbarous, and an outrage upon the age, and will declare that this government will demand the most ample reparation of any wrong which may have been committed upon any of its citizens, or upon its flag. You are confidentially informed that grave suspicions exist as to the right of the *Virginius* to carry the American flag, as also with regard to her right to the American papers which she is said to have carried. Investigation is being made. You will bear this in mind in what you say to the ministry."[2]

On the same day Mr. Fish wrote to General Sickles more at length. He advised him: "The executions would seem to have been precipitated in cold blood and vindictiveness to anticipate and prevent the interposition of any humane restraints upon the ferocity of the local authorities from the government at Madrid, or its representative in Havana. This is but another instance in the long catalogue of the defiance of the home government by those

[1] *Foreign Relations*, 1874, 977. The number was 53. [2] *Ibid.*, 927.

intrusted with authority in Cuba. . . . The promptness with which the Madrid government responded to your suggestion and forwarded instructions to the captain-general to await orders before inflicting any penalties . . . is accepted as evidence of their readiness to administer justice, and gives promise of the promptness with which they will condemn and punish the hot thirst for blood and vengeance which was exhibited at Santiago de Cuba. Condemnation, disavowal, and deprecation of the act will not be accepted by the world as sufficient to relieve the government of Spain from participation in the just responsibility for the outrage. There must be a signal mark of displeasure and punishment to which the civilized world can point. . . . You will . . . represent that the failure of some speedy and signal visitation of punishment on those engaged in this dark deed cannot fail to be regarded as approval of the act. . . . The omission to punish the acts of the 4th of November in Santiago de Cuba will be a virtual abandonment of the control of the island, and cannot be regarded otherwise than a recognition that some power more potent than that of Spain exists within that colony. . . . With regard to the *Virginius* we are still without information as to the particulars of her capture. There are conflicting representations as to the precise place . . . whether within British waters or on the high seas . . . as to whether she was first sighted within Spanish waters and the chase commenced there, or whether it was altogether in neutral waters. There is some doubt as to the right of the *Virginius* to carry the American flag, or of her right to the papers which she unquestionably carried. This is being investigated, and, of course, no admission of doubt as to the character of the vessel can be allowed until it becomes apparent that the government cannot sustain the nationality of the vessel. . . . While writing this, a telegram from Mr. Hall mentions . . . that the captain and thirty-six of the crew of the *Virginius* and sixteen others were shot on the 7th and 8th instants. Such wholesale butchery and murder are almost incredible. . . . No government deserves to exist which can tolerate such crimes. . . ."[1]

Three days after the date of the note sent to him by Mr. Fish, the Spanish minister at Washington presented two telegrams—

[1] *Foreign Relations,* 1874, 928.

one from Cuba, the other from Madrid. The contents of the former read as follows: "The *Virginius* had no crew's roll, and was wanting in the usual papers required of merchant vessels.[1] The orders from the government could not reach Santiago de Cuba in time, owing to the destruction of the telegraph wires by the insurgents. On the 12th the captain-general received a telegram from Santiago de Cuba dated the 6th, and this was the date of the first instructions from the government. On the 14th the admiral [at Havana] received the news of the executions of the 9th [8th]. Ordinary communications have been quicker than those sent by telegraph. The case of the *Virginius* is equal, or similar, to those of the *Guanaham* and *Margaret Jersey*, and the admiral assures that in the record of the proceedings, of which he already has possession, the act of piracy is fully proved, and that the crew made no secret of the truth of their hostile intent and purpose."

The telegram from Madrid said: "The government is not in receipt of sufficient particulars in reference to the case of the *Virginius*. It will act in strict conformity with international law." [2]

Two days after the peremptory instructions to General Sickles, the contents of which were unknown to the country, great meetings were held in New York and elsewhere, denouncing the seizure of the *Virginius*, the massacre of Americans, and demanding violent action against Spain. Mr. Evarts, who was later to succeed Mr. Fish as secretary of state, spoke at a meeting in New York, and expressed the popular indignation. A vast assemblage in Tammany Hall greeted with hisses the mention of the name of the secretary of state, and cried, "Down with Fish." Orders were given in Washington to put the navy on a war footing. War seemed to be in sight. Mr. Sumner pleaded against it because Spain was now a republic, and Castelar its virtual ruler.[3]

The vague and inaccurate information regarding the deplorable events in Santiago, shown in the Spanish minister's two telegrams, not received until two weeks after the occurrence, exhibits the unsatisfactory conditions which prevented the reception by the Washington government of news from Cuba, of official acts on the

---

[1] This was incorrect; the ship's papers were, on their face, entirely regular. See *Foreign Relations*, 1874, 1073.   [2] *Ibid.*, 978.
[3] Rhodes, *History of the United States*, VII, 31.

island, and the official reasons therefor. There is also needed, in order that the reader may perceive the significance of some of the sentences of the note sent, November 12, by Mr. Fish to General Sickles, that a brief exhibition be made of the government relations at that time between Cuba and Spain, hereinbefore only touched upon, and which affected the transaction of diplomatic business between Washington and Madrid, growing out of events on the island.

In the first place, there is the power which Spain conferred, in international affairs, on her governor-captain-general, in Cuba, and especially over American citizens. A learned opinion by Attorney-General Cushing, given to Secretary Marcy in 1855, in reply to his inquiry regarding official communications between agents of the United States and the governor-captain-general, is very instructive. As mentioned earlier,[1] difficulties of the same character existed at that period as in 1873. "At the present time," says Mr. Cushing, " the authority of the governor-captain-general in the island of Cuba, as also in the Philippine Islands, appears to be co-extensive with that of the old viceroys and presidents by the laws of the Indies (Zamora, *Legislacion Ultramarina*, s. voc. Cap. Gen.). Nothing can be more comprehensive than the language of the organic law, of Philip II," which said, "They who shall be appointed viceroys of Peru and New Spain . . . in all things, cases, and affairs which occur, are to do whatever appears to them, and they see to be fit, and shall provide, in the provinces of their charge, all which we might do and provide, of whatever quality and condition it may be, were they governed by us in our proper person, save such things as may be specially prohibited." (Leyes de las Indias, Lib. III, tit. 3, ley 1.)[2] The decree of Fernando VII, in 1825, it may be added, was equally comprehensive.[3] As the captain-general of Cuba and that of Puerto Rico were, in 1829, given power " to suspend, in their discretion, the functions of all foreign consuls, and even to compel them to leave the islands," Mr. Cushing was of opinion that the United States had a right to expect that the captain-general should have a corresponding

---

[1] *Supra*, 242, 253, 256, 269.
[2] Attorney-General Caleb Cushing, *Official Opinions of Attorneys-General*, VII, 559. [3] *Supra*, 224.

beneficial power, in the same relation, to quickly respond to our just requirements.[1]

Mr. Cushing's expectations were not realized in 1855, nor were they later. For one short interval the Spanish minister at Washington was authorized, in 1869, by his government to consider and, if possible, satisfy complaints presented to him by the American government of injuries to American citizens by Spanish officials in Cuba, but the authority was soon withdrawn,[2] and affairs necessarily reverted to the ancient system of demand by the American minister upon the government at Madrid, the usual reply of which was that inquiry would be made of the captain-general as to the facts. It was the vicious circle of procrastination so dear to the Oriental mind, and one in which Spain was as adept as Turkey.

On the same day (November 12) that Mr. Fish communicated with Admiral Polo de Bernabé in Washington, and despatched his telegram to General Sickles at Madrid, Señor Carvajal, the Spanish minister of state, accompanied by the under secretary of state, called on the American minister. Mr. Fish's telegram of the 12th had not yet reached the latter. Dates are important here, as throughout the narrative in this chapter.

On November 13 General Sickles wrote Mr. Fish that the minister of state had said at their interview that a partial report of the incidents attending the capture of the *Virginius* had been received, but it appeared therefrom "that the vessel was seen on the coast of Cuba, attempting to land her passengers and cargo;[3] that the pursuit began in Spanish waters,[4] and, somewhere about twenty-three miles from Jamaica, she was overtaken and captured. It was also alleged that the *Virginius* exhibited no papers; but this was subsequently qualified by the statement that her documents were not authenticated by the *visa*, or certificate, of any consul, and were, besides, irregular in other particulars; and although the report was incomplete, yet enough was known to indicate that the case would be less difficult of adjustment than was apprehended at the

[1] *Official Opinions of Attorneys-General*, VII, 561. For the political relations between Spain and her American provinces, see the arguments in the Paris Peace Conference of 1898 regarding the Cuban debt. (Moore, *International Law Digest*, I, 351–384.)
[2] *Supra*, 311. [3] This was an error. [4] This was an error.

outset, and this was a matter for sincere congratulation." General Sickles remarked to the minister of state that he had received a further communication from Washington containing additional particulars of the capture and its consequences, of which he would speak in the afternoon, when he would meet Señor Carvajal at the ministry. "It was, however," he said, "quite certain that no demand would be made by the President until trustworthy information was received of the whole case. Meanwhile, it would be satisfactory to know that this government had spontaneously taken such action in the matter as would facilitate a prompt solution of any question that might arise."[1]

Meeting at the ministry in the afternoon, as arranged, Señor Carvajal announced, "with deep regret," the reception of the news of the shooting of forty-nine of the prisoners on the 7th and 8th. He said that he had asked by cable, sent at 2 A. M., how many were American citizens. General Sickles, in pursuance of instructions, asked "whether the executive authority of Spain exercised any jurisdiction over the island, and if so, what powers belonged to it." He was answered that the minister had, heretofore, "merely expressed an opinion in saying the ordinary laws were inapplicable. There could be no doubt, however, that the executive jurisdiction was ample; and now that the revocation of the royal order of 1825[2] had deprived the captain-general of the faculty of suspending the dispositions of the supreme government, there was no reason to apprehend a repetition of the irregularities that had hitherto occurred in the administration of Cuban affairs." General Sickles said to the minister of state "that in June last, I had invited the attention of Mr. Castelar, then minister of state, to the ground taken by the authorities in Cuba, in asserting that war existed in the island, and that no other than martial law was recognized. His excellency, having replied that this government rejected any such assertion, authorizing me to convey to you that Spain did not so regard the conflict in Cuba, I begged that instructions be sent to the captain-general not to withhold from any citizen of the United States, within his jurisdiction, the protection and securities of the ordinary tribunals of justice in due

---

[1] General Sickles to Mr. Fish, November 13, 1873, *Foreign Relations*, 1874, 932.   [2] *Supra*, 224.

course of law, as provided by the seventh article of the treaty of 1795. I was assured that such orders would be given." General Sickles also reported to Mr. Fish that he "referred to a series of instances in which the Cuban authorities had exercised powers in derogation of the rights of the United States and of their citizens," and restated the responsibility which rested upon the executive government of Spain in the present case.

Mr. Carvajal, in closing the interview, said that he had hoped to have then settled the preliminaries of an adjustment, but the intelligence received "had so modified the case, as it had been considered in the council of ministers, that he must adjourn our conference until another day." General Sickles, mentioning the "profound impression" which the publication of the events of the 7th and 8th would everywhere produce, said: "The President could not be unmoved by incidents of such gravity occurring on our borders. . . . He had so far withheld any demand, believing and expecting that Spain would spontaneously hasten to offer complete reparation for what had occurred respecting the *Virginius* and her passengers. . . . I trusted not a moment would be lost in arriving at a resolution which I might convey to you [Mr. Fish] with satisfaction." [1]

On the same day (November 13) General Sickles telegraphed to Mr. Fish a short résumé of the foregoing conference with Señor Carvajal and its results.[2] On the reception, November 14, of this telegram, Mr. Fish replied to General Sickles: "Unless abundant reparation shall have been voluntarily tendered, you will demand the restoration of the *Virginius*, the release and delivery to the United States of the persons captured on her who have not already been massacred, and that the flag of the United States be saluted in the port of Santiago, and the signal punishment of the officials who were concerned in the capture of the vessel and the execution of the passengers and crew. In case of refusal of satisfactory reparation within twelve days from this date, you will, at the expiration of that time, close your legation, and will, together with your secretary, leave Madrid, bringing with you the archives of the legation. . . ." [3]

[1] General Sickles to Mr. Fish, November 13, 1873 (the second despatch of this date), *Foreign Relations*, 1874, 933.   [2] *Ibid.*, 935.
[3] Mr. Fish to General Sickles, November 14, 1873, *Ibid.*, 936.

Mr. Fish's telegram of November 12[1] did not, unhappily, reach General Sickles until November 14, the day after his friendly interview with the minister of state. Obeying its instructions, General Sickles thus, at once, passed a note to the minister of state making the demand directed. He said among other things:

"The verbal communication made to the undersigned last evening by Mr. Carvajal, at the ministry of state, coinciding in substance with the information received at Washington, must be regarded as a confirmation of the report published in Havana and Madrid on the day before yesterday. The undersigned is, therefore, directed to protest against the said act of the authorities in Cuba as barbarous and brutal, and an outrage upon this epoch of civilization; and the undersigned is likewise ordered to declare to his excellency, the minister of state, that the government of the United States will demand the most ample reparation of any wrong which may have been thereby committed upon any of its citizens or upon its flag." [2]

The reception of this note changed completely the attitude of the Spanish minister of state, who regarded its phrases as insulting to the dignity of Spain, and in whom it aroused the deepest feeling. It produced an unhappy tension which heretofore had apparently been absent. An intimation of the increased gravity of the situation might possibly have been conveyed verbally, and at first confidentially, though it is doubtful if the feeling would have been different.

Thus, on November 14, the minister of state wrote to General Sickles: "The government of the Spanish republic cannot recognize your competency to make [the protest], even as Spain would have had no such right with respect to the sanguinary acts which have happened in our own day, as well in the United States as in other nations of the old and new continents. The protest being thus rejected with serene energy, I have to fix my attention upon the harshness of style, and upon the heated and improper words you used to qualify the conduct of the Spanish authorities. . . . I would touch lightly upon this matter if I had only to occupy myself with the sting of the insult (*ofensa*), but, comprehending its intent, the government cannot consent that in anticipation of its

[1] *Supra*, 323.   [2] *Foreign Relations*, 1874, 937.

own judgment the representative of a foreign nation, even though friendly, should characterize the Spanish authorities in other terms than those which the government itself deems just, an interference always inadmissible, but still more strange when neither the cabinet at Washington, nor this of Madrid, nor yourself have at the present hour sufficient data upon which to ground a complaint, whether concerning the seizure of the *Virginius* or in relation to the subsequent occurrences. . . . You will note that, without a knowledge of the facts, it would have been at all times an act of temerity to pass judgment upon the authorities, and that until such knowledge is acquired it befits the elevation of character you have attained to consider those as guardians and representatives of the law, while the persons shot were rebels seeking to trample the law under foot, enemies of the country, and disturbers of the peace and of the rule of a sister republic. . . . You conclude by declaring, also by order of your government, that it will demand ample reparation for any offence committed upon American citizens or upon its flag. It is to be regretted that you have not maintained under this point of view of problematical reality the attitude adopted in the verbal conferences to which you make direct reference. In them you confided to the spontaneity and the cordial sentiments of the Spanish government the solution to be given to this incident, which you now, and with querulous anticipation, bring to the official arena, wherein I shall not fail to maintain steadfastly that the government of the republic is resolved that the law shall be complied with, as well in Spanish territory as in our international relations, and that no disparagement of any right will be tolerated." [1]

Señor Carvajal's violence seems to have been based upon the view that the American minister had, in the supposed haste which he had shown and in the terms he had used, gone beyond his instructions. In this, as already shown by Mr. Fish's communication preceding the date of General Sickles's note, he was mistaken, and the latter, in a reply the next day, "hastens to remove a misapprehension which seems to have led his excellency to suppose that the language of the protest, and especially the words used to

[1] Señor Carvajal to General Sickles, November 14, 1873, *Foreign Relations*, 1874, 940.

characterize the conduct of the authorities at Santiago de Cuba, were chosen by the undersigned in the expression of his own appreciation of the acts in question. . . . It may . . . be interesting to his excellency, Mr. Carvajal, to know that the language of the protest to which he takes exception is a precise transcript from the instructions received by the undersigned from his government." General Sickles's note criticised sharply the Spanish minister's remarks as to want of data. It said: "When Mr. Carvajal asserts that this government is not in possession of sufficient information respecting the capture of the *Virginius* by a Spanish cruiser, and the execution of more than fifty of the persons comprising the crew and passengers on board the vessel, it must be admitted that his authority for the statement is indisputable. . . . But when his excellency proceeds to affirm that neither the government of the United States nor the undersigned are sufficiently informed of the nationality of the *Virginius*, or of the circumstances attending her capture and the punishment inflicted on her officers, crew, and passengers by the authorities of Santiago de Cuba, to warrant a reclamation or protest against those acts, the undersigned can do no less than point out to the minister of state that he thus assumes to speak of matters not within his cognizance and beyond his means of knowledge. It is not, therefore, surprising that his excellency, while declaring that this government is without the necessary data to determine whether or not the Spanish naval and military authorities have acted within the line of their duty and of public and municipal law, at the same moment denounces the unfortunate victims of a cruel and sanguinary administration as criminals, deserving instant death, and applauds the chief actors in the bloody tragedy. In conclusion, the undersigned must observe that his excellency is also singularly unfortunate in misapprehending the forbearance of the government of the United States in forbearing the presentation of a formal demand for reparation in this transaction. It was not, as Mr. Carvajal seems to suppose, because the government of the undersigned was unable to measure the atonement due to it, but rather for the reason twice stated to his excellency, that the President wished to afford an opportunity to the government of the republic, unembarrassed by any exigency save its own sense of duty, and moved only by a noble sentiment of justice, to make ample reparation to a friendly power, as the laws and usages of nations required." [1]

Mr. Fish's telegram of the 14th had now arrived, and on the same day with the reply just quoted the demand which it called for was made in firm and unambiguous terms.[2] Following this, the same day, the American minister addressed a note to the minister of state, calling attention to the refusal of General Burriel to allow the American consul at Santiago to use the telegraph to communicate with his colleague at Kingston, Jamaica, to obtain information "material and pertinent to the defence of the persons captured," and also to the fact that when the consul-general of the United States, directed by the secretary of state to use his good offices in obtaining for American citizens aboard the *Virginius* the privileges and protection guaranteed by the treaty of 1795, had communicated his instructions to the captain-general, requesting his sanction and aid, he had received "a curt refusal." [3]

General Sickles, on November 15, telegraphed Mr. Fish that he had received an "ill-tempered note to-day from [the] minister of state, rejecting [the] protest, and saying Spain would, nevertheless, consider and decide [the] question according to law and her dignity." [4] It brought from Mr. Fish a reply which, after giving the unconfirmed report that fifty-seven others had been executed, and that but eighteen of the people of the *Virginius* would escape death, said: "These repeated violations of assurances of good-will, and of the prohibition of murder by the authorities in Santiago, increase the necessity of full and speedy reparation. There is but one alternative if denied or long deferred. If Spain cannot redress the outrages perpetrated in her name in Cuba, the United States will. If Spain should regard this act of self-defence and justification and of the vindication of long-continued wrongs as necessitating her interference, the United States, while regretting it, cannot avoid the result. You will use this instruction cautiously and discreetly, avoiding unnecessarily exciting any proper sensibilities, and avoiding all appearance of menace; but the gravity of the case admits no doubt, and must be fairly and frankly met." [5]

[1] General Sickles to Señor Carvajal, November 15, 1873, *Foreign Relations*, 1874, 941.
[2] *Ibid.*, 939. Telegram, *supra*, 329. [3] *Ibid.*, 944. [4] *Ibid.*, 938.
[5] Mr. Fish to General Sickles, November 15, 1873, *Ibid.*, 938.

On November 16 General Sickles informed the minister of state of the reception of the news (happily false) of the execution of fifty-seven others belonging to the *Virginius,* leaving but eighteen of the whole number alive. The note ended with this admonition: "The undersigned would fail to discharge an impressive and solemn duty . . . if he concealed the grave peril to which, in the judgment of the President, the friendly relations of the two countries may be exposed unless the undersigned is enabled without delay to convey to his government a satisfactory reply to the reclamations he has addressed to his excellency the minister of state."[1]

On November 17 Señor Carvajal replied: "Your communication, dated yesterday,[2] . . . contains certain deficient or erroneous preliminaries which it is proper to set right in all their integrity, so that due appreciation may be had of the attitude of the Spanish government from the time those occurrences came to its notice. On the 6th instant the capture of the vessel was known in Madrid; and at once (*en el acto*) the government sent a telegram . . . enjoining that no sentence of death should be carried into execution without the approval of said government. This order implied no doubt concerning the justice of the proceeding and the punishment;[3] it was the expression of the desire which animated the executive power to examine whether in any of these extreme cases it was possible to harmonize with the action of the law and with public safety the exercise of clemency, which prerogative is usually delegated by our colonial legislation to the captain-general. The spontaneousness of this step, anterior to any action and even to any knowledge of the matter so far as you were concerned, was recognized by the government of the United States and by yourself, as I had the honor to hear from your own lips on the 8th instant, in the conference which you call official, and which was held after you and this government had received information of the shootings of the 4th, which unfortunately took place two days before the said telegram, and of which the news did not reach Madrid until the day succeeding the despatch of the same.

[1] *Foreign Relations,* 1874, 945.
[2] This is an error. General Sickles's note dealt with here by Señor Carvajal was dated the 15th. Señor Carvajal's note did not take cognizance of that given immediately above.
[3] There had been on the 6th no information at Madrid of punishment.

"You certainly declared in that conference that your government did not take the initiative in any reclamation, and awaited until that of the Spanish republic, animated by the cordiality of the relations which exist between the two nations, and by elevated sentiments of justice, should come to a decision respecting any wrong which may have been committed against the citizens or the flag of the United States; and certainly I stated unreservedly, but without prejudice to any point of fact or of right, that the Spanish government, by its own dignity, by the estimation in which it holds the friendship of the American people, and by the respect it owes to special treaties and the rules universally admitted among cultured nations, would not await the presentation of any justified complaint, but rather, had those compacts or international laws been violated, it would declare the fact, loyally and frankly, for right and honor are never to be crushed down, nor is reason to be subordinated to dignity; but it is likewise certain that you agreed with me that the Spanish government, which only knew the facts generally, in order to appreciate the international question, the only one which might have authorized your intervention, needed to acquire a certitude as to the events and details both of the seizure and the subsequent acts; an agreement which meant neither more nor less than that the *Virginius* might be seized, and her crew and passengers condemned by Spanish tribunals (those being the facts then known), without any violation of international law or treaties; and that, on the part of the American government and on your own, there only existed a presumption that those occurrences were surrounded by circumstances capable of inflicting injury on the persons or on the dignity of your flag, by reason of not being in conformity with the proceedings of said laws and treaties; an evident sign that you ought not to have cherished the confidence, to which you refer in the first paragraph of your note, that forthwith there would be given to the government you represent complete reparation for the offence committed against its dignity and the inviolability of its flag.

"You may have nursed this mental confidence, which was never expressed, because you had a conviction that the Spanish government did not, and does not yet, share therein; but I appeal to your loyalty to establish, as the bases of these negotiations, that, in the name of the executive power on my part, and in that of your government on yours, we agree to postpone all discussion until we had a knowledge of the facts which might give rise to a debate, and until you were informed of the solution which would be spontaneously offered by the government of the Spanish republic.

"You omit to mention the second conversation we had on the 13th. . . . In this fresh conference you know what public opinion had already proclaimed—the act of justice performed on other prisoners of the steamer *Virginius* on the 7th and 8th, and the assurance possessed by the executive power, in the midst of the regret which is ever occasioned by the action of the law in this degree, even though justified by melancholy social exigencies, that its telegram of the 6th had not arrived in time to prevent the fulfilment of the sentences, and that it would suspend the execution of any other that might be pronounced. You neither added to nor took away from your declaration of the 8th, and I reiterated mine, and we parted in the same assurances, continuing the question on the same bases established in the preceding conference. In this situation, twenty-four hours afterward, I received from you the communication to which I now reply. . . . As the mere seizure of the *Virginius*, and the subjection of her crew and passengers to the Spanish tribunals, did not constitute an offence against the government of the United States, this offence must be sought in the procedure and accessory circumstances, of which the executive power is yet ignorant.

"This change of conduct and the demand of the government of the United States cannot be interpreted in any other sense than that, for its part, it has acquired this knowledge, and considers that the capture and subsequent occurrences are vitiated by reason of having failed to conform to the stipulations (of the treaty), or to international law. The government of the United States knew the disposition of the Spanish government at that time and the sentiments by which it was animated. It appeared natural that on the first of these governments deciding to hasten the solution and to terminate the period of delay agreed upon, it should have pointed out to the second these vitiations and informalities under the faith of which the violation, being proven, would have been condemned; and this procedure seemed more proper in view of the bonds which unite the two republics, than to demand, without ground of right, and in an imperious manner, a reparation whose harsh and even humiliating terms could only have been justified by great wrongs and a continued repugnance to satisfy them. . . .

"Prudence counsels both nations to suspend judgment. That the United States do not possess at the present time a legal competency to peremptorily demand a reparation is evident in many ways; but it is sufficient to say that another power [England] has presented, in a suitable manner, analogous reclamations, arising from the same affair, the grounds of which remain to be investigated; and if it were necessary to show the confusion which still reigns upon the essential facts of the seizure, we could take as an example that while you take it for granted (patent) that the *Virginius* was a regularly documented American ship, his excellency, the captain-general of the island of Cuba, asserts the contrary.

"You will observe, moreover, that only ten days have elapsed since we knew of the capture of the *Virginius*, and three since the executions of the 7th and 8th came to our knowledge and we held our last interview. The great distance, the scanty (or difficult) telegraphic communication, and the necessity of obtaining clear and precise data upon an affair complex and minute in itself combine to prevent the government of Spain from being to-day in condition to say a word on the merits of this question, it being remarkable that the United States should so suddenly overstep the bounds marked out, and in spite of its previous assent, now demand an arbitrary reparation, arbitrary, at least, at the present moment.

" Spain, in reply, limits herself to repeating her former declarations:

"1st. She will decide upon nothing to relieve the flag of the United States from an offence till she is certain the offence exists.

"2d. As the offence cannot exist except in the violation of the treaties and of international law, she again declares, as much for the sake of quieting foreign dignity as for the relief of her own conscience, that if such a violation exists by reason of the seizure of the *Virginius*, or by reason of the subsequent acts, whether her conviction of such violation be acquired by her own initiative or by a specific statement made by the government of the United States, she will be glad to repair the wrong according to its just importance, thus proving that the reign of law, be its judgments favorable or adverse, is the first essential to national honor, and that the observance of the law, and not the obstinacy born of a false idea of pride, gives the right to assume a place in the senate of cultured nations." [1]

This note, written while the Spanish government was republican in form under Castelar, and given here in almost its entirety, is peculiarly typical of Spanish official methods and of Spanish temperament. It marks the indirectness of the Oriental mind and its tendency to delay the completion of any subject in dispute. The seizure of the *Virginius* on the high seas with American papers, and the shooting of some fifty of those who had been aboard, of whom a considerable number were American citizens and British subjects, were unquestioned. No details could alter these truths. To expect that the American government, which was moved by the same feeling which stirred their countrymen to deep indignation, could await details of the courts-martial and of the executions at Santiago, in the face of these patent facts, was to expect the impossible.

"Nothing," says the Spanish publicist Olivart, in a later case of firing by a Spanish man-of-war upon an American steamer in an attempt to stop and search her, "is more dangerous to the fundamental rights of sovereignty and of the independence of states than a false and exaggerated conception of these rights." [2]

The Spanish government at this moment was governed by such total misconception. It denied a state of war, but assumed the rights of such a condition, and placed above the law of nations the edicts of its governors-general in Cuba, which were of a harshness unknown outside of Asia or Africa. Señor Carvajal not only plainly intimated that the seizure was just, which it is possible to admit, but he went far beyond: he stated that the action of General Burriel in the slaughter of his prisoners was "justified by melancholy social exigencies"; "the persons shot," he said, "were rebels seeking to trample the law under foot, enemies of the coun-

---

[1] Señor Carvajal to General Sickles, November 17, 1873, *Foreign Relations*, 1874, 947–949.
[2] *Revue Général de Droit International Public*, tome VII, 1900, 546.

try, and disturbers of the peace and of the rule of a sister republic." Too many of the Spanish rulers, and almost all of the Spanish press, were dominated by that Eastern cast of mind which sees but one really sufficient way of dealing with an enemy, and regards the punishment by death as natural and proper in such circumstances. It was the habit of ages which had to be counted with. In Spain itself, at that moment, executions were in progress, on the part of the Carlists at least, even more atrocious in character, and with even less excuse than those at Santiago.[1]

For nearly seventy years, with rare intervals, Spain had been the victim of desolating wars of invasion or of civil strife. The government was at this moment blockading its own coast and besieging one of its principal cities, Cartagena, by sea and land. Such long and bloody experiences, covering two generations, following centuries of burnings by the Inquisition; and the temperament of a race so strongly akin to the Moor and Berber, had naturally in a great degree prevented national drift toward the humaner sentiment of the age. The shooting of a few score of men assisting in carrying arms to the enemies of Spain seemed a small matter to most Spaniards. Thus in Spain the question of the legality of the seizure of the *Virginius*, and not the killing, took precedence both in the minds of the government and of the public. In the United States it was the question of the executions. This fact could not be seen by the Spanish minister of state. He could not understand the peremptory attitude of the American government on what was to him the main question—the seizure of a ship whose papers were possibly illegally obtained.

His complaint of the want of diplomatic form in the action of the American minister was perhaps justified. He had some reason to expect from the minister greater warning of such action than in the statements of the previous conferences, and the apparent want of such a courtesy, felt the more deeply by one of a race in which ceremony is a religion, roused every sentiment of opposition which had theretofore been repressed, and forced the situation into one of much greater difficulty than might have been had the instructions from Washington enabled race susceptibility to have been more carefully considered.

[1] *Foreign Relations*, 1874, 899.

On the reception of Señor Carvajal's note of November 17 the American minister telegraphed to Mr. Fish: "Regarding this as a refusal within the sense of your instruction, I propose, unless otherwise ordered, to close this legation forthwith and leave Madrid, embarking at Valencia for France, taking the secretary and archives with me."[1] Next day he telegraphed: "Popular feeling runs high here against the United States and this legation. Press violent and abusive, advising government to order me out of Spain. Last night a mob was collected to attack and sack the legation. The authorities interfered and preserved the peace."[2] On the same day he also telegraphed: "Spain asked the good offices of England. Lord Granville declined unless on the basis of ample reparation to the United States."[3] The sympathies of the British government, nineteen of whose subjects had suffered death, were necessarily, in such case, with the United States, and Mr. Layard, the British ambassador, had already been instructed to take steps toward reparation.[4]

Notwithstanding the defiance in Señor Carvajal's communications to the American minister in Madrid, the Spanish government, now convinced that the United States, should not the latter's demands be promptly met, contemplated war, caused the transfer of further negotiations to Washington by a telegram to Admiral Polo de Bernabé, its minister at Washington, stating its resolution "to abide by the principles of justice, to observe international law, to punish all those who shall have made themselves liable to punishment, regardless of their station; to ask reparation for offences that may have been done against us, and in our turn to make due reparation, if right and our own conviction should so advise us. But a knowledge of the facts is necessary to proceed with the tact and judgment required by the gravity of the case, and the news which reaches the United States must be [as] confused as that we receive here. . . . The reparations we may have to make, or those we may ask for, require time and the knowledge of facts. Assure, therefore, the government of the United States in the most positive manner that, resolved upon the preservation of the integrity of our territory and the dignity of our nation, we are also determined

[1] *Foreign Relations*, 1874, 951. [2] *Ibid.*, 954.
[3] *Ibid.*, 954. [4] *Ibid.*, 946.

strictly to comply with the principles of international law, the letter of treaties with all nations, and consequently with the American republic."[1]

This telegram was regarded as a reconsideration of the refusal to receive the protest of the United States. The demand for a proper length of time to learn the exact state of the facts was deemed reasonable by Mr. Fish. The American minister was then directed to defer his immediate departure from Madrid and await further instructions.[2] The Spanish minister at Washington was informed by Mr. Fish that a satisfactory settlement would be expected by November 26.[3]

The personal attitude of the American minister at Madrid, stirred as he had naturally been by the later notes of the Spanish secretary of state, and by the attitude of the government and the press, was now bellicose. Neither of the three written communications which he had received from the Spanish minister of state contained any expression of regret or disapproval of the capture of the ship or the slaughter at Santiago. "The press," said General Sickles, "approves the whole business, and denies that any censure or regret has been expressed by this government. The ministerial journals acquiesce."[4] General Sickles, moved by this attitude, requested Count Maffei, the Italian chargé d'affaires, to take charge of American interests and of the property of the legation, if events should demand such action, to which the Italian government consented, should application from Washington be made.[5]

On November 23 the Spanish government, by a telegram through its minister in Washington, proposed arbitration, which was declined by Mr. Fish on the ground that the subject was one of national honor, "of which the nation must be judge and custodian."[6] Another telegram was received by the minister of Spain at Washington the next day, November 24, saying: "First. Our dispositions being known, would the United States agree to wait for our solution, which would be immediate on receipt of the facts in the case? Second. Would the President, notwithstanding the

[1] Secretary of state, Madrid, to Spanish minister at Washington, November 18, 1873, *Foreign Relations*, 1874, 979.
[2] Mr. Fish to General Sickles, November 19, 1873, *Ibid.*, 955.
[3] *Ibid.*, 955. [4] Telegram, November 20, 1873, *Ibid.*, 956.
[5] *Ibid.*, 956. It was made by Mr. Fish, November 23, 1873. [6] *Ibid.*, 958.

foregoing, still insist on submitting the question to Congress? Third. Could Mr. Fish at once designate the points of offence in view of treaty stipulations and international law?"[1]

Mr. Fish answered: "Past experience in cases of reclamation for offences in Cuba will not warrant us in entering into an agreement which practically amounts to an indefinite postponement. It will be impossible for the President to refrain from communicating the facts to Congress. It is his constitutional duty to do so . . ." Mr. Fish named as the points of offence the capture on the high seas in time of peace of a regularly documented United States vessel, under the United States flag, and the conveyance of the vessel with those aboard to a port within Spanish jurisdiction, the execution of a large number of the passengers, officers, and crew, and the detention of the remainder and of the vessel. "These acts," he said, "are regarded as violations of international law and treaty stipulations."[2] This, telegraphed to Madrid, was replied to the same day in a telegram to the minister at Washington; the government, unable to understand the secondary importance of the capture, answering: "We cannot understand the precipitancy of the United States in this matter. The news is really contradictory: while Mr. Fish maintains that the vessel was an American, our minister of the colonies informs us that she carried false papers, that the captain declared that she had been fitted out and manned for the exclusive purpose of aiding the insurrection in the island of Cuba. If this were true, we would have a right to present reclamations and complaints, and we could affirm that the United States do not observe toward the Spanish republic the reciprocal friendship to which it is entitled. But in the same way that we suspend reclamations on this point, we would wish that the United States would suspend them also, on what they consider their complaints and injuries; and we think that they might consider, as an anticipation of the redress that may be due to their flag, our fixed and firm resolve to make reparation by salute and restitution of the vessel and the survivors of the crew for any offence that may be proved against the flag by the act of capture from the proceedings established in order to ascertain whether the vessel had the right or not to carry the American flag, independently of the other questions

[1] *Foreign Relations*, 1874, 983.   [2] *Ibid.*, 984.

which, in reference to these facts, the government of the two republics reserve the treatment of by diplomatic negotiations. You are authorized to make this declaration, but you will understand, and endeavor to make Mr. Fish understand, that no satisfaction would be possible if we are not first made sensible of the right with which it is demanded on account of the *Virginius*." [1]

When this was received and read to the American secretary of state by Admiral Polo on November 25, Mr. Fish replied: "The United States, in their own interests as well as in the interest of all maritime powers, cannot admit the right of any other power to capture on the high seas in time of peace a documented vessel bearing their flag. The flag which they give to a vessel must be a protection on the high seas against all aggression from whatever quarters, and they reserve to themselves the right to inquire whether the protection of that flag has been forfeited. . . . On this ground they reserve to themselves the right to inquire into the regularity of the papers of the *Virginius*, and they are prepared to make this inquiry on the execution indicated in the telegraphic despatch from his government just now read by Admiral Polo of the reparation of the indignity committed to their flag. And should Spain have complaints or reclamations . . . in consequence of the acts of the *Virginius*, when the injury to the honor of the flag of the United States is atoned for, they will be received with every purpose to do justice to Spain. . . . The Spanish cabinet cannot fail to see that the United States cannot demand less or could undertake to do more. . . ." Continuing, and showing that the papers of the *Virginius* were in due form and that she had been given the right to carry the flag, the memorandum ended: "Her papers, therefore, must continue to give her a national character, and with her flag, must be her protection." [2]

On the day of this interview between the American secretary of state and the Spanish minister, the former telegraphed the American minister at Madrid:

"If, upon the close of to-morrow, no accommodation shall have been reached in the case of the *Virginius*, you will address to the foreign office a note expressing regret at the delay of the reparation

[1] *Foreign Relations*, 1874, 984. This telegram was received by Admiral Polo at 9.45 A. M., November 25, 1873. [2] *Ibid.*, 985.

asked for, and stating that, in conformity with instructions from your government, you were under the necessity of withdrawing from Madrid, for which purpose you request the usual passport for yourself, your family, and *suite*.

"If, however, the accommodation desired should be brought about in the course of to-morrow, either here or in Madrid, you will, until otherwise directed, abstain from addressing the note adverted to.

"Should a proposition be submitted to you to-morrow, you will refer it here and defer action until it be decided upon.

"A telegram has just now been read to me by Admiral Polo, which gives reason to hope for a satisfactory accommodation.

"You will, therefore, allow the whole of to-morrow to pass before addressing your note." [1]

The same day General Sickles telegraphed: "Layard says Granville has expressed his sense of the justice and moderation of the reparation we have demanded and this has been communicated to Castelar. England reserves her reclamation for the present and endeavors to promote a settlement of the question pending between the United States and Spain." [2]

The action of England produced good results. At two o'clock on the morning of November 26 the American minister received a message from President Castelar that a note would be sent that day recognizing the principles on which the American demand was based, and promising to make the reparation required on or before December 25, if the facts elicited by the investigation making by the Spanish government should show that the *Virginius* was a regularly documented American ship.[3]

Mr. Fish's telegram of the 25th was not received at the legation at Madrid until 4.30 P. M. of the 26th. General Sickles, thus acting upon his previous instructions, and with what in view of President Castelar's message might appear somewhat undue haste, placed in the hands of the foreign minister, shortly after 2 P. M., a note borne by the secretary of legation, Mr. Adee, asking for his passports. Mr. Carvajal desired to know if a communication of the same date had reached the legation, and was informed by the secretary that none had arrived up to the moment of his

[1] *Foreign Relations*, 1874, 958.   [2] *Ibid.*, 959.   [3] *Ibid.*, 960.

leaving. The note, however, arrived at 2.30 P. M., and Mr. Carvajal was then informed that he might defer any reply until it should be renewed, if unhappily the negotiation now resumed on fresh bases failed.[1]

The Spanish note, the points of which were telegraphed by General Sickles November 26, pledged:

First. If it should be proved that the *Virginius* rightfully carried the American flag and that her papers were in regular form, her seizure would be declared illegal, the American flag would be saluted in the manner desired, and the *Virginius* with her surviving crew and passengers returned.

Second. That if it be proved that in the proceedings or sentence at Santiago there had been an essential failure to comply with the provisions of Spanish legislation or of treaties, the government would bring the authorities before the competent tribunals.

Third. Any other reclamations which may be preferred in the matter by either government to be considered diplomatically, and if an agreement should not be reached, they should be submitted to a third, named by mutual consent.

Fourth. If the 25th day of December should expire without the Spanish government's having resolved, in so far as it should come within its province, the question raised by the demand for reparation, it held itself bound to grant reparation, the same as if it had recognized the right of the government of the United States to exact it, and such reparation would be given in the form prescribed in the first and second bases.[2]

The seriousness of the situation had now come home to the Spanish cabinet, and the minister of state was using the instrumentalities of both capitals to hurry an understanding. He thus telegraphed Admiral Polo at Washington: "Negotiations renewed in Madrid. Confer again with Mr. Fish on the basis of last official note [official telegram?] and renew to him the assurances of the good faith and rectitude of our proposition, assuring him likewise that our agreement, whatever it may be, shall be beyond all doubt carried out in Cuba."[3]

On November 27 Admiral Polo called upon Mr. Fish, who read

[1] *Foreign Relations*, 1874, 959–960.   [2] *Ibid.*, 961.
[3] *Ibid.*, 987. This telegram was received November 28, 1873, at 9.15 A. M.

to him Sickles's telegram just received. The admiral was informed that the propositions just mentioned could not be accepted. Mr. Fish denied the right of any other power to visit, molest, or detain on the high seas in time of peace any American vessel; a right claimed and observed by all maritime powers; that the first proposition practically asked the United States to consent that Spain should detain the *Virginius* while she is seeking evidence to justify her act.

Admiral Polo then stated that he had received a strictly confidential and personal communication requesting to be informed if it be possible to make an arrangement whereby, if the vessel and men be given up, Mr. Fish would engage that inquiry be instituted and, if the result required, that punishment should be inflicted on those who had violated the laws of the United States, reserving, until further information, the salute to the flag. Mr. Fish, leaving the consultation for the moment, consulted the President. Returning, Admiral Polo was informed that the proposals transmitted were accepted.[1]

Next day but one, November 29, 1873, a protocol was drawn which stipulated that Spain would restore forthwith the *Virginius*, her surviving passengers and crew, and on December 25, 1873, salute the flag of the United States unless, before that date, Spain should prove that the *Virginius* was not entitled to carry the American flag, in which case the salute would be waived, and the United States would accept a disclaimer of intent of indignity to its flag in the capture of the ship.

It was agreed, besides, if it should thus be shown that the *Virginius* was not entitled to American papers and flag, the United States would take proceedings against the vessel and against those shown to be guilty, it being understood that Spain would investigate, as proposed to General Sickles, the conduct of those of her officials who had infringed Spanish laws or treaty obligations, and inflict punishment on those who had offended; other reciprocal reclamations to be the subject of consideration and arrangement, and in case of no agreement, to be the subject of arbitration should the United States Senate assent thereto.[2]

An intimation from General Sickles that unless an understanding should be reached by 3 P. M. of November 28, in accord with

[1] Cabinet Memorandum, *Foreign Relations*, 1874, 986.   [2] *Ibid.*, 987.

the terms of his note of November 15, he should be obliged to renew his request for passports, and the eagerness now shown by the Spanish cabinet for an accommodation, caused an agreement to his demand which was ratified by the council of ministers at 3 A. M. November 28, and a draft of a protocol was prepared. At noon, however, Señor Carvajal, the minister of state, sent to General Sickles a copy of a telegram just received from Admiral Polo, announcing the arrangement made with Mr. Fish, followed, a few hours later, by a note couched in somewhat effusive terms of satisfaction "in the happy termination of a question which might have had grave consequences." [1]

The rapidity with which events had moved; the activity of the Spanish minister in Washington; the information from General Sickles that he had demanded his passports, though acceding later to the request of the Spanish minister of state not to press for a reply, combined with the delays of the telegraph service, had caused Mr. Fish to suppose (though a more careful following of Sickles's telegrams might have prevented the supposition) that General Sickles had left Madrid. The reception, November 28, of General Sickles's telegram of the 26th removed this impression and Mr. Fish telegraphed the minister that, acting on the supposition of his absence, he had given the reply of the government to Admiral Polo, the substance of which he gave, adding: "Admiral Polo informs me this morning [November 28] that his government says that negotiations are renewed at Madrid. Since then I received at 4 this afternoon, your telegram of this morning announcing that you should request your passports at 3 to-day. The supposed negotiations must therefore, drop at Madrid and be conducted hereafter here." [2]

It was not, however, until December 8 that the final arrangements could be made, and then it was agreed that the *Virginius* should be given up December 16 in the harbor of Bahia Honda, with the American flag flying, instead of Santiago; this, however, not to be an admission by either party of her right to carry the flag at the time of capture, nor to prejudice the right of Spain to prove otherwise on or before December 25; that the survivors were to be delivered at Santiago on board a ship of war of the United States

[1] *Foreign Relations*, 1874, 969.   [2] *Ibid.*, 966.

within forty-eight hours after notification to the authorities of the ship's readiness to receive them, the surrender to be between the hours of 8 A. M. and 4 P. M.; that on December 25 a ship or ships of war of the United States would be in the harbor of Santiago, and that at noon the United States flag would be raised on a Spanish fort or battery, and a salute of twenty-one guns be fired, to be returned by the American man-of-war gun for gun, the salute by Spain, however, to be, on the part of the United States, spontaneously dispensed with, should the invalidity of the ship's claim to American nationality be shown on or before that date.[1]

There were serious doubts as to the possibility of compliance, by the Captain-General of Cuba, with these conditions. The Spanish volunteers in Cuba were in a very defiant attitude, and the newspaper articles were of a most inflammatory character. The government at Santiago had ordered all persons over twenty-two to enroll as volunteers.[2] On December 12, however, the *Virginius* left Havana for Bahia Honda, convoyed by the Spanish war steamer *Isabel la Catolica*, a general feeling of relief being experienced in business circles. Gold declined full ten per cent.

On December 16 the ship was delivered to Captain Whiting, chief of staff to the commander-in-chief, Admiral Case, of the North Atlantic fleet, who went to Bahia Honda in the *Despatch*. Meeting heavy weather on her way north, under convoy of the sloop of war *Ossipee*, her seams opened and despite all efforts she foundered off Cape Hatteras.[3]

The survivors of those aboard when captured were delivered at Santiago, December 18, to Captain Braine, of the sloop of war *Juniata*, and were landed at New York, December 28.

As it was fully shown by an examination at New York, which began late in November, 1873, of various persons connected with the ship, at which was present the district attorney of the United States, that the papers of the *Virginius* had been obtained fraudulently, and that she was not American-owned, the salute was omitted. The testimony secured[4] was laid before the department of

[1] *Foreign Relations*, 1874, 990. [2] *Ibid.*, 1082–1090.
[3] See Report of Naval Board of Inquiry. (*Foreign Relations*, 1875, 1148–1153.) The ship, weakly built and having had no repairs for a number of years, was wholly unseaworthy. [4] *Foreign Relations*, 1874, 991–1051.

state, and on December 11 was submitted to the attorney-general of the United States [1] for an opinion. He found that the *Virginius* belonged to General Quesada and other Cubans, and not to Patterson, who had sworn to his personal ownership when her American register was obtained. This was shown by testimony of her first captain, Shepperd, and by Señor Varona, the secretary of the Cuban Junta in New York when the ship was purchased, and who sailed in her as Quesada's chief of staff. The testimony of many others also who had served aboard was taken, and it was clear that the ship had no right to carry the American flag.

Notwithstanding her illegal use of the flag, the attorney-general held that the ship was as much exempt from capture by Spain on the high seas as though she had been lawfully registered. "Spain," said the attorney-general, "has no jurisdiction whatever over the question as to whether or not such vessel is on the high seas in violation of any law of the United States. Spain cannot rightfully raise that question as to the *Virginius*, but the United States may. . . ." [2]

The admission by Spain of the illegality of the capture, "involved of necessity not only the admission of the illegality of the capture of the crew and passengers, but admission also of the wrongfulness of the summary execution" [3] carried out at Santiago. Spain thus, by an agreement concluded at Madrid, February 27, 1875, under the government of King Alfonso, paid an indemnity of eighty thousand dollars, which was distributed by the American government to those entitled.[4] The British government likewise demanded and received compensation for the slaughter of nineteen of its subjects, holding that "there was no charge either known to the law of nations or to any municipal law, under which persons in the situation of the British members of the crew of the *Virginius* could have been justifiably condemned to death.[5]

Mr. Fish had at the outset suspicion of the nationality of the *Virginius* and warned General Sickles in the first telegram to him to speak with reserve on that branch of the case, but Mr. Fish

[1] George H. Williams.   [2] *Foreign Relations*, 1874, 1113.
[3] Mr. Fish to Mr. Cushing, February 10, 1874, *Foreign Relations*, 1875, part II, 1216.   [4] See House Ex. Doc. 15, 54 Cong., 1 Sess.
[5] Hall, *International Law*, 4th ed., 278–279. Moore, *Digest*, II, 903. Earl Granville to Mr. Layard, House Ex. Doc. 89, 44 Cong., 1 Sess., 55.

would not have covered his responsibility to the President, to Congress, and the country had he omitted to demand reparation for insult to the flag. Whoever owned the *Virginius*, she was not a pirate on the high seas when arrested by the *Tornado*. No Spanish decree could make her a pirate. Spain brought her passengers into Cuban jurisdictional waters by force and in violation of the law of nations. She had no more right to try and put them to death than if she had seized them in New York. She certainly could not, by that act of seizure, acquire lawful jurisdiction to try by summary court-martial American citizens and put them to death without permitting them to have counsel in their defence, and otherwise conforming to all the stipulations of the treaty of 1795 pertinent to the situation. Burriel's brutal and, in the light of the treaty, most stupid act, fully justified the United States in demanding from Spain immediate offer of reparation for the executions. The request for time to consider documentary details could not be considered in the state of feeling throughout the United States. The crime was murder. There was no excuse under any law, international or moral. Says the Marquis de Olivart, the Spanish publicist, so frequently mentioned herein: "If American jurists themselves confess that the visit and capture of the *Virginius* were legitimate and justified by the right of self-defence,[1] the American nationality of the pirate vessel being *prima facie* very doubtful, we must recognize with an equal frankness that the summary execution of its passengers and of a great part of its crew, by General Burriel, was a measure of unjustifiable rigor, not authorized by the needs of war, and a striking violation of the rights of American citizens in Cuba. The pretext invoked by our government, that it was a question of pirates, *enemies of the human race*, was founded on a real misunderstanding. The idea of piracy, in international law, a crime the repression of which is permitted and is even the duty of every civilized state, implies essentially the existence of the *animus furandi;* certainly the men executed at Santiago de Cuba had not this *animus*." [2]

---

[1] Such were the views of Mr. George Ticknor Curtis and Mr. Theodore Woolsey, Woolsey, *International Law*, 369.

[2] *Revue Générale de Droit International Public*, tome IV, 1897, 612. See also Hall, *International Law*, 4th ed., 278, 279.

The seizure of the ship itself raised a diplomatic question not over difficult of adjustment. But there was no calling back to life the men who had suffered death. The temper of the people throughout the United States called for action. Every available ship was commissioned or recalled from foreign stations,[1] and war would certainly have occurred but for Spain's yielding to the logic of the situation.

There remained the question of the punishment of the chief offender, General Burriel. "If the author of such a deed," said the *London Times*, "had been an Englishman, he would assuredly have been hung; yet he is still at liberty, and we believe has some sort of command."[2]

Burriel had been recalled from Cuba at the end of 1873. In April, 1874, he published[3] an elaborate justification of his acts with reference to the *Virginius* in a public letter addressed to the director of the *Revue des Deux Mondes*, which, in its issue of March 2, 1874, had severely criticised his conduct. In this, as already mentioned, he claimed as the basis of his action, the imperative orders of March 14, 1869, which had been revoked by the Spanish government,[4] upon the protest of that of the United States. The latter pressed for Burriel's punishment,[5] and the Spanish government replied that it desired and was prepared "to fulfil all the stipulations contained in the protocol of the 29th of November, 1873," but it proposed to bring the action before a court independent of political or military control.[6]

The subject rested and Burriel retired, unnoticed, "into some obscure corner of Galicia . . . humiliated by seeing that his

---

[1] By January 3, 1874, there were collected at Key West, under Rear-Admirals Case and Scott, the following ships: the frigates *Franklin, Minnesota, Wabash, Colorado,* and *Lancaster;* the corvettes *Brooklyn, Congress, Worcester, Alaska, Ticonderoga, Canandaigua, Shenandoah, Juniata, Ossipee, Wachusett, Powhatan, Wyoming, Kansas,* and *Shawmut;* the monitors *Sangus, Mahopac, Manhattan, Ajax, Canonicus,* and *Dictator;* the despatch vessel *Despatch;* the armed tugs *Pinta, Fortune,* and *Mayflower*. (Report of the secretary of the navy, 1874.)

[2] *Times*, January 26, 1876, *Ibid.*, 160.

[3] In *La Epoca*, Madrid, April 21, 1874, *Foreign Relations*, 1876, 490.

[4] Señor Ulloa, minister of foreign affairs, to Mr. Cushing, American minister, July 8, 1874, *Ibid.*, 1876, 498.

[5] *Ibid.*, 1876, 493.

[6] *Ibid.*, 512.

government is humiliated on account of his acts."[1] The delay was not surprising in view of the fact that, after six years, the inquiry into the assassination of General Prim had but passed the first stage, and was only now before the court.[2]

On August 18, 1875, however, the American minister, learning through the newspapers that Burriel had been promoted from the grade of brigadier to that of *mariscal de campo* (major-general), addressed a note to the Spanish minister of state, saying: "My government will of necessity presume that the stipulated investigation of the conduct of D. Juan Burriel and his submission to the '*juicio de residencia*' have resulted in acquitting him, not only of any violation of the municipal law of Spain, but also of any infringement of treaty stipulations—a decision that is in conflict with the explicit stipulations of treaty between the United States and Spain . . . the situation will wear an aspect of still greater gravity if, in the absence of such acquittal, . . . the Spanish government . . . shall have selected that officer for promotion on the assumption of commendableness of his acts at Santiago de Cuba."[3]

The Spanish minister of state in reply gave the exceedingly weak reason that General Burriel had been promoted through "the necessities of the war [in Spain] and of army organization," but that the government was resolved to fulfil its promises.[4] These assurances were repeated, and on April 11, 1876, Señor Calderon y Collantes, a new minister of state, sent to the American minister a copy of a letter to the minister of war recalling that a report had been called for by his predecessor from the supreme council of war, and that this in turn had called for a report from the fiscal tribunal of the branch of service in Cuba, which thus far had not been rendered.[5]

On April 21, 1876, the minister of state informed the American minister that the supreme council of war had declared itself competent to have cognizance of the cause, and that steps had been taken by the appointment of a fiscal and secretary from their own

[1] Mr. Cushing to Mr. Fish, May 17, 1875. *Foreign Relations*, 1876, 512.
[2] *Ibid.*, 455.
[3] Mr. Cushing to Señor Castro, August 18, 1875, *Ibid.*, 515.
[4] *Ibid.*, 517.
[5] Señor Calderon to the minister of war, Madrid, April 11, 1876, *Ibid.*, 531.

body. "With this," said the minister, "remains fulfilled on the part of the government of his majesty the obligation which was contracted toward the government of the United States by the . . . protocol of November, 1873. The rest remains exclusively in the charge of the supreme council . . . which, as a tribunal of justice, will proceed according to its usages and with absolute independence of the executive, in the pursuance of the principle universally recognized in countries governed by liberal institutions." [1]

In June, 1876, it was announced that the occurrences on board the *Tornado* after the capture of the *Virginius* had been referred for report to the supreme tribunal of the navy.[2] Two and a half years had thus passed before a tribunal was even discovered before which the subject could be brought. It is not surprising that Mr. Fish closed his acknowledgment of the information conveyed him with the remark that "an initiation of an investigation cannot be a performance." [3]

A second aftermath of the *Virginius* case was a reclamation for damages by Spain preferred by the Spanish minister at Washington, December 30, 1873, based upon the voluminous testimony

[1] *Foreign Relations*, 1876, 533.   [2] *Ibid.*, 535.
[3] *Ibid.*, 535. One who would study the details of the case of Burriel, his conduct in the massacre of the people of the *Virginius*, and the refusal of Spain, during three years, to punish him as it promised the United States to do, together with his letter of attempted vindication of himself, and Cushing's masterly correspondence thereon with three ministers of state of Spain, will find the record in fifty octavo pages of *Foreign Relations* for 1876. The records throw but very little more light on the case. Mr. Cushing reported on February 9, 1877, that the trial was still pending, and on the 22d of the same month, that the court was waiting for documents and evidence from Cuba; on receipt of some remarks from the department about the "slowness of the proceedings" he replied, April 4, 1877, that the slowness of proceedings in so-called state trials is proverbial in Spain, and cited examples. (See House Ex. Doc. 72, 45 Cong., 2 Sess.) Whether the case was ever decided is not of state department record. But if it be remembered that a change of administration in the United States and the pacification of Cuba took place in the same and following year, it may be surmised that the "proverbial" slowness of Spanish court was permitted to run undisturbed until Burriel, or his judges, died. Burriel died December 24, 1877. The *Diario de la Marina*, of Havana, in a notice, January 15, 1878, of his death, spoke of "the proofs of the firmness of his character" shown at Santiago, and ended: "May the earth be light upon him." Such a hope as to the judgment of posterity, can scarcely be cherished.

taken in November and December, 1873,[1] and transmitted to the American department of state with a letter summarizing the same, December 10. The main contentions on which the Spanish minister founded the claim were, that the *Virginius* sailed with false papers, including registry, crew list, and manifest; that the expedition was unlawful by reason of the imputed piratical character or purposes of the voyage, and that she carried persons connected with the revolutionary movement who were of much more importance to the insurrection than were Messrs. Mason and Slidell to the Confederate states when these latter were taken from the British steamer *Trent*.

The minister concluded with respect to all matters mentioned that he could not "but confidently expect the admission on the part of the secretary of state that the obligations of one power toward another friendly power, in whose territory there exists an insurrection to which neither party has granted belligerent rights in an international sense, are not less than those of a neutral during a regular state of war between two other countries with which the neutral is on terms of peace and friendship. The duty of efficaciously arresting beginnings, as well as preventing military expeditions from being conveyed from one country to another, in which, unfortunately, an insurrection exists, is equally obligatory in both cases, and in order to fix the measure of the efficacy referred to, the undersigned is willing, in the case of the *Virginius*, to abide by the proofs furnished and the stand taken at Geneva in the name of the United States whereby was shown the responsibility incurred by Great Britain toward the United States." [2]

Mr. Fish in reply recalled that the facts referred to him by Admiral Polo de Bernabé had only come to light in consequence of the capture of the *Virginius*, and that there was no question of the validity of her papers from any quarter when she sailed from New York; that even had it been otherwise, the falsification of the papers would have been a mere municipal offence, "subject as such to punishment by the local law of the United States, and whether so punished or not, involving no possible question or matter of

[1] *Foreign Relations*, 1874, 1008–1112.
[2] Admiral Polo de Bernabé, Spanish minister, to Mr. Fish, December 30, 1873, *Foreign Relations*, 1875, 1153.

controversy with any foreign government"; that even if this cause of reclamation "were possessed of any force in other relations," which could not be admitted, that there could be no responsibility on the part of the United States "for want of diligence or good faith, seeing that the imputed frauds were not brought to the notice of the United States by Spain and were otherwise unknown and unsuspected by the government."

As to the imputed illegal intentions of the voyage, there was no responsibility in the light of municipal law or that of the law of nations. "It is not pretended," says Mr. Fish, "that the *Virginius* was armed, equipped, or manned for war in any part of the United States; that she bore at the time, or subsequently received, any armament as a ship of war; that her build or equipment had any special military character; or, indeed, that she was intended to or ever did, in fact, act as a cruiser, piratical or other, against Spain or the subjects of Spain." As to the "inconsiderable invoice of arms or munitions of war," the destination of the ship was the neutral port of Curaçoa [near, it may be said, the coast of Venezuela, then itself in an insurrectionary state]; the voyage was on its face a perfectly lawful one. "There was no allegation or charge of any improper intent or purpose; there was nothing in the build, equipment, cargo, or destination to excite suspicion or to authorize proceedings against her at law, or detention by the President. There is no doctrine in the law of nations more universally admitted than that a neutral or friendly government cannot be rendered responsible for shipments of arms, munitions, or material of war made by private individuals at their own risk and peril, and as a private speculation. If a state of war exists, the parties concerned are unquestionably exposed to the confiscation of their goods as contraband of war, but in that case their act affords no ground for reclamation against their government."

Mr. Fish could not perceive "any analogy whatever between the case of the *Virginius* and that of the *Alabama* or other vessels fitted out in the ports of Great Britain" during the American civil war. "If there had been a state of war and the *Virginius* had been armed, equipped, and manned in the port of New York as a regular ship of war; if she had then cruised as such on the high seas, and had captured and destroyed Spanish merchantmen," such analogy would have held. But Spain "does not admit that there is a state of war, and does not pretend to represent injuries of subjects of hers, preyed upon by the *Virginius* as a cruiser, but damages to Spain as a nation or government by reason of the assumed relation of the acts of the *Virginius* to the existing insurrection in Cuba. And it is that very class of claims which, presented by the United States against Great Britain mainly in the purpose of obtaining a determination of the question, was disposed of by the arbitrators in their unanimous formal declaration that claims of this nature 'do not constitute, upon the principles of international law applicable to such cases, good foundation for an award of compensation or computation of damages between nations.' In appealing to the acts of that tribunal as authority, Spain must be considered as accepting such authority, which is conclusive as argument in opposition to the present reclamation on the part of Spain." [1]

The Spanish minister dealt with the question at much greater length, in a note of February 2, 1874, which included, besides that of the *Virginius*, the whole subject of the filibustering expeditions during the war. This was not answered until April 18, 1874, on account of the pressure of business incident to the session of Congress and a severe indisposition of the secretary of state. The two papers present a very complete history of the subject. Too voluminous to quote *in extenso* or even to summarize, it may be said that Spain held that action should be taken, such as neither of the two countries, Great Britain and the United States, which were so jealous for freedom of speech and act within the law, could have tolerated; and that the Spanish minister's argument as to the responsibility of the United States respecting the expeditions prepared within their jurisdiction, was fatally defective in that it applied only to a state of war; a state the acceptance of which, in an international sense, Spain carefully avoided.[2]

[1] Mr. Fish to Admiral Polo de Bernabé, January 9, 1874, *Foreign Relations*, 1875, 1156.

[2] "Spain," said Señor Cánovas, "cannot recognize the belligerency of rebels and bandits. It would not be desirable that she should do so. Spaniards who demand this recognition, ignore that from the moment it should exist the insurgents would be able to send to sea ships carrying the 'Lone Star' flag, make loans abroad, and have full liberty of movement such as they could

Mr. Fish, in closing his long and very able paper, said:
"During these five years this government has watched events in Cuba, perhaps not always patiently, but certainly always impartially. It has seen vessels sailing under its flag intercepted on the high seas and carried into Spanish ports. It has seen the property of its citizens embargoed and their revenues sequestrated, and when it has complained, it has met with promises of restoration; but the official assurances of Spain in that respect have in most cases not been complied with. It has seen its citizens condemned to death under the form of military law, and executed in violation of the treaty obligations of Spain. It has seen other citizens of the United States mobbed in the streets of Havana for no other reason than that they were citizens of the United States, or the accidental circumstance of the color of the dress. It has stretched its powers and interfered with the liberties of its citizens in order to fulfil all its duties as a sovereign nation toward the power which in Cuba was tolerating the evil influences of reaction and of slavery, and of 'the deplorable and pertinacious tradition of despotism' referred to by the Spanish minister of transmarine affairs, all of which made the things complained of possible. It has refrained from the assertion of its rights, under the hope, derived from the constant assurances of the government of Spain, that liberty and self-government would be accorded to Cuba, that African slavery would be driven out from its last resting-place in Christendom, and that the instruments of the Casino Español would be restrained in their violence and be made to obey law and to respect the treaty obligations of Spain."

never have without it; they would be able then to cruise at sea." Interview in the *Heraldo*, of Madrid, September 9, 1895, quoted by De Olivart, *Revue Générale de Droit International Public*, tome VII, 1900, 345.

[1] *Foreign Relations*, 1875, 1178–1213.

CHAPTER XVIII

THE CARLIST WAR.—THE ACCESSION OF ALFONSO XII.—
MR. FISH'S NUMBER 266

THE clash which had taken place of the two negotiations, the one proceeding in Washington and the other at Madrid, had the effect of bringing from General Sickles the resignation of his post. Rumors of disapproval of his conduct of the case of the *Virginius* had been published, and though Mr. Fish, in answer to Sickles's telegram of December 6, 1873, tendering his resignation, said "no dissatisfaction is expressed or intimated," and that at the moment his resignation would not be accepted as interfering with the prospects of an accommodation, the general, on December 20, renewed his request which was now granted. He presented his letters of recall early in January, Mr. Adee, the very competent secretary of legation since 1870, and later the well-known assistant secretary of state, taking over the legation as chargé d'affaires.[1]

General Sickles had discharged with marked ability and zeal, and probably with as much success as any one could have achieved under the circumstances, the difficult and trying duties of the office he had held since May, 1869. In January, 1874, Mr. Caleb Cushing was appointed to be his successor. The appointment of Mr. Cushing, who was now seventy-four years of age, was in every way fitting and one most friendly to Spain. He had won distinction in very many spheres of intellectual effort. He was graduated by Harvard College at the young age of seventeen; was a teacher there after his graduation; was many times a member of the Massachusetts legislature; a member of Congress during four terms; was the first American minister to China, with which he negotiated our first treaty with that nation; was a general in the Mexican war; a member of the Massachusetts supreme court;

[1] Mr. Adee remained as secretary until 1877, when he was transferred to the department of state at Washington. He was made assistant secretary in 1882, in which post he has ever since rendered invaluable services.

attorney-general of the United States from 1853 to 1857; was frequently employed under President Lincoln on special diplomatic missions, and was chief counsel for the United States in the Geneva arbitration for the settlement of the *Alabama* claims. He had been much in France and Spain in early life, and published as early as 1833 interesting reminiscences of his travels in both countries. He spoke a number of languages, including Spanish, with facility. Crowning his many distinguished qualities, he was on terms of intimacy and friendship with many notable Spaniards.

It is to be inferred that Mr. Cushing would not at his age have accepted diplomatic employment at Madrid, with its inhospitable climate, unless he felt that the administration at Washington had in mind an especially important work to be accomplished there, with which he sympathized and in which he thought he could succeed. He was everywhere recognized as a strong opponent of filibustering in all its various forms. On his return to Newburyport from the office of attorney-general, in 1857, he made an elaborate speech to his fellow townsmen in which he said: "I reprobate not war itself, but all irregular enterprises of war. I hold that the great issues of peace belong to the sovereign power of the Union and should not be wantonly usurped by individual rashness. I glory in the acts which it has fallen to me to perform toward the repression of all such undertakings in the United States, which require no such instruments to help them forward in their destinies in America." [1]

Mr. Cushing was known in Madrid as fiercely hostile to military expeditions against Spanish authority in Cuba, organized and conducted by the Cuban *Junta*, and it was believed that he would in every way be, as he was, *persona grata*. He did not reach Madrid until the end of May, 1874, on the last day of which month he was presented to President Serrano. Part of the delay had arisen from the necessity of going from France by Bordeaux and Lisbon, the northern part of Spain being in control of the Carlists. His general instructions from Mr. Fish of February 6, 1874, reviewed at length the history and present condition of the diplomatic relations between Washington and Madrid. They referred to several things of pressing immediate importance in which Spain had failed to make good her promises; among them, emancipation of slaves and the re-

[1] *New York Times*, April 25, 1857.

lease of embargoed estates in Cuba owned by our citizens. He was told, in effect, that the administration could not much longer go on policing the ports of the United States against the efforts of the *Junta* and holding back Congress and the country from taking into their hands remedies for the intolerable evils in Cuba. Mr. Fish went on to say: "That the ultimate issue of events in Cuba will be its independence, however that issue may be produced . . . it is impossible to doubt. If there be one lesson in history more cogent in its teachings than any other, it is that no part of America, large enough to constitute a self-containing state, can be permanently held in forced colonial subjection to Europe." He quoted Castelar, "one of the greatest and wisest of the statesmen of [Spain] or indeed of Europe," as "of a nature to command the approbation of the United States." " Let us," said Castelar, when President, "reduce to formulas our policy in America. First, *the immediate* abolition of slavery. Secondly, autonomy of the islands of Puerto Rico and Cuba, which shall have a parliamentary assembly of their own, their own administration, their own government, and a federal tie to unite them with Spain as Canada is united with England. . . . I desire that the islands of Cuba and Puerto Rico shall be our sisters, and I do not desire that they shall be transatlantic Polands." Mr. Fish added: " But of course the United States would prefer to see all that remains of colonial America pass from [a colonial] condition to the condition of absolute independence of Europe." [1]

Mr. Cushing found, on arrival at Madrid, affairs in Spain not greatly different from those in Cuba. Castelar had given way, January 2, 1874, to Marshal Serrano as president. The latter had been invested, by a decree of February 27, with dictatorial powers. Nearly all the troops of the Peninsula were concentrated in the north to re-enforce those in Viscaya, where the Carlists were besieging Bilbao with an army of twenty-five thousand men. The sending of men to Cuba was, in this crisis, suspended, and it was even proposed to take a thousand Carlist prisoners from the Cuban service and reship them to Spain for exchange.[2] "Ports not occupied by the Carlists or even likely to be menaced by them were blockaded.

[1] *Foreign Relations*, 1874, 859–863.
[2] Mr. Adee to Mr. Fish, March 4, 1874, *Ibid*, 1874, 871.

And the available naval force of Spain was inadequate to maintain an effective surveillance over two hundred miles of tempestuous coast."[1]

The siege of Bilbao, after immense effort by the republican government, was raised in May. "At the present time," said Mr. Cushing in a despatch of June 18, 1874, "the republicans continue to hold the most important positions on the seacoast of the Bay of Biscay, including uninterrupted communication by rail between Madrid and Santander. But scattered parties of Carlists are still operating in all parts of Viscaya, as well as of Guipuzcoa and of Alava. The same general state of facts occurs in Navarre, and are also in a considerable part of Catalonia, Aragon, and Valencia. From time to time these detached parties sally from their fastnesses in the mountains to levy contributions, depredate, kidnap, and murder in the contiguous regions of Old Castile, and in those of Catalonia, Aragon, and Valencia, not permanently occupied by them. Meanwhile the Carlists occupy the land frontier on the side of France, and the adjoining districts of France from Pau to Bayonne are their place of refuge, their source of supplies, and their seat of military and political conspiracy against the government of Spain. Carlists also control, or interrupt when they please, all the lines of railroad from Madrid to the northern land frontier and to the northeastern or eastern sea frontier. The direct line from Madrid to France, by the way of Irun, is permanently stopped, and the line from Barcelona by Sargossa to Madrid, has been stopped repeatedly during my short residence at Madrid, as also has been the line from Valencia to Almansa." [2]

Mr. Cushing reported the existence of martial law over wide districts; embargoes of property; suppression of news in the newspapers, and the activity of Carlist committees in France and England, both of which countries were bases of supplies and recruitment for the insurgents as well as of refuge.[3] There was as yet no official recognition by the European powers except Switzerland

---

[1] Mr. Adee to Mr. Fish, February 24, 1874, *Foreign Relations*, 1874, 867.
[2] *Ibid.*, 1874, 887.
[3] For these decrees in detail, see *Foreign Relations*, 1874, 894–897; also *Ibid.*, 1875, 1128–1135. For the complaints against France for allowing shipment of supplies, the enlistment of men for the rebel Carlists and the public activity of Carlist juntas in southern France, see Mr. Cushing's despatch of December 17, 1874, in *Foreign Relations*, 1875, 1079.

of the republican or any other government in Spain. Rumors of intervention were rife.[1]

On March 14, 1874, General José de la Concha sailed for Havana as the relief of General Jovellar, with the titles of governor-general, captain-general, and commander-in-chief. Jovellar returned to Spain and on December 29, 1874, in company with Martinez Campos, proclaimed as king, at the head of the troops at Sagunto, the son of the exiled queen Isabella, Alfonso, who at the moment was a cadet at the military college of Sandhurst, England. The next day Señor Praxédes Mateo Sagasta, president of Marshal Serrano's cabinet, issued a counter proclamation in the absence of his chief, Serrano, who was, in the words of the proclamation, "at this very moment moving the army of the north to give decisive battle against the Carlist hosts." He appealed "to all parties which bear the name of liberal to stifle in a common effort the aspirations of absolutism," and denounced "a rebellion which . . . [the government] could not favor, if it spread, any more than it could favor Carlism and demagogy."[2]

The general infection of the army, however, became at once so apparent that President Serrano advised his cabinet to acquiesce, and next day, December 31, 1874, Señor Cánovas del Castillo, as president of a regency-ministry, proclaimed Alfonso king. The well-known names of Castro, Cardenas, Jovellar, Romero Robledo, and Lopez de Ayalá, which were to reappear at intervals for many years, were among those of the new government. Castelar and Sagasta were in long eclipse. The republican government, which had been in fact but a dictatorship, had lasted two years less a month and a half.

On January 9, 1875, Alfonso reached Barcelona and on the 14th arrived in Madrid, and the era, which may be called one of stability in character of government, began which has continued to this day. The situation has been nowhere better described than by the American minister in a note to Mr. Fish. He said: "The change of government, it is true, has been brought about by military pronunciamento; but it is not competent for any party

---

[1] Mr. Cushing to Mr. Fish, July 31, 1874, *Foreign Relations*, 1874, 898; also despatch of August 14, 1874, *Ibid.*, 904.

[2] *Ibid.*, 1875, 1083.

in Spain to find fault with others in that respect. All parties, one after the other, have had recourse to conspiracy, violence, and usurpation in order to attain their personal or party ends. It was by military violence that Prim, Serrano, and Topete overthrew Queen Isabel. It was by military violence that Serrano became president by the will of Pavia. And although, on the abdication of Amadeo, the proclamation of the republic was not the act of this or that general, yet it was brought about by a not less flagrant violation of order and constitutionalism as we understand it, a mere legislative assembly of two branches having formed themselves into a constituent convention in imitation of the worst examples of the French revolution, and having then proceeded, by mere usurpation and surprise, to impose a new government on Spain. So that neither the militarism nor the illegality of the movement tends in the least degree to repel the acceptance of it in any part of the country. And quite as little repulsion is produced by the suddenness of the movement, or the brief time occupied in its consummation. On the night of the 11th of February, 1873, all Spain went to bed a monarchy and woke up, to its astonishment, a republic. In like manner, on the 2d of January, 1874, the republican dictatorship of Castelar disappeared in a night, to give place to the conservative dictatorship of Serrano. Hence, on the morning of the 31st of December, 1874, it did not appear at all extraordinary to the Spaniards, in waking up, to find that the republic had vanished and the monarchy returned with the dramatic celerity of a change of scenery at the opera. In truth, all the great actors in public affairs during the last six years, Prim, Serrano, Ruiz, Zorrilla, Figueras, Pi y Margall, Salmeran, Castelar, have lost consideration as political guides, or as governors, by the absolute failure of each successively to prevent or terminate civil war, to maintain domestic order, to regularize the public finances, to promote industry and commerce, to protect private persons and property, to introduce liberty without anarchy or conservatism without despotism, or in any other respect to establish good government in Spain." [1]

Throughout the year 1875 the main energies of Spain were given to the Carlist insurrection, which had gone on six years.

[1] Mr. Cushing to Mr. Fish, January 5, 1875, *Foreign Relations*, 1875, 1084.

The period had been one of embargoes and decrees against those affiliated with the Carlist party. Affairs in Cuba had been running the usual course, now long chronic, of petty skirmishes, slaughter of prisoners, and destruction of property.

On November 5, 1875, Secretary Fish addressed a long note to Mr. Cushing setting forth, in view of his recent communications, the determination of the President that ways and means must be found to end the devastating contest.

This elaborate state paper which in the sequel, as will hereafter appear, became known in every European foreign office by its number as "266" was called for by the democratic House on January 17, 1876. The chief part is herewith given. Mr. Fish said:

"After the expiration of more than eighteen months, it seems advisable to examine what progress has been made, and to consider our present relations with Spain.

"In reference to the arbitrary seizure and withholding of the estates and property of citizens of the United States in Cuba, under proceedings of confiscation or embargo, so called, a separate instruction was addressed to you under date of February 6, prior to your departure for your post.

"I referred therein to the general facts surrounding these cases, to the arbitrary action of the authorities, by which the property of American citizens had been seized in violation of treaty provisions in the absence of judicial proceedings, without hearing, and under such circumstances as to call for vigorous protest and demands on behalf of this government. The general facts surrounding these cases are well known.

"It is not pretended, so far as I am aware, that any legal justification for these wrongs has been attempted on the part of the authorities of Spain, or that these proceedings in Cuba are defended or upheld. On the contrary, pursuant to the decree issued by the government on the 12th of July, 1873, the illegality and indefensible character of these acts were admitted, and the embargoes were ordered to be removed and the property to be restored.

"This decree was at first received in Cuba with calm indifference, not even published or adverted to, and the proceedings of the authorities were in no notable respect changed thereby.

"At the time of the visit of Señor Soler y Pla, minister of ultramar, the decree was in some instances recognized, and some insignificant steps taken, in individual cases, to comply therewith. In general, however, it was claimed, either that encumbrances existed making a compliance therewith impossible, or the delivery was offered burdened by leases or encumbrances, and coupled with unfair conditions or demands, or delivery was avoided, on the ground that particular property was confiscated, not embargoed. In fact, the decree was treated in general with supreme indifference."

Mr. Fish then entered upon a history of the efforts of General Sickles in the period mentioned, and exhibited a series of promises and of trivial and unwarranted pretexts for delay. The kindred question of the arrest and punishment of American citizens without trial was, he said, in the same position of constant evasion except in isolated cases, "where the Spanish government has been shown that insistence on trial by courts-martial implied a state of war in Cuba which might lead to logical consequences. . . . " He went on to deliver a broadside against the conduct of Spain during a half dozen years toward the United States:

"In the cases of embargo and confiscation, not only have wrongs been long since done, but continuing and repeated wrongs are daily inflicted. The authorities of Spain in Cuba, during all this time, have been and are using the revenues of the confiscated or embargoed estates, appropriating much of the property itself, and in some cases executing long leases, or actually making sales, either on the allegation that taxes were due or without any excuse whatever.

"In the cases of arrest and punishment, citizens of the United States, in like manner, have undergone punishment because the authorities of Spain do not meet the issue and decide the question.

"Turning to the questions which arose from the capture of the *Virginius*, and the executions which followed, no extended reference is required.

"The particulars of the delivery of the vessel to this government, and the payment to both Great Britain and the United States of considerable sums as compensation for the acts of the authorities in ordering the execution of fifty-three of the passengers and crew under circumstances of peculiar brutality, have passed into history.

"So far as a payment of money can atone for the execution of these unprotected prisoners that has been accomplished.

"The higher and more imperative duty which the government of Spain assumed by the protocol of November 29, 1873, namely, to bring to justice General Burriel and the other principal offenders in this tragedy, has been evaded and entirely neglected.

"Having made this neglect the subject of a separate instruction, under this date, I abstain from further reference thereto.

"While I have no desire to detract from the settlement which was obtained or to depreciate the action of Mr. Castro, the minister of state, in the payment of the indemnity, particularly as he seemed from the first presentation of the question to be impressed with the justice of the complaint, and to regard with natural aversion the acts which gave rise to it, it is but just, in considering the general course of the authorities in Spain toward this country, to refer to the long delay in reaching an adjustment, and principally to the fact that a basis of settlement was at last reached only after every delay had apparently been exhausted.

"As you are aware, Mr. Ulloa, then minister of state, under date of August 18, 1874, and probably impelled by some pressing necessity, addressed the British chargé d'affaires at Madrid, substantially agreeing to settle the claim of Great Britain for the execution of the British subjects on board that vessel.

"The equally strong, if not stronger, claim of the United States continued to be discussed in Madrid after the promise of settlement with Great Britain had been made, and information of this adjustment reached this government a considerable time after its conclusion, and not through the authorities of Spain. Our settlement was only accomplished in the month of March following. . . .

"It would be idle to attempt to conceal the interest and sympathy with which Americans in the United States regard any attempt of a numerous people on this continent to be relieved of ties which hold them in the position of colonial subjection to a distant power, and to assume the independence and right of self-control which natural rights and the spirit of the age accord to them.

"When, moreover, this struggle, in progress on our very borders, from its commencement has involved the property and interests of citizens of the United States, has disturbed our tranquillity and commerce, has called upon us not infrequently to witness barbarous violations of the rules of civilized warfare, and compelled us, for the sake of humanity, to raise our voice by way of protest; and when, more than all, we see in the contest the final struggle in this hemisphere between slavery and freedom, it would be strange indeed if the government and people of this country failed at any time to take peculiar interest in the termination of such contest.

"In this early instruction was expressed the sincere and unselfish hope of the President that the government of Spain would seek some honorable and satisfactory adjustment, based upon emancipation and self-government, which would restore peace and afford a prospect of a return of prosperity to Cuba.

"Almost two years have passed since those instructions were issued and those strong hopes expressed, and it would appear that the situation has in no respect improved.

"The horrors of war have in no perceptible measure abated; the inconveniences and injuries which we then suffered have remained, and others have been added; the ravages of war have touched new parts of the island, and wellnigh ruined its financial and agricultural system and its relations to the commerce of the world. No effective steps have been taken to establish reforms or remedy abuses, and the effort to suppress the insurrection by force alone has been a complete failure.

"In the meantime the material interests of trade and of commerce are impaired to a degree which calls for remonstrance, if not for another line of conduct, on the part of all commercial nations.

"Whether it be from the severity and inhumanity with which the effort has been made to suppress the insurrection, and from a supposed justification of retaliation for violations of the rules of civilized warfare by other violations and by acts of barbarism, of incendiarism, and outrage, the world is witnessing on the part of the insurgents, whom Spain still claims as subjects, and for whose acts, if subjects, Spain must be held accountable in the judgment of the world, a warfare, not of the legitimate strife of relative force and strength, but of pillage and incendiarism, the burning of estates and of sugar mills, the destruction of the means of production and of the wealth of the island.

"The United States purchases more largely than any other people of the productions of the island of Cuba, and, therefore, more than any other for this reason, and still more by reason of its immediate neighborhood, is interested in the arrest of a system of wanton destruction which disgraces the age and affects every commercial people on the face of the globe.

"Under these circumstances, and in view of the fact that Spain has rejected all suggestions of reform or offers of mediation made by this government, and has refused all measures looking to a reconciliation, except on terms which make reconciliation an impossibility, the difficulty of the situation becomes increased.

"When, however, in addition to these general causes of difficulty, we find the Spanish government neglectful also of the obligations of treaties and solemn compacts and unwilling to afford any redress for long-continued and well-founded wrongs suffered by our citizens, it becomes a serious question how long such a condition of things can or should be allowed to exist, and compels us to inquire whether the point has not been reached where longer endurance ceases to be possible.

"During all this time, and under these aggravated circumstances, this government has not failed to perform her obligations to Spain as scrupulously as toward other nations.

"In fact, it might be said that we have not only been long-suffering, because of the embarrassments surrounding the Spanish government, but particularly careful to give no occasion for complaint for the same reason.

"I regret to say that the authorities of Spain have not at all times appreciated our intentions or our purposes in these respects, and, while insisting that a state of war does not exist in Cuba and that no rights as belligerents should be accorded to the insurrectionists, have at the same time demanded for themselves all the rights and privileges which flow from actual and acknowledged war.

"It will be apparent that such a state of things cannot continue. It is absolutely necessary to the maintenance of our relations with Spain, even on their present footing, that our just demands for the return to citizens of the United States of their estates in Cuba, unencumbered, and for securing to them a trial for offences according to treaty provisions and all other rights guaranteed by treaty and by public law should be complied with.

"Whether the Spanish government, appreciating the forbearance of this country, will speedily and satisfactorily adjust the pending questions, not by the issue of empty orders or decrees without force or effect in Cuba, but by comprehensive and firm measures which shall everywhere be respected, I anxiously await further intelligence.

"Moreover, apart from these particular questions, in the opinion of the President the time has arrived when the interests of this country, the preservation of its commerce, and the instincts of humanity alike demand that some speedy and satisfactory ending be made of the strife that is devasting Cuba.

"A disastrous conflict of more than seven years' duration has demonstrated the inability of Spain to maintain peace and order in an island lying at our door. Desolation and destruction of life and property have been the only results of this conflict.

"The United States sympathizes in the fact that this inability results in a large degree from the unhappy condition of Spain at home, and to some extent from the distractions which are dividing her people. But the fact remains. Added to this are the large expanse of ocean separating the Peninsula from the island, and the want of harmony and of personal sympathy between the inhabitants of the territory of the home government and those of the colony, the distinction of classes in the latter between rulers and subjects, the want of adaptation of the ancient colonial system of Spain to the present times and to the ideas which the events of the past age have impressed upon the peoples of every reading and thinking country.

"Great Britain, wisely, has relaxed the old system of colonial dependence, and is reaping the benefits in the contentedness and peaceful prosecution of the arts of peace and in the channels of commerce and of industry, in colonies which, under restraint, might have questioned and resisted the power of control from a distant government and might have exhibited, as does Cuba, a chronic condition of insurrection, turbulence, and rebellion.

"In addition to all this, it cannot be questioned that the continued maintenance, in the face of decrees and enactments to the contrary, of a compulsory system of slave labor is a cause of disquiet and of excitement to a large class in the island, as also in the United States, which the government of Spain has led us, by very distinct assurances, to expect should be removed, and which the enlightened Christianity of the age condemns.

"The contest and disorder in Cuba affect the United States directly and injuriously by the presence in this country of partisans of the revolt who have fled hither (in consequence of the proximity of territory) as to a political asylum, and who, by their plottings, are disturbers of the public peace.

The United States has exerted itself to the utmost, for seven years, to repress unlawful acts on the part of these self-exiled subjects of Spain, relying on the promise of Spain to pacify the island. Seven years of strain on the powers of this government to fulfil all that the most exacting demands of one government can make, under any doctrine or claim of international obligation, upon another, have not witnessed the much-hoped-for pacification. The United States feels itself entitled to be relieved of this strain.

"The severe measures, injurious to the United States and often in conflict with public law, which the colonial officers have taken to subdue the insurrection; the indifference, and oftimes the offensive assaults upon the just susceptibilities of the people of the United States and their government, which have characterized that portion of the peninsular population of Havana which has sustained and upheld, if it has not controlled, successive governors-general, and which have led to the disregard of orders and decrees which the more enlarged wisdom and the more friendly councils of the home government had enacted; the cruelty and inhumanity which have characterized the contest, both on the part of the colonial government and of the revolt, for seven years, and the destruction of valuable properties and industries by arson and pillage, which Spain appears unable, however desirous, to prevent and stop, in an island three thousand miles distant from her shores, but lying within sight of our coast, with which trade and constant intercourse are unavoidable, are causes of annoyance and of injury to the United States, which a people cannot be expected to tolerate without the assured prospect of their termination.

"The United States has more than once been solicited by the insurgents to extend to them its aid, but has for years hitherto resisted such solicitation, and has endeavored by the tender of its good offices, in the way of mediation, advice, and remonstrance, to bring to an end a great evil, which has pressed sorely upon the interests both of the government and of the people of the United States, as also upon the commercial interests of other nations.

"A sincere friendship for Spain, and for her people, whether peninsular or insular, and an equally sincere reluctance to adopt any measures which might injure or humble the ancient ally [1] of the United States, has characterized the conduct of this government in every step during these sad and distressing years, and the President is still animated by the same feelings, and desires above all things to aid her and her people to enter once more upon the path of safety and repose.

"It will be remembered that the President, in the year 1869, tendered the good offices of the United States for the purpose of bringing to a close the civil war in Cuba. This offer was made delicately, in good faith, and in friendship to both parties to the contest.

"General Prim, as the representative of the Spanish government, while recognizing the good faith and friendship with which this offer was made, replied:

"'We can better proceed in the present situation of things without even this friendly intervention. A time will come when the good offices of the United States will be not only useful but indispensable in the final arrangements between Spain and Cuba. We will ascertain the form in which they can be employed and confidently count upon your assistance.'

"The United States replied that its good offices for that object would be at any time at the service of the parties to the conflict. This government has ever since been ready thus to aid in restoring peace and quiet.

"The government of the United States has heretofore given expression to no policy in reference to the insurrection in Cuba, because it has honestly and sincerely hoped that no declaration of policy on its part would be required.

"The President feels that longer reticence would be inconsistent with the interests of both governments.

[1] Mr. Fish is here in error: Spain was never an ally to the United States; she was party to a war against a common enemy.

"Our relations with Spain are in that critical position that another seizure similar to that of the *Virginius*, other executions of citizens of the United States in Cuba, other wrongs of a less objectionable character even than many which have been already suffered by our citizens with simple remonstrance, or possibly even some new act of exceptional severity in Cuba, may suddenly produce a feeling and excitement which might force events which this government anxiously desires to avoid.

"The President hopes that Spain may spontaneously adopt measures looking to a reconciliation and to the speedy restoration of peace and the organization of a stable and satisfactory system of government in the island of Cuba.

"In the absence of any prospect of a termination of the war, or of any change in the manner in which it has been conducted on either side, he feels that the time is at hand when it may be the duty of other governments to intervene, solely with a view of bringing to an end a disastrous and destructive conflict, and of restoring peace in the island of Cuba. No government is more deeply interested in the order and peaceful administration of this island than is that of the United States, and none has suffered as has the United States from the condition which has obtained there during the past six or seven years. He will, therefore, feel it his duty at an early day to submit the subject in this light, and accompanied by an expression of the views above presented, for the consideration of Congress.

"This conclusion is reached with reluctance and regret.

"It is reached after every other expedient has been attempted and proved a failure, and in the firm conviction that the period has at last arrived when no other course remains for this government.

"It is believed to be a just and friendly act to frankly communicate this conclusion to the Spanish government.

"You will therefore take an early occasion thus to inform that government.

"In making the communication, it is the earnest desire of the President to impress upon the authorities of Spain the continued friendly disposition of this government, and that it has no ulterior or selfish objects in view and no desire to become a party in the conflict, but is moved solely by the imperative necessities of a proper regard to its own protection and its own interests and the interests of humanity, and, as we firmly believe, in the ultimate interest of Spain itself.

"In informing the Spanish government of these conclusions pursuant hereto, you are authorized to read this instruction to the minister of state, or to state the substance and purport thereof, as you may deem most advisable."[1]

Mr. Cushing was told in a despatch of the same date:

"It has been deemed proper to send *confidentially* a copy of instruction No. 266 to General Schenck, the minister of the United States at London, with instructions to *read* the same to Lord Derby, and to suggest to the British government that it would be agreeable to the United States, and in our opinion tend to the adjustment of the question of the pacification of Cuba, if not to the preservation of general peace, if the British government would support by its influence the position assumed by this government.

"A copy of this instruction to General Schenck is herewith enclosed.

"He has been instructed, as you will perceive, to notify the department by telegraph of the result of this communication to Lord Derby.

"Should it appear probable that the British government will enforce the position of this government, it may be wise to defer your interview with the minister of state until joint action can be agreed upon.

"Should that government hesitate, or decline, you will be at once instructed to proceed to carry out the instructions contained in No. 266. In case the government of Great Britain shall determine to support our position by its influence, proper instructions will doubtless be sent to its representative in Madrid to that effect.

"As no great delay will be occasioned thereby, it is deemed better to postpone your action in communicating these conclusions until

[1] *Report of Senate Committee on Foreign Relations Relative to Affairs in Cuba.* Report 885, 55 Cong., 2 Sess., 44-52; also House Ex. Doc. 90, 44 Cong., 1 Sess.

General Schenck shall have communicated the views of the British government, by telegraph, to the department, and telegraphic instructions can be sent you based thereon.

"A copy of instruction No. 266 will also shortly be sent to all our diplomatic representatives, *in confidence*, for their information, and the ministers to the principal European courts will be instructed to communicate its purport to the governments to which they are respectively accredited." [1]

When the contents of No. 266 were known in Europe, it was condemned by some newspapers as offensive in tone and otherwise of a character that a great European power would not venture to address to another, and that it was also in effect a warlike intervention in the affairs of an independent nation. The document, however, was not addressed to a foreign nation. If other powers than Spain were permitted to see it, the motive was to enable them to appreciate correctly the conduct of the Washington government. It contained conclusive evidence that the only purpose of Mr. Fish was to suppress doings in Cuba by individuals that were hostile and injurious to the United States. Mr. Fish sought nothing but security against future wrongs in the island. He did not deny that Americans who remained in Cuba must obey Cuban laws fairly applied under the treaty of 1795, but did demand reparation for, and future security against, maltreatment. No attack on the independence of Spain was meditated. The object was the avoidance of it. No forcible intervention was intimated unless Spain refused to restrain her officials and Spaniards in the island from injuring and annoying the United States in violation of the law of nations, or confessed inability to successfully apply such restraint. The independence given then by public law to Spain in Cuba, as to the United States in the Philippines now, is conditioned on reciprocal obligation to protect other states from preventible and unlawful injuries.

On the 16th of November, however, and before Mr. Fish's "No. 266," of the 5th of that month, had reached Madrid, Mr.

---

[1] Sen. Rep. 855, 55 Cong., 2 Sess., 52. The ministers to whom this was sent were those accredited to Russia, Germany, Austria, Italy, France, and Portugal. For the identic despatch transmitting No. 266 to these several officials see *Ibid.*, 140; for that to Mr. Schenck, *Ibid.* 152.

Cushing received a note, dated the day before, of much length from the Spanish minister of foreign affairs, Señor Calderon y Collantes, meeting in a most friendly and cordial spirit some of the demands of the United States, and repeating assurances of the trial of General Burriel, the main points of which Mr. Cushing sent in a telegram to Mr. Fish, on the same day, as follows:

"Spanish note has come in. It is eminently amicable in spirit. It concedes everything in effect or substance; disavows all trials of our citizens for things done in our country, and engages annulment of sentences with redress otherwise in any such case, which settles the confiscation cases in principle; argues that no proper case for recognition of belligerence exists in Cuba; denies that the treaty necessarily intended or implied exclusion of military tribunals, but engages royal order either for trial by civil magistrate, or for special guaranty of required securities of fair trial in every case, including lay counsel and cross-examination of witnesses; promises redress in any existing case of trial in disregard of such securities; repeats assurance of trial of Burriel; drops the *Virginius*. As the note contains alternative propositions for your consideration, it is impossible for me to act in the premises without special instructions. I send it by special messenger as far as London." [1]

Mr. Fish's No. 266 of November 5, and information that British good offices had been requested, reached Mr. Cushing on November 25. He at once telegraphed:

"You call for my opinion; I give it according to my best lights. If Great Britain co-operates, Spain will succumb in sullen despair to whatever terms the two governments may jointly dictate; but if Great Britain refuses to co-operate, Spain will conclude that she has the sympathy of all European powers, more especially as she thinks she has now gone, by her note of the 15th, to the ultimate point in each of the particular griefs of the United States. In other words, there will be war, and a popular though desperate one on the part of Spain, unless she can be convinced that the real

---

[1] MS., State Department Archives. The text of the note has never been printed, but the general purport given herewith is sufficiently supplemented by Señor Calderon's note of April 16, 1876 (Sen. Rep. 885, 55 Cong., 2 Sess., 120), to make its insertion unnecessary.

and true object of the contemplated measure is to prevent war, as I understand it to be intended. But to ward off war will be to exact the steady exercise of my personal influence here (which my colleagues tell me is great), and will require that influence to be efficiently backed by my government both here and at Washington. I am here to 'obey orders though it break owners,' as the shipmasters say. I earnestly beg you, therefore, in proportion as you desire peace, to address me specific and explicit replies in regard to certain needful instructions which I shall ask for by telegram, provided a negative answer comes from Great Britain." [1]

On the same day he wrote to Mr. Fish: "Many of the most thoughtful men in Spain really long for a foreign war as the only efficient remedy for the domestic dissensions which now distract the country. Moreover, the statesmen of the country foresee that, on the close of the war in the north, which cannot fail to come in the course of the winter, or early in the spring, there will be an army of two or three hundred thousand men to dispose of, with its officers, who will be but too much disposed to dominate in public affairs and push the civilians into the background. In addition to which there is a multitude of unthoughtful men, proud, angry, resentful, who would gladly rush into a war with the United States. Finally, there are the mercenary, the ambitious, the *declassés* and the bad, to whom war presents the usual attractions. *Multis utile bellum*, says Sallust. It is the received opinion in Spain that for the commencing period of the war she has a more efficient navy than ours. In these circumstances, if Great Britain declines to co-operate with us, Spain will, at the least, despatch to Cuba at once a large fleet, laden with troops, there to await the eventualities of diplomacy; and she may break off relations with a hostile appeal to the European powers. . . . I have no wish to exaggerate the results lately attained by me here; I cannot but think, however, that the contents of the late Spanish note, if faithfully carried out in detail, as they certainly would be, go far toward satisfying the particular reclamations of the United States." [2]

The next day, November 26, 1875, ignorant of the instruction to General Schenck in London to withhold the note, Mr. Cushing

[1] Sen. Rep. 885, 55 Cong. 2 Sess., 53.   [2] *Ibid.*, 53–54.

telegraphed: "The response of England lingers. Time passes,[1] . . . I cannot read your despatch to the Spanish minister; he does not understand English. To state its substance to him orally would be doing extreme injustice to the despatch. Why not give a copy to the Spanish minister? . . . Will you authorize me, after the Spanish minister is informed, in whatever way, of the contents of the document, to talk to him as a friend and well-wisher regarding what, in my opinion, Spain ought to do, may honorably do in this emergency?"[2]

The reception of this at Washington brought the following reply: "Schenck was instructed to delay presentation of 266, in consequence of your telegram of the 16th. The President's message will discountenance recognition of either belligerency or independence; will refer to the injuries to the United States and its citizens from the long-continued struggle and the absence of prospect of termination; will intimate intervention as an ultimate necessity, unless satisfactory results be soon reached, but will abstain from advising it at present; will refer to pending proposals not yet received here, with hope that they may afford the relief required and lead to a satisfactory settlement and removal of causes of grief; will intimate that a communication will soon be made to Congress as to the result of the proposals now on their way, and that, if it do not satisfactorily adjust all important questions, he will before long make a recommendation to Congress of the course to be pursued. The above is for your guidance in your interview with minister; be careful that it be not communicated by minister, or otherwise, to the press, or public, in anticipation of what will be done here. The instruction 266 is not intended as minatory in any sense but in the spirit of friendship, as a notice of a necessity which may be forced upon the President, but which he hopes to avoid, and desires Spain to aid him in escaping. We are sincerely desirous to preserve peace and to establish all relations with Spain on the most amicable and liberal basis, but we must be relieved and be secure as to the future, and you may give positive assurances to this effect.

[1] Referring to the need of the President's placing in his message the situation before Congress, about to meet.
[2] Telegram, Sen. Rep. 885, 55 Cong., 2 Sess., 55.

"You may give copy of 266 to minister, and may speak in the sense indicated in your telegram of yesterday, provided it be not to do away the object of the instruction. You will make the communication and present copy of instruction, without waiting for presentation in London. Schenck will to-day be instructed to read paper as soon as he can."[1]

Whatever exasperation existed on the part of either country, and whatever the attitude in general of American or Spanish politicians, there can be no question that, at the moment, both governments were fortunate in the men who were in the immediate direction of affairs. No statesman of any period was moved by sincerer or loftier motives looking to the general good than was Mr. Fish, the American secretary of state, whose influence was all-powerful with President Grant and through him with Congress. In Spain, Señor Calderon had left his congenial post of minister of grace and justice for that of the minister of state, trusting to co-operate with the American minister, a personal friend of long standing, in the hope of healing all differences.[2]

Mr. Cushing himself had long known Spain, spoke its language, and was in sympathy with its people. All these elements combined for peace, and on November 30 Mr. Cushing, as instructed, placed in the hands of Señor Calderon No. 266, saying:

"This despatch is not conceived in any minatory sense, but, on the contrary, in the spirit of friendship, as a notice of a pressing necessity, which may force the hand of the President in given circumstances from which he desires to save himself, and desires Spain to aid him in escaping them. He sincerely desires to maintain peace and to establish the relations of the United States with Spain upon the most friendly and liberal bases, provided they contain satisfaction for the present and security for the future; and I am authorized, to this end, to offer the most positive assurances to the government of his majesty." Mr. Cushing also at the same time gave the short synopsis of the President's annual message to Congress, sent in Mr. Fish's telegram of the 27th.[3]

The paper was received by Señor Calderon in the spirit for which Mr. Fish had hoped, and in which Mr. Cushing assured

[1] Telegram, November 27, 1875, Sen. Rep. 885, 55 Cong., 2 Sess., 56.
[2] Ibid., 62. [3] Ibid., 58.

it to be intended. "Mr. Calderon," said Mr. Cushing, "has carefully read your 266; admits its grievances; is opposed in principle to sequestration of property of foreigners; condemns the delays of redress; will take up and promptly settle each case; will remove all cause of complaint as to treaty; reprobates conduct of local authorities in Cuba as more injurious to Spain than to the United States."[1]

The annual message of President Grant of December 7, 1875, which became a classic on the subject of Cuba, did much to create a not unfavorable impression in Europe of Mr. Fish's proposal. It opened the question with a statement of the complete success of the department of state in obtaining all it sought as pecuniary reparation in the affair of the *Virginius* by the prompt payment of eighty thousand dollars, which had been distributed among the American passengers and crew, or the families of those who died. It then went on to say, among other things:

"While conscious that the insurrection in Cuba has shown a strength and endurance which make it at least doubtful whether it be in the power of Spain to subdue it, it seems unquestionable that no civil organization exists which may be recognized as an independent government capable of performing its international obligations and entitled to be treated as one of the powers of the earth. A recognition, under such circumstances, would be inconsistent with the facts, and would compel the power granting it soon to support by force the government to which it had really given its only claim of existence. In my judgment, the United States should adhere to the policy and principles which have heretofore been its sure and safe guides in like contests between revolted colonies and their mother country."

The President reproduced the arguments of his previous messages to Congress against the recognition of belligerency, which he still regarded "as unwise and premature," and "at present indefensible as a measure of right." He said: "Each party seems quite capable of working great injury and damage to the other . . . but they seem incapable of reaching any adjustment. . . . Under the circumstances, the agency of others, either by mediation or by intervention, seems to be the only alternative which must,

[1] Telegram, December 4, 1875, Sen. Rep. 885, 55 Cong., 2 Sess., 61.

sooner or later, be invoked for the termination of the strife. At the same time, while thus impressed, I do not, at this time, recommend the adoption of any measure of intervention. I shall be ready at all times, and as the equal friend of both parties, to respond to a suggestion that the good offices of the United States will be acceptable, to aid in bringing about a peace honorable to both. It is due to Spain, so far as this government is concerned, that the agency of a third power, to which I have adverted, shall be adopted only as a last expedient. Had it been the desire of the United States to interfere in the affairs of Cuba, repeated opportunities for so doing have been presented in the last few years, but we have remained passive, and have performed our whole duty and all international obligations to Spain with friendship, fairness, and fidelity, and with a spirit of patience and forbearance which negatives every possible suggestion of desire to interfere or to add to the difficulties with which she has been surrounded."

He referred to the Spanish proposals of November 15,[1] not yet received in their full text, with the hope that they would "lead to a satisfactory adjustment," and concluded with the statement that if disappointed in such a hope, he should feel it his duty to make a further communication to Congress during the pending session, "recommending what may then seem to me to be necessary." [2]

The President did not make a further communication on the subject. The House at this time was controlled by the democrats. The important point was the reservation by the President, in his own hands, of action in Cuban affairs. The situation was much akin to that to come in 1898. Had he at this moment yielded to Congress the determination of what should have been done, there would almost certainly have been war.

The President and his secretary of state responded frankly, as Mr. Cushing asked, in regard " to the real and true object" of No. 266. They gave the specific and needful replies to Mr. Cushing's inquiries. He was authorized to give a copy of No. 266 to the Spanish minister of state. He was authorized "to talk to him as a friend," provided the object of No. 266 be not done away with. Something was accomplished for the United States, but not that which was essentially needful. Spain, profuse in her promises

[1] *Supra*, 374, 375.   [2] Richardson, *Messages and Papers*, VII, 332.

in October and November, obtained that which she sought: a conservative tone in the President's message.

Meanwhile, on December 2, 1875, came an intimation that Great Britain could not be relied upon to help Mr. Cushing. Mr. Layard, the British ambassador at Madrid, called upon Mr. Cushing and expressed readiness to back him, but not until "our respective governments should have settled on a line of action and instructed us to that effect. He expresses great discontent at the failure of Spain to pay attention to the various claims, thirteen in number, presented by him in behalf of his government, and says that the situation will be untenable here without some improvement in the conduct of the business of the ministry of state. He thinks Great Britain has abundant cause of her own to interfere in the affairs of Cuba under her slave-trade treaties with Spain." [1]

Madrid did not fail to realize the meaning of that! It had weight with the Spanish minister of state, who later spoke to Mr. Cushing "of the political necessity of abandoning the old colonial system and of promptly bringing about emancipation of the slaves." He added that if it were in his power to speak directly to the American secretary of state he would beg to ask him explicitly, as a friend, the precise thing which he would wish Spain to do under the mediation of the United States, with the assurance that, if just or practicable, "Spain would be but too glad to do it, as well in her own interest as in good-will toward the United States, and in the consciousness that the United States and Spain are by commercial ties inseparably associated in the question of the tranquillity and prosperity of Cuba." [2]

A few days after this conversation there was a leader in the *London Times* on No. 266, which probably expressed controlling English opinion. It ran thus:

"It will be very difficult to answer an indictment so formidable in itself and ending in so mild a demand. The purists of international law may at once be warned off the field of discussion. They may say that the United States has no more right to dictate how Spain shall govern Cuba than Spain has to order the reorgani-

[1] Mr. Cushing to Mr. Fish, December 3, 1875, Sen. Rep. 885, 55 Cong., 2 Sess., 59.
[2] Mr. Cushing to Mr. Fish, January 16, 1876, *Ibid.*, 78.

zation of the South. They may say that the American citizens who live in Cuba went there at their own risk, and must bear the inevitable penalties of civil war. Much the same fate, it may be pleaded, would have come to any Spaniards who had owned property in Virginia during the war between the North and the South, and yet they would have received no redress. Nor, it might be added, were either the Confederate or the Federal cruisers particularly respectful of foreign rights in their efforts to destroy each other. But these arguments are fit merely for lecture-rooms. The practical answer is that the general rules of international usage, conveniently called international law, can be applied only to ordinary cases of warfare. Since there is no international parliament, each nation is justified in defending its interests by exceptional measures when they are attacked in an exceptional manner. . . . America is acting with at least as much moderation as this country would display if Cuba were as near to Cornwall as it is to Florida. In such a case we should require Spain to protect the property of our countrymen and to take the obvious means of restoring her colony to a state of peace, by abolishing slavery and allowing the Cubans to rule themselves." [1]

It will be remembered that Mr. Fish informed Mr. Cushing on November 5, 1875, that a copy of No. 266 will "shortly be sent to all our diplomatic representatives *in confidence* for their information, and the ministers at the principal European courts will be instructed to communicate the purport to the governments to which they are respectively accredited." The minister at London was directed to read it to Lord Derby and to suggest that it would be agreeable to the United States "if the British government would support by its influence the position assumed by this government." No. 266 was brought to the attention of the continental powers, but not in the same terms as to Great Britain, the suggestion being made "that should these governments . . . see fit to urge upon Spain the necessity for abandoning or terminating the contest in Cuba, such a course would be satisfactory to this government and conducive to the interests of all commercial nations." [2]

[1] *London Times*, January 26, 1876.
[2] Moore, *Digest*, VI, 99. See also note, *Supra*, 374.

But Great Britain's action finally was distinctly against giving aid to Mr. Cushing, Lord Derby declaring "that if nothing were contemplated beyond an amicable interposition having peace for its object, the time was ill-chosen and the move premature." [1]

At the time of the writing of the foregoing in the *Times*, and of Lord Derby's declaration to Mr. Schenck, and of the saying to Mr. Cushing by the Spanish minister of state that he would like to ask Mr. Fish explicitly for "the precise thing which he would wish Spain to do under the circumstances," the President's message of December, 1875, was in Europe. If by its aid a reasonably good diplomatic instinct had been applied to the interpretation of No. 266, the result, with the Spanish government in the frame of mind expressed in Señor Calderon's note of November 15,[2] and as soon as the Carlists should be defeated as they were soon to be, must have been that which the administration at Washington sought: a full amnesty to the rebels in Cuba, a cessation of fighting, a release of embargoed estates, a faithful observance of the stipulations of the treaty of 1795, a liberal local government in the island with nominal sovereignty retained by Spain, and gradual emancipation of the slaves. The *Times* may have been correct in describing that as a "mild demand," but it also should have been intelligent and frank enough to say that if the property or person of a foreigner was injured unlawfully during the war of secession reparation was made to him.

The real difficulties in Cuba grew out of two insurrections, the primary one that of Yara in 1868; the second grew out of the domination of the captain-general by the *Casino Español* and the Spanish volunteers, and the consequent disregard of the government at Madrid. What the President of the United States demanded in No. 266 was that, so far as American citizens were concerned, Madrid should make its authority in Cuba, and quick obedience to its orders, a reality.

On January 21, 1876, the President sent to the House of Representatives, on its request, a copy of No. 266 and cognate papers. On the next day the House asked for copies of any correspondence with any European government during the year 1875, other than

[1] Mr. Schenck to Mr. Fish, January 28, 1876, Sen. Rep. 885, 55 Cong., 2 Sess., 162.
[2] *Supra*, 375.

Spain, relative to Cuba. The President replied that there had been none.[1]

Meanwhile and subsequently there was criticism of the administration, for its violation of the "Monroe doctrine" in what it had done. The documents sent to Congress in 1876, those furnished twenty years later in the period of the second Cuban rebellion, and the information of the contents of notes from the state department to our ministers abroad, set forth in 1906 in the digest of international law so ably edited by Mr. John Bassett Moore,[2] give the details of what occurred. They make apparent that No. 266 had simply been communicated to European governments and conversations had taken place regarding it between our representatives and those governments, as well as between Mr. Fish and the ministers of those governments at Washington. This exhibit clearly shows that the only object of Mr. Fish was that which he had described to Mr. Cushing in the note to him of November 5, 1875. It may possibly be now thought that under the present interpretation of the Monroe doctrine there was, in 1875, a violation of it; but certainly the author of that doctrine, John Quincy Adams, could not have been of that opinion in 1826 had the facts been before him. He was then President, and his secretary of state, Mr. Clay, on May 26 of that year, instructed the American minister at St. Petersburg to ask the Russian government to aid in bringing about peace between Spain and her colonies, with especial reference to safeguarding Cuba from attack by Colombia and Mexico.[3]

However that may be, the inference is that offering to the great European powers an opportunity to advise Spain, in the greatest of her many great difficulties, was salutary, although nearly all drew back from the suggestion. From the point of view of these powers, whose interests were so much less than those of the United States, there were for the moment fair reasons for their own inaction. The Duke Décazes, the French foreign minister, said: "The great obstacle to any result lies in the powerlessness of the government of the young Alphonso. That weakness as regards

---

[1] Richardson, *Messages and Papers*, VII, 357.   [2] Moore, *Digest*, VI, 92–105.
[3] *Supra*, 207; also Moore, *Digest*, VI, 447, where are many references to the subject at this earlier period.

this particular question arises from a general condition (*ensemble*) of affairs in Spain. Many circumstances together have produced such a situation that, although the Spanish government might wish to take such steps as were proposed—tending to self-government and emancipation in Cuba—it does not do it. It would fail if it attempted a policy which could be used against it with Spanish people. The northern provinces disturbed by the Carlists and Cuba with its insurrection are both held with difficulty. The young king's government must move with exceeding care. Besides, there is doubt of the power of the home government to enforce its will. . . . The young king dare not commence his reign with a failure (*défaillance*). . . . If the Spanish government allowed the Carlists a pretext to assume to be the champions of the preservation of the colony of Spain it would increase its embarrassments. There is the recent letter of Don Carlos, proposing to subdue the rebellion in Cuba; the Spanish people (*ces pauvres diables Espagnols*) take it for serious and do not see the ridiculous side of it." [1]

Portugal feared for her independence and the establishment of an Iberian Union as compensation to Spain should the latter lose Cuba.[2] Italy, only, of all the powers, offered to instruct her minister to urge the expediency of Spain's fulfilling duties to the United States and pacifying Cuba, without specifying measures.[3]

While the moment may not have been altogether favorable, eastern Europe, besides the reasons mentioned, being in the ferment which in a little more than a year was to develop into the Russian-Turkish war, it is not wholly unjust to suppose that while the concert of the powers was accustomed to act upon questions of such a character affecting Europe, it was not quite ready to admit the United States, a country without dynastic relations with Europe, to its intimacy upon a question so remotely affecting them as that of Cuba. There could be seen in this reserve the jealousy of the entrance to its councils of a comparatively new power, so recently out of the throes of a great civil war, during which it had the real friendship of but one [4] and the marked enmity of two of the most power-

---

[1] Mr. Hitt, chargé d'affaires, to Mr. Fish, December 10, 1875, Sen. Rep. 885, 55 Cong., 2 Sess., 143.
[2] Mr. Moran, minister to Portugal, to Mr. Fish, December 31, 1875, *Ibid.*, 171.
[3] Mr. Fish to Mr. Cushing, December 20, 1875, *Ibid.*, 65.   [4] Russia.

ful. As to England, the significant fact, alluded to in No. 266, is not to be forgotten that, as early as August, 1874, Spain consented to make pecuniary reparation (withheld from the knowledge of the United States) for British subjects on the *Virginius* who were put to death, but reparation for citizens of the United States, slain under the same circumstances, was delayed and refused for seven months thereafter.

Nor would it have been unnatural if recent incidents growing out of the American case and the Geneva award, checked at London to aid at Madrid one, who as Mr. Cushing, had been so conspicuous in pursuing Great Britain on account of the Confederate cruisers. As events turned, the one country to suffer from the apathy shown by Europe was Spain.

CHAPTER XIX

THE END OF THE TEN YEARS' WAR

On February 3, 1876, the American minister received from Señor Calderon a memorandum giving a review of the Cuban situation, which had been sent, as a reply to Mr. Fish's No. 266, to the Spanish representatives near European governments as well as to the minister at Washington. It was an able presentation of the Spanish side of the question. Señor Calderon showed that of the leaders of the secession movement, all of whom were Cubans, not one was now living. Of those who succeeded them in command not one was a Cuban. Maximo Gomez, the principal, was a Dominican, as was Modesto Diaz; Rulof was a Pole; the person known as El Inglesito, an Englishman. "Their forces," he said, "now consist of negroes, mulattoes, Chinese, deserters from the battalions which were formed provisionally in Santo Domingo during our brief rule there, and a few independent bodies which were formed in Spain during the most disorderly period of the revolution. . . . It may be confidently asserted that there are to-day not more than eight hundred white natives of Cuba with arms in their hands in the insurgent ranks. The consequence of this radical change in the elements of the insurrection is, that what could be considered, in the beginning, as a struggle for independence has now assumed a character of ferocity, and become a war of races and of devastation, which it was not before. Wherever a band of insurgents make their appearance they steal and plunder everything that they can lay their hands on and set fire to the crops and buildings. . . . Not a single instance can be pointed to in which such a deed has been committed by our troops. . . . It is easy to estimate what would be the consequences, not only for Spain but for the world at large, of the triumph (which is fortunately quite impossible) of such an insurrection. If such a triumph were once gained through the efforts of the negroes, mulattoes, and adventurers, the power would be in their hands; they would establish such a government as their capacity would permit, and, far from being the commencement of an era of peace for the island and of security for the interests of Europe and America, it would be the utter ruin of them all and the end of all civilization. . . . The triumph of Spain would soon be followed by the judicious but total abolition of slavery, which still exists in Cuba in spite of the sincere wishes of his majesty's government; it would insure the administrative reforms which have been offered to the island; it would open the door to the representation of the inhabitants in the Congress of Deputies; and finally, it would speedily bring to pass what will in vain be sought by other means."

He referred to the measures already carried out in Puerto Rico as a guarantee of Spain's intentions. He mentioned as a surety of putting down the insurrection the presence in Cuba of 45 ships with 135 guns and 2,426 seamen; and in the army, a total of 273 general officers, 3,054 officers, 68,115 soldiers, 8,475 horses, 462 mules, and 42 field-pieces, shortly to be added to by 10,370 men who had embarked for the island, making a total regular force of over 78,000 men. In addition, there was a force of volunteers of over 50,000.

He stated that in the western department the sugar estates had increased in number instead of diminishing; there were in the west, which was the great sugar district, 1,070, while in the central department there were but 102, and in the east 200. He showed that the real wealth of the island as well as the great mass of the population was in the west, as yet but little disturbed by the insurrection; that the receipts from duties were constantly increasing, and that the general commerce of the island with the world had not suffered in volume.[1]

That the sympathies of the American minister were with Señor Calderon is clear. "Spain," he said, "is willing enough to confide in us if we will let her. The proof of that is found not in profession (although that we have), but in the analysis of the diplomatic relations of Spain with other powers contained in previous despatches. In fine, whatever causes of grief or jealousy she has against us, she

[1] For this memorandum in full, see Sen. Rep. 885, 55 Cong., 2 Sess., 92–96.

has greater against others. Nevertheless, she is now anxious and suspicious with regard to the United States. She knows that thousands of bad Spaniards (called Cubans), having a holy horror of the smell of gunpowder, have fled to 'snug harbor' in New York, Key West, and New Orleans, have been dedicating themselves there for years, by distribution of bonds, by speeches, newspapers, solicitations, exaggerated claims, violations of law, and in every other possible way, to the task of embroiling the two governments in war, and are the efficient authors of all our troubles with her, directly or indirectly, including the tragedy of the *Virginius*. I dread emigrant rebels. . . . God forbid that these dishonored men, who prate of the independence of Cuba, without manliness or courage to fight for it, preferring the safer occupation of trading in bogus bonds and calumniating the President and yourself, should succeed in making our country the instrument of their rancorous hatred of their own country." [1]

The views of Señor Calderon were, said Mr. Fish, received with "sincere gratification" by President Grant. Meeting the former's invitation for a "frank statement concerning the precise thing which the United States would advise or wish Spain to do," Mr. Fish continued: "In the first place the President desires emphatically to disabuse the mind of the government and people of Spain of the existence of any desire on the part of the government of the United States for the acquisition of Cuba. . . . Whatever grounds may be supposed to have existed in the past evincing such desire, there are at this time no considerations, moral, social, political, or financial, which are regarded . . . as making the acquisition of Cuba by the United States either desirable or convenient. The President, moreover, desires in an equally emphatic manner to express the desire of the United States to maintain a firm, solid, and enduring peace with Spain and to remove every disturbing question which embarrasses or which can threaten the relations of the two countries. . . . You will, in the name of the President, state that his earnest wish is:

"First. The mutual and reciprocal observance of treaty obligations, and a full, friendly, and liberal understanding and inter-

[1] Mr. Cushing to Mr. Fish, February 21, 1876, Sen. Rep. 885, 55 Cong., 2 Sess., 96–99.

pretation of all doubtful treaty provisions, wherever doubt or question may exist.

"Second. Peace, order, and good government in Cuba, which involves prompt and effective measures to restore peace, and the establishment of a government suited to the spirit and necessities of the age; liberal in its provisions, wherein justice can be meted out to all alike, according to defined and well-established provisions.

"Third. Gradual but effectual emancipation of the slaves.

"Fourth. Improvement of commercial facilities and the removal of the obstructions now existing in the way of trade and commerce."

The despatch further dwelt, at length, upon the impossibility of Spain's conquering a peace by force of arms; upon the example of Great Britain toward her colonies; upon the contentedness of Puerto Rico under its new conditions, and "amicably, sincerely, and earnestly" suggested "the immediate adoption of measures founded on a declaration of complete and entire amnesty, with an invitation to all Cubans to return at will, and to all those in arms to return to peaceful occupations, guaranteeing to all immunity in person and property for acts of rebellion, such declaration to be accompanied by the adoption and proclamation of the necessary measures to provide a just and liberal government, with large powers of local and self-control, under proper municipal organizations, suited to the colonial possessions of an enlightened distant power at the present day."

The paper, which continued at some length, was, while sympathetic and most friendly in tone, one of entire frankness and plain speaking, in perfect accord with the character of both President Grant and the secretary of state, and an earnest endeavor to point the way to a settlement of a gloomy and desperate situation.[1]

The President's message and the general attitude of the American government had their effect, "modifying and mollifying to a very sensible degree the opinions and feelings as well of the Cuban Spaniards as of the Peninsula Spaniards. As to the former, it has awakened them from the dream of immediate independence. Moreover, they desire to put a stop to the incendiary operations

[1] Mr. Fish to Mr. Cushing, March 1, 1876, Sen. Rep. 885, 55 Cong., 2 Sess., 102–106.

of the insurgents in Cuba, which they see tend to render the island as useless to them as to Spain and the United States." [1]

But nothing as yet came of the Spanish promises. Such energies as Spain had, now that the Carlist war was ended, went to the re-enforcement of the army in Cuba. In July 15,000 men were sent, additional to the not less than 86,000 already there.[2]

Mr. Cushing, in the same month, summed up the situation in words of soundest sense in a despatch to Mr. Fish, which needs to be quoted in full:

"MADRID, *July* 11, 1876.

"SIR: Will you permit me to make some observations of a consolatory tendency in reference to the non-success of your earnest efforts to meliorate the condition of things in Cuba?

"1. You encounter, in the first place, the indisposition of either party to the contest in Cuba to listen to the counsels of wisdom and friendship. It is the very predicament described by a late writer in the following words:

"'There are conjunctures in history in which reasoning and the attempt at persuasion fail. Where opposition is irreconcilable, where each party is striving heart and soul for an object, which the other looks upon as ruin and ignominy to himself, there can be no arbitrament but force. The ruler must show his power to rule, the subject must show his power to win independence.'

"Is not this true? Is there any example in history in which rebellions have yielded to reason—when either the sovereign or the rebellious subjects could be persuaded to cease from strife, until after the one or the other party had been vanquished?

"We in the United States have possessed parliamentary institutions for more than three centuries—not one only, as might be inferred from the rejoicings of the late Fourth of July. We think we are—we are—imbued with all the instincts of order, peace, and good government.

"Now, would we of the North have listened to any suggestion from abroad to desist from the effort to put down secession by force of arms? Would our insurgent fellow-citizens in the South have

---

[1] Mr. Cushing to Mr. Fish, March 2, 1876, Sen. Rep. 885, 55 Cong., 2 Sess., 108.

[2] Mr. Adee to Mr. Fish, July 22, 1876, *Foreign Relations*, 1877, 516.

been persuaded to lay down their arms by any promises, assurances, or even concrete acts on the part of the government of the Union?

"Again, going back to our own insurrection against Great Britain, would any proposition of hers, or even enacted measures for better administration of the colonies have influenced us to make peace? Or could Great Britain yield to us until defeated in all quarters, and completely disheartened, by the combined forces of the United States, France, Spain, and the Netherlands?

"With enlightened zeal you have labored thanklessly for the peace and welfare of Cuba and of Spain herself, and if you have not been able to effect all the good you desire, it is only because you have had to encounter impediments of moral impossibility in the nature of things.

"2. In the second place, my residence in Spain has enabled me to appreciate the true cause and character of maladministration in Cuba. It is that the governors are incapable of conducting and the governed equally incapable of receiving good government. They are all Spaniards alike, as General Prim so often said, whether you call them Peninsulars or Cubans. And (to say nothing of the colored population) it is not the best of the Spaniards, Creole or Peninsular, which constitutes the population of Cuba.

"Now, has there been maladministration in Cuba? So there has been in Spain herself. Have there been rebellions in Cuba, guerilla warfare, burnings, sacking of towns, military executions, deportations, embargo of private property, banishments, suspension of suffrage, arbitrary domination of captains-general? So all these things have been occurring in Spain. She has had naught else for more than sixty years but alternations betwixt anarchy and despotism. The few periods of comparative, but transient, tranquillity she has enjoyed during the reign of Queen Isabel were due to the mere usurpation of two great generals, Narvaez and O'Donnell, to whose administrations of the sword men look back now as to the halcyon days of Spain. Since the dethronement of Queen Isabel—that is, during the very period of the civil war in Cuba—there has not only been civil war in Spain, but, simultaneous therewith, a rapid succession of provisional and experimental governments, each destitute of inherent stability, and every one of which subsisted only by means of irresponsible dictatorships, except that of King Amadeo alone, who fell simply, as men say, because he was the only man in Spain scrupulously faithful to his oath and obstinately adhesive to the constitution of the country.

"And yet, constitutionally honest as he was, his ministers betrayed him and assassins (not yet punished) fired on him on a bright moonlit evening in one of the most frequented and brilliantly lighted streets of Madrid. Possibly if Prim had not been assassinated in the street (by men, they also not yet punished), Spain might have been saved from her extremest days of misery, the cantonal insurrection; but that is doubtful, since the misfortunes of Spain and of Cuba are conditions of the national character, as manifested alike in Spain and in all Spanish America.

"For, let me repeat, the governors and the governed, all the same in race, and with defects aggravated in the latter by tropical life and by association with slaves, are at least equally to blame for the calamities of Cuba.

"In fine, looking at the subject from the point of view of the interests of the United States, which alone is of account in the face of a civil contest where both parties are deaf to the counsels of friendship and to considerations of sympathy and humanity, it seems to me that we have much to lose and nothing to gain by compromising ourselves in the matter of Cuba, it being superabundantly evident that, whether as to Lopez and his companions laboring professedly to betray their country to a foreign nation for the promotion of slavery, or in the case of Aldama and his associates, laboring to betray it to the same nation for the gratification of personal resentment and ambition, they all have but one thought as respects us, namely, to make a cat's-paw of our government, while ready to emulate, on the earliest possible opportunity, the 'sublime ingratitude' of Schwartzenberg."[1]

The only forward step for the moment was the signing, January 12, 1877, by Señor Calderon and Mr. Cushing, of a protocol which, later, was to have much weight in the relations of Spain and the United States. It was declared to be a "declaration on both sides as to the understanding of the two governments in the premises and respecting the true application of [existing treaties]," and

[1] Sen. Rep. 885, 55 Cong., 2 Sess., 127.

thus was clearly understood as not setting aside any part of such treaties as was claimed later by Spanish authorities in Cuba.

The distinction established by the protocol was as follows:

1. "No citizen of the United States residing in Spain, her adjacent islands, or her ultramarine possessions charged with acts of sedition, treason, or conspiracy against the institutions, the public security, the integrity of the territory, or against the supreme government, or any crime whatsoever, shall be subject to trial by any exceptional tribunal, but exclusively by the ordinary jurisdiction, except in the case of being captured with arms in hand.

2. "Those who, not coming within this last case, may be arrested or imprisoned, shall be deemed to have been so arrested or imprisoned by order of the civil authority for the effects of the law of April 17, 1821, even though the arrest or imprisonment shall have been effected by armed force.

3. "Those who may be taken with arms in hand and who, therefore, are comprehended in the exception of the first article, shall be tried by ordinary council of war in conformity with the second article of the hereinbefore-mentioned law; but even in this case the accused shall enjoy for their defence the guarantees embodied in the aforesaid law of April 17, 1821."

Article 4 recites these guarantees which thus gave the right to all such as mentioned in the second and third paragraphs to name attorneys or advocates, who should have access to them at suitable times (Art. 20 of the law of 1821); a right to a copy of the accusation and a list of witnesses for the prosecution who should be examined in the presence of the accused, his attorney, and advocate (Art. 23); the right to compel such witnesses as they may desire to appear and testify in person or by deposition (Art. 22); the right to present such evidence as they may deem proper (Art. 26); to be present in open court and make their defence orally or in writing, by themselves or by an advocate (Art. 24). The sentence to be referred to the territorial court or to the captain-general, according as the trial has taken place before an ordinary judge or a court-martial.[1]

---

[1] In full, *Foreign Relations*, 1877, 496. For the law of 1821, see Cong. Record, 54 Cong., 2 Sess., 2227.

For a discussion of this very important document, see Olivart, *Revue Générale de Droit Internationale Public*, vol. VII, 1900, article "Le Différend

General Jovellar had returned to Cuba as governor-general, early in 1876. In October of the same year the appointment of General Martinez Campos as commander-in-chief of the army of operations was made public; an essential change from the system which had always theretofore obtained of combining this command with the duties of the governor-general.

General Campos went to Cuba with a prestige and popularity, both in Spain and in the island, which promised well, and with a complete and energetic support from the government such as no previous commander had had. A loan of $15,000,000 was contracted on Cuban account, and 24,800 troops were despatched to Cuba during this month. "Another such effort," said the American chargé d'affaires, "as the present one cannot reasonably be expected or even hoped for from Spain in her actual circumstances. And the result, it is felt, must be commensurate with the effort. It will not do for Spain merely to hold her own to the west of the *trocha* and on the coasts during this campaign; she must *win* or face the consequences."[1]

The result was that Spain won. General Martinez Campos

Hispano-Americain au Sujet de la Question Cubaine." The Spanish negotiators were the Duke of Tetuan and Señor Cánovas. The protocol, as Señor de Olivart well says, "was the effect and not the cause of the situation in Cuba; it was the consequence," referring to the "shameful and criminal massacre" of the *Virginius* prisoners, "of the faults (*turpitudes*)" of the Spanish governors.

The words in the protocol "residing in Spain, her adjacent islands, or her ultramarine possessions," were later, as will be seen, to give much trouble; a difficulty, from the American point of view, only avoided by the absence of this qualification in Article 7 of the treaty of 1795, which as a treaty held as against the protocol. It should be stated that this protocol was never officially promulgated either in Spain or Cuba, a fact which itself produced much misunderstanding. This failure was the more pronounced as the final paragraph was a declaration from Señor Calderon y Collantes that "in order to afford to the government of the United States the completest security of the sincerity and good faith of his majesty's government in the premises, command will be given by royal order for the strict observance of the terms of the present protocol in all the dominions of Spain, and specifically in the island of Cuba. The minister of ultramar assured a little later the American chargé d'affaires of its immediate promulgation (see Mr. Adee to Mr. Evarts, June 28, 1877, *Foreign Relations*, 1877, 512), but it seems not to have been known in Cuba or Spain until it appeared in the American papers, after the breaking out of the insurrection of 1895.

[1] Mr. Adee to Mr. Fish, October 10, 1876, *Foreign Relations*, 1876, 473.

and General Jovellar were both broad-minded and patriotic men. Both, and particularly the former, had much sympathy with the Cubans in their causes of discontent. In October, 1877, several of the prominent Cuban leaders surrendered. These offering to lay before those still in arms the question of general pacification, were tried by the order of Gomez as traitors and were executed. The capture, however, in the same month, of the Cuban president, Don Tomas Estrada Palma, and of several who constituted the main part of the so-called government, the mild and considerate treatment of these and the evident success of General Campos in his campaign, caused the appointment of a committee of the revolutionists to make proposals for peace. On February 10 an agreement was reached at Zanjon, in the Camaguey, signed by Campos largely on his own responsibility and by Vicente Garcia and Maximo Gomez on the part of the Cubans, by which were accorded to Cuba the same political privileges as Puerto Rico: oblivion of the past; a general pardon to all who had taken part in the revolutionary movement, including those under trial, those suffering sentences in or out of the island, or who had been deserters from the Spanish army. Any one desiring to leave Cuba could do so. Slaves and Asiatic colonists, men and women, with the insurrectionary force, were declared free who should present themselves before March 31, 1878; compensation for such slaves was granted owners who had remained loyal, in conformity with the law of gradual emancipation already applied to Puerto Rico.[1]

The ten years' contest was at an end. The diplomacy of the United States resumed its usual course of conflict over questions of commerce and occasional complaints on the part of Spain, mostly groundless, of attempted filibustering. The fiscal policies of both were essentially equally vicious, so that whatever the complaint of one, it could readily be offset by an almost equally just complaint of the other. Rarely has there been such opportunity for the use of *tu quoque*.

It seems clear that in asking for the political conditions of Puerto Rico the revolutionary leaders were asking for what they did not understand. Nor did Campos know any better. In the course of

[1] Senate Doc. 79, 45 Cong., 2 Sess., 16.

the negotiations that preceded the agreement, he telegraphed General Jovellar: ". . . This is the question: Neither they nor I know the difference between the constitution that rules at present in Puerto Rico and the constitution of the Peninsula. What we wish is, that whenever the Spanish constitution be changed for a more liberal or more conservative one, Cuba shall be treated in the same way as Spain. It is important, however, to know the differences, and I hope your excellency may inform me of them, if you know them, or have the means of finding out."

General Jovellar answered the same day, February 9: "I am very sorry not to be able to give you the details of the existing differences between the system of government of Puerto Rico and that of the peninsular provinces, as I have not paid special attention to the subject; but as the essential things for the prosperity of a people are the development of provincial and municipal life, the representation in legislative bodies, and a fair administration of justice, and whereas concerning all these points the laws are the same, we may say that the provinces in question are fundamentally assimilated." The agreement was thus made in the dark.

No one can question the earnestness and wisdom of the views of Martinez Campos respecting Cuba. He was, so far as the island was concerned, the one effective Spanish statesman of his period. No words could be finer in spirit than those of his report of the events leading to the peace. And they were meant. They breathed a lofty patriotism, a kindness of character, an understanding of conditions such as were shown by few other Spaniards of his time.

"Since the year 1869," he said, "when I landed on the island with the first re-enforcements, I was preoccupied with the idea that the insurrection here, though acknowledging as its cause the hatred of Spain, yet that hatred was due to the causes that have separated the colonies from the mother country, augmented, in the present case, by the promises made to the Antilles at different times (1812–1837 and 1845), promises which have not only not been fulfilled, but, as I understand, have not been permitted to be so by the Cortes, when at different times their execution has been begun. . . . When one day after another passed without hopes being satisfied, but, on the contrary, the greater freedom permitted now and then by a governor were more than cancelled by his successor; when they were convinced that the colony went on in the same way; when bad officials and a worse administration of justice more and more aggravated difficulties; when the provincial governorships, continually growing worse, fell at last into the hands of men without training or education, petty tyrants who could practise their thefts and sometimes their oppressions because of the distance at which they resided from the supreme authority, public opinion, until then restrained, began vehemently to desire those liberties which, if they bring much good, contain also some evil, and especially when applied to countries that have so peculiar a life of their own, and are without preparation for them. A people sometimes vehemently desires what is not best for it—the unknown—and when everything is denied aspire to everything. So it happened here. . . .

"For my own part, had the responsibility been mine, free of the Cortes, and empowered to decide for the government of his majesty, on condition of at once rendering an account, I would have ventured everything. On the 7th of November, 1876, there would have appeared in the *Havana Gazette* the disembargo of estates, a general pardon, the assimilation of Cuba with Spain, orders to treat prisoners well; and, to show that this was not weakness but strength, there was the argument of my *one hundred thousand bayonets*. Public opinion I should have little regarded. Perhaps the war might have ended some time ago. It was policy; but war is made with policy. It was the flag with the motto of liberty. Or take away the flag and give, once for all, the liberty which must at last be given. When we are strong we are able and ought to be generous. Perhaps some will ask how I offered the terms which I reported on the 30th of January, and will add that better might have been obtained. At present, I suppose so, but I understand by advantageous terms for the government what contributes to satisfy the desires and aspirations of the people; I proposed the first condition, because I believe they must fulfil it. I wish that the municipal law, the law of provincial assemblies, and representation in the Cortes should be established. . . . The law of labor is to be settled, the question of labor supply, the necessary changes of property are to be studied, the fearful and unsustainable problem of slavery is to be studied before foreign nations impose a solution of it upon us, the penal code is to be studied and the province of the courts to be defined, the form of contributions and assessment of taxes determined and some attention paid to schools and public works. All these problems whose solution concerns the people must be solved after hearing their representatives, not by the report of juntas chosen through favoritism or for political reasons. They cannot be left to the will of the captain-general, the head of a department, or the colonial minister, who generally, however competent, do not know the country.

"I do not wish to make a momentary peace; I desire that this peace be the beginning of a bond of common interests between Spain and her Cuban provinces, and that this bond be drawn continually closer by the identity of aspirations and the good faith of both. Let not the Cubans be considered as pariahs or minors, but put on an equality with other Spaniards, in everything not inconsistent with their present condition."[1]

In the non-fulfilment of such aspirations lies, as truly said by Martinez Campos, the history of Cuban discontent.

But Campos was in advance of his country and of the conservative party, of which he was a member. When he returned to Spain he laid before the Cánovas cabinet, May 19, 1878, his plan of legislation in a paper as frankly outspoken as that previously quoted. He said: "The promises never fulfilled, the abuses of all sorts, the neglect of public improvements, the exclusion of the natives from all branches of the administration, and many other faults were the causes of the insurrection. The belief, shared in by all our governments, that the people could be terrified into subjection and that it was a point of dignity not to make concessions until the last shot had been fired—these factors, I believe, have kept up the insurrection. By the continuation of such a system we never would have come to an end, even though we had packed the island with soldiers. It is necessary, if all wish to avoid our ruin, to adopt frankly liberal measures. I believe that Cuba cannot constitute an independent state; she is more than prepared to con-

[1] For this interesting report, made February 18, 1878, see *Foreign Relations*, 1879, 944–951.

stitute a Spanish province. And let there be a stop to the coming of office-holders—all Spaniards. Let the natives have their share and give some stability to the tenure of office."[1]

But the governing powers of Spain were no more ready to listen to these words of a wise soldier than they were ready, twenty years later, to listen to the wise seaman whom she forced to carry her only fleet to destruction.

Cánovas, who represented all the conservatism of Spain, was unwilling to accept such views. In the spring of 1879 he made way for Campos as prime-minister; but the latter was illy supported by his colleagues, nor was there any large public sentiment in Spain which came to his support. He thus resigned in December of the same year. Cánovas again came to power and a bill was pushed through in the absence of the extremists of both sides, who withdrew from the chamber in company with the representatives of Cuba.[2] A new legislative regimen was declared and nominally a new departure was made in colonial administration by which, in the letter of the law, Cuba was given the status of a province of the Peninsula.

But the right of representation in the Cortes was made a mockery by means thoroughly effective both in restricting the return of repsentative Cubans and in rousing their animosity. The franchise was limited to those paying a tax of twenty-five dollars, with the exception that all government employees and all persons connected with mercantile companies were entitled to registration in any case. As practically all belonging to the first of these classes and a very large proportion of the second were Spaniards, and as none but the wealthier Cubans could pay such a tax, the result was to throw the elections into the hands of the peninsular party, and thus nearly all the representatives were Spaniards, who, in some cases, had never been in Cuba. Of the twenty-four deputies and fifteen senators elected in 1884 but eight were Cubans. A somewhat similar disproportion held throughout. In 1896, of the twenty-eight aldermen of Havana but one was a Cuban. That the Cuban representatives in the Cortes in 1897 " were returned by General Weyler at the dictation of Señor Cánovas can be proven, if

[1] Merchan, *The Causes and Justification of the War*, 407.
[2] Hume, *Modern Spain*, 535.

necessary, by the recorded testimony of Señor Sagasta, who made at the time a sharp protest based upon that fact." [1]

A liberal party had been founded in Cuba on the conclusion of the peace whose principles were, in general, those which had been advanced by the Cuban representatives in the abortive commission of 1867, the failure of which had brought about the ten years' war. A second party, termed the union constitutional, was also formed, with a programme differing but little from that of the liberal, but ending finally as a party of strong reactionaries, dominated wholly by the peninsular element, which, speaking in a general sense, wanted no reform. The liberal party was a Cuban organization and it so remained.

The union constitutionalists made, in the first instance, a declaration of principles which all but extremists could accept. "It called for the liberty of the press, the right of petition, of peaceful public meeting, of assimilation in political rights to the other provinces of Spain, of special laws with relation to the particular interests of Cuba, for improved morality in public administration, and for new laws which would be efficacious in securing judicial responsibility. On the economic question it pronounced for customs reforms, special protection for the agricultural production of the island and for the tobacco industry, suppression of export duties, a rational reduction of the imports, especially on the necessaries of life, and a liberal commercial treaty with the United States on the basis of reciprocity. It favored the abolition of slavery on the terms of Moret, but with modifications suitable to the condition of the country. It also favored immigration under the direction of the government as the basis of free contract. . . .

"The artificial nature of the two organizations, formed mechanically as part of a new political regimen, was soon lost. Their growth was along natural lines. The union constitutionals modified or ignored their original economic precepts. Then they became jealous of the integrity of Spanish institutions in the Antilles. The control passed away from the original supporters. The intransigentes [2] at first had looked with contempt on the group of

[1] Mr. Hannis Taylor, minister to Spain 1893–1897, "A Review of the Cuban Question," *North American Review*, November, 1897.
[2] The ultra-Spanish party.

union constitutionals. They began by criticising its assumptions and combating its principles. They ended by dominating the organization."[1] In fact it was a simple drift back to the primal elements of Cuban and Spanish, the former of which desired and preached autonomy, the latter opposing it nominally as a death-blow to the national unity, but in reality as an end of bureaucratic privilege.

"How far Spanish statesmen comprehended the Cuban movement for autonomy must remain undetermined. Emilio Castelar wanted no transatlantic Poland. Yet his republican principles did not carry him to the length of advocating complete home-rule for Cuba. Moret, who was to formulate the system when it came to be proposed (1897), at that time was giving it little support. Praxédes Sagasta, in the regular changes of power which made him the ruler of Spain alternately with Cánovas del Castillo, never suggested home-rule for Cuba. The pendulum swinging between these two prime-ministers sometimes vibrated with hope of broader and truer parliamentary government for Spain itself, sometimes remained in equilibrium, but never swung loose from the orbit of colonial subjection. Sagasta was up and Cánovas was down; the liberal party had its vague and hesitating schemes for the Antilles. Cánovas was up and Sagasta was down; the conservative party had liberal legislation in view and nothing came of it. If in the farcical election of deputies from Cuba to the Cortes the government in power occasionally permitted an autonomist to be chosen, it was merely good-natured tolerance. If the autonomists at times sent delegations to Madrid and were represented by resident committees, this was treated as a colonial chimera not worthy of serious attention. Cánovas had his policy of assimilation by which Spaniards and Cubans were to approach one another in their political rights. But he never yielded his ground that autonomy meant separation of Cuba from the Peninsula. And what he called the national actualities, the need of supporting the bureaucratic classes, was always a bar to the real insular government of Cuba by its own people."[2]

Had Cuba been met at this time in a liberal spirit in which such

[1] Pepper, *Tomorrow in Cuba*, 7, 8, 11.
[2] *Ibid.*, 16, 17.

a term is understood in England or the United States, there can be little question that the island would have become again faithful to the mother country. The blood, the traditions, the literature, the social affiliations were Spanish; it only required a reasonable treatment to cause such bonds to resume their natural influence, but it cannot be repeated too often that of this Spain, as Spain, was incapable. However much it was desired by certain broad-minded and advanced Spaniards, the inertia of the conservative mass was too great to be moved. A reformist party was organized in Cuba in 1893 to which many Spanish liberal-minded residents of the island attached themselves, but the harm already worked in the interval since the peace of El Zanjon was too great for such to influence the trend of events.

Again quoting Mr. Pepper: "The analysis of the legislation and of the decrees of 1878 and subsequent years shows that in essence there was little dilution of what had always been the cardinal principle of Spanish colonial government. This was military rule. The paths were sometimes crooked, the passages wound into labyrinths of cedulas, decrees, orders, edicts, circulars, and bandos. They brought up at the same barrier. The beginning and the end was the governor-general exercising his military functions as captain-general. After 1878 Cuba had good, bad, and indifferent captains-general. Their character was reflected in the administration of the island."[1] The overtaxation, the rapacity, national and individual, remained the same.

At the very bottom of the difficulty was the earliest concept of the relation of the American possessions to the Spanish crown. In theory, the Spanish provinces of America had been integral parts of Spain and stood to the crown as did the provinces of the Peninsula. It was this theory which, in large degree, stood in the way of a real autonomy such as that of the Dominion of Canada. This theory, however, did not prevent a financial treatment which laid upon Cuba the whole burden of the war. The budget for the year 1878–79 rose to $46,594,000. It gradually decreased, being in 1885–86, $34,169,000, and thereafter was about $26,000,000. In 1895 the debt of the island was $295,707,264, the interest on which was $9.79 for each inhabitant. This included a debt of Spain

[1] Pepper, *Tomorrow in Cuba*, 5.

to the United States; the expenses of the occupation, from 1861 to 1865, of Santo Domingo; the cost of the expedition in 1861 to Mexico; the cost of the war with Peru. The cost of the legation and consulates in the United States was borne by Cuba, even to the secret-service money of the legation; $2,192,795 were paid in pensions, a subsidy of $471,836 was paid to the Transatlantic Company; $96,800 a year went to support the ministry of the colonies at Madrid.

Cuba in 1894 was paying $6,197,135 (or 23.18 per cent. of the budget for the year of $26,733,219) for the support of the army employed solely in Cuba, and $1,094,071 for the navy; $12,933,970 went chiefly for interest on the debt; $826,922 for public improvements, though but eighty-eight miles of highway had been built in twenty-eight years; $182,000 were assigned to public instruction.

Said Estrada Palma, vouching for the statement from which the foregoing is taken and the general truth of which is incontestable: "The hopes . . . held out [by the Spanish government] have never been realized. The representation which was to be given the Cubans has proved to be absolutely without character; taxes have been levied anew on everything conceivable; the offices in the island have increased, but the officers are all Spaniards; the native Cubans have been left with no public duties whatsoever to perform except payment of taxes to the government and blackmail to the officials; without privilege even to move from place to place in the island except on the permission of governmental authorities.

" Spain has framed laws so that the natives have substantially been deprived of the right of suffrage. The taxes levied have been almost entirely devoted to support the army and navy in Cuba, to pay interest on the debt that Spain has saddled on the island, and to pay the salaries of the vast number of Spanish office-holders, devoting only $746,000 for internal improvements out of the $26,-000,000 collected by tax. No public schools are within reach of the masses for their education. All the principal industries of the island are hampered by excessive imposts. Her commerce with every country but Spain has been crippled in every possible manner, as can readily be seen by the frequent protests of ship-owners and merchants.

" The Cubans have no security of person or property. The

judiciary are instruments of the military authorities. Trial by military tribunals can be ordered at any time at the will of the captain-general. There is, besides, no freedom of speech, press, or religion."[1]

The whole is a monstrous showing; whatever Cuban deserts, Cuban woes were very real. With unfortunate economic conditions added, it is not surprising that at the end of seventeen years revolt was again active, the outbreak being set for February 24, 1895.

Again it must be said that one finds the difficulties of the situation—apparently, to the Anglo-Saxon mind, so easy of solution—in the Spanish character itself: in its inability to understand the meaning or at least the application of free and representative government.

Using the words of a most qualified observer regarding Spain, what purported to be national elections were always controlled by the political party holding the executive power, which so manipulated the electoral machinery as to predetermine the result. The people looked listlessly on while the government officials, aided by the *caciques*,[2] employed all the necessary methods to return as many of the government nominees as its managers deemed necessary; and if any officious person attempted to object he was simply sent to jail. As both parties employed the same means there was no recrimination. The natural result was that the national assemblies thus chosen possessed no real political authority; they were simply dead bodies into which the living spirit of popular approval never entered, and as such, of course, they could not confer upon ministries the right to rule. The fact that a Spanish ministry was supported by overwhelming majorities in both branches of the Cortes was considered no reason why it should continue in power if a coterie of military officers or a combination of newspapers made an adverse demonstration at Madrid. The administration of affairs was still carried on under the old bureaucratic system by certain notables named by the crown, who called upon the phantom body known as the Cortes to clothe their acts in forms of legality. In the light of these incontestable facts, it is easy to understand that Spain could not give to her colonies what

[1] For these documents, see Sen. Rep. 885, 55 Cong., 2 Sess., 1–42.
[2] The local party leaders.

she did not herself enjoy—popular government as it is understood throughout the world.¹

Combined with this general situation was the powerful personality of the minister who held Spain in his hand, Señor Cánovas, "at heart a Spaniard of the past, an absolutist, a Cardinal Ximenes de Cisneros, masquerading in the garb of the nineteenth century, and yet . . . he clearly understood that even in Spain the ancient principles of absolutism must be concealed beneath the constitutional forms that prevail to-day. . . . I cannot doubt that it was his settled purpose to govern the remaining colonies of Spain under the old paternal system, conceding nothing in the way of real autonomy except a few empty forms, so designed as to conceal his real purpose." ²

The Maura law submitted in 1893 had failed, says the same authority, through the genuineness of the attempt. That framed by Señor Abarzuza passed both houses of the Cortes unanimously in February, 1895. Ten days later began the Cuban revolt. "The plain and simple explanation of that event is to be found that the passage of the sham Abarzuza law finally convinced the Cuban leaders that no real amelioration of their condition was to be expected from the mother country. . . . The only thing like a local legislature that it proposed to create was a 'council of administration,' half of whose members were to be appointed by the crown, the other half elective." The governor-general could suspend the council as a whole or could suspend individual members so long as a quorum remained. In any case the council was simply advisory. "Whatever it might do, it was expressly declared to be subject 'to the supervision and to the powers inherent in the sovereignty of the nation, which are reserved by law to the supreme government.' " ³

But added to the disappointment in the passage of so futile an effort at autonomy was the great influence of the economic situation. Four-fifths of Cuba's wealth was in sugar, for which the United States was practically her one purchaser. When the reciprocity of a few years ended, in 1894, the island, ground between the mill-

¹ Mr. Hannis Taylor, minister to Spain, 1893–97, "A Review of the Cuban Question," *North American Review*, November, 1897.
² *Ibid.* ³ *Ibid.*

stones of both American and Spanish protection, was naturally deeply disturbed by the revulsion from wealth to comparative poverty. It became almost impossible for the cane sugar to compete with the beet; great numbers of Cuban laborers were deprived of work. When revolt came, excited in great degree by enforced idleness, it was natural that they should join the insurgent ranks. The United States are thus not guiltless of the horrors of the revolt to come in 1895. The greed of American and Spanish protectionists was, in fact, at the bottom of Cuban revolt and largely responsible for the loss of the hundreds of millions of money and the many thousands of lives which the war involved.

The declaration was the result of a deliberate preparation of which the soul was José Marti. More than two hundred clubs were formed in the United States, Mexico, and in Central and South America, every member of which contributed a tenth or more of his earnings. Naturally the greater amount came from the Cubans in the United States, but money came from every country where there were Cuban residents or Cuban sympathizers. At the beginning of 1895 the agitators were supposed to have ready a million dollars.[1]

The serious character of the new movement was at once recognized in Spain, and Martinez Campos, as the one best able to meet the situation, left Madrid April 3, 1895, and on April 16 relieved General Calleja as governor-general. Campos came with unlimited powers and credit, and with the promise of every support from the home government, an earnest of which was in the despatch, before his departure, of seven thousand troops as a first reenforcement to the thirteen thousand (a third of whom were ineffectives) in the island when the revolt began. The provinces of Santiago, Santa Clara, and Matanzas had already been declared, March 4, in a state of siege by his predecessor.

The revolt he now faced, however, was very different to that of twenty years before, in extent, in resources, and, above all, in determination. Spain herself, however, was changed from the anarchic kingdom of the earlier period. While the old abuses of *empleomania* and administrative corruption were still as active as

---

[1] Quesada, *Free Cuba*, 473. Benton, *International Law and Diplomacy of the Spanish American War*, 25. *North American Review*, vol. 166, 560.

ever, there was permanency at the head and a cessation of civil war. Spain was thus free to bend all her energies to the suppression of the new rising, and from the moment of first action showed an amazing energy in the despatch of troops and in the general support of the war, which, could the energy and expense have been diverted to happier ends, would have transformed the face of the land of Spain, and have brought wealth and happiness, instead of the reverse, to her people.

Maximo Gomez, who had returned to Cuba from his native island of Santo Domingo, was made the Cuban commander-in-chief, and while the struggle was markedly different in its greater humanity to prisoners from that of the ten years' war, it was to be one of ruthless devastation and destruction of property, as the following proclamation so clearly shows:

"GENERAL HEAD-QUARTERS OF THE ARMY OF LIBERATION,
"NAJASA, CAMAGUEY, *July* 1, 1895.

"TO THE PLANTERS AND OWNERS OF CATTLE RANCHES:

"In accord with the great interests of the revolution for the independence of the country and for which we are in arms:

"Whereas, all exploitations of any product whatsoever are aids and resources to the government that we are fighting, it is resolved by the general-in-chief to issue this general order throughout the island, that the introduction of articles of commerce, as well as beef and cattle, into the towns occupied by the enemy is absolutely prohibited. The sugar plantations will stop their labors, and whoever shall attempt to grind the crop, notwithstanding this order, will have their cane burned and their buildings demolished. The person who, disobeying this order, will try to profit from the present situation of affairs, will show by his conduct little respect for the rights of the revolution of redemption, and therefore shall be considered as an enemy, treated as a traitor, and tried as such in case of his capture.

"MAXIMO GOMEZ, *the General-in-Chief*."[1]

[1] Nevertheless, throughout the country preparations were made for the grinding of the crop. A peremptory order, of which the following is a copy, was then issued on November 6:

HEAD-QUARTERS OF THE ARMY OF LIBERATION,
TERRITORY OF SANCTI SPIRITUS, *November* 6, 1895.

Animated by the spirit of unchangeable resolution in defence of the rights of the revolution of redemption of this country of colonists, humiliated and despised by Spain, and in harmony with what has been decreed concerning the subject in the circular dated the 1st of July, I have ordered the following:

ARTICLE I. That all plantations shall be totally destroyed, their cane and out-buildings burned, and railroad connections destroyed.

ART. II. All laborers who shall aid the sugar factories—these sources of supplies that we must deprive the enemy of—shall be considered as traitors to their country.

ART. III. All who are caught in the act, or whose violation of Article II shall be proven, shall be shot. Let all chiefs of operations of the army of liberty comply with this order, determined to unfurl triumphantly, even over ruin and ashes, the flag of the republic of Cuba.

In regard to the manner of waging the war, follow the private instructions that I have already given.

For the sake of the honor of our arms and your well-known courage and patriotism, it is expected that you will strictly comply with the above orders.

M. GOMEZ, *General-in-Chief.*

To the chiefs of operations: Circulate this.

On the 11th of November the following proclamation was issued:

HEAD-QUARTERS OF THE ARMY OF LIBERATION,
SANCTI SPIRITUS, *November* 11, 1895.

TO HONEST MEN, VICTIMS OF THE TORCH:

The painful measure made necessary by the revolution of redemption drenched in innocent blood from Hatuey to our own times by cruel and merciless Spain will plunge you in misery. As general-in-chief of the army of liberation it is my duty to lead it to victory, without permitting myself to be restrained or terrified, by any means necessary to place Cuba in the shortest time in possession of her dearest ideal. I therefore place the responsibility for so great a ruin on those who look on impassively and force us to those extreme measures which they then condemn like dolts and hypocrites that they are. After so many years of supplication, humiliations, contumely, banishment, and death, when this people, of its own will, has arisen in arms, there remains no other solution but to triumph, it matters not what means are employed to accomplish it.

This people cannot hesitate between the wealth of Spain and the liberty of Cuba. Its greatest crime would be to stain the land with blood without effecting its purposes because of puerile scruples and fears which do not concur with the character of the men who are in the field, challenging the fury of an army which is one of the bravest in the world, but which in this war is without enthusiasm or faith, ill fed and unpaid. The war did not begin February 24; it is about to begin now.

The war had to be organized; it was necessary to calm and lead into the proper channels the revolutionary spirit always exaggerated in the beginning by wild enthusiasm. The struggle ought to begin in obedience to a plan and method more or less studied, as the result of the peculiarities of this war. This has already been done. Let Spain now send her soldiers to rivet the chains of her slaves; the children of this land are in the field, armed with the weapons of liberty. The struggle will be terrible, but success will crown the revolution and efforts of the oppressed.

MAXIMO GOMEZ, *General-in-Chief.*

Señor Estrada Palma adds, in his letter of December 7, 1895, to Mr. Olney, in which these appear: "The reasons underlying this measure are the same which caused this country to destroy the cotton crop and the baled cotton in the South during the war of secession." . . . The action of the insurgents is perfectly justified because it is simply a blockade, so to speak, on land— a prevention of the gathering, and hence the export of the [sugar crop] with, naturally, a punishment for the violation thereof. (Sen. Rep. 885, 55 Cong., 2 Sess., 14, 15.)

CHAPTER XX

THE FILIBUSTERING CASES.—THE "ALLIANÇA" INCIDENT.—
THE ANNUAL MESSAGE OF 1895

THE intimate commercial relations of Cuba with the United States, in which the former found four-fifths of its market, and the educational facilities which attracted many Cuban youths, naturally caused the presence there at all times of great numbers of Cubans. Many of these had taken up permanent residence and were favorite and influential persons in American society. This, with the fact that it was the only large producer, in the Americas, of arms and warlike stores, together with the proximity of the intricate system of Florida keys and waterways, made the United States the natural base of Cuban supply and Cuban intrigue. There was thus at once thrown upon the American government the renewal of its duty of the preservation of its neutral obligations in circumstances of much greater difficulty than in the previous insurrection, through the acquired experience of the Cubans, their much greater command of money, and an antecedent preparation far beyond that of the previous revolt. So complete had been this preparation that four expeditions were attempted at the very outbreak of insurgency, all of which, however, were thwarted by the action of the American government. The whole force of cruising revenue vessels in the Atlantic was directed to this work, and this was later supported by a large number of ships of the navy, the unfortunate *Maine* being of this number.

From New York to the Mexican border was a coast to be guarded of 5,470 miles, more than double that of Cuba. Much of this was of great intricacy, the Florida keys in especial affording long and sparsely settled stretches of this character.

On June 12, 1895, President Cleveland issued a proclamation which was, in effect, a recognition of a state of insurgency temporarily beyond the control of Spain.[1] It gave warning that all vio-

[1] Wilson, *Lecture on Insurgency*, Naval War College, 1900, 6. Benton, *Int. Law and Diplom. of Sp. Am. War*, 35.

lations of the neutrality laws of the United States would be rigorously prosecuted.[1]

The cases which came before the courts turned chiefly upon the expression "within the territory of the United States" and the construction of what constituted "any military expedition." The latitude given to these in some of the earlier charges of the courts gradually narrowed until the master and two mates of the Danish steamer *Horsa* were indicted and convicted in the district court of the eastern district of Pennsylvania. This case, with the rulings of the judge of the district court and the final decision of the Supreme Court, on an appeal by the defendants, fully illustrates the attitude and action of the American government.

The following was shown in evidence before the court: The *Horsa*, sailing under the Danish flag, the officers Danish subjects,

[1] The law is Section 5286 of the Revised Statutes. "Every person who, within the territory or jurisdiction of the United States, begins or sets on foot, or provides or prepares the means for, any military expedition or enterprise to be carried on from thence against the territory or dominions of any foreign prince or state, or of any colony, district, or people, with whom the United States are at peace, shall be deemed guilty of a misdemeanor and shall be fined not exceeding three thousand dollars and imprisoned not more than three years." "Title LXVII of the Revised Statutes, headed 'Neutrality,' embraces eleven sections, from 5281 to 5291 inclusive. Section 5281 prohibits the acceptance of commissions from a foreign power by citizens of the United States within our territory to serve against any sovereign with whom we are at peace. Section 5282 prohibits any person from enlisting in this country as a soldier in the service of any foreign power, and from hiring or retaining any other person to enlist or go abroad for the purpose of enlistment. Section 5283 deals with fitting out and arming vessels in this country in favor of one foreign power as against another foreign power with which we are at peace. Section 5284 prohibits citizens from the fitting out or arming, without the United States, of vessels to cruise against citizens of the United States; and Section 5285, the augmenting the force of a foreign vessel of war serving against a friendly sovereign. Sections 5287 to 5290 provide for the enforcement of the preceding sections, and Section 5291, that the provisions set forth shall not be construed to prevent the enlistment of certain foreign citizens of the United States." (Chief-Justice Fuller in opinion delivered in Wiborg *et als.* Plaintiff in Error *vs.* the United States, October term, 1895.) The first neutrality laws date from June 5, 1794, Section 5286 (R. S.) being section five of the first act. They were given their final forms April 20, 1818, when section five of the first act was carried forward as section six of the later act. There was a law, limited to two years, passed in 1838, of a more stringent character which applied only to countries, conterminous with the United States. For this, the cause of passage and suggestion of Spain for renewal and extension, see *Infra*, 515.

was engaged in the fruit business for John D. Hart & Co., and cleared at Philadelphia, November 9, 1895, for Port Antonio, Jamaica. Just before sailing her captain received a written message, the purport of which, he later testified, was: "After I passed the [Delaware] breakwater, to proceed north near Barnegat and await further orders." He thus on arrival anchored off Barnegat Light, between three and four miles off shore, a matter of no difficulty, in good weather in the shallow sea of the New Jersey coast. He was now outside of United States jurisdiction. On the same evening a steam-lighter, *J. S. T. Stranahan*, left Brooklyn carrying some cases of goods and two boats taken aboard during the evening. The lighter received below Staten Island during the night between thirty and forty men, apparently Cubans or Spaniards. She ran down to Barnegat, saw the *Horsa*, which had hoisted a white flag, and ran up a similar one. The passengers, cases of goods, and life-boats were put aboard the *Horsa*. The cases were shown to have contained rifles, swords, machetes, a Maxim gun, cartridge belts, medicines, and bandages. Arms were divided among the men, who were drilled on the passage south toward Jamaica, the course to which passes near the eastern end of Cuba. On nearing this point the passengers left the ship in the two boats brought from Brooklyn, with all the ammunition and arms they could carry, and the *Horsa* proceeded to Port Antonio, throwing overboard some boxes of ammunition which had been left by her passengers. On her return to the United States the captain and the two mates were indicted, and tried as mentioned before the Federal court.

The government had failed to convict in preceding cases which differed in no important principle from that of the *Horsa*. The judge in the latter case charged the jury, after explaining the indictment, as follows: "The evidence heard would not justify a conviction of anything more than providing the means for or aiding such military expedition by furnishing transportation for the men, their arms, baggage, etc. . . . To convict them you must be fully satisfied by the evidence that a military expedition was organized in this country, to be carried out as and with the object charged in the indictment, and that the defendants, with the knowledge of this, provided means for its assistance and assisted it as before stated.

"Thus you observe the case presents two questions: First, was such military expedition organized here in the United States? Secondly, did the defendants render the assistance stated here with knowledge of the facts?

"In passing on the first question it is necessary to understand what constitutes a military expedition within the meaning of the statute. For the purposes of this case it is sufficient to say that any combination of men organized here to go to Cuba to make war upon its government, provided with arms and ammunition, we being at peace with Cuba, constitutes a military expedition. It is not necessary that the men shall be drilled, put in uniforms, or prepared for efficient service, nor that they shall have been organized as, or according to, the tactics or rules which relate to what is known as infantry, artillery, or cavalry. It is sufficient that they shall have combined and organized here to go there and make war on the foreign government, and have provided themselves with the means of doing so. I say 'provided themselves with the means of doing so' because the evidence here shows that the men were so provided. Whether such provision, as by arming, etc., is necessary, need not be decided in this case. I will say, however, to counsel, that were that question required to be decided I should hold that it is not necessary.

"Nor is it important that they intended to make war as an independent body or in connection with others. Where men go without combination and organization to enlist as individuals in a foreign army they do not constitute such military expedition, and the fact that the vessel carrying them might carry arms as merchandise would not be important."

The Supreme Court, on the appeal, held that these views of the district judge were correct as applied to the evidence.

The jury was also instructed by the district judge that the master and mates were not guilty if they were ignorant of the fact that they were to transport the men in question until the arrival of the ship off Barnegat, outside the three-mile limit. In such event, the ship being a foreign vessel and beyond our jurisdiction at such a point, they could not be held to be guilty. "If, however, they entered into an arrangement here to furnish and provide the means of transportation, and provided it, they are guilty, if this was a military expedition, although the men were not taken aboard and the transportation did not commence until the ship anchored off Barnegat," a view also held by the Supreme Court, which also concluded that "the *Horsa's* preparation for sailing and the taking aboard of the two boats at Philadelphia constituted a preparation of means for the expedition or enterprise." [1]

The lower courts being bound by the definitions of the Supreme Court, the rigor of its findings made Cuban attempts thereafter much more difficult; and more particularly as President Cleveland used the decision as the basis of a second proclamation, July 27, 1896, declaring that the "neutrality laws of the United States have been the subject of authoritative exposition by the tribunal of last resort, and it has thus been declared that any combination of persons organized in the United States for the purpose of proceeding to and making war upon a foreign country with which the United States are at peace, and provided with arms to be used for such purpose, constitutes a 'military expedition or enterprise' within the meaning of said neutrality laws, and that the providing or preparing of the means for such 'military expedition or enterprise' which is expressly prohibited by said laws, includes furnishing or aiding in transportation for such "military expedition or enterprise.'"

The proclamation also called attention to the fact that by express enactment, "if two or more persons conspire to commit an offence against the United States any act of one conspirator to effect the object of such conspiracy renders all the conspirators liable to fine and imprisonment."

There was no mistaking the tone and purpose of this pronouncement, and though the Cuban emissaries were far from abandonment of their efforts, they were driven to devices such as were exemplified in the case of the *Laurada*, which, proceeding from Wilmington, Del., August 5, 1896, with clearance for Port Antonio, Jamaica (the main *entrepôt* of the fruit trade), took on board off Barnegat, in the open sea, from three tugs awaiting her,

[1] House Doc., 326, 55 Cong., 2 Sess. The judgment against the captain, Wiborg, was affirmed; that against the mates, Petersen and Johansen, was reversed on the view that there was no adequate proof to show that they had knowledge of the ship's orders or movements when the vessel was in American jurisdiction.

some passengers, among whom were the well-known filibusters Nuñez and Roloff, and some cases of arms and warlike stores. She went to the small and isolated guano island of Navassa, about thirty-five miles off the western end of Hayti, and which was under the jurisdiction of the United States. She expected to meet here the tugboats *Three Friends*, the *Commodore*, and *Dauntless*. Only the latter, which had left Brunswick, Ga., August 12, "in spite," as reported by the collector, "of the closest surveillance," and had taken aboard some hundred men at Woodbine, appeared.

The *Dauntless* carried the men and supplies from the *Laurada* to Cuba, distant ninety miles, making two trips. The *Laurada* completed her voyage and returned to the United States. Hart, the president and manager of the fruit company to which she belonged, and Murphy, her captain, were indicted for violation of the neutrality law. Hart was condemned to two years' imprisonment and a fine of five hundred dollars. Murphy was acquitted. An appeal in the case of Hart resulted in an affirmation of the judgment, and an opinion from the court that went beyond any previous decision in rigor. The judge held that "a combination of a number of men in the United States, with a common intent to proceed in a body to a foreign country and engage in hostilities, either by themselves or in co-operation with the others, against a power with which the United States is at peace, constitutes a military expedition when they actually proceed from the United States, whether they are then provided with arms or intend to secure them in transit. It is not necessary that all the persons shall be brought into personal contact with each other in the United States, or that they shall be drilled, uniformed, or prepared for efficient service."

"The decision," says Benton, "clearly established the principle that, to secure a conviction in the courts of the United States, it would not be necessary to show that the defendant had provided the means for carrying the expedition to Cuba, but that if he provided the means for any part of its journey with knowledge of its ultimate destination and of its unlawful character, he was guilty." [1]

"Providing the means for carrying a known military expedition to an island over which the United States has jurisdiction, as one

[1] Benton, 54, 55. Moore, *Digest*, VII, 911-916.

stage of its journey, with knowledge of its final hostile destination," was thus made an offence under the statute.[1]

Though the final conviction of Hart, March 18, 1898, came too late to affect filibustering materially, it was additional evidence of the desire and intention of the American government to deal strictly with evasions of the law in question, and of its good-will toward Spain. The failures to convict in the cases which had arisen in the first stage of the conflict, through the narrowness of definitions by the courts, were, in view of those of the later period, just causes of Spanish dissatisfaction; but in any case there was no just ground for complaint against the American government itself for want of energy, or as to watchfulness or willingness to proceed against violators of the law, whenever possible. That it was much hampered by the sympathies of the population, which extended to all classes, and which it may be taken for granted caused too lenient views to be taken by many officials of the customs and affected the action of the latter favorably to the Cubans, is unquestionable, and that there were cases in which Spain might justly have demanded damages is scarcely to be questioned. The leanings of a whole people, however, are too strong to be always successfully encountered by a government in the administration of its laws. These leanings were the result of Spanish action in Cuba itself, and not of enmity to the Spanish people. The American people were deeply moved through a sentiment which, whether well or ill based, was in itself an evidence of their humanity and kindliness. The action of the national government and its officers, thus so strongly adverse to the drift of national feeling, was distinctly on a high plane of honor and disinterestedness.

Furthermore, "it is not the purpose of the principles governing neutral aid to belligerents to make insurrection impossible or directly to aid governments in maintaining the *status quo*. No more are they formulated to throttle sympathy and to forbid such comfort and support as individuals may desire to give. They accomplish their purpose when they prevent what is technically known as 'direct military aid,' 'armed expeditions,' 'ships of war fitted out,' or use of sail for belligerent purposes in aid of either one of the belligerents. The contention at present is that

[1] Moore, *Digest*, VII, 915.

there is a limit to the obligations of a neutral as to the enforcement of neutrality; that its duty is not one of perfect vigilance." [1]

Nor should the inertness of Spain herself in the matter be overlooked. Expeditions landed with scarcely an attempt at prevention on the part of Spanish cruisers or garrisons. With proper energy, with 67 vessels of all classes in Cuba, and with more than 200,000 men available on land, the coast should have been securely guarded and every landing-place made impossible to an invader. Instead, the Cuban authorities leaned almost wholly upon the American government for prevention, there being but one seizure afloat by the Spanish, that of the *Competitor*, during the three years of the insurrection.

Of the 71 expeditions of which there is report, but 5 were stopped on the coast of Cuba by the Spanish. The United States authorities stopped 33, the English 2; 4 were prevented by storms; 27 were successful. Nearly all the vessels were but small tugs of less than 100 tons. Only 4 were larger ships: the American *Laurada* of 899 net tons; the English Bermuda of 823; the Norwegian *Leon* of 490, and the Danish *Horsa* of 459. The responsibility for the last three rested largely with the consuls of the nations to which they belonged, as they could not have left American ports without their consent. The *Bermuda* made 5 trips, the *Horsa* 2. The *Three Friends*, a tug of 89 tons, made 8, the *Dauntless*, of 77 tons, made 12.

Said the secretary of the treasury, speaking of an expedition by the *Laurada*, in February, 1897: "If the Spanish patrol of 2,200 miles of Cuban coast had frustrated one-half the number of the expeditions that were frustrated by the United States authorities along a coast-line of 5,470 miles, not one man nor one cartridge would have been illicitly landed in Cuba from the United States in the past two years and a half. In this particular instance the vessel landed her men and arms unmolested for two days in a prominent seaport [Banes], though all Cuban seaports have been reported under Spanish control, and though the Spanish authorities had been informed of her landing and even minutely of the situation of torpedoes which had been laid for her protection." [2]

[1] Benson, 62, citing Woolsey, *American Foreign Policy*, 37.
[2] Letter of the secretary of the treasury, November 30, 1897. House Doc. 326, 55 Cong., 2 Sess., 10 and 18.

It was the proximity of the United States and not merely Cuban energy, supported by the popular good-will of the country, which made the Union the principal source of Cuban supply. Exactly the same elements that made the close and extensive commercial relations in time of peace caused the active commerce in war material in the time of war. Had the American government been successful in preventing absolutely the illegal part of such traffic it would have been transferred to other countries, and supplies of arms and men would have gone from England and France to Cuba, as, through the proximity of these countries to Spain, they went thence to the Carlists in far greater degree than from the United States to the Cubans. The traffic, in so far as the employment of vessels and men was concerned, was a mere question of money. The inducements would have been the same to the Englishman or Frenchman, and with the same result; the only difference would have been the larger expense to the Cuban committees. The suppression of such committees in Great Britain more particularly would have been as difficult as in the United States. Both countries are extremely jealous of trespassing upon the right of speech or action. The Cuban Junta of New York had its counterpart in the Carlist committee of London. It was impossible in countries of such liberalism to suppress either, or for any political party to propose so doing.

However much the abuse of such liberty by the Cubans in the United States may be deplored, it is impossible not to admire the self-sacrifice shown by the whole body, in the heavy contributions they were called upon to make, and the energy, courage, and ability exhibited by the leaders in the hazardous efforts, and their remarkable persistency in the face of such frequent disaster. This much must be granted them by the fair-minded. It is a fine page in the history of their island.[1]

Scarcely had revolt begun but that Spanish officials showed, by firing upon the mail steamer *Allianca*, one of the line between New York and Colon, passing through the Windward Passage

[1] For a full list, so far as known, of the vessels engaged in filibustering, and the Spanish view of this question, see the Marquis de Olivart, "Le Différend entre l'Espagne et les États Unis, au Sujet de la Question Cubaine," *Revue Générale de Droit International Public*, tome V (1898), 358–422.

twice weekly, the same fatuity of conduct in ignoring the need of not uselessly arousing American feeling adversely as had been shown in the previous contest.

The *Alliança* was on her homeward voyage. Sighted off Cape Maysi by the cruiser *Venadito*, March 8, the latter, distant, by the commander's own account, a mile and a half from shore and a like distance from the *Alliança*, fired a blank shot. To this the *Alliança* paid no attention, nor did she do so to the two projectiles fired later. She continued her course, her speed soon carrying her beyond further risk of interference. By her captain's statement she was six miles from shore, a distance evidently much nearer the truth, as the mile and a half stated by the Spanish captain as his own distance would be a most unlikely proximity to land, at such a point, for a cruising vessel. Mr. Gresham, the American secretary of state, telegraphed Mr. Hannis Taylor, the American minister at Madrid: "The Windward Passage, where this occurred, is the natural and usual highway for vessels plying between [northern] ports of the United States and the Caribbean Sea. Through it several lines of American mail and commercial steamers pass weekly within sight of Cape Maysi. They are well known, and this voyage embraces no Cuban port of call. Forcible interference with them cannot be claimed as a belligerent act, whether they pass within three miles of the Cuban coast or not, and can under no circumstances be tolerated when no state of war exists. This government will expect prompt disavowal of the unauthorized act and due expression of regret on the part of Spain, and it must insist that immediate and positive orders be given to Spanish naval commanders not to interfere with legitimate American commerce passing through that channel." [1]

On presenting this, in audience with the minister of state, March 16, Mr. Taylor was informed, as usual, that on reception of official information from Cuba the minister would adopt, "according to the principles of international law and without prejudice to the authority which he has a right to exercise in the territorial waters of Cuba, the proper measures if an involuntary wrong has been committed against the government of the United States." [2] "I was

[1] Telegram, March 14, 1895, *Foreign Relations*, 1895, 1177.
[2] *Ibid.*, 1179.

promised," said Mr. Taylor, "that this preliminary answer should be followed by a specific and formal reply to your demand the moment the facts can be obtained from Cuba by telegraph."[1]

On March 24, 1895 the Duke of Tetuan became minister of state, and promised "to consider the *Alliança* incident before everything."[2] A month passed, and the American secretary of state pressed for reply. On April 18 it was acknowledged that the *Venadito* fired upon the *Alliança* when the latter was outside the three-mile limit, and on May 16 the act was disavowed in a note from the minister of state,[3] which was accepted at Washington, "without conceding that the exact location of the *Alliança* at the time the shot was fired can be considered a controlling circumstance."[4]

[1] *Foreign Relations*, 1895, 1178.   [2] *Ibid.*, 1180.   [3] *Ibid.*, 1184.
[4] Acting secretary of state Uhl to American minister, June 5, 1895, *Ibid.*, 1185. In discussing this question with the Spanish authorities, Mr. Taylor had adopted as his guide the instructions in 1880 of Mr. Evarts, then secretary of state, to General Fairchild, minister at Madrid, relative to the visit and search of four American schooners in rapid succession between May and June of that year, all of which claimed to be not less than six miles distant from the Cuban coast, and two of them much more. Said Mr. Evarts: "The question does not appear to this government to be one to be decided alone by the geographical position of the vessels, but by the higher considerations involved in this unwonted exercise of search in a time of peace; and to a greater extent than the existing treaty of 1795 between the two nations, in its eighteenth article, permits it to be exercised even in time of recognized public war, that article permitting visitation only, with inspection of the vessels' sea letters, and not search. These interferences with our legitimate commerce do not even take the form of revenue formality performed by the revenue vessels of Spain, but carry in their methods most unequivocal features of belligerent searches made by the war vessels of Spain. From the unhappy history of the events of the last ten years in and about the waters of the Antilles it is only too cogently to be inferred that these proceedings of Spanish war vessels assume a right thus to arrest our peaceful commerce under motives not of revenue inspection, but of warlike defence. In this aspect of the case it may well be doubted whether, under cover of revenue investigation to intercept smuggling or other frauds, jurisdictional power within the limit of the recognized maritime league could be invoked in time of peace to justify the interference of Spanish cruisers with lawful commerce of nations passing along a public maritime highway, in a regular course of navigation which brings them near the Cuban coast, though not bound to its ports. It is not to be supposed that the world's commerce is to be impeded, and the ships of foreign and friendly nations forced to seek an unwonted channel of navigation. . . ."

Reverting to the larger question of right of search on the high sea, Mr. Evarts continued: "This government never has recognized, and never will recognize any pretence or exercise of sovereignty on the part of Spain, beyond

"Known only in a vague and confused way by the reports in the foreign press, the incident and its solution had awakened in Spain scarcely any public interest. It was only about the end of August that this was moved. At this time a Polish adventurer, Count Hobkirk, stating himself to have been a passenger of the *Aliança,* published in a newspaper an account [which he stated to be] supported by the assertions of Señor Muruaga, the Spanish minister at Washington, and by 'interviews' even of the captain of the *Venadito,* affirming that the ship was the property of a well-known filibuster, filled with warlike stores; that she was in Spanish waters, and very near the shore. The satisfaction conceded to the United States by the Spanish government was then criticised with the greatest vehemence. When, in the early days of September, the president of the council declared to a journalist that, war not existing, it was not possible to exercise the right of search, either within or without the territorial waters, and that one could only demand in these waters the character of the ship and prevent her entry into ports and places not open to commerce, the whole Spanish press stupidly cried against the abdication of the sovereign rights of Spain and the humiliation of the national honor.

"Such a misunderstanding of the principles of the law of nations was the most melancholy proof of the ignorance and presumption which were to lead Spanish opinion to the final conflict. The most popular evening journal of Madrid, the *Heraldo,* wrote, September

the belt of a league from the Cuban coast, over the commerce of this country in time of peace. This rule of the law of nations we consider too firmly established to be drawn into debate, and any dominion over the sea outside this limit will be resisted with the same firmness as if such dominion were asserted in mid-ocean."

Spain had, for more than a hundred years, established both for the Peninsula and her oversea possessions two leagues as the measure of maritime jurisdiction. This regulation Mr. Evarts regarded as applicable to revenue regulations only against smuggling, and to be taken in the same light as the revenue regulations of the United States, in force since 1799, which "not only allow but enjoin visitation of vessels bound to our ports within four leagues from land." (Mr. Evarts to General Fairchild, August 11, 1880, *Foreign Relations,* 1880, 922–927.) Spain had previously advanced this claim, and much correspondence with the American government had taken place in 1863, with the result that the latter had offered to submit the question to the King of the Belgians. Though a convention was made to this effect, the question was never submitted. For this subject of jurisdiction over the Marginal Sea, see Moore, *Digest,* I, 698–735.

14, 1895, that Señor Cánovas would have certainly held other principles and have given a different solution to the affair of the *Alliança* 'if he had not been profoundly deceived as to two things: the effective power of the republic of Washington and the decadence which he thinks inevitable of the country whose fate he holds in his hands.' One was to see two years later who was deceived in this regard; unfortunately, Señor Cánovas was no longer of this world to recall it to the Madrid journal." [1]

The quotation thus given by Señor Olivart to mark the folly of the press, shows not only ignorance of the terms of the treaty of 1795, but the incapacity for any real appreciation of the case. However much may be granted to the necessities of self-defence, such necessity could hardly be evident in the case of a large steamship, one of several (the appearance of which must have been perfectly familiar to the commander of the cruiser), standing her usual northerly course at high speed, past the extreme eastern end of Cuba, where no harbor existed. The act of the Spanish commander was simply one of utter want of judgment and wholly inexcusable from any point of view.

Almost coincident with the *Alliança* affair the question of the payment of the large claim of Mr. Mora, an American citizen, whose extensive estates in Cuba had been confiscated during the ten years' war, assumed an acute form, and did much to disturb Spanish feeling. The claim was one which had been brought before the commission established by the convention of 1871. In

---

[1] The Marquis de Olivart, *Revue Générale de Droit International Public*, tome VII (1900), 544–546. The principal owner of *El Heraldo* was Captain Moreu, who commanded the *Cristóbal Colón* in 1898. This paper published an interview with Señor Cánovas, September 9, 1895, in which the latter expressed on the subject the very correct views of international law to which the paper took such exception. The *Imparcial* also said, September 12, 1895, referring to the government: "They will not be able to escape the humiliation imposed on Spain in the *Alliança* affair; they will not be able to repair the injustice committed against the commander of the *Venadito*. It is not less certain that Spain can and ought to scrutinize and detain all ships which give reason for suspicion. *There is nothing established against this right.* Admitted by writers, mutually signed in the treaty of 1795, ratified in 1869 (1877), this has neither been modified nor weakened by any later treaty; it has its foundation in the law of self-defence. Against all that they knew but one offset . . . the power of the United States. But the dignity of Spain is still greater than the power of the United States."—*Ibid.*, 456.

November, 1886, Señor Moret made a formal offer to pay the sum of $1,500,000 as a full and definite indemnity, which was accepted by the United States, and a formal agreement was made. But the Spanish Chambers having refused to accord the necessary credit the money remained unpaid. The principal reason for the refusal of the Cortes was the existence of still larger Spanish claims for the cession of Florida and for indemnities to Spanish subjects for injuries during the American civil war. On March 16, 1894, a project of a convention of arbitration of these claims was presented by the American minister at Madrid,[1] but at the same time declaring expressly that the payment of the Mora indemnity would not be submitted to the proposed arbitration, and that the definitive arrangement of this latter could no longer be awaited.

A note from the American minister, on December 28, 1894, stating that he was "instructed to respectfully, yet firmly, insist upon a reply, without further delay,"[2] to his communication in the matter six months previous, brought reply that "when the occasion arrives the Cortes will be disposed to vote the necessary credit . . . provided such vote coincides with the decision of the United States to settle the pending Spanish claims."[3]

The passage of a joint resolution in Congress, approved March 2, 1895, requesting the President to insist upon this payment, with interest from December, 1886;—its presentation to the Spanish government by the American minister, June 18;[4] and a note from the American secretary of state to the Spanish minister at Washington, "still more energetic and truly comminatory,"[5] brought an ending of the matter. Mr. Olney's proposal to Señor Dupuy de Lome was for an immediate payment of a half of the claim, and the remainder on January 1, 1896. It ended: "If the Cortes shall take such action as both the law and the justice of the case as well as the true interests of Spain require, a long-standing grievance and source of irritation between the two countries would be happily removed. If such action is refused, it would

---

[1] *Foreign Relations*, 1894. (Appen. 442. Draft of proposed convention, *Ibid.*, 435–438.)
[2] *Ibid.*, 1895, 1160. [3] *Ibid.*, 1161. [4] *Ibid.*, 1895, 1165.
[5] De Olivart, *Revue Générale de Droit International Public*, tome VII, 551.

leave the United States to consider what course its honor and interests and the due protection of its citizens call for." [1]

"But the Spanish government could not dream of sending to the parliament, which was hostile to it, a question which the preceding cabinets had not succeeded in resolving with friendly majorities. Thus the legislature closed July 1 without being consulted." [2] On July 17 it was determined in the council of ministers to offer to execute the stipulation of 1886 by three payments of a half million Spanish dollars each, the form and time of payment to be the subject of ulterior arrangement.[3] By a memorandum agreed upon at Boston, August 10, signed by the secretary of state, the Spanish minister, and the representatives of Señor Mora and of all interested, Spain agreed to pay the $1,500,000 in Spanish gold by September 15, 1895, which offer was accepted as in full of all demands. On August 19 a royal decree opened an extraordinary credit with the ministry of the colonies, to be covered by the floating debt of Cuba and to be submitted to the Cortes on their first meeting. On the date set payment was made in Washington, the sum finally received amounting in American gold to $1,449,000.[4]

One can well recognize that the pressure of the American government at this time for such an amount of money could not be taken otherwise than as a grievance by Spain. The sum was one which Spain at no time was able to pay without difficulty, and still less at a moment when the resources of the country were so heavily strained by the immense efforts it was making, with revolt also active in the Philippines, to increase her force in Cuba which was rapidly becoming a gulf into which was to be swept whatever wealth had come from the comparative prosperity of the previous fifteen years of Cuban and peninsular peace.

President Cleveland in his annual message, December 2, 1895, made an appeal to the country for support of the laws. "Whatever," he said, "may be the traditional sympathy of our countrymen as individuals with a people who seem to be struggling for larger autonomy and greater freedom, deepened, as such sympathy

[1] *Foreign Relations*, 1895, 1196.
[2] De Olivart, *Revue Générale de Droit International Public*, tome VII, 551.
[3] Señor de Lome to Mr. Olney, July 17, 1895, *Foreign Relations*, 1895, 1170.
[4] Five Spanish *duros* are equal to $4.83 American.

naturally must be, in behalf of our neighbors, yet the plain duty of their government is to observe in good faith the recognized obligations of international relationship. The performance of this duty should not be made more difficult by a disregard on the part of our citizens of the obligations growing out of their allegiance to their country, which should restrain them from violating as individuals the neutrality which the nation of which they are members is bound to observe in its relations to friendly sovereign states."

He referred to the case of the *Alliança* as an act "promptly disavowed, with full expression of regret and assurance of nonrecurrence of such just cause of complaint, while the offending officer was relieved of his command. Military arrests of citizens of the United States in Cuba had occasioned frequent reclamations. Where held on criminal charges their delivery to the ordinary civil jurisdiction for trial had been demanded and obtained in conformity with treaty provision, and where merely detained by way of military precaution under a proclaimed state of siege, without formulated accusation, their release or trial had been insisted upon. The right of American consular officers in the island to prefer protests and demands in such cases having been questioned by the insular authority, their enjoyment of the privilege stipulated by treaty for the consuls of Germany was claimed under the most-favored-nation provision of our own convention and was promptly recognized." [1]

He announced the settlement of the Mora claim, and mentioned the conclusion of an arrangement in January, 1895, brought about by the enforcement of differential duties against United States exports to Cuba and Puerto Rico, and the immediate claim thereupon for the benefit of the minimum tariff of Spain in return for the most favorable treatment permitted by our laws as regarded the productions of Spanish territory. He noted that "vigorous protests against excessive fines imposed on our ships and merchandise by the customs officers of these islands for trivial errors have resulted in the remission of such fines in instances where the equity of the complaint was apparent, though the vexatious practice had not been wholly discontinued." [2]

---

[1] For the correspondence covering these cases, see *Foreign Relations*, 1895, 1209–1214.

[2] Richardson, *Messages and Papers of the Presidents*, IX, 636–637.

CHAPTER XXI

CASES OF AMERICAN CITIZENS.—WEYLER SUCCEEDS CAMPOS.—WEYLER'S PROCLAMATIONS.—CUBA IN THE SENATE.—THE SPANISH MINISTER USES THE NEWSPAPERS.—SEÑOR CÁNOVAS.—SENATE DEBATE

THE difficulties arising from the arrest of American citizens of Cuban birth, many of whom had merely taken out American citizenship *ad hoc*, were, by the wise prescience of Señor Cánovas, avoided in most cases during 1895 by expulsion from the island, instead of bringing them before the courts and submitting to the terms of the protocol of 1877, which were so irritating to Spanish sentiment through the precautions thus established against summary action.[1]

Señor Cánovas was happily supported throughout the year, by the humanity and excellent judgment of General Campos, though individual cases of extreme hardship arose through the harshness and arbitrary action of subordinate Spanish officers. In the cases of three of the Ansley family and a Mr. Somers, in September, the American government took marked exception to their treatment. "The right of Spain," said Mr. Olney, "as of every other sovereign state to expel aliens need not be discussed. If the right be conceded in its fullest extent, the mode of its exercise may be so harsh, unreasonable, and oppressive as to give just ground of complaint, and was so beyond all doubt in the four cases now under consideration. Whether there be regard to the arbitrary character of the decree of deportation, to the successive steps by which it was apparently proposed to be enforced, to the separation of husbands and fathers from dependent families, or to the constrained abandonment of the latter in destitute circumstances to the tender mercies of strangers, the proceedings at every stage and in every particular seem to have been characterized by wilful disregard, not merely of the rights of American citizens, but of the dictates of

[1] *Supra*, 226.

common humanity. This government cannot be expected to look upon such proceedings except with indignation, nor to pass them over without remonstrance." [1]

"It was only in the first months of 1896 that this moderation and this mildness of action [to which it must be said the above was an exception] began to change, when General Weyler succeeded Marshal Martinez Campos in Cuba. Misinterpreting the prudent policy of Señor Cánovas, the new governor-general held for two or three months in close solitary confinement a moderate number [seven] of individuals whom he had caused to be arrested without ever arriving at declaring against them the existence of any crime." [2]

Such difficulties were, however, in the main determined with tact and judgment. Spain, as so frequently mentioned, had much reason for suspicion and complaint in regard to the large number of Cubans who had taken out American citizenship merely for protection in Cuba, a phase of nationalization, be it said, which had existence elsewhere, as in Germany, Turkey, and Morocco, and which everywhere gave the United States much trouble. A notable instance was that of Julio Sanguily, who had been a brave and efficient officer in the insurgent army during the ten years' war, who claimed to have been an American citizen since 1889, and was residing in Havana.[3] He was arrested February 24, 1895, accused of conspiracy on the ground of a statement in a letter found on the person of Señor Coluna addressed to Señor Betancourt, one of the insurgent leaders, in which he declared himself unable to put "himself at the head of the work of redemption" for want of funds, and through a letter found later in the cravat of a Señor Azcuy who had been arrested, but who seizing the letter had so chewed it that it was partially illegible. It was held by the court that this letter was by Sanguily and was an appointment by him of Azcuy as a colonel in the insurgent army.

Brought first before a military court, on the ground that Sanguily had not, as required, inscribed himself in Havana as an American

[1] Mr. Olney to Señor de Lome, September 27, 1895, *Foreign Relations*, 1895, 1230. Señor de Olivart finds this particular remonstrance "*tout à fait légitime,*" *Revue Générale*, vol. VII, 567.

[2] De Olivart, *Ibid.*, 565.

[3] Senator Hoar stated in specific terms that Sanguily's naturalization was fraudulent, *Cong. Record*, 54 Cong., 2 Sess., 2239.

citizen, the case later, on demand of the American government, was transferred to a civil tribunal in November, 1895, under the provisions of the treaty of 1795 and the protocol of 1877. He was found guilty and sentenced to imprisonment for life or, in case the penalty should be remitted, to absolute deprivation of civil rights and subjection to the vigilance of the authorities during his lifetime.

The arrest and trials had attracted great attention in the United States, and in December, on a resolution of Senator Call, of Florida, the Senate called for the papers from the department of state. Appeal was taken by Sanguily to the Supreme Court at Madrid. This latter decreed a new trial, which began December 21, 1896, and ended by his being sentenced to perpetual imprisonment. He was finally, through the good offices of the department of state, released February 25, 1897, on condition that he would leave the island and not return before the termination of the war. Sanguily signed a pledge given on his "own free will and without compulsion on the part of any one," "sacredly" affirming "to the United States and to Spain that if . . . released by the pardon of the latter government he would "leave and remain away from Cuba and "not aid directly or indirectly the present insurrection."[1]

"It is with reason," says Señor de Olivart, "that President Cleveland in his message of December 2, 1895, was able to speak of the tact shown by the two governments in their relations. . . . In some forty cases there was but one where condemnation was pronounced and still this sentence was not executed. The protocol of 1877, so vexing to Spanish sovereignty, was in the end interpreted on one side and the other, in a conciliatory manner, and with moderation; it was only later in the grave affair of the *Competitor* that pacific relations were in danger. At the period now in question (1895–96) two other proofs of the good feeling between the two states may be cited—without speaking, besides, of the perfect correctness with which the United States tried then to prevent the filibustering expeditions to Cuba and the infractions of the law of neutrality.

[1] *Foreign Relations*, 1896, 844, in which 96 pages (750–846) are devoted to this case. See also De Olivart, *Revue Générale de Droit International Public*, VII, 569–573. De Olivart also states, "as a fact well known," that Sanguily, some days after the rupture between Spain and the United States, joined the Cuban army.

On one hand, the American government recognized fully the true principles on the subject of the responsibility of Spain regarding damages caused by the destruction committed in Cuba by the insurgents during the autumn and winter of 1895. On the other, the Madrid government, correcting the misunderstanding of General Martinez Campos, recognized not less fully . . . the right of the American consuls, in virtue of the clause of the most favored nation (a like right being expressly conceded to Germany) of presenting to the Spanish authorities of Cuba their complaints and observations touching the execution of the treaties."[1]

On January 18, 1896, Campos, having failed in the field, was forced by the attitude of the peninsular party in Havana to give up his office. In his farewell of that date to the army he said: "I have not been fortunate in my endeavors as commander, despite your bravery and sufferings. As governor I have failed to pursue the war policy which the constitutionalist and reformist parties desired me to follow and which my conscience prevented me from carrying into effect";[2] this policy having been too mild, too conciliatory for the volunteers and other extremists who, in Havana, controlled the situation. General Marin took over affairs, pending the arrival of General Weyler, shortly appointed to succeed, and Campos, two days later, left for Spain, arriving at Coruna February 3, to meet not only coldness but insult from the populace. "A majority of the newspapers here," said a despatch from Madrid, "are indignant with General Campos for suggesting that autonomy should be granted to the Cubans. They declare that the suggestion is an insult to the nation after the sacrifices it has made."[3]

At this time the insurgents were in the immediate vicinity of Havana. All efforts had failed to confine them to the eastern provinces, and thenceforward the great sugar estates of the island were at their mercy, but little of which was shown. The well-being of the island was to be wrecked until it should become valueless to the Spaniards. Already its production had fallen off in value $55,000,000. On January 10, 1896, Gomez issued a circular: "Inasmuch as the work of grinding sugar is now suspended in the

[1] De Olivart, *Revue Générale de Droit International Public*, VII, 573–574.
[2] Telegram to *New York Herald* from Havana, January 18, 1896.
[3] Telegram, Madrid, February 4, 1896, *New York Herald*.

western districts the burning of cane fields is prohibited. The boiling houses and machinery of sugar estates shall be destroyed in case their owners or managers shall attempt to resume work, notwithstanding this order for the protection of property." How ruthlessly this last was obeyed was seen in the gaunt walls and blackened ruins scattered everywhere throughout the sugar districts of the unfortunate island at the end of the war.[1] The fact that Campos had endeavored to save these by guarding them with detachments of his men, which thus weakened the army for offensive action, was one of the causes of Spanish popular complaint.

General Weyler came with a new determination. The war was to be ruthless in character. He proclaimed: "I take charge with the confidence, which never abandons a cause, of preserving the island for Spain. I shall always be generous with those who surrender, but will have the decision and energy to punish rigorously those who in any way help the enemy. Without having in mind any political mission, I would not oppose the government of his majesty when in its wisdom, having peace in Cuba, it should think convenient to give this country reforms with the same spirit of love in which a mother gives all things to her children. Inhabitants of the island of Cuba, lend me your help. So you will defend your interests, which are the interests of the country."

Again appears the unfortunate attitude of mind that reform must follow pacification instead of being a means toward it.

On February 16 General Weyler issued three proclamations: one ordering all inhabitants of the district of Sancti Spiritus and the provinces of Puerto Principe and Santiago de Cuba to concentrate in places which were military head-quarters; forbidding travel within the radius of operations without a pass, and ordering the vacation of all commercial establishments in the country districts.

A second delegated the judicial attributes of the governor-general to the commanders-in-chief of the first and second corps and to the general of the first division in Puerto Principe; declared that

---

[1] For the character of this destruction and incidentally for evidence of the value of American holdings in the island, see the letter of Messrs. E. Atkins & Co., of Boston, December 9, 1895, regarding the ruin on their estates worked by the insurgents, *Foreign Relations*, 1895, 1217.

prisoners caught in action would be subjected to the most summary trial without any other investigation except that indispensable for the objects of the trial. If the sentence were deprivation of liberty, the culprit was to be brought to Havana for final judgment. No sentence of death was to be carried out without the authority of the captain-general, except where no means of communication existed or in cases of insult to superiors or of military sedition.

The third declared all subject to military law who propagated any notice or assertion favorable to the rebellion; who destroyed or damaged railways, telegraphs, or other means of communication; all incendiaries; all who facilitated the supply of arms or ammunition; telegraphers who divulged army information; those who through the press or otherwise reviled the prestige of Spain or her army; those who extolled the enemy or supplied the enemy with horses, cattle, or other resources; who acted as spies; who served as guides; who adulterated army food or conspired to alter prices; who used explosives, and those who communicated with the enemy by homing pigeons, fireworks, or other signals. "The offences enumerated," said clause 14, "when the law prescribes the death penalty or life imprisonment, will be dealt with most summarily." [1]

The tide of popular feeling in the United States was now rapidly rising. A great democracy, the education of whose mass usually ends with the public school, and whose library, later, is the newspaper, does not reason with a volume of international law in its hand or trouble itself, if the question takes form in its mind at all, with what seems to it minor distinctions which weigh not at all with its prejudices and sympathies. For a hundred years the American democracy had been in antagonistic contact with Spanish rule in Louisiana, in Florida, in Mexico, and it knew but one mode of settlement of the difficulties which had thus arisen; a mode which had swept Spanish authority from huge empires of territory which constitute to-day more than half the dominion of the Union. At the same time it had seen the same authority driven from the remainder of North America and from the whole of South America. It was to be expected that in such a question as that of Cuba, its base of reasoning would be the inherited views of these many

[1] For the full text of these edicts see *Cong. Record*, 54 Cong., 1 Sess., 2345-46.

generations, and that its starting-point would be that Spain was in the wrong. When to this was added the destruction of a great commerce, and a daily account, too often in overlurid form, of Cuban happenings, but which frequently in the calmest statement was deeply harrowing, it was impossible that American popular sympathy should not go to a people fighting for relief from a political system which some thoughtful Spaniards themselves believed unbearable.

This sympathy found its natural reflex in Congress, the great majority of the members of which were, equally with the public, convinced that the situation demanded action from the American government; it has to be added that many favoring action were not too accurate as to "the laws of war" which they so often recalled, and to which they appealed so strongly as a reason for interference. Thus, on the first day of the new Congress, December 3, 1895, Senator Call, of Florida, offered a resolution recognizing Cuban belligerency, and, protesting against the character of the war, demanded that the President take measures to assure its being carried on in a civilized manner.[1] Senator Allen, of Nebraska, followed with a resolution which included the independence and annexation of Cuba, the purchase of all the islands in the neighborhood of the United States, the prompt and effective observation of the Monroe doctrine in "its purity and primary intentions," and a firmer and prompter policy in the protection and maintenance of the rights of American citizens abroad. Senator Kyle, on January 13, 1896, asked that the President be authorized to receive the accredited representatives of the Cuban patriots after verifying the fact that they had an established place of government.

These propositions, referred to the committee on foreign relations, brought a report from the majority, January 29, 1896, which declared that "Congress would welcome with satisfaction the concession by Spain of complete sovereignty" to the people of Cuba, "and would cheerfully give to such voluntary concession the cordial support of the United States." It spoke of the damage to American interests; stated that the United States had always met "with vigor, impartiality, and justice" the difficult task of supporting its neutrality; that the devastation of the war now

[1] *Cong. Record*, 54 Cong., 1 Sess., 205.

waged "creates strong grounds of protest against the continuance of the struggle . . . which is rapidly changing the issue to one of existence on the part of a great number of the native population"; that "it becomes a duty of humanity that the civilized powers should insist upon the application of the laws of war recognized among civilized nations to both armies."

The report then proceeded to declare, despite the fact that such persons had been so frequently declared in the proclamations of the Presidents to have no right to the protection of their own government, that "as our own people are drawn into the struggle on both sides . . . their treatment when wounded or captured . . . should not be left to the revengeful retaliations which expose them to the fate of pirates or other felons." It ended by declaring that "the inability of Spain to subdue the revolutionists by the measures and within the time which would be reasonable when applied to occasions of ordinary civil disturbance is a misfortune that cannot be justly visited upon the citizens of the United States, nor can it be considered that a state of civil war does not exist, but [or] that the movement is a mere insurrection and its supporters a mob of criminal violators of the law, when it is seen that it requires an army of 100,000 men and all the naval and military power of a great kingdom even to hold the alleged rebellion in check.

"It is due to the situation of affairs in Cuba that Spain should recognize the existence of a state of war in the island, and should voluntarily accord to the armies opposed to her authority the rights of belligerents under the laws of nations.

"The Congress of the United States recognizing the fact that the matters herein referred to are properly within the control of the Chief Executive until, within the principles of our Constitution, it becomes the duty of Congress to define the final attitude of the government of the United States toward Spain, presents these considerations to the President in support of the following resolution: *Resolved by the Senate* (the House of Representatives concurring), That the present deplorable war in the island of Cuba has reached a magnitude that concerns all civilized nations to the extent that it should be conducted, if unhappily it is longer to continue, on those principles and laws of warfare that are acknowledged to be obligatory upon civilized nations when engaged in open hostilities, including the treatment of captives who are enlisted in either army; due respect to cartels for exchange of prisoners and for other military purposes; truces and flags of truce; the provision of proper hospitals and hospital supplies and services to the sick and wounded of either army.

"*Resolved, further*, That this representation of the views and opinions of Congress be sent to the President; and if he concurs therein that he will, in a friendly spirit, use the good offices of this government to the end that Spain shall be requested to accord to the armies with which it is engaged in war the rights of belligerents, as the same are recognized under the law of nations." [1]

It is clear that the newspaper reports of inhumanity had had a deep effect upon the minds of the committee; that whatever cause might exist for its action, there was an underlying feeling that a continuance of the savagery of the war, whether on the part of the one or other side, must cease. How this was to be brought about by a recognition of belligerency is scarcely to be seen. The resolution in itself was vague and valueless except as an opinion on the part of the majority of the committee that affairs in Cuba were deplorable.

Senator Cameron submitted from the minority of the committee a review of the ten years' war and of the circumstances which had caused the United States to proclaim their right to intervene. "As was said by Mr. Fish," said the report, "the mere offer on our part to mediate as between the contending forces was in itself a concession of belligerency and a recognition of the existence of that condition. But for various reasons this argument was not pressed by our government," the main of these being the expectancy of concessions from Spain to Cuba; the civil war in Spain; the irritation on account of the activity of Cubans in the United States; the pressing questions of reconstruction in the South, and the difficulties at the time of the negro problem. The report recalled that Spain had recognized the belligerency of the South before a battle had been fought; reviewed the declarations of General Campos; cited the reports of the consul-general in Havana in 1885 declaring the island under an unparalleled tyranny, and that "what with governmental oppression and illegal tyranny,

[1] Senate Report 141, 54 Cong., 1 Sess.

emancipation, brigandage, low prices for sugar and high taxes on everything, the ruin of the island is already almost consummated."

"The danger and scandal of the situation," said the report, "have been such as can be compared with nothing but the condition of Armenia. . . . The precedents are clear, and if our action were to be decided by precedents alone, we should not be able to hesitate. The last great precedent was that of the [American] civil war. . . . In that instance, without waiting for the outbreak of hostilities further than the bloodless attack on Fort Sumter and its surrender, April 13, 1861, the British government issued its proclamation of neutrality on the 13th of May following, before it received official information that war existed except as a blockade of certain insurgent ports. The French government acted in concert with Great Britain, but delayed the official announcement until June. The Spanish government issued its proclamation of belligerency June 17; and the first battle of the war was not fought until July 21, or known at Madrid until August. . . ."

The report recalled the defeat of Campos, "the military possessions of the whole eastern half of the island" by the insurgents (the important fact that the ports were an exception was overlooked), and stated that they had gained military control of the western provinces (again overlooking the very important question of the towns and ports). It continued: "If the government of the United States still refrained from recognizing the belligerency of the insurgents after this conclusive proof of the *fact*, the reason doubtless was that in the absence of any legal complication the question became wholly political, and that its true solution must lie not in a recognition of belligerency but in a recognition of independency. In 1875, when the situation was very far from being as serious as it is now, President Grant, after long consideration of the difficulties involved in public action, decided against the recognition of belligerency as an act which might be delusive to the insurgents, and would certainly be regarded as unfriendly by Spain. He decided upon a middle course. The documents above quoted show that he proposed to the Spanish government a sort of intervention which should establish the independence of Cuba by a friendly agreement. In doing so he not only recognized both parties to the conflict as on an equal plane, but he also warned Spain that if such mediation should not be accepted, direct intervention would probably be deemed a necessity on the part of the United States.

"Spain preferred to promise the insurgents terms so favorable as to cause for a time the cessation of hostilities. Since then twenty years have passed. The insurrection, far from having ceased, has taken the proportions of a war almost as destructive to our own citizens as to the contending parties. The independence of Cuba was then regarded by the President of the United States as the object of his intervention, and has now become far more inevitable than it was then. Evidently the government of the United States can do no less than to take up the subject precisely where President Grant left it, and to resume the friendly mediation which he actually began, with all the consequences which would follow its rejection."

The review ended with the offer of a resolution very different to the colorless formula of the majority, and which was perfectly definite as to intention, viz.: "That the President is hereby requested to interpose his friendly offices with the Spanish government for the recognition of the independence of Cuba." [1]

On February 5 Senator Morgan brought from the majority of the committee a substitute for their proposition of January 29, as follows: "That in the opinion of Congress a condition of public war exists between the government of Spain and the government proclaimed and for some time maintained by force of arms by the people of Cuba; and that the United States of America should maintain a strict neutrality between contending powers, according to each all the rights of belligerents in the ports and territory of the United States." [2]

The debate, which began February 20, at first chiefly upon the relative constitutional powers of the executive and of Congress as to the recognition of belligerency and independence, and which occupied most of the period February 25–28, brought on the 28th a severe speech from Senator Sherman, who quoted from the *New York Journal* an article which purported to be a translation from a book by one Enrique Donderio [Donderis], a Spaniard,

---

[1] Senate Report 141, 54 Cong., 1 Sess.
[2] *Cong. Record*, 54 Cong., 1 Sess., 1317.

"who," said Mr. Sherman, "was so horror-stricken with the awful crimes he saw committed, that he fled to the United States and there compiled his manuscript."[1] The account, which should have been unbelievable on its face, but which was read as veritable history by Senator Sherman, made of Weyler (later shown not to have been at the period in the field at all) a monster of unheard-of brutality and coarseness. To have given credence to statements of such character; to unfold with dramatic earnestness at such a time and place and on such evidence unbelievable horrors which, "if they had been true, would have made the Spanish general the greatest monster of history," naturally causes one to doubt the wisdom of the senator uttering them. It was not a happy augury for the appointment soon to be made to the post of secretary of state, now of such extreme importance.

On February 28, 1896, were passed by the Senate the amended resolution offered by Senator Morgan February 5, and the resolution of Senator Cameron altered to read: "That the friendly offices of the United States should be offered by the President to the Spanish government for the recognition of the independence of Cuba." There were 64 yeas and but 6 nays, 19 not voting.

The resolutions of the House which called directly for intervention if necessary[2] passed, March 2, by 262 to 17 votes, brought a

[1] For Senator Sherman's speech, see *Cong. Record*, 54 Cong., 1 Sess., February 28.

[2] "*Resolved*, That in the opinion of Congress a state of public war exists in Cuba, the parties to which are entitled to belligerent rights, and the United States should observe a strict neutrality between the belligerents.

"*Resolved*, That Congress deplores the destruction of life and property caused by the war now waging in that island, and believing that the only permanent solution of the contest, equally in the interest of Spain, the people of Cuba, and other nations, would be in the establishment of a government by the choice of the people of Cuba, it is the sense of Congress that the government of the United States should use its good offices and friendly influence to that end.

"*Resolved*, That the United States has not intervened in struggles between any European governments and their colonies on this continent; but from the very close relations between the people of the United States and those of Cuba in consequence of its proximity and the extent of the commerce between the two peoples, the present war is entailing such losses upon the people of the United States that Congress is of opinion that the government of the United States should be prepared to protect the legitimate interests of our citizens, by intervention if necessary."—*Cong. Record*, 54 Cong., 1 Sess., March 2, 1896, 2342.

conference committee of the two houses, which on the 5th reported in favor of the House resolution. The question, now again before the Senate, was, through the opposition of Mr. Hale to immediate action, set as the order of the day for March 9. The new debate lasted two weeks.

The news of the discussion in Congress brought a climax of feeling in Spain, shown forcibly in Madrid, but more particularly in Barcelona, where the American consulate was attacked. The Madrid government presented formal regrets for the occurrence, and an offer of complete reparation, with the assurance that every necessary disposition had been taken at the capital to protect the American legation and the person of the minister.[1]

That the loose defamation of Spain, both in the Senate and House, by men of prominence and leading, who were naturally more fully quoted than were the more conservative, should have caused such demonstrations, and have brought the Spanish press to call for war, is certainly not a cause for surprise. There were, fortunately, some in both houses of Congress of saner mind than those quoted, but the general tone of the debates, violent, loose as to facts and, in marked instances, as to law, did no credit to Congress or the country.

Señor Dupuy de Lome, the Spanish minister, had entered the field by the publication, in the *New York Herald* of February 23, 1896, of the Spanish view, declaring the existence of "a conspiracy in order not to present to the Americans . . . the Spanish side of the question." When he left Spain, he said, in March, 1895, in the same steamer with Campos, the mulatto leaders, the brothers Maceo, had not reached Cuba. He learned of their coming on reaching Puerto Rico. Gomez and Marti arrived from Santo Domingo a few days later. For nearly two months only the black

---

[1] De Olivart, *Revue Générale de Droit International Public*, VII (1900), 604. De Olivart gives the following as published in the Madrid *El Liberal* of March from Barcelona: "The mob arrived at the United States consulate. The rioters, hissing and shouting, '*Abajo los tocineros Americanos*' (down with the American pig-killers), threw stones and potatoes, which broke many windows of the consulate residence. They then went to the prefecture and the residence of the captain-general where they tore up a Spanish flag. They returned again to the consulate. They were at least 15,000; they had a very lively struggle with the police, and finished by tearing to pieces an American flag."—(De Olivart, *Ibid.*, 604.)

leaders Moncada and Rabi, and Masso, "a white and honest Cuban," were at the head of small bands aided by "noted highwaymen and robbers like Matagas, Mirabal, and Miro, the latter a renegade Spaniard who fought during the Carlist war in Spain on the side of absolute monarchy, and now fights against his own country for a republic." He had been of the opinion when he reached New York that the revolt would be ended before the rainy season began.

He thought it necessary to state clearly that the revolution had been imported. "All the representative leaders were and have been abroad, and have obeyed the junta which has been established in New York and which had more than one hundred and fifty revolutionary clubs, the greater part of them being in the United States. The revolution is not a popular uprising of a discontented nation. It is a filibustering movement, principally of demagogues without standing in the island, who have nothing to lose and are trying their chances."

The conservative or union-constitutional party, he said, had had its way; Cuba was now treated as a part of Spanish territory. All the three parties, the most extreme of which, the autonomist, wanted home-rule the same as Canada, were, under the law of 1895, represented in the Spanish Cortes, under the same laws as the Spanish home provinces themselves, there being a deputy for each forty-five thousand inhabitants and two senators for each of the six provinces; and, besides, "senators representing the universities and the business interests of the island." He dwelt upon the great effect of the economic conditions, for which Spain was not responsible, in causing the uprising: the abolition of slavery, the competition, with its European bounty system, of the beet root; the abolition of the reciprocity treaty by Congress and the consequent increased duty on sugar in the United States which had all tended to depress Cuban industry and throw out of employment men on the plantations; the increased duty on cigars and the decreased duty on leaf tobacco had also tended to injure the island industries, and caused the migration of many to the United States, where they had become part of the revolutionary juntas.

"I am sure," said Señor Depuy de Lome, "that it will amaze the American people to know . . . that the persons leading the present revolution from New York are American citizens. Every one of them has sworn allegiance to the American flag and constitution, and when they went to Cuba the first thing with which they were provided was an American passport. It is very strange that American citizens are conducting a war against a country with which the United States is at peace. . . . It will also seem very strange to the honest American citizen that the president of what they call the Cuban republic is a naturalized citizen of the United States, and that only two of those whom he calls his ministers or secretaries are not naturalized citizens of the United States . . . and the most extraordinary thing is that those American citizens do not ask and do not intend to be annexed to the United States."

After a somewhat lengthy review of the military conditions of the preceding twelve months, he said: "I am of the same opinion as President Van Buren when he said [referring to events in 1837 on the Canadian frontier], 'Our laws are insufficient to prevent invasions of neighboring powers,' and of the same opinion as President Buchanan, when he, as chairman of the committee on foreign relations, expressed the opinion that 'the duty of good neighborhood and the preservation of peace along the borders require that the rights of our citizens under the law of nations should be abridged in furnishing arms, etc., to insurgents.'[1] If the laws were different it would have been impossible for the jury to declare in Wilmington, Delaware, that a body of men caught in the moment of embarking, under cover of the night, with belts full of cartridges, with arms, and ammunition and with letters for the Cuban leaders in the field, were not a military expedition. It would have been impossible for a jury in Charleston, South Carolina, to declare that Captain Hughes, of the *Laurada*, who took out of port a party of men with guns, arms, and ammunition, and who suffered those men to be drilled during the voyage and had them landed in a deserted place on the Cuban coast, was not guilty of transporting a military expedition. It would have been impossible to return the arms and ammunition found hidden in a barn on a deserted key, near Cedar Key. And it would have been impossible for the *Commodore* to make her extraordinary voyage, which has taken from the middle of August to the middle of February to go from New London, Connecticut, to Charleston, South Carolina,

[1] *Benton's Debates*, vol. XIII, pp. 638–641.

where she lies with a full cargo of war material. It would have been also impossible to discharge the men arrested in the schooners *Lark* and *Antoinette*, or to have set free the expedition of Collazo when the men returned to Key West after their failure and after having camped for several weeks at Cape Sable, Florida. Different laws would have made it impossible for Calixto Garcia and his men, sent to sea in a death trap, the *Hawkins*, and miraculously saved, to return to New York, to conspire again publicly, and to try again to reach Cuba. It would have been impossible for the Cuban revolutionary junta to remain unchecked, making the United States its basis of operations against a country with which the United States is at peace."

He refrained from discussing the question of belligerency more than to say that he held the same opinions as those held by Mr. Adams when in London during the civil war; by Lincoln and Seward; by Grant, Fish, and Evarts. He recalled the Spanish decree of June 17, 1861, acknowledging the belligerency of the South, article 5 of which forbade "the transportation of effects of war . . . as well as the carrying of papers or communications for belligerents." "Transgressors," said the article, "shall have no right to the protection of my government."

He claimed that the Cubans were taxed less *per capita* than the people of Spain, and that "all is forgotten about the majority of Cubans who are loyal to Spain; about the foreigners, principally Americans, who declare that they can only be protected by Spain, and about the many thousands, not to say hundreds of thousands, of Spanish-born citizens who went to Cuba when mere children, who with their thrift and economy have expanded the resources of the island." He concluded with a question, which had undoubted point: "I will only ask impartial persons to compare Cuba with many other countries, from the Rio Grande to Cape Horn, and see if there is more liberty, order, and good government, and if Spanish Cuba is not more free and happy than many other nations which are independent. As to the commercial relations with the United States, I will only say that Cuba under the Spanish régime buys sixty per cent. more than Mexico, more than Canada, and taking into consideration the population of the countries, more than all the South American republics combined."

The newspaper account of infamous actions attributed to General Weyler and read by Mr. Sherman in the Senate, February 28, as veritable history, aroused Señor Dupuy de Lome to a second newspaper article, in which he showed that the newspaper had itself injected the name of Weyler into the translation of its account from the pamphlet of forty-three pages by Donderis, in which Weyler's name was not even mentioned. He showed the origin of the report of the killing of 43,500 prisoners by the Spanish to have come from a remark by General Sickles, at the time minister to Spain, who, August 16, 1872, quoting the statement of the *Imparcial*, of Madrid, that "from the beginning of hostilities in Cuba 13,600 insurgents have been killed in battle and 43,500 taken prisoners," added on his own account, "it is believed that all prisoners of war are shot or garroted." Referring to Senator Lodge's reading of the report in the Madrid *El Liberal*, January 29, of General Weyler's parting words at Cadiz, "I propose to exterminate the filibusters," Señor de Lome showed that *El Liberal* had used a colloquial word which could only be translated "to clean out." [1] Continuing, Señor de Lome said: "I have before my eyes a summary of charges of inhumanity in connection with the war of the rebellion in the United States. . . . I am sure that many of them are false, most of them exaggerated, some necessary, others unavoidable. . . . In an English paper of those days I read the following opinion of the American civil war: 'Stripped of its trappings, it is a mere quarrel for territory. The antagonists are acting like Delawares and Pawnees. War to the knife, pushed to absolute extermination, is what they have resolved on, and people breathe a language of massacre and extermination.'" [2]

The passage by the House, on March 2, of its own resolutions, brought a conference committee of the two chambers: Sherman, Morgan, and Lodge of the Senate, and Hitt, McCreary, and Adams of the House. The result, an almost immediate agreement that the Senate should recede and adopt the House resolutions, was reported March 5, 1896. Through the opposition of Mr. Hale, the consideration of the report was deferred to March 9, when Mr. Hale began the debate by declaring his unalterable resolution

[1] *Limpiar*, to clean, to scour; as *limpiar ropa*, to wash clothes.
[2] *Cong. Record*, 54 Cong., 1 Sess., 2591.

to oppose the recognition of belligerency. He referred to Señor de Lome's paper, arousing thereby strong objections from several senators to the reading of communications of an unofficial character from foreign ministers in the United States. The objection was however withdrawn, Señor de Lome's good faith, his moderation, and his personal popularity inclining most to pass over what was in itself a transgression in diplomacy. Senator Gray's question weighed much in the determination. "Suppose," he said, "some member of Parliament . . . had said that it was a matter of history . . . that when Major André was executed, or before he was executed, he was tortured by General Washington, had his eyes burned out with red-hot irons, do you suppose that the American ambassador in London might not, with perfect propriety, point out either that the history was an unauthentic one, or that a mistake had been made in the reading of such a grewsome and false statement?" [1]

Senator Hale quoted from "one of the last issues of the [New York] *World*" a despatch from its correspondent in Cuba, Mr. William Shaw Bowen: "General Weyler has, in my opinion, been grossly traduced. I should add that I feel confident that it is owing to misinformation, to erroneous prejudice, to systematic attacks on him personally by interested enemies that the people of the United States and their public representatives have formed a monstrously erroneous opinion about the governor-general. . . . I am astonished to perceive how unacquainted with the true conditions are the public men of Washington." [2] He quoted from the *New York Journal*, strongly pro-Cuban: "So effectual has been the work of the insurgent general [Maceo] that thirteen towns held by the Spaniards have been destroyed and the rich tobacco lands throughout the province have been laid waste. Practically all the island west of Havana is a wilderness. . . . Whole towns have been obliterated or reduced to a heap of ashes and their inhabitants are wandering helpless over the face of the country, without a place to lay their heads or wherewithal to be clothed, and many of them starving." 'If I vote alone," said Mr. Hale, "I shall vote for no resolution which gives aid and

[1] *Cong. Record*, 54 Cong., 1 Sess., 2633.
[2] *Ibid.*, 2591.

comfort to the red-handed foray of this guerilla leader, whose exploits are so exultingly chronicled as I have read them here."

He quoted from the *New York World*, in this instance a message by cable, March 6, from Señor Cánovas: "We have as yet no official notification of the intentions of the American government, and cannot, therefore, take cognizance of, or protest by vote against, any of the proceedings of the Senate and House of Representatives of the United States. Nor have we sounded the European powers or courts regarding their support in any form. All we have done is to show to the American government and to Minister Taylor that we have endeavored to enforce respect for the American legation and consulates, repressing so sternly the disturbances that we have ordered the Madrid, Granada, Barcelona, and Valencia universities closed, and we will close all universities, schools, and establishments whose students dare to make demonstrations hostile to the United States. We will send to prison and prompt trial all the authors and promoters of such disturbances. We believe they are prompted by the advanced republicans. Nothing will be omitted on our side to show our desire to preserve cordial relations with America. . . . The situation now is one of extreme delicacy. Indeed I cannot define how far it is possible for the government of Spain to permit amicable and careful mediation of a foreign power, however honorable and disinterested it may be, without incurring the grave risk of being accused of submitting to outside interference, pressure, and dictation in the midst of a civil war. The United States are a great power, and until they recognize the object and encourage the aims of the insurrectionists in Cuba they are friendly to Spain. After the recognition of the belligerents in Cuba by the United States it would be impossible for the government of Spain to accept the good offices of President Cleveland, or to permit any interference whatever.

"Nevertheless, I still hope some means will be found by the President to avoid alienating the friendly relations with the United States, which Spain has shown this week she prizes highly. I am fully alive to the significance and the possible consequences of the vote of the United States Congress to the rebels as well as to Spain in her relations with the United States, especially in connection with the right of search on the high seas and in the matter of privateers and filibustering expeditions.

"The only new and seemingly warlike preparations yet made by Spain are made simply with a view to equipping a fleet of war ships and transatlantic steamers to chase filibusters and to guard the coasts of Cuba. That is the sole object in view. General Weyler having said that he had enough troops, only the usual reliefs will be sent to Cuba until autumn, and no naval demonstration is contemplated."

Señor Cánovas deprecated the misapprehension of Weyler's character and methods; before the latter left for Cuba his views had been approved, and he had only acted in harmony with the requirements of the war. He declared himself determined to carry out the administrative political reforms "as soon as the pacification of the island permits and even such economical tariff reforms as may be consistent with the interests of both the colony and the mother country. But it is," he said, "impossible to attempt reforming during a civil war or any foreign pressure in the present condition of the island. When Marshal Campos was sent to Cuba as governor-general, . . . he soon discovered that it was impossible to do so." Señor Cánovas ended declaring that "we cannot admit that the slightest ground exists for the recognition of the belligerency of the Cuban insurgents."[1]

This very important and frank declaration of policy was fitly described by Senator Hale as a credit to the Spanish government, under sore temptations to be querulous and complaining and to use retaliatory language.[2] Its publication was wise and opportune.

Following this with an appeal from Castelar for peace, Mr. Hale said: "I will not contrast the tone of these communications of these great men representing Spain, with the interest and fate of her government and her future depending, and with much temptation to exacerbation of spirit—I will not contrast the language in which they are couched or the spirit which pervades them with certain other declarations to which some of us have listened."[3] It was well-merited reproof to the extravagant declamation both in the Senate and House, which was but too frequently of a character which sober thought could not commend, and "the heat, rapidity,

[1] *Cong. Record*, 54 Cong., 1 Sess., 2593.   [2] *Ibid.*, 2593.   [3] *Ibid.*, 2594.

and carelessness" of which, Mr. Hoar declared, had "almost turned the Senate of the United States, I will not quite say, into a mob."[1]

Mr. Hoar showed the insufficiency of the evidence to justify the action contemplated, but he did more; he said: "Our honorable friends come in here and shrink—I will not say flinch—from sending their declaration where it alone can have any political effect. They undertake to make this utterance in a way that will accomplish all the mischief that it is capable of and have none of its vigor, potency, or effect. It is not the act of the American people. It is not binding on a single American citizen. It is not binding on the President. It is not binding on either House of Congress. It is not binding on any member of Congress. It is not binding for any future year. It is a declaration to which the constitution adds, in letters that cannot be effaced, 'This means nothing; it has no power.' The President of the United States alone can give it life and vigor and potency and authority, and the committee, when they wrote the word 'concurrent' at the top of that resolution, wrote in brief these words: 'It is distinctly to be understood that this is a Pickwickian resolution, without vigor or potency or meaning.' We have not dared to tell Spain that we recognize the insurgents as belligerents and are prepared to take the consequences. We have not dared to give the President of the United States the constitutional authority to protect any American citizen. We give Spain the right of search in terms, but if she undertakes to exercise it, we can turn upon her and say, 'This did not mean anything. It was . . . merely moot court debate, brought in to see which member of the Senate or of the other House could make the most eloquent and inspiring speech; but it had no constitutional effect on the great question of peace or foreign policy or international relations. . . .' There is but one organ in this country to foreign countries, and that is the executive. He cannot declare war and he cannot make laws regulating commerce except as a part of the legislative powers of the country, but everything else is his. It is for him to make treaties; it is for him to appoint and receive ambassadors, and it is for him, as it has been the custom of this country for a hundred years, to determine the question of recognition or belligerency."[2]

[1] Speech, March 11, 1896, Cong. Record, 54 Cong., 1 Sess., 2680.   [2] *Ibid.*, 2683.

Mr. Hoar's remark concerning the moving cause of over declamation must however not be taken too literally. Undoubtedly the presidential election of the coming fall had weight, but back of all was a very real feeling of deep indignation with the events in Cuba and of very real sympathy with the Cubans. While there had been intemperate statement, the foreign relations committee of the Senate had had access to the documents of the department of state which policy forbade making public, and had at least assured itself of the necessity of having Congress declare its state of mind, which was all that a concurrent resolution could effect. Mr. Sherman showed that there was even some notable Spanish opinion in support of the view that it was Spain's duty to stop the war. He quoted the former Spanish minister of state, Señor Pi y Margall, who a few months before had said: "Let us be just to the men who to-day are fighting us in Cuba. We ought long ago to have granted them the autonomy to which they have an undeniable right; we should have kept them united to the Peninsula by the single tie of common interests, national and international. How much blood and treasure we would have been spared by such a course! We were urged to it by reason, by right, by our self-interest, by the thought of the vast colonial empire we have lost. Unfortunately, for nations even more than for individuals, the force of habit is irresistible. Nothing could make us give up our old policy, a policy discredited by disaster to ourselves and to others. If there is now a war in Cuba the fault is ours and ours alone. . . . The compromise with which we shall have to terminate the present war, if Cuba does not prove stronger than we, let us make now while we are still the more powerful and our generosity cannot be branded as weakness. . . . Seventeen years ago we gave them freedom; let us now give them autonomy. Let us make them masters and arbiters of their own destinies. Let us leave them to rule themselves in all matters pertaining to their internal life—political, administrative, and economic. . . . Against such conduct the sentiment of patriotism is invoked. But above the idea of country rises that of humanity; and above both that of justice. Cuba is the grave of our youth in these deplorable wars. . . . It is irritating to read and to hear, day after day, that it is necessary to send to Cuba regiment after regiment in order to make an end of the rebels and to leave the sovereignty of the nation firmly planted and established. . . . The sovereignty of the nation! Must the nation to be sovereign drain the life of the groups composing it? Does its sovereignty necessarily carry with it the slavery of the colonies? Its sovereignty is limited to the national interests. It must be confined to a form which will permit relations between the mother country and the colonies to exist." [1]

The long debate in the Senate did not end until March 23, when it resolved to stand by its own resolutions. On this same date Senator Mills, of Texas, offered a resolution which, coming from such a source, shows the extent to which feeling had risen. The first section of this resolution directed the President to request Spain to grant Cuba "such local government as they may wish"; the second was the forerunner of a very similar one to come two years later: "In case Spain shall refuse to grant to the inhabitants of Cuba the rightful power of local self-government, then the President of the United States is hereby directed to take possession of the island of Cuba with the military and naval forces of the United States and hold the same until the people of Cuba can organize a government deriving its just powers from the consent of the governed, and arm and equip such military force as may be necessary to protect them from invasion." [2]

The House on April 6, 1896, by a vote of 287 to 27 (80 not voting), accepted the Senate's resolutions, though not without a prolonged debate. Mr. Boutelle, of Maine, was one of the small number who stood firmly in opposition to the movement. He quoted a letter of March 23 by twenty-five Spanish residents of New York which declared that Cuba and Puerto Rico, in being allowed to send more than sixty members to the Spanish parliament, had, in such a representation, a greater liberty than was enjoyed by Canada or Jamaica; that Cuba with a territory the size of Pennsylvania, and a population of 1,500,000, was taxed but $22,000,000; less than the taxation for municipal purposes alone of the city of New York; that while Cuba's taxable property was about that of Boston, it was taxed at less than half the rate in either Boston or New York; that every province had its legislature and every municipality its council;

[1] Madrid, *El Don Quijote*, July 12, 1895. *Cong. Record*, 54 Cong., 1 Sess., 2726.
[2] *Ibid.*, 3077.

that the great majority of the people of Cuba "having got what reforms they asked are satisfied to remain in the Spanish empire." [1]

All this may have been; but the actuality of conditions was now such that the only thing possible to Spain to prevent American intervention was, if not wholly to sever connection with the island, to grant it a measure of autonomy which should make it as free of the mother country as was Canada of England, and thus remove the impression of injustice which was the foundation of American sympathy.

[1] *Cong. Record,* 54 Cong., 1 Sess., 3551.

CHAPTER XXII

THE ATTITUDE OF THE CLEVELAND ADMINISTRATION DEFINED.— THE CASE OF THE "COMPETITOR"

THOUGH the concurrent resolution just passed had no legal weight beyond giving form to the sentiment in Congress and was in nowise mandatory upon the President, and though the better class of opinion throughout the Union, as shown in the press, was opposed to such action as declaring a state of belligerency which did not exist and at the same time demanding the independence of Cuba, and thus practically declaring victory to rest with the insurgents,[1] a vote, and by such majorities, could not be wholly ignored. It had the effect of bringing from the American government an official and solemn document on the subject of intervention in a note to the Spanish minister from Mr. Olney, April 4, 1896.

In transmitting this note, Señor de Lome said: "When one considers the numerous resolutions of the two houses of Congress, the popular agitation, the tide of public opinion, superficial but widespread, which has been inspired against Spain by our enemies, the attitude of the press and what it has been asking and is asking even to-day—nay, more, what has been demanded and is demanded even now of the President of the republic—we can do no less than admire the high qualities of rectitude and honor, the fearlessness and the respect toward the legitimate rights of Spain shown in this note addressed by this government through me to the government of his majesty."[2]

This note, so complete an exposition of the attitude of the American government, needs to be given in full.

[1] De Olivart, *Revue Générale*, vol. IX (1902), 162.
[2] Señor Enrique Dupuy de Lome, to the Spanish minister of state, April 10, 1896, *Spanish Diplomatic Correspondence and Documents*, 4.

"Department of State,
"Washington, *April* 4, 1896.
"Señor Don Enrique Dupuy de Lome.

"*Sir:* It might well be deemed a dereliction of duty to the government of the United States, as well as a censurable want of candor to that of Spain, if I were longer to defer official expression as well of the anxiety with which the President regards the existing situation in Cuba as of his earnest desire for the prompt and permanent pacification of that island. Any plan giving reasonable assurance of that result and not inconsistent with the just rights and reasonable demands of all concerned would be earnestly promoted by him by all the means which the Constitution and laws of this country place at his disposal.

"It is now some nine or ten months since the nature and prospects of the insurrection were first discussed between us. In explanation of its rapid and, up to that time, quite unopposed growth and progress you called attention to the rainy season, which, from May or June until November, renders regular military operations impracticable. Spain was pouring such numbers of troops into Cuba that your theory and opinion that, when they could be used in an active campaign, the insurrection would be almost instantly suppressed, seemed reasonable and probable. In this particular you believed—and sincerely believed—that the present insurrection would offer a most marked contrast to that which began in 1868, and which, being feebly encountered with comparatively small forces, prolonged its life for upward of ten years.

"It is impossible to deny that the expectations thus entertained by you in the summer and fall of 1895, and shared not merely by all Spaniards, but by most disinterested observers as well, have been completely disappointed. The insurgents seem to-day to command a larger part of the island than ever before. Their men under arms, estimated a year ago at from ten to twenty thousand, are now conceded to be at least two or three times as many. Meanwhile, their discipline has been improved and their supply of modern weapons and equipment has been greatly enlarged, while the mere fact that they have held out to this time has given them confidence in their own eyes and prestige with the world at large. In short, it can hardly be questioned that the insurrection, instead of being quelled, is to-day more formidable than ever and enters upon the second year of its existence with decidedly improved prospects of successful results.

"Whether a condition of things entitling the insurgents to recognition as belligerents has yet been brought about may, for the purposes of the present communication, be regarded as immaterial. If it has not been, it is because they are still without an established and organized civil government having an ascertained situs, presiding over a defined territory, controlling the armed forces in the field, and not only fulfilling the functions of a regular government within its own frontiers, but capable internationally of exercising those powers and discharging those obligations which necessarily devolve upon every member of the family of nations. It is immaterial for present purposes that such is the present political status of the insurgents, because their defiance of the authority of Spain remains none the less pronounced and successful and their displacement of that authority throughout a very large portion of the island is none the less obvious and real. When in 1877 the president of the so-called Cuban republic was captured, its legislative chamber surprised in the mountains and dispersed, and its presiding officer and other principal functionaries killed, it was asserted in some quarters that the insurrection had received its death-blow and might well be deemed to be extinct. The leading organ of the insurrectionists, however, made this response:

"'The organization of the liberating party is such that a brigade, a regiment, a battalion, a company, or a party of twenty-five men can operate independently against the enemy in any department without requiring any instructions save those of their immediate military officers, because their purpose is but one, and that is known by heart, as well by the general as his soldier, by the negro as well as the white man or the Chinese, viz., to make war on the enemy at all times, in all places, and by all means; with the gun, the machete, and the firebrand. In order to do this, which is the duty of every Cuban soldier, the direction of a government or a legislative chamber is not needed; the order of a subaltern officer, serving under the general in chief, is sufficient. Thus it is that *the government and chamber have in reality been a superfluous luxury for the revolution.*'

"The situation thus vividly described in 1877 is reproduced to-day. Even if it be granted that a condition of insurgency prevails and nothing more, it is on so large a scale and diffused over so extensive a region, and is so favored by the physical features and the climate of the country, that the authority of Spain is subverted and the functions of its government are in abeyance or practically suspended throughout a great part of the island. Spain still holds the seaports and most, if not all, of the large towns in the interior. Nevertheless a vast area of the territory of the island is in effect under the control of roving bands of insurgents, which, if driven from one place to-day by an exhibition of superior force, abandon it only to return to-morrow when that force has moved on for their dislodgment in other quarters. The consequence of this state of things cannot be disguised. Outside of the town, still under Spanish rule, anarchy, lawlessness, and terrorism are rampant. The insurgents realize that the wholesale destruction of crops, factories, and machinery advances their cause in two ways. It cripples the resources of Spain on the one hand; on the other, it drives into their ranks the laborers who are thus thrown out of employment. The result is a systematic war upon the industries of the island and upon all the means by which they are carried on, and whereas the normal annual product of the island is valued at something like eighty or a hundred millions, its value for the present year is estimated by competent authority as not exceeding twenty millions. Bad as is this showing for the present year, it must be even worse for the next year, and for every succeeding year during which the rebellion continues to live. Some planters have made their crops this year who will not be allowed to make them again. Some have worked their fields and operated their mills this year in the face of a certain loss, who have neither the heart nor the means to do so again, under the present even more depressing conditions. Not only is it certain that no fresh money is being invested on the island, but it is no secret that capital is fast withdrawing from it, frightened away by the hopelessness of the outlook. Why should it not be? What can a prudent man foresee as the outcome of existing conditions except the complete devastation of the island, the entire annihilation of its industries, and the absolute impoverishment of such of its inhabitants as are unwise or unfortunate enough not to seasonably escape from it. The last preceding insurrection lasted for ten years and then was not subdued, but only succumbed to the influence of certain promised reforms. Where is found the promise that the present rebellion will have a shorter lease of life, unless the end is sooner reached through the exhaustion of Spain herself? Taught by experience, Spain wisely undertook to make its struggle with the present insurrection short, sharp, and decisive; to stamp it out in its very beginning by concentrating upon it large and well-organized armies—armies infinitely superior in numbers, in discipline, and in equipment to any the insurgents could oppose to them. Those armies were put under the command of its ablest general as well as its most renowned statesman—of one whose very name was an assurance to the insurgents both of the skilful generalship with which they would be fought and of the reasonable and liberal temper in which just demands for redress of grievances would be received. Yet the efforts of Campos seem to have utterly failed, and his successor, a man who, rightfully or wrongfully, seems to have intensified all the acerbities of the struggle, is now being reenforced with additional troops. It may well be feared, therefore, that if the present is to be of shorter duration than the last insurrection, it will be because the end is to come sooner or later through the inability of Spain to prolong the conflict, and through her abandonment of the island to the heterogeneous combination of elements and of races now in arms against her. Such a conclusion of the struggle cannot be viewed even by the most devoted friend of Cuba and the most enthusiastic advocate of popular government, except with the gravest apprehension. There are only too strong reasons to fear that, once Spain were withdrawn from the island, the sole bond of union between the different factions of the insurgents would disappear; that a war of races would be precipitated, all the more sanguinary for the discipline and experience acquired during the insurrection; and that, even if there were to be temporary peace, it could only be through the establishment of a white and a black republic, which, even if agreeing at the outset upon a division of the island between them, would be enemies from the start, and would never rest until the one had been completely vanquished and subdued by the other.

"The situation thus described is of great interest to the people of the United States. They are interested in any struggle anywhere for freer political institutions, but necessarily and in special measure in a struggle that is raging almost in sight of our shores. They are interested, as a civilized and Christian nation, in the speedy termination of a civil strife characterized by exceptional bitterness and exceptional excesses on the part of both combatants. They are interested in the non-interruption of extensive trade relations which have been, and should continue to be, of great advantage to both countries. They are interested in the prevention of that wholesale destruction of property on the island which, making no discrimination between enemies and neutrals, is utterly destroying American investments that should be of immense value and is utterly impoverishing great numbers of American citizens. On all these grounds and in all these ways the interest of the United States in the existing situation in Cuba yields in extent only to that of Spain herself, and has led many good and honest persons to insist that intervention to terminate the conflict is the immediate and imperative duty of the United States. It is not proposed to now consider whether existing conditions would justify such intervention at the present time, or how much longer those conditions should be endured before such intervention would be justified. That the United States cannot contemplate with complacency another ten years of Cuban insurrection, with all its injurious and distressing incidents, may certainly be taken for granted. The object of the present communication, however, is not to discuss intervention, nor to propose intervention, nor to pave the way for intervention. The purpose is exactly the reverse—to suggest whether a solution of present troubles cannot be found which will prevent all thought of intervention by rendering it unnecessary. What the United States desires to do, if the way can be pointed out, is to co-operate with Spain in the immediate pacification of the island on such a plan as, leaving Spain her rights of sovereignty, shall yet secure to the people of the island all such rights and powers of local self-government as they can reasonably ask. To that end, the United States offers and will use her good offices at such time and in such manner as may be deemed most advisable. Its mediation, it is believed, should not be rejected in any quarter since none could misconceive or mistrust its purpose. Spain could not, because our respect for her sovereignty and our determination to do nothing to impair it have been maintained for many years at great cost, and in spite of many temptations. The insurgents could not, because anything assented to by this government which did not satisfy the reasonable demands and aspirations of Cuba, would arouse the indignation of our whole people. It only remains to suggest that, if anything can be done in the direction indicated, it should be done at once and on the initiative of Spain. The more the contest is prolonged, the more bitter and more irreconcilable is the antagonism created, while there is danger that concessions may be so delayed as to be chargeable to weakness and fear of the issue of the contest, and thus be infinitely less acceptable and persuasive than if made while the result still hangs in balance, and they could be properly credited, in some degree at least, to a sense of right and justice. Thus far Spain has faced the insurrection sword in hand, and has made no sign to show that surrender and submission would be followed by anything but a return to the old order of things. Would it not be wise to modify that policy and to accompany the application of military force with an authentic declaration of the organic changes that are meditated in the administration of the island with a view to remove all just grounds of complaint? It is for Spain to consider and determine what those changes would be. But should they be such that the United States could urge their adoption as substantially removing well-founded grievances, its influence would be exerted for their acceptance, and, it can hardly be doubted, would be most potential for the termination of hostilities and the restoration of peace and order to the island. One result of the course of proceeding outlined, if no other, would be sure to follow, namely, that the rebellion would lose largely, if not altogether, the moral countenance and support it now enjoys from the people of the United States.

"In closing this communication, it is hardly necessary to repeat that it is prompted by the friendliest feeling toward Spain and the Spanish people. To attribute to the United States any hostile or hidden purposes would be a grave and most lamentable error. The United States has no designs upon Cuba and no designs against the sovereignty of Spain. Neither is it actuated by any spirit of meddlesomeness nor by any desire to force its will upon another nation. Its geographical proximity and all the considerations above detailed compel it to be interested in the solution of the Cuban problem, whether it will or no. Its only anxiety is that the solution should be speedy, and by being founded on truth and justice should also be permanent. To aid in that solution it offers the suggestions herein contained. They will be totally misapprehended unless the United States be credited with entertaining no other purpose toward Spain than that of lending its assistance to such termination of a fratricidal contest as will leave honor and dignity unimpaired at the same time that it promotes and conserves the true interests of all parties concerned.

"I avail myself, etc.,
"RICHARD OLNEY."[1]

This very important document, temperate, wise, and abounding in good counsel, the sending of which at this moment was evidently dictated by an administration which wished Spain well and which frankly but in the most friendly manner set before the Spanish government the realities of the situation, was carried to Madrid by one of the secretaries of the Spanish legation at Washington. A full month intervened between its arrival and the sending of a reply, May 22, 1896.

In the meantime two important events occurred: The one, the capture by an armed launch of the schooner *Competitor* and her crew of five men, which had just landed an expedition of fifty-nine men near Punta Berracos, west of Havana, and the sentence to death of the crew by a summary court-martial, regardless of existing conventions as to the trial of the Americans aboard; the other, the reading, on May 11, at the opening of the Spanish parliament, of a speech from the Queen Regent, which practically anticipated the reply of the American note, and, no doubt, was so intended.

After an historical summary of the contest, the speech, says De Olivart, proclaimed "that the Spanish nation was always ready to pardon and to make peace; that, in the unanimous opinion of all true friends of Spain in the Antilles, an immediate application of

[1] *Spanish Corres. and Docs.*, 4–8.

reforms and a change of political organization while the strife was in full vigor, far from favoring the solution of the problem, would but make it more difficult.[1] One has to consider from the government's point of view that the insurrectionist forces were already much weakened, and, if they were not more so, it was by reason of the protection and aid which the insurgents received from abroad and from the chimerical hope that one day, misunderstanding the law of nations, their cause would be taken in hand by a great nation. Having said this, the Queen Regent solemnly affirmed that 'once the insurrection reached an end, it would be indispensable, in order that a solid peace should be established, to give the Antilles an administrative and economic personality which would render the part taken by the country in its own affairs easy and expeditious, all the while safeguarding the rights of Spanish sovereignty and leaving intact the conditions necessary to its maintenance; it is to this end that the efforts of the government shall tend.' "[2]

Almost at the same moment the Cuban president, Estrada Palma (at New York, be it said), was putting forth a manifesto which declared that "with few exceptions the idea could come to no one in the United States of supporting any project destined to put an end to the actual strife which should not have as a base the independence of Cuba." He continued: "It is useless to speak of reforms and even of a large autonomy. To hold such language would be to create illusions and lose time which could be profitably used to avoid the ruin and desolation of the island. The revolution is powerful, it is incarnate in the Cuban people, and there exists no power, neither Spanish nor human, which can arrest it in its course."[3]

The queen's speech foreshadowed, as mentioned, the reply to the American note. This reply, though signed by the Duke of Tetuan as foreign minister, was of course the work of the forceful head of the ministry, Señor Cánovas. Dated at Madrid, May 22,

[1] Says Señor de Olivart in a note to his discussion of this speech: "The events which occurred in the last days of 1897 and the early ones of 1898 show the justice of this affirmation, which seemed when made paradoxical." He ignores that there was to intervene a full year and a half of struggle of increasing bitterness.
[2] De Olivart, *Revue Générale de Droit International Public*, IX (1902), 169.
[3] In the *Republica Cubana*, May 14, 1896, De Olivart, *Ibid.*, 170.

1896, it was embodied in a note from the Spanish minister at Washington to Mr. Olney, June 4. The original, in full, was as follows:

"Madrid, *May* 22, 1896.

"Excellency: In due course I received your excellency's despatch of the 10th of last April, accompanied by the original note of Mr. Olney, of the 4th of the same month, regarding the Cuban situation, and by the literal translation which your excellency has made of said note.

"The importance of the communication from the government of Washington has led the government of his majesty to examine it with the greatest care, and to postpone an answer until such times as its own views on the complicated and delicate Cuban question should be made public. In this way the previous voluntary decisions of the Spanish government may serve, as they are now serving, as the basis of the reply. The ample and liberal purposes made known to the Cortes by the august lips of his majesty in the speech from the throne permit the taking up of the matter in all sincerity.

"The government of his majesty fully appreciates the noble frankness with which the government of the United States has advised it of the very definite views it has formed touching the juridical impossibility of recognizing the Cuban insurgents as belligerents. Indeed, those who are fighting in Cuba against the integrity of the Spanish mother country do not possess any qualifications which entitle them to the respect or even the consideration of other nations; they do not possess—as the secretary of state expresses it—an established and organized civil government, with a known seat and administration of defined territory; and they have not succeeded in permanently occupying any town, much less any city, large or small. It is impossible, therefore—as the secretary of state also said, voluntarily, and with great legal acumen—for the Cuban insurgents to perform the functions of a regular government within their own frontiers, and much less to exercise the rights and fulfil the obligations that are incumbent on all the members of the family of nations. Moreover, their systematic campaign of destruction against all the industries of the island, and the means by which the campaign is carried on, would of itself be sufficient to keep them without the pale of the rules of international law universally recognized and applicable to the case, leaving to them the character to which they are entitled by their acts of vandalism and destruction.

"No less gratifying to the government of his majesty has been the explicit and spontaneous declaration that the government of the United States seeks no advantage in connection with the Cuban question, its only wish and purpose being that the ineluctable and lawful sovereignty of Spain be conserved and even strengthened through the submission of the rebels, which, as the secretary of state himself declares, is of paramount necessity to the Spanish government in order to maintain its authority and honor. No less could have been expected from the lofty sense of right cherished by the government of the United States, and the government of his majesty recognizes with pleasure all the weight carried by the emphatic declarations of Mr. Olney touching the sovereignty of Spain and the decision of the United States not to do anything derogatory to it. In view of so correct and so friendly an attitude it is unnecessary to discuss, as Mr. Olney remarks, the hypothesis of intervention, which would be inconsistent with the aforesaid views.

"There can be no greater accuracy of judgment than that displayed by the secretary of state touching the future of the island of Cuba in the event, which cannot and shall not be, of the insurrection terminating in its triumph. As Mr. Olney says, with much reason, such a termination of the conflict would be looked upon with the most serious misgivings, even by the most enthusiastic advocates of popular government, because, as he rightly adds, with the heterogeneous combination of races that exist there the disappearance of Spain would be the disappearance of the only bond of union which can keep them in balance and prevent an inevitable struggle among the men of different color, contrary to the spirit of Christian civilization. The accuracy of the statement of the secretary of state is the more striking as, owing to the conditions of population on the island, no part of the natives can be conceded superiority over the others, if the assistance of the European Spaniards is not taken into account.

"The island of Cuba has been exclusively Spanish from its discovery; the great normal development of its resources, whatever they are, whatever their value, and whatever they represent in the community of mankind, is due entirely to the mother country; and even at this day, among the diverse groups that inhabit it, whatever be the stand-point from which the question is examined, the natives of the Peninsula are absolutely necessary there for the peace and advancement of the island.

"All these reasons clearly demonstrate that it is not possible to think that any benefit can come to the island of Cuba except through the agency of Spain, acting under her own convictions, and actuated, as she has long been, by principles of liberty and justice. The Spanish government is aware that, far from having justice done it on all sides on these points, there are many persons obviously deceived by incessant calumnies who honestly believe that a ferocious despotism prevails in our Antilles, instead of one of the most liberal political systems in the world being enjoyed there now, as well as before the insurrection. One need only glance over the legislation governing the Antilles—laws which ought to be sufficiently known in the United States at this day—to perceive how absolutely groundless such opinions are. A collection of the Cuban newspapers published in recent years would suffice to show that few civilized countries then enjoyed in an equal degree freedom of thought and of the press—the foundation of all liberty.

"Naturally the government of his majesty and the people of Spain wish and even long for the early pacification of Cuba. In order to secure it they are ready to exert their utmost efforts and at the same time to adopt such reforms as may be useful or necessary and compatible, of course, with their inalienable sovereignty, as soon as the submission of the insurgents be an accomplished fact. It is truly gratifying to me here to observe that our opinions on this point coincide with those of the secretary of state.

"No one, on the other hand, is more fully aware of the serious evils suffered by Spaniards and aliens in consequence of the insurrection than the government of his majesty. It realizes the immense injury inflicted on Spain by the putting forth, with the unanimous co-operation and approbation of her people, of such efforts as were never before made in America by any European country. It knows, at the same time, that the interests of foreign industry and trade suffer—as well as the Spanish interests—by the system of devastation of the insurgents. But if the insurrection should triumph the interests of all would not merely suffer, but would entirely and forever disappear amid the furors of perpetual anarchy.

"It has already been said that in order to avoid evils of such magnitude the cabinet of Madrid does not and will not confine itself exclusively to the employment of armed force. The speech from the throne, read before the national representation, promised, *motu proprio*, not only that all that was previously granted would be carried into effect as soon as opportunity offers, but also, by fresh authorization of the Cortes, all that which may appear to be necessary to amplify and extend the original reforms, to the end that both Antilles may, in the administrative department, enjoy a *personnel* of a local character; that the intervention of the mother country may be dispensed with in their domestic affairs, with the limit merely that the rights of sovereignty be not impaired, or the powers of the government to preserve the same. This solemn promise, guaranteed by the august word of his majesty, will be fulfilled by the Spanish government with a true liberality of views. The foregoing facts, being better known every day, will make it patent to the just people of other nations that Spain, far from proposing that her subjects in the West Indies should return to a régime unfit for the times, when she enjoys such liberal laws, would never have withheld these same laws from the islands but for the incessant separatist conspiracies, which compelled her to look above all to self-defence.

"Under the promises thus made I entertain the confidence that the government of the United States will readily see that Spain, while grateful in the highest degree for the kind advice bestowed, has forestalled it for a long time past. It follows, therefore, as a matter of course, it will comply with it in a practical manner as soon as circumstances make it possible. But Mr. Olney will have seen by the public press that already the insurgents, elated by the strength which they have acquired through the aid of a certain number of citizens of the United States, have contemptuously repelled, through the medium of the Cubans residing in that country, any idea that the government of Washington can intervene in the contest, either with its advice or in any other manner, on the supposition that the declarations of disinterestedness of the government of the United States are false, and that it wishes to get possession of that island in the future. Hence it is evident that no success would attend such possible mediation, which they repel, even admitting that the mother country would condescend to treat with its rebellious subjects, as one power with another, thus certainly jeopardizing its future authority, detracting from its natural dignity, and injuriously affecting its independence, for which it has always shown so jealous a care in all times, as history teaches. In brief, there is no effectual way to pacify Cuba apart from the actual submission of the armed rebels to the mother country.

"Notwithstanding this, the government of the United States could, by use of proper means, contribute greatly to the pacification of the island of Cuba. The government of his majesty is already very grateful for the intention of the United States to prosecute the unlawful expeditions of some of its citizens to Cuba with more vigor than in the past, after making a judicial investigation to determine the adequacy of its laws, when honestly enforced. Still, the high moral sense of the government of Washington will undoubtedly suggest to it other more effectual means of preventing from henceforth what is now the case, the prolongation of a struggle so close to its borders and so injurious to its commerce and trade (which Mr. Olney justly deplores) being especially due to the powerful assistance which the rebellion finds in the territory of the great American Republic, against the wishes of the larger part of its population. The constant violation of international law is especially manifest on the part of Cuban emigrants, who care nothing for the losses suffered in the interim by the citizens of the United States and of Spain through the prolongation of the war.

"The Spanish government, on its part, has already done much and will do more each day in order to achieve so desirable an end, by endeavoring to correct the mistakes of public opinion in the United States and by exposing the plots and calumnies of its rebellious subjects. It may well happen that the declarations recently made in the most solemn form by the government of his majesty concerning its intentions for the future, will also contribute in large measure to gratify the wish expressed by Mr. Olney that all the people of the United States, convinced that the right is with us, will completely cease to extend unlawful aid to the insurgents.

"If, with such an object in view, the government of the United States—which shows itself so hopeful that the justice of Spain may be recognized by all—should desire additional information to that it already has upon the Cuban question, the government of his majesty will have the greatest pleasure in supplying it with the most accurate details. When the government of the United States shall once be convinced of our being in the right, and that honest conviction shall in some manner be made public, but little more will be required in order that all those in Cuba who are not striving merely to accomplish the total ruin of the beautiful country in which they were born, being then without hope of outside aid and powerless by themselves, will lay down their arms.

"Until that happy state of things has been attained, Spain, in the just defence not only of her rights, but also of her duty and honor, will continue the efforts for an early victory which she is now exerting, regardless of the greatest sacrifices.

" In these terms you will reply to the above-mentioned note from Mr. Olney.
"Dios, etc.,
"The Duke of Tetuan."

Señor de Lome wrote, June 11, 1896, to the Spanish minister of state: "The secretary of state, whom I have seen to-day, has shown himself very reserved, understanding that the note contains a courteous refusal to the government of his majesty to accept the good offices of the United States, and showing an interest in being informed at the proper time of the discussion of matters concerning the island, and the propositions of law which are presented to the Cortes, because he believes that the situation here and in Cuba must be bettered." [1] This last was an ominous sentence, the weight of which neither Señor Cánovas nor Señor de Lome seemed to appreciate.

The American note was, indeed, the turning-point of the affairs of Spain. Its rejection meant, could only mean as a finality, the forcible intervention by the United States, and war. The Spanish

[1] *Spanish Diplomatic Correspondence*, 1896–1900, 13.

government saw in the American proposals, despite the earnest assurances to the contrary, a desire to acquire the island. It looked back over the three-quarters of a century, which had begun with a frank declaration of covetousness, which had culminated in the Ostend manifesto, and to the repeated wishes to acquire the island which had only ceased with the war between the States in 1861. It was unable to recognize the changed attitude toward Cuba of the American mind, already more than sufficiently concerned with a race question of its own, and which desired no addition to such a weighty difficulty as was involved in Cuban annexation.

It was again the question of *pundonor*, the sensitiveness which would not brook the interference of a foreign power with the affairs of Spain. But interference of some sort was certain. The only question was whether it should be friendly and in support of Spain's dominancy, or unfriendly and disruptive of her American dominion. Señor Cánovas, though no doubt he did not forecast the latter as a result of the despatch of the minister of state of May 22, deliberately, in his ignorance of the American mind, risked the latter alternative. A country, the king of which had in 1823 invited the occupancy of its entire territory by a foreign army which was to hold the land for years from the Pyrenees to Cadiz, could well afford the friendly aid and counsel, to be given in all confidence, which the American department of state stood ready to offer. Had an autonomy been offered on principles thus agreed upon, meeting, as it necessarily must have done in order to be approved, Anglo-Saxon ideas of free government, a non-acceptance by the Cubans would have totally destroyed American sympathy. The result in such case, it is not too much to say, would have been a deep revulsion of American feeling. Every moral aid possible on the part of the United States would have been at the command of Spain. There can scarcely, despite the pronouncement of Estrada Palma for nothing short of independence, have been any question as to the result.

As it was, the note sounded the knell of Spanish dominion in Cuba. The Spanish minister in Washington was warned by the American secretary of state, in a friendly conversation going beyond the usual limits of official reserve, of the danger of awaiting the coming to power of a new administration, which might not be able to hold so well in hand the forces antagonistic to Spain. But Cánovas, with mind cast in the same mould with that of Philip II, was determined to first assert the authority of Spain over the insurgents, as Philip was determined to assert the authority of a unified religion over all races of the Peninsula, whatever the cost to Spain. Ruin followed the policy of the one as of the other. [1]

[1] Says the Marquis de Olivart: " From confidential information which we have received (and which we are ready to rectify if it is not exact) we are led to believe that General Martinez Campos and the minister of state himself, the Duke of Tetuan, had been partisans of a different reply in the first days of the discussion of the American proposition at Madrid. They would have preferred that, in one form or another, the proposition made by the government of the United States should be accepted." (*Revue Générale de Droit International Public*, IX (1902), 171.)

CHAPTER XXIII

THE CASE OF THE "COMPETITOR."—THE ANNUAL MESSAGE OF 1896.—THE ACTION IN CONGRESS

THE affair of the *Competitor* came to accentuate the gravity of Spain's decision. This schooner, April 20, 1896, had cleared from Key West for Port Lemon, Fla., with twenty-four passengers; her crew was composed of the master, Laborde; Gildea, mate; Leavitt and Barnett, seamen; and Gurk, the cook. There was also aboard a young man from Kansas, named Melton, a newspaper correspondent.

Off Cape Sable, April 22, if we are to believe the affidavits of the master, mate, and Melton, which in the circumstances need to be taken with doubt, the passengers took charge by force, went to Cape Sable, and there received twenty-five others, with arms and ammunition. The schooner reached the north shore of Cuba at Point Berracos, some seventy miles west of Havana, April 25, and there landed her passengers and material. Shortly after she was sighted by the Spanish armed launch, *Mensajora*. There were aboard the schooner at this moment, Laborde, Gildea, Melton, and three passengers, Vedia, Masa, and Quesada. The two seamen and the cook had gone ashore.[1] Laborde, Gildea, and Quesada attempted to escape by swimming ashore; the two first were seized in the water, but the last was drowned. All the others were taken to Havana where they arrived May 29.

Laborde claimed to be born in New Orleans of Cuban parents; Gildea, born in Liverpool, was a British subject, but both were entitled under article 171 of the American Consular Regulations to American protection.[2] The consul-general at once demanded that the case should come under the terms of the treaty of 1795 and the protocol of 1877.

[1] The seamen were captured on May 11 and taken to Havana.
[2] This article, based on statutes, reads:
"That the circumstance that the vessel is American is evidence that the

The extended and active correspondence of the next few days (from the 7th to the 9th of May) developed the views of the judge-advocate that "foreigners without distinction of nationality are subject to the laws and courts of Spain for crimes committed within Spanish territory"; that whatever interpretation "may be given to the treaty and its meaning given by the protocol, this [latter] from its beginning declares it only embraces resident American citizens, and these only in the case of not being arrested with arms in hand," circumstances which he claimed "do not concur in the present case." He also assumed that foreigners must be inscribed in the register of the provincial governments and at their consulates in order to be regarded residents, and that the law of April, 1821, invoked by the consul-general was derogated by Spanish laws of subsequent enactment.[1]

The judge-advocate finally extended his views sufficiently to declare the protocol of 1877 an expression only of private opinion; that it was not "even an addition nor complement of any pre-existing treaty,"[2] to all of which the consul-general steadily replied that the treaty of 1795 was still existent, that the protocol could in no wise detract from the force of the treaty, and that in the interpretation of the protocol the latter must "conform to the treaty, and not the treaty to the protocol."[3]

The summary court proceeded with the case and on May 8 pronounced sentence of death upon all with the exception of the man Masa. But already, in response to a request from Washington, May 1, telegraphic instructions had arrived from Madrid

crew on board are such, and that in every regularly documented vessel, the crew will find their protection in the flag which covers them."

The British consul-general, requesting Consul-General Williams, May 8, to extend his aid to Gildea, said: "As I understand the *Competitor* is an American vessel, it appears to me that you alone are competent to intervene." On hearing, on the 8th, of the sentence of death, Mr. Gollan (the British consul-general) wrote the governor-general and admiral requesting suspension of execution until he could telegraph the British Foreign Office. On the 9th the admiral informed him that, in deference to his wishes, he had telegraphed the government at Madrid. On the 10th he was informed that the execution had been suspended and that the case had been remitted to the supreme council of war. *Foreign Relations*, 1896, 731, 732.

[1] Judge-advocate to commander-in-chief of West Indian Station (under whom the case came), May 7, 1896, Senate Doc. 79, 54 Cong., 2 Sess., 211.
[2] *Ibid.*, 216. [3] *Ibid.*, 209–217.

suspending all executive action until examination could be made as to the citizenship of the prisoners,[1] and the entire record shortly after was ordered sent to Madrid for review, the final outcome being the release, November, 1897, of all the prisoners, including the two seamen escaped ashore who were captured May 11.

But this unhappy case, which, if dealt with with greater judgment, would probably have helped the cause of Spain, aroused deepest feeling in Cuba, the Peninsula, and the United States. Both at Havana and Madrid the public demanded that the prisoners be shot as pirates, while in Washington it was seized upon as a new and terrible case of martyrdom of heroes of Cuban liberty and independence.[2]

Before the question had become imminent, Senator Call, on May 5, demanded that Congress should request the President to protest against the execution of the *Competitor* prisoners, and endeavor to obtain for them the treatment of prisoners of war. Senator Morgan made a violent speech, May 15, ending in declaring that all relations should be suspended with the Spanish government until the proceedings of the court at Havana should have been annulled. The resolution which he offered, calling for the correspondence in the case, was adopted by the committee on foreign affairs and by the Senate, but the President refused to communicate the correspondence. On June 3 and 5 Senator Morgan appealed to the statutes giving all citizens of the United States abroad the protection of their government,[3] declaring that every day passed by the *Competitor* prisoners in confinement and under sentence of death was a day of black dishonor for the United States.[4]

As just said, less precipitancy and a greater regard for existing treaties by the Havana authorities would have saved much to Spain. The able publicist so often quoted, and who has dealt with the subject of Spanish and American differences throughout in so broad and enlightened a way, finds them, without reserve, in the wrong. The application of the procedure of the summary court-

---

[1] Mr. Taylor to Mr. Olney, May 4, 1896, Senate Doc. 79, 54 Cong., 2 Sess., 202.
[2] De Olivart, *Revue Générale de Droit International Public*, IX (1902), 195.
[3] Sections 2000 and 2001.
[4] *Cong. Record*, June 5, 1896, p. 6718.

martial "supposes," he says, "that the capture is proven at the instant of the perpetration of the crime, or during an uninterrupted pursuit, or finally because effects or instruments which show participation in the crime are found upon the accused; [the summary court thus] can only apply in a case where the crime is punishable by death or perpetual chains. The *Competitor* was arrested; pursuit was then impossible. As to arms, none were found but in the pocket of Vedia; Melton [Laborde] and Gildea were absolutely disarmed in the water. . . . The prisoners having surrendered on demand and having offered no resistance, an inferior punishment, by two degrees, had to be applied: submission to the procedure of a summary court was thenceforward no longer possible. If considered as executive agents they were still less punishable, for in this case they could only be condemned to prison under article 231.

"The allegations of the assessor were erroneous. It is not possible to refuse the character of an international treaty to the protocol of 1877, by reducing it to a simple diplomatic conversation. Besides, it cannot be said that trial by a summary court gives the same guarantees of justice and defence as does an ordinary court-martial. We must maintain . . . that the Spanish courts had to hold to their substantial laws of procedure. It was no less the duty of the government to suspend the execution of a judgment the accord of which with existing international stipulations was doubtful. It was indisputable that judgment had been pronounced despite the provisions of the protocol and of almost all the articles relative to American citizens taken arms in hand. It was the very grave situation which was had in view at the time of the signature of the agreement. It was equally certain that in the trial the rules of the law of 1821[1] had not been followed. It may well be allowed that this was abrogated, so far as Spanish law was concerned, by later laws; but in international law it bound Spain so far as the citizens of the United States were concerned. The only point truly doubtful was this: Was the protocol applicable to individuals non-resident in Spanish territory, but coming there only to commit a crime? At first view, both good sense and patriotism would

[1] For the decree in full, establishing this law, see *Cong. Record*, 54 Cong., 2 Sess., 2227.

incline one to say no. If the real soldiers of the expedition, and in great number, had been taken, very few Spaniards would have dared to sustain that a contrary solution would have been admissible. Consul [-General] Williams and Mr. Olney replied that a treaty gives the same rights to subjects of the two contracting states. Consequently the guarantees of a *fair trial* being assured to all Spaniards *finding themselves* in the territory of the Union, an identic situation had to be allowed to all Americans *finding themselves* in Spanish territory, whatever the time and reason of their presence. The argument has a certain force. One should, nevertheless, make some difference between the tourist and traveller (cases cited by the Americans) who, *being* in a foreign land, commit a crime or mix in a conspiracy, and the filibuster who carries aid and succor to a revolt.

"The important point to our mind," continues the Marquis de Olivart, "was the general spirit of the protocol. This, in effect, had for its object to protect *completely*, by avoiding the precipitate action and the severities of the Spanish military authorities, the American citizens concerned in attempts against the sovereignty of Spain. It thus derogated a fixed principle of international law, by virtue of which no account of nationality should be taken in repressing such crimes. This it was that irritated the dignity and good sense of the Spaniards. But once the exception admitted, it mattered little that the foreign individual thus privileged came openly to fight a nation friendly to his own, or did so secretly, in violating the sacred laws of hospitality. It is evident that if the point in question had been a clause of an ordinary treaty, such as article 7 of the treaty of 1795, the pretension of the American government would have been inadmissible. On the other hand, in presence of an unfair stipulation (*une stipulation de mauvaise foi*), if one can thus express himself in speaking of the protocol, one had to undergo the consequences of this want of candor (*mauvaise foi*). It had to recognize that trial by an ordinary court-martial under the forms of the laws of 1821 was the worst which could happen to an American citizen brought before Spanish tribunals." [1]

It was most unfortunate that this excellent common-sense should not have been recognized in the beginning. Whatever the general

[1] De Olivart, *Revue Générale de Droit International Public*, IX, 200.

principle of international law (and it is unquestionably correctly stated by the distinguished and candid author quoted), the exception (and it practically was an exception in favor of Americans in view of the unlikelihood of reversed conditions) was a necessity to the preservation of peace. It was the precipitancy mentioned which the American government was so anxious to avoid; and its curbing was in the interest of Spain far more than in its own. To have allowed the continuance of such precipitancy as that in the case of the *Virginius* sufferers; to have yielded full swing to the Oriental idea that death swiftly dealt was the only true means of repression, would have been, throughout the insurrection, to court war between Spain and the United States. The Spanish home government had come to see this; the official in Cuba could never be brought to open his eyes fully to it. It was the tenacious holding to this view of sudden and severe vengeance by the latter which, more than all else, the effects of reconcentration excepted, finally brought war in 1898.

"Hasty in form and excessively severe *au fond*," says De Olivart, "the sentence of death [in the case of the *Competitor* crew] was wisely and prudently suspended by Señor Cánovas. Thus was put off for two years the opening of hostilities. The decision of the supreme council of war taken in the last days of August, 1896, which ordered a new trial of the case by an ordinary court-martial was a yielding to equity and law. It showed, besides, that excessive severity and harshness are much less efficacious than respect for law. For the first time one has not forgotten that to go step by step in affairs in which foreigners are interested, and as a consequence their governments, is nevertheless, to go faster.

"The matter here rested. It was out of mind during the rest of the governments of Señor Cánovas and of Mr. Cleveland, and during a part of those of Mr. McKinley and Señor Sagasta. In November, 1897, the accused were liberated. This compromise, express or tacit, was the only solution possible at the moment. A new trial would have ended either in the acquittal of the three terrible pirates, or at most, and this would have been about the same thing, their condemnation to very light penalties. Such a solution would have exasperated public opinion at Havana and Madrid to a paroxysm; Madrid could never have been persuaded of its justice; to have confirmed the first sentence and caused its execution, would have given to the jingoes and insurgents a pretext of war. It is the *ridiculus mus* of the fableist which emerges from the whole of this affair. It teaches us but one very melancholy lesson. It shows clearly what Spain could do after three years' watch of its coast by the navy: the capture of one empty vessel and the arrest of two swimmers and three filibusters, one of whom had to be pardoned in order to condemn the others . . . *on paper.*"[1]

But it taught more: it showed the ineradicable idea in the mind of the Spanish official that death without delay must be measured out to certain offenders despite treaties or conventions. Nor were the offences over heinous to the world at large; but they were such as to which the Spaniard and his forbears had been accustomed to applying the last penalty. It mattered little what the rest of the world called piracy or rebellion; to him, and under his decrees in Cuba, the five unarmed men of the *Competitor* were both pirates and rebels, though no robbery or violence upon the sea, which alone under the law of nations constitutes piracy, had been committed; and no allegiance to the King of Spain was claimed by the authorities to exist in the case of three at least, without which there could be no rebellion. The game was not worth the candle. The *Competitor* affair, small in itself, was made momentously large by folly, and went far to fix in the American mind an idea of Spanish bloodthirst and cruelty which had its reflex in the declaration, in the platform of the Republican convention which in June nominated Mr. McKinley for president, of the "best hopes" for the "full success" of the Cuban insurgents, and the expression of the belief that "the United States should actively use its influence and good offices to restore peace and give independence to the island."[2] This conviction was soon to be made ineradicable by the effects of the decree which, first ordering a partial concentration of the rural population of Cuba,[3] was later to be made general.

[1] De Olivart, *Revue Générale de Droit, International Public*, 202.
[2] McKee, *National Conventions and Platforms*, 303.
[3] This decree was as follows:

HAVANA, October 21, 1896.

Don Valeriano Weyler y Nicolau, Marquis of Teneriffe, Governor-General and Captain-General of this Island, and General in Chief of its Army, etc.:
I order and command:
First. All the inhabitants of the country or outside of the line of fortifications of the towns shall, within the period of eight days, concentrate them-

In strict fairness one is obliged to say that the merciless plundering by the insurgents of loyalist plantations, the burning of cane fields, and the ruthless destruction of costly estates, whether belonging to loyalists or to sympathizers with the insurrection, or to Cuban or foreign owners, the protection of which by detachments of Spanish troops took largely from the efficiency of the army, called for action of drastic character. The grievous error of the Spanish government was in disregarding the precautions which should have been taken to feed the people thus herded together. Apparently none such were taken. Driven into the garrisoned places, their huts burned, their fields destroyed, their live stock driven away or killed, without adequate shelter, or in most cases without shelter of any kind, without agricultural tools for cultivating the zones set aside in some instances for cultivation, the wretched people, unclothed, unfed, and under appalling unhygienic conditions, died at a rate which, long kept up, would have gone far toward the depopulation of Cuba.

That such a policy was not needed in order to create a most difficult situation may be seen by the last annual message of President Cleveland, December 7, 1896, in which he set forth in kindly language, but in terms of justifiable strength, the serious character of affairs. The message said:

". . . It is difficult to perceive that any progress has thus far been made toward the pacification of the island or that the

selves in the town occupied by the troops. Any individual who after the expiration of this period is found in the uninhabited parts will be considered a rebel and tried as such.

Second. The extraction of provisions from the towns, and their transportation from one town to another by land or water without permission of the military authority of the point of departure, is absolutely prohibited. The infringers will be tried and punished as abettors of the rebellion.

Third. The owners of beeves should transport them to towns or their vicinity, to which end they will be given proper protection.

Fourth. At the expiration of the period of eight days, which in each municipal district shall be counted from the publication of this proclamation in the head town of same, all insurgents who present themselves shall be placed at my disposal for the purpose of fixing them a place where they shall reside, serving them as a recommendation if they furnish news of the enemy which can be made use of, if the presentation is made with firearms, and more especially if it be collective.

Fifth. The provisions of this proclamation are only applicable to the Province of Pinar del Rio. VALERIANO WEYLER.

situation of affairs as depicted in my last annual message has in the least improved. If Spain still holds Havana and the seaports, and all the considerable towns, the insurgents still roam at will over at least two-thirds of the inland country. If the determination of Spain to put down the insurrection seems but to strengthen with the lapse of time, as is evinced by her unhesitating devotion of largely increased military and naval forces to the task, there is much reason to believe that the insurgents have gained in point of numbers and character and resources, and are none the less inflexible in their resolve not to succumb without practically securing the great objects for which they took up arms. If Spain has not yet re-established her authority, neither have the insurgents yet made good their title to be regarded as an independent state. Indeed, as the contest has gone on, the pretence that civil governments exists on the island, except so far as Spain is able to maintain it, has been practically abandoned. Spain does keep on foot such a government, more or less imperfectly, in the large towns and their immediate suburbs. But, that exception being made, the entire country is either given over to anarchy or is subject to the military occupation of one or the other party. It is reported, indeed, on reliable authority, that, at the demand of the commander-in-chief of the insurgent army, the putative Cuban government has now given up all attempt to exercise its functions, leaving that government confessedly (what there is the best reason for supposing it always to have been in fact) a government merely on paper.

"Were the Spanish armies able to meet their antagonists in the open, or in pitched battle, prompt and decisive results might be looked for and the immense superiority of the Spanish forces in numbers, discipline, and equipment could hardly fail to tell greatly to their advantage. But they are called upon to face a foe that shuns general engagements, that can choose and does choose its own ground, that, from the nature of the country, is visible or invisible at pleasure, and that fights only from ambuscade and when all the advantages of position and numbers are on its side. In a country where all that is indispensable to life in the way of food, clothing, and shelter is so easily obtainable, especially by those born and bred on the soil, it is obvious that there is hardly a limit to the time during which hostilities of this sort may be prolonged. Meanwhile, as in all cases of protracted civil strife, the passions of the combatants grow more and more inflamed and excesses on both sides become more frequent and more deplorable. They are also participated in by bands of marauders, who, now in the name of one party and now in the name of the other, as may best suit the occasion, harry the country at will and plunder its wretched inhabitants for their own advantage. Such a condition of things would inevitably entail immense destruction of property, even if it were the policy of both parties to prevent it as far as practicable. But while such seemed to be the original policy of the Spanish government, it has now apparently abandoned it and is acting upon the same theory as the insurgents—namely, that the exigencies of the contest require the wholesale annihilation of property, that it may not prove of use and advantage to the enemy.

"It is to the same end that, in pursuance of general orders, Spanish garrisons are now being withdrawn from plantations and the rural population required to concentrate itself in the towns. The sure result would seem to be that the industrial value of the island is fast diminishing, and that unless there is a speedy and radical change in existing conditions it will soon disappear altogether. That value consists very largely, of course, in its capacity to produce sugar, a capacity already much reduced by the interruptions to tillage which have taken place during the last two years. It is reliably asserted that should these interruptions continue during the current year and practically extend, as is now threatened, to the entire sugar-producing territory of the island, so much time and so much money will be required to restore the land to its normal productiveness that it is extremely doubtful if capital can be induced to even make the attempt.

"The spectacle of the utter ruin of an adjoining country, by nature one of the most fertile and charming on the globe, would engage the serious attention of the government and people of the United States in any circumstances. In point of fact, they have a concern with it which is by no means of a wholly sentimental or philanthropic character. It lies so near to us as to be hardly separated from our territory. Our actual pecuniary interest in it is second only to that of the people and government of Spain. It is reasonably estimated that at least from $30,000,000 to $50,000,000 of American capital are invested in plantations and in railroad, mining, and other business enterprises on the island. The volume of trade between the United States and Cuba, which in 1889 amounted to about $64,000,000, rose in 1893 to about $103,000,000, and in 1894, the year before the present insurrection broke out, amounted to nearly $96,000,000. Besides this large pecuniary stake in the fortunes of Cuba, the United States finds itself inextricably involved in the present contest in other ways both vexatious and costly.

"Many Cubans reside in this country, and indirectly promote the insurrection through the press, by public meetings, by the purchase and shipment of arms, by the raising of funds, and by other means, which the spirit of our institutions and the tenor of our laws do not permit to be made the subject of criminal prosecutions. Some of them, though Cubans at heart and in all their feelings and interests, have taken out papers as naturalized citizens of the United States, a proceeding resorted to with a view to possible protection by this government, and not unnaturally regarded with much indignation by the country of their origin. The insurgents are undoubtedly encouraged and supported by the widespread sympathy the people of this country always and instinctively feel for every struggle for better and freer government, and which, in the case of the more adventurous and restless elements of our population, leads in many instances to active and personal participation in the contest. The result is that this government is constantly called upon to protect American citizens, to claim damages for injuries to persons and property, now estimated at many millions of dollars, and to ask explanations and apologies for the acts of Spanish officials, whose zeal for the repression of rebellion sometimes blinds them to the immunities belonging to the unoffending citizens of a friendly power. It follows from the same causes that the United States is compelled to actively police a long line of sea-coast against unlawful expeditions, the escape of which the utmost vigilance will not always suffice to prevent.

"These inevitable entanglements of the United States with the rebellion in Cuba, the large American property interests affected, and considerations of philanthropy and humanity in general have led to a vehement demand in various quarters for some sort of positive intervention on the part of the United States. It was at first proposed that belligerent rights should be accorded to the insurgents—a proposition no longer urged because untimely and in practical operation clearly perilous and injurious to our own interests. It has since been and is now sometimes contended that the independence of the insurgents should be recognized. But imperfect and restricted as the Spanish government of the island may be, no other exists there, unless the will of the military officer in temporary command of a particular district can be dignified as a species of government. It is now also suggested that the United States should buy the island, a suggestion possibly worthy of consideration if there were any evidence of a desire or willingness on the part of Spain to entertain such a proposal. It is urged, finally, that, all other methods failing, the existing internecine strife in Cuba should be terminated by our intervention, even at the cost of a war between the United States and Spain—a war which its advocates confidently prophesy could be neither large in its proportions nor doubtful in its issue.

"The correctness of this forecast need be neither affirmed nor denied. The United States has, nevertheless, a character to maintain as a nation, which plainly dictates that right and not might should be the rule of its conduct. Further, though the United States is not a nation to which peace is a necessity, it is in truth the most pacific of powers and desires nothing so much as to live in amity with all the world. Its own ample and diversified domains satisfy all possible longings for territory, preclude all dreams of conquest, and prevent any casting of covetous eyes upon neighboring regions, however attractive. That our conduct toward Spain and her dominions has constituted no exception to this national disposition is made manifest by the course of our government, not only thus far during the present insurrection, but during the ten years that followed the rising at Yara in 1868. No other great power, it may safely be said, under circumstances of similar perplexity, would have manifested the same restraint and the same patient endurance. It may also be said that this persistent attitude of the United States toward Spain in connection with Cuba unquestionably evinces no slight respect and regard for Spain on the part of the American people. They in truth do not forget her connection with the discovery of the western hemisphere, nor do they underestimate the great qualities of the Spanish people, nor fail to fully recognize their splendid patriotism and their chivalrous devotion to the national honor.

"They view with wonder and admiration the cheerful resolution with which vast bodies of men are sent across thousands of miles of ocean, and an enormous debt accumulated, that the costly possession of the Gem of the Antilles may still hold its place in the Spanish crown. And yet neither the government nor the people of the United States have shut their eyes to the course of events in Cuba, nor have failed to realize the existence of conceded grievances, which have led to the present revolt from the authority of Spain—grievances recognized by the Queen Regent and by the Cortes, voiced by the most patriotic and enlightened of Spanish statesmen, without regard to party, and demonstrated by reforms proposed by the executive and approved by the legislative branch of the Spanish government. It is in the assumed temper and disposition of the Spanish government to remedy these grievances, fortified by indications of influential public opinion in Spain,[1] that this government has hoped to discover the most promising and effective means of composing the present strife, with honor and advantage to Spain and with the achievement of all the reasonable objects of the insurrection.

"It would seem that if Spain should offer to Cuba genuine autonomy—a measure of home-rule which, while preserving the sovereignty of Spain, would satisfy all rational requirements of her Spanish subjects—there should be no just reason why the pacification of the island might not be effected on that basis. Such a result would appear to be in the true interest of all concerned. It would at once stop the conflict which is now consuming the resources of the island and making it worthless for whichever

[1] "In this," says Señor de Olivart, "Mr. Cleveland was deceived. Spanish opinion, supported and directed by the newspapers, which, almost without exception, wished war and promised the chastisement of the rebels and of their protectors, did not demand the reforms, which they considered as a humiliating and useless remedy."—Note, *Revue Générale de Droit International Public*, XII (1905), 488.

party may ultimately prevail. It would keep intact the possessions of Spain without touching her honor, which will be consulted rather than impugned by the adequate redress of admitted grievances. It would put the prosperity of the island and the fortunes of its inhabitants within their own control, without severing the natural and ancient ties which bind them to the mother country, and would yet enable them to test their capacity for self-government under the most favorable conditions. It has been objected on the one side that Spain should not promise autonomy until her insurgent subjects lay down their arms; on the other side, that promised autonomy, however liberal, is insufficient because without assurance of the promise being fulfilled.

"But the reasonableness of a requirement by Spain of unconditional surrender on the part of the insurgent Cubans before their autonomy is conceded is not altogether apparent. It ignores important features of the situation—the stability two years' duration has given to the insurrection; the feasibility of its indefinite prolongation in the nature of things, and as shown by past experience; the utter and imminent ruin of the island, unless the present strife is speedily composed; above all, the rank abuses which all parties in Spain, all branches of her government, and all her leading public men concede to exist and profess a desire to remove. Facing such circumstances, to withhold the proffer of needed reforms until the parties demanding them put themselves at mercy by throwing down their arms, has the appearance of neglecting the gravest of perils and inviting suspicion as to the sincerity of any professed willingness to grant reforms. The objection, on behalf of the insurgents, that promised reforms cannot be relied upon must of course be considered, though we have no right to assume, and no reason for assuming, that anything Spain undertakes to do for the relief of Cuba will not be done according to both the spirit and the letter of the undertaking.

"Nevertheless, realizing that suspicions and precautions on the part of the weaker of two combatants are always natural and not always unjustifiable—being sincerely desirous in the interest of both as well as on its own account that the Cuban problem should be solved with the least possible delay—it was intimated by this government to the government of Spain some months ago that if a satisfactory measure of home-rule were tendered the Cuban insurgents and would be accepted by them upon a guarantee of its execution, the United States would endeavor to find a way not objectionable to Spain of furnishing such guarantee. While no definite response to this intimation has yet been received from the Spanish government, it is believed to be not altogether unwelcome, while, as already suggested, no reason is perceived why it should not be approved by the insurgents. Neither party can fail to see the importance of early action, and both must realize that to prolong the present state of things for even a short period will add enormously to the time and labor and expenditure necessary to bring about the industrial recuperation of the island. It is therefore fervently hoped on all grounds that earnest efforts for healing the breach between Spain and the insurgent Cubans, upon the lines above indicated, may be at once inaugurated and pushed to an immediate and successful issue. The friendly offices of the United States, either in the manner above outlined or in any other way consistent with our Constitution and laws, will always be at the disposal of either party.

"Whatever circumstances may arise, our policy and our interests would constrain us to object to the acquisition of the island or an interference with its control by any other power."

The President sounded a deep note of warning, saying:

"It should be added that it cannot be reasonably assumed that the hitherto expectant attitude of the United States will be definitely maintained. While we are anxious to accord all due respect to the sovereignty of Spain, we cannot view the impending conflict in all its features, and properly apprehend our inevitably close relations to it and its possible results, without considering that by the course of events we may be drawn into such an unusual and unprecedented condition as will fix a limit to our patient waiting for Spain to end the contest, either alone and in her own way, or with our friendly co-operation.

"When the inability of Spain to deal successfully with the insurrection has become manifest and it is demonstrated that her sovereignty is extinct in Cuba for all purposes of its rightful existence, and when a hopeless struggle for its re-establishment has degenerated into a strife which means nothing more than the useless sacrifice of human life and the utter destruction of the very subject-matter of the conflict, a situation will be presented in which our obligations to the sovereignty of Spain will be superseded by higher obligations, which we can hardly hesitate to recognize and discharge. Deferring the choice of ways and methods until the time for action arrives, we should make them depend upon the precise conditions then existing; and they should not be determined upon without giving careful heed to every consideration involving our honor and interest or the international duty we owe to Spain. Until we face the contingencies suggested, or the situation is by other incidents imperatively changed, we should continue in the line of conduct heretofore pursued, thus in all circumstances exhibiting our obedience to the requirements of public law and our regard for the duty enjoined upon us by the position we occupy in the family of nations.

"A contemplation of emergencies that may arise should plainly lead us to avoid their creation, either through a careless disregard of present duty or even an undue stimulation and ill-timed expression of feeling. But I have deemed it not amiss to remind the Congress that a time may arrive when a correct policy and care for our interests, as well as a regard for the interests of other nations and their citizens, joined by considerations of humanity and a desire to see a rich and fertile country, intimately related to us, saved from complete devastation, will constrain our government to such action as will subserve the interests thus involved and at the same time promise to Cuba and its inhabitants an opportunity to enjoy the blessings of peace. . . ."

Congress, however, was inclined to go farther. On December 21, 1896, Senator Cameron reported from the majority of the committee on foreign relations a joint resolution: "That the independence of the republic of Cuba be, and the same is hereby, acknowledged by the United States of America," and "That the United States will use its friendly offices with the government of Spain to bring to a close the war between Spain and the Republic of Cuba." The resolution was accompanied by an elaborate and able report upon the general subject of recognition, citing all previous cases in Europe and America.

After an analysis of those of Europe, the report said: "From this body of precedent it is clear that Europe has invariably asserted and practised the right to interfere, both collectively and separately, amicably and forcibly, in every instance, except that of Poland, where a European people has resorted to insurrection to obtain independence. The right has been based on various grounds: 'impediments to commerce,' 'burdensome measures of protection and repression,' 'requests' of one or both parties 'to interpose,' 'effusion of blood,' and 'evils of all kinds,' 'humanity' and 'the repose of Europe' (Greek treaty of 1827); 'a warm desire to arrest with the shortest possible delay the disorder and the effusion of blood' (protocol of November 4, 1820, in the case of Belgium); 'his own safety or the political equilibrium on the frontiers of his empire' (Russian circular of April 27, 1849, in the case of Hungary); 'to safeguard the interest and honor' and to 'maintain the political influence' of the intervening power (French declarations of 1849–50 in regard to the States of the Church). Finally, in the latest and most considerable, because absolutely unanimous act of all Europe, simply the 'desire to regulate' (preamble to the treaty of Berlin in 1878, covering the recognition of Servia, Roumania, Montenegro, and Bulgaria)."

The report also referred to "the declaration of Lord John Russell on the part of the British government in the House of Commons, May 6, 1861, in which he announced that the law officers of the crown had already 'come to the opinion that the Southern Confederacy of America, according to those principles which seem to them to be just principles, must be treated as a belligerent.' This astonishing promise of belligerency to an insurrection which had by the latest advices at that time neither a ship at sea nor an army on land, before the fact of war was officially known in England to have been proclaimed by either party, was accompanied by a letter of the same date from Lord John Russell to the British ambassador at Paris, in which he said that the accounts which had been received from America were 'sufficient to show that a civil war had broken out among the states which lately composed the American Union. Other nations have therefore to consider the light in which, with reference to the war, they are to regard the confederacy into which the Southern states have united themselves; and it appears to her majesty's government that, looking at all the circumstances of the case, they cannot hesitate to admit that such confederacy is entitled to be considered as a belligerent invested with all the rights and prerogatives of a belligerent.'

"On May 8 the French minister 'concurred entirely in the views of her majesty's government' and pledged himself to the joint action. . . . We know that early as March, 1861, the French minister at Washington advised his government to recognize the Confederate States, and in May, he advised it to intervene by forcibly raising the American blockade. Mercier's recommendation was communicated to Russell, who entertained no doubt as to the right of intervention, either diplomatic or military, even at that early moment when the serious operations of war had hardly begun.

" 'There is much good sense in Mercier's observations [wrote Russell to Palmerston, October 17]. But we must wait. I am persuaded that if we do anything it must be on a grand scale. It will not do for England or France to break a blockade for the sake of getting cotton; but in Europe powers have often said to belligerents: 'Make up your quarrels. We propose to give terms of pacification which we think fair and equitable. If you accept them, well and good. But if your adversary accepts them and if you refuse them, our mediation is at an end, and you must expect to see us your enemies.' "[1]

The offer of the resolution "caused much excitement. Stocks fell and the financial interests of the great Eastern cities rose in wrathful opposition. They declared without any reservation that 'war would unsettle values'—a horrid possibility not to be contemplated with calmness by any right-thinking man. The error of the financial interests was in thinking that war would 'unsettle values.' That which 'unsettled values' was the Cuban question, and so long as that remained unsettled, 'values' would follow suit."[2]

[1] Senate Report, 1160, 54 Cong., 2 Sess.
[2] Lodge, *The War with Spain*, 19.

CHAPTER XXIV

CUBA IN CONGRESS.—THE NEW ADMINISTRATION.—RECONCENTRATION

THE numerous joint resolutions offered at this time in the Senate bore witness to the trend of popular sentiment. On December 9, 1896, Senator Mills, of Texas, introduced a joint resolution that the President be directed to take possession of Cuba and hold the same until the people of Cuba could organize "a government deriving its powers from the consent of the governed."[1] Senator Call, of Florida, offered a joint resolution recognizing the independence of Cuba,[2] and on the same date Senator Cullom, of Illinois, whose character and reputation gave weight to his action, proposed to resolve "that the extinction of Spanish title and the termination of Spanish control of the islands at the gateway of the Gulf of Mexico are necessary to the welfare of those islands and to the people of the United States."[3] On December 21 Senator Hill, of New York, offered a joint resolution declaring "that a state of public war exists in Cuba, and that the parties thereto are entitled to and hereby are accorded belligerent rights . . . and the United States will preserve a strict neutrality between the belligerents."[4] Later, on February 4, 1897, Senator Allen, of Nebraska, in another joint resolution showed himself eager that "United States battle-ships should be sent without delay to Cuban waters to enforce upon Spain the elimination of all unusual and unnecessary cruelty and barbarity" in the conduct of the war.[5] Memorials were received from the legislatures of Louisiana, Nebraska, South Carolina, and Wyoming, favoring belligerent rights, or Cuban independence.[6]

---

[1] *Cong. Record*, 54 Cong., 2 Sess., 39. [2] *Ibid.*, 39. [3] *Ibid.*, 60.
[4] *Ibid.*, 355. [5] *Ibid.*, 2226.
[6] *Ibid.*, 130, 1088, 1638, 1419.

The firm attitude of the Cleveland administration, and the announcement by Mr. Olney, the secretary of state, that no attention would be paid to a joint resolution of recognition of belligerency or independence of Cuba even if passed by both houses over the President's veto, as the right of recognition rested solely with the executive and the resolution would only be "the opinion of certain eminent gentlemen," [1] brought congressional action for the moment to a nullity, the question, through the influence of the speaker, Reed, not even being considered by the House.

By the end of 1896 over 160,000 men of all arms and ranks had, since the outbreak, been sent to Cuba; an amazing effort which spoke in strongest terms for the efficiency of the Spanish war office. But the ability of Cuban finance to meet such an effort was in inverse ratio to the volume of war traffic. The $76,000,000 of imports from Cuba to the United States in 1894 had fallen to $40,000,000 in 1896, and to $18,000,000 in 1897. The exports from the United States to Cuba were now but $8,000,000, a third of what they were four years before. The continuance of the struggle clearly meant ruin to the island.

In the last days of 1896, France, Great Britain, and Germany combined to counsel Spain to accept the good offices of the United States with a view to assure a prompt termination of the war. Spain refused the invitation,[2] but it had its effects in a decree dated December 31, 1896, granting Puerto Rico an elective provincial assembly, and on February 6, 1897, was published the long-looked-for decree establishing " . . . as soon as the state of war in Cuba will permit it," what was, from the Spanish point of view at least, a reformed system of government for both the Spanish islands.[3]

But whatever the influences which had brought Señor Cánovas (for it was he who was the actual government of Spain) to this point, his delayed action was but another unhappy example of the fatal habit of procrastination of his race. It came at the very end of Mr. Cleveland's term of office and at a moment when his administration, which had shown itself so desirous of doing strict justice to Spain, and which took a liberal view of the projected

[1] The *Evening Star* (Washington).
[2] Le Fur, *Etude sur la Guerre Hispano-Américaine de* 1898, 12.
[3] For the decree, see *Spanish Diplom. Cor.*, 21–23.

reforms, was powerless. Moved by the general satisfaction expressed in Washington, the Spanish minister, with natural exultation and hope in his heart, wrote home: "The opinion of the secretary of state—which is also that of the President of the Republic—concerning the reforms is, that they are as extensive as could be asked and more than they expected. This is also the opinion of most of the principal politicians who have not been openly unfriendly to us—including many of those who have great influence in the new administration, and Mr. McKinley himself. The press which began to attack them without knowing them has lately been silent in the matter. The Cuban question is to-day dead in Congress and before the public, and to this is to be attributed the little excitement the matter is creating here." He adds: "I should not conceal that I note a certain tendency to inaction on the part of the secretary of state during the little time that remains to him in the discharge of his office."[1]

But whatever the Spanish view of its liberality or that of the American administration—and it was, in fact, weighted with reservations and conditions which nullified markedly its liberal provisions—the Cuban leaders were determined to have none of it. Señor Estrada Palma "reiterated his emphatic assertion that the Cubans would accept independence only. Rather than allow Spain any voice in the government of Cuba the Cubans would suffer death and the devastation of the island." The reforms, he said, "amount to nothing. They are practically the same that were voted before the war broke out. If the Cubans did not then accept them and rose in arms, can they be expected to accept them now?" Said another: "If real autonomy, such as Canada has from Great Britain, had been offered to us before the war it would have been accepted. Do you think it would be fair or just to those who have fought and fallen for independence for us to outrage their memories by such terms as these?"[2]

The bellicose attitude of so large a number of members both of the Senate and the House, the evident strong sympathy of Congress and the American people in general, the support of so large a por-

[1] Señor Dupuy de Lome to the Spanish minister of state, February 13, 1897, *Spanish Diplom. Cor.*, 24.
[2] *New York Herald*, February 5, 1897.

tion of the American press, could not but fix the hopes of the Cubans and determine them in their demand for independence. In the circumstances the issue of any decree of autonomy short of one akin to that of Canada, which would have disarmed criticism, was a useless waste by Spain of time and energy. Perhaps, in the mind of Cánovas, steeped as it was in the absolutist spirit of ancient Spain, it was so intended; if not so, it was a mind unequal to appreciating the effect of an attempt to leave in the new law a loophole for exerting so much of the personal power which existed in the old régime.

The close of the Cleveland administration was a period of protests regarding the treatment of American citizens (all but one, it should be said, of Cuban birth), who had been arrested for complicity with the insurgents. Special feeling had been aroused by the death, under strong suspicions of cruelty, of Richard Ruiz, a dentist of American citizenship, who, with his wife and children, lived at Guanabacoa, four miles from Havana. He had been arrested February 4, for suspected complicity in an attack on a railway train but two and a half miles from Havana on January 16, 1897. He was confined for thirteen days without being allowed communication with any one, and at the end of this time was found dead in his cell. Consul-General Lee reported, after an examination of the case, that Ruiz was arrested on a false charge; that he was kept *incomunicado* for three hundred and fifteen hours in violation of treaty rights which limited such confinement to seventy-two hours; that he died from congestion of the brain produced by a blow on top of the head, whether given by the jailer or produced by his own maniacal act could not be decided.[1]

In the end, however, all were released, nor can it be said that, excepting the case of Ruiz, there was undue delay on the part of Spain in meeting the American demands, or undue harshness of treatment.[2] The *Competitor* prisoners had already all been freed in December, 1896. The notorious Sanguily, whose detention had caused much inflammatory discussion in Congress, and had created much ill-deserved sympathy throughout the Union and the authen-

---

[1] Report of Consul-General Lee, May 31, 1897.
[2] For the correspondence on this subject see *Foreign Relations*, 1897, 483 et seq.

ticity of whose citizenship was denied by such an authority as Senator Hoar, was released February 25, 1897.[1]

The Cleveland administration closed with the preservation of the *status quo*. It left a most vigorous patrol of the southern coasts by the navy and revenue marine against filibustering expeditions;[2] it had pressed to a successful conclusion in the courts the actions against transgressors of the neutrality laws,[3] the decisions in which made escape in the future much more difficult;[4] it had upheld throughout American rights, and had preserved not unkindly relations with Spain; it closed with the general commendation and support of the country as to its conduct of our foreign relations.

On March 4, 1897, Mr. McKinley succeeded Mr. Cleveland whose independence in judgment had shown strongly throughout his administration in stemming the tide of emotional feeling in the Cuban question. Mr. Cleveland by character and temperament stood as a leader of public opinion; Mr. McKinley as a follower. The two men, equally conscientious, were marked examples of these two schools of statesmanship, which have had historic recognition from the time of Moses and Aaron: the one felt it a duty to resist a popular demand not in accord with his judgment; the other equally felt it a duty to yield.

The change in the personality of the secretary of state was no less momentous. At no moment since the civil war did the department of state more need a vigorous and able head, but Mr. Olney, one in temperament and character with his chief, was succeeded by Senator John Sherman, who not only had been conspicuous in the Senate in his attacks, sometimes of an illogical and inconsiderate character, upon Spanish policy and conduct in Cuba, but whose infirm health, soon to become painfully evident, combined with advanced age, now seventy-four years, made the appointment one to be justly criticised. Mr. Sherman's appointment, even had

---

[1] Sanguily was arrested at Jacksonville, Fla., April 7, 1897, charged with attempting to fit out a filibustering expedition. The charge seems to have been not pressed.

[2] One has but to examine the newspaper files of 1897 to be assured of the activity and zeal of this patrol. The American ships were, in fact, doing the duty which should have been done by the Spanish navy on the Cuban coast.

[3] The owner of the steamer *Laurada* was sentenced in March, 1897, to two years in prison and $500 fine. [4] *Vide supra.*

he been in vigorous health and equal to the heavy duties of his office, was in the critical condition of affairs, on account of his previous pronounced antagonistic views to Spanish procedure, a blow to peace. The mere fact that Mr. Sherman from the earlier days of the ten years' war had fulminated so vigorously against Spain's dominion in Cuba, and, too, with so little knowledge of the subject that he was in 1873 even ignorant of so important an international document as the treaty of 1795,[1] made his appointment, in the critical condition of affairs, a mistaken one. That the appointment was a concession to certain political adjustments in his state, of a decidedly personal nature, did not add to the political morality of the appointment. The affairs, however, of the department of state soon passed into the hands of the assistant secretary, Mr. Day, later to become secretary, and virtually such from the beginning of his service in the department.

The new Congress called together at once after the inauguration of the new President to discuss the tariff became also, in the Senate at least, a field for effort led by Senator Morgan, of Alabama, in favor of the recognition of Cuban belligerency. His resolution, introduced April 1, was passed May 20, by a vote of 41 to 14, 33 senators not voting. Introduced in the House it was referred to the committee on foreign affairs "when it should be appointed," but as Speaker Reed did not appoint the committee, action was never taken.

The question of the reconcentrados was now becoming one of first importance. A wave of strongest sympathy was sweeping over the United States, moved by the reports of the sufferings and deaths caused, so far as the press informed the people, by the system established by General Weyler. It was the feeling thus engendered against Spain which gradually moved the country toward war. It is necessary that the justice of this feeling, which took powerful hold of the great mass of Americans and affected the President and Congress, should be examined.

Within the first six months of the insurrection a series of orders were issued, as has been seen,[2] by the insurgent leaders which practically decreed the cessation of labor in Cuba. In case of disobedience, they commanded a devastation which, as carried

[1] *Supra*, 307.   [2] *Supra*, 408.

out, has no parallel in history in savage destructiveness. It ruined what was practically Cuba's one support, the production of sugar. Should any plantation attempt to grind, the cane was to be burned and the buildings demolished. One, to understand the destruction and fear which followed these edicts, has but to note the fact that production fell from 1,004,264 tons in 1894–95, to 225,221 in the following year. The guards furnished by the Spanish authorities availed little; their mere presence was a signal of ruin, for in the dry weather and high winds of the grinding season it was "a simple matter for one person (who can easily conceal himself in the tall cane) to start a conflagration that [would] unless promptly extinguished, destroy hundreds of acres in a few hours."[1] The sad pictures of gaunt walls and chimneys, remnants of once splendid establishments which could be seen throughout central and western Cuba, were witness to the shocking waste of capital and production which these orders brought.

It is thus upon the insurgents themselves that, primarily, the burden of the miseries of the great unemployed mass of Cubans must be laid; for Cuba, through the action of its own sons, became a land of enforced idleness. Thus, even before concentration was ordered, large numbers of laborless people had assembled in the towns in search of work and food. Of work there was none, and food was to be had only by charity. The Spanish officials, until General Weyler's order of reconcentration was issued, were not officially responsible for affording aid, nor were they usually in a position to do so, the food supply of the Spanish army itself being at all times during the war a difficult and very uncertain problem. Many of the unemployed men, as already said, joined the insurgents; the greater part of these unhappy poor were women and children.

General Weyler's proclamation ordering concentration had now, on Mr. McKinley's advent to office, been in force a year. The great increase, caused by this order, of demoralized, poverty-stricken, and shiftless humanity, crowded with the wreck of their slight belongings into the small Cuban towns, could, in the inability of the Spanish government to furnish them food, but result in ap-

[1] Mr. Owen McGarr, American consul at Cienfuegos, to department of state, January 10, 1898, Senate Doc. 230, 55 Cong., 2 Sess. 28.

palling mortality. Though the decree had been issued February 16, 1896, it was not until December 1 of that year that zones of cultivation were ordered set aside for these miserable people, who had so little means with which to cultivate; and even now persons whose husbands or fathers were with the insurgents, were excepted from the permission to till the zone.

Cuban and Spaniard thus alike were responsible for the misery which was to sweep off nearly 200,000 people of the island.[1] Had either of the antagonists justification for action involving such terrible results? That Spain was justified, in the light of public law, was to be judicially announced four years later, by an American commission itself, which held, subject to certain limitations and restrictions, neither of which applied to Spain in Cuba, that "it is undoubtedly the general rule of international law that concentration and devastation are legitimate war measures."[2]

Not only had concentration thus the support of international law, but it had American precedent itself in an order, by General Thomas Ewing, August 25, 1863, by which the inhabitants of a large district of Missouri were directed to remove from the region within fifteen days.[3] Nor, though it met but two years later, did the Hague convention, signed July 29, 1899, by the delegates of fifteen nations, including the United States, make mention of concentration among things prohibited.[4] Nor did Great Britain hesitate to use the same methods in the war of 1899–1902, with results much less tragic than in Cuba, through England's greater resources and better administration.

It must be admitted that Spain was legally within her rights; that she was so under the greater law of humanity, is a larger and more difficult question, though it is but fair to her to bear in mind

[1] The last Spanish census was in 1887 and gave 1,631,687 as the population in that year. The report of the census of 1899 says: "The number of inhabitants was certainly not overstated (p. 72)." The latter census, taken in October, 1899, gave a population of 1,572,797. "It is probable, therefore, that the direct and indirect losses by the war and the reconcentration policy, including a decrease of births and of immigration, and an increase of deaths and emigration, reached a total not far from 200,000."—*Census of Cuba*, 1899, p. 72.

[2] Rules of the Spanish Treaty Claims Commission (rule 8), announced November 24, 1902, Senate Doc. 25, 58 Cong., 2 Sess., 7.

[3] *Ibid.*, 125.   [4] *Ibid.*, 124. Nor has any yet been made.

that the great mass of the people concentrated would have remained on the land, employed and fed, had the insurgents permitted. Both Cuban and Spaniard must thus, as just said, bear the weight of this great destruction of life, but with a difference in responsibility. The Spanish action was legalized action; the insurgent devastation, which was the forerunner and real cause of Spain's action, was warranted by no rule of war; for no rule covers the remote and problematic effect sought by the insurgents; viz., cutting off the monetary support of Cuba to Spain and thus rendering it, at some remote and indefinite period, an undesirable possession.

The rules governing American armies in the field allow: "Of all destruction of property and obstruction of the ways and channels of traffic, travel, or communication, and of all withholding of sustenance or means of life from the enemy." "War," they again say, "is not carried on by arms alone. It is lawful to starve the belligerents, armed or unarmed, so that it leads to the speedier subjection of the enemy."[1]

But, on the part of the insurgents, there was no question of starvation or subjection of a besieged enemy; it was one of producing a desert which the Spaniards might not care to retain. By no rule of international law, by no law of military necessity, can their action be upheld.

Nor as ex-Senator Chandler, one of the commission on the Spanish Treaty Claims, showed, were the United States in a position to accuse Spain of cruelty without the *riposte* from her of *tu quoque*, which was soon to come forcibly. He quoted General Sherman's proposal to "sally forth to ruin Georgia,"[2] and Grant's order to Sheridan, August 16, 1864: "If you can possibly spare a division of cavalry, send them through Loudon County to destroy and carry off the crops, animals, negroes, and all men under fifty years of age, capable of bearing arms. . . . All male citizens under fifty years of age can fairly be held as prisoners of war, not as citizen prisoners. If not already soldiers, they will be made so the moment the Rebel army gets hold of them."[3] And again, Sheridan's own report, October 7, 1864: "I have destroyed 2,000 barns filled with wheat, hay, and farming implements; over 70 mills filled with

---

[1] General Order No. 100. See Spanish Treaty Claims Commission, p. 124.
[2] Sherman, *Memoirs*, II, 159.   [3] *Ibid.*, I, 486.

flour and wheat; have driven in front of the army over 4,000 head of stock, and have killed and issued to the troops not less than 3,000 sheep. . . . To-morrow I will continue the destruction of wheat, forage, etc., down to Fisher's Hill. When this is completed the valley from Winchester up to Staunton, 92 miles, will have but little in it for man or beast." [1]

The rules agreed to by three of the five members of the Treaty Claims Commission, emphasized by the documents quoted by ex-Senator Chandler, require us, in fairness, to admit that the charges against Spain of violation of the law of nations, so far as concentration and devastation are concerned, cannot be upheld. It must thus be conceded that the administration, in communications to Congress and in its correspondence, was, in some of its statements of unjustifiable procedure, not in accord with existing international law or established usage in war. However honorable to our government and people were the more humane views of the rules of war so frequently put forward in public documents and speeches, they could, when differing from established international law, hold, for the rest of the world, no more than could Spain's singular definition of piracy which she had so frequently advanced.[2]

On May 6, 1897, the President, moved by the consular reports of destitution and suffering of a large number of American citizens, estimated at from six to eight hundred, sent a special message advising the appropriation of fifty thousand dollars for their relief and the transportation to the United States of those who wished to return. A bill in accord with this was passed and approved by the President May 24.

The general acceptance by the American press of the view of Spanish cruelty added to the public feeling, and no doubt aided in bringing from the secretary of state a note to the Spanish minister of a very warm, vigorous, and, it must be said, ill-advised statement,

[1] *Official Records, Union and Confederate Armies*, series I, vol. XLIII, part I, pp. 30, 31. Quoted by ex-Senator William E. Chandler, Spanish Treaty Claims Commission, in Senate Doc. 25, 58 Cong., 2 Sess., 130–133. For quotations as to limitations of devastation, see *Ibid.*, 134, 135. See also Flack, *Span.-Amer. Dip. Relations, Preceding War of* 1898, Johns Hopkins University Studies, 1906.

[2] The Treaty Claims Commission (3 to 2) refused to accept the declarations of the executive as conclusive in questions of international law. (Report, p. 99.)

for it both traversed international law, and, by confining animadversions to one alone of the contesting parties, and to the less guilty, was manifestly unfair. Mr. Sherman said:

"No incident has so deeply affected the sensibilities of the American people or so painfully impressed their government as the proclamations of General Weyler, ordering the burning or unroofing of dwellings, the destruction of growing crops, the suspension of tillage, the devastation of fields, and the removal of the rural population from their homes to suffer privation and disease in the overcrowded and ill-supplied garrison towns. The latter aspect of this campaign of devastation has especially attracted the attention of this government, inasmuch as several hundreds of American citizens among the thousands of concentrados of the central and eastern provinces of Cuba were ascertained to be destitute of the necessaries of life to a degree demanding immediate relief, through the agencies of the United States, to save them from death by sheer starvation and from the ravages of pestilence.

"From all parts of the productive zones of the island, where the enterprise and capital of Americans have established mills and farms, worked in large part by citizens of the United States, comes the same story of interference with the operations of tillage and manufacture, due to the systematic enforcement of a policy aptly described in General Weyler's bando of May 27 last as 'the concentration of the inhabitants of the rural country and the destruction of resources in all places where the instructions given are not carried into effect.' Meanwhile, the burden of contribution remains, arrears of taxation necessarily keep pace with the deprivation of the means of paying taxes, to say nothing of the destruction of the ordinary means of livelihood, and the relief held out by another bando of the same date is illusory, for the resumption of industrial pursuits in limited areas is made conditional upon the payment of all arrears of taxation and the maintenance of a protecting garrison. Such relief cannot obviously reach the numerous class of concentrados, the women and children deported from their ruined homes and desolated farms to the garrison towns. For the larger industrial ventures, capital may find its remedy, sooner or later, at the bar of international justice, but for the labor dependent upon the slow rehabilitation of capital there appears to be intended only the doom of privation and distress.

"Against these phases of the conflict, against this deliberate infliction of suffering on innocent non-combatants, against such resort to instrumentalities condemned by the voice of humane civilization, against the cruel employment of fire and famine to accomplish by uncertain indirection what the military arm seems powerless to directly accomplish, the President is constrained to protest, in the name of the American people and in the name of common humanity. The inclusion of a thousand or more of our citizens among the victims of this policy, the wanton destruction of the legitimate investments of Americans to the amount of millions of dollars, and the stoppage of avenues of normal trade—all these give the President the right of specific remonstrance; but in the just fulfilment of his duty he cannot limit himself to these formal grounds of complaint. He is bound by the higher obligations of his representative office to protest against the uncivilized and inhuman conduct of the campaign in the island of Cuba. He conceives that he has a right to demand that a war, conducted almost within sight of our shores and grievously affecting American citizens and their interests throughout the length and breadth of the land, shall at least be conducted according to the military codes of civilization. . . . If the friendly attitude of this government is to bear fruit it can only be when supplemented by Spain's own conduct of the war in a manner responsive to the precepts of ordinary humanity and calculated to invite as well the expectant forbearance of this government as the confidence of the Cuban people in the beneficence of Spanish control." [1]

The Spanish minister, while forwarding the note to his home government, and quick to recognize the injustice of applying to Spain alone, views which with even greater force applied to the conduct of the insurgents, himself made a reply protesting against "the partiality and exaggeration of the information" received by the American government "and which is doubtless the cause of the attitude which it has now assumed." After appealing to the history of our own civil contest, he said: "Allow me further to say that the sufferings and hardships of the non-combatants have been mainly due to the system and the policy pursued by the insurgents when they invaded the central and western provinces. They then

[1] Mr. Sherman to Señor Dupuy de Lome, June 26, 1897, *Spanish Diplom. Cor.*, 25.

burned crops, destroyed dwellings, and set fire to the towns which they found without garrisons, and compelled all loyal persons, or those who did not sympathize with them and aid them, to seek refuge in the forts which surrounded the cities."

After discussing the question of exaggeration and misconception at some length, he ended with that demand of the impossible ever present in the Spanish mind, and the impossibility of which, in a free nation, it could never be brought to understand. He said:

"If the American people, to whose philanthropic sentiments reference is made in your excellency's note of June 26, understood, from a dispassionate examination of this question, that the insurrection lives for evil only, and, instead of encouraging it by holding out the fallacious hope of assistance, which is the basis of all its trust, would counsel peace; if, instead of aiding and abetting the violations of law which are constantly committed by the Cuban emigrants organized here for the purpose of making war upon a nation friendly to the United States, they would aid the Federal government in its efforts to prevent the departure of filibustering expeditions, which render this long and desolating war possible, all the evils would very soon cease which are deplored by his majesty's government and by all Spaniards, as well as by the President and people of the United States." [1]

The reply of the Spanish minister of state himself, August 4, 1897, was an enlargement of the contentions already advanced by Señor Dupuy de Lome. He said:

"The secretary of state supposes, in his note, that among the thousands of Spanish reconcentrados who have been compelled to transfer their abode from the country to the towns and fortified inclosures there are hundreds of North Americans who, owing to the want of the means of subsistence, have had to be assisted by their government; and yet its own official experience could have shown it the great mistake in the reports relative to this point, since, when the time arrived for the distribution of the sums voted by the Federal parliament at the request of the President of the Republic, its consuls found hardly any North American citizens actually in need, to such an extent that at the time that the secretary of state addressed you the note of June 26 they had only succeeded in using

[1] Señor Dupuy de Lome to Mr. Sherman, June 30, 1897, *Spanish Diplom. Cor.*, 27.

among them six thousand dollars of the fifty thousand dollars appropriated for that benevolent object, including the amount appropriated for bringing them home. The very men who reported the evil were, therefore, those who were called upon to correct the mistake, since, upon investigating the evil closely, they were finally compelled to admit, in obedience to the irresistible force of facts, that there had been much more imagination than reality in the reports. The case of the said concentrated North Americans applies perfectly to the other suppositions in Mr. Sherman's note to which I am replying, and if it were possible to make an official verification of the whole of it, like that which was made in the case of the apportionment of the assistance, the injustice of the charges which are made would be rendered equally evident.

"It cannot be denied, it is true, that interests are injured, sufferings caused, and the normal conditions of labor and property changed by General Weyler's proclamations, as they would be by all others issued in similar cases by generals in the field, but this is owing to the imperative duties arising from circumstances; and they are likewise animated by a truly humane purpose—that of putting as speedy an end as possible to the struggle by securing the complete submission of the insurgents, and, as its consequence, the re-establishment of the law wrongfully disturbed by them. The object of some of these proclamations is to deprive the rebels of the means which they employ in the prosecution of their plans; others are intended to protect the inhabitants of the country who are loyal to Spain from the outrages, misery, and robberies to which they are subjected by the rebels, by the express orders of their commanders; and both objects are equally lawful and necessary, although in their application they may, as has been said, injure certain private interests, as these must everywhere and always be subordinated to the superior claims of the community and the state.

"All civilized countries which, like Spain at present, have found themselves under the harsh necessity of resorting to arms to crush rebellions, not always so evidently unjustifiable as that of Cuba, proceed and have proceeded in the same manner. In the United States itself, during the war of secession, recourse was had to concentrations of peaceable inhabitants, to seizures and confiscation of property, to the prohibition of commerce, to the destruction of all agricultural and industrial property, particularly of cotton and tobacco, without the safeguard of their foreign flags, in the case of the important factories of Roswell, for instance, sufficing to save them; to the burning of entire cities; to the ruin and devastation of immense and most fertile regions—in short, to the destruction of all the property of the adversary, to the abolition of constitutional rights by the total suspension of the writ of habeas corpus, and to the development of a military and dictatorial system which, in the states opposed to the Union, lasted many years after the termination of the bloody contest.

"There are found at every step, not only in the most reliable historians, including North American patriots,—the staunch champions of the Union—but also in the official documents published in Washington and in the reports and memoirs published by the illustrious generals who conquered, orders, measures of severity, and acts of destruction not only similar to, but even more severe than, those which General Weyler has found himself forced to issue in Cuba.

"Hunter's and Sheridan's invasion of the valley of the Shenandoah, of which it was said, to show its total ruin, that 'if a crow wants to fly down the valley he must carry his provisions with him' (Draper, vol. III, p. 408); the expedition of General Sherman, that illustrious and respected general, through Georgia and South Carolina; the taking of Atlanta and the subsequent expulsion of non-combatants—women and children—and their concentration at remote distances; the shootings at Palmyra; the burning of Columbia; the horrors connected with the treatment of the prisoners and peaceable suspects who were confined together in the warehouses and prisons at Richmond and Danville, and, more particularly, in the prisons at Andersonville, where, according to official data, more than twelve thousand perished; and many other incidents of that horrible struggle, that genuine contest of Titans which put the wisdom and vigor of the North American people to so severe a test, furnish an eloquent, though mournful, example of the distressing but unavoidable severity which accompanies war, even when it is carried on by armies educated in a republic and directed, from the summit of the civil power and the military command, by personalities so famous, so honored, and so devoted to duty and human liberty as Lincoln and Grant.

"The invincible General Sherman explained on various occasions the supreme justice of these acts, and in perusing his memoirs and the official reports which he addressed to the directing council of war at Washington are found remarkable statements as to the severity with which it is necessary to proceed against the enemy to make the operations of the military forces efficient and successful. 'War is war,' said this able general, 'and the tremendous responsibility for civil wars rests upon their authors and upon those who are their direct or indirect instruments.' And when replying to the city council of Atlanta this wise leader also said:

"'You can not condemn war with more horror than I; war is cruelty personified, . . . but I shall not recoil from any sacrifice until I have brought it to an end. . . . The Union must maintain its authority to the extent of its ability. If it yields it is lost, and that is not the will of the nation. Recognize the Union and the authority of the national government, and then this army which is now devastating your fields, houses, and roads for military purposes will be your protector.'

"Lofty and patriotic views, which his majesty's government does not hesitate to appropriate and to apply to Cuba.

"It may well be—and his majesty's government hastens to admit it—that, in spite of the reliability of the sources from which the foregoing statements relative to the war of secession have been drawn, there may be some exaggeration in them, too; but in that case that very fact would prove the danger of forming a settled opinion as to matters equally important without seeking to inform ourselves of the facts, and trusting merely to the reports of others, however truthful they may appear. . . . Nor can the devastation of its landed wealth, unless we close our eyes to the evidence, be attributed to the Spanish authorities as their own peculiar system; it was the insurgents that, in obedience to the instructions of their principal leader, Maximo Gomez, began by burning sugar-cane plantations and destroying the cane mills, making extensive use of dynamite for this purpose and for the destruction of the railroads, and boasting that they would carry desolation and ruin everywhere. They were the ones, also, who reduced these cruel practices to a system, and destroyed even the cattle, the basis of subsistence, if they found more than they needed at the time—all this in the vain hope of inducing Spain to abandon the island upon seeing it in ashes and incapable of furnishing her with supplies of any kind, as if right and honor were of no importance in the eyes of civilized nations. In a circular of Maximo Gomez, dated Sancti-Spiritus, November 6, 1895, it was ordered that the sugar mills should be entirely destroyed, their sugar cane and the outbuildings burned, and their railroads torn up; that any laborer lending the assistance of his arms to the sugar mills should be considered a traitor; and that the penalty of death should be inflicted upon all who failed to execute these atrocities. Not less than one hundred and twenty mills (bateyes) suffered the terrible consequences of this atrocious order. If we add to this the blowing up of bridges and trains, the systematic dispersion of their bands, without ever fighting for victory and honor, and, above all, the use of explosive projectiles, which civilized and international conventions repudiate, the inhuman procedure of the rebels will be fully shown.

"Moreover, we must bear in mind that this system of the total destruction of Cuban property has always been advocated by the filibustering junta at New York, composed, in great part, of naturalized North Americans, and that this very junta has issued the most cruel orders; so that, by a most amazing coincidence, the authors of the admittedly abominable devastation which, according to the secretary of state, has so greatly aroused the sympathies of the North American people, are citizens of the Union and organizations working without hinderance in its bosom. . . ."

The despatch concluded, declaring that Spain expected to persevere in this system, resolved to establish the new régime now ordered. The minister of state also expected that the Washington cabinet would "doubtless see that the truly humane and reasonable course" was to co-operate with Spain " by putting an end to the existence of the public and organized direction which [the revolt] receives from [the United States] and without which the rebellion would long ago have been entirely subdued by arms."[1]

[1] The Duke of Tetuan to Señor Dupuy de Lome, August 4, 1897, *Spanish Diplom. Cor.*, 29–33.

There is no denying the force of the Spanish argument. It must necessarily be considered a complete reply to the contention of the American secretary of state that the desolation of Cuba was wholly or even mainly the work of the Spanish administration, and also as to the right under international law to concentration. Nor in the face of the occurrences of the American civil war, with its stoppage of commerce and the reduction thereby to starvation-point of the cotton operatives of Great Britain, could mere injury to commerce be made a just ground of intervention.

While the assertions of Secretary Sherman's paper cannot be justified, either in law or precedent, American feeling had, however, justification in the carelessness for results shown by the Spanish authorities in concentrating the people with what must have been full knowledge of their inability to support them, and the delay in effort to establish zones of cultivation which should have at once been taken in hand. Nor can the general advance in humane feeling during what was now a whole generation after the American civil war be ignored.

All reports, official and other, gave a most melancholy account of the condition of the Cubans. They were but the forerunners of the still more harrowing details of the next year given with such emphasis in the consular and other reports from the island. Says a correspondent accompanying a Spanish column and whose statements thus have the undenied verity of a censored document: "The misery among the pacificos at San Cristobal was appalling. Their only shelter consisted of huts of palmetto leaves. They slept on the ground. They have no money, and were it not for the rations given them by the Spanish alcalde they must have perished. I visited the spot where they receive their food at noon on the day of my arrival. There I found hundreds of emaciated women and children gathered around four great caldrons of soup, which they took away with them in old tin cans or in any receptacle they could lay their hands on.

"In many cases the fathers, husbands, and brothers of these wretched persons were with the insurgents; but give the Spanish authorities credit for the fact that they fed all alike as far as possible, after providing for the troops. The supplies dealt out were meagre, but it was the best the alcalde could do. . . .

"From San Cristobal I went, according to directions, to Los Palacios, or the Palaces. What a mockery was the name! Better might it have been called the City of Ruins—burnt to the ground by the insurgents. A city of leaves had arisen from the ashes of a city of stone. A large area enclosed by fortifications, built for the most part of loose stones and railroad iron, was covered largely by the inevitable huts of palmetto leaves, and the largest edifices consisted of thatched roofs built across the half-burned walls of antebellum buildings.

"The 'hotel' where I stayed was of such a character. Its one large room served as reception-room, dining-room, and bedchamber for myself, my interpreter, two priests, three sick soldiers, and two civilians. Rats ran riot at night and fleas and other insects held high carnival. For a Gehenna on earth commend me to Los Palacios under present conditions.

"While waiting for Weyler's column, which had made a détour to the southward, I had a chance to talk to many pacificos within the line. They one and all bear testimony to what has already been said, that neither Cuban nor Spanish regular troops harm women or children, unless through accident when they get in line of fire.

"That the Spanish have slaughtered male pacificos found between lines in cold blood and in large numbers is true, but I was surprised to learn that the insurgent general Bermudez is as much feared by pacificos as Weyler. One woman told me how Bermudez had hanged her brother because he was unwilling to give up his horse to the insurgents. Bermudez took the horse and sent the man where he didn't need one. In fact, there was no difference of opinion as to Bermudez's cruelty, and on one occasion he narrowly escaped being executed by Maceo for his sanguinary work in spite of the great general's orders."[1]

The report, October 15, 1897, of the American consul at the important port of Matanzas, but sixty miles east of Havana, is but one of a series from consuls, naval officers, and Red Cross observers, all persons of highest character and veracity in whose statements it was impossible not to confide. Said Mr. Brice, the consul mentioned:

[1] *New York Herald*, January 4, 1897.

"Over two thousand (I have the list of names) have died in this city—want of food—since January 1 up to October 1, 1897. Since the latter date the daily average death-rate has been over forty-five persons. Sixty-two died last Sunday; of these fifty-seven from actual starvation. Normal death-rate of Matanzas city prior to Weyler's concentration order, six persons daily (not including soldiers).

"In the interior towns of the province the situation is beyond belief. In some towns one-third to one-half the population has disappeared. . . .

"Local authorities are powerless and unable to cope with the situation. Cities and towns are bankrupt and can give little or no relief to the starving thousands. Last Monday morning six to seven hundred starving women unexpectedly raided the market and carried off everything in sight. . . . Allow these people to go out into the country and plant crops, and in less than sixty days all will be well and starvation a thing of the past."[1]

Though there was no doubt some exaggeration in Consul Brice's report, and a very great exaggeration in the supposed number of deaths during the whole period,[2] the situation was appalling enough to arouse the sympathies of any people. Commander (later rear-admiral) Converse, commanding the cruiser *Montgomery* visiting Matanzas, reported February 6, 1898: "The present population of the city of Matanzas is variously estimated to be from 50,000 to 60,000 (including the reconcentrados). In the city of Matanzas there have been between 11,000 and 12,000 deaths (ascribed to starvation and incident diseases) during the past year, and the rate is increasing daily. In October, 1897, there were 974 deaths; in November, 1,260; and in December, 1,733. Reports from the cemetery show that at the present time the daily death-rate averages 46.[3]

---

[1] *Foreign Relations*, 1898, 596.

[2] Viz. 500,000 as against the 200,000 estimated by the census officials in 1899 (*supra*, 493).

[3] This would be an annual death-rate of about 300 per thousand, or nearly one-third of the population. At the end of November, 609 deaths were reported for the week in Havana and its suburb Regla; an annual rate of 158 per thousand. (*New York Times*, November 28, 1897. Report by Inspector Brunner to Surgeon-General Wyman of the Marine Hospital Service.)

"Within the city limits there are at present about 14,000 people absolutely without food and clothing. Of these 11,000 live in the streets of the city and are wholly without homes or shelter. The remaining 3,000 live in three small villages, located on three hills just beyond the built-up portion of the city. Each village contains about 1,000 persons who live in small huts constructed of palm branches. . . . Most of them are women and children, and they are all emaciated, sick, and almost beyond relief, unless they could have the benefit of regular treatment in the hospitals. They are dying in the streets for want of food, one body having been passed by myself on the occasion of my official visit to the civil authorities and another having been seen by other officers of the ship.

"The distress is no longer confined to the original reconcentrados (the laboring country people, most of whom have already perished), but has now extended to the better classes, who before the war were in moderately comfortable circumstances. Those now begging in the streets are, for a large part, well-to-do people or their children, and the citizens of Matanzas are themselves beginning to suffer for the actual necessaries of life, having drained their resources to supply the urgent needs of the thirty thousand or more reconcentrados who have been quartered upon them.

"The citizens of Matanzas have established three places where they issue rations of . . . cooked rice and fish. . . . Every day about nine hundred people receive a meal. It is needless to add that this supply is entirely inadequate for the large number (fourteen thousand) of destitute starving people within the city limits. . . .

"The Spanish authorities have rendered some assistance to the starving, and on two occasions gave one thousand dollars toward the relief fund. This was but a small amount, but it is said to have been all that the government could give. . . .

"The urgent necessity for immediate relief and assistance cannot be exaggerated. Whenever the officers of the Montgomery landed they were constantly followed by clamoring crowds of starving men, women, and children, importuning them in the most heart-rending manner for food, for the want of which they are dying. . . ."[1]

[1] Commander Converse to the secretary of the navy, February 6, 1898, *Foreign Relations*, 1898, 669. See also Captain Sigsbee's report, February

8, 1898, *Ibid.*, 671. Also the reports of consuls in Cuba, Senate Doc. 230 ("Consular Correspondence Respecting the Condition of Reconcentrados in Cuba," etc.), 55 Cong., 2 Sess. See also the article "The Cuban Insurrection," by G. C. Musgrave (an Englishman), in *the Contemporary Review*, July, 1898. The account, by Mr. Musgrave, of the conditions are more harrowing than any even of the American reports. He says: "Even in Havana city, where they can beg in the streets, and where food was never scarce among the residents as in less-favored towns, I have seen children lick the blood off the stones at the shambles, and all the inhabitants of Los Fossos [the point where the reconcentrado were herded] that had strength to crawl hastened one day to the beach to fight over the putrid carcass of a cow that had washed ashore" (p. 7). His account is very terrible throughout and is a very severe arraignment of Spanish procedure and policy.

CHAPTER XXV

THE NEW AMERICAN ADMINISTRATION.—A LIBERAL SPANISH GOVERNMENT.—MR. McKINLEY'S FIRST ANNUAL MESSAGE

ON September 13, 1897, Mr. Hannis Taylor presented his letters of recall and General Stewart Lyndon Woodford [1] his letters of credence as American minister at Madrid.

The instructions of the new minister, after a short history and statement of conditions, declared in plain words the unity of the administration with Congress in feeling and intention. They said: "In the judgment of the President the time has come for this government to soberly consider and clearly decide the nature and methods of its duty both to its neighbors and itself. . . . [It] has labored and is still laboring under signal difficulties in its administration of its neutrality laws. It is ceaselessly confronted with questions affecting the inherent and treaty rights of its citizens in Cuba. It beholds the island suffering an almost complete paralysis of many of its most important commercial functions by reason of the impediments imposed and the ruinous injuries wrought by this internecine warfare at its very doors; and above all it is naturally and rightfully apprehensive lest some untoward incident may abruptly supervene to inflame passions beyond control and thus raise issues which cannot be avoided.

"In short, it may not be reasonably asked or expected that a mere policy of inaction can be safely prolonged. There is no longer question that the sentiment of the American people strongly demands that if the attitude of neutrality is to be maintained toward these combatants, it must be a genuine neutrality as between combatants fully recognized as such in fact as well as in name. The problem of recognition of belligerency has been often presented, but

---

[1] General Woodford had been an officer of volunteers during the civil war, from 1862 to 1865. He received a brevet as brigadier-general.

never perhaps more explicitly than now. Both houses of Congress adopted, by an almost unanimous vote, a concurrent resolution recognizing belligerency in Cuba, and, latterly, the Senate, by a large majority, has voted a joint resolution of like purport, which is now pending in the House of Representatives.

"At this juncture our government must seriously inquire whether the time has not arrived when Spain, of her own volition, moved by her own interests and by every paramount sentiment of humanity, will put a stop to this destructive war and make proposals of settlement honorable to herself and just to her Cuban colony and to mankind. The United States stands ready to assist her and tender good offices to that end.

"It should by no means be forgotten that besides and beyond the question of recognition of belligerency, with its usual proclamation of neutrality and its concession of equal rights and impartial imposition of identical disabilities in respect to the contending parties within our municipal jurisdiction, there lies the larger ulterior problem of intervention, which the President does not now discuss. It is with no unfriendly intent that this subject has been mentioned, but simply to show that this government does not and cannot ignore the possibilities of duty hidden in the future, nor be unprepared to face an emergency which may at any time be born of the unhappy contest in Cuba. The extraordinary, because direct and not merely theoretical or sentimental, interest of the United States in the Cuban situation cannot be ignored, and if forced the issue must be met honestly and fearlessly, in conformity with our national life and character. Not only are our citizens largely concerned in the ownership of property and in the industrial and commercial ventures which have set on foot in Cuba through our enterprising initiative and sustained by their capital, but the chronic condition of trouble and violent derangement in that island constantly causes disturbance in the social and political condition of our own people. It keeps up a continuous irritation within our own borders, injuriously affects the normal functions of business, and tends to delay the condition of prosperity to which this country is entitled.

"No exception can be taken to the general proposition that a neighboring nation, however deeply disturbed and injured by the existence of a devastating internal conflict at its doors, may be constrained, on grounds of international comity, to disregard its endangered interests and remain a passive spectator of the contest for a reasonable time while the titular authority is repressing the disorder. The essence of this moral obligation lies in the reasonableness of the delay invited by circumstances and by the effort of the territorial authority to assert its claimed rights. The on-looking nation need only wait 'a reasonable time' before alleging and acting upon the rights which it, too, possesses. This proposition is not a legal subtlety, but a broad principle of international comity and law.

" The question arises, then, whether Spain has not already had a reasonable time to restore peace and been unable to do so, even by a concentration of her resources and measures of unparalleled severity which have received very general condemnation. The methods which Spain has adopted to wage the fight give no prospect of immediate peace or of a stable return to the conditions of prosperity which are essential to Cuba in its intercourse with its neighbors. Spain's inability entails upon the United States a degree of injury and suffering which cannot longer be ignored. Assuredly Spain cannot expect this government to sit idle, letting vast interests suffer, our political elements disturbed, and the country perpetually embroiled, while no progress is being made in the settlement of the Cuban question. Such a policy of inaction would in reality prove of no benefit to Spain, while certain to do the United States incalculable harm. This government, strong in its sense of right and duty, yet keenly sympathetic with the aspirations of any neighboring community in close touch with our own civilization, is naturally desirous to avoid, in all rational ways, the precipitation of a result which would be painfully abhorrent to the American people. . . .

" You are hereby instructed to bring these considerations as promptly as possible, but with due allowance for favorable conditions, to the attention of the government of her majesty the queen regent, with all the impressiveness which their importance demands, and with all the earnestness which the constantly imperilled national interests of the United States justifies. You will emphasize the self-restraint which this government has hitherto observed until endurance has ceased to be tolerable or even possible for any longer indefinite term. You will lay especial stress on the unselfish friendliness of our desires, and upon the high purpose and sincere wish of the United States to give its aid only in order that a peaceful and enduring result may be reached, just and honorable alike to Spain and to the Cuban people, and only so far as such aid may accomplish the wished-for ends. In so doing you will not disguise the gravity of the situation nor conceal the President's conviction that, should his present effort be fruitless, his duty to his countrymen will necessitate an early decision as to the course of action which the time and the transcendent emergency may demand.

"As to the manner in which the assistance of the United States can be effectively rendered in the Cuban situation, the President has no desire to embarrass the government of Spain by formulating precise proposals. All that is asked or expected is that some safe way may be provided for action which the United States may undertake with justice and self-respect, and that the settlement shall be a lasting one, honorable and advantageous to Spain and to Cuba, and equitable to the United States." [1]

The new minister found a changed condition in Spanish politics. The forceful and able man who had hitherto been the government of Spain for many years as much as Richelieu had embodied, in his day, that of France, was no more. Señor Cánovas had been murdered by an Italian anarchist on August 8. Señor Azcárraga became the head of a ministry *ad interim*, to be succeeded on October 4 by a new ministry, with Señor Sagasta at its head, Señor Gullon, minister of state, and Señor Moret, minister of ultramar. These names were in themselves a promise of a new order in Cuba; a promise made doubly sure by the manifesto [2] of their party which had been issued when in opposition, June 24, 1897, and in which they declared themselves as ever eager for a policy as to Cuba differing from that of the conservatives, and as having "initiated and developed a policy before—and long before—the insurrection broke out, and it did so expressly to avoid and prevent it. To this policy responded, and by this purpose were inspired, the reforms of Señor Maura, which, had they not met with such parliamentary

[1] Instructions to Gen. Woodford, July 16, 1897, *Foreign Relations*, 1898, 558.
[2] Published June 24, 1897, in the evening paper *El Correo* (*The Post*) of Madrid. For this, see *Foreign Relations*, 1898, 592, 593.

obstacles and they been enacted, could have been reasonably applied, and, we rightfully believe, would have averted the disasters and prevented the horrors of the present insurrection." The manifesto was an augury of a change which was to be loyally attempted.

The new government was in the face of a most serious situation. "Sagasta before taking office declared that the financial situation was deplorable, if not desperate. . . . It is confessed that the troops in Cuba are six months in arrear in their pay and there is no money to send them. . . . Never before in the world's history has a nation made such sacrifices and put forth such an effort to subdue revolting colonies as has Spain since 1895. Between November, 1895, and May, 1897, no less than 181,738 men, 6,261 officers, and 40 generals have been sent to Cuba. Counting the garrisons already in the island, the total fighting force must have been hard on 225,000 men. In addition and during the same period, Spain has had to send 28,000 men to the Philippines. It is safe to say that no nation in modern or in ancient times ever sent across the seas so many of her fighting men in her own ships in the same length of time. It has been a supreme and unequalled display of energy, but it has been fruitless. . . . The pity of it all is that Spain has spent every power, has exhausted herself, and yet has not quickly ended the rebellion. In other words, the insurgent policy has triumphed in both its great aims; Spain is baffled and breathless; sympathy for Cuban independence has risen to great heights in the United States and is rising higher every day. . . . It is clear that the new ministry intends to try . . . the plan of placating by reforms and a grant of autonomy while still making a show of crushing out opposition by force. It is a question if this is not too late—if the change will not mean to the insurgents a final confession of weakness, and cause them to stand more stubbornly than ever for independence. . . . If so, Sagasta's task will be the difficult one of inducing the Spanish people to submit to the inevitable. He may be aided or he may be hampered by the attitude of our own government. At present, we must confess, a diplomatic collision and a rupture appear the most probable. But whichever way Spain turns the dilemma that confronts her is most cruel; and no one possessed of the historic imagination can fail to see pathos in the situation to-day of the nation that, three centuries ago, was at the head of Europe and of civilization." [1]

On September 18, 1897, General Woodford had his first interview with the Spanish minister of state, still the Duke of Tetuan, to whom he read the essential part of his instructions. The interview was one of nearly three hours, "friendly in manner, positive in meaning." He pressed the necessity of early peace and informed the minister that the Spanish government should give, "before the first of November next, such assurance as would satisfy the United States that early and certain peace can be promptly secured, and that otherwise the United States must consider itself free to take such steps as its government should deem necessary to procure this result, with due regard to our own interests and the general tranquillity." [2]

On September 23, 1897, the American minister presented the formal note, promised during the interview, practically a transcript of his instructions. Six days later, September 29, the ministry resigned, and on October 6 their successors were announced: Sagasta, president of the council; Gullon, minister of state; Moret, minister of the colonies.

Meanwhile the British, French, Russian, and German ambassadors at Madrid had severally called upon the new American minister for information as to the attitude and intentions of his government, and had received from him a full and frank expression of the views embodied in his instructions. In answer to a question from the French ambassador, General Woodford made a reply which unquestionably was the mind of the American administration: that we "sought neither annexation nor a protectorate, but only peace." [3]

Señor Gullon, the new minister of state, replied to General Woodford's note on October 23. He said, very truly, as shown by the manifesto of his party just mentioned:

"The present government of his majesty is now most advantageously situated for investigating the points referred to and for securing the pacification of Cuba on the proper basis, since its own character, the antecedents of those who compose it, and the public

[1] *The Nation*, October 17, 1897.
[2] *Foreign Relations*, 1898, 567.   [3] *Ibid.*, 1898, 580.

and solemn promises which in the past and of its own sole initiative it has made to the representatives of the country involve, in the colonial policy of Spain and in the manner of conducting the war, a total change of immense scope, which must exercise considerable influence upon the moral and material situation of the Greater Antilla. . . . [It] is determined to put into immediate practice the political system which the present president of the council of ministers announced to the nation in his manifesto of the 24th of June of this year. The acts accomplished by the present government, notwithstanding the short time which has elapsed since its elevation to power, are a secure guarantee that not for any one nor for anything will it halt in the path which it has traced, and which, in its best judgment, is that which will bring us to the longed-for peace.

"To military operations, uninterrupted for a single day and as energetic and active as circumstances demand, but ever humanitarian and careful to respect all private rights as far as may be possible, must be joined political action honestly leading to the autonomy of the colony in such a manner that upon full guarantee of the immutable Spanish sovereignty shall arise the new personality which is to govern itself in all affairs peculiar to itself by means of an executive organization and the insular council or chamber. . . .

"In order to realize this plan, which it advocates as a solemn political engagement voluntarily assumed while its members were in opposition, the government of his majesty proposes to modify existing legislation so far as necessary, doing so in the form of decrees to admit of its more speedy application, and leaving for the Cortes of the kingdom, with the co-operation of the senators and deputies of the Antillas, the solution of the economical problem and a patriotic and fair apportionment of the payment of the debt. . . ."

Señor Gullon, having thus stated the views and intentions of his government, remarked that while General Woodford's note stated that the President felt it his duty to make the strongest effort to contribute effectively toward peace, he did not state the measures he proposed to take. The minister himself had views as to what these should be, but they were simply a reiteration of a demand which the American government was already doing its utmost, under the law, to meet; his proposition being that while Spain should "continue to put forth armed efforts, at the same time decreeing the political concessions which she may deem prudent and adequate," the United States should "exert within their borders the energy and vigilance necessary to absolutely prevent the procurement of the resources of which from the beginning the Cuban insurrection has availed itself from an inexhaustible arsenal."

Señor Gullon, recurring to the unwise terms of President Taylor's proclamation in 1850, which gave such an opening to cruel and bloody action by Spanish officials in Cuba, proceeded to say how this should be done: "That while condemning by means of an energetic proclamation those violating the Federal laws and aiding the insurrection in Cuba, [the President] notify all American citizens doing so that they cannot henceforth count upon the diplomatic protection of the government of Washington in however grave a situation their wrongful conduct may place them. By thus abandoning to their fate those who infringe the fundamental statutes of the Union and openly conduct illegal filibustering expeditions, and by energetically and constantly restraining those who convert Federal territory into a field of action for reprehensible filibustering schemes, by exacting, lastly, of all superior and subordinate officials the strictest fulfilment of their duties in all that relates to the laws of neutrality, the President would do more toward peace than is possible by any other means or procedure whatever. If, however, it be alleged that the powers of the executive are limited on this point, we must recall the doctrine advanced by the United States before the arbitral tribunal of Geneva, according to which 'no nation may, under pretext of inadequate laws, fail in the fulfilment of its duties of sovereignty toward another sovereign nation.'"

He then cited, as an instance of what might be done, the act of March 10, 1838, passed on account of the difficulties on the Canadian border, which had arisen through the McKenzie rebellion,[1]

[1] The first two of the nine sections of this act (with the salient points italicized) were as follows: "Sec. 1. That the several collectors, naval officers [etc.] . . . of the United States shall be and they are hereby respectively authorized

adding: "He who is not disposed to grant the means does not earnestly desire the end in view; and in this case the end—to wit, peace—will be attained by the United States exerting itself energetically to enforce with friendly zeal the letter and spirit of its neutrality laws."

Señor Gullon reviewed the depressed military situation of the insurgents, the more tranquil conditions, and the better agricultural prospects of the western part of the island, and declared that a change of attitude toward the combatants, in the circumstances

and required to seize and detain *any vessel, or any arms or munitions of war* which may be provided or prepared for any military expedition or enterprise against the territory or dominions of any foreign prince or state, or of any colony, district, or people *coterminous with* the United States and with whom they are at peace, . . . and retain possession of the same until the decision of the President be had thereon, or until the same shall be released as hereinafter directed.

"Sec. 2. That the several officers mentioned in the foregoing section shall be and they are hereby respectively authorized and required to seize *any vessel or vehicle, and all arms and munitions of war, about to pass the frontier of the United States for any place within any foreign state or colony, coterminous with the United States,* when the character of the vessel or vehicle shall furnish probable cause to believe that the *said vessel or vehicle, and the quantity of arms and munitions, or other circumstances shall furnish probable cause to believe* that the said vessel or vehicle, arms or munitions of war, are intended to be employed by the owner or owners thereof, *or any other person or persons*, with his or their privity, in carrying on any military expedition [etc., as in Sec. 1]. . . . Provided that nothing in this act contained be so construed as to extend to or interfere with any trade in arms or munitions of war, conducted in vessels by sea with any port or place whatsoever, or with any other trade which might have been lawfully carried on before the passage of this act, under the law of nations and the provisions of the act hereby amended."

Such a law even if made permanent and extended to cases beyond sea would not have effected more than that of 1818, which, so far as it concerned the main question with Spain, forbade to "provide or prepare the means for any military expedition or enterprise to be carried on" from the United States. The gist of the whole matter was in the thoroughly established usage common to all countries and held to with great tenacity, particularly by the United States and Great Britain, of traffic in arms and in munitions of war, these being subject to seizure outside the country of origin under given circumstances. Had the United States at this juncture applied the law of 1838 to Cuban circumstances (a thing impossible to have brought about), and even had the efforts for prevention of supply to the Cubans been thoroughly effective, the latter would have turned to Great Britain or elsewhere. The United States were simply the most convenient source. (For a discussion of the law of 1838, which differs from the view here expressed, see George Bemis, *American Neutrality*, Little, Brown & Co., 1866; for the law in full, Niles's *Register*, LIV, 50; or Stat. V., 212. See further references in Moore's *Digest*, VII, 920.)

described "would be so ungrounded, so unjust, so unjustifiable, so contrary to the correct procedure of the Washington cabinet under circumstances when discrimination was much more difficult, that it must be rejected as utterly improbable. Whatever passions may, at a given moment, blind the judgment of a deliberative chamber in countries like the United States, where right and justice always triumph, the executive power will act as a secure safeguard, of whose fitness and energy any doubt would be offensive. . . .

"It is timely to remember that the American government had to admit in its note of April 4, 1896, that it was impossible to recognize the belligerency of the rebels at that time, although the insurrection was in a much more flourishing condition, and that, if Spain were withdrawn from the island of Cuba, the sole bond of union between the many heterogeneous elements in the island would disappear, which proves the necessity of her presence and the absurdity of the idea that there can be any other organization in the island possessing the attributes of lawful international personality. The insurgents, as has already been said on another occasion by his majesty's government, have always been and still are without real civil government, fixed territory, courts of their own, a regular army, coasts, ports, navy, everything that the principal American writers on international law and statesmen require as preliminary to the discussion of a recognition of belligerency. The rebel bands never fight for honor and victory, nor do they even defend themselves; they hide behind the dense thickets of the tropical soil and sally with impunity when the situation is temporarily in their favor. Under these circumstances it is impossible to admit that there can be a change in the attitude of the United States toward the combatants in Cuba.

"As his majesty's government has decided, freely and deliberately, to establish autonomy in Cuba, there arises by the force of circumstances the case foreseen by the eminent Mr. Cleveland in his message of December 7, 1896; and, admitting the continuing international accountability (solidarity) of the governments which succeed each other in a country, it can not be doubted that the present most worthy President will agree with his predecessor that no just reason exists for conjecturing that the pacification of the island of Cuba will fail to be effected upon this basis. The government of his majesty the King of Spain expects with confidence from the rectitude, love of peace, and friendship of the President of the United States that he will aid it in this noble and humane undertaking, and that he will exert himself energetically to prevent the insurrection from receiving from the United States the moral and material aid which gives it its only strength and without which it would have already been subdued or would certainly be subdued very speedily.

"It is, therefore, above all, indispensably necessary that the President should decide upon his course toward Spain so far as regards the Cuban problem, and that he should state clearly whether he is ready to put a stop absolutely and forever to those filibustering expeditions which, by violating with the greatest freedom the laws of friendship, injure and degrade the respect which the American government owes to itself in the discharge of its international engagements."

Señor Gullon now made reference, very mistakenly, as will be seen, to a late occurrence, saying in language hardly becoming the situation: "There must be no repetition of such lamentable acts as the last expedition of the schooner *Silver Heels*, which left New York in spite of the previous notification of his majesty's legation at Washington and before the eyes of the Federal authorities, because it is only thus that the peaceful intentions of the United States government will be proved and that the friendly understanding to which I have referred will be possible."

He declared "the advances and improvements" in Cuba, "which the Washington cabinet itself, not many months ago, in an official note, declared would be 'most potential' for the termination of hostilities, and for bringing about a change in the tendencies and feelings, not of the North American government, but of the very people of the United States on this subject, are also realized by the voluntary initiative of the mother country."

Señor Gullon ended, saying: "Her majesty's government, now and always faithful to the ties of affection which unite it with the United States, and cherishing, moreover, the firm intention of drawing them closer, in reply to the courteous wishes expressed of your excellency, will be most happy to have your excellency state whatever you may think proper, with entire liberty, and in the form that you may deem most fitting with regard to the alternatives mentioned, or upon any other points, with the assurance that your excellency's views, opinions, or assertions will always be heard with friendly interest, and will be respected so far as may be permitted to a government by primary and permanent duties, the neglect of which the Madrid cabinet cannot imagine that so respectworthy and so friendly a nation as the United States will advise." [1]

The attitude of mind, evident throughout Señor Gullon's paper, and ever that of the Spanish cabinet, of whatever complexion, could not be changed either by evidence or argument. It could not see that American law could not go beyond existing statutes without contravening what, in Anglo-Saxondom, were esteemed established rights; that the rights of free speech, free discussion in the press, and of public meeting were rights which no government such as that of the United States could suppress or would attempt to suppress; that the American government, the first which ever enacted a neutrality law, stood on unassailable ground in its declaration; that "a friendly government violates no duty of good neighborhood in allowing the free sale of arms and munitions of war to all persons, to insurgents as well as to the regularly constituted authorities, and such arms and munitions, by whichever party purchased, may be carried in its vessels on the high seas without liability to question by any other party. In like manner its vessels may freely carry unarmed passengers, even though known to be insurgents, without thereby rendering the government which permits it liable to a charge of violating its international duties. But, if such passengers, on the contrary, should be armed and proceed to the scene of the insurrection as an organized body, which might be capable of levying war, they constitute a hostile expedition which may not be knowingly permitted without a violation of international obligation." [2]

Nor would the Spanish government recognize the great lengths to which the American government had gone in its endeavors to

[1] Señor Gullon to General Woodford, October 23, 1897, *Foreign Relations*, 1898, 582.

[2] Mr. Fish to Admiral Polo de Bernabé, Spanish minister, April 18, 1874, *Ibid.*, 1875, 1190. Quoted by Mr. Sherman to General Woodford, November 20, 1897, *Ibid.*, 1898, 610.

suppress filibustering. "The Spanish reply," said the secretary of state, "appears to be unaware or heedless of the magnitude of the task which this government has performed and is still performing with the single purpose of doing its whole duty in the premises. To give a proof of this I need but cite the work of our navy toward the enforcement of the municipal obligations of neutrality. Since June, 1895, our ships of war have, without intermission, patrolled the Florida coast. At various times the *Raleigh, Cincinnati, Amphitrite, Maine, Montgomery, Newark, Dolphin, Marblehead, Vesuvius, Wilmington, Helena, Nashville, Annapolis,* and *Detroit* have been employed on this service.

"Starting with one ship having Key West as its head-quarters, the number on continuous duty was gradually increased to four, without counting additional service performed as special occasion demanded at other seaboard points. At the present time a vessel with head-quarters at Pensacola patrols the coast from the northwest as far south as Tampa, another with head-quarters at Key West patrols the coast from Tampa around to Miami on the east side, and a third with head-quarters at Jacksonville patrols the Atlantic coast from Miami to Georgia. The action of these regularly stationed ships is at all times concerted. Their commanders are ordered to communicate directly with one another, with the United States district attorneys in Florida, with the custom-house officials in that state, and with the commanding officers of the several revenue-cutters likewise on duty in that quarter. Acting upon the information thus received, they take such immediate action as they may deem advisable or necessary in order to prevent the violation of the neutrality laws.

" In addition to this stated detail on the Florida coasts, vessels belonging to the North Atlantic station have been sent at different times to the various Atlantic ports north of Georgia at the request of the Spanish minister and the department of state or upon receipt of information from the department of justice or the treasury department concerning reported filibustering expeditions. Many hundreds of official letters and telegrams record the orders given to these vessels and the action had by their commanders. It may be asserted, in short, that every vessel of the navy which could practically be employed in the shallow waters of the Florida coast has been detailed for this work, while for a time two revenue-cutters were transferred to the navy department to assist, besides the efficient co-operation of the regularly stationed cutters under the orders of the treasury department.

"No less degree of activity has marked the operations of the treasury department and the department of justice. Every means at lawful command have been employed by them in co-operation to enforce the laws of the United States. Alertness in every regard has been peremptorily enjoined upon all officials, high and low, and has been sedulously practised by them.

"In the light of these undisputable facts, and with this honorable record spread before him, the President is constrained to the conviction that nothing can be more unwarrantable than the imputation of the government of Spain that this government has in any wise failed to faithfully observe and enforce its duties and obligations as a friendly nation." [1]

The animadversions of Señor Gullon in the case of the *Silver Heels* were equally unjust. The escape of this schooner, October 16, 1897, with an expedition from New York was wholly due to to the officiousness of the Spanish officials themselves, on whose pressing request and against the judgment of the United States authorities, the treasury officials waited aboard the revenue-cutter in the stream, instead of seizing the schooner, as the latter had wished, at her wharf. She thus escaped under cover of the night.[2]

The desire of the new government of Spain to meet the views of that of the United States, and its earnestness in the question of reform, were shown by its decision October 6, to recall General Weyler, and in the steps taken to issue an autonomistic constitution for Cuba. General Blanco thus relieved General Weyler as governor-general, on October 31, 1897. Weyler left the same day in the mail steamer, *Montserrat,* for Spain. Before leaving he received a deputation and said among other things: "I had expected my release from the time of the death of Señor Cánovas, not believing that any political leader would be strong enough to sus-

---

[1] Secretary of state to American minister, November 20, 1897, *Foreign Relations*, 1898, 603–611. General Woodford to Señor Gullon, December 20, 1897, *Ibid.,* 653.   [2] See *Foreign Relations,* 1898, 611–615.

tain me when the United States and the rebels were together constantly demanding that Spain should come to a settlement"; a speech which was near to bringing him before a court-martial. He disembarked at Barcelona, where he met an enthusiastic reception, the Catalan protectionists being inimical to the new government on account of the fiscal autonomy now to be granted Cuba; in itself one of the strongest proofs of the sincerity of the Sagasta cabinet.

General Blanco at once attempted an alleviation of concentration, issuing a decree, November 13, 1897, that the *reconcentrados* be furnished a daily ration, the sick attended to, and agricultural and industrial labor reorganized as rapidly as circumstances would allow.

Those owning or leasing farms were, however, obliged to show that they had the means of working them; ordinary laborers were obliged to pass the night in the fortified place of the estate on which they labored, and owners were obliged to build centres of defence for the zones of cultivation, in the outer lines of which would be a defensive force of the army. Owners and laborers were allowed to carry arms for their defence; boards were ordered to be organized for the protection and care of those who could not meet the conditions for going again into the fields.[1]

It would have been impossible, even had circumstances favored, to remedy at once the woful conditions established by the two combatants during these nearly three wretched years. But circumstances did not favor. Thus a month later the American consul at Matanzas was reporting that "the scenes of misery and distress daily observed are beyond belief. . . . General Blanco's order . . . is inoperative and of no avail." Later on in the same report he gave a very good reason. The attitude of the insurgents made betterment impossible. The consul said: "A few plantations are grinding cane. In every case they are heavily guarded by Spanish troops, and have paid insurgents for so doing. Was shown a letter from insurgent chief to owner of large plantation, in which price demanded for grinding was two thousand centones (ten thousand six hundred dollars United States gold). It was paid."[2]

[1] Senate Doc. 230, 55 Cong., 2 Sess., 6.
[2] Consul Brice, Matanzas, December 17, 1897, *Ibid.*, 30.

But this was not the worst. The consul at Santiago wrote: "[I] inclose herewith an order issued by command of General Maximo Gomez . . . forbidding the grinding of the sugar crops for the years 1897 and 1898. In this part of Cuba, so far as I can learn, all idea of making a sugar crop is entirely abandoned. I regret to say that the stoppage of industries, from present appearances, will not halt at the sugar crop, but coffee and other agricultural crops fall under the same ban. I had hoped that after the reconcentration order was revoked by the energetic action of the present administration, we would find no trouble in reinstating American industries; but it appears that all the benefits that should have accrued to our citizens are thwarted by the insurgents who refuse to allow them to return to their sugar, coffee, and other estates. The Pompo Manganese mines, owned by Americans, which would at the present time be a very profitable investment if allowed to operate, are also being held up by the same power." He ended by saying: "It is beyond the power of my pen to describe the situation in eastern Cuba. Squalidity, starvation, sickness, and death meet one in all places. Beggars throng our doors and stop us in the streets. The dead in large numbers remain over from day to day in the cemeteries unburied." [1]

Three weeks later Consul Barker reports from Sagua la Grande: "One sugar-mill is running, not without interruption, with chances of making one-fourth of a crop. Another—just started up—was attacked yesterday by a band of insurgents, killing fourteen and wounding five of the guerrillas paid by the estate to protect the operatives. Seven laborers were killed, the insurgents leaving two of their dead." [2]

In the face of such orders and of such deeds, the letter addressed to President McKinley and purporting to be signed by the insurgent commander-in-chief, under whose directions such atrocities were enacted, was deeply false both in statement and spirit. The letter said: "However true and minute may be the reports you have heard, never will you be able to form a just conception of all the bloodshed, the misery, the ruin, and sorrow caused to afflicted Cuba to obtain her independence; and how the despotic spirit of

[1] Consul Hyatt, January 12, 1898, Senate Doc. 230, 55 Cong., 2 Sess., 38.
[2] Report, January 31, 1898.

Spain, irritated to the last degree before the most just of all rebellions, has revelled in the most implacable destruction of everything, lives and property." It continued later in a phrase which shows an extraordinary faculty of stifling one's moral perceptions, saying: "The revolution as master of the country has never prohibited any citizen, whatever his nationality, from earning his living." [1]

The deliberate destruction of the support of a people and the inhumanity shown in the orders of Gomez are deep stains upon the conduct of the Cuban cause. In 1894 there were more than three hundred and fifty sugar-mills in the island, many of which were great and costly establishments. Few of these escaped injury and, says an English authority, "about one-half were either totally destroyed or so thoroughly wrecked as to render necessary their almost complete reconstruction." [2] Such wreckage of property was in itself brutal; but when it involved, as it did to vast numbers of working people, deprivation of work and consequent suffering and death on a gigantic scale, it rises to the height of a crime which no ruler of military procedure can condone. Historic truth demands the setting forth of the fact that Cuban and Spaniard were alike regardless of the misery caused by their methods and of its extent. [3]

On November 25, 1897, three decrees were signed by the queen regent; the two first extended to the Antilles all rights enjoyed by peninsular Spaniards; the second established in the island the electoral laws of Spain (neither of these required the consent of the Cortes); the third, granting autonomy, required such consent.

The right was given to frame the insular budget both as to revenues and expenditure; to set apart the Cuban share of the national budget, which latter was to be voted by the national Cortes with the assistance of the Cuban members; to initiate or

[1] This letter with a translation was handed in at the office of the American consul-general at Havana by an unknown messenger, and forwarded by Consul-General Lee to Washington, February 15, 1898. (Sen. Doc. 230, 55 Cong., 2 Sess., 25.)

[2] Robinson, *Cuba and Intervention*, 97.

[3] Mr. Robinson, just quoted above, estimates that of the 3,000,000 cattle in Cuba before the war, ninety per cent. were slaughtered by the opposed forces. As the Cuban farmer depended chiefly upon oxen for his agriculture, the effect of this slaughter was most disastrous. (*Ibid.*, 96.)

take part in commercial treaties affecting Cuban interest; to accept or reject commercial treaties made without Cuban participation; to frame the colonial tariff, acting in accord with the peninsular government in scheduling articles of mutual commerce between the mother country and the colonies.[1] It fell short of Canadian autonomy in that the Canadian governor-general performs all his executive acts by and with the advice and consent of a council of ministers who are the leaders of the majority in the lower house, are thus created by it, as is the British cabinet, and must reflect the popular will. In any case, however, the decrees were far more liberal than anything theretofore offered; their very liberality was to cause their overthrow.[2]

The fact of the signing of the decrees, telegraphed from Madrid November 26, reached Washington in time for lengthened mention in the President's message, sent on the convening of Congress, December 6. The message dealt with Cuban affairs at great length. It declared that "The cruel policy of concentration . . . initiated February 16, 1896 . . . has utterly failed as a war measure. It was not civilized warfare. It was extermination."

Unconscious, apparently, of the true status of this subject in usage and in the rules of war, the President continued: "Against this abuse of the rights of war, I have felt constrained, on repeated occasions, to enter the firm and earnest protest of this government. There was much of public condemnation of the treatment of American citizens by alleged illegal arrests and long imprisonment awaiting trial or pending protracted judicial proceedings. I felt it my first duty to make instant demand for the release or speedy trial of all American citizens under arrest. Before the change of the Spanish cabinet in October last, twenty-two prisoners, citizens of the United States, had been given their freedom."

The President continued with a résumé of the correspondence between General Woodford and the Spanish minister of state, and declared the Spanish charge of failure by the United States to perform its international duties wholly "without any basis in fact. It could not have been made," he said, "if Spain had been cognizant of the constant efforts this government has made at the

[1] *Nation*, December 9, 1897.
[2] For these decrees in full, see *Foreign Relations*, 1898, 616–644.

cost of millions, and by the employment of the administrative machinery of the nation at command to perform its full duty according to the law of nations. That it has successfully prevented the departure of a single military expedition or armed vessel from our shores in violation of our laws would seem to be a sufficient answer. . . . Of the untried measures [of pacification] there remain only recognition of the insurgents as belligerents; recognition of the independence of Cuba; neutral intervention to end the war by imposing a rational compromise between the contestants, and intervention in favor of one or the other party. I speak not of forcible annexation, for that cannot be thought of. That by our code of morality would be criminal aggression."

The President quoted, at much length, President Grant's message of December 7, 1875, with full acceptance of its conclusions regarding recognition. He gave a synopsis of the newly decreed law for Cuba, saying: "That the government of Sagasta has entered upon a course from which recession with honor is impossible can hardly be questioned; that in the few weeks it has existed it has made earnest of the sincerity of its professions is undeniable. I shall not impugn its sincerity, nor should impatience be suffered to embarrass it in the task it has undertaken. It is honestly due to Spain and to our friendly relations with Spain that she should be given a reasonable chance to realize her expectations and to approve the asserted efficacy of the new order of things to which she stands irrevocably committed. She has recalled the commander whose brutal orders inflamed the American mind and shocked the civilized world. She has modified the horrible order of reconcentration, and has undertaken to care for the helpless and to permit those who desire to resume the cultivation of their fields to do so, and assures them of the protection of the Spanish government in their lawful occupations. She has just released the *Competitor* prisoners heretofore sentenced to death, and who have been the subject of repeated diplomatic corespondence during both this and the previous administration. Not a single American citizen is now in arrest or confinement in Cuba of whom this government has any knowledge."

The message ended with a phrase that could not be misunderstood, saying: "The near future will demonstrate whether the indispensable condition of a righteous peace, just alike to the Cubans and to Spain as well as equitable to all our interests so intimately involved in the welfare of Cuba, is likely to be attained. If not, the exigency of further and other action by the United States will remain to be taken. When that time comes that action will be determined in the line of indisputable right and duty. It will be faced without misgiving or hesitancy. . . . If it shall hereafter appear to be a duty imposed by our obligations to ourselves, to civilization, and humanity to intervene with force, it shall be without fault on our part and only because the necessity for such action will be so clear as to command the support and approval of the civilized world." [1]

The conservative Spanish view of the message is shown in a telegram from the minister at Washington, December 8, which said: "The greater part of the newspapers—among them many which have constantly demanded intervention in Cuban matters—compliment the message . . . and consider its tone very conservative and its tendency pacific which will assure security to the country by not bringing on a crisis. . . . Although there is much in it that is annoying, it is explicable in view of the sentiment of the Congress. To the democrats and opponents of the President, the message has seemed without force. Taylor [ex-minister to Spain] . . . says that the message is the most short-sighted and discreditable of the United States." [2]

The general impression in Spain was one at least not of dissatisfaction; the crisis had been tided over, and the announcement that the new autonomy was to have a fair trial was an offset to the threats which could be of value only in case of its failure. "It was remarked with reason that it was singular to see a government arrogate the right of distributing praise and blame to the authorities of a foreign nation. General Weyler, who was particularly aimed at in the presidential message, made violent protestation, in the form of an address to the queen regent, against this intrusion into the affairs of a foreign country. He was de-

---

[1] President McKinley, annual message, December 6, 1897, *Foreign Relations*, 1897, XI–XXI.

[2] De Lome to minister of state, December 8, 1897, *Spanish Cor. and Docs.*, 51.

nounced before a council of war on account of this, which might have given cause for grave diplomatic difficulties; but the United States, where, it must be borne in mind, attacks of this kind were almost of daily occurrence, had the good taste to attach no importance to this act of one who had become a private person."[1]

[1] Le Fur, *Étude sur la Guerre Hispano Américaine*, 15. Weyler's protest appeared in the *Paris Temps*, 2–3, January, 1898.

CHAPTER XXVI

CUBAN RELIEF.—HAVANA RIOTS.—THE INTERCEPTED LETTER AND RESIGNATION OF DUPUY DE LOME.—DESTRUCTION OF THE "MAINE"

WHATEVER the cause of Cuban suffering, the situation was one to call for sympathy from the coldest heart. The President took the initiative, and on December 24, 1897, the eve of the day which most appeals to kindly feeling among the Christian nations, a circular was sent from the department of state announcing that "in deference to the earnest desire of the government to contribute effective action toward the relief of the suffering people in the island of Cuba, arrangements have been perfected by which charitable contributions in money or the kind can be sent to the island by the benevolently disposed people of the United States." It was arranged with the Cuban authorities to admit all such articles free of duty. Consul-General Lee was directed to receive the offerings and to co-operate with the local authorities and the charitable boards in their distribution. The response was immediate and effective. The Red Cross Society lent its aid, both in contribution and in management, the president of the society, Miss Clara Barton, going herself with an excellently organized staff to Cuba.[1]

Though nothing beyond what has been already said is needed to show the necessity of such relief in general, a few words may be quoted from the report, January 18, 1898, of Consul Brice at Matanzas, which show that misery had extended to all classes.

---

[1] The earlier shipments were carried to Havana free of cost by the Ward line of steamships. Later the naval supply steamer *Fern* was used for the outlying ports, twelve thousand persons applied for relief on the first day of issuing rations. (See Miss Clara Barton, in *North American Review*, May, 1898, p. 554.) The aid thus rendered was continued until the outbreak of hostilities and did much to relieve the misery of the population.

Declaring that there were 90,000 people in the province of Matanzas alone in a starving condition, he added: "There are thousands of families (of the better classes, formerly well-to-do) who to-day are living on one meal a day, and that very scant. They have sold or pawned furniture, jewelry, clothing, etc., to eke out an existence, until all is gone or nearly so. . . . The daughter of a former governor of this province was seen begging in the streets (incognito) of this city. Many of these people call on me privately at my residence asking and praying for God's sake to be remembered when this relief comes from the United States."[1]

It was under such conditions that General Blanco had taken office. His earnest efforts to relieve distress, which included the appropriation of $100,000 for this purpose, a special tax on real estate in Havana, which by November 27 had already reached the amount of $88,000, and the formation of relief committees wherever the Spanish authorities had power, availed little against the disinclination of many subordinate officers to help forward autonomy. Both Spaniard and Cuban were against it. The consequence even of a message of peace to the Cubans in the field meant death to the messenger.[2] Said Consul Hyatt at Santiago de Cuba: "Personal appeals of provincial governors and other important officers have been made earnestly and often to the same individuals. . . . Wholesale removals of Spanish officers from civil positions are made by sweeping orders with instructions to fill their places with Cuban autonomists. About a week since came an order dismissing every employee of the custom-house in this city, to take effect as soon as proper autonomists could be found to fill their places. As yet only two have been named. . . . It is given out that sometime in the month of February there will be an election held for . . . sixty members of the council of administration, while seventeen additional ones are to be appointed by the governor-general. . . . The Cuban leaders declare that they will neither

[1] Senate Doc. 230, 55 Cong., 2 Sess., 31.
[2] Consul Hyatt to Assistant Secretary of State Day, January 1, 1898, Senate Doc. 230, 55 Cong., 2 Sess., 31. The trial by a summary court-martial and execution of Colonel Ruiz of the Spanish army for an endeavor to lay such a message before his friend Colonel Aranguren, of the Cuban forces, was a notable case in point. (See Pepper, *To-morrow in Cuba*, 86.)

make nominations nor go near the polls."[1] Less than a month later the same official could say: "Extremists of both sides seem able to dominate the sentiments of their respective parties. . . . Autonomy is already a dead issue."[2] It is not unfair to say that the state of affairs in the island was now not far from anarchic.

On January 12 Consul-General Lee telegraphed that serious riots were occurring in which mobs led by Spanish officers had attacked the offices of the newspapers advocating autonomy. The palace was reported heavily guarded and the consulate protected by armed men. Next day he telegraphed: "After a day and night of excitement, all business suspended, and rioting. Everything quiet at this hour. City heavily guarded. Soldiers protect public squares and threatened points. Mobs shouted yesterday, 'Death to Blanco, and death to autonomy,' while '*Viva* Weyler' was frequently heard. Contest between Spanish factions. Attention has not been directed to other issues. Heard once yesterday of a few rioters shouting a proposal to march to our consulate. Presence of ships may be necessary, but not now." Later in the day he was more uncertain as to the control by General Blanco of the situation. "If demonstrated he cannot maintain order, preserve life, and keep the peace, or if Americans and their interests are in danger ships must be sent, and to that end should be prepared to move promptly. Excitement and uncertainty predominate everywhere."[3]

On the next day the consul-general reported: "All quiet"; nor was there a renewal of the rioting. "The recent disorders," said General Lee, "are to be primarily attributed to a group of Spanish officers who were incensed at articles appearing in three of the newspapers of Havana, *El Reconcentrado, La Discusion,* and *El Diario de la Marina.* . . . It is probable that the Spanish officers were first provoked by the denunciations of Weyler in the columns of one of these papers, and determined to stop it, and afterward, being supported by the mob, turned the demonstration into an antiautonomistic affair. . . . The intense opposition to [the autonomistic plan] arises from the fact that the first appointment of officers to put into form its provisions were made generally outside of their

[1] Mr. Lee to Mr. Day, January 8, 1898, Sen Doc. 230, 55 Cong., 2 Sess., 38.
[2] *Ibid.,* February 1, 1898, 41.
[3] Telegram, January 13, 1898, *Foreign Relations,* 1898, 1025.

party in order to show the Cubans in arms that autonomy was instituted for their benefit and protection.[1]

The decision made early in the winter to send south what was known as the North Atlantic Squadron, whose area of duty was the Atlantic coast and the Caribbean, had caused an inquiry on December 16, 1897, from the Spanish minister of state to Señor Dupuy de Lome as to its mission. This was in itself entirely peaceful; it had already been detained in the bleak northern waters during two winters, in deference to Spanish sentiment and to the detriment of efficiency and health, and it was in no sense unreasonable that it should now be sent to the warmer waters of the Gulf of Florida, an admirable exercising ground specially adapted as such through its calms and the shallowness which allowed anchorage many miles from land. The Spanish minister was informed that the decision to send the squadron had been made some time before, and that its usual drills had been resumed in southern waters in order not to arouse excited public sentiment, and also with the purpose of demonstrating that the situation had improved, and to avoid the demand for ships to go to Cuba.[2]

While events just mentioned gave reason for concern for the safety of the many Americans resident in Havana, the departure of the squadron at Hampton Roads, assembled in anticipation of its southern cruise, was not hastened; nor was there necessity for so doing as there was already ample force in Florida waters, engaged in looking after filibusters, to render assistance in case of need.[3]

The riots, though the result of party antagonism among the Spaniards themselves, had greatly disturbed American feeling, a change which the Spanish minister at Washington was quick to recognize. He telegraphed Madrid, January 14, 1898, that while no ships would be sent, the change of "sentiment has been so abrupt, and our enemies, influenced by it, so numerous, that any sensational

[1] Mr. Lee to Mr. Day (confidential), January 18, 1898, Senate Doc. 230, 55 Cong., 2 Sess., p. 20.

[2] Señor Dupuy de Lome to Señor Gullon, December 16, 1897, *Spanish Cor. and Docs.*, 52.

[3] The vessels at or near Key West were the battle-ship *Maine*, cruiser *Montgomery*, torpedo-boats *Cushing*, *Ericsson*, and *Dupont*, and several revenue vessels. The original purpose, however, of the *Maine* was to have a ship at hand which could render assistance to Americans, should need arise, in Havana.

occurrence might produce a change and disturb the situation."[1] Two days later Señor Dupuy de Lome telegraphed: "The news from Havana has not improved; if it continues it will cause the situation here to change. The sensational press is just as it was in the worst period, and the government and cabinet seem to have lost all faith in Spain's success, and, to some extent, to have lost tranquillity. I have just had a conference with the head of staff of the *Herald*, a person of importance here and generally well informed. He told me that in view of recent events the President has stated that, according to information he has received, autonomy in Cuba has come to nothing; that grave disorders are feared in Havana and throughout the island, and that, if the disorders are repeated, he had determined to land troops from the war vessels to protect the consulate. He asked me what would be done if that occurred. I told him that it would mean fighting; that Spain would never submit to what was done in Korea and Crete . . . it indicates a state of things that would have been impossible a week ago."[2] The minister of state at once replied that Señor Dupuy de Lome had "very properly considered" the eventuality reported to him "as intolerable."[3]

Havana continued calm, the Spanish minister telegraphed January 24, 1898, that in "a long and important conference," on the same date with Mr. Day, he was informed that "the President had not departed in any way from the attitude set forth in the message, which left the Spanish government in entire liberty to develop its policy." Later, the same day, the minister was told that the result of his morning conference "and the reports concerning the commercial negotiations confirmed by Woodford have been so satisfactory that the President has determined to send the *Maine* to Havana as a mark of friendship, and the secretary of the navy would so state to the press . . . the sending of the vessel simply as a visit must be taken as an act of friendly courtesy, and not looked upon in any other aspect; that the President believes it has been a mistake not to have had an American war vessel visit Cuba in the past three years, because now what is a fresh proof of international courtesy is looked upon as a hostile act. The secretary

[1] Señor Dupuy de Lome to Señor Gullon, *Spanish Cor. and Docs.*, 64.
[2] *Ibid.*, 65.   [3] *Ibid.*, 65.

of the navy has given to the press the following statement: 'The rumors which were current yesterday regarding the movements of the fleet and disturbances in Havana are far from having foundation. Circumstances have become so normal, the situation so quiet, and relations so cordial that our war vessels are to renew their friendly visits to Cuban ports, entering and leaving those ports to go to ports of other neighboring friendly countries. The first vessel to make a visit of this kind will be the *Maine*.' "[1]

The Spanish minister of state, while commending Señor Dupuy de Lome's discussion with Mr. Day, replied: "The attitude of that government does not completely satisfy me, because it does not heed your excellency's request that the outcome of autonomy be awaited, nor does it publish its unalterable determination to continue in the path of peace, scorning or overcoming every agitation to the contrary which may be set in motion. Bearing in mind that the evidence of the important acts initiated and already realized by the insular government of Cuba is apparent to all, the government of the United States ought to inaugurate toward Spain a more considerate, frank, and favorable policy than that proclaimed in the presidential message. Until this happens and we are satisfied in regard to Lee, we shall endeavor to maintain ourselves as heretofore in the most correct path." He cordially accepted the state-

---

[1] Señor Dupuy de Lome to Señor Gullon (telegram), January 24, 1898, *Spanish Cor. and Docs.*, 68.

General Lee was informed by telegram, January 24: "It is the purpose of this government to resume friendly naval visits at Cuban ports. In that view the *Maine* will call at the port of Havana in a day or two. Please arrange for a friendly interchange of calls with the authorities."

Lee answered the same day: "Advise visit be postponed six or seven days to give last excitement more time to disappear. Will see authorities and let you know result. Governor-general away for two weeks. I should know day and hour [of] visit."

To this Assistant Secretary of State Day replied on the same date: "*Maine* has been ordered. Will probably arrive at Havana some time to-morrow. Cannot tell hour; possibly early. Co-operate with authorities for her friendly visit. Keep us advised by frequent telegrams."

On January 25, before the ship's arrival, at 11 A. M., Lee telegraphed: "At an interview authorities profess to think United States has ulterior purpose in sending ship. Say it will obstruct autonomy, produce excitement, and most probably a demonstration. Ask that it is not done until they can get instructions from Madrid, and say that if for friendly motives, as claimed, delay unimportant." (Sen. Doc. 230, 55 Cong., 2 Sess., 84, 85.)

ments regarding the visit of the *Maine,* and added that "to reciprocate such friendly and courteous demonstrations, we shall arrange also that vessels of our squadron may visit the ports of the United States in passing to and from the island of Cuba." [1] On the same date as that of this message the *Maine* anchored in Havana harbor, with no unusual or untoward incident. [2]

Three days later at the annual diplomatic dinner at the White House the Spanish minister reports that the President, after the dinner, requested the minister to sit with him and the English, German, and French ambassadors, although there were nine other ministers having precedence. On rising the President approached Señor Dupuy de Lome and said: "I see that we only have good news; I am well satisfied with what has occurred in the House and with the discipline of the Republicans. You, who comprehend this, will understand this, and will understand how strong our position is and how much it has changed and bettered in the past year; you have no occasion to be other than satisfied and confident." "This sincere declaration," said Señor de Lome in the telegram which he sent the minister of state next day, "was witnessed by all the foreign diplomats." [3]

On February 1, 1898, Señor Gullon replied to the American minister's note of December 20, 1897. He complained that the satisfaction from the statements "giving eloquent expression to the recognition of the irreproachable procedure of Spain is to a great extent destroyed or diminished by the blame cast upon the predecessors of the present government, and still more so by the fact that the numerous and incredible excesses committed by the Cuban insurgents are confounded in the same category with the conduct of the regular army," a criticism the justice of which cannot be denied. The minister protested that his government could not consent to a foreign cabinet's making use of party struggles or re-

[1] Señor Gullon to Señor Dupuy de Lome (telegram), January 25, 1898, *Spanish Cor. and Docs.,* 69.

[2] The *Maine* arrived without any demonstration, the usual visits were made and returned, and everything, in so far as the visit was concerned, was normal. Two German naval vessels were also at Havana.

On February 18, three days after the destruction of the *Maine,* the Spanish armored cruiser *Vizcaya* arrived at New York where she remained a week and then went to Havana. [3] *Spanish Cor. and Docs.,* 71.

criminations as a basis for its views in its diplomatic relations, as they were "domestic matters entirely foreign to the judgment or decision of other nations." He said not very appositely: "The more expressive and earnest the congratulations with which you admit that the Spanish government has drawn the plans and laid the foundations of a noble structure in Cuba, so much the less justifiable and so much [the] less intelligible is the hint" that the United States could only reasonably be expected by Spain to maintain its present attitude until facts should prove that the indispensable requisites to a peace, fair and just to all concerned, should be attained.

Continuing, he said: "The Spanish government assuredly did not admit that reasons of proximity or damages caused by war to neighboring countries might give such countries a right to limit, to a longer or shorter period, the duration of a struggle disastrous to all, but much more to the nation in which it breaks out or is maintained." He referred to his note of October 23, 1897, as proving that while anxiety for peace or friendly suggestions might be expressed, "never and under no circumstances" could foreign intrusion or interference be justified. Spain would, he said, act upon these honorable principles, "just as the United States nobly acted upon them" in 1861. He cited the instructions of Mr. Seward to the American minister at Paris, April 22, 1861, as constituting "a notable example for all countries which, like Spain, value their honor above all else, even to (the execution of) the declared purpose to 'struggle with the whole world,' rather than to yield to pressure from without."[1]

The minister declared that while the radical reforms instituted were in progress, "it is certainly not the time for the United States government to substitute for its former offers of its good offices hints of a change of conduct in the event of more or less remote contingencies, and to base this notification of its change not only upon the contingency of a material success . . . but upon its own estimate of the success itself."

He cited Calvo's statement that "international law does not merely oblige states to prevent their subjects from doing anything to the detriment of the dignity or interests of friendly nations or governments; it imposes upon them, in addition, the strict duty

[1] Presidents' Messages and Docs., 1861-65, 200.

of opposing within their own territory all plots, machinations, or combinations of a character to disturb the security of countries with which they maintain relations of peace, friendship, and good harmony."[1] Under this, he stated, had been addressed the request to Washington "on numerous occasions to prevent, with a firm hand, the departure of filibustering expeditions against Cuba, and to dissolve or prosecute the Junta which is sitting publicly in New York, and which is the active and permanent centre of attacks upon the Spanish nation." In this connection, he said that all that the Spanish government had allowed itself to do was "to suggest the means of rendering real and effectual those obligations which are derived from true friendship, such as the Spanish government understands it, either by the proclamation of the same nature and as emphatic as those which illustrious predecessors of the illustrious President, Mr. McKinley, thought themselves called upon to publish under similar circumstances, or by the severe application of the regulations in force, or by their amendment or enlargement, as occurred in the act of March 10, 1838."[2]

The watchfulness "during the last few months along the extended coasts of America" was recognized "with genuine gratitude." The paper closed with a declaration of the "firm resolution [of the Spanish people and government] to maintain their legitimate and traditional sovereignty in the island of Cuba at every hazard," and with an appeal to the United States to recognize the changed conditions saying: "It is only in this formula of colonial self-government and Spanish sovereignty that peace, which is so necessary to the Peninsula and to Cuba, and so advantageous to the United States, can be found."[3]

The movement southward of the American squadron continued to give much concern to the Spanish government. Señor Gullon

---

[1] Calvo, *Le Droit International*, §1298, III, 156. [2] *Supra*, 515 (note).
[3] Señor Gullon to General Woodford, February 1, 1898, *Spanish Cor. and Docs.*, 71–78. Also *Foreign Relations*, 1898, 658. To this note no return was ever made; a few weeks later General Woodford, in an interview with Señores Gullon and Moret, informed them that he regarded the note as a serious mistake; that he would advise all possible delay in answering it; and that whether the answer would be pleasant or disagreeable must depend entirely on practical results in Cuba. General Woodford to President McKinley, February 26, 1898, *Foreign Relations*, 1898, 664.

telegraphed Señor Dupuy de Lome, February 8, 1898: "The display and concentration of naval forces near Havana and in the waters near the Peninsula (Spain), and the persistency with which the *Maine* and *Montgomery* remain in the Greater Antilles are causing increasing anxiety and might, through some mischance, bring about a conflict. We are trying to avoid it at any cost, making heroic efforts to maintain ourselves in the severest rectitude." [1]

Even while the Spanish minister of state was sending this, the first serious blow was being given to the improved understanding between the two governments. At the same moment of Señor Gullon's despatch, Señor Dupuy de Lome was telegraphing that a letter sent by him to Señor José Canalejas, the editor of the Madrid *Herald*, who had been visiting the United States, but was now inspecting conditions in Cuba, had been intercepted, and Señor Dupuy de Lome was informed of its prospective publication next day in a New York paper.[2] While not remembering the "humiliating" terms in which, the paper claimed, he had spoken of the President, he said: "It may be true, and my position here would be untenable. I notify your excellency in order that you may decide upon the course best for the queen and Spain, without considering me in any way." [3]

The publication was made on February 9, as promised. While undated, internal evidence showed it to have been written about the middle of December, 1897. It began with some frank truths, saying: "The situation remains here the same. Everything depends on the political and military outcome in Cuba. The prologue of all this, in this second phase of the war, will end the day when the colonial cabinet shall be appointed, and we shall be relieved in the eyes of this country of a part of the responsibility for what is happening in Cuba, while the Cubans, whom these people think so immaculate, will have to assume it. Until then

---

[1] *Spanish Cor. and Docs.*, 80.

[2] The American minister at Madrid was informed by Señor Moret, minister of ultramar, that the letter had been stolen from the Havana post-office by a Spanish clerk in the office and who was a spy in the service of the insurgents. General Woodford to President McKinley, March 4, 1898, *Foreign Relations*, 1898, 676.

[3] Señor Dupuy de Lome to Señor Gullon, February 8, 1898 (telegram), *Ibid.*, 80.

nothing can be clearly seen, and I regard it as a waste of time and progress by a wrong road to be sending emissaries to the rebel camp, or to negotiate with the autonomists who have as yet no legal standing or to try and ascertain the intentions and plans of this government. The [Cuban] refugees will keep on returning one by one, and as they do so, will make their way into the sheepfold, while the leaders in the field will gradually come back. Neither the one nor the other had the courage to leave in a body, and they will not be brave enough to return in a body."

The letter continued with the first of the two passages which were notably objectionable. "The message has been a disillusionment to the insurgents, who expected something different; but I regard it as bad [for us]. Besides the ingrained and inevitable ill-breeding (*groseria*) with which is repeated all that the press and public opinion in Spain have said about Weyler, it once more shows what McKinley is, weak and a bidder for the admiration of the crowd, besides being a would-be politician (politicastro) who tries to leave a door open behind himself while keeping on good terms with the jingoes of his party."

The second, following at some interval, was regarded more gravely than even the animadversions against the President, "by reason of the want of candor which appeared to underlie the proposition for a reciprocity arrangement with the autonomous government of Cuba, which [Dupuy de Lome] shortly afterward brought forward and advocated with much profession of earnestness."[1] It read: "It would be very advantageous to take up, even if only for effect, the question of commercial relations, and to have a man of some prominence sent hither in order that I may make use of him here to carry on a propaganda among the senators and others in opposition to the Junta and to try and win over the refugees."[2]

[1] Secretary of state to General Woodford, February 23, 1898, *Foreign Relations*, 1898, 1018.
[2] For the letter in full, see Moore's *Digest*, VI, 176, 177. A paragraph intervening between the two quoted said: "I do not think sufficient attention has been paid to the part England is playing. Nearly all the newspaper rabble that swarms in your hotels are Englishmen and while writing for the *Journal*, they are also correspondents of the most influential journals and reviews of London. It has been ever so since this thing began. As I look at

Mr. Day, calling upon the Spanish minister, was informed by the latter that the letter was his; "that as minister from Spain, [he] could say nothing, but claiming right to express [his] opinion privately, as, with such frequency and less discretion, the American agents have done." In his telegram conveying this conversation, Señor Dupuy de Lome added: "My position, you will see, cannot be what it was before; I do not believe I can continue here."[1]

On the next day, February 10, 1898, the minister of state telegraphed: "In accordance with your excellency's urgent initiative, in view of recent incidents and before any manifestation on the part of the United States government could be provoked, the acceptance of your excellency's resignation was adopted and communicated to the representative of the United States."[2]

A telegram stating that the immediate recall of the offending minister was expected had been sent on the 9th, but was not received by General Woodford until the next day. On calling in the afternoon upon the minister of state to whom the message was read, he found the action just mentioned already taken, and telegraphed that the resignation had been proffered and accepted by cable before the interview. On February 14, General Woodford called attention in a note to the minister of state that although it was the fourth day since their interview, he had "not yet had the satisfaction of receiving any formal indication that his majesty's government regrets and disavows the language and sentiments which were employed and expressed" in Señor Dupuy de Lome's letter. Hoping and believing that the Spanish government had not received the text, he enclosed the two offending paragraphs.[3] Señor Gullon replied the next day that the Spanish government "with entire sincerity lamented the incident." He however deprecated the stress laid upon the second paragraph quoted as objectionable, which, written at a date now relatively distant, could not be used to throw doubt upon the good faith in such negotiations of the Spanish government, which, "with respect to the new colonial régime and the projected treaty of commerce, gave it, England's only object is that the Americans should amuse themselves with us and leave her alone, and if there should be a war, that would the better stave off a conflict which she dreads, but which will never come about."

[1] *Spanish Cor. and Docs.*, 81.
[2] Señor Gullon to Señor Dupuy de Lome, *Ibid.*, 81. [3] *Ibid.*, 83.

such evident proofs of its real designs and of its innermost convictions that it does not now consider compatible with its prestige to lay stress upon or to demonstrate anew the truth and sincerity of its purposes and the unstained good faith of its intentions."[1] The American government recognized that the safety of the ministry did not permit it to go further in open concession and the incident was closed by a note from the American minister, February 19, stating his government's satisfaction with Señor Gullon's reply.[2]

"The publication of the letter," says a personal and confidential note from Assistant Secretary Day to General Woodford, on March 3, "created a good deal of feeling among Americans, and but for the fact that it was a private letter, surreptitiously, if not criminally obtained, it might have raised considerable difficulty in dealing with it diplomatically. . . . If a rupture between the countries must come, it should not be upon any such personal and comparatively unimportant matter."[3]

The assistant secretary could well mention the incident as "comparatively unimportant," for at 9.40 P. M., February 15, the *Maine* had been blown up in Havana harbor, with the loss of two officers and two hundred and fifty-eight men.

The ship had been lying in the harbor just three weeks. There had been question of her removal for sanitary reasons, and the assistant secretary of state, telegraphing this on February 4, had also said: "Should some vessel be kept there all the time? If another sent, what have you to suggest as to kind of ship?" To this Consul-General Lee had replied the same day: "Do not think slightest sanitary danger to officers or crew until April or even May. Ship or ships should be kept here all the time now. We should not relinquish peaceful control of situation, or conditions would be worse than if vessel had never been sent. Americans would depart with their families in haste if no vessel in harbor, on account of distrust of preservation of order by authorities. If another riot occurs, [it] will be against the governor-general and autonomy, but might include anti-American demonstration also. First-class battle-ship should replace present one if relieved, as object-lesson

---

[1] Señor Gullon to General Woodford, February 15, 1898, *Spanish Cor. and Docs.*, 84.   [2] *Ibid.*, 85.   *Foreign Relations*, 1898, 680.

and to counteract Spanish opinion of our navy, and should have torpedo-boat with it to preserve communication with admiral."[1]

The *Maine*, in consequence of this opinion, remained. On the occurrence of the disaster there was immediate expression to the American minister at Madrid of deep sympathy from the Spanish government, Admiral Camara bearing from the minister of marine a special message of sympathy from the Spanish navy. The Spanish minister at Washington presented personally the expression of grief of the queen regent, and warm messages of condolence were received from Governor-General Blanco and the alcalde of Havana. The recovered dead, after lying in state in the civil government building of Havana, were buried at the Havana cemetery in ground presented to the United States. "They were escorted to the cemetery by representatives of all military, naval, and civil organizations, and foreign consular officers, and through a vast concourse of people spreading over the route."[2] The survivors were cared for at the hospitals with every kindness.[3]

The "court of inquiry" of three members and a judge-advocate, customary under the American naval regulations in cases of accidents to ships, was ordered to inquire into the disaster. The members were Captains Sampson and Chadwick and Lieutenant-Commander Potter, all of the squadron which had been engaged in drills in the Gulf of Florida, with head-quarters at the Dry Tortugas, and Lieutenant-Commander Marix, sent from Washington as judge-advocate. The court left for Havana on the 20th of February in the lighthouse steamer *Mangrove*, aboard which, while in Havana, the members of the court lived and carried on their duties. The tender *Fern*, the coast-survey steamer *Bache*, and the cruiser *Montgomery*, were ordered to Havana to assist the court in various ways and to aid in caring for the survivors of the *Maine*. In the call made by the members of the court of inquiry on their arrival upon Governor-General Blanco, any examination beyond the ship's side was objected to by the latter, and the Spanish authorities

---

[1] *Foreign Relations*, 1898, 1027. The torpedo-boat *Cushing* was sent February 11, but remained only two days.

[2] Sigsbee, *The Maine*, 110.

[3] For the expressions of condolence from Spanish authorities and the replies thereto, see *Foreign Relations*, 1898, 1029-1035.

instituted an examination by their own people, which was carried on simultaneously with that of the American court.

The gravity of the situation and the responsibility resting on the court was fully felt by the members. The situation precluded any haste and the inquiry was carried on deliberately, carefully, and searchingly for twenty-three days, and with every effort to reach a fair and just finding.

Necessarily the destruction of a battle-ship and two-thirds of her people would be an appalling event under any circumstances. "For a brief time," as said the President in his message, "intense excitement prevailed" in the United States, but with the exception of a certain class of newspapers, the general attitude was in every way to be praised. Said the *Nation:* "The admirable conduct of the government officials at Washington renders the course of the sensational press in this city [New York] the more shameful by contrast. . . . It speaks well for the good sense of the masses that so little effect has been produced by all this stuff. It is evident that a large proportion of the public refuses to take the sensational newspapers seriously." [1]

[1] *The Nation*, February 24, 1898, p. 139.

CHAPTER XXVII

THE FIFTY MILLION BILL.—EXCHANGE OF VIEWS AT MADRID.— SPAIN'S FATAL PROCRASTINATION

THE Spanish government now complained seriously of Consul-General Lee. Señor Moret, minister of ultramar, during a frank conversation with the American minister, on March 1, requested by the former, insisting that autonomy was making real and effective progress, that it was winning the business classes, the planters, and all the great middle class to its support, said, "it will surely succeed if it can have the sympathy of the American consul-general at Havana and the friendship of the United States." "Moret," said General Woodford, reporting the conversation, "believes that General Lee's home and legation are centres of sympathy for the insurrection, and that through General Lee's conversation, reports, and general personal and official influence the insurrection is helped and autonomy retarded." On leaving he handed General Woodford a memorandum which said: "Spain cannot consider him a reliable man and is entitled to say that his reports are misleading and untrustworthy. Consul Lee freely admits that he is corresponding with the insurgents and openly avows that he is deadly against autonomy. The insular government distrusts him as well, and is much inclined to solicit his recall." To this reply came by telegram of the next day: "The President will not consider any proposal to withdraw General Lee. Even a suggestion of his recall at this time would be most unfortunate from every point of view. Our information and belief is that throughout this crisis General Lee has borne himself with great ability, prudence, and fairness." [1] General Woodford was able to reply on March 4 that there would be no suggestion of recall of Consul-General Lee; "the minister fully appreciates the situation." [2]

The death-blow to autonomy was given on March 9 in the appro-

[1] *Foreign Relations*, 1898, 675, 676.   [2] *Ibid.*, 676.

priation by Congress, without a dissentient vote, of fifty million dollars, "for the national defence and for each and every purpose connected therewith, to be expended by the President, and to remain available until January 1, 1899." [1]

It was now impossible that the insurgents, with hopes raised to highest pitch by action which could to them have but one meaning, should now yield to Spain's offers. Coming so quickly upon the dismissal of a trusted minister and the destruction of the *Maine*, it was as a knell to Spain's hopes for Cuba. The news in Spain, said General Woodford, writing to the President on the date of the passage of the act, "has not excited the Spaniards—it has stunned them. To appropriate fifty millions out of money in the treasury, without borrowing a cent, demonstrates wealth and power. Even Spain can see this. To put this money, without restriction and by unanimous vote, absolutely at your disposal demonstrates entire confidence in you by all parties. The ministry and the press are simply stunned." [2] Two days later the new minister of Spain to Washington, Señor Polo de Bernabé, was at his post, and telegraphed, "In spite of the supremeness of this measure, the situation at the moment appears more tranquil, while still of undeniable gravity," [3] an opinion which could not have much value so long as the effect in Cuba should not be taken into account. On March 12 the minister telegraphed that he had been received by the President, "who made a most gracious address. I fear, nevertheless, that the acts will not bear out the words." [4]

The American minister throughout had had correspondence with the President, to whom he wrote frequently and at great length, as well as to his direct superior, the secretary of state. On March 17 he wrote the former in a letter numbered forty-three: "With the exception of Minister Moret and those whom his splendid courage and personal magnetism inspire and control, I do not think that any thoughtful man in Madrid now believes that autonomy, and what is euphemistically called 'influencing rebel chiefs,' and military operations combined, can practically suppress the

[1] *Cong. Record*, 55 Cong., 2 Sess., p. 2631.
[2] *Foreign Relations*, 1898, 684.
[3] Señor Polo de Bernabé to minister of state, March 10, 1898, *Spanish Cor. and Docs.*, 90. [4] *Ibid.*, 91.

rebellion *before the rainy season begins.* Señor Sagasta, an experienced statesman, a loyal Spaniard, and a faithful friend of the queen . . . waits hoping against hope. I think he would do anything for peace that Spain would approve and accept. Señor Gullon evidently doubts whether peace can be maintained. . . . [On] February 7 I . . . reported that the present ministry had decided that they have made all the concessions to the United States that they can make without endangering their own power and the continuance of the present dynasty; that they will do no more and will fight if what they have done does not secure our continued neutrality. In my No. 33 of February 19 [the numbers referred to the letters to the President], I confirmed my belief in the disposition and decision of the Spanish government to make no further concessions . . . [Señor Moret's admission] that the delay of one month in dissolving the old Cortes and convening the new one was due to the request of the insular government, throws much light upon the Cuban question."

The minister continued: "To-day I have more hope in possible peace than I have had since I sailed from New York. The unanimous passage of the Cannon [fifty million dollars] bill at Washington and the reception of the news here in Madrid, give me this hope. . . . The thought of sale is to-day in the air of Madrid. . . . I think the largest shareholders of the Spanish debt will soon advise the sale. But Señor Moret has now made a speech . . . in which he has taken very positive ground that autonomy will succeed. His speech is clever and strong; but . . . even he may change. . . . I believe that Spain, tired out and exhausted, threatened with practical famine, and confronted with the immediate necessity of tremendous outlay, would thank the queen for her wisdom and courage should she dare to part with Cuba without war, and would sustain her even if she were compelled to change her ministry to secure this result." After analyzing the prospect of continued famine and anarchy throughout the summer, he said: "I am thus, reluctantly, slowly, and entirely a convert to the American ownership and occupation of the island. . . . I therefore ask your permission to treat [if we could purchase at a reasonable price] . . . should the opportunity ever be presented."[1]

[1] General Woodford to President McKinley, March 17, 1898, *Foreign Relations,* 1898, 685.

It was but the next day that he again wrote the President (No. 44) at great length, saying: "At noon I learned that the council of ministers had held long and heated meeting; that the ministers of war and navy had advised immediate action by Spain, urging that each day of delay increased our preparation for war and lessened any chance of Spanish success; that Moret had argued for peace; that Sagasta had finally and positively declared for peace on any terms at all consistent with Spanish honor; that the peace party had triumphed and that the ministers of war and navy had withdrawn their threats of possible resignation." Later in the day General Woodford had an interview of an hour and a half with Señor Moret, who requested that the talk should be as between "Mr. Woodford and Mr. Moret, as he thought the time had come for a full and free understanding between us in the interest of peace." Señor Moret asked: "Can you not, and will you not ask your President to advise the insurgents to lay down their arms and accept autonomy?" General Woodford replied: "I cannot; you would not accept our good offices last autumn, and the self-respect of my government forbids our tendering them again except at the official request of Spain, and such request, to be efficient now, should leave us a very free hand."

Requested by Señor Moret to "talk freely. . . . If we can understand each other fully we can work together for peace, and that is what my unhappy country needs," General Woodford, after referring to the oncoming rainy season and the continuation of disorder and suffering, said: "The Spanish flag cannot give peace; the rebel flag cannot give peace; there is but one flag and one power that can secure peace and compel peace; that power is the United States and that flag is our flag." Encouraged by Señor Moret, he gave his views, mentioning that they were wholly personal and without authority: "The United States to pay a fixed sum for the purchase of the island; a part of such price to be retained as a fund for the payment of all claims due from the United States to Spain or to Spanish citizens, and from Spain to the United States or citizens of the United States"; the claims to be determined by a commission; the agreement to sell need not be published, the public memorandum might only provide for adjustment of all differences, with the Queen of Great Britain as arbitrator.

Señor Moret asked if serious opinion in the United States would be willing to purchase Cuba; also whether it was thought the United States would be willing to guarantee the Cuban debt if independence were granted, which would be a practical protectorate, and what General Woodford thought would be the effect upon Spain if she were to part with the island.

He was answered that it was believed that the great body of thoughtful Americans were as opposed to immediate annexation as General Woodford himself was; "that after all the excitement of temporary and passionate discussion our people think carefully and act deliberately." General Woodford rehearsed the exaggerated views as to the reduction of Cuban population from 1,600,000 to no more than 1,200,000, and "that many careful judges fixed the present population and soldiers at less than 1,000,000"; restated the condition of devastation and prevention of commerce still prevailing, and mentioned his belief "that the most conservative public opinion in the United States would not justify" the President or government "in delaying action beyond a very early day, and that since we must act, I believed that our people would prefer to buy rather than suffer the pains of war, since purchase or war must result in the same thing—the occupation and ownership of the island. As to guarantee of the Cuban debt and practical protectorate over the island, . . . many of our people would prefer this to occupation and ownership," but General Woodford hoped this would not be the solution, on account of "syndicate deals and private financial operations."

"As to the effect upon Spain . . . the business men and the plain people . . . are tired of a useless and exhausting war; that Spain had lost Cuba; that if autonomy succeeded in securing peace, the autonomisitc government would each year ask and get larger and larger independence; that disagreement would probably come over the distribution of the present debt, and that certain quarrels would arise over future contributions by Cuba to the expenses of the home government; that if autonomy succeeded, a new nation would be created and that nation could not be expected to continue subject and tributary to Spain; that when the autonomic government resisted there would be rebellion which Spain could neither coax nor coerce."

At the close Señor Moret said: "Substantially, I do not commit myself to details. The right way can be found if we will both do our best, and I will work with you for peace, and I am sure we shall get together as to details. This must be confidential between us, for we are not talking as officials." [1]

The next day, March 19, General Woodford sent a telegram to the President, after having shown it to Señor Moret, who said that without being able to approve it officially he would personally work with the American minister to secure the results which the latter had indicated. The telegram said: "Unless report on *Maine* requires immediate action, I suggest that nothing be decided or done until after the receipt of my personal letters 43, 44, and 46, which my second secretary of legation will carry from Gibraltar, Monday, March 21. I also suggest that you authorize me to tell the queen informally, or any minister indicated by her, that you wish final agreement before April 15. If you will acquaint me fully with general settlement desired, I believe Spanish government will offer without compulsion, and upon its own motion, such terms of settlement as may be satisfactory to both nations. Large liberty as to details should be offered to Spain, but your friendship is recognized and appreciated, and I now believe it will be a pleasure to Spanish government to propose what will probably be satisfactory to you." [2]

The minister sent, the same day, the No. 46 referred to in his telegram. He said: "Señor Moret said to me this morning that justice to the queen required him to assure me in the most positive manner that she had not been privy to or cognizant of any suggestion that she wished to talk with me about any possible cession of Cuba, either to the insurgents or to the United States; that she wished to hand over his patrimony unimpaired to her son when he should reach his majority, and that she would prefer to abdicate her regency and return to her Austrian home rather than be the instrument of ceding or parting with any of Spain's colonies. . . . I am sure that Mr. Moret regards this [parting with Cuba] as inevitable and is only seeking the way in which to do it and yet save Spanish honor. He will probably find the way to do it even if he

[1] *Foreign Relations*, 1898, 688–692.
[2] *Ibid.*, 692.

has to sacrifice himself. I hope this last may not be necessary. I do not believe it will be. . . ."[1]

The historian who has carefully studied the documents which have been made public cannot resist the conclusion that the secretary of state was very early convinced that the guns would, sooner or later—the sooner the better—have to be invoked to blow away obstacles that resisted diplomacy, but that President McKinley was reluctant to take the step because he felt that with sufficient time his diplomatic efforts could bring peace to Cuba. General Woodford, as seen, zealously seconded the optimism of the President. The next day Assistant Secretary Day informed the minister: "President is at loss to know just what your telegram 19th covers. Whether loss of *Maine* or whole situation. [The unanimous report that *Maine* was blown up by submarine mine] must go to Congress soon. Feeling in the United States very acute. People have borne themselves with great forbearance and self-restraint last month. President has no doubt Congress will act wisely and immediate crisis may be avoided, particularly if there be certainty of prompt restoration of peace in Cuba. *Maine* loss may be peacefully settled if full reparation is promptly made such as the most civilized nation would offer. But there remain general conditions in Cuba which cannot be longer endured, and which will demand action on our part unless Spain restores honorable peace which will stop starvation of people and give them an opportunity

---

[1] *Foreign Relations*, 1898, 693. The turn of opinion in Spain had already found voice in a portion of the press, the *Nacional*, of Madrid, proposing that the island be sold to the United States, the Spanish debt ($400,000,000) pertaining to it to be assumed by the Union, Spain to enjoy for a certain time her tariff privileges, and that life and property of Spaniards in the island be guaranteed. The proposal to assume such a debt would have made acceptance of the island impossible. Says the *Nation* (March 10, 1898): "The chances of such a step are not one in a hundred. The truth is that if the island were offered to us as a free gift we should be by no means in haste to accept it. . . . The spur that pricks us on has been the spectacle of a people near our shores fighting for independence. . . . It may be a mistaken one in the sense that we have too hastily assumed that the insurgents are the people of Cuba, but it is not soiled with the desire of gain."

These words, in the view of the present writer, fairly express the attitude of the American mind of the period. Spain's attitude was colored throughout by the idea that the United States wished Cuba for its own purposes. Time has shown the falsity of this view.

to take care of themselves and restore commerce now wholly lost. April 15 is none too early date for accomplishment of these purposes. Relations will be much influenced by attitude of Spanish government in *Maine* matter, but general conditions must not be lost sight of. It is proper that you should know that, unless events otherwise indicate, the President, having exhausted diplomatic agencies to secure peace in Cuba, will lay the whole question before Congress. Keep President fully advised, as action of next few days may control situation." [1]

On March 21 the minister telegraphed that he had had no intimation of the character of the report on the *Maine* previous to the word just received, so that the *Maine* was not in consideration in anything which he had sent. The subject had never been discussed between the Spanish government and himself.[2] On March 22 he had an interview with Señor Moret in which, speaking unofficially, he informed the latter of the reception of a reply to his telegram of March 19, shown Señor Moret. General Woodford mentioned that the report on the *Maine* was now in the hands of the President, but that he himself was not authorized to disclose its character or conclusions. He repeated to Señor Moret the purport of the remainder of the telegram just received, and said: "I will telegraph immediately to the President any suggestion that Spain may make, and I hope to receive within a very few days some definite proposition that shall mean immediate peace."[3] In the telegram reporting the interview General Woodford mentioned that he had arranged an interview with the minister of state for March 23, and asked instructions in case he should be asked to suggest what might be acceptable to the President. He received none until three days after.

The ministers met, as arranged, on the 23d. Señor Moret, who spoke English, and who thus, frequently, in the interest of accuracy, acted as interpreter, was present at this interview and conveyed to the minister of state the repetition by General Woodford of that which the latter had already stated to himself. Señor Gullon replied that his government had not received the text of the Spanish

[1] *Foreign Relations*, 692. (March 20, 1898.)   [2] *Ibid.*, 695.
[3] General Woodford to President McKinley (telegram), March 22, 1898, *Ibid.*, 696.

report, and in the absence of any statement from the minister "as to the character of the American report he could not discuss the matter, but that the Spanish government would certainly do whatever right and justice should require when [it] should have full knowledge of all the facts." He then said that he was surprised at the apparent change in the attitude of the United States as indicated by the statement just made, and added that he would be glad to have the minister tell him why it was presented at the present time.

General Woodford replied that "the United States has not varied its attitude since I came to Spain last September. My first words to her majesty when I was presented at San Sebastian were the sincere expression of the desire of the United States for peace in Cuba and peace between Spain and the United States. Peace seemed to be made possible by the removal of General Weyler, by the attempted change in the methods of conducting the war, and by the proffer of autonomy to the island. I believe that the present Spanish government was sincere in the efforts it indicated. . . . The peace . . . has not been secured . . . and the time has come when the United States must, in the interest of humanity and because of the great and pressing commercial, financial, and sanitary needs of our country, ask that some satisfactory agreement be reached within a very few days which will assure immediate and honorable peace."

General Woodford, saying that "neither the present judgment of the civilized world nor the final judgment of history would excuse the United States in longer permitting the present condition of affairs in an island lying within one hundred miles of our coast," continued at some length respecting Cuba's dark conditions, closing his remarks with the statement of the telegram that "the great and controlling questions of humanity and civilization require that permanent and immediate peace be established and enforced."

Señor Gullon, repeating" that Spain might be relied upon to do what is right and just and honorable in the matter of the *Maine,*" expressed his belief that the insurrection would be practically suppressed before the rainy season began; that all the rebel leaders, with the exception of a few chiefs, were willing now to submit if the United States would only advise them to do so, and that if we would withhold intervention until the beginning of the rainy season he believed that he could assure the government of the United States that the rebellion would then be ended and that autonomy would be assured in its successful operation. He added that the Spanish government is ready to enlarge and increase the present grant of autonomy in all honorable ways that will add to its efficiency and guarantee its success.

"He then," says General Woodford, "asked if I would not telegraph my government to withhold action until the beginning of the rainy season." General Woodford, after saying that he "had come reluctantly but positively to the judgement that autonomy could not give peace to Cuba in any reasonable time," said, "kindly, but firmly, that I did not believe the delay for which he asked to be possible and that my government wished immediate and honorable peace; and I repeated that unless some satisfactory agreement is reached within a very few days the President must submit the whole question to Congress." [1]

On the following day (March 24) Señor Moret, who was now eager for, and optimistic as to the possibility of, an adjustment, called by prearrangement upon the American minister, the interview being purely personal and in no sense official. He proposed that the question of "an early and honorable peace" be submitted to the Cuban congress, to meet May 4, and that the Spanish government give the congress all necessary authority to negotiate and conclude such peace.

"I asked him," said General Woodford, "what about military operations in Cuba between now and May 4? He replied an immediate armistice or truce to be enforced by the Spanish government upon its army, provided the United States can secure the acceptance and enforcement of like immediate truce by the insurgents.

"I then asked, supposing the insular government and Congress cannot arrange terms for permanent peace with the insurgent government before the 15th of next September, which will be the end of the rainy season? He replied that he would personally advise his minister that the government of Spain and the United States should in such event jointly compel both parties in Cuba to

[1] General Woodford to Secretary Sherman, No. 189, March 25, 1898, *Foreign Relations*, 698–701.

accept such settlement as the two governments should then jointly advise, such terms to be arranged . . . before the 15th of next September. He told me that the minister for foreign affairs would probably communicate some such proposition to me officially to-morrow (Friday), in answer to my official statement of yesterday. I replied that I could give him no assurance or intimation as to whether such proposition would be acceptable to you." [1]

On March 25, in an interview requested by Señor Gullon with General Woodford, the former "was very earnest in his desire that the report . . . on the subject of the *Maine* should not be sent to Congress but should be held as the subject of diplomatic adjustment between the two governments. He assured me," says General Woodford in his account of the interview, "that Spain would do in this matter whatever was just and right. He repeated the suggestion, made informally by Señor Moret the day before, of leaving the question of peace to the insular government. General Woodford asked if his government would be willing to grant an immediate and effective armistice, or truce, provided the insurgents on their part would agree to and enforce the same. Señor Gullon replied that he could not give a final answer without consulting his associates, but that personally he feared that such an armistice was impossible." [2]

Again was Spain to suffer from the fatal habit of procrastination. Had her government now done what it was to grant a fortnight later, in terms independent of action by the insurgents, the situation might have been saved. The report of the court upon the *Maine* was not to go to Congress for yet three days. Had the President in his message transmitting this been able to append the words in which, on April 11, he announced the order from Spain to General Blanco to suspend hostilities, affairs would have had a very different color, and the message of April 11 might never have been sent in the fateful form in which it went. Instead, the Spanish minister of state sent to the American minister, Friday evening, March 25, a vague memorandum, which Señor Moret declared to the latter to

---

[1] General Woodford to President McKinley (telegram), March 24, 1898, *Foreign Relations*, 697.

[2] General Woodford to Secretary Sherman, March 25, 1898, *Ibid.*, 701.

mean "that the question of an early and honorable peace shall be submitted by the Spanish government to (the) Cuban congress on May 4, and that (the) Spanish government will give [the] Cuban congress all necessary authority to negotiate and conclude peace, provided such authority shall not diminish or interfere with the constitutional power vested by the Cuban constitution in the central government." He said, states the American minister, "that if we asked for immediate armistice he believes Spanish government will grant and enforce armistice on sole condition that insurgent government does same. If you approve these suggestions and believe they will lead to immediate peace, I ask authority to put these two direct questions to Spanish minister for foreign affairs: First, Does your memorandum mean exactly what the minister for colonies says, employing his precise words? Second, Will you decree and enforce immediate armistice until the end of the rainy season if insurgent government will do the same? I believe that if immediate peace can be secured now, lasting until September 15, hostilities will not be resumed. I expect to see Minister Moret this (Saturday) evening at my house."[1]

Accompanying the vague memorandum translated into understandable terms by Señor Moret was a second part, which mentioned an unfortunate request from the wrecking company employed on the *Maine* to recover the bodies and examine the wreck. This request, conveyed by Captain Sigsbee to the governor-general, was for permission to employ dynamite to blow away some of the upper works for the easier recovery of the dead. Finding that the object was mistaken—as being to destroy the ship and thus "annihilate the only proofs" of cause, the request was immediately withdrawn. The memorandum said: "Even without seeing in the request of the captain of the *Maine* any other meaning than that personally expressed in the petition signed by him, the Spanish government considers as utterly unjustifiable and inadmissible the resolution which submits to a political assembly the report drawn up by the official American board of inquiry. . . . As yet nothing is known of the report of the Spanish commission. After having invited in vain the United States naval officers to take part

[1] General Woodford to President McKinley (telegram), March 25, 1898, *Foreign Relations*, 1898, 703.

in its labors and go through the necessary investigations conjointly with its members, it has finished and drawn up its conclusions with a complete knowledge of the scene of a disaster so deplorable and painful for all Spaniards. One of the principal, if not the principal, bases of judgment is therefore wanting for every individual or body of men who may wish to weigh the facts with perfect impartiality. Under these circumstances, to place before a popular deliberating assembly, without correction, explanation, or counterproof of any kind, a report which, issued by the fellow-citizens of the members of that body, must necessarily meet with approval inspired rather by sentiment than by reason, is not only to resolve beforehand a possible future discussion, but apparently reveals an intention of allowing national enthusiasm, commiseration, or other like natural and comprehensible feelings, so frequently found in all numerous and patriotic assemblies, to form an *a priori* judgment not founded on proof, and to reject, before even knowing its terms, any affirmation which may give rise to doubt or seem distasteful. The most elementary sense of justice makes it . . . a duty to previously examine and discuss in an atmosphere of absolute calmness two different inquiries tending to one common end." [1]

The several communications of the last few days from the American minister caused the sending by the Spanish government of telegrams, on March 24 and 25, to the representatives of Spain abroad for the information of the governments to which they were accredited. The first set forth the situation as described by the American minister, the protest against a reference of the *Maine* report to Congress, and the necessity of knowing the sentiments and wishes of the insular congress in order "to assure an immediate and satisfactory peace to the Cubans." The second directed the representatives to inform the governments to which they were accredited of the circumstances and to ask their "friendly offices in order that the Preisdent of the United States may retain under Federal [executive] control all questions affecting the relations or differences with Spain in order to bring them to an honorable conclusion. So convinced is Spain," continued the circular, "of her right in this matter and of the prudence with which she is

[1] For both parts of this memorandum, see *Foreign Relations*, 1898, 702.

acting that, if the aforesaid suggestion does not avail, she will not hesitate to at once ask the counsel of the great powers and, in the last resort, their mediation to adjust the pending differences, which differences in the near future, may disturb a peace that the Spanish nation desires to preserve, as far as its honor and the integrity of its territory will permit, not only on its own account, but because war once begun affects all other powers of Europe and America." [1]

It was not until March 26 that Mr. Day telegraphed a reply to General Woodford's request of the 22d for instructions. He said: "The President's desire is for peace. He cannot look upon the suffering and starvation in Cuba save with horror. The concentration of men, women, and children in the fortified towns, and permitting them to starve, is unbearable to a Christian nation geographically so close as ours to Cuba. All this has shocked and inflamed the American mind, as it has the civilized world, where its extent and character are known. It was represented to him in November that the Blanco government would at once release the suffering and so modify the Weyler order as to permit those who were able to return to their homes and till the fields from which they had been driven. There has been no relief to the starving except such as the American people have supplied. The reconcentration order has not been practically superseded. There is no hope for peace through the Spanish arms. . . . More than half the island is under control of the insurgents. . . . We do not want the island. The President has evidenced in every way his desire to preserve and continue friendly relations with Spain. He has kept every international obligation with fidelity. He wants an honorable peace. He has repeatedly urged the government of Spain to secure a peace. She still has the opportunity to do it, and the President appeals to her from every consideration of justice and humanity to do it. Will she? Peace is the desired end. For your own guidance, the President suggests that if Spain will revoke the reconcentration order and maintain the people until they can support themselves, and offer the Cubans full self-government with reasonable indemnity, the President will gladly assist in its consummation. If Spain should invite the United States to mediate for peace and the insurgents would

[1] For the first telegram, see *Spanish Cor. and Docs.*, 95; for second, *Ibid*, 98.

make like request, the President might undertake such office of friendship."[1]

On March 26, also, a summary of the report of the court of inquiry was telegraphed by the state department to General Woodford. The telegram ended: "Upon the facts thus disclosed a grave responsibility appears to rest upon the Spanish government. The *Maine*, upon a peaceful errand, and with the knowledge and consent of that government, entered the harbor of Havana, relying upon the security and protection of a friendly port. Confessedly she still remained, as to what took place on board, under the jurisdiction of her own government, yet the control of the harbor remained in the Spanish government which, as the sovereign of the place, was bound to render protection to persons and property there, and especially to the public ship and the sailors of a friendly power. The government of the United States has not failed to receive with due appreciation the expressions of sympathy by the government of the queen regent. . . . This fact can only increase its regret that the circumstances of the case, as disclosed by the report of the board of inquiry, are such as require of the Spanish government such action as is due where the sovereign rights of one friendly nation have been assailed within the jurisdiction of another. The President does not permit himself to doubt that the sense of justice of

---

[1] *Foreign Relations*, 1898, 704. The assistant secretary of state would seem somewhat in error in view of the official statements from the governor-general of Cuba, sent on this date by the Spanish minister at Washington to the secretary of state (but which no doubt had not been received when the telegram was sent), that there had been no relief to the starving in Cuba except that supplied by the American people. General Blanco mentioned that $100,000 had been distributed on November 23, 1897, and $50,000 on March 2, 1898. His report continued: "The zeal of the local governors and alcaldes was invoked, those authorities being invited to set an example, which they have done with a devotion worthy of all praise. In this manner private charity being stimulated, and with the confidence of official support, likewise took active measures, organizing productive boards, economical kitchens, and beneficent associations, . . . thus contributing greatly to the alleviation of the suffering." He, as well as the provincial governors in their reports, gratefully acknowledged the relief which had come from the United States. (For these reports, see *Foreign Relations*, 1898, 705–710 and 714–717.) On March 28 it was arranged that supplies could be sent to the reconcentrados by the American government, to be conveyed and distributed under the same conditions as the private supplies which had been sent. (*Ibid.*, 717.)

the Spanish nation will dictate a course of action suggested by the friendly relations of the two governments."[1]

On Sunday, March 27, Mr. Day telegraphed General Woodford: "Believed the *Maine* report will be held in Congress for a short time without action. A feeling of deliberation prevails in both Houses of Congress. See if the following can be done:

"First. Armistice until October 1. Negotiations meantime looking for peace between Spain and insurgents through friendly offices of President United States.

"Second. Immediate revocation of reconcentrado order so as to permit people to return to their farms, and the needy to be relieved with provisions and supplies from United States, co-operating with authorities so as to afford full relief.

"Add if possible:

"Third. If terms of peace not satisfactorily settled by October 1, President of the United States to be final arbitrator between Spain and insurgents.

"If Spain agrees, President will use friendly offices to get insurgents to accept plan."[2]

On the evening of the day (March 25) that the memorandum expressing willingness to submit the question of peace to the Cuban congress was received, General Woodford was called upon by Señor Moret, who informed him that Señor Sagasta, the president of the council of state, "would be glad to talk with him informally on the subject of an immediate suspension of hostilities in Cuba through the means of an armistice or truce." General Woodford telegraphed for instructions, acknowledging at the same time the reception of the state department's telegram of March 26, and asking the meaning of the words "full self-government" and "with reasonable indemnity" used therein. He added: "Under Spanish constitution, ministry cannot recognize independence of Cuba or part with nominal sovereignty over Cuba. Cortes alone can do this, and Cortes will not meet until April 25. If I can secure immediate and effective armistice or truce between Spanish troops and insurgents, to take effect on or before April 15, will this be satisfactory?" He mentioned the possibility of submission of the question of peace to the Cuban congress, and continued: "If I

[1] *Foreign Relations*, 1898, 1036.   [2] *Ibid.*, 712.

can secure these two things, with absolute and immediate revocation of concentration order, may I negotiate? I believe that an immediate armistice means present and permanent peace. Also, I believe that, negotiations once open between insurgents and the Cuban government, some arrangement will be reached during the summer which the Spanish government will approve, and that Cuba will become practically independent and pass from Spanish control." [1]

This was answered next day. "Full self-government with indemnity would mean Cuban independence." For the answer to the remainder of the inquiry General Woodford was referred to the state department's telegram of Sunday the 27th, adding: "Very important to have definite agreement for determining peace after armistice, if negotiations pending same fail to reach satisfactory conclusions." A second telegram followed, saying: "Important to have prompt answer on armistice matter." [2]

[1] General Woodford to secretary of state, March 27, 1898, *Foreign Relations*, 1898, 713.
[2] Mr. Day to General Woodford, March 28, 1898, *Foreign Relations*, 1898, 713.

CHAPTER XXVIII

THE REPORT ON THE "MAINE" BEFORE CONGRESS.—RESOLUTIONS IN CONGRESS.—SPANISH PROPOSITIONS

ON March 28 the President sent the report of the court of inquiry to Congress with a special message dignified and reserved in tone, and which was strictly confined to a presentation of the facts and statements before him.[1] It ended with the final sentence quoted in the state department telegram of March 26,[2] adding: "It will be the duty of the executive to advise the Congress of the result [of Spain's action in the premises], and in the meantime deliberate consideration is invoked." The report was referred without debate to the committee on foreign affairs. The House adjourned. On this same date the Spanish minister at Washington transmitted to the secretary of state a résumé of the findings of the Spanish court, declaring the ship destroyed by an internal explosion. The

[1] The report signed on March 21, 1898, on board the battle-ship *Iowa* (of which the senior member of the court, Sampson, was captain) found that "the *Maine* was destroyed by the explosion of a submarine mine, which caused the partial explosion of two or more of the forward magazines. The court has been unable to obtain evidence fixing the responsibility for the destruction of the *Maine* upon any person or persons." (For the finding in full see Senate Doc. 207, 55 Cong., 2 Sess.; also Sigsbee, *The Maine*, Appendix A.) The finding was based chiefly upon the fact that "at frame 17 the outer shell of the ship from a point eleven and a half feet from the middle line of the ship and six feet above the keel when in a normal position, has been forced up so as to be now about four feet above the surface of the water, and therefore about thirty-four feet above where it would be had the ship sunk uninjured," also that the outside bottom plating was bent into a reversed V-shape, and at frame 18 the vertical keel was broken in two, and the flat keel bent into an angle similar to that just mentioned. This break was about thirty feet above its normal position. It was impossible to the court to conceive such lifting effects upon a ship's bottom from an interior explosion, a judgment borne out by the results of the explosions of the forward magazines in the Spanish ships destroyed in the battle of Santiago, where there was no disturbance of the ships' bottoms. It is to the mind of the present writer also impossible to conceive that the bottom of the *Maine* could

[2] *Supra.*

weight of the finding was, however, greatly weakened by the statement that "the divers, when examining the hull of the *Maine*, could not see its bottom as it was buried in the mud"; whereas, in fact, the state of the bottom, so clearly described by the American court, was the essential element in the latter's finding.

The presentation to Congress of the report of the court brought next day a flood of joint resolutions, among the more important of which were those of Senators Frye and Foraker, both of which demanded the withdrawal of the Spanish forces and the recognition of the independence of Cuba.[1] The resolution of the former repeated the technical error so frequently made, that "the warfare for the past three years has been conducted by the Spanish government in violation of the rules of civilized warfare." That of Senator Foraker, while giving the reason for interference, held insufficient in international law, that the war was "destructive of the commercial and property interests of the United States," was

be bent as described by any lurching forward of the after body of the ship as it sank in the shallow water. For this sank so slowly that no such effort could have bent the heavy girder formed by the strong cellular bottom of the *Maine*, strengthened as this was by the vertical keel and six longitudinals.

It should also be mentioned that the scantling of the *Maine* was far heavier than that of any other ship in the service.

That an interior explosion may be caused by an exterior one was shown conclusively in the Russian-Japanese war, in the cases of Admiral Makaroff's flag-ship, the *Petropavlovsk*, and of the Japanese battle-ship *Hatsuse*.

The writer would also mention that when the court was ordered, he was one of two members who thought the explosion internal. Both were convinced otherwise against their prepossessions.

The incompleteness of the Spanish examination on which was found an internal explosion, is shown by the statement (Sen. Rep. 885, 55 Cong., 2 Sess., 625) of the principal Spanish diver, that "the bilge and keel of the vessel throughout its entire extent were buried in the mud, but did not appear to have suffered any damage," a statement in most complete disaccord with the facts. It should be noted that the total work of the Spanish divers was but seventeen and a half hours, as shown by the records in the Spanish report.

Even if proof which seemed so conclusive to the American court of inquiry had not existed, it is difficult to reconcile with the theory of accident the destruction of an American man-of-war at such a time and in such a place, by the only occurrence of such a character known in American naval history. That a ship peculiarly safe as to her arrangement of magazines, with no powder aboard except that known to be of stable character (the usual brown powder of the period), with all her high explosives, as gun-cotton, in the after part of

[1] *Cong. Record*, 55 Cong., 2 Sess., 3293.

much more correct in terming it cruel, barbarous, and inhuman, if he meant to apply these words to the conduct of both parties to the contest.

On March 28 the American minister had an official interview with Señor Gullon. He read to the latter the summary of the report of the court of inquiry on the loss of the *Maine*, and left an official note giving the summary and stating the expectancy by the United States, "that the sense of justice of the Spanish nation will dictate a course of action suggested by the friendly relations between the two governments."[1] At this interview General Woodford requested a conference next day (March 29) between himself and Señores Sagasta, Gullon, and Moret. The conference, the details of which are given in the minister's letter of March 29 to the President, was opened by the reading, by General Woodford, of the following statement:

"The President instructs me to have direct and frank conversa-

---

the ship where no explosion took place, and with a crew of officers and men in a special state of watchfulness, should have waited until her arrival in Havana to undergo this extraordinary and most exceptional experience through accident aboard, seems now to the writer, though unthought of then, to transcend the bounds of probabilities to such degree that this is almost sufficient of itself to settle the question as against interior accident, apart from the reasons which seemed to the court conclusive.

The presence of the *Maine* was regarded undoubtedly by a large number of the Spanish in Havana as a threat; she commanded the city; she was a great fortress planted in their midst which completely dominated the city and harbor. It required but a fanatic to anticipate a situation which to some no doubt seemed likely, and there were many such in Havana who wished war in any case. It must be remembered that the general attitude of the Spanish mind was one of extreme and foolish contempt for the military power of the United States, and that a desire to precipitate war, joined with unreasoning hatred, only needed an opportunity which combined in itself the serious weakening of an enemy's power, revenge for supposed injuries, and a dramatic stroke dear to such a temperament. Nor is it impossible to suppose that some of the Cuban side should, in their desire to force a war, have been concerned. That the Spanish government was in anywise responsible for the detonation of the fateful fuse, except through want of precautions against such action, is not and was not by any member of the board for a moment supposed.

The writer, as a member of the court, would welcome an examination of the wreck by a complete exposure of it as it lies. It could only result in substantiating the description of the injuries by the court, whose examination was too complete to leave chance of serious error.

[1] American minister to secretary of state, March 28, 1898, *Ibid.*, 1040.

tion with you about the present condition of affairs in Cuba, and present relations between Spain and the United States.

"The President thinks it is better not to discuss the respective views held by each nation. This might only provoke or incite argument and might delay and possibly prevent immediate decision.

"The President instructs me to say that we do not want Cuba.

"He also instructs me to say, with equal clearness, that we do wish immediate peace in Cuba. He suggests an immediate armistice, lasting until October 1, negotiations in the meantime being had looking to peace between Spain and the insurgents, through the friendly offices of the United States.

"He wishes the immediate revocation of reconcentration order, so as to permit the people to return to their farms and the needy to be relieved with provisions and supplies from the United States, the United States co-operating with the Spanish authorities so as to afford full relief."

Señor Sagasta replied, agreeing that discussion of views would be inopportune and useless, stated that the present government was arranging to furnish employment for those of the reconcentrados able to work and to supply the necessities of the feeble and of the women and children. He accepted the assistance of the United States in this work. He expressed his appreciation of the manner in which the President had presented the subject [of the *Maine*] to Congress, and added that he believed his method of dealing with this question would enable the two governments to examine and adjust the matter in some way honorable and fair to both nations. He was in thorough accord with the President in desiring an early and honorable peace. He suggested that there were difficulties in the Spanish situation in the Peninsula which General Woodford, as a stranger, could hardly understand, which made it almost impossible for the Spanish government to offer such an armistice, but that if it were asked by the insurgents it would be at once granted; that the insular congress would meet on May 4, when the insular government could make such a proposition; that only six weeks would intervene before that time, and he hoped the United States, which had waited so long, would now wait for these few weeks; that the offer of autonomy had been accompanied by firm declaration that Spain would employ military operations in aid of civil reforms; that these operations were being successfully conducted, and that he hoped that the rebellion would be largely reduced before the Cuban congress met.

General Woodford replied substantially that the sober sense of the American people insisted upon immediate cessation of hostilities; that the recent speech of Senator Proctor,[1] one of the most reliable of American public men, had so convinced public sentiment, that longer prosecution of the war must now be prevented.

On a request for answer to the two suggestions of the statement (an immediate armistice and revocation of the concentration order), it was arranged that there should be a meeting on Thursday afternoon (March 31) at the office of the president of the council.

"I then," says General Woodford, "sat down at Señor Sagasta's desk and wrote the following telegram which I have sent you in cipher:

" No. 60. Have had conference this afternoon with the president of the council, the minister for foreign affairs, and minister for colonies [Señores Sagasta, Gullon, and Moret]. Conference adjourned until Thursday afternoon, March 31. I have sincere belief that arrangement will then be reached, honorable to Spain and satisfactory to the United States and just to Cuba. I beg you to withhold all action until you receive my report of such conference, which I will send Thursday night, March 31.

"I had Señor Moret." continued General Woodford, "read this telegram and translate it twice to his colleagues so that there could be no misunderstanding as to its language and meaning."

In the evening Señor Moret called upon the American minister and said that "he thought the latter had made positive and favorable impression on President Sagasta's mind; that the ministers would meet [March 30] for discussion; that a further meeting

---

[1] In the Senate, March 17, 1898. Mr. Proctor had just returned from a visit to Cuba, whither he had gone to make acquaintance at first hand with affairs. His visit was wholly unofficial and unsuggested by any one. His account of conditions outside Havana was one of "desolation and distress, misery and starvation." He found the accounts of the condition of the reconcentrados not overdrawn, and of the hospitals he said: "It is not within the narrow limits of my vocabulary to portray it." Coming from one universally esteemed for character, sound sense, and reticence of statement, the speech, as General Woodford rightly said, had a great effect upon public sentiment.

would be held . . . March 31, under the presidency of the queen, and that he hoped a satisfactory adjustment would be reached at our adjourned conference to be held Thursday afternoon.[1]

The assistant secretary of state made reply to General Woodford's telegram (No. 60) the day it was sent and received. He said: "It is of the utmost importance that the conference be not postponed beyond next Thursday and definite results then reached. Feeling here is intense." He added next day: "Your No. 60 is encouraging, but vague as to details. The United States cannot assist in enforcement of any system of autonomy."[2]

General Woodford returned: "There will be no delay beyond Thursday, March 31. If definite results are not then reached I shall close negotiations."[3] Mr. Day answered at once:

"You should know and fully appreciate that there is profound feeling in Congress, and the gravest apprehension on the part of most conservative members that a resolution for intervention may pass both branches in spite of any effort that can be made. Only assurance from the President that if he fails in peaceful negotiations he will submit all the facts to Congress at a very early day, will prevent immediate action on the part of Congress. The President assumes that whatever may be reached in your negotiations to-morrow will be tentative only, to be submitted as the proposal of Spain. We hope your negotiations will lead to a peace acceptable to the country."[4]

One immediate effect of the conference of March 29 was the complete revocation of the reconcentration orders, by proclamation of Governor-General Blanco, on March 30. The act gave good augury for the meeting which was to take place next day, but the fates were against it. The meeting was held as arranged at 4 P. M. Señor Gullon handed General Woodford the Spanish propositions, which dealt separately with each of the subjects before them, as follows:

"CATASTROPHE OF THE 'MAINE.'—Spain is ready to submit to an arbitration the differences which can arise in this matter.

"RECONCENTRADOS.—General Blanco, following the instruc-

[1] *Foreign Relations*, 1898, 718–721.   [2] *Ibid.*, 718.
[3] General Woodford to Mr. Day, March 30, 1898, *Ibid.*, 721.
[4] Mr. Day to General Woodford, March 30, 1898, *Ibid.*, 721.

tions of the government, has revoked in the western provinces[1] the bando relating to the reconcentrados, and although this measure will not be able to reach its complete developments until the military operations terminate, the government places at the disposal of the governor-general of Cuba a credit of three million of pesetas [six hundred thousand dollars], to the end that the countrymen may return at once and with success to their labors.

"The Spanish government will accept, nevertheless, whatever assistance to feed and succor the needy may be sent from the United States in the form and conditions agreed upon by the assistant secretary of state, Mr. Day, and the Spanish minister in Washington.

"PACIFICATION OF CUBA.—The Spanish government, more interested than that of the United States in giving to the Grand Antilla an honorable and stable peace, proposes to confide its preparation to the insular parliament, without whose intervention it will not be able to arrive at the final result, it being understood that the powers reserved by the constitution to the central government are not lessened and diminished.

"TRUCE.—As the Cuban chambers will not meet until the 4th of May, the Spanish government will not, on its part, find it inconvenient to accept at once a suspension of hostilities asked for by the insurgents from the general-in-chief, to whom it will belong in this case to determine the duration and conditions of the suspension." [2]

A circular telegram sent the same day to Spanish representatives abroad said: "If these bases of argument, which meet in great part McKinley's demands and are the limit of our concessions and efforts to preserve peace, are to be accepted at Washington, the valued good offices of the sovereign (or president of republic) and government to which you are accredited ought to be immediately determined upon and put into effect at once, if, as we hope by the reports from your excellency, they desire to co-operate to effect the preservation of peace and the reasonable protection of our rights." [3]

---

[1] This was an error in so far as General Blanco's actual action was concerned. His proclamation of March 30 declared reconcentration terminated "throughout the island." (See *Foreign Relations*, 1898, 738, for the order in full.)
[2] *Spanish Cor. and Docs.*, 107; *Ibid.*, 726.   [3] *Spanish Cor. and Docs.*, 108.

The bases did indeed "meet in great part McKinley's demands," but not in the most essential; that is, action looking to immediate cessation of hostilities, for nothing could be more vain at this moment than expectancy that a truce would be asked for by the insurgents. General Woodford expressed to the Spanish ministers at the conference that the final proposition would not be acceptable. "Taken," he said, "in connection with the one relating to the 'pacification of Cuba,' [it] does not mean immediate or assured peace. It means, when read with the other, continuation of this destructive, cruel, and now needless war."[1]

"The conference," telegraphed the minister to the President, "has turned as I feared on a question of punctilio. Spanish pride will not permit the ministry to propose and offer an armistice; which they really desire because they know that armistice now means certain peace next autumn. I am told confidentially that the offer of armistice by the Spanish government would cause revolution here. Leading generals have been sounded within the last week and the ministry have gone as far as they dare go to-day. I believe the ministry are ready to go as far and as fast as they can and still save the dynasty here in Spain. They know that Cuba is lost. Public opinion in Spain has steadily moved toward peace. No Spanish ministry would have dared to do one month ago what this ministry has proposed to-day."[2]

This telegram was at once an expression of the American minister's disappointment, an attempt to excuse the inaction of the Spanish ministry, and the transmission of a covert hope that the American government would give Spain another opportunity.

The president of the home-rule government of Cuba, Señor José Maria Galvez, now took part in the question, become so deeply momentous and acute, in a telegram sent through the governor-general to Washington, which was a protest against any effort of the American government to force upon Cuba any form of government without the consent of its people, and an expression of the hope that the President of the United States would aid in the re-establishment of peace in Cuba under the sovereignty of the

[1] General Woodford to Mr. Day, March 31, 1898, *Foreign Relations*, 1898, 727.
[2] Telegram, March 31, *Ibid.*, 727.

mother country.¹ A manifesto was, at the same time, issued by the home-rule government to the people of Cuba to join in the realization of peace and concord.²

Affairs were, however, sweeping with a torrential force which only one thing could stay: a declaration that, for the time at least, no more shot were to be fired by Spain. The Vatican, kept informed evidently by Archbishop Ireland (now in Washington by order of the Pope to work for peace),³ appreciated this if Spain did not, and the Spanish ambassador near the Holy See telegraphed from Rome that he was informed that "the President of the republic desires to reach a settlement, but he is finding himself helpless against Congress. The difficulty lies in who should ask for a suspension of hostilities. The President . . . seems well disposed to accept the offices of the Pope; and the latter, willing to aid us, inquires, first, if the intervention of his holiness to ask the armistice would save the national honor; second, if such intervention would be acceptable to her majesty and the government."⁴

Señor Gullon replied to the ambassador: "The moment the United States government is disposed to accept the aid of the Pope, Spain and her government will gladly accept his mediation," promising "further to accept the proposal that the holy father shall formulate a suspension of hostilities; informing his holiness that for the honor of Spain it is proper that the truce should be accompanied by the retirement of the American squadron from the waters of the Antilles, in order that the American republic may also show its purpose not to support—voluntarily or involuntarily— the insurrection in Cuba,"⁵ a not surprising request in view of the proportions of the fleet now assembled at Key West.

Señor Gullon, calling at once upon the American minister, by a not unnatural error mentioned the offer of the Pope as made at the suggestion of President McKinley. He gave General Woodford to understand that his government would accede to the Pope's desire; but going so far, said General Woodford in telegraphing the inter-

¹ *Foreign Relations*, 1898, 728.   ² *Ibid.*, 731.
³ Polo de Bernabé to minister of state, April 4, 1898, *Spanish Cor. and Docs.*, 111.
⁴ Señor Merry del Val to minister of state, April 2, 1898, *Ibid.*, 109.
⁵ Telegram, April 3, 1898, *Ibid.*, 110.

view, "asks that the United States will show its friendship for Spain by withdrawing our war-ships from the vicinity of Cuba and from Key West as soon as the armistice has been proclaimed. That the Spanish government will continue this armistice so long as there are any reasonable hopes that permanent peace can be secured in Cuba. He asks your immediate answer as to withdrawal of war-ships at once after proclamation of armistice. I still believe that when armistice is once proclaimed hostilities will never be resumed and that permanent peace will be secured. If under existing conditions at Washington you can still do this, I hope that you will.

"The Austrian ambassador," he continued, "has heard me read this despatch and says he will guarantee that Spain will do this. . . . I know that the queen and her present ministry sincerely desire peace and that the Spanish people desire peace, and if you can still give me time and reasonable liberty of action, I will get you the peace you desire so much and for which you have labored so hard." [1]

The immediate reply to General Woodford from Washington was that "the President has made no suggestions to Spain except through you. He made no suggestions other than those which you were instructed to make for an armistice to be offered by Spain to negotiate a permanent peace between Spain and insurgents, and which Spain has already rejected. An armistice involves an agreement between Spain and insurgents which must be voluntary on the part of each, and if accepted by them would make for peace. The disposition of our fleet must be left to us. An armistice to be effective must be immediately proffered and accepted by insurgents. Would the peace you are so confident of securing mean the independence of Cuba? The President cannot hold his message longer than Tuesday." [2]

On April 4 General Woodford was informed that "Congress may very possibly take decisive action [at] middle or end of this week," and was directed to notify consular officers to arrange to leave Spain in case of rupture of relations.[3] He was also instructed the

[1] Telegram, April 3, 1898, *Foreign Relations*, 1898, 732.
[2] Mr. Day to General Woodford, April 3, 1898 (telegram), *Ibid.*, 732.
[3] *Foreign Relations*, 1898, 733.

next day, "In case of necessity intrust the legation to British embassy."[1]

On April 5 General Woodford telegraphed the President: "Should the queen proclaim the following before 12 o'clock noon of Wednesday, April 6, will you sustain the queen, and can you prevent hostile action by Congress?

" 'At the request of the holy father, in this passion week, and in the name of Christ, I proclaim immediate and unconditional suspension of hostilities in the island of Cuba.

" 'This suspension is to become immediately effective so soon as accepted by the insurgents in that island, and is to continue for the space of six months, to the 5th of October, 1898.

" 'I do this to give time for passions to cease, and in the sincere hope and belief that during this suspension permanent and honorable peace may be obtained between the insular government of Cuba and those of my subjects in that island who are now in rebellion against the authority of Spain.

" 'I pray the blessing of Heaven upon this truce of God, which I now declare in His name and with the sanction of the holy father of all Christendom.'

"Please read this in the light of all my previous telegrams and letters. I believe this means peace, which the sober judgment of our people will approve long before next November, and which must be approved at the bar of final history.

"I permit the papal nuncio to read this telegram, upon my own responsibility and without committing you in any manner. I dare not reject this last chance for peace. I will show your reply to the queen in person, and I believe that you will approve this last conscientious offer for peace."[2]

[1] *Foreign Relations*, 1898, 734. [2] *Ibid.*, 734.

CHAPTER XXIX

SPAIN'S PRACTICAL ACCEPTANCE OF AMERICAN DEMANDS.—COLLECTIVE NOTE OF THE FOREIGN POWERS.—THE PRESIDENT'S MESSAGE.—THE JOINT RESOLUTION OF CONGRESS.—THE DECLARATION OF WAR

SPAIN had now practically accepted the American demands in full, unless Mr. Day's telegram of March 25, mentioning "full self-government with reasonable indemnity," which his telegram of March 28 defined as meaning Cuban independence, and which was given as the basis on which the President would "assist in [the] consummation [of peace]," was to be considered a demand for immediate independence.[1] But the minister's message brought a telegram, sent at midnight of March 5, which he could hardly consider encouraging, and which apparently shows that the die was already considered cast. It said: "The President highly appreciates the Queen's desire for peace. He cannot assume to influence the action of the American Congress beyond a discharge of his constitutional duty in transmitting the whole matter to them with such recommendation as he deems necessary and expedient. The repose and welfare of the American people require restoration of peace and stable government in Cuba. If armistice is offered by the government of Spain the President will communicate that fact to Congress. The President's message will go to Congress tomorrow. It will recount the conditions in Cuba; the injurious effect upon our people; the character and conditions of the conflict, and the apparent hopelessness of the strife. He will not advise the recognition of the independence of the insurgents, but will recommend measures looking to the cessation of hostilities, the restora-

[1] This was communicated unofficially but never officially to the Spanish government.

tion of peace and stability of government in the island in the interests of humanity, and for the safety and tranquillity of our own country." [1]

This was transmitted at once to the Spanish minister of state. The sending of the presidential message was, however, postponed through the presentation that day to the President of a collective note by the representatives of Great Britain, Germany, France, Austria-Hungary, Russia, and Italy, making "a pressing appeal to the feelings of humanity and moderation of the President and of the American people in their differences with Spain. They earnestly hope," continued the note, "that further negotiations will lead to an agreement which, while securing the maintenance of peace, will afford all necessary guarantees for the re-establishment of order in Cuba." [2]

The President's reply after recognizing the good-will which prompted the action continued in terms which could leave little doubt as to the action to be advised to the Congress. He said: "The government of the United States appreciates the humanitarian and disinterested character of the communication now made on behalf of the powers named, and for its part is confident that equal appreciation will be shown for its own earnest and unselfish endeavors to fulfil a duty to humanity by ending a situation the indefinite prolongation of which has become insufferable." [3]

Three days later the representatives of the greater European powers made a like visit to the Spanish minister of state; their suggestion that Spain should accede to the solicitation of the Pope, and their belief that the suspension of hostilities was "compatible with the honor and prestige " of the Spanish arms, caused the order, the same day (April 9), for the suspension of hostilities.[4]

Meanwhile, on April 6, General Woodford received a telegram saying: "The President's message will not be sent to Congress until next Monday, to give the consul-general at Havana the time he urgently asks to insure safe departure of Americans," a word which caused General Woodford to withdraw his note of that day to Señor Gullon, and to express a hope, in his answer to Washington, "that this will also give the Spanish government the time in

[1] *Foreign Relations*, 1898, 735. [2] *Ibid.*, 1898, 740. [3] *Ibid.*, 741.
[4] Spanish *Cor. and Docs.*, 114.

which to issue a frank and effective proclamation of such an armistice as may lead to an early and honorable peace." [1]

On April 7 General Woodford caused to be corrected in the Madrid newspapers misstatements as to the movements of members of the legation and his family. The communication ended by saying: "[General Woodford] is working for peace, and, despite all rumors to the contrary, he still hopes that peace will be kept between the United States and Spain and that peace will very soon be again established in Cuba—a peace that shall be based upon absolute justice, with protection to the great American interests in that island and with the maintenance of the honor of Spain."

He gave the next day to the American and English correspondents at Madrid an interview saying: "I have never lost my faith; and doubtful as conditions seem to-day, I still believe that these great and good purposes of my President may be secured. I shall not desist from my labors for a just and honorable peace until the guns actually open fire; and my faith is still strong that war, with all its horrors, can be averted. Enough blood has been shed in Cuba already, and I cannot believe that the closing hours of the nineteenth century will be reddened by conflict between Spain and the United States. My country asks for peace based upon conditions that shall make peace permanent and beneficent, and I have faith that Spain will yet do what is necessary to assure justice for Cuba, and with justice peace is certain." [3]

On April 9 he followed up a telegram stating that the Spanish propositions had not been modified, sent early in the day, by a later one announcing that authority to proclaim an armistice had been cabled to Governor-General Blanco, information of action on which was formally conveyed next day by Señor Polo de Bernabé to Mr. Day.[4]

General Woodford apparently now satisfied that the goal for which he had so earnestly striven had been reached, telegraphed the President: "In view of the action of the Spanish government, . . . I hope that you can obtain full authority from Congress to do whatever you shall deem necessary to secure immediate and permanent peace in Cuba by negotiations, including the full power to employ

---

[1] *Foreign Relations*, 1898, 743, 744.   [2] *Ibid.*, 745.   [3] *Ibid.*, 745.
[4] *Ibid.*, 747. For text of proclamation, see *Ibid.*, 750.

the army and navy, according to your own judgment, to aid and enforce your action. If this be secured I believe that you will get final settlement before August 1 on one of the following bases: Either such autonomy as the insurgents may agree to accept or recognition by Spain of the independence of the island, or cession of the island to the United States. I hope that nothing will now be done to humiliate Spain, as I am satisfied that the present government is going, and is loyally ready to go, as fast and far as it can. With your power of action sufficiently free, you will win the fight on your own lines." [1]

The crux of the situation lay in the phrase of the last sentence—"with your power of action sufficiently free." But this freedom, the retention of which, if peace was to be preserved, was a necessity, the President now, though his diplomacy had been crowned with all the success the American envoy at Madrid had hoped for, had determined to yield, evidently convinced that war could be the only real solution. The question once referred to Congress, it would have required, in order to prevent warlike action, a calmness of judgment and discussion which it was impossible to find in the majority of a large popular body stimulated, through the three years of the Cuban strife, by a highly wrought popular sentiment. Congress equally with the great majority of the American people had been brought to view the immediate extinguishment of Spanish dominion in the island a necessity. President Grant, facing a situation of like character in the ten years' war, had, supported by Mr. Fish, unyieldingly determined to keep hold of the reins of diplomacy. President Cleveland had been equally firm in holding a like course. Had either, in the critical moments of their administrations, transferred the Cuban question to Congress, war would have been the result.

This, naturally, was clear to President McKinley. There were clearly but two courses open: one to put aside the diplomatic success attained and act upon the view that anything short of an immediate abrogation of Spanish authority in Cuba was a useless continuation of an unbearable situation, and thus advise its immediate discontinuance; the other, in the new light of the Spanish declaration of a suspension of hostilities, to withhold such advice for

[1] Telegram, April 10, 1908, *Foreign Relations*, 1898, 747.

the moment and, instead, to lay before Congress the diplomatic correspondence, in full, of the last three weeks, and advise Congress that he proposed to await the results of the armistice now declared.

The President chose the former course; the best, judged by our knowledge to-day, for Spain, for Cuba and for the United States. On April 11, 1898, he sent his message to Congress.

After a general statement of the conditions repeated so frequently in the messages of his predecessors and in his own, the President mentioned the efforts, including those of Spain, made to relieve suffering, and then said:

"The war in Cuba is of such a nature that short of subjugation or extermination a final military victory for either side seems impracticable. The alternative lies in the physical exhaustion of the one or the other party, or perhaps of both—a condition which in effect ended the ten years' war by the truce of Zanjon. The prospect of such a protraction and conclusion of the present strife is a contingency hardly to be contemplated with equanimity by the civilized world, and least of all by the United States, affected and injured as we are, deeply and intimately, by its very existence.

"Realizing this, it appeared to be my duty, in a spirit of true friendliness, no less to Spain than to the Cubans, who have so much to lose by the prolongation of the struggle, to seek to bring about an immediate termination of the war. To this end I submitted on the 27th ultimo, as a result of much representation and correspondence, through the United States minister at Madrid, propositions to the Spanish government looking to an armistice until October 1 for the negotiation of peace with the good offices of the President.

"In addition, I asked the immediate revocation of the order of reconcentration, so as to permit the people to return to their farms and the needy to be relieved with provisions and supplies from the United States, co-operating with the Spanish authorities, so as to afford full relief.

"The reply of the Spanish cabinet was received on the night of the 31st ultimo. It offered, as the means to bring about peace in Cuba, to confide the preparation thereof to the insular parliament, inasmuch as the concurrence of that body would be necessary to reach a final result, it being, however, understood that the powers reserved by the constitution to the central government are not lessened or diminished. As the Cuban parliament does not meet until the 4th of May next, the Spanish government would not object, for its part, to accept at once a suspension of hostilities if asked for by the insurgents from the general-in-chief, to whom it would pertain, in such case, to determine the duration and conditions of the armistice.

"The propositions submitted by General Woodford and the reply of the Spanish government were both in the form of brief memoranda, the texts of which are before me, and are substantially in the language above given. The function of the Cuban parliament in the matter of 'preparing' peace and the manner of its doing so are not expressed in the Spanish memorandum; but from General Woodford's explanatory reports of preliminary discussions preceding the final conference it is understood that the Spanish government stands ready to give the insular congress full powers to settle the terms of peace with the insurgents—whether by direct negotiation or indirectly by means of legislation does not appear.

"With this last overture in the direction of immediate peace, and its disappointing reception by Spain, the executive is brought to the end of his effort."

The President then referred to his acceptance in his message of December, 1896, of the views of President Grant in 1875, showing the recognition of the independence of Cuba to be indefensible and impracticable. "Nothing," he said, "has occurred to change my view in this regard." In support of this he also quoted the words of President Jackson in his message of December 21, 1836, on the proposed recognition of Texas, in which Jackson said: "Prudence . . . seems to dictate that we should still stand aloof and maintain our present attitude . . . at least until the lapse of time or the course of events shall have proved beyond cavil or dispute the ability of the people of that country to maintain their separate sovereignty and to uphold the government constituted by them."

"They are," said Mr. McKinley, " evidence that the United States, in addition to the test imposed by public law as the condition of the recognition of independence by a neutral state (to wit, that the revolted state shall 'constitute in fact a body politic, having a government in substance as well as in name, possessed of the elements of stability,' and forming *de facto*, 'if left to itself, a state among the nations, reasonably capable of discharging the duties of a state'), has imposed for its own governance in dealing with cases like these the further condition that recognition of independent statehood is not due to a revolted dependency until the danger of its being again subjugated by the parent state has entirely passed away. . . .

"I said in my message of December last, 'It is to be seriously considered whether the Cuban insurrection possesses beyond dispute the attributes of statehood which alone can demand the recognition of belligerency in its favor.' The same requirement must certainly be no less seriously considered when the graver issue of recognizing independence is in question, for no less positive test can be applied to the greater act than to the lesser; while, on the other hand, the influences and consequences of the struggle upon the internal policy of the recognizing state, which form important factors when the recognition of belligerency is concerned, are secondary, if not rightly eliminable, factors when the real question is whether the community claiming recognition is or is not independent beyond peradventure.

"Nor from the stand-point of expediency do I think it would be wise or prudent for this government to recognize at the present time the independence of the so-called Cuban republic. Such recognition is not necessary in order to enable the United States to intervene and pacify the island. To commit this country now to the recognition of any particular government in Cuba might subject us to embarrassing conditions of international obligation toward the organization so recognized. In case of intervention our conduct would be subject to the approval or disapproval of such government. We would be required to submit to its direction and to assume to it the mere relation of a friendly ally.

"When it shall appear hereafter that there is within the island a government capable of performing the duties and discharging the functions of a separate nation, and having, as a matter of fact, the proper forms and attributes of nationality, such government can be promptly and readily recognized and the relations and interests of the United States with such nation adjusted.

"There remain the alternative forms of intervention to end the war, either as an impartial neutral by imposing a rational compromise between the contestants, or as the active ally of the one party or the other.

"As to the first, it is not to be forgotten that during the last few months the relation of the United States has virtually been one of friendly intervention in many ways, each not of itself conclusive, but all tending to the exertion of a potential influence toward an ultimate pacific result, just and honorable to all interests concerned. The spirit of all our acts hitherto has been an earnest, unselfish desire for peace and prosperity in Cuba, untarnished by differences between us and Spain, and unstained by the blood of American citizens.

"The forcible intervention of the United States as a neutral to stop the war, according to the large dictates of humanity and following many historical precedents where neighboring states have interfered to check the hopeless sacrifices of life by internecine conflicts beyond their borders, is justifiable on rational grounds. It involves, however, hostile constraint upon both the parties to the contest as well to enforce a truce as to guide the eventual settlement.

"The grounds for such intervention may be briefly summarized as follows:

"First. In the cause of humanity and to put an end to the barbarities, bloodshed, starvation, and horrible miseries now existing there, and which the parties to the conflict are either unable or unwilling to stop or mitigate. It is no answer to say this is all in another country, belonging to another nation, and is therefore none of our business. It is specially our duty, for it is right at our door.

"Second. We owe it to our citizens in Cuba to afford them that protection and indemnity for life and property which no government there can or will afford, and to that end to terminate the conditions that deprive them of legal protection.

"Third. The right to intervene may be justified by the very serious injury to the commerce, trade, and business of our people, and by the wanton destruction of property and devastation of the island.

"Fourth, and which is of the utmost importance. The present condition of affairs in Cuba is a constant menace to our peace, and entails upon this government an enormous expense. With such a conflict waged for years in an island so near us and with which our people have such trade and business relations—when the lives and liberty of our citizens are in constant danger and their property destroyed and themselves ruined—where our trading vessels are liable to seizure and are seized at our very door by war-ships of a foreign nation, the expeditions of filibustering that we are powerless to prevent altogether, and the irritating questions and entanglements thus arising—all these and others that I need not mention, with the resulting strained relations, are a constant menace to our peace, and compel us to keep on a semiwar footing with a nation with which we are at peace.

"These elements of danger and disorder already pointed out have been strikingly illustrated by a tragic event which has deeply and justly moved the American people. I have already transmitted to Congress the report of the naval court of inquiry on the destruction of the battle-ship *Maine* in the harbor of Havana during the night of the 15th of February. The destruction of that noble vessel has filled the national heart with inexpressible horror. Two hundred and fifty-eight brave sailors and marines and two officers of our navy, reposing in the fancied security of a friendly harbor, have been hurled to death, grief and want brought to their homes and sorrow to the nation.

"The naval court of inquiry, which, it is needless to say, commands the unqualified confidence of the government, was unanimous in its conclusion that the destruction of the *Maine* was caused by an exterior explosion, that of a submarine mine. It did not assume to place the responsibility. That remains to be fixed.

"In any event the destruction of the *Maine*, by whatever exterior cause, is a patent and impressive proof of a state of things in Cuba that is intolerable. That condition is thus shown to be such that the Spanish government cannot assure safety and security to a vessel of the American navy in the harbor of Havana on a mission of peace, and rightfully there.

"Further referring in this connection to recent diplomatic correspondence, a despatch from our minister to Spain, of the 26th ultimo, contained the statement that the Spanish minister for foreign affairs assured him positively that Spain will do all that the highest honor and justice require in the matter of the *Maine*. The reply above referred to of the 31st ultimo also contained an expression of the readiness of Spain to submit to an arbitration all the differences which can arise in this matter, which is subsequently explained by the note of the Spanish minister at Washington of the 10th instant, as follows:

"'As to the question of fact which springs from the diversity of views between the reports of the American and Spanish boards, Spain proposes that the facts be ascertained by an impartial investigation by experts, whose decision Spain accepts in advance.'

"To this I have made no reply."

The President then quoted at some length President Grant's opinion expressed in his message of 1875, that "the agency of others, either by mediation or by intervention, seems to be the only alternative which must sooner or later be invoked for the termination of the strife," and also quoted the similar views expressed by President Cleveland in his last annual message in 1896, and in his own in 1897. He then said:

"The long trial has proved that the object for which Spain has waged the war cannot be attained. The fire of insurrection may flame or may smoulder with varying seasons, but it has not been and it is plain that it cannot be extinguished by present methods. The only hope of relief and repose from a condition which can no longer be endured is the enforced pacification of Cuba. In the name of humanity, in the name of civilization, in behalf of endangered American interests which give us the right and the duty to speak and to act, the war in Cuba must stop.

"In view of these facts and of these considerations, I ask the Congress to authorize and empower the President to take measures to secure a full and final termination of hostilities between the government of Spain and the people of Cuba, and to secure in the island the establishment of a stable government, capable of maintaining order and observing its international obligations, insuring peace and tranquillity and the security of its citizens as well as our own, and to use the military and naval forces of the United States as may be necessary for these purposes.

"And in the interest of humanity and to aid in preserving the lives of the starving people of the island I recommend that the distribution of food and supplies be continued, and that an appropriation be made out of the public treasury to supplement the charity of our citizens.

"The issue is now with the Congress. It is a solemn responsibility. I have exhausted every effort to relieve the intolerable condition of affairs which is at our doors. Prepared to execute every obligation imposed upon me by the constitution and the law, I await your action."

Only now, however, did the President mention the yielding by Spain to all demands officially placed before her, saying with a terseness which could only be held to mean that the concession came too late:

"Yesterday, and since the preparation of the foregoing message, official information was received by me that the latest decree of the Queen Regent of Spain directs General Blanco, in order to prepare and facilitate peace, to proclaim a suspension of hostilities, the duration and details of which have not yet been communicated to me.

"This fact with every other pertinent consideration will, I am sure, have your just and careful attention in the solemn deliberations upon which you are about to enter. If this measure attains a successful result, then our aspirations as a Christian, peaceloving people will be realized. If it fails, it will be only another justification for our contemplated action."

It is needless to dwell upon the many and various resolutions brought forward in each House, beginning April 13; referred to the committees on foreign affairs, reported, and debated until on April 19 (though the legislative day was the 18th), final action was taken on a joint resolution, of which that reported on April 13 by the Senate committee on foreign affairs was the basis. The report of this committee was prefaced by many pages dealing with the general question of Cuba, but first with the destruction of the *Maine*.

It regarded this "as only a single incident in the relations" with Spain, and "if that calamity had never happened the questions between the United States and that government would press for immediate solution." It considered that it "was compassed either by the official act of the Spanish authorities or was made possible by negligence on their part so willing and gross as to be equivalent in culpability to positive criminal action."

The control of Spain over the western part of the island was declared a "dominance over a desolation which she herself has created." Elaborate argument was made in justification of recognition and intervention, but, notwithstanding, the majority of the committee evaded the question of recognition in the joint resolution offered, which was as follows:

"Whereas the abhorrent conditions which have existed for more than three years in the island of Cuba, so near our own borders, have shocked the moral sense of the people of the United States, have been a disgrace to Christian civilization, culminating, as they have, in the destruction of a United States battle-ship, with two hundred and sixty-six[1] of its officers and crew, while on a friendly visit in the harbor of Havana, and cannot longer be endured, as has been set forth by the President of the United States in his message to Congress of April eleventh, eighteen hundred and ninety-eight, upon which the action of Congress was invited: Therefore,

"*Resolved*, by the Senate and House of Representatives of the United States of America in Congress assembled: First. That the people of the island of Cuba are, and of right ought to be, free and independent.

"Second. That it is the duty of the United States to demand, and the government of the United States does hereby demand, that the government of Spain at once relinquish its authority and government in the island of Cuba and withdraw its land and naval forces from Cuba and Cuban waters.

"Third. That the President of the United States be, and he hereby is, directed and empowered to use the entire land and naval forces of the United States, and to call into the actual service of the United States the militia of the several states, to such extent as may be necessary to carry these resolutions into effect."

Four members of the committee, while "cordially" concurring in the report, favored "the immediate recognition of the republic of Cuba, as organized in that island, as a free, independent, and sovereign power," and reported an amendment of the first paragraph by inserting after the word independent: "and the govern-

[1] An error; the number was two hundred and sixty.

ment of the United States hereby recognize(s) the republic of Cuba as the true and lawful government of that island." [1]

Debate in the Senate lasted until late Saturday, April 16. The amendment of the minority of the committee was adopted by a vote of 51 to 37, the dissentients being 33 republicans and 4 democrats. Ten republicans voted with the majority. An amendment offered on the 16th by Senator Teller disclaiming any intention on the part of the United States of seeking sovereignty or dominion over Cuba was agreed to without a division. The resolutions as amended were passed by a vote of 67 to 21, 24 republicans voting with the democrats and populists in the majority; 19 republicans and 2 democrats forming the minority. Sunday intervened.

The House on Monday, the 18th, wisely and fortunately, but somewhat surprisingly, it must be said, considering its more popular character, struck out, through the exertions of the republican leaders, the resolution of recognition. The adherence of the Senate, when the bill was returned, to its original vote caused twice a reference to conferences, the final result being that at 1.20 A. M. of April 19 a joint resolution from the conference committee was adopted in the Senate by a vote of 42 to 35, and at 2.40 o'clock in the House by 311 to 6. Twelve senators and 38 representatives did not vote. The resolution, prefaced as it originally came from the Senate committee on foreign affairs, was as follows:

"*Resolved*, by the Senate and House of Representatives of the United States of America in Congress assembled: First. That the people of the island of Cuba are, and of right ought to be, free and independent.

"Second. That it is the duty of the United States to demand, and the government of the United States does hereby demand, that the government of Spain at once relinquish its authority and government in the island of Cuba, and withdraw its land and naval forces from Cuba and Cuban waters.

"Third. That the President of the United States be, and he hereby is directed and empowered to use the entire land and naval forces of the United States, and to call into the actual service of the United States the militia of the several states, to such an extent as may be necessary to carry these resolutions into effect.

[1] *Senate Report*, 885, 55 Cong., 2 Sess.

"Fourth. That the United States hereby disclaims any disposition or intention to exercise sovereignty, jurisdiction, or control over said island except for the pacification thereof, and asserts its determination when that is accomplished to leave the government and control of the island to its people."

The resolution was signed by the President at 11.24 A. M. of April 20.

Within a few minutes (at 11.35 A. M.) the secretary of state received a note from the Spanish minister stating that, the passage of the joint resolution and its signing by the President making his continuance in Washington impossible, he requested his passports, announcing that Spanish interests would be looked after by the French ambassador and Austro-Hungarian minister.[1] He left Washington the same evening for Canada, having first telegraphed his action to the Spanish minister of state.

The resolution was telegraphed to the American minister at Madrid with directions "to immediately communicate" it to the government of Spain, with the formal demand which the resolution embodied, with the addition that "if by the hour of noon on Saturday next, the 23d day of April, instant, there be not communicated to this government by that of Spain a full and satisfactory response to this demand and resolution, whereby the ends of peace in Cuba shall be assured, the President will proceed without further notice to use the power and authority enjoined and conferred upon him by the said joint resolution to such extent as may be necessary to carry the same into effect."[2]

The Spanish minister of state, before the instructions telegraphed could be acted upon, and in order "to avoid receiving the American ultimatum,"[3] sent to General Woodford a note stating that "the President having approved a resolution of both chambers of the United States, which in denying the legitimate sovereignty of Spain and in threatening armed intervention in Cuba, is equivalent to an evident declaration of war, the government of his majesty has ordered its minister in Washington to withdraw without loss of time from American territory with all the *personnel* of the legation.

---

[1] *Foreign Relations*, 1898, 765.   [2] *Ibid.*, 762.

[3] Señor Gullon to Spanish representatives abroad, April 21, 1898, *Spanish Cor. and Docs.*, 136.

By this act the diplomatic relations which previously existed between the two countries are broken off, all official communication between their representatives ceasing, and I hasten to communicate this to your excellency in order that on your part you may make such dispositions as seem suitable." [1]

General Woodford, acknowledging the reception of the note, announced to Señor Gullon that he had directed all the consular representatives of the United States in Spain to turn over their consulates to the British consuls and leave Spain at once, and that he himself had placed the affairs of his legation in the hands of the British embassy, which would have the care of American interests. He ended with: "I now request passports and safe-conduct to the French frontier for myself and the *personnel* of this legation. I intend leaving at four o'clock for Paris." [2]

At daylight the next morning, April 22, Admiral Sampson's fleet was crossing the narrow sea between Key West and Cuba, with orders to blockade the Cuban coast from Cardenas to Bahia Honda on the north and Cienfuegos on the south. Two days later, on April 24, Admiral Dewey received orders to proceed at once to the Philippines and "capture or destroy" the Spanish squadron.

On April 25 it was enacted by the American Congress: "That war be, and the same is hereby declared to exist, and that war has existed since the 21st day of April A. D., 1898, including said day, between the United States of America and the kingdom of Spain."

The appeal had at last been made to the law of force on which has ever depended, and apparently for ages will depend, the arbitrament of the greater questions of life. Though nearly twenty centuries have passed since the great preachment of peace, more than ever are land and sea under martial threat. The facts of the universe are stronger than human theory. If we acknowledge an Almighty oversight of our world, who shall say that the existence of war and preparation for war are immoral and not in the intention of things? If this be allowed, war of itself cannot be

---

[1] Señor Gullon to General Woodford, April 21, 1898, *Spanish Cor. and Docs.*, 135.
[2] *Ibid.*, 135.

the great evil; the evil is in the horrors, many of which are not necessarily concomitant. Militant operations have been softened equally with those of civil justice, and the war now beginning between the United States and Spain was one in which these greater horrors were largely to be absent. The combatant forces almost alone were to suffer, and they in moderate degree. At least the short struggle ended the immensely greater evils of the contest between Cuban and Spaniard.

The war was the final act in the struggle for supremacy between Anglo-Saxons and men of the Latin race in North America, in which Philip, Elizabeth, Drake, Howard, Chatham, Vernon, Wolf, Montcalm, Washington had, all, a part. The expedition of the Great Armada; the murderous early struggles in Carolina and Florida; the seven years' war which drove France from the American continent, were but acts in the drama the culmination of which, in 1898, left the Anglo-Saxon and the American in Mexico masters of the whole of the northern continent. It was the end of a race struggle which had lasted full three hundred years.

Spanish dominion in America, in which there had been much both of glory and of shame, with splendid episodes of heroic endeavor, noble self-abnegation, and great attainment, was to end in the final sacrifice, nobly met, in the sea which had through generations witnessed so many conflicts of the two races.

Though Spain was to lose her American dominion, she was not to lose the good-will and kindly regard of the American people, linked as these are with her by the chain wrought by the great discoverer, and to whom Spain must ever be the land which has made so much of the history of the Western world. Those who know Spain know a country in which kindliness, courtesy, and simplicity of character much more than offset the want of the more energetic qualities on which modern life lays so great store; and in those who have this knowledge there can but be the wish for, in time to come, the peace and prosperity which through so many centuries have failed to be her portion, and that Spanish statesmanship to come will meet the true deserts of the Spanish people.

INDEX

ABARZUZA, Spanish statesman, author of Cuban law passed Feb., 1895, 406.

Act, the Mobile, 70; practically withdrawn by proclamation, 71.

Act, strengthening neutrality act, passed March 3, 1817, 123.

Adams, John, 27.

Adams, secretary of state, 1817, 124; concerning charges in Baltimore against privateers, 122; best equipped and ablest statesman who has held the office, 124; correspondence with De Onis, re treaty, 124; opposes yielding Texas, 125; supports Jackson, 134; overbears opposition, 134; reply to Spanish minister, 134; reply to Pizarro, 135-137; reply silenced European comment, 137; preserves Northwest to U. S., 139; land grants by Spain in Florida, 139; holds delay in ratification of treaty unjustified, 142; sharp reply to Vives, 145; re South American independence, 150; reply, April 6, 1822, to Spanish minister's protest re South American recognition, 153; re South American revolutionary governments, 155; re privateers and pirates, 180; instruction to Nelson, American minister in Spain, 1823, 180; Cuba indispensable to Union, 183; fears British occupancy of Cuba, 185; does not believe Holy Alliance could restore Spanish dominion in South America, 195; anticipates Monroe declaration in informing Russian minister, July 15, 1823, that "American continents are no longer subjects for any new colonial establishments," 198; views of stand to be taken, 198; author of Monroe doctrine, 198 (note); answer to Russian minister, Nov. 27, 1823, a full exposition of American policy, 199; opposes touching European situation in message of 1823, 200; reasons for joining in Panama congress, 209, 210; action sound, 210; president, message, Dec. 6, 1825, notifies Congress of proposed action re Panama congress and nominates envoys thereto, 209; second message on Panama congress, 213, 214.

Addington informs Mr. King New Orleans might be occupied by England, 46.

Aix-la-Chapelle, meeting of alliance at, Oct. 1, 1818, 160; sovereigns present, 160; the two protocols, 161, 162.

Albemarle, Lord, 13.

Alexander, Emperor of Russia, 107; directs minister in Washington to "plead cause of peace," 144; religious exalté, 156; wholly subservient to Metternich, 171.

Allen H., minister to Chile, 155.

Allen, William Vincent, Senator, offers joint resolution re Cuba, 486.

Alliança, case of, fired on by *Venadito*, 419-423; discussion by Olivart, 422, 423.

Amadeo, called to throne of Spain, Nov., 1870, 282; abdication of, Feb. 11, 1873; election of, 305 (note); king from January, 1871, to February, 1873, 313.

Ambrister, Lieutenant, 116; accompanies Woodbine in endeavor to arouse Indians, 125; executed by Jackson, 130; violent feeling in England, 130, 137.

Amelia Island, 115; seized by adventurers, led by Sir Gregor McGregor, 125.

America (U. S.), humiliation of, through failure to follow Gallatin's advice, 89; ships seized, 90; a victim, 104; true course to arm, to occupy Texas and let war come if it would, 105; affairs tending to war with Great Britain, 114; American slavery bulwark of Spain in Cuba and Puerto Rico, 215.

America, South, why Spanish in character instead of Anglo-Saxon, 111; lost to Great Britain, 111.

America, Spanish, secession precipitated by Spaniards of Spain, 110.

Amistad, extraordinary case of, 270 (note).

Anderson, R. C., minister to Colombia, 155; nominated envoy to Panama congress, 209; did not attend, dying at Bogota, 214.

Anduaga, Don Joaquin de, Spanish minister, protests against recognition of South American independence, 153; Adams's reply, 153, 154.

Appalachicola, fort on, great value of stores, 118.

Aranda, Count, boundaries proposed by, in 1782, 25; often declared France mistaken in encouraging American independence, 27.

Arbuthnot tried and hanged by Jackson, 130; serious character of act, 130; execution near to bringing war with Great Britain, 131, 136.

Armstrong General John, minister to France, writes Monroe that France will side with Spain, 82; advises Jefferson to occupy Texas, 86, 92; arrival of defi-

INDEX

nite propositions from French government, 93; new proposition from French emissary, 94; receives note re Santo Domingo, 97, 98; beseeches government to take positive ground, 99; to French government, declining alliance, 100.

Aury, "Commodore," seizes Fernandina as a conquest of Mexican republic, 126.

Austria dominates largely Italy, 170; treaty binding Naples to monarchical institutions, 170; moves 85,000 men into Italy and suppresses Naples and Piedmont revolutions, 172; action in Italy but prelude to designs as to Spain, 173; results in Italy, 173.

Autonomy in Cuba, $50,000,000 appropriation death-blow to, 545.

Avenero, Spanish admiral, 232 (note).

Azara, Spanish minister to Paris, unable to state if the Floridas were included in cession to France, 44.

Azcárraga succeeds Cánovas as minister of state *ad interim*, 511.

BARKER, consul at Sagua la Grande, reports laborers killed by insurgents, 523.

Barrancas, Fort, 116; taken by Jackson, 131.

Barton, Miss Clara, in Cuba, 529.

Bathurst, Lord, letter to Castlereagh, re Canning's objections to action of Holy Alliance, 168–170.

Baton Rouge seized, 112.

Bayou Pierre, strong Spanish garrison at, 102.

Becerra, minister of state *ad interim*, cold reception of U. S. proposals, 299; unfortunate absence of Prim and Silvela, 299; bitterly opposed to propositions, 299; requests withdrawal of Sickles's note of Sept. 3, 300; while accepting good offices of U. S., bases rejected, 301.

Bedoya, Serrano, 282.

Belligerency, recognition of, demanded in U. S., 286; report upon, by majority of Senate committee on foreign affairs, Dec. 21, 1896, 483–485.

Benton, Senator, on Panama congress, 212.

Berlin decree, 99.

Bermuda, British filibustering steamer, 418.

Bernadotte to command Louisiana expedition, 44.

Bernadotte, King of Sweden, 160.

Bernstorff, Prussian representative at Aix-la-Chapelle, 160.

Berthier, ordered to prepare Santo Domingo expedition, 48.

Berrien, Senator, on Panama congress, 812.

Beurnonville, General, 50.

Bill for $2,000,000 for Floridas passed, 97.

Billy Butts, American schooner carrying arms, etc., to *Virginius*, 315.

Black Warrior, mail steamer and cargo seized at Havana for alleged violation of customs laws, 255; impossible to find excuse for action, 256; despatch regarding, to Soulé, 257; Spain's attitude, 258; matter arranged by owners with Cuban authorities, 259.

Blanco, Guzman, connection with *Virginius*, 315.

Blanco y Erenas, Don Ramon, marquis of Pena Plata, succeeds Weyler, Oct. 31, 1897, 522; attempts alleviation of concentration, 522; non-success, 522; efforts to relieve distress, 530; opposition to his policy of reform, 530; complete recall of concentration orders, 566.

Bland, Theodoric, a commissioner to South America, 149.

Blockade, of New York, 92; of Spanish main, declared by Spanish authorities, 179; protest against by American and British commanders, 180.

Bolivar, 149; treaty with Marshal Morillo, 1820, 179; circular calling a congress to include Spanish-American states and U. S., 205; objects of Panama congress, 210, 211.

Bonaparte, Joseph, 45.

Bonaparte. See Napoleon.

Boone, Daniel, 30.

Boundaries, nothing could be clearer, 69; proposed in cabinet meeting, Nov. 12, 1805, 92, 94.

Boutelle, Charles Addison, M. C., speech of, on Cuba, 449.

Bowdoin, James, to succeed Pinckney at Madrid, 82, 84, 98.

Brest, 48.

Brice, U. S. consul, Matanzas, report of conditions at, 504, 505; Blanco's order re concentration ineffective, 522; report of misery in Matanzas, 529, 530.

British occupancy of the Floridas feared, 113; British protest against U. S. occupancy of West Florida, 113.

Brougham, praises Monroe declaration, 202.

Buchanan, James, secretary of state, despatch proposing to buy Cuba, 221–223; minister to England, to ascertain views of British government re Cuba, 253; to bring to notice continuance of slave-trade, 253; member of Ostend conference, 261; president; continued recommendation to purchase Cuba a painful demonstration of inability to read signs of the times, 272.

Buenos Ayres, declares for Fernando and against France, May 25, 1810, 149; declares independence, July 9, 1816, 149.

Bulgary, Count, Russian minister to Spain, requested by Spanish minister of state to call upon American minister, 143.

INDEX

Bullock, captain of *Black Warrior*, hauls down flag, 256.
Burr, schemes of, 100; intrigues with British minister, 101; turns to Spanish minister, 101.
Burriel, General, governor of Santiago; defence of, 322. See *Virginius*, case of, 351-353.
Butler, Robert, commissioner, receives transfer of Florida, 147.

CABALLERO DE ROSAS, GENERAL, Captain-General of Cuba, in place of Dulce, 290; issues unwarranted decrees, 290; decrees modified on protest of U. S., 292.
Cabinet, action of, on Jefferson's proposals for joining with Great Britain, 57; memoranda of, 92; accepts Napoleon's terms, 94; terms agreed upon in, re Spanish question, 94; English, almost wholly Tories, 168; Canning announces in, opposition to Aix meeting, 168; Monroe's, except Adams, think Jackson wrong, 134.
Cadiz, 48; merchants of, 109.
Calderon, Señor, Spanish minister of state, sends note to American minister, Nov. 15, 1875, meeting U. S. demands, 375, 379; memorandum from, Feb. 3, 1876, 387, 388; signs protocol of 1877, 393.
Calhoun, stimulates panic re Holy Alliance, 195.
Call, Wilkinson, senator, re *Competitor*, 470; offers joint resolution, 486.
Cambrian, British frigate, outrageous conduct of, 104.
Cameron, James Donald, senator, reports joint resolution acknowledging Cuban independence, Dec. 21, 1896, 483; report on precedents, 483-485; excitement following offer of resolution, 485.
Campos, General Martinez, his patriotic declaration, 397-400; prime-minister in 1879, 400; resigns, 400; again sent to Cuba, April, 1895, with unlimited powers and credit, 407; humanity and excellent judgment of, 427; succeeded by Weyler, 428, 430.
Canada yielded, 1763, to Great Britain, 13.
Canalejas, Señor José, editor *Madrid Herald*, letter to, from De Lome, intercepted, 538.
Canning, George, cabinet minister, 107; announces opposition to the policy of the Holy Alliance, 168; letter from Lord Bathurst to Castlereagh discussing Canning's opposition, 168-170; final English attitude due to, 170; succeeds Castlereagh as prime-minister, 174; adds forcibly to Wellington's instructions, 174; note to ambassador at Paris declaring separation of Spanish colonies an accomplished fact, 178; instructions to minister at Madrid, 181; "double character of Spain," 181; sends British squadron to Cuban waters, 186; note to Rush mentioning intentions of Holy Alliance, 187; views as to combined action of England and U. S., 187, 188; writes Rush and has interview, 188; defence of inaction in Spain, 190; explanation to Rush of long silence, 196; disclaims desire for any portion of Spanish possessions, 196; objects to Monroe's declaration on account of the Northwest, 203.
Cánovas del Castillo, president of commission on Cuban reforms, 277; unwilling to accept liberal views of Campos and resigns, 400; again in power, 400; new laws for Cuba ineffective, 400; characterization of, 406; wise action re U. S. citizens, 427; cable message to *N. Y. World*, quoted by Senator Hale, 445, 446; in ignorance of the American mind risked American unfriendliness by rejecting good offices of U. S., 466; assassinated, Aug. 8, 1897, 511.
Capo d'Istria, Russian representative at Aix-la-Chapelle, 160.
Captain-General of Cuba, action re *Crescent City* and *Ohio*, 246-249; his authority an irresponsible one, 248, 249; above the law, 249; Spain opposed to alterations in status of, 254; much-desired commercial treaty impossible, 254; examination of relations between, and agents of U. S., 326.
Carácas, junta of, proclaimed treasonable, 110; elects supreme junta, 1810, 148; destruction by earthquake causes temporary failure of revolution, 149; U. S. Congress votes $50,000 for earthquake sufferers, 149 (note).
Carmichael, William, chargé d'affaires, Madrid, instructions to, 1792, 35.
Carondelet, governor of Louisiana, propositions of, to intriguers, 39.
Carron, British sloop of war, 116.
Carvajal, Spanish minister of state re *Virginius* (which see), 320, 321, 322, 328, 329, 330, 331, 332, 333, 334-338, 340, 344.
Casa Calvo, to leave New Orleans, 93.
Casa Yrujo, Marquis of. See Yrujo.
Cass, Lewis, secretary of state, 236 (note).
Castelar, president of republic, 313; telegram from, re *Virginius*, ordering non-imposition of death penalty without reference to Spain, 319; deeply moved by executions, 321, 322.
Castlereagh, to Rush, re execution of Arbuthnot and Ambrister, 130; prime-minister, represents Great Britain at Aix-la-Chapelle, 160; commits suicide, 174.
Cevallos, Spanish minister of state, refers U. S. to France, 62; severe remarks to Pinckney, 75; much alarmed by Pinckney, 75; appeals to French minister, 75;

discloses French note forbidding discussion of French spoliations, 82; discusses Louisiana boundary, 82; feels secure under ægis of Napoleon, 83; states boundary acceptable to Spain, 83; informs American minister that De Onis was empowered to open negotiations re Florida, 124.
Chadwick, Captain French Ensor, member *Maine* court of inquiry, 542.
Champagny, 99, 100.
Chandler, William Eaton, ex-senator, on laws of war in report of Spanish treaty claims commission, 493, 494.
Charles IV, King of Spain, 37, 42; abdication of, 106.
Charles V the cause of Spain's ruin, 8.
Chateaubriand, French foreign minister, note giving reasons for French action, 177.
Chesapeake, attacked by *Leopard*, 104.
Chile, revolution begins, 1810, 149.
Citizens, American, cases of, in Cuba, 427; mildness of proceedings against changed under Weyler, 428; cases determined in main with tact and judgment, 428.
Claiborne, governor of Louisiana, 63, 93; described by French prefect, 101.
Clark, George Rogers, capture of Kaskaskia, 24, 37.
Clay, Henry, M. C., attacks in Congress Jackson's course, 138; opposes yielding Rio Grande as boundary, 139; motion of, 1818, for appropriation for minister to Rio de la Plata lost, 151; renews motion in 1820, without result, 152; same defeated, 1821, 152; secretary of state; sees minister of Mexico, Central America, and Colombia re Congress, 205; U. S. cannot be party to existing war with Spain, 205; aims of Spanish-American states, 205; despatch urging Spain to accept situation, 206, 207; despatch to minister in Russia to engage Russia to influence Spain to stop war against revolted colonies, 207; Spain's reply, 207; reply of, to explanation by South American republics re proposed conference, 209; "seizure of Cuba," by England or France, "would mean war," 216.
Cleveland, Grover, president, proclaims rigorous prosecution of transgressions of neutrality law, 411; second proclamation of, July 27, 1896, 415; annual message, Dec. 2, 1895, 425, 426; last annual message, Dec. 7, 1896, 475-483; close of administration a period of protests re treatment of American citizens, 489; succeeded by President McKinley, 490.
Clinch, Colonel, attacks negro fort, 120.
Clubs, Cuban, more than 200 in the Americas, 407.
Colonies, trade of, perquisite of parent state, 90.

Colorado River offered as west boundary by American envoys, 83; boundary, 94.
Commission, to South America, sails in frigate *Congress*, Dec. 4, 1817, 150; reports from, Nov. 1, 1818, 150.
Commission, royal, sits in Spain on Cuban reforms; Cánovas del Castillo, president of, 277; economic propositions of, 278; reports Jan. 30, 1867; proposals of commission, 278, 279; final result, fatal to Spain in issuance of decree of Feb. 12, 1867, antagonistic to commission's views, 279; bitter denunciations of, in Cuba, 279; political reforms proposed, 279, 280; favored by Serrano, 280, 281; 1867, plans presented for abolition of slavery in Cuba and Puerto Rico, 281; only result of commission increased taxation, 281; turning-point of Cuban and Spanish relations, 281.
Commodore, filibuster tug, 416.
Competitor, filibustering schooner, the only filibustering vessel seized by Spain during war, 418; history of, 468; captured, 468; persons seized, 468; case of, 469-474; condemnation of crew, as "pirates," 469; release of, Nov., 1897; feeling aroused by case in Spain, 470; action in Congress, 470; De Olivart's discussion of case of, 471-474; "the *ridiculus mus* of the fabulist," 474; case made momentous by folly, 474, 489.
Concentration, its standing in international law examined, 491-495; effect of, 492, 493; U. S. precedent, 493; used by British in Boer war, 493; number of deaths, 493 (and note).
Concha, General José de la, captain-general, 237; appointed governor-general, etc., of Cuba, 362.
Congress of Holy Alliance, See Holy Alliance.
Congress, U. S. proposes to yield claim of navigation of Mississippi below 31°, 20; instructions of re peace negotiations disregarded by American commissioners, 26; effect which would have resulted from following instructions of, 26; refers Spanish treaty to new federal government,;34; House unalterably determined not to yield navigation of Mississippi, 52; debate on Jackson's course, 138; joint resolution, expressing friendly interest in South American independence, 148; debates on Panama congress, 211, 212; Southern opposition overborne, 213; nominations of envoys to Panama confirmed, 213; great emotion in, re Cuba, 306; Senator Morgan's resolution, passed in Senate, recognizing Cuban belligerency, did not come before House through action of speaker, 491; resolutions, Senate, 433; report of Senate committee on foreign relations, 433, 434; the resolution

INDEX

593

offered by majority of committee, 434, 435; minority report and resolution, 435–437; majority offer substitute for their previous resolution, 437; speech of Senator Sherman, 437, 438; Senate passes resolutions, Feb. 28, 1896, 438; resolutions in House passed March 2, 438; text of, 438 (note); passage of resolutions causes climax of feeling in Spain, 439; House passes Senate resolutions, 449; Senate, joint resolution reported from majority of committee on foreign relations recognizing Cuban independence, 483; report accompanying same, 483–485; excitement following offer of resolution, 485; question of Cuban recognition not brought to vote in House, 487; Senate, resolution offered by Mr. Morgan for recognition of Cuban belligerency, 491; passes bill appropriating $50,000 (approved May 24, 1897) for relief of Americans in Cuba, 495; appropriates $50,000,000 March 9, 1898, for national defence, 545; death blow to autonomy, 545; Spain stunned, 545; action in, on President's message of April 11, 1898, 583–585; war declared to exist since April 21, 1898, 586.

Consul(s) American, at Santiago reports complete anarchy, 289; British, appointed for South American ports, 197; question of, in Cuba, 218; no new Spanish, received exequators, 112; Spanish, office of, at New Orleans attacked by mob, 239; event characterized by secretary of state, 239; vice-, at Santiago, insulting action toward, by General Burriel, 317.

Convention, ratification of re Spanish claims refused by Spain, 71.

Converse, Commander, U. S. N., reports conditions at Matanzas, 505, 506.

Copenhagen, 115.

Coppinger, Don José, governor transfers Florida, July 10, 1821, 146.

Cordoba, banished, 282.

Cortes, permanent commission of, on transmarine affairs opposed to treating with any foreign power re Cuba, 301.

Creeks, destructive blow against, 117; treaty with, by Jackson, 117.

Creole, of Lopez expedition, confiscated, 233.

Crescent City, brings news of executions of members of Lopez expedition, 239; refused privileges of port, 246; ordered to leave port without landing mails or passengers, 247; order suspended, 247; U. S. protest, 247, 248.

Crimean war removes American apprehension re Cuba, 260.

Crittenden, Colonel, W. S., with Lopez expedition, 1851, 237; captured and executed, 237.

Cuba, might have been a Spanish Canada, 12; seizures in, of American property, 96; saved to Spain by slave power of U. S., 111; future of, in doubt, 182; fear of French occupancy, 182; Adams on Cuba, 183–186; importance of, to U. S., 183; desire of U. S. that Cuba should remain Spain's, 186; U. S. nervous as to British intentions re Cuba, 186; independence of, opposed by the South, 206; desirability of annexation to U. S., 215; Adams on, 215; Jefferson on, 215, 216; efforts of U. S. to preserve *status quo*, 216; seizure of, by England or France, would mean war, 216; despatch from Duke of Alcudia arouses suspicion re Cuba, 216, 217; questions of consuls in, 218; proposition of Polk administration to buy, 221; purchase by U. S. would have been fiercely resisted, 223; never assumed serious form, 223; edict of 1825 governing, 224; early discontent in, 225; government of, remained a despotism, 228; in 1850, 228–229; salaries paid by, 229; trade of, and revenues, 229; revolt begins, 229; increased tyranny, 246; interference with American shipping, 246; question of sale of, reopened by U. S., 260; question of purchase practically dead by 1856, 271; statesmanship of both Spain and U. S. at period re Cuba sadly astray, 271; last bill for purchase of, offered by Slidell, 1859, 272; antagonism to joining U. S. in, 274; extensive character of slave-trade in Cuba in 1864, 274; impetus to sugar production, 274; organization of volunteers in, 275; great political influence of clubs and volunteers, 275; letter, signed by 24,000 Cubans, to Serrano, 275; a commission established in Madrid, to consider reforms in, 276; bases of Cuban demands, 276, 277; passions aroused by failure of Spain to adopt recommendations of commission in 1867, 279, 281; increased taxation only result of commission in 1867, 281; turning-point in relations with Spain, 281; insurrection beginning Oct. 1868, 282; time ill chosen, 283; negotiations for peace made impossible by assassination of Arango, 284; civil war spread through island, 284; extraordinary decrees issued in, 284, 285; decrees antagonize treaty of 1795, 285; New York junta issues bonds payable on independence, 285; junta in U. S. demands recognition of belligerency, 286; troops in, 306; law of emancipation, 312; not allowed by volunteers to be published for two years, 313; examination of government relations between, and Spain, 326; vicious circle of procrastination, 327; war ends, 396; terms of peace signed by Campos and

594 INDEX

by Garcia and Gomez, Feb. 10, 1878, 396; Campos on affairs of, 397–400; new laws for, ineffective, 400; parties in, 401, 402; Cuba in the Spanish parliament, 402; analysis of legislation of 1878, 403; Cuban finance, 404; influence in 1895 of economic situation, 406; ground between American and Spanish protection, 407; greed of protectionists at bottom of revolt of 1895, 407; situation in Cuba, 430, 431; situation in, at end of 1896, 487; extension of decree to, granting provincial legislative assembly when state of war would permit, 487; satisfaction in Washington, 488; Estrada Palma on decree, 488; devastation in, chiefly due to orders of insurgent chiefs, 492; melancholy condition of, 503–507; report of same in *N. Y. Herald*, 503, 504; report of consul at Matanzas, 504; report of Commander Converse, 505, 506; destruction of sugar mills, 524; brutality of action, 524; decrees, Nov. 25, 1897, extending to Antilles all rights of Spaniards, 524; riots in Havana, 531.

Cullom, Shelby Moore, Senator, offers joint resolution re Cuba, 486.

Cushing, Commander of Wyoming. See *Virginius*.

Cushing, Caleb, attorney-general, report upon status of Governor-General of Cuba, 326; vicious circle of procrastination, 327; appointed minister to Spain, 358; his special fitness, 358, 359; reaches Madrid, end of May, 1874, 359; instructions to, 359, 360; finds Spain in same condition as Cuba, 360, 362; on change of government in Spain, 363; 373; receives, Nov. 16, 1875, note from Señor Calderon meeting U. S. demands, 375; telegram, Nov. 25, to Mr. Fish, "Spain will succumb in sullen despair," 375, 376; letter of same date, 376; receives and communicates No. 266 and a telegram of Nov. 27 re President's message, 378; is received by Señor Calderon in friendly spirit, 379, 380; help of England cannot be relied upon, 381; on Spain and the Cubans, 388, 389, also 391–393; arranges protocol of 1877, 394.

DALLAS, 93.

Daniells, Edward, tarred and burned to death, 119.

Dauntless, filibuster tug, 416, 418.

Day, William Rufus (assistant secretary of state, March, 1897, secretary of state, April 26, 1898), 491; on De Lome letter, 541; informs Woodford general conditions in Cuba cannot be longer endured, 550, 551; to Woodford, detailing attitude of U. S. government, 557; sends summary of *Maine* report, 558; to Woodford, "See if following can be done," 559; meaning of term "full self-government," 561; to Woodford, "profound feeling in Congress"; hopes negotiations will lead to peace acceptable to country, 566; telegram of March 5 in reply to Woodford's sending queen regent's proposed proclamation, 572; re armistice and disposition of fleet, 570; informs Woodford possible decisive action at "middle or end" of week; arrange for consular officers to leave in case of rupture, 571.

Décazes, Duke, French foreign minister, reasons for not interfering in Spanish affairs, 385.

Decree, of Berlin, 99; of Milan, 99; of reform, by Cadiz regency, 109; revocation of, 109; forbidding alienation of property in Cuba, 285.

Decrees by Napoleon, effect of, 92.

Decrès, instructions as to boundaries of Louisiana, 68; instructions to Laussat re boundaries, 69.

Deposit, right of, at New Orleans annulled, 1802, 51.

Depredations, by Spanish, 95; Spain's conduct authorized warlike action, 105.

Derby, Lord, foreign minister, re interference in Cuba, regards "time ill-chosen and move premature," 383.

Devastation in Cuba chiefly due to orders of insurgent chiefs, 492.

Dulce, General, banished, 282; Governor-General of Cuba, Jan. 4, 1869, 283; cold reception of, 283; extraordinary powers, 283; forced to issue blood-thirsty decrees, 284; driven from Cuba by volunteers, 290.

Duponceau, P. S., gives opinion, 72.

Dupuy de Lome, Enrique, Spanish minister to U. S., in Mora claim, 424; publishes statement in *New York Herald*, Feb. 23, 1896, 439–443; second newspaper article, 443; objections in Senate to such publication, 444; transmitting the Olney note with high praise, 451; interview with Mr. Olney re reply to the Olney note, 465; satisfaction re feeling in Washington over decree granting legislative assembly to Cuba when war would permit, 488; inquiry re movement of squadron south, 532; disturbed by events in Havana, 533; reports conference with Mr. Day, 533; telegraphs encouraging remarks of President, 535; intercepted letter to Canalejas, 538; 539; statement to Mr. Day, 540; telegram, offering resignation, 540.

Duval, circuit judge, "feeble, inefficient," domineered over by Pinkney, 122.

EMBARGO, ignoble answer to British insults, 104.

England, time to recognize magnanimity of government of, in terms of peace

INDEX

of 1783, 27; meditates emancipation of Spanish America, 45; relations with, explained, 90; only flag, except American, on the sea, 90; invokes "rule of 1756," 90; seizes American ships, 90; commerce of, "languid and prostrate" through relaxation of rule of 1756, 91; not in human nature for, to endure trade situation, 91; course of, called for war, 104; loses an empire on the Plate, 106; swept into bloody torrent, 170; affairs tending to war with U. S., 114; fear of action of, justified action of U. S. in the Floridas, 116; U. S. declares war against, 116, proposition to, of joint recognition of Buenos Ayres, 144; refuses any plan to re-establish Spanish authority in South America which would involve use of force, 164; circular note from, opposing Metternich system, 168; opposes *in toto* claims enunciated at Troppau, 172; foreign office issues circular note re Holy Alliance 173; similarity of relations of, and those of U. S with Spain, 179; rights by treaty of 1810, 179; powerful squadron in Carribean alarms U. S. re Cuba, 186; offers to guarantee Cuba to Spain, 187; reception in, of Monroe's message of 1823, with general satisfaction, 202; newspaper comment in, 202, 203; abolishes slavery, 1830, 220; gives Spain £400,000 as compensation for abolishing slave-trade, 220; slave-trade continues, 220; takes concurrent action with France and orders squadron to prevent filibustering by force, 241; identic notes proposing declaration re Cuba, 241, 242, 243; takes higher plane re Cuba, on account of slave-trade, 254.

Enna, Spanish general, killed by Lopez expedition, 237.

Envoys, American, threaten Spain with war, 83; state ultimate conditions, 83; end negotiation, 84.

Erving, G. W., sent to Madrid as chargé d'affaires, 84; left Madrid 1810, 112; made minister 1814, 112: directed to present points of redress and indemnity, 123.

Essex, ship, case of, 91; secondary effect of decision in case of, 92; frigate, attack on at Valparaiso, included in U. S. claims, 124.

Estrada Palma, Cubans would accept independence only, 459; re new decree, reiterates that independence only will satisfy Cubans, 488.

Evarts, speaks at New York meeting, denouncing seizure of *Virginius*, 325; secretary of state, instructions to minister at Madrid, in 1880, re visit and search of four American schooners, 421 (note).

Everett, A. H., minister to Spain, 217.

Everett, E., reply to identic notes, re Cuba, of England and France, 243-245; reply to Lord John Russell, 246 (note).

Expedition, British, intended to restore New Orleans to Spain, 117.

Expeditions, filibustering, many from England to aid Venezuela, 238 (note); "military," the question of, 412, 415, the law, 412; filibustering, number stopped, 418; secretary of treasury on prevention of, 418.

FELICIANA, West, convention of, 112; West Florida independence declared, 112.

Fernandina, seized by Commissioner Matthews, 115; a nest of smugglers, 115; Spanish garrison surrender, 115; occupation maintained until May, 1813, 116.

Fernando VII, abdication of Charles IV in favor of, 106, 110, 112; returned to Spain, 1814, 121; refused Cadiz constitution, 121; reverted to absolutism, 121; crowning act to decree death to any one who spoke in favor of constitution, 121; appeals to Louis XVIII for aid of Holy Alliance, 174; requests French troops to remain in Spain, 208; murderous activity of, basis of continuance of French occupation, 224; restores ancient law of succession, 225; questions of succession, 226; dies, Sept. 29, 1833, leaving widow, queen-governess, 226.

Fillmore, President, message condemning filibustering expeditions, 238.

Fish, Hamilton, secretary of state, 287; confronted by *Alabama* and Cuban questions, 287; formulated rule applicable to both situations and held President to same, 287; protests against decrees in Cuba, 288; agrees with forcible language of Hoff's report and directs minister to solemnly protest against barbarous conduct of war, 289; protests against decrees of Caballero de Rosas, 291; decrees modified, 292; good offices of U. S. tendered to Spain, 292, 293; bases of, 293; declination may involve recognition of belligerent rights to Cubans, 294; President ready to advise to guarantee sum Cuba should pay, 294; declares terms suggested by Spain impossible of attainment, 296; despatch on subject, 297, 298; new terms suggested, offer of which to be withdrawn if not accepted by Oct. 1 (1869), 298; new basis proposed of action re Cuba, 301; Cuban contest cannot end without abolition of slavery, 304; holds proclamation signed by President granting belligerency, 307; states action of Cuban agents in U. S. had decreased American sympathy, 308; No. 266, Nov. 5, 1875, to Cushing, 364-

596 INDEX

373; encloses copy of instruction to Schenck, minister to England, 373; copy of No. 266 sent in confidence to all diplomatic representatives, 374; character of No. 266, 374; telegram to Cushing re President's message and No. 266, 377; in *Virginius* case, 323, 325, 327, 329, 330, 333, 340, 341, 342, 343, 344, 345, 346, 347, 349, 353, 354, 356, 357; only object of in No. 266, 384; emphatic declaration re supposed desire of U. S. for Cuba, what the administration desires, 389, 390, See also *Virginius*.

Florida Blanca, Count, Spanish minister of foreign affairs, objects to use of Mississippi by U. S., 17.

Florida exchanged, 1763, for Havana, 13; way seems clear to acquirement of, 98; a nest of piracy, 127.

Florida, East, temporary occupation of, 116.

Florida, West, facts regarding ownership, 64; question of ownership a burning dispute, 64; American claim to, discreditable, 66; seizures in, of American property, 96; northern boundary, under England, parallel of 32° 28', 15; to be a part of Orleans territory, 113.

Floridas, extraordinary population of the, 112.

Flushing, 48.

Folch, Don Vicente, Governor of Florida, decides to deliver West Florida to U. S., 113; only means to save from ruin, 113.

Foronda, Valentino de, succeeds Yrujo, 111.

Forsyth, John, new minister to Spain, 140; carries new treaty, 140; instructions to, 140; notes between, and Spanish minister of state, 141; authorized to extend time of ratification of treaty, 141; requests "immediate, explicit, and unequivocal reply," 143; threatening note from, 143.

Fort Bowyer, attack upon by British repulsed, 117.

Fort, Negro, centre of raids on Georgia frontier, 118; its suppression demanded, 119; destroyed, 120.

Fort Scott, massacre of soldiers and women on way to, 127.

Foster, Augustus I., British minister, protests against action in West Florida, 114; letter to British foreign minister, 115.

Fowltown, attack on, 127.

France, as early as 1781, looks to restitution of Louisiana, 26; seizes American shipping and carries to Spanish ports, 40; will side with Spain in event of rupture, 82; dictates terms for Florida, 83; seizes American ships, 90; opened colonial ports in 1793, 90; her own carriers swept from the sea, 90; proposes terms re Florida, 94; intrigue with, ended, 100; concession to, re Florida, fails, 103; swept into bloody torrent, 107; remonstrates with Spain, 144; proposes Bourbon prince for Buenos Ayres, 150, 151; offer accepted by Buenos Ayres contingent on action of Great Britain, 151; failure of, 151; demands admission to quadruple alliance, 161; French army moved to Pyrenees, 174; assists Fernando with money to foment counter revolution, 174; Urgel regency take refuge in, 174; demands release of Fernando and abrogation of Spanish constitution, 176; king's speech announcing invasion of Spain, 178; occupation of Spain 178; war with Spain makes Cuban question important to U. S., 186; administration journal, *L'Étoile*, denounces message of 1823, 202; powerful squadron of, in West Indies causes alarm, 208; explanation requested by U. S., 207; takes concurrent action with England, and orders squadron to prevent filibustering by force, 241; identic notes proposing declaration re Cuba, 241, 242, 243.

Francisco de Borja, court-martial aboard, 317.

Franklin, B., opposes yielding of Mississippi navigation, 22; advises Jay to leave Spain, 24; 27.

Frere, John Hookham, British minister at Madrid, 50.

Fry, Joseph, captain of *Virginius*, 314; shot, Nov. 7, 1873, with thirty-six others, 317.

GAINES, GENERAL EDMUND P., builds Fort Scott, near Florida boundary, 119; ordered to Amelia Island, 127; instructed, if necessary, to cross Florida border against Indians, 128.

Gallatin, general views of situation in letter to Jefferson, 87; urges building a navy, 88; his views, truest statesmanship, 89, 93; advocates true and statesmanlike course, 105.

Galvez, governor of Louisiana, captures Pensacola, March 9, 1781, 24.

Galvez, José Maria, president of Cuban home-rule government, 568.

Garcia, Calixto, Cuban general, in the Hawkins expedition, 442.

Gardoqui, Diego de, first Spanish envoy, 30; has grounds for hoping to regain Louisiana, 30; denies right to Mississippi navigation, 32; returns to Spain, 1789, 34; again Spanish negotiator, 1793; his impressions of U. S., 36.

Genet, French minister, enlists men in West to act against Spain, 37.

Georgiana (and *Susan Loud*), of Lopez expedition, seizure at Contoy Island, 233; release demanded at Havana by American consul and Captain Randolph, of *Albany*, 233; Commodore Morris, special commissioner of state department, to demand release of prisoners 233; crew and passengers tried as "pirates," 233; U. S. would view their punishment as an *outrage* upon its rights, 233; Spanish minister of state insists upon right of capture, 234; American minister denies right of seizure in waters of friendly power, 234; argument of Spanish minister of state, 234, 235; stand of American minister 234, 235; Spain qualifies expeditionaries as "pirates," 235; passengers for California released, 235; crew sentenced, 235; American demands cause pardon, 235; vessels confiscated though no state of war and there could be no prize court, 235; extraordinary apathy of state department, 236; importance of cases, 236; capture of *Virginius* less flagrant, 236.

Gerard, French minister to U. S., 17.

Germany swept into bloody torrent, 107.

Gildea, British subject, mate of *Competitor* (which see), 468.

Glenn, district-attorney, Baltimore, "weak and incompetent," 122.

Godoy, Prince of the Peace, signs treaty with U. S., Oct. 27, 1795, 37, 48; appeal to vanity of, 82; offers war or peace, 84, 85; agrees to refer Florida negotiation to Paris, 99, 107.

Gollan, British consul-general at Havana, letter to U. S. consul-general re British subject aboard *Competitor*, 469 (note).

Gomez, Maximo, made Cuban commander-in-chief, 408; cruel orders of, 408–410; extraordinary letter attributed to 523.

Government, American, conscious of lending itself to immoral scheme re Florida, 104.

Graham, John, a commissioner to South America, 149.

Grant, President, since March 4, 1869, 287; orders capture of all concerned in violating eighth section of act of 1818, 292; signs proclamation granting belligerent rights to Cubans, 307; held by Mr. Fish, 307; annual message Dec. 7, 1875, 379, 380; administration criticised re supposed violation of Monore doctrine, 384; General, quoted by Ex-Senator Chandler in question of rules of war, 494.

Gravina, Admiral, Spanish ambassador at Paris, 77.

Gray, George, Senator, defends Dupuy de Lome's publication, 444.

Great Britain. See England.

Greece revolts, 174.

Grenville, Lord, signs treaty with U. S., 1794, 37.

Gresham, W. Q., secretary of state, telegram to American minister, Madrid, re firing on *Allianca*, 420; acceptance of Spain's disavowal, 421.

Gullon, new minister of state, 511; replies to American minister's note, October 23, 1897, 513–519; reference to amendment in 1838 of U. S. neutrality laws, 515; replies, Feb. 1, 1898, to American minister's note of Dec. 20, 1897, 535–537; on De Lome incident, 540; discusses situation with American minister, 552–557; subject of the *Maine*, 554–556; important meetings with American minister, 564–566; the President's demands presented, 564; re Vatican's movement for peace, 569; accedes to Pope's request, 569; hopes withdrawal of U. S. fleet, 570; U. S. declines this last, 570.

Gun-boats, Jefferson's, 105; absurdity of, 105; Spanish, held on Peru's protest, 300; release of, 300.

HALE, EUGENE, SENATOR, speech on Cuba, 444–446.

Hardenburg, Prussian representative at Aix-la-Chapelle, 160.

Harrison, Benjamin, Governor of Virginia, 31.

Hart, condemnation of, under neutrality act, 416.

Havre, 48.

Hawkins, filibustering steamer, lost, 442.

Hay, John, secretary at Madrid, 287.

Hayne, Senator, on Panama congress, 213.

Henley, Captain J. D., U. S. N., reports character of Aury's followers, 126; hoists American flag at Fernandina and causes Aury to withdraw, 127.

Hermes, British sloop of war, 116; loss of, 117.

Hill, David B., Senator, offers joint resolution re Cuba, 486.

Hoar, George Frisbie, Senator, speech on recognition of Cuban belligerency, 447, 448.

Hoff, Rear-Admiral, U. S. N., reports re Speakman and Wyeth, 289.

Holy Alliance, how formed, 156; a religious rhapsody, 156; text of, 157 (note); all powers, except Turkey and Spain, requested to join, 158; apparent harmlessness deceptive, 159; inception, 159 (note); the protocols of Aix-la-Chapelle, 161; proposed mediation of, in affairs of South America, 164; argument against joining, by U. S., 165; meet at Troppau, Oct. 9, 1820, 170; resolved not to recognize governments produced by rebellion, 171; moves to Laybach, 172; Canning's opinion of, 173; main question now Spain and revolted American provinces, 174; would follow France's procedure in Spain, 175; British representative protests, 176, tenor of instructions to representatives at Madrid, 176; representatives, except English, with-

INDEX

draw from Madrid, 177; designs of, re South America, 187, 188.
Hornet, sloop of war, carries new minister to Spain, 140; returns to U. S., 141; again at Cadiz, 143; arrival produces anxiety, 143; leaves for U. S. Oct. 20, 1819, without signature of treaty, 143.
Horsa, Danish steamer, case of, 412–415.
Houston, district judge, "feeble, inefficient," domineered over by Pinkney, 122.
Hoyas banished, 282.
Hubbert, R., accompanies McGregor in seizure of Amelia Island, 125; dies of mortification, 126.
Hyatt, consul at Santiago, reports failure of autonomy, 530.

IBERIAN, a Semite, 4; akin to Kabyl, 4.
Indians, southern, begin war assisted by Georgia negroes, 127.
Ingersoll, Jared, gives opinion, 72.
Innes, Judge, deep in Spanish plot, 39.
Instructions to envoys, of March 2, 1803, express no desire to go beyond the Mississippi, 54, 55.
Insults, ignoble answer of U. S. government to, 104.
Insurgents, Cuban devastation chiefly due to, 492.
Insurrection, of second of May at Madrid, 106; forerunner of dissolution of Spanish empire, 106; swept into bloody torrent, 107; duties of neutrals in cases of, 417.
Ireland, Archbishop, his efforts for peace, 569.
Isabel I, religious fervor of, 9.
Isabella II, born, Oct. 10, 1830, 226; heirship brings Carlist war, 226.

JACKSON, British minister, lends himself to Burr's views, 101;
Jackson, General Andrew, treaty with Creeks, 117; expels British from Pensacola, 117; commands southern division, 118; calls attention of Spanish governor to nuisance of Negro Fort, 119; ordered to take personal command and conduct war against Seminoles, 128; letter to President Monroe, urging seizure of East Florida, 128; enlists 1,000 militia, 128; occupies St. Marks, 129; report, 129; sends garrison to Pensacola, 129; conduct of, in cases of Arbuthnot and Ambrister a violation of international law and good sense, 130; receives remonstrance from governor of Pensacola, 131; takes Pensacola, 131; attacks and takes Fort Barrancas, 131; directs Gaines to seize St. Augustine, 132; organizes Pensacola district as if a U. S. province, 132; (in Adams's reply to Pizarro), 136; public feeling with, 138; debate on, in Congress, 138; appointed governor of Florida, 147.

James I, "King of Spain greater than u all," 9.
Jay, John, envoy to Madrid, 1780, 17; embarrassing situation of, 19; perplexed by instructions from Congress, 21; informs Spanish minister of action of Congress, 22; submits basis of treaty yielding Mississippi navigation and guaranteeing Spanish dominions in North America, 23; limits offer in proposed treaty thus saving situation, 23; leaves Spain for Paris, June, 1782, 25; 27; secretary for foreign affairs, receives powers to treat with Gardoqui, right to Mississippi navigation stipulated 32; advises yielding Mississippi navigation for thirty years, 32; signs British treaty, 1794, 37.
Jefferson, Thomas, vice-president, 1798, writes Madison of serious situation, 40; president, stirred by proposed occupancy of New Orleans by France, 46; bellicose letter to Livingston, 46; letter to Dupont de Nemours, 47; weak message to Talleyrand, 48; powerless between Spain and France, 50; annual message, 1802, 53; special message on cession of Louisiana, Jan. 11, 1803, 54; leans to British alliance, 57; not eager for westward expansion, 70; agrees in expediency of leaving things *in statu quo*, 76; 80; timidity prevents accepting Armstrong's advice, 86; extraordinary view of relations with Spain, 87; thoughts turn to a British alliance, 87; sounds cabinet, 87; letter to Madison re suggested alliance, 87; now leans to occupancy of Texas, 89; suggestions in letter to Madison, 89; turns from English alliance, 92; bold words regarding Napoleon, 92; turns to France, 92; report of cabinet meeting, 92; acts upon Talleyrand's advice, 94; warlike annual message of 1805, 95; meets Miranda, 102; favoring Miranda would have hazarded friendship of France, 103; such action not in reason, 103; stifled conscience and threw over constitutional scruples re Florida, 104; course of administration worse than war, 105; not a statesman in true sense, 105; a navy "a ruinous folly," 105; the gunboats, 105; 107; view of right of every nation to change government, 154; small regard to such principle by European powers, 154; answers Monroe, favoring joining with England in declaration, 190; Cuba most interesting addition which could be made to Union, 191.
Jesuits, restoration of, demanded, 109.
Jovellar, "everything to be subordinated to war," 314; with Martinez Campos, proclaims Alfonso XII, 362.
Joyeuse, 48.

INDEX

Junta, Cuban, such committees difficult of suppression both in U. S. and England, 419.

Juntas formed in Spain, 108; central junta at Cadiz, 108; formation of provincial juntas; acts of self-preservation, 109; declare for Fernando VII, 109; contribute millions to central junta in Spain, 109; of Carácas proclaimed treasonable, 110.

KENTUCKY, people of, look to Mississippi as their proper highway to ocean, 30.

King, Rufus, minister to England, sends rumors of cession of Louisiana to France, 43; sends copy of French-Spanish treaty of 1801, 43; probable plans of Great Britain, 45; regards affairs of U. S. and Spain serious, 102; Miranda's projects welcome aid in case of war, 102.

King of Spain, makes great grants of land in Florida, 139; held void by U. S., 139.

Krudener, Madame, "friend and guide," of Alexander, 156, 158.

LABORDE, master of *Competitor*, 468.
Latouche-Treville, 48.
Laurada, case of, 415-416; 418.
Laussat, French prefect of Louisiana, 63, 68; only duty was to deliver Louisiana to the U. S., 68.
Lawyers seldom good administrators, 79.
Layard, British ambassador, action of, under direction of government, re slavery, aids U. S. proposals, 304; at Madrid, 340; 381.
Leander, ship, furnished Miranda, 102.
Leander, British frigate, outrageous conduct of, 104.
Leclerc to command Santo Domingo expedition, 48.
Lee, Consul-General Fitzhugh, on Ruiz case, 489; to receive charity offerings and co-operate with Cuban authorities, 529; reports riots in Havana, 531; telegrams re visit of *Maine*, 534 (note); on retention of *Maine* at Havana, 541; complained against by Spain, 544; President declares, has "borne himself with great ability, prudence, and fairness," and will not consider withdrawal, 544.
Leo XIII, takes part in endeavor to preserve peace, 569.
Leon, Norwegian filibuster, 418.
Leopard, British man-of-war, fires on *Chesapeake*, 104.
Lersundi, a reactionary, made captain-general of Cuba, May 30, 1866, 282.
Letona banished, 282.
Little Belt, British sloop of war, fired into by *President*, frigate, 114.
Livingston, Robert R., minister to France, gets evasive replies from Talleyrand, believes Floridas are given to France, French armament preparing to take possession of Louisiana, 44; convinced Floridas not included, 45; informs Joseph Bonaparte U. S. has no wish to go beyond Mississippi, 45; nominated minister plenipotentiary jointly with Monroe, 54; presses subject of purchase east of Mississippi, 57; informs Talleyrand U. S. desires only New Orleans and Floridas, 58; changes his mind regarding West Florida, 65; advises Madison to claim to Perdido, 66; joins Monroe in advising to claim West Florida, 66; forced to maintain that Spain had retroceded West Florida without knowing it, etc., 68; to Madison re French demands, 80 (note).

Livingston, Edward, gives opinion, 72.
Loomis, Jairus, sailing-master, in command of convoy from New Orleans, 119; assists in attack on negro fort, 120; blows up negro fort, 120.
Lopez, Narciso, organizes revolt 1848, 230; expedition in 1849 suppressed, 230; Taylor's proclamation, 230; expedition organized 1850, 230; offers leadership to Quitman, 230; expedition sails in *Creole*, *Georgiana*, and *Susan Loud*, April 25, 1850, 231; rendezvous off Yucatan, 231; lands at Cardenas and surprises garrison, 231; re-embarks, disappointed in support, 231; starts for Key West, 231; discovered and pursued by *Pizarro*, 232; expedition disperses, 232; Lopez arrested but released, 233; second expedition, 1851, 237; events of, 237; Lopez garroted at Havana, 237; execution as "pirates," of many of the men, 237; sentences of others, 237; release of remainder, 237; final release of all survivors, 238; criminality of expedition strongly condemned by administration, 238; message of President Fillmore, 238; such expeditions not unknown elsewhere, 238; execution of members of expedition causes intense excitement, 239; riot in New Orleans, 239; satisfaction demanded by Spain, 239.
Lorient, 48.
Loss, American, through seizure of ships, enormous, 91.
Louisiana, ceded by France to Spain, 1763, 13; transfer made public, 1764, 13; rumors of transfer to France, 1801, 43; transfer to France delayed, 48; order for delivery signed at Barcelona, Oct. 15, 1802, 50; treaty of cession, April 30, 1803; 60; sum paid by U. S. for, 60; west of Mississippi forced upon us, 60; transfer wholly act of Napoleon, 60; precautions to secure delivery, 62; delivered Nov. 30, 1803, 63; 79; proposed to cede from Rio Bravo to Guadeloupe

600   INDEX

(Texas), 92; 95; seizures in, of American property, 96; population disaffected, 101; ready to turn to France or Spain, 101; serious feeling in French-Spanish population, 102.

Luffborough, midshipman, killed with two of his men, 119.

McGillivray, half-breed, desires Spanish protection, 31.

McGregor, Sir Gregor, adventurer, seizes Amelia Island, 125; deposed by "Commodore" Aury, 126.

McKean, J. B., gives opinion, 72.

McKee, John, commissioner with G. Matthews to accept surrender of East Florida, if offered, 114.

McKinley, William, President, succeeds Cleveland, 490; special message re relief of Americans in Cuba, 495; bill for same approved May 24, 1897; annual message of Dec. 1897, 525–527; issues circular, Dec. 24, 1897, calling for contributions for relief of Cuban distress, 529; encouraging remarks to Spanish minister, 535; answer, March 5, 1898 to General Woodford's telegram forwarding queen regent's proposed proclamation, 572; receives collective note of powers, 573; reply to same, 573; message of April 11, 1898, 576–582; action justified by events, 576; signs on April 20, the joint resolution of April 19 (legislative day, April 18), 585.

Mackintosh, Sir James, protests in parliament against passage of foreign enlistment bill, 238 (note).

Madison, James, despair of, on account of proposed closure of Mississippi, 33; letter to Jefferson respecting same 34; secretary of state, instructs Livingston respecting anxiety to obtain the Floridas, 43; instructs Charles Pinckney in Madrid, May, 1802, 44; to guarantee Spanish territory, 44; writes Pinckney re withdrawal of deposit, 51; replies to Yrujo re cession of Louisiana, 62; letter to Pinckney re boundaries, 67; instructions of, April, 1804, to Monroe and Pinckney, 73; weak explanation of Mobile act, 76; 80; "Spain must swallow claim," 81; advises Monroe to use skilful appeal to fears of Spain, 82; to Monroe re Pinckney's recall, 82; not blind to truth re West Florida, 85; 87; writes Armstrong of "venal suggestions" of French functionaries, 92; writes Armstrong and Bowdoin to express views conciliating France, 98; to Armstrong, refusing Napoleon's demands, 100; meets Miranda, 102; statement of course re Miranda, 103; 107; President, proclamation taking possession of West Florida, 112; sends confidential message to Congress advising enabling President to occupy East Florida, 114; Matthews action makes a "distressing dilemma," 115; special message recommending strengthening neutrality act, 123; expresses in message, Nov. 5, 1811, interest in South American developments, 148; writes Monroe favoring joining England in declaration re Holy Alliance, 193, 194; favors declaration also re Greece, 195.

Maine, to go to Havana, 534; telegrams re visit, 534 (note); destruction of Feb. 15, 1898, 541; burial of dead at Havana and honors shown, 542; court of inquiry, 542; report on, sent to Congress, 561, 562; Spanish report on, 562; report of court, 561–563 (note).

Marbois, Barbé, Count of, conference with Napoleon, 59.

Marcy, secretary of state, directs Soulé to open question of sale of Cuba should opportunity offer, 268; repudiates Ostend manifesto, 269.

Maria Cristina, widow of Fernando VII, queen regent, 226.

Marti José, soul of Cuban revolt of 1895, 407.

Mason, John Y., minister to France, member of Ostend conference, 261.

Matanzas, terrible conditions at, 505, 506.

Matthews, George, commissioner, with I. McKee, instructed to accept surrender of East Florida if offered, 114; oversteps instructions in seizing Fernandina, 115; not policy of U. S. to wrest Florida from Spain, 115; powers revoked, 115; situation not changed, 115.

Maura, Spanish statesman, law submitted in 1893, failed through genuineness of attempt, 406.

Melton, American correspondent aboard *Competitor* (which see), 468.

Mensajora, Spanish armed launch, captures *Competitor*, 468.

Message, Dec. 3, 1805, 95; Dec. 9, 1805, 96; of Dec. 3, 1805, a play for benefit of France, 96; to be taken to heart by Spain, 97; annual, Dec., 1869, 307; special, June 13, 1870, 307–311; Cleveland's annual, Dec. 2, 1895, 425, 426; annual, Dec. 7, 1896, 475–483; of President McKinley sending report on *Maine*, 561, 562; of April 11, 1898, 576–582.

Metternich, represents Austrian government at Aix-la-Chapelle, 160; *deus ex machina* of Holy Alliance, 162; a character fraught with evil, 163; 172.

Mexico, revolts, 1820, 149; aims in combination with South American states to wrest Cuba and Puerto Rico from Spain, 205; Vera Cruz falls to Mexican forces, 1825, 206; calls on U. S. to fulfil pledge of 1823, 208.

Milan decree, 99.

"Military" expeditions. See Expeditions, "military."

Militia to be organized, 96.
Mills, Roger Quarles, Senator, resolution of, re Cuba, 449; offers joint resolution, 486.
Minister, French, view of character of U. S. government, 104.
Minister, Spanish, well informed of attitude of France, 81; had knowledge of Burr's plans, 101; recommends watching Burr, 101; remarks re Wilkinson, 101; has full knowledge of Miranda's preparations, 103; warns Spanish main, 103; demands satisfaction for events at New Orleans, 239.
Ministers, foreign, both England and U. S. fortunate in, at time of Holy Alliance, 197; of Mexico, Central America, and Colombia. See Clay re Panama Congress, 205. See Depuy de Lome.
Miralles, Don Juan de, Spanish agent, 1779, to U. S., 17; letter to Congress, Nov. 24, 1779, urging capture of Florida, 17.
Miranda, Francisco de, 100; history of, 102; comes to U. S. in 1805, 102; excellent standing with prominent men, 102; writes Madison a compromising letter, 102; expedition leaves New York, 102; expedition fails, 103; reappears in Venezuela, 149; surrenders and dies in Spain, July 14, 1816, 149.
Miro, Spanish governor, treaty of, with Indians, 31; 39.
Mississippi River, free to Great Britain and France by treaty of 1763, 14; to close outlet to American Southwest meant war or independence, 30; the, value to West, 35; vital to the West, 52; 93.
Mississippi, territory of, 95.
Mobile, 95.
Monroe James, nominated as joint envoy with Pinckney to Spain, 54; nominated minister extraordinary, 54; joins Livingston in advising to claim West Florida, 66; basis of action, 76; ordered to Madrid without delay, 76; leaves London *en route* for Madrid, 79; fatuous idea of influencing Napoleon, 79; letter to Talleyrand, 79; leaves Paris for Madrid, 79; learns before leaving Paris that West Florida is not included in cession to France, and claims for spoliations excluded by treaty of 1800, 80; negotiation opened by himself and Pinckney, 81; only alternative to return to London or submit to French terms, 83; leaves Madrid, May 26, 1805, 84; arrives Paris, June 20; London, July 23, "conscious of failure," 84; secretary of state, makes vigorous reply to British protest re Florida, 114; mention of Florida question to French minister, 115; warns Jackson re involving government in contest with Spain, 117; reiterates claim to Florida, 122; never doubted that Louisiana extended to Rio Bravo, 122; enterprises of revolutionists forestalled, 122; president, 124; letter to, from Jackson inexplicably disregarded, 128; thinks Jackson acted against instructions, 134; nervously anxious to conclude treaty (1819), 139; Texas might have been saved, 139; views of importance of treaty of 1819, 140, 141; if treaty not ratified proposes action by Congress, 142; remarks in annual message, 142 (note); secretary of state, Dec. 19, 1811, acknowledges receipt of declaration of Venezuelan independence, 148; president, on South America in annual message, 1818, 150; message March 8, 1822, recognizing South American independence, 152; protest by Spanish minister, 153; writes Jefferson and Madison for advice re Rush's dispatch, 190; thinks should meet Canning's proposal, 191; unsettled as to course re Canning's proposal, 195; in sketch of message, 1823, lays more stress on European than South American situation, 200; carried away by sympathy for Greece, 200; protest by Adams, 200; message of Dec. 2, 1823, 200-202.
Monroe Doctrine, Adams the true author, 198 (note); as it appears in message, Dec. 2, 1823; 200-202; declaration of, decisive, 204; Mr. Fish accused of violating, in sending No. 266, 384.
Montevideo, 110.
Montmorency, Duke of, puts three questions to allied conference, 174; answer of allies, 175.
Montreal, 107.
Moors, number of, driven from Spain, 5; resident race, 6; expulsion of, 1609, 9.
Mora, Antonio Maximo, claim of, 423-425; settled, 425.
Morales, Spanish commander in Venezuela, brutal decree of, 179.
Moret, new minister of ultramar, 511; discussions with American minister, 551-557; important meetings with, 564-566; the President's demands presented, 564.
Morgan, Senator, John Tyler, speech re *Competitor* prisoners, 470; resolution in favor of Cuban belligerency, April 1, 1897, 491; passed Senate, May 20, 491; did not come to vote in House, 491.
Morier, British chargé d'affaires, protests against occupancy of West Florida, 113.
Morris, Gouverneur, speech calling for war, 56; advocates strong navy, 56 (note); minister to France, letter to, from Jefferson re right of nations to change government, 154.
Morris, Commodore Charles. See *Georgiana*.

NAPLES adopts Spanish constitution July 2, 1820, 166; King of, invited to Troppau, 171; absolutism restored by Austria and Holy Alliance, 172; question of, arouses British feeling, 173; Canning's speech on, 173.
Napoleon, price paid by, for Louisiana, 42; fails to obtain Floridas, 43; opens minds of commissioners to true destiny of U. S., 45; reverses proclamation of freedom to blacks, 49; orders preparation of Louisiana armament, 49; thwarted by Godoy, 50; disquieting remarks of, to British Ambassador, March, 1803, 57; decides to transfer Louisiana, 58; views as to Louisiana, 59; broken promise of, re transfer of Louisiana, 61; good policy to put obscurity in question of boundary, 65; determined that, if Florida ceded, U. S. must pay, 80; changes menace from England to Austria, 93; his schemes demand money, 93; *en route* for Austria, 94; attempted propitiation of, 97; angry because of American support of blacks in Santo Domingo, 97; holding Florida as bait for alliance, 98; informs Talleyrand that Charles IV declines to alienate Florida, 98; commands American intercourse with Santo Domingo to cease, 98; order obeyed by passage of bill Feb. 28, 1806, 98; determined to force U. S. to take sides against England, 99; directs Champagny as to terms on which will aid U. S., 99; offers Florida if America join France, 99; throws over question of Florida, 100, 104; imagination reached too far, 106; 107, 111, 112.
Natchez, a Spanish post, 29.
Natchitoches, Spanish force close to, 102.
Navarro, Don Diego Joseph, Captain-General of Cuba, 17.
Navy, effect of putting afloat naval force, 105; what it would have saved, 106; placed on war footing re *Virginius*, 325; French, powerless, 105; Spanish, a negligible quantity, 105.
Negro fort destroyed, 120.
Nesselrode, Russian representative at Aix-la-Chapelle, 160.
Neutrality law of 1838, 515, 516 (note).
Neuville, De, French minister, 141; to influence U. S. to preserve peace with Spain, 144; startled by proposal of South American independence, 150.
New Orleans, 104; riot in, 239; Spanish consulate attacked, 239.
New York at times a blockaded port, 104.
Nichols, Lt.-Col. Edward, hoists British flag with Spanish in Pensacola forts, 116; proclamation to Kentuckians, 116; proclamation described by Adams, 116; returns to Florida, 118; makes treaty with Seminoles, 118; builds fort in Florida, 118; leaves for England, 118, 136.

Niobe, British man-of-war. See *Virginius*.
North, the, demands trade facilities with Spain, ready to sacrifice West, 33; favors yielding Mississippi navigation, 33.
Note, collective, of the powers presented to President, 573; President's reply, 573; collective, of powers to Spain, advising accepting Pope's proposal of suspension of hostilities, 573.
Nuñez, filibuster, 416.

OFFICERS, SPANISH, to leave New Orleans, 93.
Ogden, Samuel, aids Miranda, 102.
Ohio, mail steamer, treatment of, at Havana, 248, 249.
Olivart, Marquis de, publicist, on misconception of sovereign rights, 338; discussion of protocol of 1877, 394, 395 (note); discussion of *Alliança* case, 422, 423; on Spanish-American situation, 429; on speech of Queen Regent, 458, 459; on *Competitor* case, 471-474.
Olney, Richard, secretary of state, energetic note re Mora claim, 424; important note of April 4, 1896, to Spanish minister, tendering good offices of U. S., 452-458; note praised by minister, 451; Dupuy de Lome's interview with, 465; Spanish reply a declination of good offices of U. S., 460, 465; U. S. note a turning-point for Spain, 465, 466; succeeded as secretary of state by Mr. Sherman, 490.
Onis, Chevalier Don Luis de, U. S., refused to receive him as minister until status of Spain should be decided, 112; received as minister, 1815, 112; demands return of West Florida to Spain, 121; calls attention to fitting out of privateers in U. S. ports, 121; states desire of Spain to arrange differences, 123; contentions re treaty, 124; 135; new note from, renewing negotiations, 135.
Orders in council, effect of, 92.
Orleans, territory of, 95.
Ostend, meeting of ministers at, Oct. 9, 1854, 262; the manifesto, 262-267.
Oswald, 27.

Pampero, in Lopez expedition, 236.
Panama congress, chap. XI, 205; circular from Bolivar, 205; terms on which U. S. will take part, 209; meets June 22, 1826, 214; no representative from U. S., 214; adjourned to Tucubaya, Mexico, but never met, 215.
Parker, Commodore, special commissioner at Havana, 237; obtains release of some of Lopez expedition, 237; opinion of Cuban situation, 237.
Parma, offered Spain for Florida, 50.
Patterson, John F., nominal owner of *Virginius*, 314.
Peace, negotiations for, begun 1782, 25.

INDEX

Pensacola, occupied by British, 116; a centre of distribution of arms to Indians, 117; taken by Jackson, 131.
Percy, W. H., captain R. N., 116.
Peru, no movement toward revolt until 1819, 149; protest against delivery of Spanish gun-boats built in U. S., 300; case similar to Spain's protest of year before, 300; Prim says war with, absurd and foolish, 300; release of gun-boats, 300.
Philip II, expels Moors, 1609, 9.
Philippines, 109.
Pichon, French minister, 62.
Piedmont revolution, March 10, 1821, 172.
Pierce, President, message re *Black Warrior*, 256.
Pinckney, Charles, Minister to Spain, 51, to negotiate the enlarging of rights and interests in the Mississippi and territories eastward, 54; presses Spain, 73; threatens war, 74; creates panic in Mediterranean, 75; negotiation opened by himself and Monroe, 81; recalled, 84.
Pinckney, Thomas, minister to England, appointed negotiator at Madrid, 1795, 37.
Pinkney, William, lawyer, domineers over judges, 122.
Piracy in Caribbean, 97.
Pirates, swarms of, from Cuba, 180.
Pitt, William, British premier, 78; interested in Miranda, 102.
Pi y Margall, president of republic, 313; minister of state on Cuban rights, 448, 449.
Pizarro, minister of state, note to Ewing, minister, with threat of war, 135.
Pizarro, Spanish steamer, intention to seize *Virginius*, 316.
Pocock, Admiral, 13.
Poinsett, Joel, appointed agent to Buenos Ayres, 149; instruction to, 149; minister to Mexico, 155.
Poletica, Russian minister to U. S., directed to "plead cause of peace," 144; instructed to approach U. S. government re joining Holy Alliance, 165.
Polignac, French ambassador, London, spoken to by Canning with great plainness, 196; defines views of France, 196; proposes consideration of combined action by allies, 197.
Polly, ship, decision regarding, 90.
Polo de Bernabé, Admiral, Spanish minister at Washington, re *Virginius* (which see), 323, 324, 325, 327, 340, 341, 343, 345, 346, 347, 353–356.
Polo de Bernabé, new Spanish minister to Washington, 545; leaves Washington April 20, 1898, 585.
Population, rapid flow of, to West, 35.
Porter, David D., lieutenant U. S. N., commanding *Crescent City*, 246.

Portugal, adopts Spanish constitution, August 20, 1820, 168; fears for her independence, 385.
Potter, Lieutenant Commander William Parker, member *Maine* court of inquiry, 542.
Power, Thomas, 39.
Pragay, Hungarian, with Lopez expedition, 237.
Price, Dr., favors control of Mississippi valley by men of English blood, 27.
Prim, an exile in France, 282; one of new government, 282; mention, 283; liberal views of, 295; explains views re conditions of concessions, 296, 297; unfortunate absence when U. S. proposals were handed in, 299; "must wait a year or two," 299; war with Peru "absurd and foolish," 300; "not another shot will be fired in it," 300; U. S. propositions now a general topic of discussion, 302; broad views of, 302; his life to be the forfeit, 305; shot Dec. 27, 1870, died Dec. 30, 313.
Privateers, French, use Spanish ports as their own, 40; swarms of, 121; Baltimore and Charleston largely concerned in fitting out, 122; indictments in Baltimore, 122; list of, illegally fitted out, furnished, 123; akin to pirates, 180.
Proclamation of Madison, taking possession of West Florida, 112.
Proclamation of belligerency, signed by President Grant, held by Mr. Fish, 307.
Protocol signed at Troppau, 171; circular, giving "short view of first results," 171.
Protocol of 1877, 394; discussion of, 394, 395 (note); in case of *Competitor*, 468–474; discussion of, by de Olivart, 471–474.
Protocols by allies, Aix-la-Chapelle, 1818, 161, 162.
Puerto Rico, seizures in, of American property, 96; saved to Spain by slave power of U. S., 111; project for reforms brought forward, 303; American minister assured these would be extended to Cuba when hostilities should cease, 303; new laws relating to, 312; emancipation of slaves, 312; an elective provincial assembly granted Dec. 31, 1896, 487.
Puñon Rostro, Count of, immense grants of land to, 139.
Purre, Don Eugenio, takes possession of St. Joseph, 23.

QUEBEC, made a governmental district, 1763, 14.
Queen Regent, speech of, 458, 459; foreshadows reply to Olney note, 459; signs decrees, Nov. 25, 1897, extending to Antilles all rights of Spaniards, 524; not privy to any suggestion of cession of

604 INDEX

Cuba, 549; proposed proclamation suspending hostilities, 571; reply of U. S., 572.

RAWLE, WILLIAM, gives opinion, 72.
Randolph, Edmund J., secretary of state, 1794, fears separation of Kentucky, 36.
Randolph, John, chairman of committee, informed of need of $2,000,000 appropriation, 97; told by Madison that we must give France money or "take a Spanish or French war," 97; proposition regarded by, a base prostration of national character, 97.
Recognition, right of, rests solely with President, 487.
Reconcentrados, question of, now of first importance, 491; justice of feeling re, examined, 491-495.
Reconcentration, Weyler's first decree, Oct. 21, 1896, 474, 475 (note); the Spanish error involved, 475; revoked entirely, 566.
Red Cross in Cuba, 529.
Reed, Thomas Brackett, speaker of House, 491.
Reform, appeal for reforms by Spain's American provinces, 109; character of, demanded, 109.
Regency, the, in Spain, 108; folly of, 109; madness of, 110.
Relations of Spain and U. S. comparatively quiet from 1855 to 1868, 273.
Religious fanaticism, instigated by Fernando and Isabella, 8.
Republic, declared in Spain, Feb., 1873, 313.
Resolutions, joint, granting Cuban belligerency, introduced, Jan., 1870, 307; passed House, lost in Senate, 311; offered in Senate acknowledging Cuban independence, Dec. 21, 1896, 483; excitement following, 485; numerous joint, offered re Cuba, 486; of Senator Morgan re Cuban belligerency passed Senate May 20, 1897, 491; did not come before House, 491.
Revolt against Napoleon, 108.
Rhea, John, insurgent president, West Florida, writes proposing incorporation with U. S., 112.
Rights, neutral, annulled, 99.
Rio Bravo, west boundary of Louisiana, 68.
Rios Rosas, banished, 282.
Riot at New Orleans, 239.
Riots in Havana, 531; American feeling disturbed by, 532.
Rochefort, 48.
Rochester, Wm. B., nominated secretary to mission to Panama congress, 209.
Rodas banished, 282.
Rodney, Cæsar A., commissioner to South America, 149; minister to Argentina, 155.

Roloff, filibuster, 416.
Ruiz, Richard, case of, 489.
Rule of 1756, 90; greatly relaxed, 91.
Rules of war, 493.
Rush, note to, from Canning re Holy Alliance, 167, 188; has interview with Canning, 188; offers to join with Canning if South American independence recognized, 189; views of, 189; writes six despatches and letters re proposed declaration, 195; disappointed in Canning's silence, 196; on reception of Monroe's message in England, 203.
Russell, Lord John, reply to Everett's note re Cuba, 245; re recognition of belligerency of Confederate government, 484, 485.
Russia objects to giving Parma to Spanish prince, 50; remonstrates with Spain, 144; supplies ships to Spain for South American expedition, 166; issues circular note re Spanish revolution, 166, 167; ominous warning of note, 168; unsatisfactory reply of, to Clay's despatch requesting aid re Spain, 208.

SACO, opinion of, regarding Cuba's need of autonomy, 227.
Sagasta, Praxédes Mateo, mention, 283; proclamation vs. action proclaiming Alfonso XII, 362; head of new ministry, 511; important meetings with American minister, 564-566; the President's demands presented, 564; Spanish propositions, 567.
St. Cyr, French ambassador, ordered to press Spain to deliver Louisiana, 49; promise to Spain never to alienate Louisaina, 50.
St. Mary's River, 115.
St. Michael, fort at Pensacola, 116; taken by Jackson, 131.
Salmeron, president of Spanish republic, 313.
Samaná, bay, French expedition arrives January, 1802, 48.
Sampson, Captain William Thomas, president of *Maine* court of inquiry, 542.
Sanguily, Julio, case of, 428, 429; released Feb. 25, 1897, 490.
Santo Domingo, trade of, 97; act prohibiting trade with, 98.
Saunders, Spanish agent, threatening letter of, 35.
Scott, Sir William, decision of, re ship *Polly*, 90; effect of decision re *Essex*, 91; reverses decision regarding continuous voyage, 91; condemns ship *Essex*, 91.
Seaboard in a state of anxiety, 96.
Seamen, a thousand yearly impressed from American ships, 104.
Seaports to be furnished with cannon, 96.
Sebastian, chief justice, in Spanish pay, 39.
Seizures of American property in Cuba, etc., 96.

INDEX

Seminole war, 127.
Senate, ratifies treaty of 1819, Feb. 19, 1821, 146. (See Congress and Resolutions.)
Sergeant, John, nominated envoy to Panama congress, 209; did not attend, 214.
Serrano, Duke de la Torre, letter to, signed by 24,000 Cubans, 275; favors reform, 275; declares Cuban aspirations legitimate, 281; banished, 282; head of new government, 282; mention, 283.
Serrurier, French minister, 115.
Sevier, ex-governor of Franklin, writes Spanish governor of desire by Southwest, of Spanish protection 31.
Shelburne, 27.
Shepperd, F. E., first captain of *Virginius*, 315.
Sheridan, General Philip H., quoted by ex-Senator Chandler in question of rules of war, 494, 495.
Sherman, Senator John, inconsiderateness of action in moving for belligerency, 307 (note); speech on recognition of Cuban belligerency, 437, 438; speech quoting Pi y Margall, Spanish minister of state, 448, 449; succeeds Mr. Olney as secretary of state, 490; appointment criticised, 490, 491; note to Spanish minister, June 26, 1897, re suffering in Cuba, 496, 497; Spanish minister's reply, 497; instructions to General Woodford, 508–511; despatch, replying to Señor Gullon's note of Oct. 23, 1897, showing enforcement of neutrality obligations, 520, 521.
Sherman, General William Tecumseh, quoted by ex-Senator Chandler in question of rules of war, 494.
Shipowner, American, despair of, 99.
Shipping American, takes trade of British, 90; American, prospered amazingly, 90; interference with American, by Spain continued, 250.
Ships, American, 90; seizure of, in large numbers, 91; armed for Santo Domingo trade, 97; superfluous equipment of reaches Santo Domingo blacks, 97; sequestered could be released by taking sides with France, 99; American. seized by British, 104; natural prey, 104,
Short, William, American commissioner, instructions to, 1792, 35.
Sickles, General, Daniel E., minister to Spain, 287; reports conversations with Prim, 296, 297; sends new propositions valid until Oct. 1, 298; unfortunately obliged to hand in U. S. proposals while Prim and Silvela absent, 299; withdraws note of Sept. 3, 302; report of Spanish conditions, 303; re *Virginius* (which see), 320, 321, 327, 328, 329, 330, 332, 333, 334, 340, 341, 343, 344, 345, 346, 347, 349; tenders resignation, 358; discharged trying duties with marked zeal and ability, 358; succeeded by Caleb Cushing, 358.
Sigsbee, Captain Charles Dwight, of *Maine*, 555.
Silvela, Spanish minister of state supports Santiago officials, but enjoins mercy and humanity on captain general, 290; declares intention to give self government to Cuba, 295; unfortunate absence when U. S. proposals handed in, 299.
Skinner, postmaster at Baltimore, indicted re privateering, 122.
Slavery, plans for abolition of, in Cuba, presented by commission in 1867, 281; contest in Cuba must end slavery, 304.
Slave-trade in full vigor in Cuba notwithstanding Spain's treaty with England, 220.
Smith, Adam, favors control of Mississippi valley by men of English blood, 27.
Smith, William, surveyor of customs. N. Y., warm friend of Miranda's, 102,
Smith, William, purser of *Crescent City*, accused of maligning captain-general, 246; ship refused courtesies of port on account of, 246.
Soulé, Pierre, minister to Spain, 251; an improper appointment, 251; instructions to, 252, 253; reports Spanish situation re U. S., 254; sharp note re *Black Warrior*, 258; regards outrage on owners insignificant compared with that on flag, 260; declares Spain does not fear our resentment, 261; member of Ostend conference, 261; resigns, 269.
South America, states of, combine to wrest Cuba and Puerto Rico from Spain, 205.
Spain, decadence due to inaptitude for administration and government, 11; effort to keep pace with democratic spirit stifled by French invasion of 1823, 12; gives France 1,000,000 francs for America, 1776, 15; disinclination to aid U. S. revolution, 15, 16, 17; immense possessions under treaty of 1763, 15; hope of weakening English race, 15; policy in American revolution, 16; fears American example, 16; declares war against Great Britain, May 3, 1779, 16; attitude of Spain, 16; powerless to aid U. S., 17; fleet ill-manned, ill-equipped, 17; never ally of U. S., 17; makes known her views, 18; denies right of U. S. to use the Mississippi, 18; wishes America to build ships for Spanish use, 19; desires exclusive use of Gulf of Mexico, 20, 21; seizes St. Joseph, 23; disappointment of, in recognition of American independence, 27; claims 32° 28' as northern boundary of Florida, 29; extends posts to Natchez and Walnut Hills, 29; accepts American situation, Feb. 22, 1783, 27; sinister position of, with regard to America, 28; again

ready to treat, 1791, 35; proposed guarantee of territory by U. S. 44; objects to transfer of Louisiana, 61; renounces opposition to same, 63; strong case of 72; war declared against England, 81; minister declares American terms inadmissible, 84; strained relations of U. S. with, 84; seizes American ships, 90; Talleyrand proposes frightening, 93; terms to, 93; no intention of yielding Texas, 102; follows Berlin decree, 104; nationality effaced, 106; "The Regency," 108; independent action of River Plate region against, in 1810, 110; thenceforward ally of Great Britain, 111; revolt against Napoleon brings peace with Great Britain, 111; influence of occupancy of, by French, 111; recognizes the Floridas as lost to her, 123; policy recognized of giving the Floridas for as much of Texas as U. S. would yield, 123; first conditions of, re Florida treaty, included return of all Louisiana west of the Mississippi, 124; unable to preserve peace on borders of Gulf of Mexico, 127; minister of, demands reparation for Jackson's conduct in Florida, 132, 133; proposes new negotiator, 143; General Vives selected, 143; revolution of 1820, 146; new government reconciled to treaty, 146; king signs order transferring Florida, Oct 24, 1820; forces of, in Venezuela successful until 1819, 149; declines any mediation which would not guarantee restoration of her South American dominion, 164; offers general amnesty to South Americans, 164; conditions of, 164; expedition organized to subdue South America, 166; never sailed, 166; destitution and misrule in, 166; French consuls in West Indian ports, 182; immediate concession to British demands, 182; American claims of like character not settled until 1834, 182 (note); opens Cuba to trade, 182; urged by U. S. to accept situation, 206; "would never abandon claim to ancient and rightful possessions," 207; informed "Cuba must in no event and under no pretext pass into the possession of or under protection of" any other European power, 217; American complaints against, 218; cost of French occupation borne by, 218, 219 (note); reasons for refusing to receive American consuls, 219; request for guarantee of continued possession declined, 219; proposition to, in 1848, to buy Cuba, 221; rejects same, 223; edict of 1825, re Cuba, 224; the Salic law, 225; constitution and parliament established, 226; Cuban and Puerto Rican representatives denied seats in Parliament, 227; this denial foundation of Cuban revolt, 227; policy of delay re *Black Warrior*, 258, 259; offers mixed commission re American claims, which is refused by U. S. as some are not of character to submit to such tribunal, 270; convention agreed upon in 1860, 270 (note); relations of, with U. S. comparatively quiet, 1855–1868, 273; wasting strength in useless adventures, 273; reason for, personal, 273; joins England and France in Mexican expedition, 273, withdraws from Mexico, 273; failure to adopt recommendations of commission, in 1867, fatal to, 279, 281; turning-point in relations with Cuba, 281; a volcano in unrest, 282; revolution begins Sept., 1868, 282; Isabella dethroned and deported, 282; Serrano, Prim, Topete, and Sagasta, heads of new government, 282; tender to, of good offices of U. S., 293; bases of, 293; declination may involve recognition of belligerent rights to Cubans, 294. President ready to advise to guarantee sum Cuba should pay, 294; intimates willingness to accept good offices of U. S. on certain bases, 295; Mr. Fish declares terms incapable of attainment, 296; refuses good offices of U. S. on terms proffered, 301; marked signs of changed attitude of, 303; adjustment nearly in reach, 303; loses great opportunity, 304; fundamental difficulty in, herself, 304; woful condition of, 305; errs in sending so many infantry to Cuba, 306; amazing energy shown, 306; special powers conferred on minister at Washington re Cuban affairs, and withdrawn, 311, 312; new laws re Puerto Rico, 312; law of emancipation, 312; republic declared Feb., 1873, 313; part of coast declared blockaded, 313; state of, 313; low credit of, 314; examination of government relations between, and Cuba, 326; vicious circle of procrastination, 327; mollifying effect in, of President's annual message of 1875, 390; ends Cuban war, 395; terms of peace, 396; new legislative regimen for Cuba, 400; observations on Spanish cabinets, 402; cost of Spanish government in Cuba, 404; government of Spain described, 405; inertness in preventing landing of expeditions in Cuba, 418; but one seizure made afloat, 418; climax of feeling on account of passage of belligerency resolutions in Congress, 439; consulate in Barcelona attacked, 439; note on riot, 439; only thing which would prevent American intervention in Cuba, 450; speech of queen regent, 458, 459; reply to the Olney note, 460–465; reply a declination of American good offices, 465; the Olney note a turning point for, 465, 466; agitation in, re *Com-*

INDEX

petitor, 470; decree granting elective provincial assembly to Puerto Rico, with extension to Cuba when state of war would permit, 487; refusal of good offices offered by France, Great Britain, and Germany, 487; minister of state, reply of, Aug. 4, 1897, to the American secretary of state, 498-502; Spain expects to persevere in present course, 502; new ministry [in, 511; previous party manifesto promises new order in Cuba, 511; serious situation of new ministry, 512; Spain's great efforts, 512; decrees signed, Nov. 25, 1897, extending all rights of Spaniards to Antilles, 524; condolences re destruction of *Maine*, 542; circular notes to representatives, 556; presents final propositions, 567; sends circular telegram to representatives, March 30, 1898, 567, 568; practical acceptance of demands of U. S., 572; receives collective note of powers advising acceptance of Pope's proposals for a suspension of hostilities, 573.

Spaniard, a Moro-Iberian, 6; great qualities of, 6, 7.

Spanish, the, qualities of, 10.

Spanish-America, explanation by republics of, re proposed conference, 208; Clay's reply, 209.

Speakman, Charles, shot at Santiago, 289.

Spoliations, French, 94.

Squadron, North Atlantic, to go South, 532; movements of, give concern to Spain, 537, 538.

Supreme Court, ruling of, 414, 415.

Surplus, Gallatin advises spending two or three millions of, in ships, 105.

Susan Loud, of Lopez expedition. See *Georgiana*.

TACON, CAPTAIN-GENERAL OF CUBA, 227.

Talleyrand, Prince, again agent of cession of Louisiana to France, 42; seeks to put limits to extension of U. S., 43; his venality, 48; hints that whole of Louisiana may be had, 58; remarks on boundary of Louisiana, 65; miscarriage of effort to recover Louisiana for France, 77; Louisiana to be a wall of brass against U. S. and England, 77; note to Spanish ambassador re American claims, 77; informs Spain that U. S. claims for French spoliations must not become "subject of a new discussion," 78; report to emperor, 81; "unjust pretensions of U. S. to West Florida" 81; Monroe has note of, denying right to West Florida, 82; unsigned note from, to American minister, 93; advises frightening Spain, 93; writes American minister with indignation re Santo Domingo, 97; directs French ambassador at Madrid to obtain transference of negotiation to Paris, 98; 107.

Taylor, Hannis, American minister, Madrid, 420; adopts as guide in *Alliança* case the instructions of Mr. Evarts in 1880 to Fairchild, American minister, re visit and search of four American schooners, 421 (note); presents letter of recall, Sept. 13, 1897, 508.

Tecumseh, 117.

Tennessee, people of, look to Mississippi as their proper highway to ocean, 30.

Tetuan, Duke of, in the *Alliança* case, 421; Spanish minister of state, reply to the Olney note a declination of American good offices, 460-465; minister of state, reply Aug. 4, 1897, to secretary Sherman's note, 498-502.

Texas, part of Louisiana, 69; to be hypothecated by Spain, 94.

Thames, battle of, 117.

Three Friends, filibuster tug, 416, 418.

Thurston, writes Washington of scheme to place West under British protection, 37.

Times, London, upholds Monroe declaration, 202; leader in, 381, 382.

Topete, Admiral, squadron of, raises flag of revolt at Cadiz, Sept. 10, 1868, 282; one of new government, 282; mention, 283.

Tornado, Spanish man-of-war, captures *Virginius*, Oct. 31, 1873, 317.

Toulon, 48.

Toussaint l'Ouverture, 48.

Trade, controlled by American ships, 91.

Trafalgar, 99, 105.

Treaty of 1763, 13, limits assigned by, 13; provisional, Nov. 30, 1782, 25; secret article of, between U. S. and Great Britain, 29; of 1783, yielded the Floridas to Spain without mention of limits, 29; with Spain, arguments for, 38; of 1800 between France and U. S., 42; of St. Ildefonso, 1800, ceding Louisiana to France, 42; of 1819, terms proposed by each party, 124; negotiation of, with Spain, renewed, 138; propositions of Spain and U. S., 138; signed, Feb. 22, 1819, 139; opposition of Clay to giving up Texas, 139; question of land grants, 140; of 1819, obstacle to ratification of by Spain, the question of South American recognition, 144; of 1819, accepted by Spain, 146; ratified by Senate, 146; ratifications exchanged, Feb. 22, 1821; of Nov. 20, 1815, sixth article of, real basis of Holy Alliance, 160.

Troops, Spanish, in Red River region, 102.

Troppau, meeting at, of Holy Alliance, Oct. 9, 1820, 170; personages at, 170; Alexander's remarks at, 171; protocol signed at, 171; King of Naples invited to, 171.

Turreau, General, French minister to U. S. instructions to, re boundaries, 78; in-

formed of attitude of France re spoliation claims, 78.
Tuyll, Baron, Russian minister, declaration to, by Adams, 198; note from, Oct. 3, 1823, 198; Adams's reply to, Nov. 27, 1823, a full exposition of U. S. policy, 199.

UHL, acting secretary of state, 421.
United States, difficulties with Spain began with independence, 13; claim to navigation of Mississippi, under treaty of 1763, 14; boundaries under treaty of 1783 due to disregard of instructions from Congress, 26; at end of war finds outlets of all its rivers leading to Gulf of Mexico in hands of Spain, 30; abortive efforts toward a treaty with Spain, 30, 37; treaty of 1795, 37, 38; shipping seized by Spain and France, 40; half of territory of, despoiled of Spanish empire, 41; the cession of Louisiana, 46–60, (see Jefferson, Livingston, Madison, Monroe, Napoleon, Talleyrand, etc.); the world's carrier, 90; the only flag except England's on the sea, 90; ports of, entrepots for European goods, 91; French proposals for arrangement with Spain, 94; only nation to find splendid and inexhaustible booty in ruin of Spanish empire, 107, 108; to reckon with Spain as ally of Great Britain, 111; the treaty of 1819, 123, 138–146 (see Spain; also Adams, De Onis, Monroe, Vives); on firm ground in claiming to Rio Grande, 124; South American independence, chap. VIII; government of, wholly frank regarding attitude toward South America, 155; invited to join in mediation between Spain and South America, 164; declines any action short of recognition of independence, 164; declines joining Holy Alliance, 165; membership in Holy Alliance offered, 165; similarity of relations of, with those of England with Spain, 179; the Monroe doctrine, chap. X (see Adams, Canning, Monroe, Rush); desire that Cuba should remain Spain's, 186; nervous as to British intentions re Cuba, 186; looks askance at Cuban independence, 206; the South opposed to a free Cuba, 206; urges Spain to accept situation, 206; letter from Clay on Spanish American situation, 206, 207; the Panama congress, chap. XI (see Adams); declares could not consent to occupation of Cuba and Puerto Rico by other power than Spain, "under any contingency whatever," 208; policy of re Panama congress, opposed by South as meaning freedom to slaves in Cuba, 211; minister to Madrid, 1840, directed to inform Spain she may depend on U. S. for preservation of Cuba and Puerto Rico, 220; proposition of Polk administration to buy Cuba, 221; purchase of Cuba would have been fiercely resisted through growing anti-slavery sentiment, 223; never assumed serious form, 223; firm ground taken in 1858 re rights of vessels, 236; submission to surveillance over Cuba by French and English squadrons impossible, 241; reply to identic notes re Cuba, of France and England, 243–245; remonstrances of, re interference with shipping, 247–250; extraordinary reply of Spain as to powers of captain-general, 249; decided attitude in *Black Warrior* case, 257; empowers minister to open anew the question of sale of Cuba, 260; refuses mixed commission re claims, 270; convention agreed upon in 1860, 270 (note); relations of with Spain, comparatively quiet, 1855–1868, 273; use of, by Cubans and principles involved, 286; the Grant administration, 287–394 (see Caleb Cushing, Fish, Grant, Polo de Bernabé (admiral), Prim, Sickles, Spain); tenders good offices to Spain, 293; bases of, 293; declination may involve recognition of belligerent rights to Cubans, 294; President ready to advise to guarantee sum Cuba should pay, 294; terms on which good offics of, would be given, not accepted, by Spain, 301; reclamations against Spain presented, 312; The *Virginius* case, 314–357 (see *Virginius*); reserve of European cabinets toward advances of, 385; why basis of Cuban intrigue and supply, 411; the Cleveland administration and the Cuban war, 411–489 (see Cameron, Cleveland, Congress, Dupuy de Lome, Morgan, Olney, Sherman, Cuba, Spain); exertions of, to repress filibustering, 411; proclamation declaring violations of neutrality laws would be rigorously prosecuted in effect a recognition for a state of insurgency, 411; popular feeling rising, re Cuba, 432; the McKinley administration and Cuba (see Cameron, Congress, Day, Dupuy de Lome, Hale, Hoar, McKinley, Morgan, de Olivart, Sherman, Reconcentrados, Woodford, Cuba, Spain); declares war with Spain, 585.
Upshur, on preservation of Cuba to Spain, 221.
Urgel, Seo de, regency set up at, 174.

VALDES, CAPTAIN-GENERAL GERONIMO, bando of, 228.
Valmaseda, Count of, brutal proclamation of, 285.
Valparaiso, 107.
Varona, Cuban agent, testimony re ownership of *Virginius*, 349.
Vatican, attempts to preserve peace, 569; telegram from Spanish ambassador to Madrid, 569.

INDEX

Venadito, Spanish steamer, fires on *Aliança*, mail steamer, 419.
Venezuela, sends U. S. word of severance from Spain, 148.
Verona, Congress of allies at, 175; no stranger allowed at, 175.
Viar, Spanish agent threatening letter of, 35.
Victor to command expeditionary army to Louisiana, 68.
Villaret, 48.
Virginius, capture of, Oct. 31, 1873, 314; history of, 314–317; 53 of crew shot, 317; protest of captain of *Niobe*, 318; Burriel's reply, 318; protest of Commander Cushing of *Wyoming*, 319; treatment of protests of American, British, and French consuls, 319; President Castelar telegraphs, before knowledge of executions, that death penalty must not be imposed without approval of Cortes, or sanction of executive, 319, 320; Mr. Fish telegraphs American minister: "If an American citizen wrongfully executed, U. S. will require most ample reparation," 320; steps which minister had already taken, 320; Spanish minister of state calls on American minister and expresses deep regret on hearing of executions, 321; President Castelar "greatly moved," 321; Mr. Fish in note to Spanish minister asked him to relieve anxiety as to news "too shocking to be credible," 323; telegraphs minister, Madrid, Nov. 12, to protest against action, if confirmed, as "brutal, barbarous, and an outrage upon the age," and to demand most ample reparation; warns that grave suspicions exist as to right of *Virginius* to carry American flag, 323; letter to minister, 323, 324; Spanish minister at Washington receives two telegrams, 325; mass meetings in New York and elsewhere; Mr. Evarts speaks at New York; Mr. Fish denounced; navy ordered on war footing; war in sight, 325; inaccurate reports reach Spain, 327; Spanish minister of state informs American minister "with deep regret" of shooting of 49 prisoners, 328; the conference of the two ministers, 328, 329; minister telegraphs belief that Spain would spontaneously offer reparation, 329; Mr. Fish telegraphs ultimatum, Nov. 13, 329; American minister on reception of telegram of 12th sends note, Nov. 14, embodying same, 330; Spanish minister of state returns an indignant note, 330, 331; his error, 331; American minister's reply, 331, 332; he renews demands, Nov. 15, in terms of ultimatum sent Nov. 13, 333; calls attention to Burriel's conduct to consul at Santiago, 333; Mr. Fish telegraphs, Nov. 15: "If Spain cannot redress outrages, U. S. will," 333; note from American minister warning Spanish government, 334; note, Nov. 17, from minister of state declaring limits to which Spain will go, 334–338; American minister proposes to leave Madrid; British ambassador demands reparation, 340; Spain now convinced of danger of war, 340; transfers negotiations to Washington, 340; telegram to Spanish minister proposing new terms of arrangement, 340; American minister directed to defer departure from Madrid, 341; Spain, Nov. 23, proposes arbitration, 341; U. S. refuses, as subject was one of national honor, 341; Spain's telegram of Nov. 24 asking if U. S. would await her solution on receipt of facts, if President would withhold reference to Congress, and if points of offence could be designated, 341, 342; Mr. Fish's reply, 342; Spain cannot understand precipitancy of U. S., must be satisfied of right of *Virginius* to flag, telegram Nov. 24, 342, 343; Mr. Fish replies U. S. must reserve right to inquire into question of right of *Virginius* to flag, Nov. 25, 343; telegraphs minister Nov. 25, if accommodation not reached on close of to-morrow, withdraw from Madrid, 344; minister telegraphed, Nov. 25, Lord Granville expresses through minister his sense of moderation of the demands, 344; on Nov. 26, Spain recognizes principles of American demand, 344, 345; American minister requests passports before reception of Spain's note, but notifies reply may be deferred, 344, 345; Spanish proposals declined; new ones proffered by Admiral Polo accepted, 346; protocol drawn, Nov. 29, 1873, 346; minister of state informs U. S. minister of arrangement, 347; final arrangements Dec. 8, 347, 348; *Virginius* delivered to U. S. at Bahia Honda, Cuba, Dec. 16, 1873, 348; survivors delivered at Santiago Dec. 18, 348; *Virginius* papers proved fraudulent, 348, 349; attorney-general holds that she was, notwithstanding, exempt from capture; that only the U. S. could raise the question, 349; Spain pays indemnity of $80,000, 349; England demands and receives indemnity for the slaughter of 19 subjects, 349; remarks, 350; case of General Burriel, 351, 353; Spain's claims for damages, 353, 354; Mr. Fish's complete answer, 354, 357.
Vives, General, appointed minister to U. S., 143; presents credentials April 12, 1820, 145; presents note "opening and almost closing negotiation," 145.
Vives, denies having stated to Gallatin that he had authority to deliver Florida, 146.

Vizcaya arrives at New York, 535 (note). Volunteers, power in Cuba in hands of, 284.

Voyage, direct, not allowed, 90; what constituted direct voyage, 90.

WALNUT HILLS (Vicksburg), a Spanish post, 29.

War, imminent between France and Great Britain, 57; message of 1805 received by public as equivalent to declaration of, 95; some things worse than, 105; declaration of by U. S. against England, June 18, 1812, 116; against Spain, April 18, 1898, 585.

Washington, fears separation of Western states, 31; letter to Governor Harrison, 1784, 31, 37; hopes new treaty with Spain will quiet West, 39; having a navy would have saved capture of, 106.

Webster, on preservation of Cuba to Spain, 1843, 221; replies to Spanish minister re New Orleans riot, 239.

Wellesley. See Wellington.

Wellington, Duke of, ready to invade South America, 111; lands in Portugal instead of South America, 111; at Aix-la-Chapelle, 160; alone represents Great Britain at Verona, 174; instructions to, 174, 217, 219.

West Florida. See Florida, West.

West, hatred of Spaniard as natural as of Indian, 41; impossible to accept Spain's control of way to sea, 41.

Weyler y Nicolau, Valeriano, marquis of Teneriffe, succeeds Campos as governor-general of Cuba, 430; proclamations of, 431, 432; relieved by Blanco, Oct. 31, 1897, 521; remarks near bringing court-martial, 521, 522; protests against criticism in President's message, 527.

White, Senator, on Panama congress, 213.

White, Commander Edwin, of U. S. S. *Kansas*, protects *Virginius*, 316; action approved, 316 (note).

Whitlock, English general, surrender of, 106.

Whitworth, Lord, British ambassador, 57.

Wilkinson, General James, paid agent of Spain, 35; receives money from Spain, 39; commissioner with Claiborne to receive transfer of Louisiana, 63; base character of, 63; deep in Burr's conspiracy, 101.

Williams, consul-general at Havana, letter to, from British consul-general re British subject aboard *Competitor*, 469 (note).

Woodbine, Captain, 116; accompanies McGregor in seizure of Amelia Island, 125, 137.

Woodford, General Stewart L., presents letters of credence as U. S. minister at Madrid, Sept. 13, 1897, 508; instructions to, 508–511; presents note, Sept. 23, 1897, 513; called on for information by the several ambassadors at Madrid, 513; note replied to, Oct. 23, 513; re the De Lome letter, 540; Spain stunned by $50,000,000 appropriation of March 9, 1898, 545; his number 43 to President hoping peace, 546; his conversations with Señor Moret, 547–549; meetings with Spanish ministers, 551–557; answer to inquiry for instructions, 557; receives telegram, re *Maine*, 558; asks instructions, 559, 560; pressed for answer, re armistice, 561; important meetings with Spanish ministers, 564–566; presents President's demands, 564; sends details of conferences with Spanish ministers, 564–567; sends Spanish propositions, 568; Spain's attitude a question of punctilio and means continuation of war, 568; reports acceptance by Spanish government of Pope's proposal for armistice with request for withdrawal of U. S. fleet from vicinity of Cuba, 569, 570; receives reply, 570; telegraphs proposed proclamation of Queen Regent suspending hostilities: "I believe this means peace," 571; reply to same, 572; causes corrections of newspaper misstatements in Madrid, 574; sends telegram, April 9, announcing armistice ordered, 574.

Wyeth, Albert, shot at Santiago, 289.

YARA, pronunciamiento, Oct. 10, 1868, 282.

Yrujo, Marquis of Casa de, Spanish minister, adverse to intendant's action, re deposit, 51; states re-establishment of right of deposit, 52; protests of, against transfer of Louisiana, 61; angry comment on Mobile act, 70; thorn in side of government, 71; obtains opinions upon hypothetical case, 72, 76; presence at Washington disagreeable, 93.

ZABALA, banished, 282.

Zea Bermudez, Spanish minister in Russia, informs Russia of adoption of constitution, 166.